Learning the Internet for Business

Chris Katsaropoulos
Kathy Berkemeyer
Don Mayo
Cathy Vesecky

Acknowledgments

This book is dedicated to:

My mother-in-law, Gail Richardson. Thanks for all your encouragement and support. Also, thanks again to Jennifer Frew. It's always a pleasure working with you. *Chris*

Jack for his love, patience, support, and sense of humor. *Kathy*

Kathy B—sorry I missed you in the last one. *Don*

Otto and Sally. *Cathy*

Managing Editor	**Technical Editors**	**English Editor**	**Layout and Design**	**Internet Simulation Production**
Jennifer Frew	Monique Peterson Jennifer Frew Cathy Vesecky	Monique Peterson	Shu Y. Chen Paul Wray Maria Kardasheva Midori Nakamura	Scott Kopitskie

Published by DDC Publishing, Inc.

Internet address: ***http://www.ddcpub.com***

ISBN: 1-56243-587-6
Cat No. Z-27

10 9 8 7 6 5 4 3 2 1

Printed in the United States of America.

Contents

Introduction vi

Learning the Internet Simulation CD-ROM viii

Log of Exercises x

Understanding the Internet x

Lesson 1: Microsoft Internet Explorer 1

Exercise 1 2
- The Active Desktop in Internet Explorer 4.0
- Install the Windows Desktop Update
- Customize The Active Desktop
- The Internet Explorer Channel Bar
- Restore the Active Desktop

Exercise 2 12
- Start Internet Explorer 4
- Internet Explorer Screen
- Get Help
- Exit Internet Explorer

Exercise 3 22
- Standard Toolbar Buttons
- Open a World Wide Web Site from the Address Bar
- Open a World Wide Web Site Using the File Open Dialog Box
- Back and Forward
- Stop a Search
- Return to Your Home Page

Exercise 4 30
- Internet Explorer Main Search Page
- AutoSearch from Address Bar

Exercise 5 38
- Open and Add to the Favorites Folder
- Open Web Sites from the Favorites Folder
- Delete Favorites
- Create New Folders in the Favorites Folder
- Move Favorites from Folder to Folder
- File Favorites
- Edit Favorites

Lesson 2: Netscape Navigator 51

Exercise 1 52
- About Netscape Navigator
- Start Netscape Navigator
- The Home Page
- The Navigator Screen
- Netscape Help
- Hypertext Links
- Image Maps
- Exit Netscape Navigator

Exercise 2 62
- The Navigation Toolbar
- Open World Wide Web Sites
- Stop a Load or Search
- Status Bar
- Return to the Home Page
- Change the Default Home Page

Exercise 3 70
- History List
- Bookmarks
- Bookmarks Window
- Add Bookmarks
- Open a Bookmarked Web Site
- Delete Bookmarks
- Create Bookmarks from the History List

Exercise 4 78
- Netscape Navigator Main Search Page
- Start Search from Location Field

Lesson 3: Search Engines and Search Sites 85

Exercise 1 86
- Searching vs. Surfing
- Search Sites
- Search Basics

Exercise 2 94
- Keyword Searches
- Refine a Search
- Get Help
- Yahoo! and AltaVista Alliance

Exercise 3 106
- Operators
- Boolean Operators
- Grouping Operators
- Case Sensitive Searches
- Major Search Engines and Operators

Lesson 4: E-mail 115

Exercise 1 116
About Electronic Mail
Launch Outlook Express
Configure Outlook Express to Send and Receive Mail
Exercise 2 128
Outlook Express Main Window
Compose New Messages
Send Messages
New Message Toolbar
Exercise 3 138
Retrieve New Messages
The Mail Window
Read Messages
Delete a Message
File a Message
Save a Message
Print a Message
Reply to a Message
Forward a Message
Exercise 4 150
Launch Netscape Messenger
Configure Messenger to Send and Receive E-mail
Exercise 5 158
The Message List Window
Compose New Messages
Send Messages
Message Composition Toolbar
Exercise 6 166
Get New Messages
Read Messages
Delete a Message
File a Message
Bookmark a Message
Save a Message
Print a Message
Reply to Mail
Forward Mail

Lesson 5: Finding News and Information 179

Exercise 1 180
Jump Online at AOL.com
Web Resources at MSN.com
News and Entertainment at the Pathfinder Network
Exercise 2 194
Check Business News with BusinessWeek Online
Check Business News with Forbes Digital Tool
Use the NewsHound Push Service
Exercise 3 206
Research Investments with Morningstar
Check Interest Rates with Bank Rate Monitor
Exercise 4 216
Find Business Capital with MoneyHunter
Exercise 5 224
Find Legal Information at the Legal Information Institute
Consult OSHA Regulations at the OSHA Web Site
Find Tax Information with IRS Digital Daily

Lesson 6: Operations 237

Exercise 1 238
Search for Commercial Real Estate with NetProperties
Search for Residential Real Estate with HomeScout
Make Relocation Decisions with HomeBuyer's Fair
Exercise 2 252
Hire Employees or Find a Job with America's Job Bank
Exercise 3 262
Find Business Resources at the Small Business Administration
Manage a Small Business with Edge Online Business Tools
Exercise 4 272
Research Computer Purchases with CNET
Purchase a Computer Online
Troubleshoot Computer Problems with The Tech Support Guy
Exercise 5 284
Send and Track Packages with the United States Postal Service
Cut Your Phone Bill with TRAC
Exercise 6 294
Master Common Tasks with Learn2
Look up Words with Merriam-Webster Online
Find Historical Documents at the National Archives
Find the Correct Time for Any City in the World
Use Financial Calculators
Exercise 7 308
Plan Travel with Microsoft Expedia
Book Travel with Expedia's Travel Agent
Exercise 8 320
Find a Restaurant with Zagat Survey
Get Directions with MapQuest
Check the Travel Forecast with Intellicast

Lesson 7: Sales and Marketing 331

Exercise 1 332
Improve Target Marketing with American Demographics
Research Target Markets with U.S. Census Bureau
Exercise 2 342
Develop Sales Leads with SalesLeads USA
Research Companies with Hoover's Online
Exercise 3 354
Locate Clients with BigBook
Find People with Four11
Find Company Web Sites with WebSitez
Exercise 4 366
Improve Sales Techniques with SalesDoctors Magazine
Get the Most out of Trade Shows with Trade Show News Network
Exercise 5 376
Develop a Target Mailing List with List Merchant
Search for Mailing Lists and Market Online with American List Council

Exercise 6 388
Sell to the Government with Commerce Business Daily
Exercise 7 396
Find International Sales Resources with MSU-CIBER
Find Trade News with Trade Information Center
Locate Trade Leads with Global Marketplace
Translate Foreign Languages with travlang

Lesson 8: Creating a Company Web Page 409

Exercise 1 410
Use Word's Web Publishing Tools
Design Your Web Site
Word 97 Web Page Templates
Create a Basic Home Page
Exercise 2 416
Enter New Text in a Web Page
Work with Tables
View Table Borders
Insert Table Rows or Columns
Exercise 3 422
Character Formatting
Change Text Colors
Paragraph Formatting
Online Layout View
Web Page Preview
Use Web Page Styles
Exercise 4 428
Save a Document as a Web Page
Create Bulleted Lists
Create Numbered Lists
Exercise 5 434
Create and Insert Hyperlinks
Edit Hyperlinks
Exercise 6 440
Copy Hyperlinks
Paste as Hyperlink
Exercise 7 442
Create a Web Page with the Blank Web Page Template
Create a New Table
Merge and Split Cells
Exercise 8 448
Work with Horizontal Lines
Add Colors to Tables
Add Background Textures
Exercise 9 454
Create a Feedback Form
Work in Form Design Mode
Add Controls to Forms
Modify Controls and Control Properties
Exercise 10 460
Insert Graphics Files
Use the Clip Gallery
Supply Alternate Text
Exercise 11 466
Add Marquees
Add Animation
Exercise 12 470
Insert Videos
Add Background Sound

Appendixes 475

Appendix A 476
Introduction
Origins of Viruses
Categories of Viruses
Virus Symptoms
Appendix B 478
Essential Downloads
Internet Explorer
Netscape Navigator
TUCOWS
Shareware.Com
The Jumbo Download Network
VDOLive Video Player
Adobe Acrobat Reader
Shockwave
Appendix C 481
Glossary
Appendix D 488
Post Web Sites to a Server
Save All Your Web Site Files in One Folder
Use Relative Hyperlinks
Contact Your Internet Service Provider
Use Personal Web Server
Appendix E 490
Troubleshooting

Index 496

This Book is Designed for You...

if you are just beginning to use the Internet and would like to begin exploring the business applications of the World Wide Web. Instead of just telling you about the Internet and the Web, this book offers easy to follow exercises that actually show you how business on the Internet works.

You will learn how to:

- Use the Web for business management, sales, and marketing.
- Use Microsoft Internet Explorer and Netscape Navigator, the two most popular Web browsers available today.
- Enter addresses to get to business Web sites all over the world.
- Organize and save addresses to sites you want to access again.
- Navigate the Web using hyperlinks.
- Use search engines and business Web sites to find information on a wide range of topics, products, etc.
- Compose and send e-mail.
- Understand Internet terms.
- Create a corporate Web page using Microsoft Word 97 for Windows.

This book assumes that you have some general knowledge and experience with computers, and that you already know how to perform the following tasks:

- Use a mouse (double-click, etc.).
- Make your way around Microsoft Windows 95 (copy, paste, print, etc.).
- Install and run programs.

If you are completely new to computers as well as the Internet, you may want to go through DDC's **Learning Microsoft Windows 95** before you go through the exercises in this book.

If you are completely new to Microsoft Word 97, you may want to go through DDC's **Word 97 Visual Reference Basics** before you go through Lesson 8 on creating a company Web page.

What Do I Need to Use This Book

This book assumes that you already have a basic understanding of computers. Ideally, you should have access to an Internet Service Provider so that you can go "live" on the Web to explore the Web sites featured in the book.

Though a few of the exercises in the book are best performed live on the Web, the majority of the exercises should be completed using the Web simulation on the CD in the back of the book.

Please read over the following list of must haves to ensure that you are ready to be connected to the Internet. How to get connected to the Internet is not covered in this book.

- A computer (with a recommended minimum of 16 MB of RAM) and a modem port.
- A modem (with a recommended minimum speed of 14.4kbps, and suggested speed of 28.8kbps) that is connected to an analog phone line (assuming you are not using a direct Internet connection through a school, corporation, etc.).
- Established access to the Internet through an online service such as AOL, independent Internet service provider, etc.
- Access to the browser applications: Microsoft Internet Explorer 4.0 and/or Netscape Navigator 4.0 *(if you do not currently have these applications, contact your Internet Service Provider for instructions on how to download them.)*
- A great deal of patience. The Internet is a fun and exciting place. But getting connected can be frustrating at times. Expect to run into occasional glitches, to get disconnected from time to time, and to experience occasional difficulty in viewing certain Web pages or features. The more up-to-date your equipment and software are, however, the less difficulty you will probably experience.

How to Use this Book

Introduction

Before you start Lesson 1, read the brief Understanding the Internet section of this Introduction. It will give you some basic concepts and terminology that will make understanding the Web easier.

Lessons 1-8

The exercises in each topic contain two parts:

Notes
Explain and illustrate Internet or Web page concepts and tools being introduced.

The right column on each page frequently contains hints, notes, cautions, and definitions.

Cautions and warnings that alert you of potential pitfalls

Hints and additional notes on an Internet or Word 97 feature.

Definitions of Internet and Web page terminology.

Exercise Directions
Explain and illustrate how to complete the exercise. Most exercises will make use of the DDC Web simulation located on the CD that accompanies this book.

The simulation is a unique feature that assures that the notes and exercise steps in this book remain consistent with what you see on screen—despite possible changes to actual Web sites.

After you complete an exercise that uses a simulated site, you will be given the actual Internet address of the Web site featured in the exercise.

✓ *Web Search questions in Lessons 1-7 give you a chance to test your ability to find information on the Internet.*

✓ *Thought questions in Lessons 5-7 encourage you to think about the information you find in your traveling in the Web.*

✓ *A few exercises ask you to go online to see how the Internet works live.*

✓ *Exercises for Lesson 8, Creating a Company Web Page, use data files supplied on the CD.*

Appendixes

Viruses What they are and how to avoid them.

Glossary A list of Internet terms with definitions.

Essential Downloads Great software you can get free on the Web.

Publishing Your Web Pages An overview of the process used to load Web pages on a server for access via the Web.

Troubleshooting Help for common pitfalls you may encounter when creating Web pages.

Data and Solution Files

Data files for completing the Exercises in Lesson 8 are provided on the accompanying CD-ROM. The data files include Word 97 documents you use to create Web pages as well as graphics, video, sound, and animation files used to build the Web pages.

Important Note: Building a Web page or Web site in Word requires that all of the Web site's files be stored in the same folder. You will create a separate folder on your computer system for storing all the Word 97 and Web page document files you create as you work through the Lesson 8 Exercises.

The files you create and store in your folder will be used in subsequent exercises to build a complete, integrated Web site. Please consult your instructor about the best location on your computer system for storing your Web site folder.

Please read the installation directions on page vi to learn how to access the book's files. Solutions disks may be purchased separately from DDC Publishing.

The Solution disk may be used for you to compare your work in Lesson 8 with the final version or solution on disk. Each solution filename begins with the letter "S" and is followed by the exercise number and descriptive filename. For example, **S03TRY** would contain the final solution to the exercise directions in exercise three.

A directory of data disk and solutions disk filenames are provided in the Log of Exercises (see page viii).

✓ *Saving files to a network may automatically truncate all filenames to a maximum of eight characters. Therefore, though Windows 95 allows for longer filenames, a maximum of only eight characters with a three-character file type extenstion can be saved to a network drive.*

The Teacher's Manual

While this book can be used as a self-paced learning book, a comprehensive Teacher's Manual is also available. The Teacher's Manual contains the following:

- Lesson objectives
- Exercise objectives
- Related vocabulary
- Points to emphasize
- Web search solutions
- Company Web page solutions

What's Included on the CD-ROM

The DDC Internet Simulation CD-ROM

The Internet is constantly changing, constantly reinventing itself. As a result, there are no guarantees. For example, a Web site you visit today may not look the same or, for that matter, may not even exist tomorrow. Obviously this can be frustrating.

To ensure that steps in many exercises in this book will yield the results that are illustrated, simulations of sites will be used. These simulated sites can be found on the DDC Internet Simulation CD-ROM.

The **Learning the Internet Simulation CD-ROM** is designed to be used in conjunction with *Learning the Internet for Business*. It simulates actual Internet sites so that you are not required to log onto the Internet in order to learn. That means no modems, no connection time or fees, no wandering to other Internet sites. The simulation also ensures consistent results for each exercise regardless of Web site updates, revisions, relocation and removal.

The exercises on the CD-ROM follow the exercises in the book in sequential step-by-step order. For example, if you start an exercise and skip a step or click the wrong object or item, the program will not proceed to the next step or you will receive an error message.

How to Install the Internet Simulation Program

1. Close any applications that may be running.
2. Place the CD in your CD-ROM drive.
3. Click Start on the Desktop. (Windows 95, Windows 98, Windows NT 4.0)
4. Click Run... and type: *CD-ROM drive letter*:\SETUP.EXE
5. Click OK to start the installation wizard.
6. Click Next > in the **Welcome** screen.
7. In the **User Information** screen that appears, enter your name and a Company (or school) name; then click Next >.

   ✓ *Be sure to enter something in the Company text box, or you won't be able to go to the next screen.*
8. In the **Choose Destination Location** window, accept the directory that is suggested, or click Browse... and select another directory. Click Next >.
9. In the **Select Program Folder** window, accept the name for the Program Folder or assign a different name, and then click Next >.

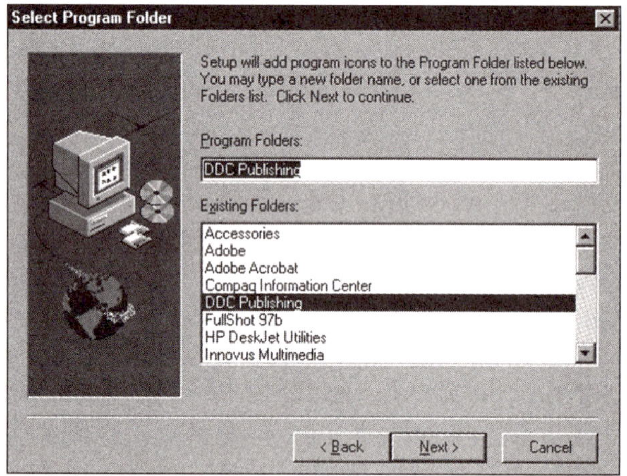

10. In the **Start Copying Files** window, review the settings. If you want to change any setting, click the < Back button and make the desired changes. If you are satisfied with the current settings, click Next >.
11. The Install Wizard will set up the simulation.
12. Click Finish to complete the installation.

Launch the Internet Simulation

✓*Important: To run the simulation you must have the CD in your CD-ROM drive.*

1. Click Start on the desktop.
2. Select **Programs**.
3. Select the **DDC Publishing** directory.

   If you created another directory for the DDC files, select that directory.
4. Click Learning the Internet for Business to launch the simulation.
5. Select the exercise that corresponds with the exercise in the book.

Minimum System Requirements for Internet Simulation Program

Software	Windows 95, Windows 98, or Windows NT 4.0 (or higher)
Disk Space	50MB available hard disk space.

Multimedia Internet Browser Tutorial

For the new user of the Internet, the CD-ROM includes basic computer-based training on how to navigate the Internet using a browser. A browser is a program that helps manage the process of locating information on the World Wide Web. The tutorial introduces the concepts and then shows you how to apply them. (*See installation instructions below.*)

IMPORTANT*: If at any time you see a warning message similar to the one below, click* ***No To All*** *to proceed with the installation.*

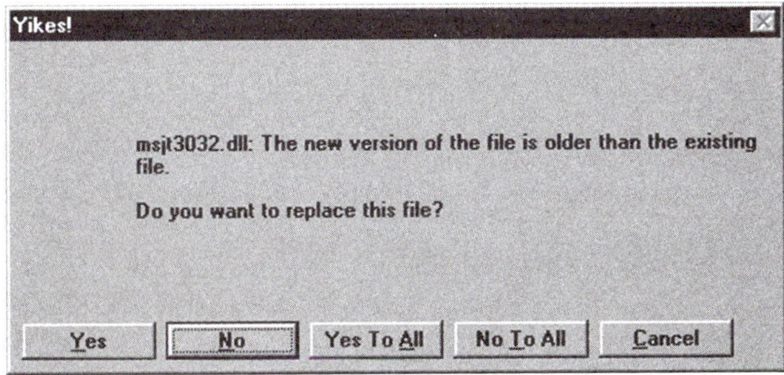

1. **To install from Windows 95:**

   Click Start on the desktop and click Run....

   OR

   To install from Windows NT:

   Go to Program Manager in Main, click File.
2. In the Run window, begin program installation by typing:

   CD-ROM drive letter:\NETCBT\SETUP
3. Click NEXT at the Setup Wizard screen.
4. At the following screen, click Next > to create a DDCPUB directory for storing program files. Then click YES to confirm the directory choice.
5. At the following screen, allow the default folder to be named ***DDC Publishing***, and click Next >.
6. At the next screen, choose one of the following options based on your individual system needs:

   NOTE: A ***Typical*** *installation is standard for most individual installation.*

   - **TYPICAL:** installs a minimum number of files to the hard drive with the majority of files remaining on the CD-ROM.

     NOTE: With this installation, the CD must remain in the CD-ROM drive when running the program.
   - **CUSTOM:** installs only those files that you choose to the hard drive. This is generally only recommended for advanced users of Innovus Multimedia software.
   - **SERVER:** installs the programs on a network server.
7. Click Next > to begin copying the necessary files to your system.
8. Click OK at the Set Up status Window and then click YES to restart Windows.

To launch the program, place the CD in the CD-ROM drive, click Start on the Windows 95 desktop, select **Programs**, **DDC Publishing**, and then select **NETCBT**.

Lesson 8: Creating a Company Web Page

Exercise	Filename	Data File	Solution File
1	Verity	--	S01Verit.html
2	Verity	--	S02Verit.html
3	Verity	--	S03Verit.html
			S03Web.html
4	Menu	04Menu.doc	S04Menu.html
5	Verity	--	S05Verit.html
	Menu	--	S05Menu.html
	Calendar	05Calend.html	S05Calen.html
6	Verity	--	S06Verit.html
	Menu	--	S06Menu.html
	Calendar	--	S06Calen.html
7	Info	--	S07Info.html
	Verity	--	S07Verit.html
8	Info	--	S08Info.html
9	Feedback	--	S09Fdbck.html
10	Verity	--	S10Verit.html
	Feedback	--	S10Fdbck.html
		Book1.wmf	Book1.wmf
		Books1.wmf	Books1.wmf
11	Verity	--	S11Verit.html
		Burstani.gif	Burstani.gif
12	Verity	--	S12Verit.html
		Count.avi	Count.avi
		Melorise.wav	Melorise.wav

Understanding the Internet

Basics

The Internet – What is it?

The Internet is a world-wide network that connects several thousands of businesses, schools, research foundations, individuals, and other networks. Anyone with access can log on, communicate via e-mail, and search for various types of information.

Internet History

The Internet began in 1969 as ARPAnet, a project developed by the US Department of Defense. Its initial purpose was to enable researchers and military personnel to communicate in the event of an emergency.

How to Access the Internet

Most people access the Internet by using a modem, communication software, and a standard phone line to dial in. Direct access is also available through most colleges and universities and through some large organizations and corporations.

If you plan to use a dial in connection to the Internet you will need to sign up with a public or private Internet Service Provider, or an online Service such as America Online, CompuServe, or Delphi. For a certain fee, such services generally provide you with a Web browser, an e-mail account, a pre-determined number of hours for Internet access time (or unlimited access at a higher fee), and various other features.

Common Uses of the Internet

- Communicate world-wide via e-mail.
- Use the World Wide Web to order products, read reviews, obtain stock quote information, make travel arrangements, do research for work or school projects, etc.
- FTP to a computer site to download or upload shareware items (software, fonts, games, etc.).
- Access a Search Engine to help you find Internet Sites on news articles that relate to a particular topic, subject, or product you need information about.

Internet Terms

The following is a list of basic terms that will help you start to understand the Internet. Please refer to the detailed glossary in the back of the book for those terms not covered below.

World Wide Web (WWW)
The WWW is a user-friendly system for finding information on the Internet through the use of hypertext and hypermedia linking.

Hyper links
On the Web, some words or graphics appear in a different **color**, are <u>underlined</u>, or **<u>both</u>**. This distinction indicates that the item is a link to another Web page or another Web site. Clicking your mouse on one of these links takes you to a new page with related information.

Home Page
All Web sites begin with a Home Page. A Home Page is like a table of contents. It usually outlines what a particular site has to offer and contains links that can connect you to other Web sites.

Network
Networks are groups of computers or other devices that are connected in such a way that they are able to share files and resources. The Internet is a global network of networks.

Browsers
Web browsers are graphic interface programs that provide simple techniques for viewing and searching the WWW. Browsers work in conjunction with the connection you establish to the Internet via your Internet service provider. The browser programs referred to in this book are Netscape Navigator and Microsoft Internet Explorer.

URL (Uniform Resource Locators)
A URL is a WWW address. It is a locator that enables the WWW system to search for linked sites.

E-Mail (Electronic Mail)
By far the most popular feature on the Internet, e-mail is a communication system for exchanging messages and attached files. E-mail can be sent to anyone in the world as long as both parties have access to the Internet and an Internet address to identify themselves.

Search Engines
Software programs that "surf" through the Internet for a given topic of information, catalog the results, and display descriptions of the suggested sites. Examples of search engines are Yahoo and AltaVista.

Internet Service Provider (ISP)
Companies that provide a dial-up connection to the Internet as well as other Internet services.

✓ *America Online, Prodigy, and CompuServe are online services that also provide access to the Internet.*

FTP (File Transfer Protocol)
File transfer Protocol is an Internet protocol that enables one computer to transfer files to another. An FTP site is a host computer that commonly contains executable application files, as well as documents, images, and multimedia files. An Internet Web browser will allow you to log into most FTP sites.

Many FTP sites are maintained by universities. Some are operated by companies that distribute their software (Netscape and Microsoft both maintain FTP sites). Not every software title is on the Internet, but three types are commonly available for download: freeware, shareware, and beta releases.

Viruses – Caution!
The Internet is a breeding ground for viruses (see *Appendix B*). Computer viruses are nasty little commands or programs hidden in executable program files. Some viruses won't cause any damage, but those that do can cause a loss of data and time.

Internet Cautions

ACCURACY: Be cautious not to believe everything on the Internet. Almost anyone can publish information on the Internet, and since there is no Internet editor or monitor, some information may be false. All information found on the World Wide Web should be checked for accuracy through additional reputable sources.

SECURITY: When sending information over the Internet, be prepared to let the world have access to it. Computer hackers can find ways to access anything that you send to anyone over the Internet, including e-mail. Be cautious when sending confidential information to anyone.

VIRUSES: These small, usually destructive computer programs hide inside of innocent-looking programs. Once a virus is executed, it attaches itself to other programs. When triggered, often by the occurrence of a date or time on the computer's internal clock/calendar, it executes a nuisance or damaging function, such as displaying a message on your screen, corrupting your files, or reformatting your hard disk.

Lesson 1:
Microsoft Internet Explorer

Exercise 1

- The Active Desktop in Internet Explorer 4.0
- Install the Windows Desktop Update
- Customize The Active Desktop
- The Internet Explorer Channel Bar
- Restore the Active Desktop

Exercise 2

- Start Internet Explorer 4
- Internet Explorer Screen
- Get Help
- Exit Internet Explorer

Exercise 3

- Standard Toolbar Buttons
- Open a World Wide Web Site from the Address Bar
- Open a World Wide Web Site Using the File Open Dialog Box
- Back and Forward
- Stop a Search
- Return to Your Home Page

Exercise 4

- Internet Explorer Main Search Page
- AutoSearch from Address Bar

Exercise 5

- Open and Add to the Favorites Folder
- Open Web Sites from the Favorites Folder
- Delete Favorites
- Create New Folders in the Favorites Folder
- Move Favorites from Folder to Folder
- File Favorites
- Edit Favorites

Exercise 1

- The Active Desktop in Internet Explorer 4.0
- Install the Windows Desktop Update
- Customize The Active Desktop
- The Internet Explorer Channel Bar
- Restore the Active Desktop

NOTES

The Active Desktop in Internet Explorer 4.0

- **Internet Explorer 4** is more than an updated browser. It contains the Active Desktop, which lets you customize your Windows 95 desktop to take advantage of constantly changing Internet content and the convenience of Web navigation tools, such as single-click links and Back and Forward buttons. When you install Explorer 4, you have the option of installing the Windows Desktop Update, which contains the Active Desktop feature.

  ✓ *The exercises in this book assume that you have installed the Windows Desktop Update.*

- The **Active Desktop** significantly alters the way you access the Internet and can change some of the ways you are used to working in the Windows 95 environment. For instance, you can access a Web page directly from the Start menu. Or, set your desktop to display in Web style, with single-click links to files, folders, and programs. You will learn more about customizing the Active Desktop in this exercise. Illustrated on the following page is an example of how the desktop looks when displayed in Web style.

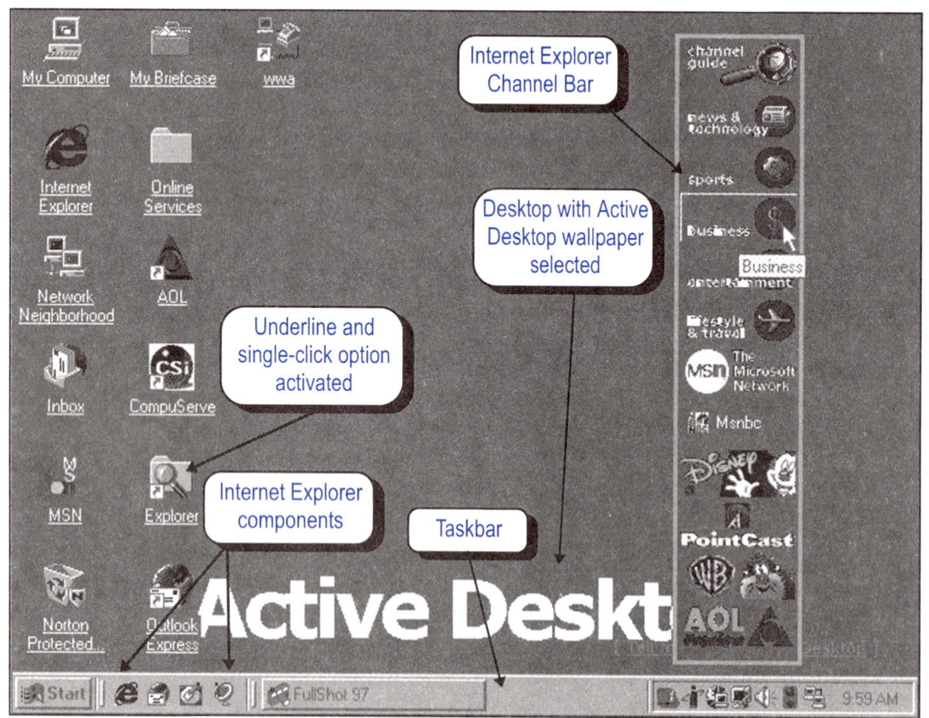

NOTE

Internet Explorer is not just an Internet browser, it's an Active Desktop that integrates Windows and the Internet. If you install the Active Desktop component, you will notice changes to your Windows 95 desktop and Windows Explorer. This lesson will touch briefly on how the Active Desktop functions.

Install the Windows Desktop Update

- You must have the **Windows Desktop Update** installed in order to use the Active Desktop. To determine if the Windows Desktop Update has been installed, first open the Control Panel and double-click on Add/Remove Programs. Select Microsoft Internet Explorer 4.0 then click Add/Remove. The Internet Explorer 4.0 Active Setup dialog box opens. If you see the message **Add Windows Desktop Update from Web site**, select it and continue to install it. If you *do not* see this option, then the Windows Desktop Update is already installed. Click **Cancel** and close all open windows to return to the desktop.

  CAUTION: *Be sure that you do not select the option to uninstall Internet Explorer 4.0.*

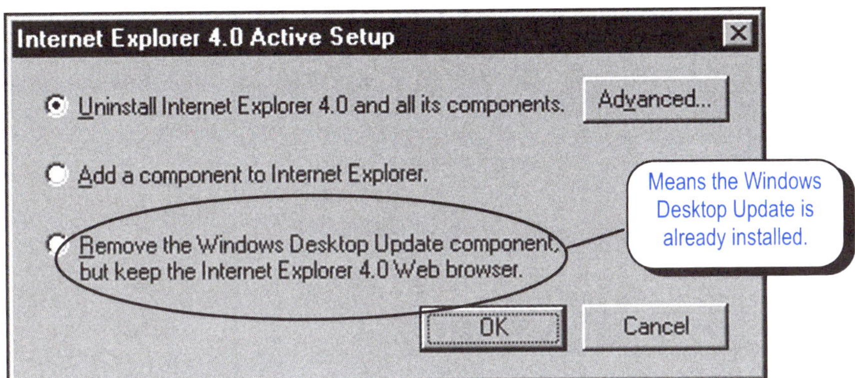

Customize The Active Desktop

- When the Windows Desktop Update is installed, you can set the Active Desktop to display folders and programs in Web style format or in classic Windows 95 style format.

Web Style

- If you select the Web style format, all folders, shortcuts, documents, etc. will respond to a single-click. Note the illustration below of the Control Panel window with the Web style feature activated.

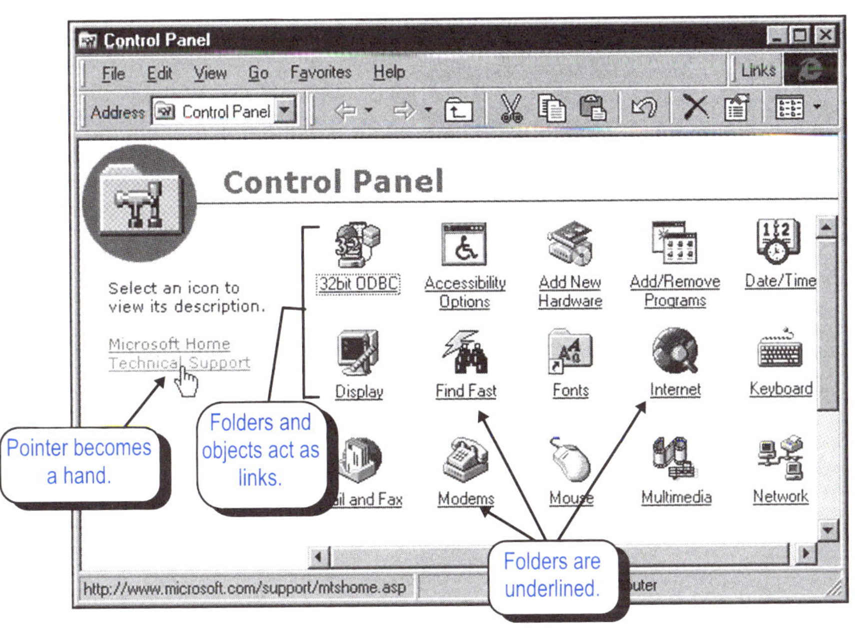

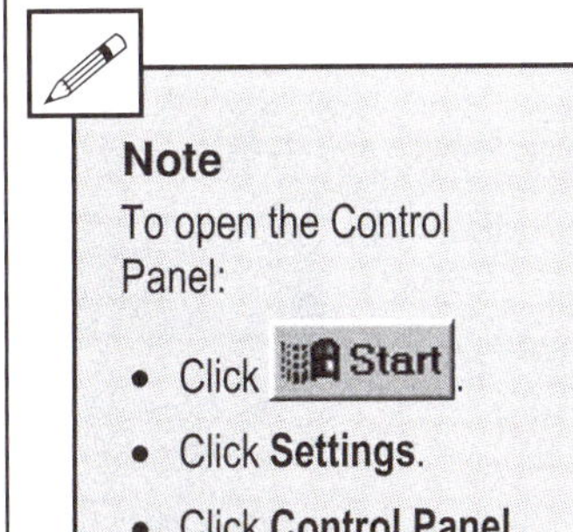

Note

To open the Control Panel:

- Click **Start**.
- Click **Settings**.
- Click **Control Panel**.

Note

The single-click option can be distracting for many users. Though you might be accustomed to using the single-click option when you are working online. You might not like it when you are working in other applications (Word, Excel, PowerPoint, etc.). You can disable this feature by doing the following:

- Click **Start**.
- Select **Settings**.
- Click **Folder Options**.
- Click **Custom, based on setting you choose**.
- Click **Settings**.
- Click **Double-click to open an item (single-click to select)**.
- Click **OK** and then click **Apply** to return to desktop.

- To turn on the Active Desktop's Web style, click **Start** on the taskbar and select Settings, Folders & Icons or Folder Options.

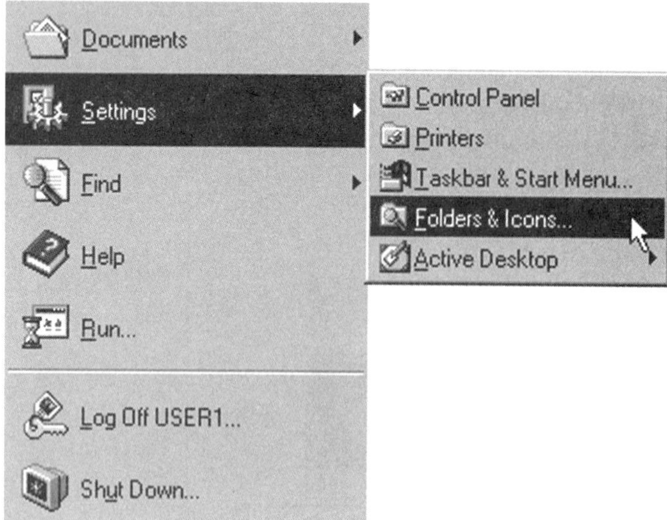

- In the Folder Options dialog box that follows, select Web style and click OK.

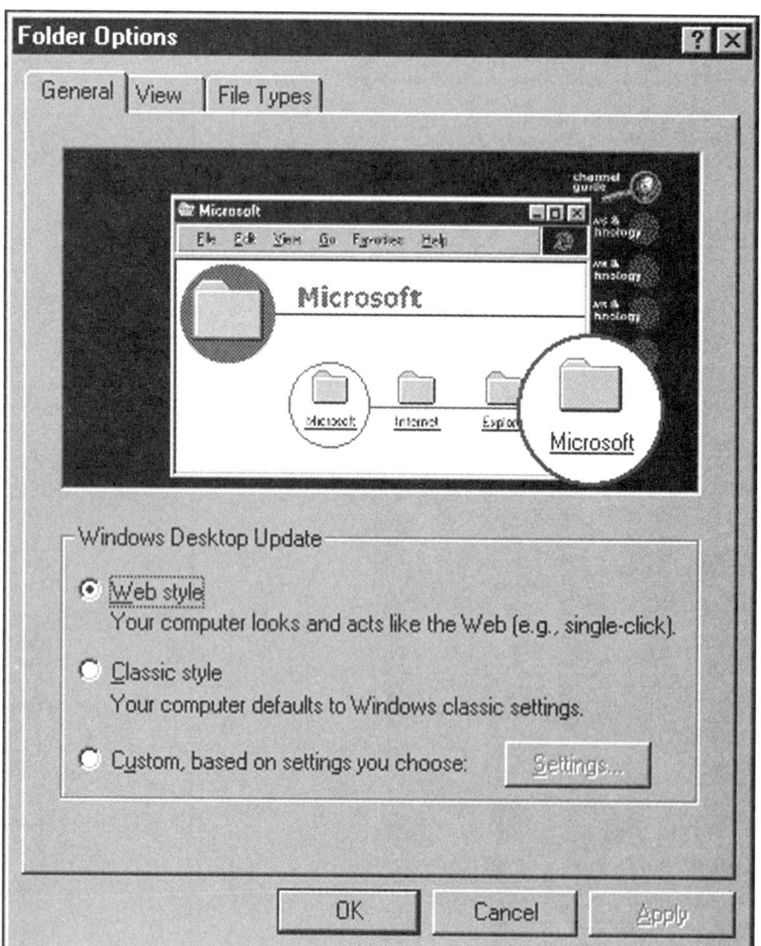

✓ *The exercises in this book assume that you have selected the Web style option as illustrated above.*

- If you are using the Web style feature for your Active Desktop, you can use any Web (HTML) page as your desktop background. To apply the default HTML wallpaper installed with Internet Explorer 4, right-click on the Windows 95 desktop, click Active Desktop, then Customize my Desktop.

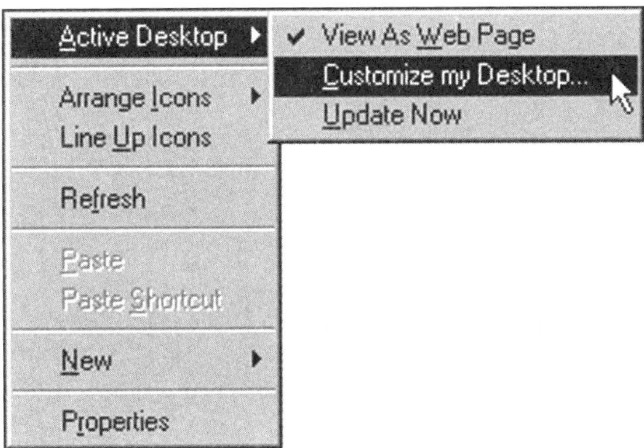

- In the Display Properties dialog box that follows, click the Background tab and select wallpapr from the list box (it is probably at the end of the list of available wallpapers).

✓ *This Property dialog box may be familiar to you if you have made changes to backgrounds (wallpaper), set screen savers, or made other adjustments to the appearance of your desktop.*

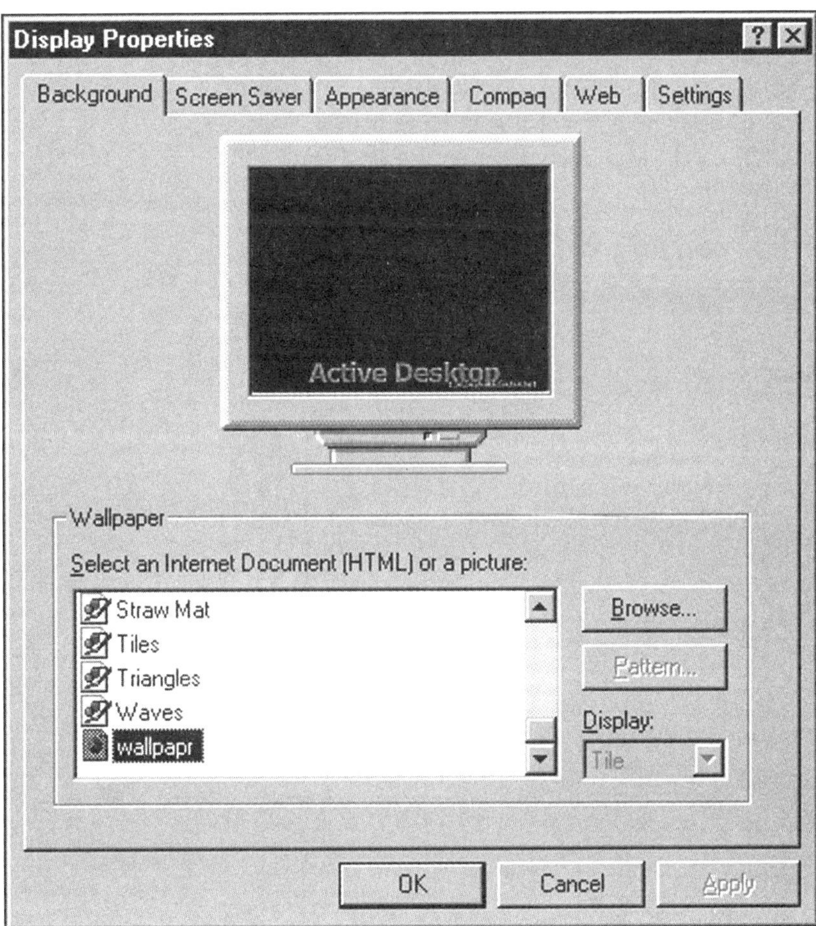

Classic Windows 95 Style

- If you prefer the traditional look and feel of Windows 95 to the new Web style format, you can select the Classic style option in the Folder Options dialog box to apply it to your desktop and folders. Note the illustration below of the Control Panel window as it looks when Classic style selected.

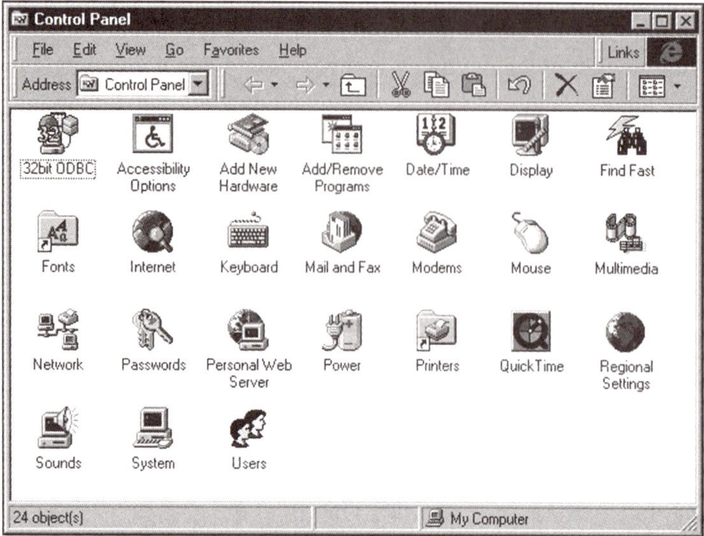

- Note, however, that even when you select the Classic style for your desktop, certain changes will still be apparent if you have installed the Active Desktop with Internet Explorer 4. Notice the differences in the menu structure and toolbars before and after installing the Active Desktop as illustrated below. These changes affect the Windows Explorer, Control Panel, Recycle Bin, and My Computer windows. You will also find differences in your Start menu.

Windows Explorer before installing Explorer 4

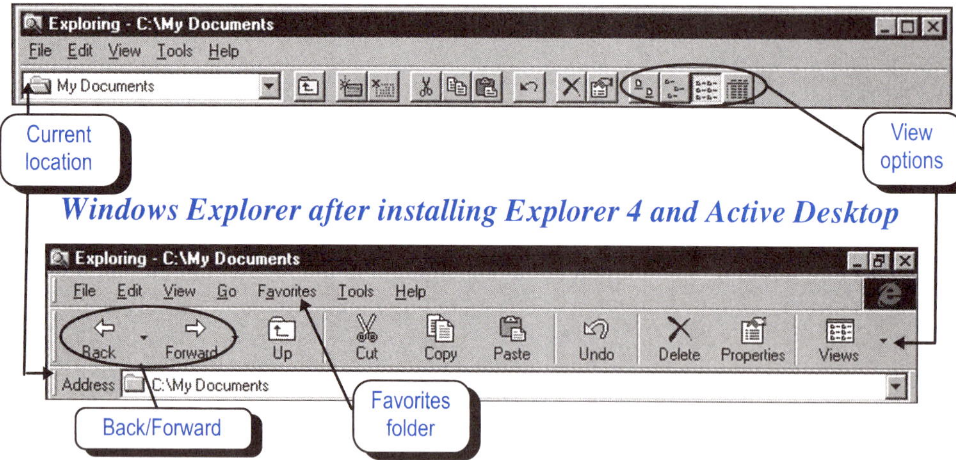

✓ *This illustrates changes that occur after installing Explorer 4 and the Active Desktop and setting the Folders option set to Classic. (The Web style feature has been deselected.)*

- The following changes occur in the Windows Explorer, Control Panel, My Computer, and Recycle Bin folders if you install the Active Desktop with Explorer 4:
- **Favorites** is added to the Menu bar. The Favorites folder is a place where you can store Web site addresses. Additional Internet options have also been added to some of the menus.
- **Go** is added to the Menu bar. The Go menu allows you to go directly from the current window to other applications or windows, such as your Internet Home page or search page, the Outlook Express mail program, your address book, or the My Computer window.
- The **Address bar** indicates the folder that is currently open.
- Move handles appear at the front of each toolbar and Menu bar.
- Additional toolbar buttons appear. **Back** and **Forward** can be used to navigate to and from folders and documents that you have accessed in the current session. These buttons will appear on the Internet Explorer toolbar as well.
- The View options are now on a drop-down menu accessed from the Views button on the toolbar.
- Four additional buttons are added to the taskbar:

Launches the **Internet Explorer browser**. An additional shortcut to launch Internet Explorer is on the desktop.

Launches **Outlook Express**, the e-mail portion of Explorer 4 *(see Lesson 4)*.

Click to toggle back and forth between the desktop and any window you may have open.

Click to view **channels** *(see page 8)*.

Combined Styles

- If you prefer, you can select a combination of some Web style and some Classic style features for your desktop. To do so, select the Custom option in the Folder Options dialog box and then click the Settings button.

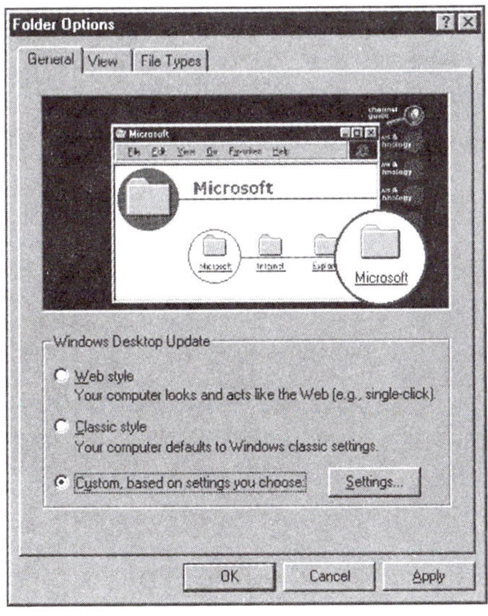

- In the Custom Settings dialog box that follows, select the desired features.

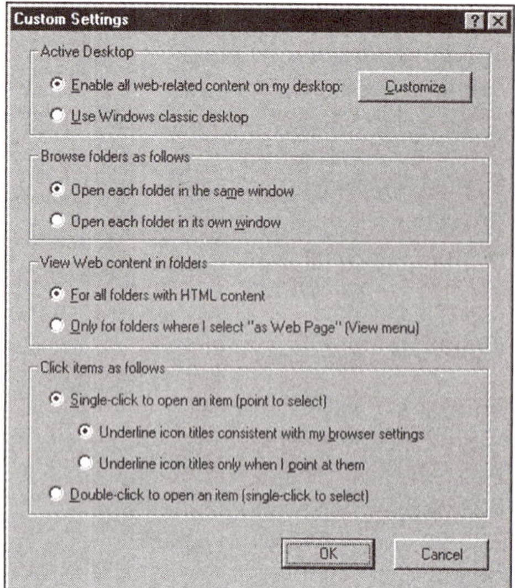

- For example, to combine single-click functionality with the Classic Windows 95 desktop, select the Use Windows classic desktop option and the Single-click to open an item option. Or, to activate the Web style desktop but retain the traditional double-click functionality, select Enable all web-related content on my desktop and Double-click to open an item.

The Internet Explorer Channel Bar

- One of the most noticeable features of the Active Desktop is **The Internet Explorer Channel bar**. It displays by default when you set the desktop to Web style. A **channel** is a Web site that can deliver content from the Internet directly to your computer. You can "subscribe" to a channel and customize how and when content is updated. All the Channels installed on your computer display on the Channel bar even if you haven't subscribed to them. You can also add channels to the Channel bar.
- If you want to use the Web style desktop but do not want the Channel bar displayed by default, you can turn it off. To do so, right-click on the desktop and select Active Desktop, then Customize my Desktop. In the Display Properties dialog box on top of the following page, click the Web tab and deselect the Internet Explorer Channel Bar check box.

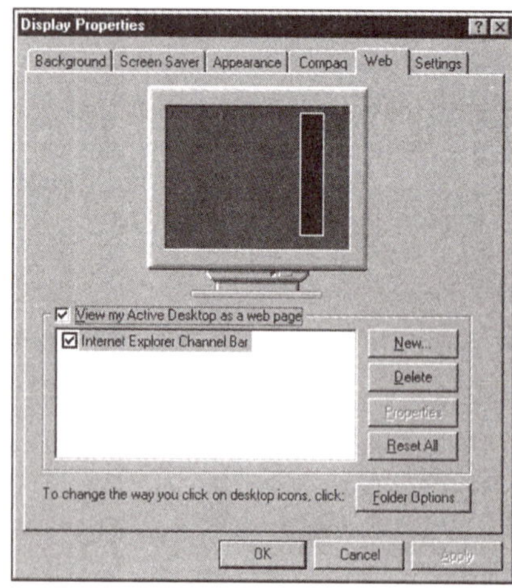

Restore the Active Desktop

- Occasionally, the Active Desktop will not function correctly and you may see the following screen.

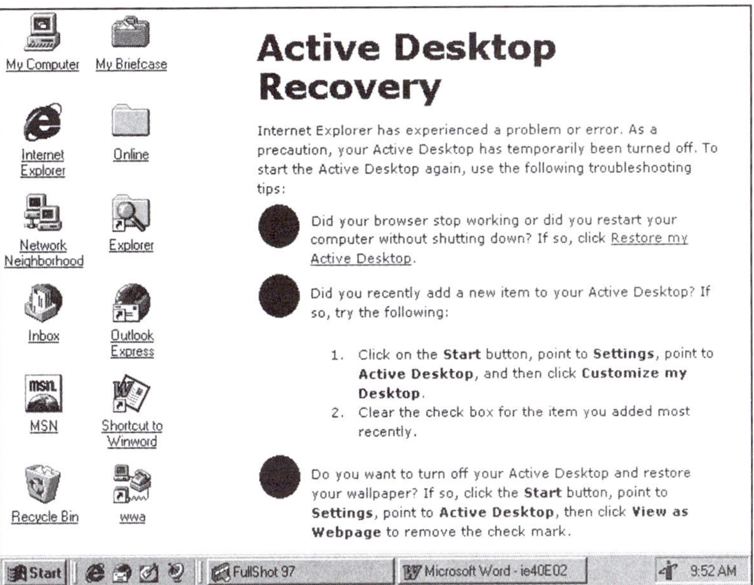

- Select the desired action and continue. If you choose to restore the Active Desktop, the following message will appear:

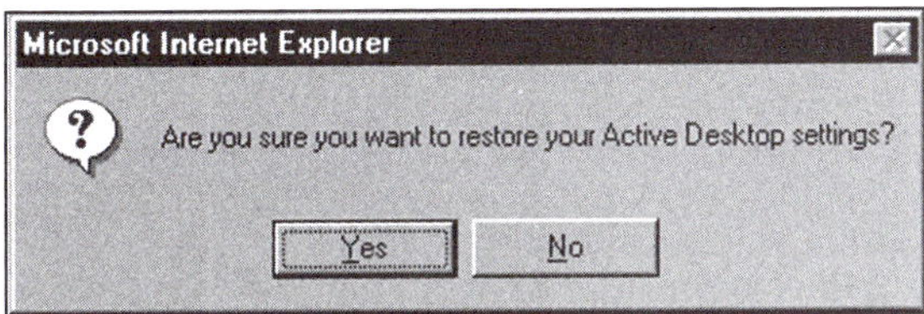

Click Yes to restore your Desktop settings. If the Active Desktop does not function correctly, you may have to adjust settings or remove recent additions to the desktop.

In this exercise, you will configure the Active Desktop, examine some of the ways that the Active Desktop changes the Windows 95 environment, and learn how to return to the Classic Windows 95 desktop.

✓ *This exercise assumes that you have done a standard installation of Internet Explorer 4.0, with the Windows Desktop Update (the Active Desktop) included and the Web style desktop selected.*

EXERCISE DIRECTIONS

1. Start Windows 95 and do the following:
   a. Click Start on the taskbar.
   b. Select Settings, Folders & Icons or Folder Options.
   c. Select Web style if it is not already selected and click OK.
2. Right-click on the Windows 95 desktop and select Properties. Click the Background tab and be sure that wallpapr is selected. Click OK. *(It is probably at the end of the list of available wallpapers.)*

   ➲ *Your desktop should now look like this illustration.*

3. Move the mouse pointer over the Internet Explorer icon on the desktop.

   ➲ *The pointer changes to a hand and a description of Explorer displays.*

   ✓ *If an explanation doesn't appear, move the pointer to an empty area on the desktop, click once, and then point to the Internet Explorer icon.*

4. Move the pointer over the My Computer folder and click once to open.

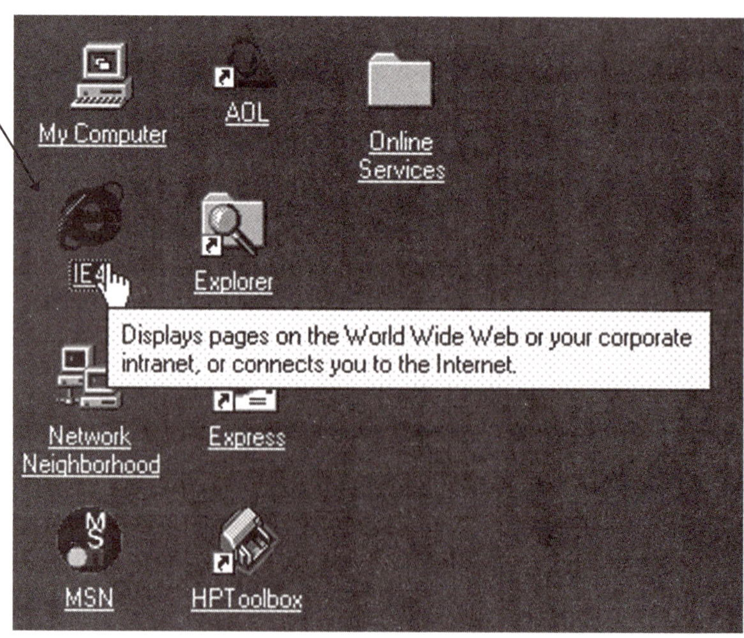

5. Point to, but do not click, on the **Printers** folder.
   ✓ *Note the description that displays on the left side of the window*

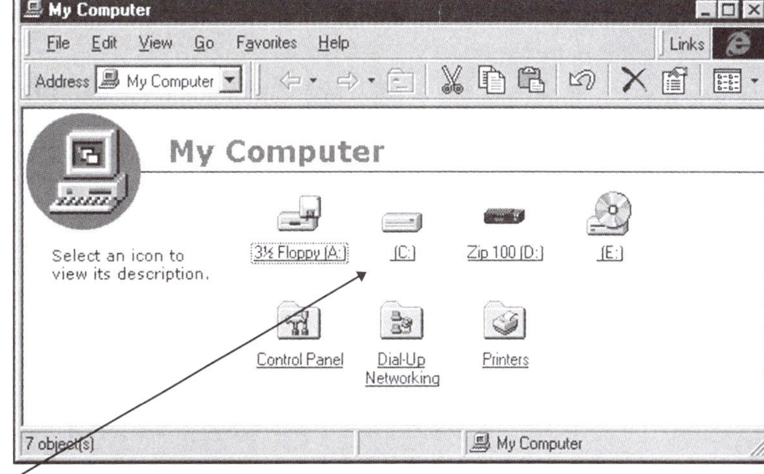

6. Point to, and click once on the **[C:]** drive icon.
   ✓ *Note the description that displays (in the illustration).*
7. Click View on the Menu bar.
8. Deselect as Web Page.
   ✓ *Note the change in the My Computer folder. Also, note that the toolbar and the Menu bar do not change.*
9. Click the arrow next to the Views button on the toolbar and select **as Web Page**.
   ✓ *You may need to maximize the My Computer window to display the Views button.*
10. Close My Computer and return to the Windows 95 desktop.
    ✓ *The rest of the exercises in this lesson assume that you are using the Active Desktop with the Web style option selected and single-click option activated. If you want to use the Classic setting, you will be able to complete all the exercises in this lesson, but you will often need to double-click when the directions indicate single-click.*

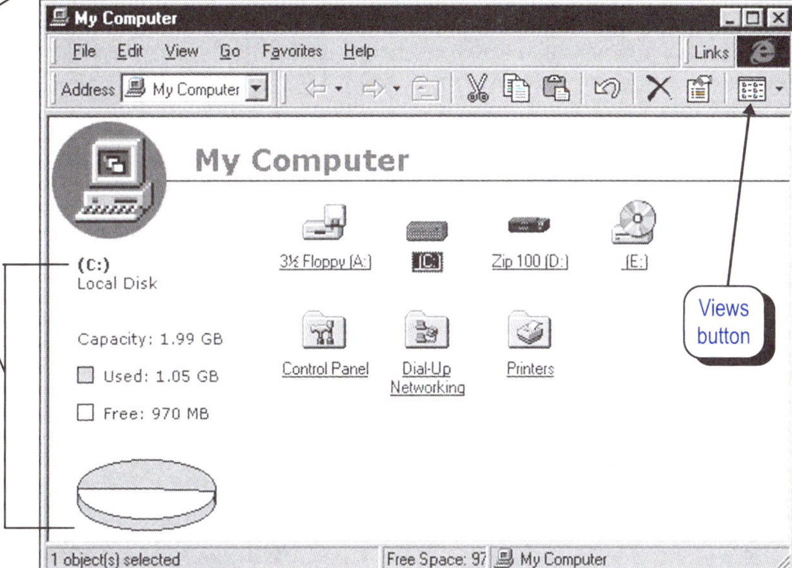

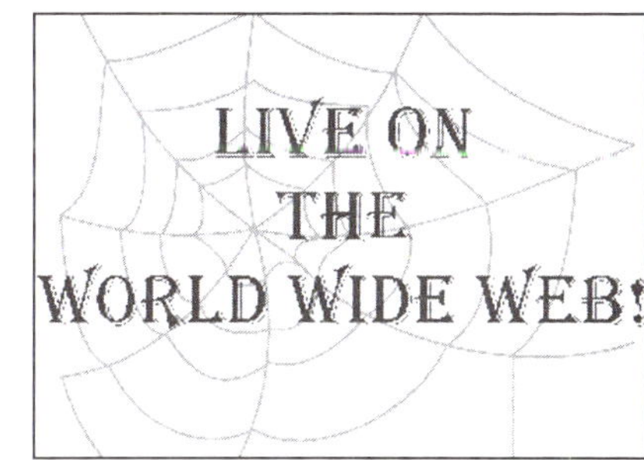

Internet Explorer Home Page
http://www.microsoft.com/ie

Microsoft Corporation Home Page
http://www.microsoft.com

Internet Computing Magazine
http://www.zdnet.com

Exercise 2

■ Start Internet Explorer 4 ■ Internet Explorer Screen ■ Get Help ■ Exit Internet Explorer

NOTES

Start Internet Explorer 4

- When you first install Internet Explorer, if you are using the Active Desktop, you may see the message illustrated below when you turn on your computer. If you are familiar with Explorer 3, you may want to select number 1 to take a tour of the new features in Explorer 4. Number 2 will provide information about Channels.

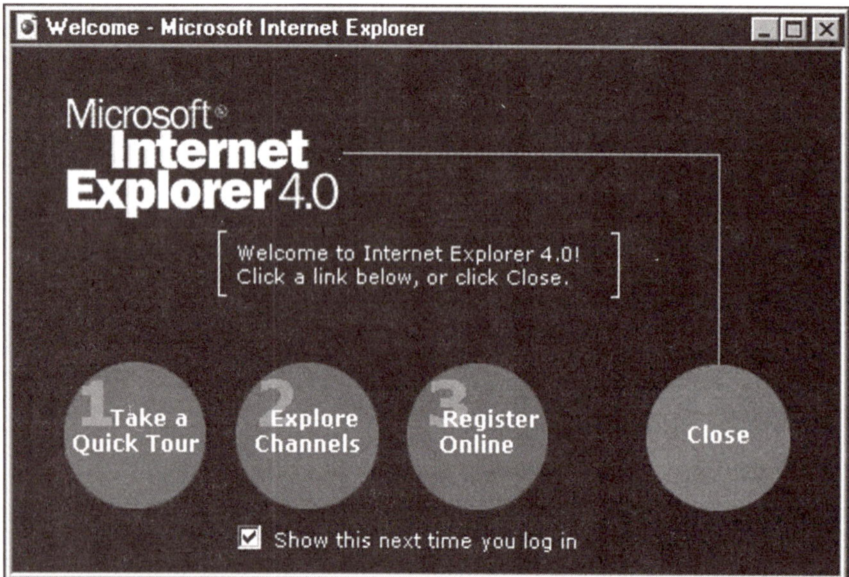

- To start Internet Explorer, do one of the following:
  - Click [Internet Explorer] on the Desktop.
  - Click [e] on the taskbar.
  - Click [Start], then select Programs, Internet Explorer, and click Internet Explorer.

✓ *Since there are so many variables involved in establishing a connection to the Internet, this book assumes that you have already established an Internet connection. If you are having trouble with an Internet connection, contact your Internet Service Provider, of if you are working on a Local Area Network, contact your network administrator.*

Internet Explorer Screen

- When you connect to the World Wide Web using Internet Explorer, the first screen that displays is the Home page. The term Home page can be misleading since the first page of any World Wide Web site is called a Home page. This first page is sometimes referred to as the Start page.
- You can change (customize) the first page that you see when you connect to the Internet.
- The Internet Explorer screen contains features that will be very helpful as you explore the Internet. Some of these features are constant and some change depending on the Web site visited or the task performed. Note the description of each screen part below and on the following pages.

  ✓ *Because Web pages are constantly changing, the page that you see when you are connected may be different from the one illustrated below.*

Parts of the Internet Explorer Screen

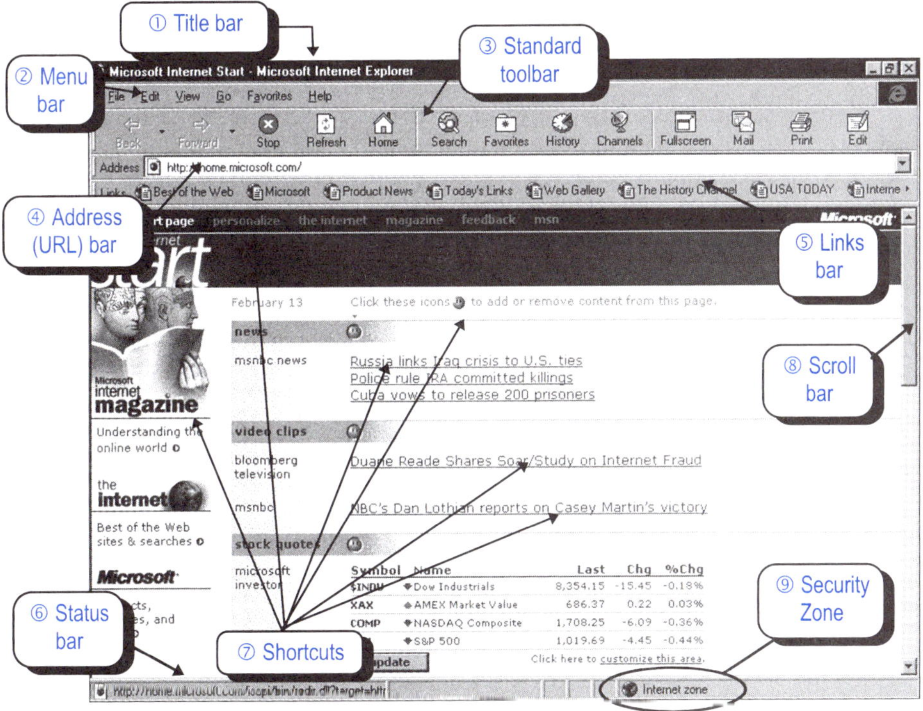

① Title bar Displays the name of the program (Internet Explorer) and the current Web page, in this case Microsoft's Internet Start page. You can minimize, restore, or close Explorer using the buttons on the right side of the Title bar.

② **Menu bar** Internet Explorer commands and dialog boxes can be accessed from the various menus listed on the Menu bar.

The Internet Explorer icon on the right side of the Menu bar rotates when action is occurring or information is being processed.

③ **Standard toolbar** Displays buttons for frequently performed tasks such as loading, moving between, and printing Web pages.

✓ *If the Standard toolbar does not display, select View from the Menu bar and click Toolbars, Standard Buttons.*

④ **Address (URL) bar** Displays the electronic address (URL) of the current Web page or the file path if the current document is located on your hard or external disk drive. You can click in the Address bar, type a new address and press Enter to go to the address location. You can also start a search from this line (see Exercise 4 in this lesson). If you click on the arrow at the right end of the address line, you will see the last 25 URLs and file paths that you have entered.

✓ *If the Address bar does not display, select View, Toolbars, Address Bar.*

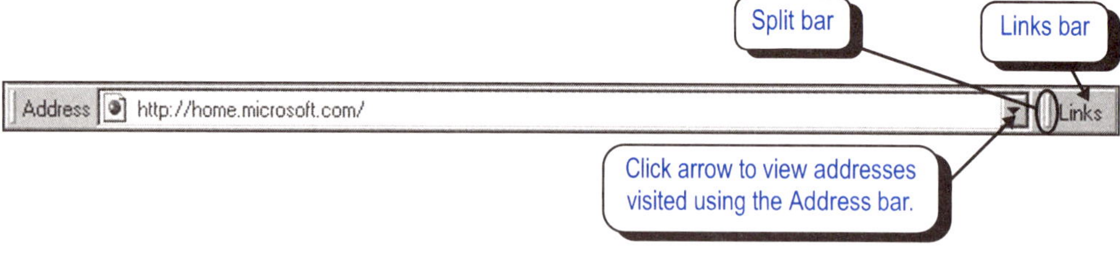

⑤ **Links bar** The Links bar, containing links to various Microsoft sites, is concealed on the right side of the Address bar.

✓ *If the Links bar does not display, select View, Toolbars, Links.*

Drag the split bar that separates the Links and Address bars to the left to display the contents of the Links bar on the Address bar as in the illustration on the following page.

Note

You can rearrange the Menu bar, Standard toolbar, Address bar, and Links bar as desired by clicking and dragging on a pull handle.

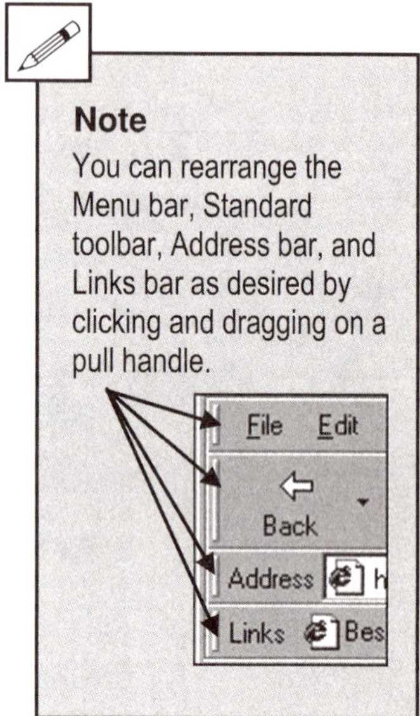

Drag the split bar down to display the contents of the Links bar directly below the Address bar, as in the illustration below.

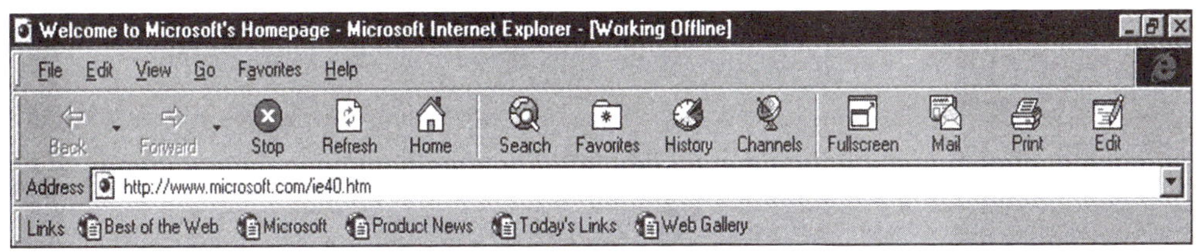

You can also double-click the Links button to display the current links on the Address bar. Double-click again to extend the Links bar further and hide the Address bar, as in the illustration below.

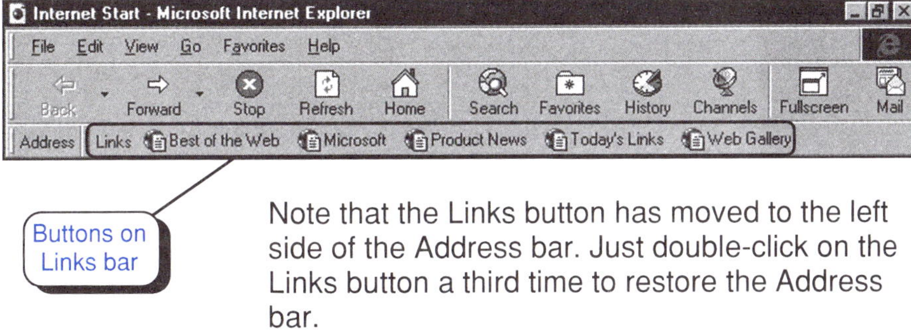

Note that the Links button has moved to the left side of the Address bar. Just double-click on the Links button a third time to restore the Address bar.

⑥ **Status bar** Displays the status of the current link or download. When you place the mouse pointer over a hyperlink, the Status bar displays the URL of the link.

✓ *If the Status bar does not display, select View, Status Bar.*

⑦ **Shortcuts** Click on shortcuts (also called hyperlinks) to move to other Web sites. Shortcuts are usually easy to recognize. They can be underlined text, text of different colors, "buttons" of various sizes and shapes, or graphics. An easy way to tell if you are pointing to a shortcut is by watching the mouse pointer as it moves over the page. When it changes to a hand 👆 you are on a shortcut.

When you point to a shortcut, the full name of the Web site will appear on the Status bar.

⑧ **Scroll bars** Click scroll arrows or drag scroll bars to move the screen view horizontally or vertically, as in all Windows applications.

⑨ **Security Zone** Displays the security zone for the current site. You can assign a Web site to one of four security zones, depending on how much you trust it to be free from viruses and other damaging content. The Internet Zone is the default. Internet Explorer applies a different level of security protection to each zone.

Get Help

- The Help menu offers a number of ways to get assistance with Internet Explorer, including online support from Microsoft.

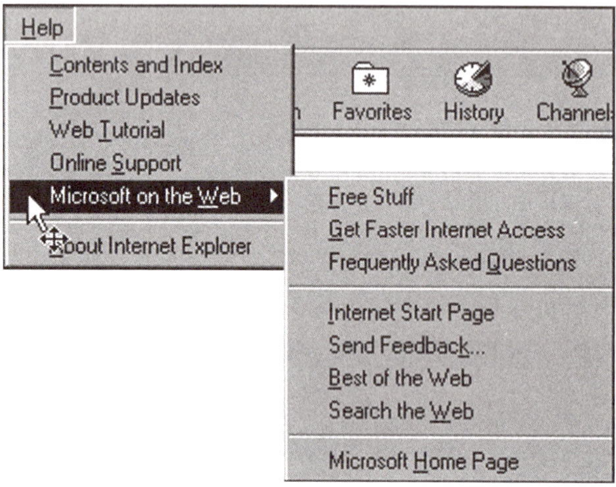

Contents & Index

- To open the Help Contents and Index feature, click Help on the Menu bar, then select Contents and Index. **Contents** offers an overview of Microsoft Internet Explorer and general information on how to use it effectively. Click on a book icon next to a topic to display a list of subtopics. Click a subtopic to display its contents in the right-hand panel of the Help window.

Click a book icon to display subtopics.

Click a subtopic to display its contents in right-hand panel.

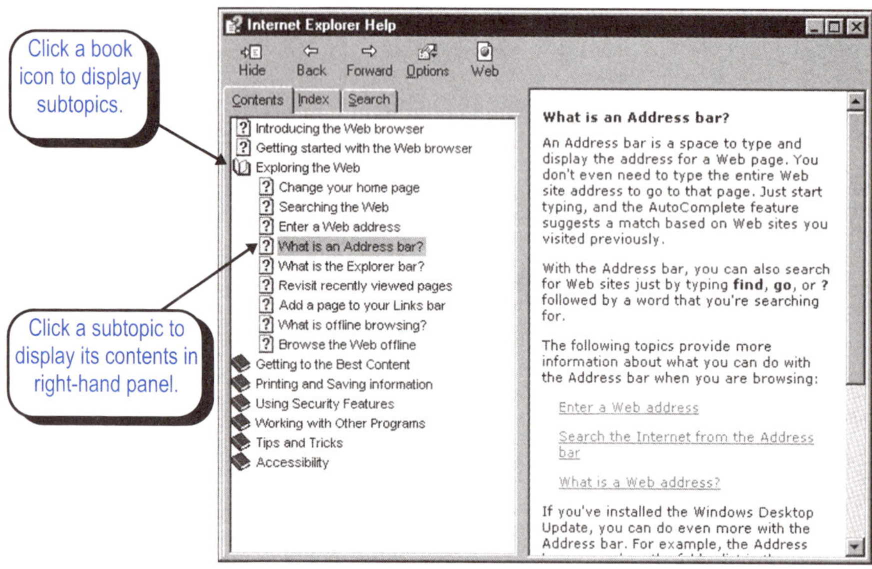

- The **Index** and **Search** features of Help let you look for information on specific functions and topics.
- When you click on the **Index** tab, a two-part dialog box appears. To find a desired topic by name, begin typing the first few letters of the topic in the text box. As you type, the list box in the left panel of the Help window displays index entries that match what you type. When a likely entry appears in the list, click it and then click the Display button at the bottom of the Help dialog box or simply double-click the entry.

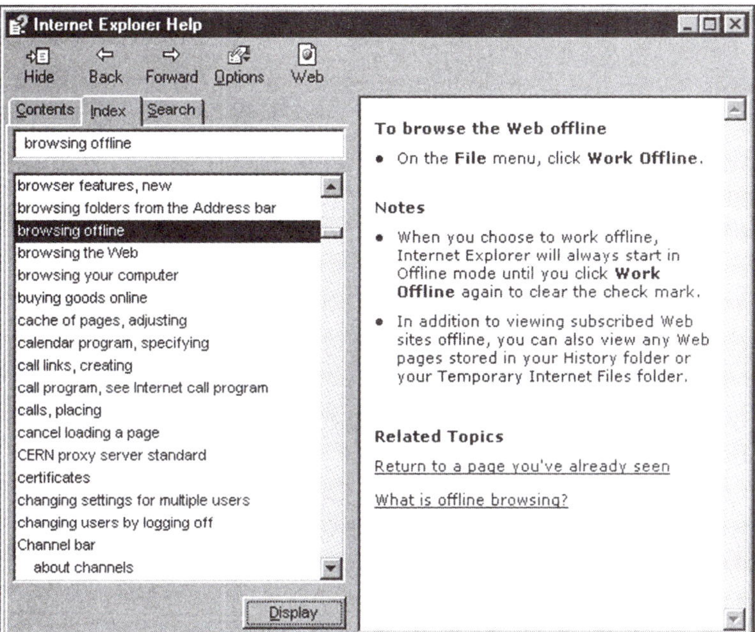

- To search for a topic by keyword, click the **Search** tab. Type in a word to find and then click List topics to view the available help topics that contain the keyword. Select a topic to view and click Display. Click the Close button (x) in the top right of the Help windows or press the Escape key to exit Help.

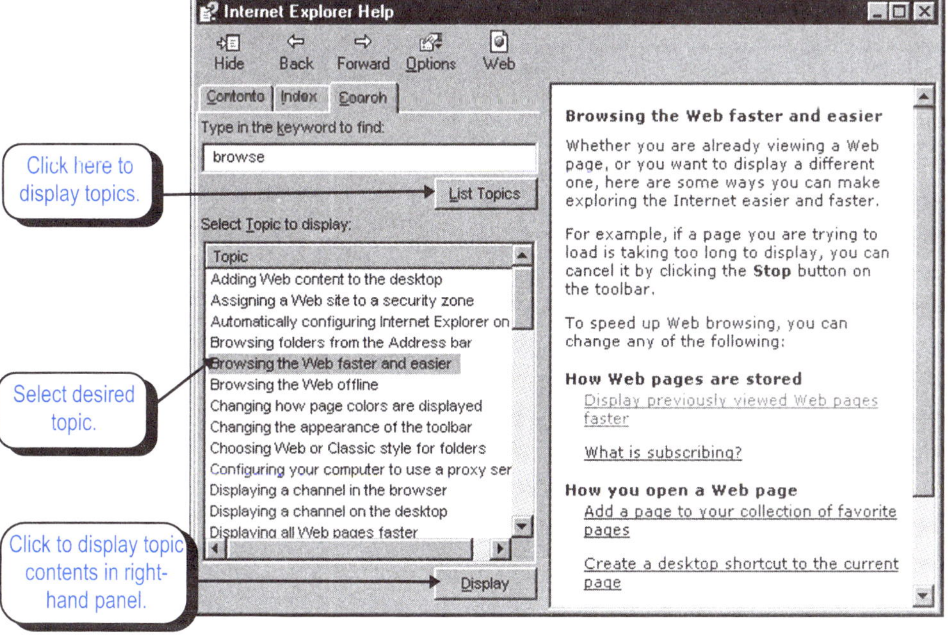

- The buttons on the Help toolbar in the Internet Explorer Help dialog box let you perform various actions to navigate the Help screens easily.

  - **Hide (Show)** conceals and reveals the list of help topics that appear in the left panel of the Help window.
  - Click **Back/Forward** to move among the Help topics you've opened in the current Help session.
  - Click **Options** to select from a drop-down menu of navigation options (Back, Forward, Stop, Refresh, Customize, and Print).
  - The **Web** button will give you information on the Internet Explorer Home User Web site and contains a link that will connect you directly to that site.

Exit Internet Explorer

- Exiting Internet Explorer and disconnecting from your service provider are two separate steps. It is important to remember that if you close Internet Explorer (or any other browser), you must also disconnect (or hang up) from your service provider. If you don't disconnect, you'll continue incurring charges.
- To exit Internet Explorer, click File, Close, or click the Program Close button (X) in the upper-right corner of the Explorer window.

In this exercise, you'll examine an Internet Explorer page and access the Help feature.

Note: *To ensure consistent results, this exercise uses simulated sites. The real URLs appear at the end of the exercise.*

Web Search

Search for answers to the following questions using the Web sites you will visit in the Web simulation exercise.

1. Name the five links under the Products & Services heading on the Microsoft home page.

 ____

2. Which of the items on the Edit menu appear to be active?

 ____

3. When you minimize Explorer, which icons remain on the desktop?

 ____

4. What are the three tab options available in the Internet Explorer Help dialog box?

 ____

EXERCISE DIRECTIONS

1. Launch the Internet simulation. From the Main Menu, select Lesson 1, then select Exercise 2.
2. Use the scroll bar or scroll arrows to move up and down the current Web page.
3. Point to the File menu and click once to open it.
4. Notice the options available on the File menu.
5. Move the mouse pointer over the other menus, click on each one, and note the options on each menu.
6. Look at the Title bar and make a note of the name of the current Web page.

 ✓ ***Microsoft Internet Explorer*** *will follow the name of the current page.*

7. Click the Minimize button to reduce Explorer to a button on the taskbar.
8. Notice a connected button on the taskbar that indicates that you are connected to the Internet. Click on this button to find out connection information.
9. Locate the minimized Web page on the taskbar and click to restore it.

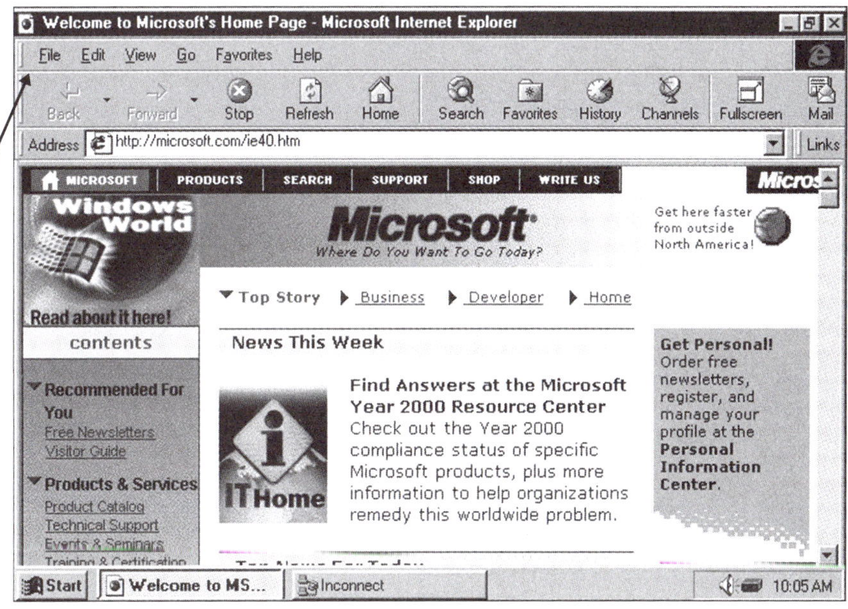

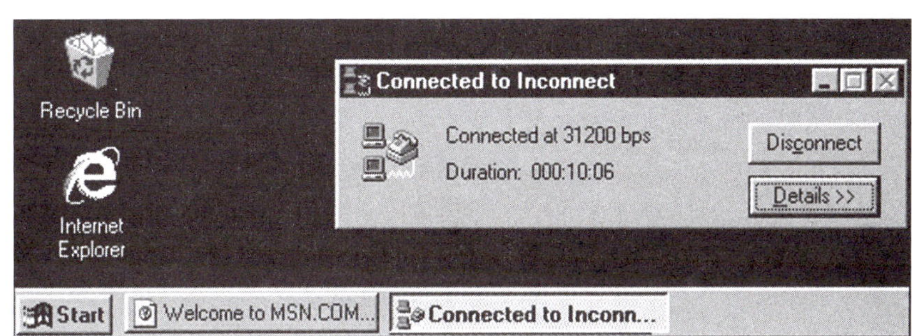

10. Click on the Help menu and do the following:
    a. Click Contents and Index.
    b. Click the Index tab.
    c. Click in the text box and type *start page* and click Display.
    d. Select **Changing your home page** in the Topics Found dialog box and click Display.
       ✓ *The steps required to change your start page appear on the right of the Explorer Help window.*
    e. Click the Hide button on the Help toolbar to conceal the list of topics.
    f. Click the Show button on the Help toolbar to reveal the Index tab and list of topics.
    g. Click the Back button on the Help toolbar to return to the previous Help topic.
    h. Click the Close button ☒ to return to Internet Explorer.
11. Click the Help menu again and select Web Tutorial.
12. Click the link TO PERSONAL COMPUTING.
13. Click Home on the Standard toolbar to return to your Home page.
14. Continue on to the next exercise

    OR

    Exit from the simulation.

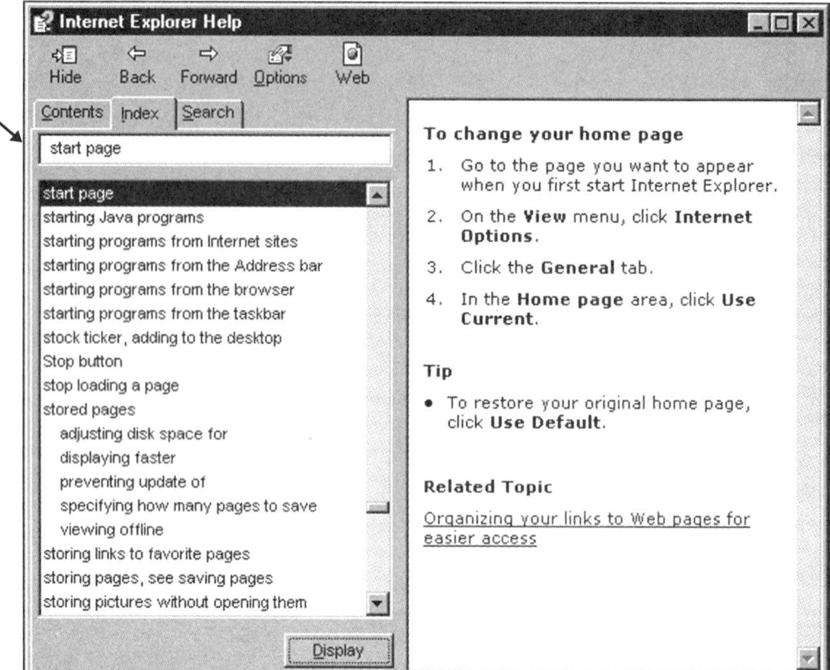

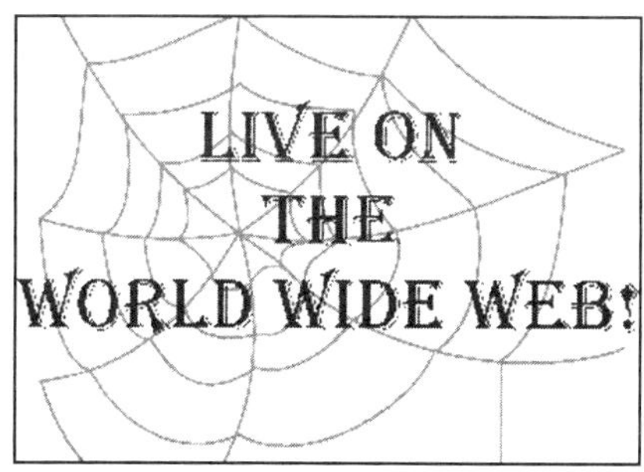

Microsoft Online Internet Magazine
http://home.microsoft.com/reading/default.asp

Internet Society's History of the Internet
http://www.isoc.org/internet-history/

The World Wide Web History Project
http://www.webhistory.org/home.html

Microsoft's Best of the Web
http://home.microsoft.com/exploring/exploring.asp

Exercise 3

- Standard Toolbar Buttons
- Open a World Wide Web Site from the Address Bar
- Open a World Wide Web Site Using the File Open Dialog Box
- Back and Forward ■ Stop a Search ■ Return to Your Home Page

NOTES

Standard Toolbar Buttons

- The **Internet Explorer Standard toolbar** displays buttons for frequently used commands. If the Standard toolbar is *not* visible when you start Explorer, open the View menu, select Toolbars, then select Standard Buttons. A description of each button's function follows below.

Moves you backward through previously viewed Web pages.

Moves you forward through previously viewed sites.

✓ *The Back and Forward buttons are available only if you have moved back and forth through multiple Web pages in the current Internet session.*

Interrupts the opening of a page that is taking too long to display.

✓ *Delays can be expected with pages that are filled with graphics, audio, or video clips.*

Reloads the current page.

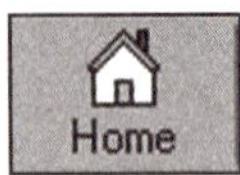

Returns you to your Home page.

Opens the Explorer bar, allowing you to select from a number of Search services with a variety of options. Click the Search button again to close the Explorer bar.

Opens the Explorer bar and displays the Web sites that you have stored using the features available on the Favorites menu. You will learn how to add to and organize Favorites in Exercise 5. Click the Favorites button again to close the Explorer bar.

Opens the Explorer bar and displays links to Web sites that you have visited in previous days and weeks. You can change the number days that sites are stored in your History folder. Click the History button again to close the Explorer bar.

Displays the list of current channels in the Explorer bar. Click again to close the Explorer bar.

Conceals the Menu bar, text titles, Status bar, and Address bar to utilize as much screen space as possible when viewing a Web site. Click the Fullscreen button again to restore the menu, titles, Status bar, and Address bar.

Displays a drop-down menu with various e-mail and news group options. You will learn about Outlook Express e-mail options in Lesson 4. (News groups will not be covered in this text.)

Sends a copy of the current page to your printer.

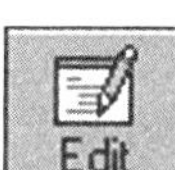

Opens a copy of the current page in the FrontPage Express program, where you can edit and save it to your hard drive. (FrontPage Express will not be covered in this text.)

Open a World Wide Web Site from the Address Bar

- Click in the Address bar and start typing the address of the Web site you want to open. If you have visited the site before, Internet Explorer's **AutoComplete** feature will try to guess the correct address and automatically finish entering it on the Address bar. If the suggested URL is the correct address, press Enter to go to it. If it is not the correct address, continue typing in the Address bar to overwrite it. To see other possible matches, click the down arrow to the right of the Address bar. If you find the address you want, click on it, and Explorer 4 will connect to it.

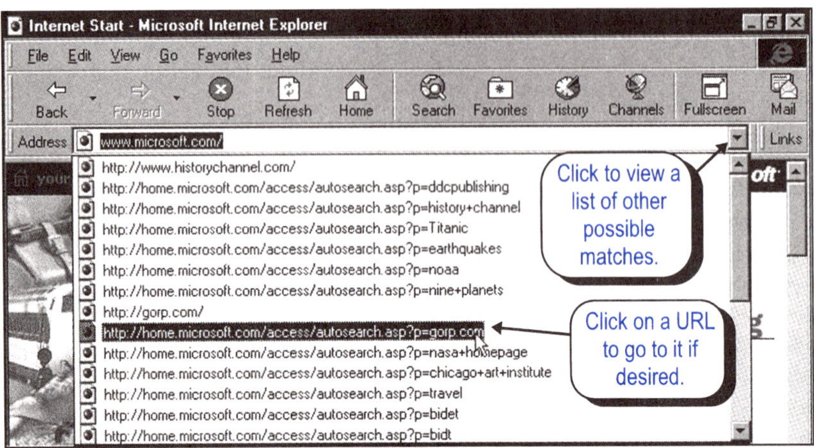

- If you prefer, you can turn off the AutoComplete feature. To do so, open the View menu, select Internet Options, and click the Advanced tab. Deselect the Use AutoComplete check box in the Browsing area of the dialog box.

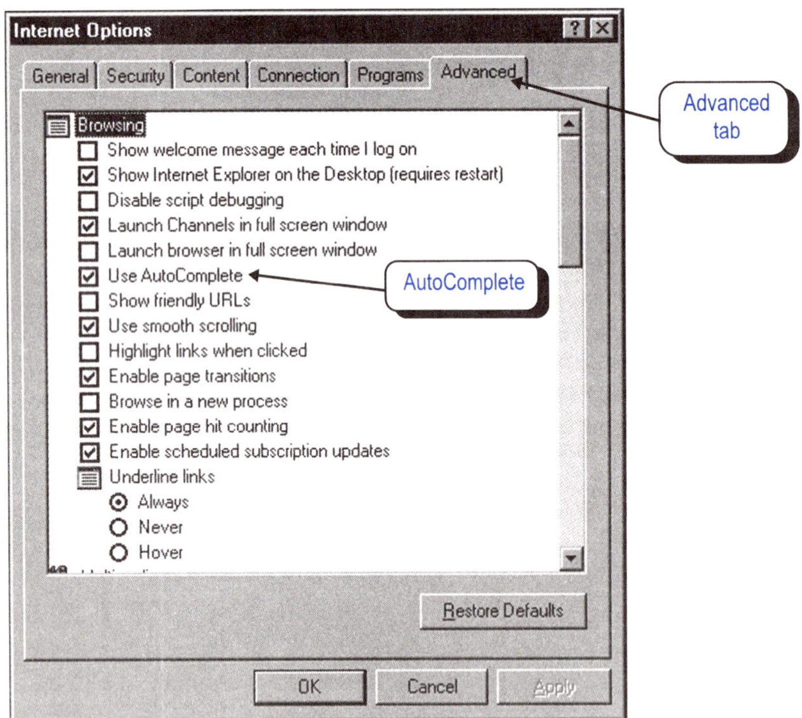

Note

You can also type in a file path in the Address bar to open a document located on your hard drive or floppy disk.

Note

You can set Internet Explorer to search for similar addresses automatically when it can't locate the one you entered. To select this option, do the following:

- Open **View**.
- Click **Internet Options**.
- Click **Advanced** tab.
- Scroll down and locate the **Searching** section.
- Select the desired options.

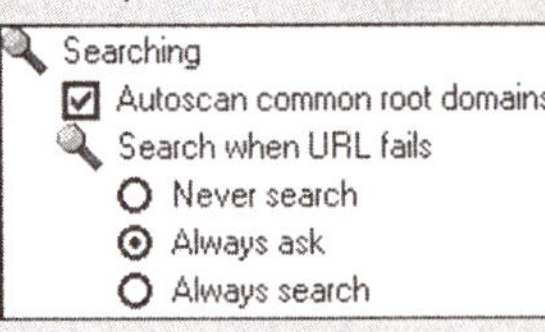

- Click **OK** to return to Internet Explorer.

Note

If you have a local file from your hard drive open in the Explorer window, the drop-down menu below the Address bar will list drives and folders on your hard drive, rather than recently visited URLs.

Open a World Wide Web Site Using the File Open Dialog Box

- Select File, Open, and start entering the exact address of the site you want to open. If AutoComplete is turned on and Explorer finds a potential match for the site, it will automatically display it on this line. If the match is the site that you want to open, press Enter to go there. If the match is not correct, continue typing the desired address to overwrite the suggested URL and then press Enter. If you want to see other possible matches, click the down arrow in the Open dialog box, select a different address, and then press Enter to go to the site.

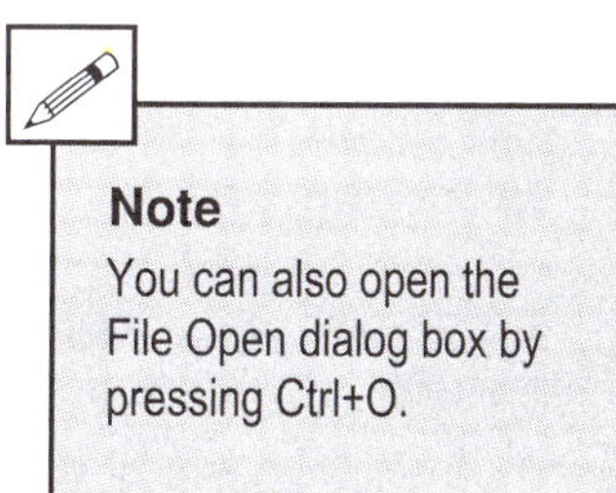

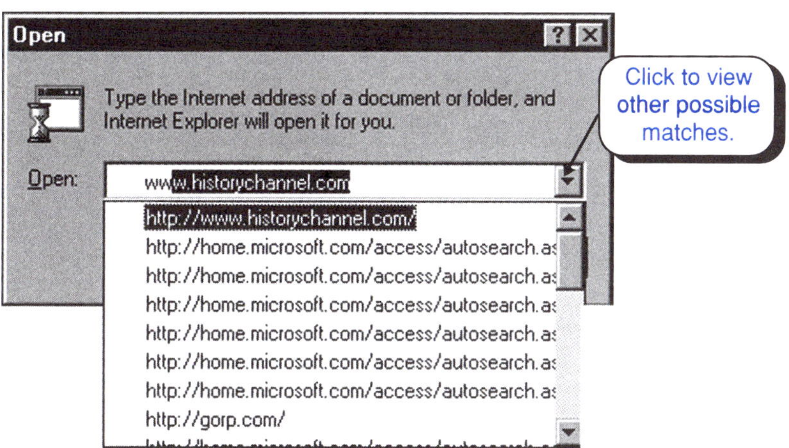

✓ *Other ways of opening Web sites will be explored in this lesson. Lesson 3 will explain in detail how to search for sites whose exact addresses you do not know.*

Back and Forward

- **Back** and **Forward** buttons are quick ways to return to sites that you have visited in the current session. If you have opened multiple sites and want to avoid clicking Back or Forward continuously to find a site, you can click the down arrow next to the Back or Forward button and select a link from the list.

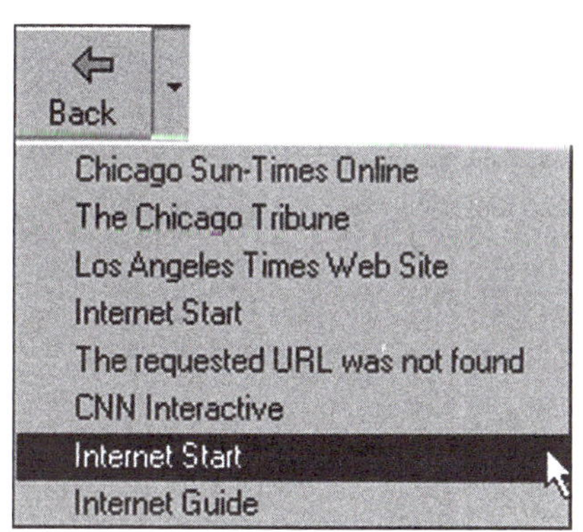

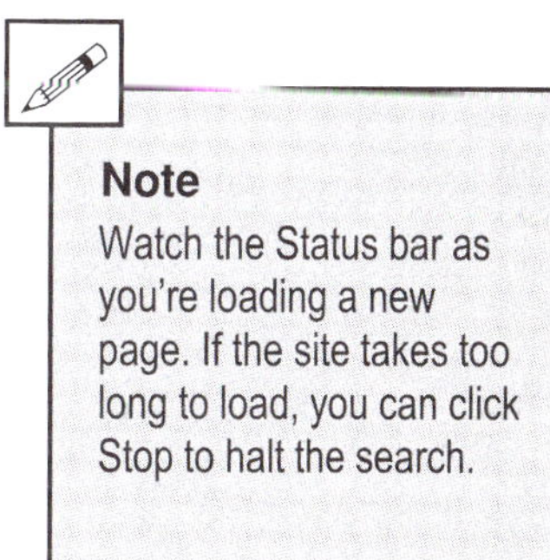

- When you first open Internet Explorer, the Back and Forward buttons will be dimmed since you have not yet opened any Web sites.

Stop a Search

- The length of time a Web page takes to open depends on the speed of your modem, the number of graphics on the page you are opening, and the speed of your computer. As you gain more experience exploring Web sites, you will develop a sense for download time and when a site is taking too long to open. If you want to interrupt the downloading of a page, click the **Stop** button Stop. Even if you stop a search, you may still be able to navigate the site if all the text has been downloaded.
- You will receive a variety of messages and signals as a Page downloads on your computer.
  - The Status bar Finding site: www.ddcpub.com will tell you what is currently happening.
  - Images will start to "appear" on screen.
  - Graphics placeholders will appear.
  - The status indicator on the left side of the Status bar will indicate how much of the page is downloaded.

Return to Your Home Page

- When you click the **Home** button Home on the Standard toolbar, you will return to your Home or Start page, the page that you see when you first start Internet Explorer. You can also return to your Home page by selecting Home Page on the Go menu.

In this exercise, you will use some of the navigational tools of Internet Explorer to open Web sites, interrupt searches, and get back to your Home Page.

Note: To ensure consistent results, this exercise uses simulated sites. The real URLs appear at the end of the exercise.

Web Search

Search for answers to the following questions using the Web sites you will visit in the Web simulation exercise.

1. After you enter an address in the Open dialog box, what three options are available?

 ____

2. When you click the down-arrow next to the Forward button, what options are available.

 ____

3. When you click the down-arrow at the end of the Address line, name the four addresses that appear.

 ____

EXERCISE DIRECTIONS

1. Launch the Internet simulation. From the Main Menu, select Lesson 1, then select Exercise 3.
2. Open the File menu and select Open.
3. On the Address line, type the following and press Enter: *http://www.si.edu*

 ➲ *The Smithsonian Institution Home page appears.*
4. Move your pointer over the page and note how it changes to a hand when it is over a hyperlink.
5. Find the link to Museums – Organizations and click once on it.

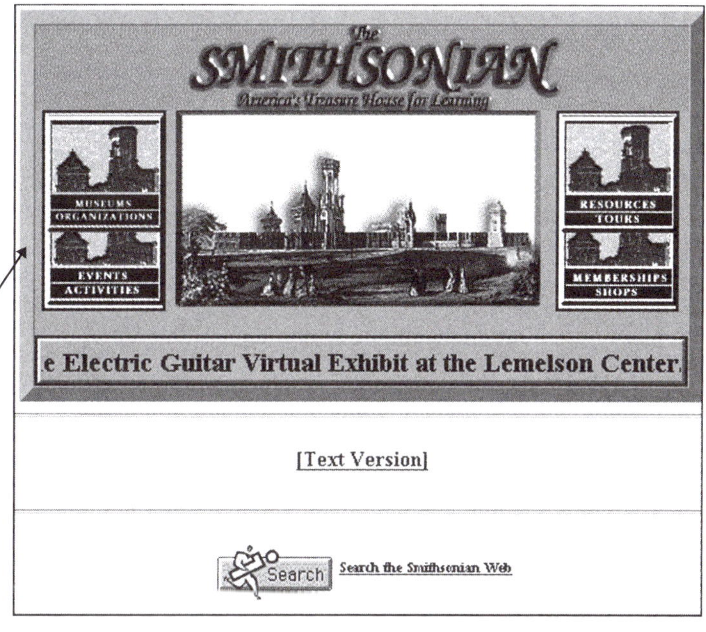

6. Scroll down and click the link to A Map of the Mall and do the following:

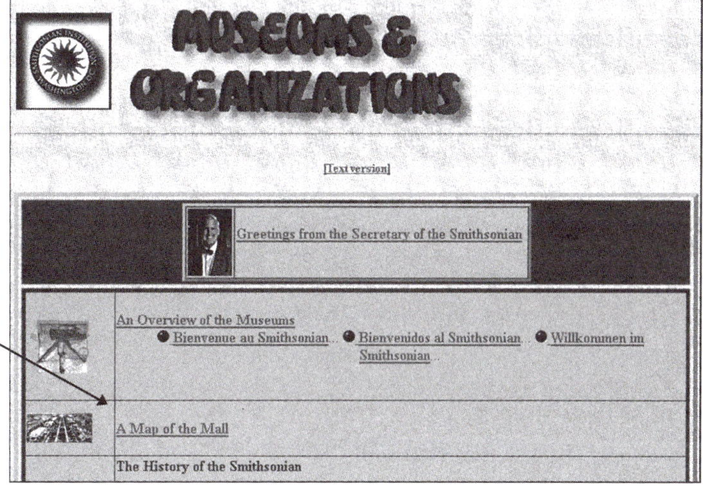

a. Scroll down and click on the <u>American History</u> building (illustrated at right).
b. Click the Back button once to return to the Map of the Mall.
c. Click the arrow next to the Back button and note the series of links that displays. Click **The Smithsonian Institution Home Page**.

➲ *The Forward button is no longer dimmed.*

d. Click the arrow next to the Forward button and click on **National Museum of American History**.

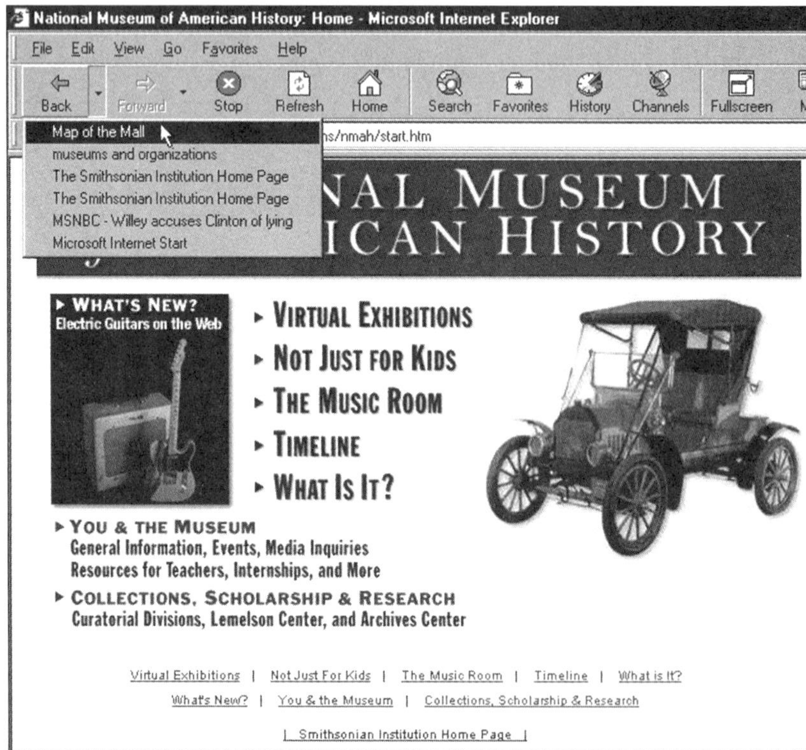

7. Click once in the Address bar. The entire address will automatically be highlighted. Start typing the following address: *www.si.edu.*

   ➲ *Explorer will suggest a possible match. Since you have just visited this site, the suggested address is correct.*

8. Click the down arrow at the end of the Address line to view the number of addresses that are possible matches.
9. Accept the *www.si.edu* address by pressing Enter.
10. Open the File menu, select Open and do the following:

    a. Type the following on the Address line and then press Enter: *http://www.noaa.gov.*
    b. Let the page start to load, but then click the Stop button before the page is fully downloaded.

    ✓ *Note the* ▣ *symbol that indicates a graphic.*

11. Click the Home button to return to your Start page.
12. Continue on to the next exercise

    OR

    Exit from the simulation.

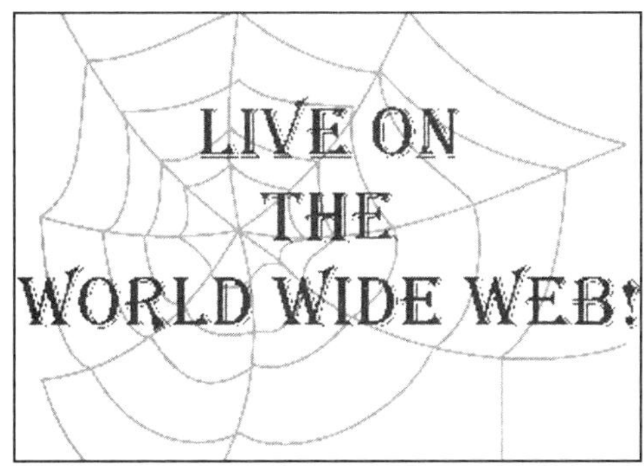

The Smithsonian Institution Home Page
http://www.si.edu

The History Net
http://www.thehistorynet.com

The History Place
http://www.historyplace.com

Hyper History Online
http://www.hyperhistory.com

Links to the Past
http://www.cr.nps.gov

Exercise 4

■ Internet Explorer Main Search Page
■ AutoSearch from Address Bar

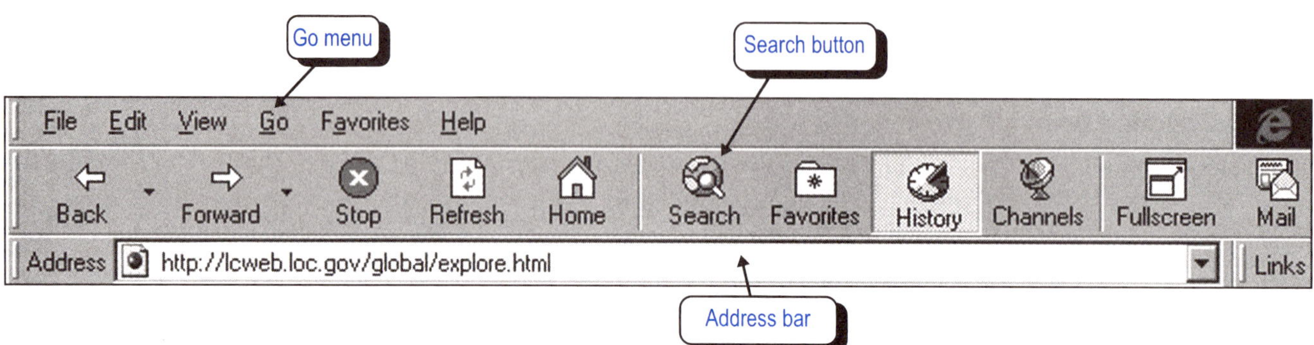

NOTES

Internet Explorer Main Search Page

- Explorer offers a variety of search options that you can access directly from the Standard toolbar. You may already be familiar with search providers, such as Yahoo!, Lycos, and AltaVista. These sites function a bit like a library, cataloguing, classifying, and organizing the information available on the Internet to make it accessible.
- To access the Internet Explorer search page, click the **Search** button [Search] on the Standard toolbar or click Search the Web on the Go menu. The Explorer bar will open on the left side of the screen, with a search provider automatically selected. Enter a search topic in the text box and click the appropriate button such as *Find, Seek, Go Get It, or Search*. The results of the search will display in the Explorer bar. Note the illustration on the next page.

  ✓ *Because Microsoft is constantly updating its Web sites, the search page that you see may differ from the one in the following illustration, and search procedures may vary.*

Note

Adjust the width of the Explorer bar by moving your pointer over the edge of the window between the Explorer bar and the Web page on the right side of the screen. When the pointer becomes a double-arrow, click and drag to the left or right.

Note

If you are using Microsoft Network, the main search page for Microsoft will open when you select Search the Web from the Go menu. Contact Microsoft if you want to change this.

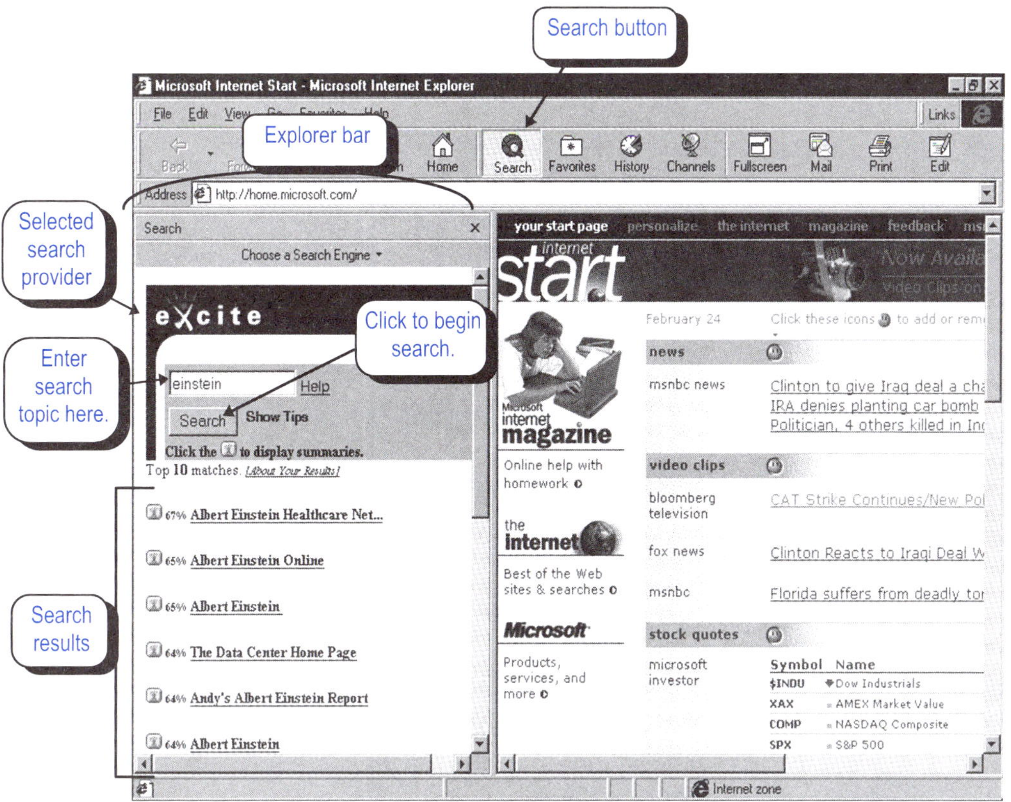

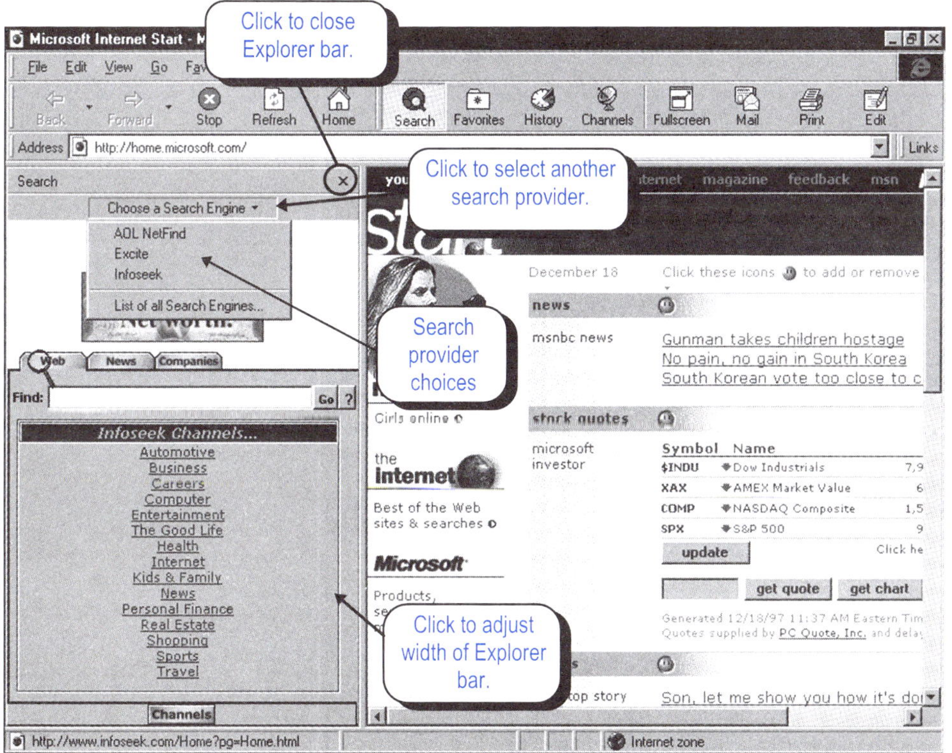

- You can choose a different search provider by clicking the arrow next to the Choose a Search Engine box and selecting a different Search service from the drop-down menu.

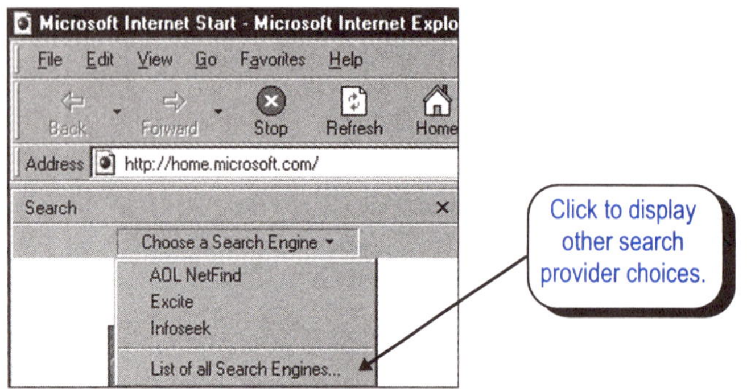

- To view a list of all the available search services, select List of all Search Engines from the drop-down menu. The list of all available search providers will appear in the Pick a Search Engine page on the right side of the screen, categorized by the types of searches they perform. The Explorer bar will remain on the left side of the screen.
- You can also access the Pick a Search Engine page from the Menu bar by selecting Go, Search the Web.
- If you click the close box on the Explorer bar or click the Search button again, the Explorer bar will close and the Pick a Search Engine page will fill the screen.

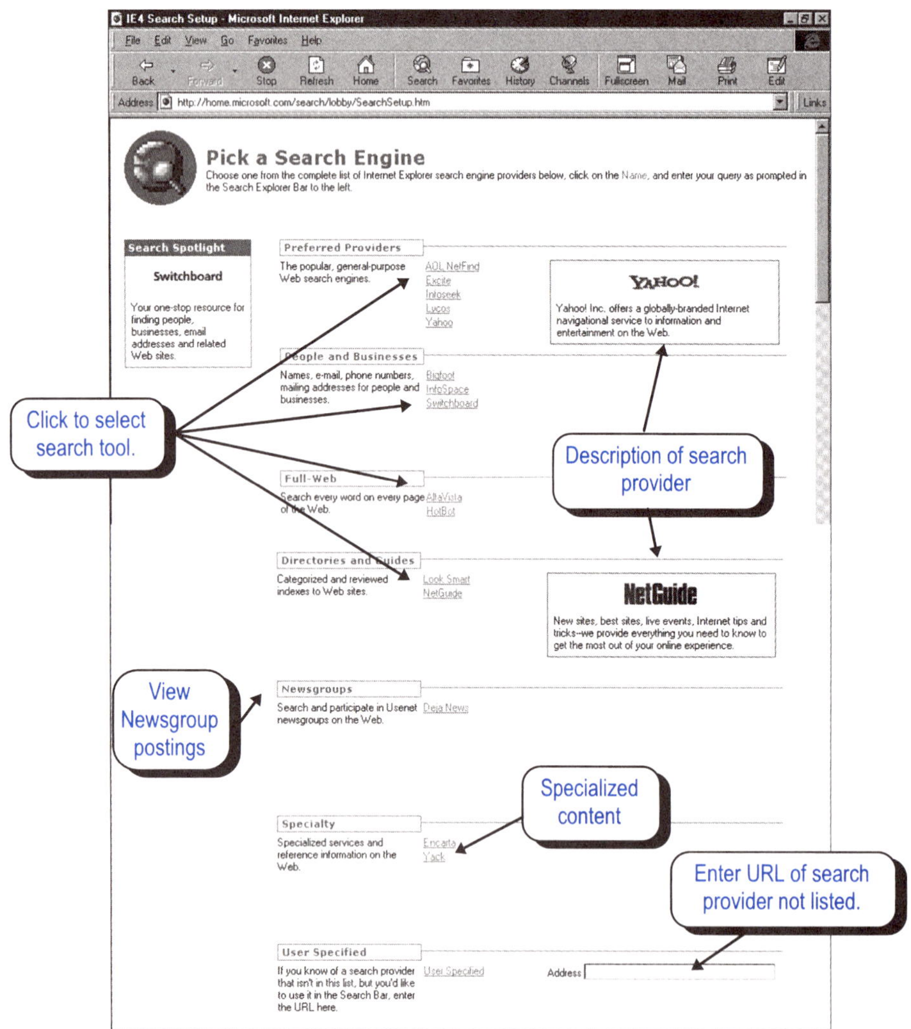

- When you select a search provider, it will open in the Explorer bar on the left of the screen. Enter your search text in the appropriate box and click the corresponding search button.

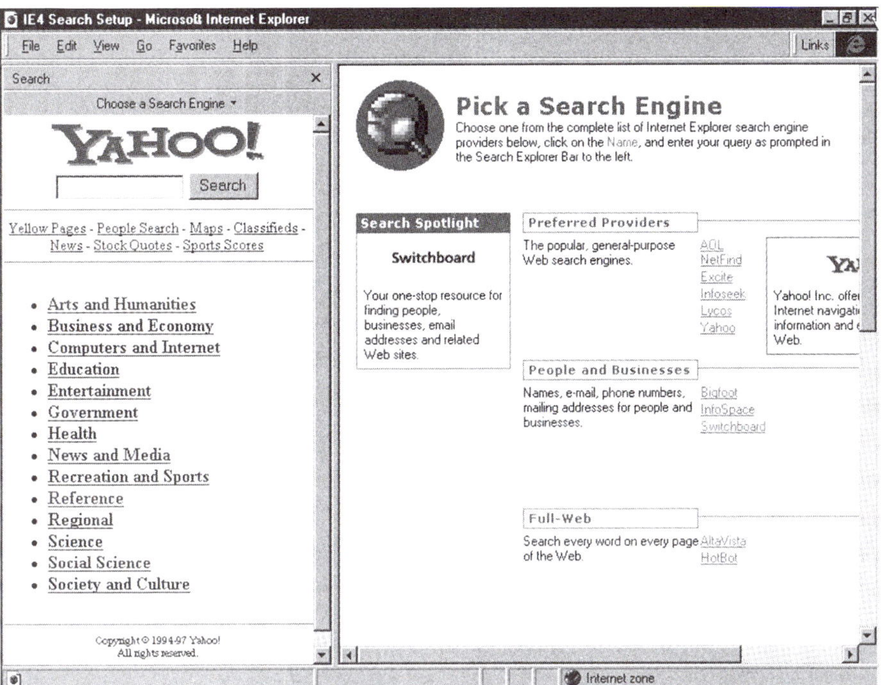

AutoSearch from Address Bar

- In addition to displaying and entering addresses in the Address bar, you can use **AutoSearch** to perform a quick search directly from the Address bar.

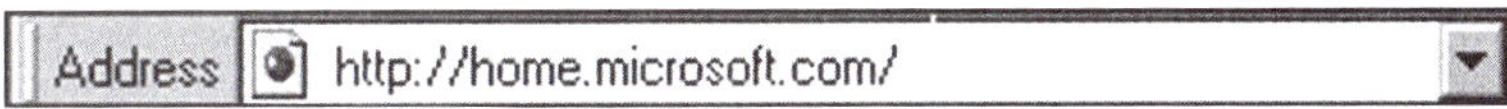

Click once in the Address bar and type **go**, **find**, or **?** and press the spacebar once. Type the word or phrase you want to find and press Enter. For example, if you want to search for information about the year 2000, type "Find the year 2000" on the Address bar and press Enter.

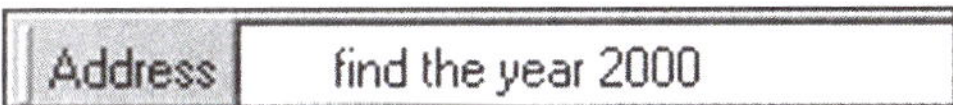

You'll know AutoSearch has found a search provider when the Status bar displays the message, "Connecting to site...". The results of your search will display with bold key words in the list of links that are relevant to your search string.

- AutoSearch uses only one search provider. If you want to refine your search or see if other search providers will give you different results, click the Search button on the Standard toolbar. Select a Search provider from the Choose a Search Engine drop-down list in the Explorer bar to access a different Search provider.

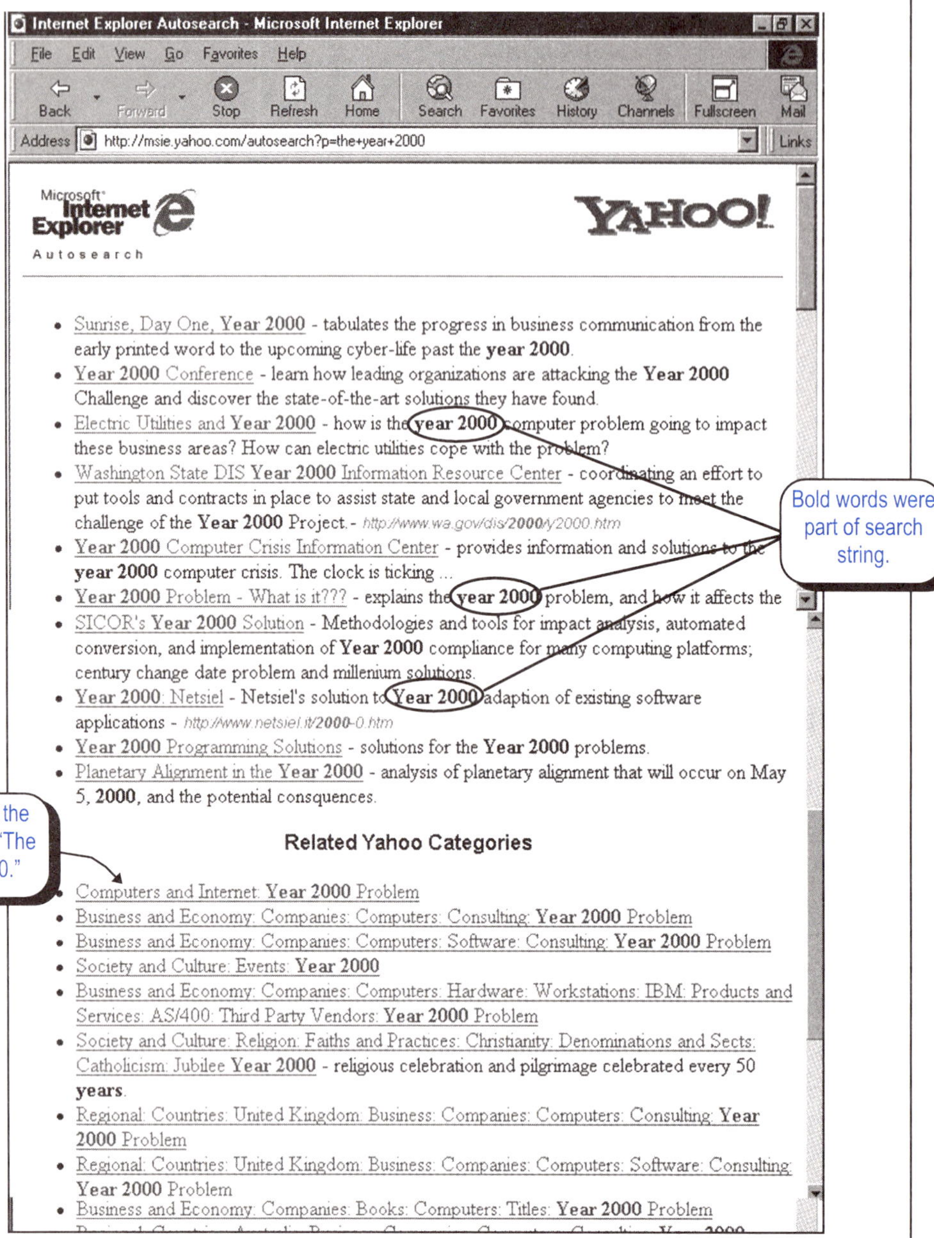

In this exercise, you will conduct a search using AutoSearch and the Internet Explorer main search page to find information about skiing and accommodations in a Colorado ski area.

Note: To ensure consistent results, this exercise uses simulated sites. The real URLs appear at the end of the exercise.

Web Search

Search for answers to the following questions using the Web sites you will visit in the Web simulation exercise.

1. List five links that result from the go ski areas search.

   ____

2. How many Hotels & Inns are based in Frisco?

   ____

3. How many guestrooms are there in the Wellington Inn?

   ____

EXERCISE DIRECTIONS

1. Launch the Internet simulation. From the Main Menu, select Lesson 1, then select Exercise 4.
2. Click in the Address bar.
3. Type the word *go* followed by the words *ski areas* (use all lowercase letters) then press Enter.

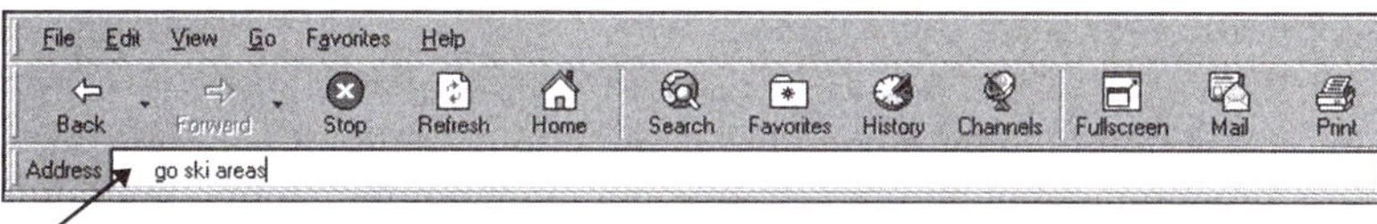

4. Scroll down and view the variety of links that contain the search topic.

   ✓ *Note that the words* ski *and* areas *are in bold in the list of results.*

5. Click in the Address bar again and type *find ski areas Colorado* and press Enter.

   ➲ *The results of the search displays; the key search words are in bold.*

6. Scroll down and click on the link to Regional: U.S. States: Colorado: Recreation and Sports: Skiing: Ski Areas.

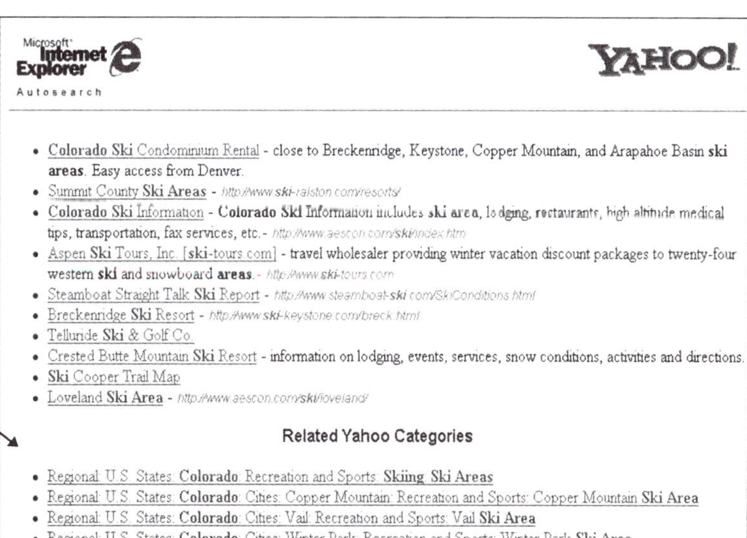

➲ *This page gives you more specific links about Colorado ski areas.*

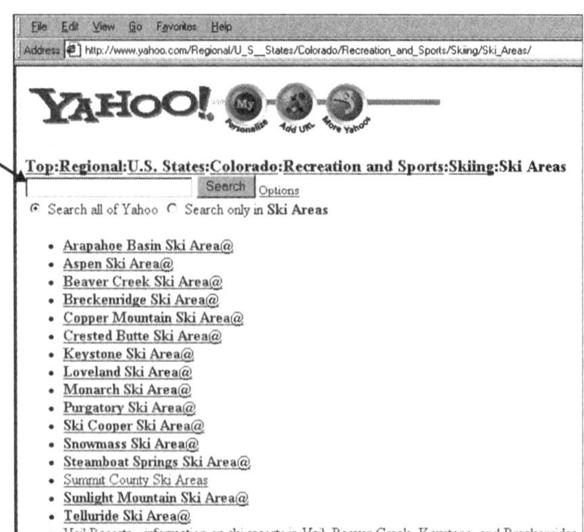

7. Click the Search button on the Standard toolbar to open the Explorer bar.
8. Type the following in the Excite Search textbox and press Enter: *lodging+breckenridge+lodging.*
   ✓ *Be sure to use the plus signs with no spaces when you enter the search topic. This tells the search engine to display only those sites that include all of the search items.*

   ➲ *The results of your search will appear in the Explorer bar on the left side of the screen. Excite displays results ten at time in decreasing order of confidence rating.*
   A result rated close to 100% has a good chance of containing what you want.

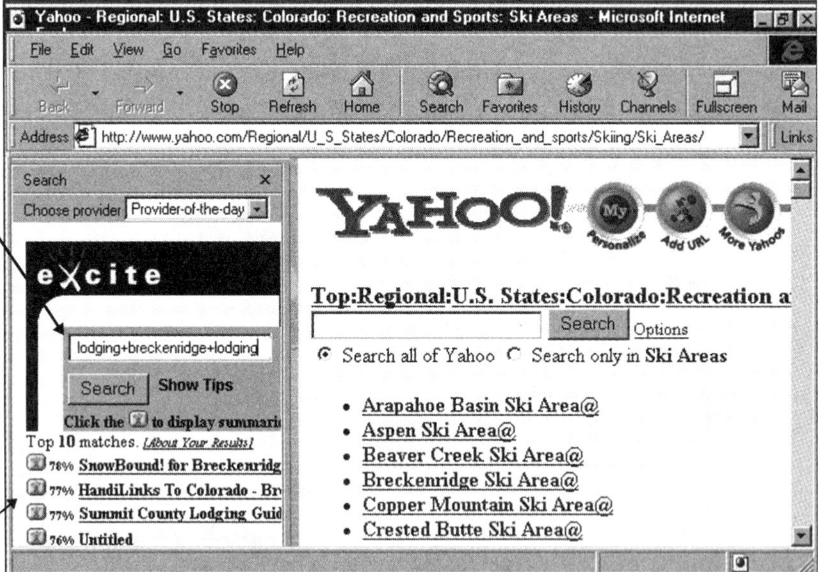

9. Click on the Summit County Lodging Guide.

   ➲ *The selected Web site will open on the right side of your screen.*

10. Click the Close box in the Explorer bar to close it.
11. Scroll down and click the link to the Wellington Inn, Winter Information.

    ➲ *The Home page for The Wellington Inn displays.*

12. Click the Back button once to return to the Summit County Lodging information page.
13. Continue on to the next exercise

    OR

    Exit from the simulation.

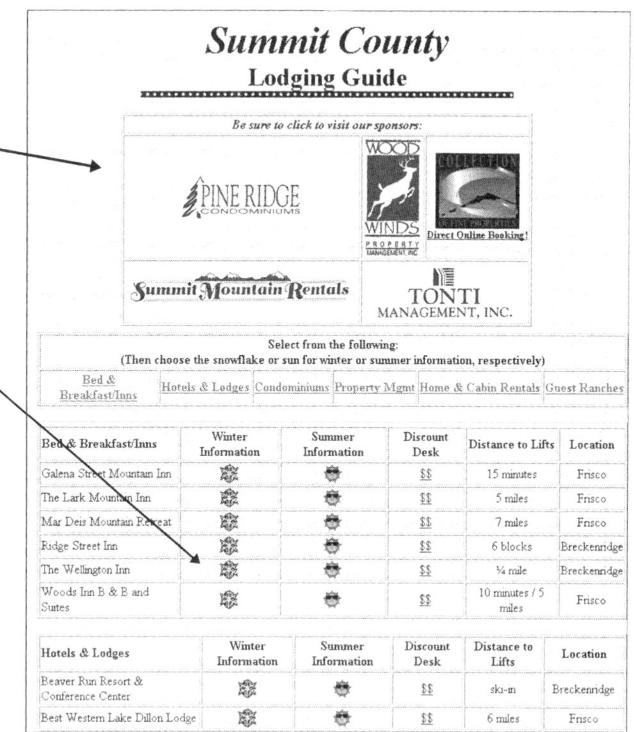

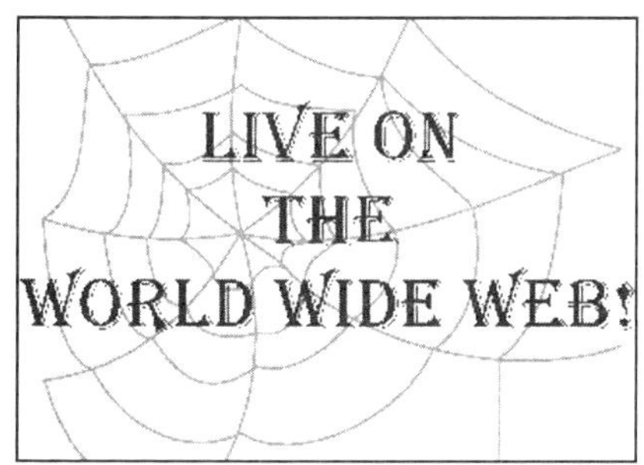

Cool Trails
  http://www.cooltrails.com/

National Scenic and Historic Trails [gorp.com]
  http://www.gorp.com/gorp/resource/us_trail/nattrail.htm

USA Skiing – Ultimate Destinations
  http://www.usa-skiing.com/

Epicurious Traveler
  http://travel.epicurious.com/

Exercise 5

- Open and Add to the Favorites Folder
- Open Web Sites from the Favorites Folder ◆ Delete Favorites
- Create New Folders in the Favorites Folder
- Move Favorites from Folder to Folder ■ File Favorites
- Edit Favorites

NOTES

Open and Add to the Favorites Folder

- As you spend more time exploring the Web, you will find sites that you want to visit frequently. You can store shortcuts to these sites in the **Favorites folder**. When you want to go to a site whose address is stored in the Favorites folder, click the **Favorites** button on the Standard toolbar, or click the Favorites menu. Then click on the shortcut to the desired site.
  - To add a site to the Favorites folder, first open the desired Web site.
  - Click on the Web page icon in the Address bar and drag it onto the Favorites button on the Standard toolbar. Or, drag it onto the Favorites menu, which will open for you to drag the icon to the desired destination.

  ✓ *The Web page is added to the Favorites list.*

  OR

  - Open the desired Web site.
  - Click the Favorites menu and select Add to Favorites, or right-click anywhere on the Web page and select Add to Favorites.
  - The following dialog box appears.

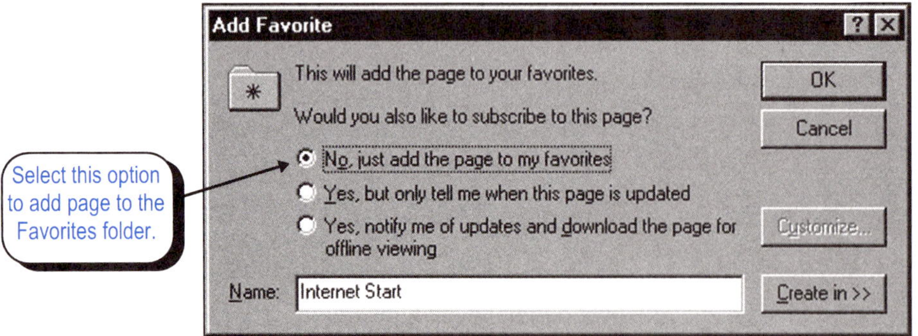

  - The name of the Web page appears in the Name box. You can change the name, if desired, by clicking in the Name box and overwriting the existing text.

Note

You can add a site to the Favorites folder without connecting to it. Just right-click on a hyperlink to the desired site and select Add to Favorites.

- In the Add Favorite dialog box, there are three ways you can respond to the question, "Would you also like to subscribe to this page?" Subscribing to a page means you can schedule automatic updates to that site.
  - No, just add the page to my favorites
    Puts a shortcut to the Web site in your Favorites folder.
  - Yes, but only tell me when this page is updated
    Explorer will alert you when an update to the site is available.
  - Yes, notify me of updates and download the page for offline viewing
    Explorer will automatically download and update to your computer.

  ✓ *In this exercise, you will only work with the first option.*
- Click OK to add the Web address to the Favorites folder.

✓ *The Web page is added to the Favorites list.*

Open Web Sites from Favorites Folder

- Opening a favorite site is quick and easy. First, click the Favorites button [Favorites] on the Standard toolbar to display the contents of your Favorites folder in the Explorer bar.

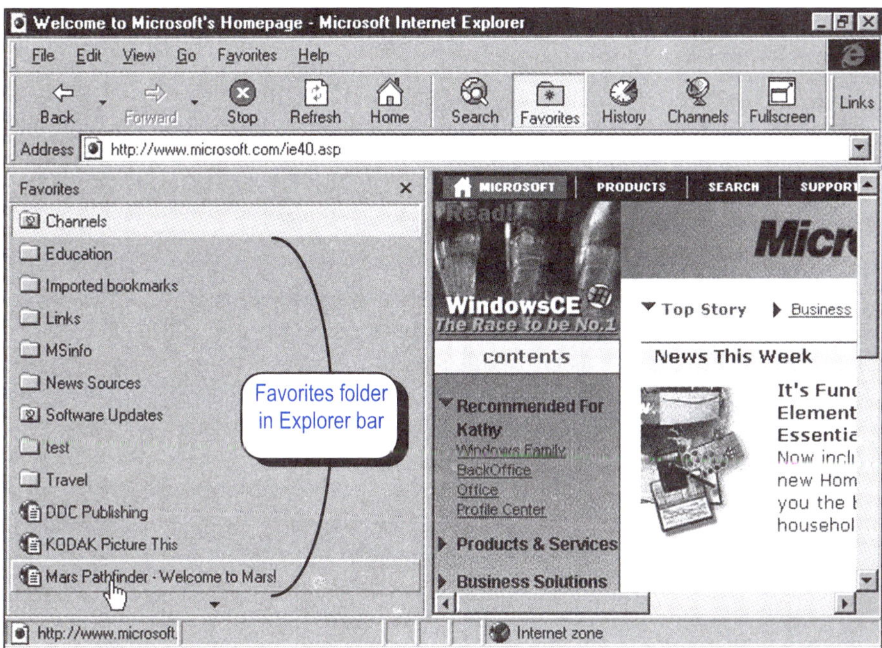

- Next, click on a site to open. Or, click on a folder to display its contents and then select a site. You can close the Explorer bar by clicking the Close button (X) in the upper-right corner of the bar, or by clicking on the Favorites button on the Standard toolbar.

- You can also open a favorite site by clicking on the Favorites menu and selecting a folder and/or site from the drop-down list that displays.

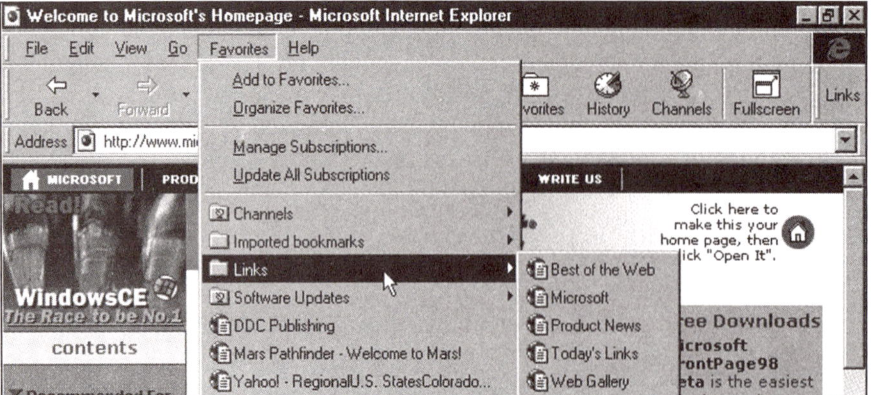

Delete Favorites

- Favorites may be deleted at anytime. For example, you may wish to delete a Web site that no longer exists or remove one that is no longer of interest to you.
- To delete a favorite do the following:
  - Click Favorites.
  - Click Organize Favorites.
  - In the Organize Favorites window, select the favorite you want to delete.

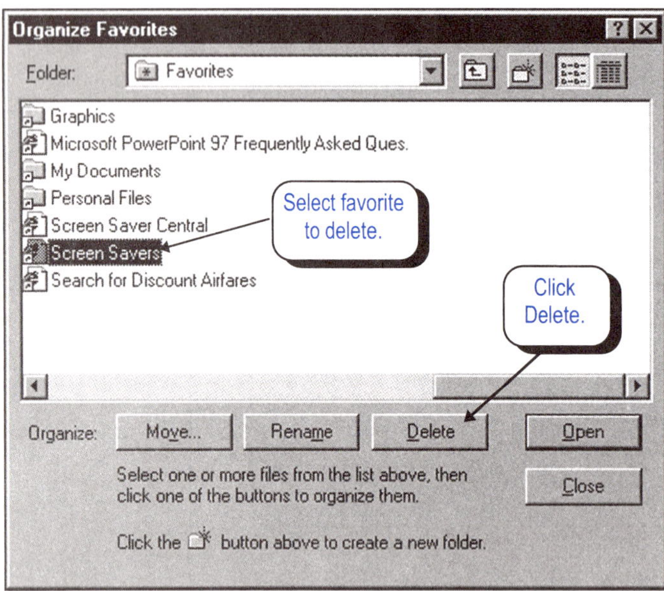

  - Click the Delete button.

    OR

    Press the Delete key.

    OR

    Right-click on the selected favorite and choose Delete from the shortcut menu.

Create New Folders in the Favorites Folder

- It won't take long for your Favorites folder to grow quite long. Just as you create folders for your word processing, spreadsheet, and other files, you can create folders to organize your favorite Web addresses.
- You can create new folders before or after you have saved sites in your Favorites folder.

To create a new favorites folder:

- Click Favorites and select Organize Favorites to open the Organize Favorites window.
- Click the Create New Folder button (shown in illustration below).

- Type the name of the new folder and press Enter.

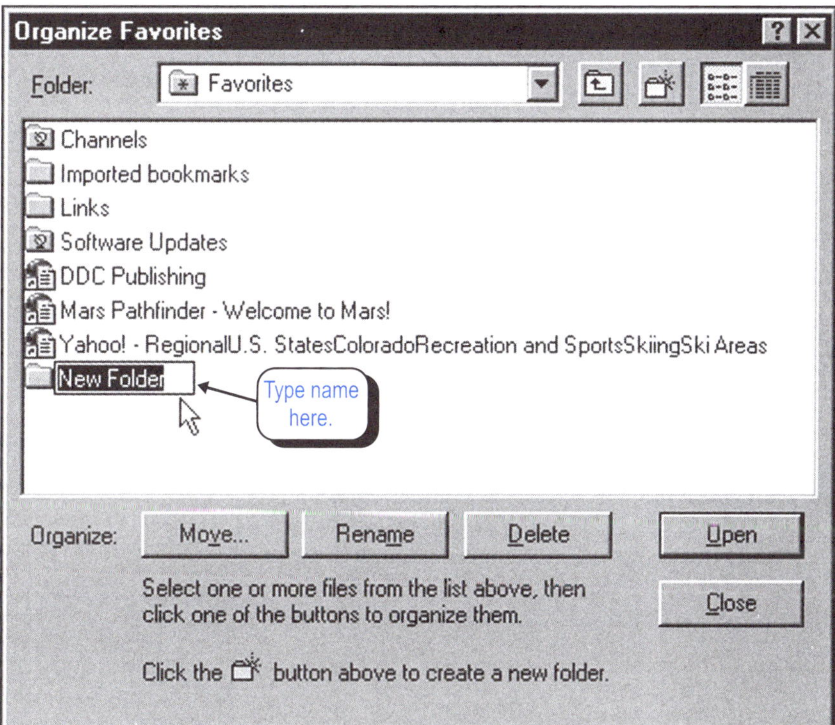

Move Favorites from Folder to Folder

- You can move favorites from folder to folder in either the Organize Favorites window or the Explorer bar simply by dragging and dropping.

To move favorites in the Explorer bar:

- Click the Favorites button on the Standard toolbar to open the Favorites list in the Explorer bar.

- Click and drag the desired favorite to the destination folder. Release the mouse when you are pointing to the desired folder.

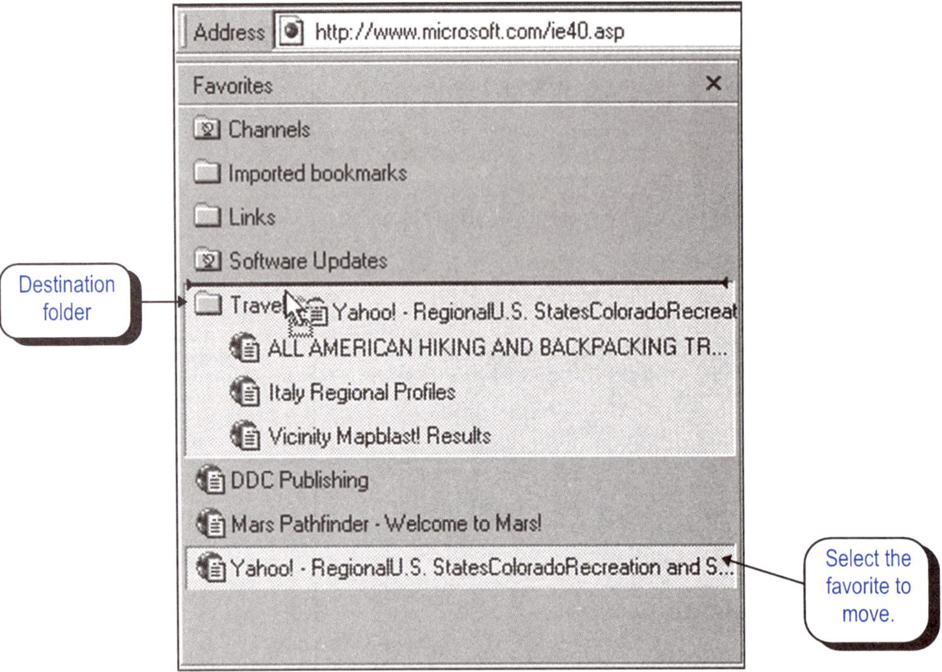

✓ *The favorite is placed in the new folder.*

- You can also drag and drop folders in the favorites list. When you move a folder, its contents move with it.

To move favorites in the Organize Favorites window:

- Click Favorites.
- Select Organize Favorites to open the Organize Favorites window.
- Click once on the desired favorite to highlight it and, while still holding down the left mouse button, drag the highlighted favorite to the desired folder. When the destination folder becomes highlighted, release the mouse button and drop the favorite on top of the folder.

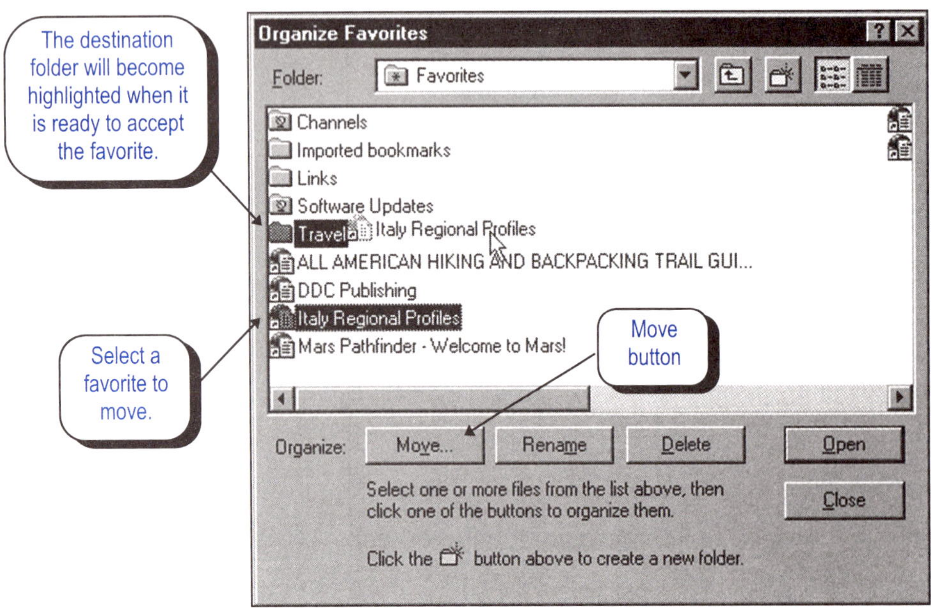

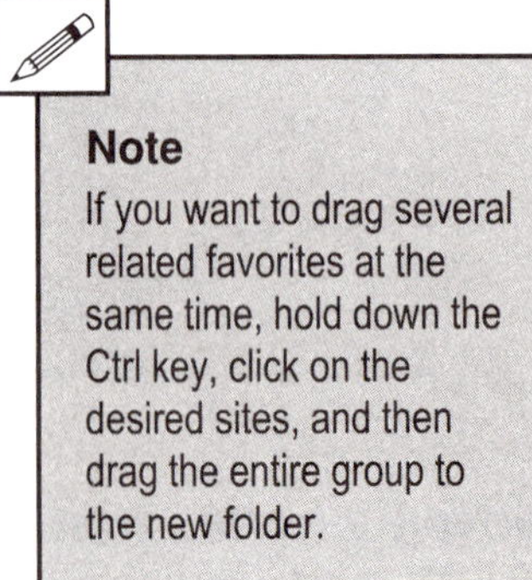

Note

If you want to drag several related favorites at the same time, hold down the Ctrl key, click on the desired sites, and then drag the entire group to the new folder.

- You can also move favorites in the Organize Favorites window by selecting the desired sites and clicking the Move button at the bottom of the window.
- In the Browse for Folder dialog box that follows, click the desired destination folder and click OK.

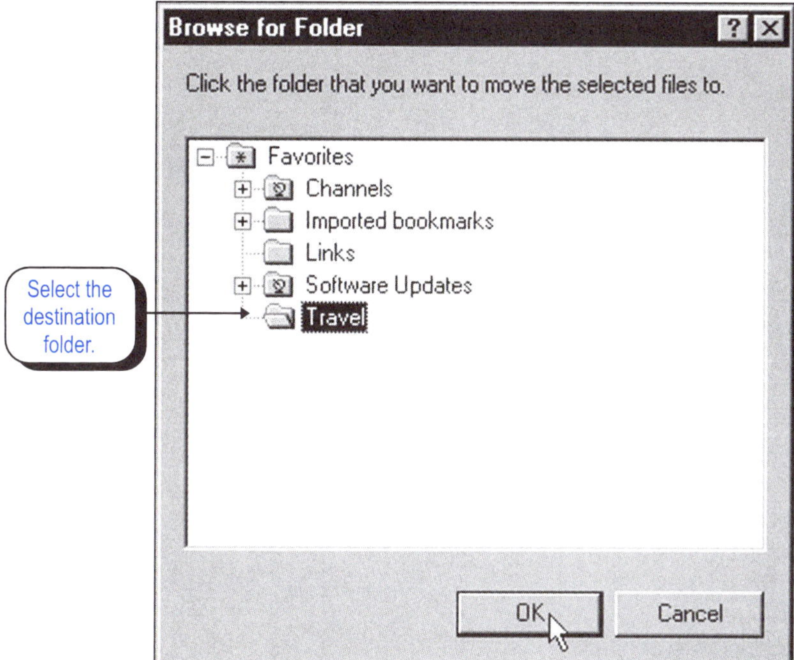

✓ *The address names will be grayed for a few moments as the move is completed.*

File Favorites

- Once you have created folders within your Favorites list, you can file favorites as you create them. To do so, open to the Web page you want to mark as a favorite, click on the Favorites menu, and select Add to Favorites.
  - In the Add Favorite dialog box, click the Create in button to display the contents of your Favorites folder.

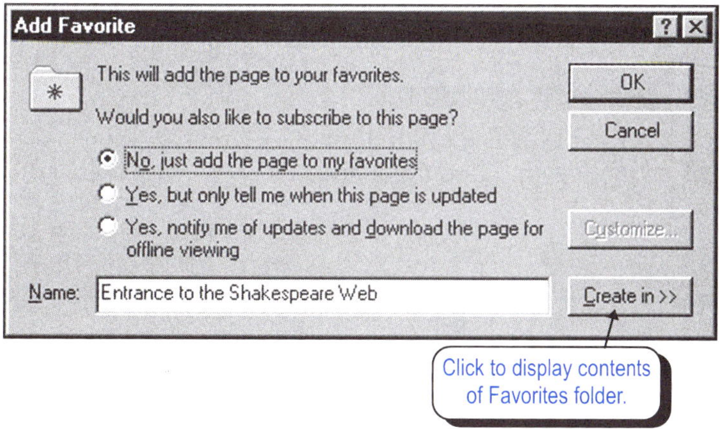

• From the list that displays, select the desired destination folder and click OK. The favorite will be automatically added to the selected folder.

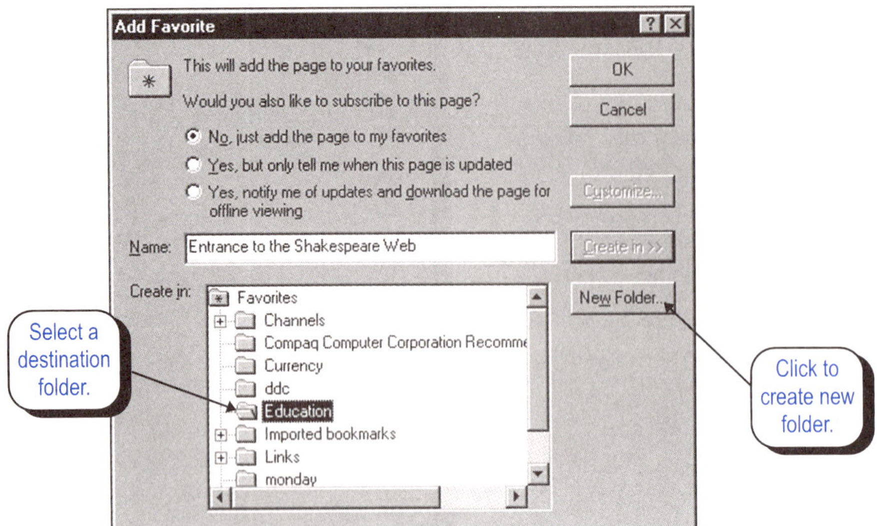

OR

To create a new folder in which to store the new favorite, click the New Folder button. In the Create New Folder dialog box that displays, enter a folder name and click OK twice. The new favorite is automatically added to the new folder.

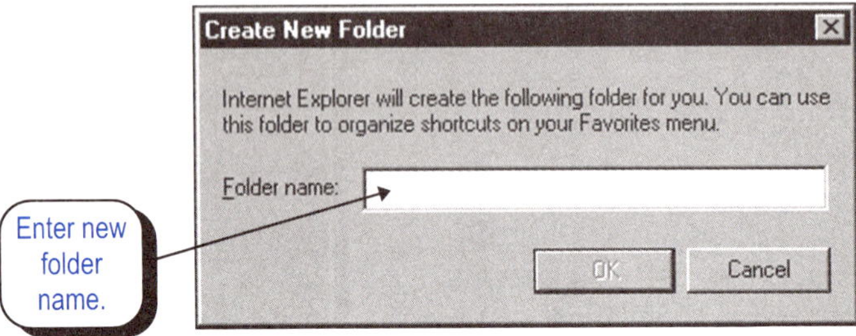

Edit Favorites

- After adding a site to your Favorites folder, you may find that you need to change its URL and/or name. For example, if a Web site URL changes, you'll need to change the URL stored in the Favorites folder. Or, you may find that the name automatically assigned to the favorite when you created it is not clearly identifiable.
- In either case, you will need to edit the favorite as follows:
  - Display the Favorites list by clicking the Favorites button on the Standard toolbar or by clicking the Favorites menu and selecting Organize Favorites.
  - Select the favorite to edit.
  - Right-click on the selected favorite.

To change the name of a favorite:

- Select Rename from the shortcut menu.

Organize Favorites Window *Favorites in Explorer Bar*

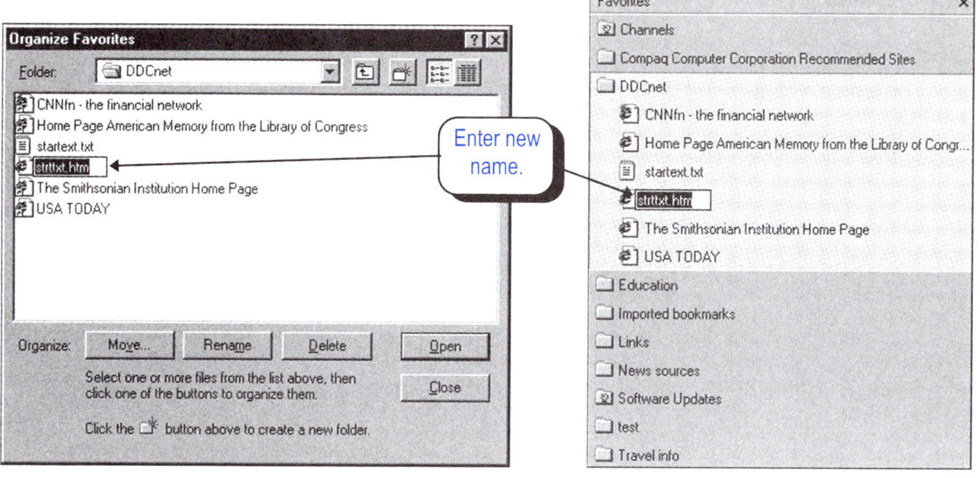

- Type the new name and press Enter.

To change the URL of a favorite:

- Select Properties from the shortcut menu.
- In the dialog box that follows, click the Internet Shortcut tab.

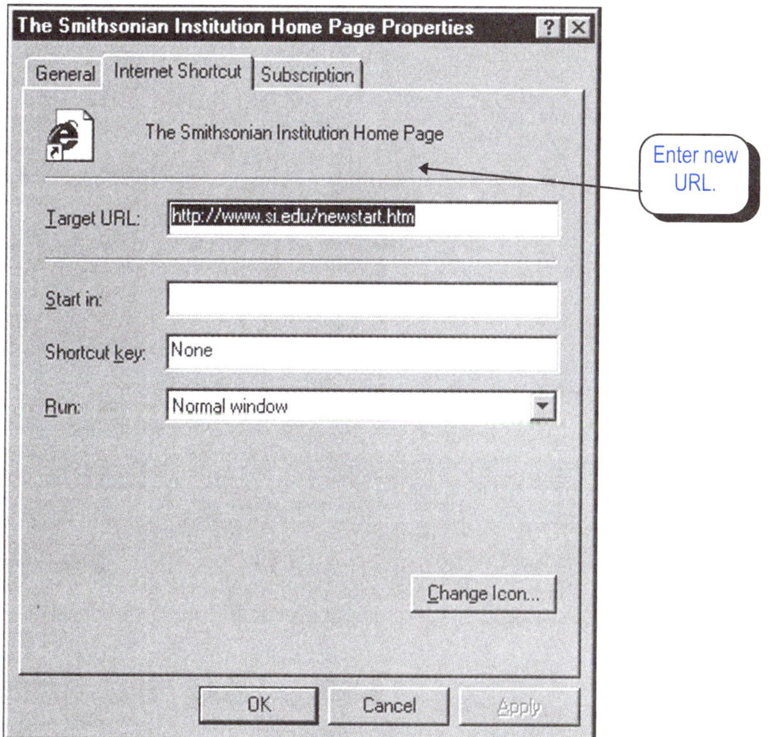

- Click in the Target URL text box and type the new URL.
- Click OK.

In this exercise, you will add Web addresses to your Favorites folder, create new folders, and move and delete addresses.

Note: *To ensure consistent results, this exercise uses simulated sites. The real URLs appear at the end of the exercise.*

Web Search

Search for answers to the following questions using the Web sites you will visit in the Web simulation exercise.

1. List the first five links that result from the search on find library of congress

 ____

2. On the American Memory Collection Search page, what are the five categories that you can use to limit your search?

 ____

3. Name the options that you see when you right-click on a Favorite in the Explorer bar?

 ____

EXERCISE DIRECTIONS

1. Launch the Internet simulation. From the Main Menu, select Lesson 1, then select Exercise 5.
2. Click in the Address bar and type the following and press Enter: *find library of congress*.
3. Scroll down and click the following:

 Government: Legislative Branch: Agencies: Library of Congress link.
4. Click the link to American Memory from the Library of Congress.

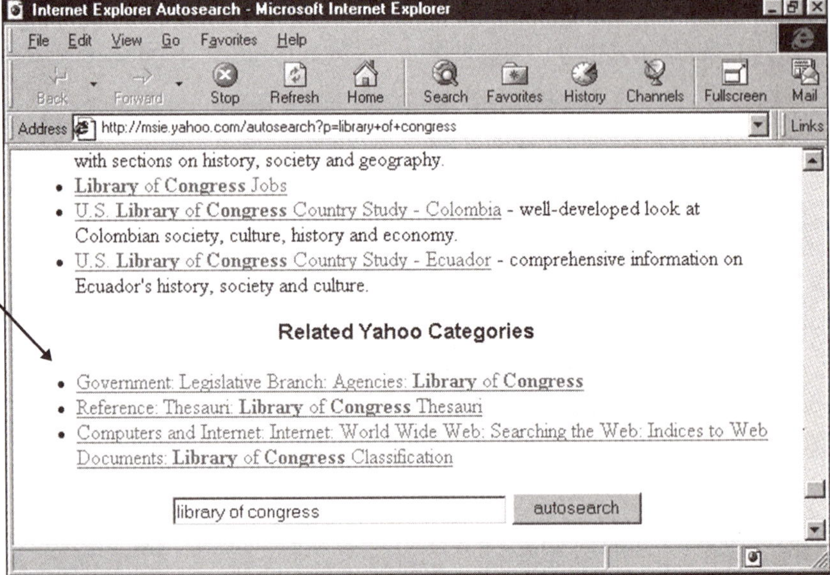

➲ *The Home page for The American Memory from the Library of Congress opens.*

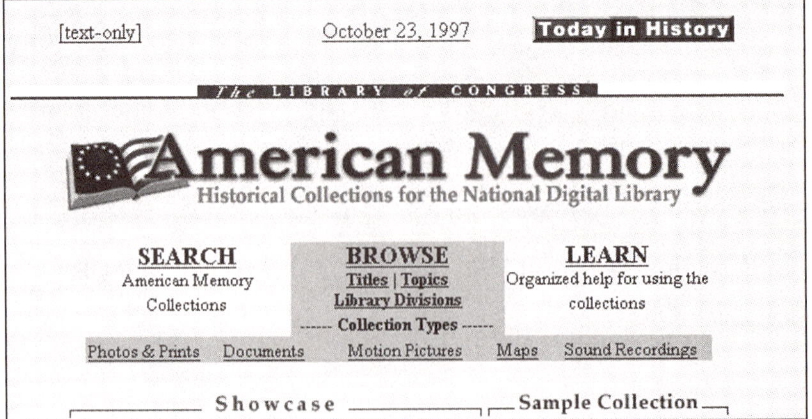

5. Click the Favorites menu and click Add to Favorites.

   ➲ *The Add Favorite dialog box appears.*

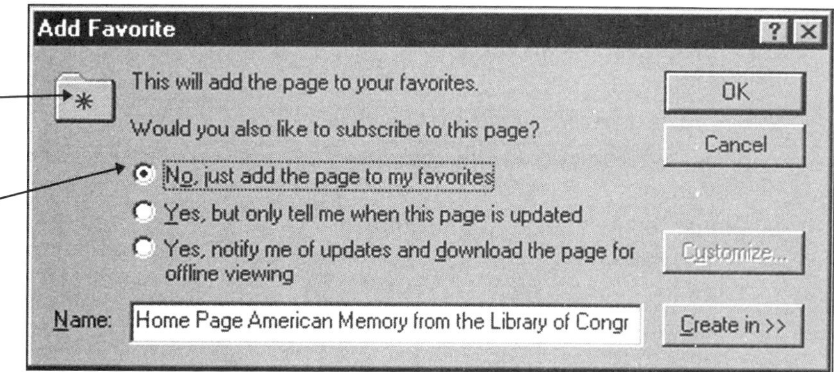

6. The first option, **No, just add the page to my favorites**, is selected, so click **OK** to add this page to your Favorites folder.
7. Click Home to return to your Home page.
8. Click the Favorites button on the toolbar to open the Favorites folder in the Explorer bar.
9. Click on the link to Home Page for The American Memory from the Library of Congress.
10. Close the Explorer bar.
11. Click the link to SEARCH American Memory Collections.

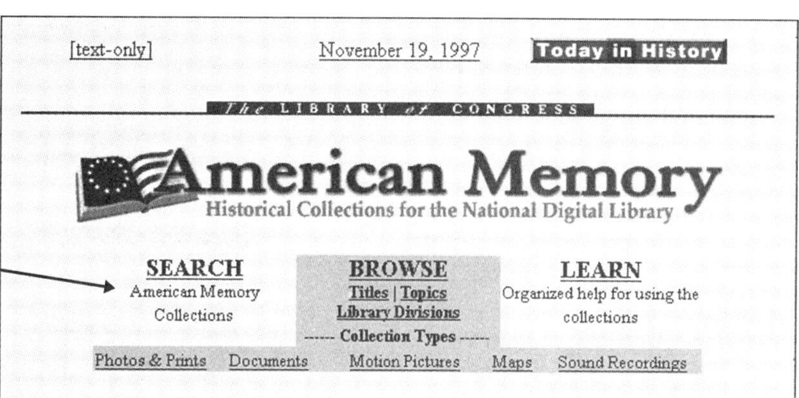

12. Add this page to your Favorites folder.

    ✓ *Note that you can add any page to the Favorites folder, not just the opening page.*
13. Use the Address bar to find the Home page for the Smithsonian Institution:
    a. Type *find smithsonian institution* in the Address bar and press Enter.

       ➲ *A list of search results displays.*

    b. Click on the first link to Smithsonian Institution.
14. Click the Favorites menu and select Add to Favorites. Then do the following:
    a. In the Add Favorite dialog box, select **No, just add the page to my favorites**; then click the Create in button.
    b. Click New Folder.
    c. Name the new folder *DDCnet* and click OK.
    d. Click OK to add the site to the new folder.
15. Click Home to return to your Start page.

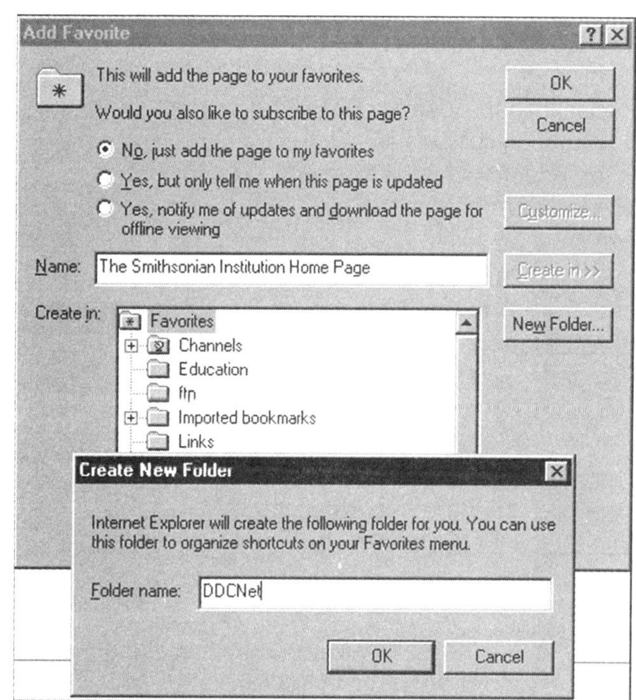

16. Click Favorites on the menu, select Organize Favorites and do the following:
    a. In the Organize Favorites dialog box, click the New Folder button.
    b. Name the new folder *Education* and press Enter.
    c. Click the Close button
    d. Click the Favorites button on the Standard toolbar to open the Explorer bar and note that the folder you just created is listed.
    e. Close the Explorer bar.

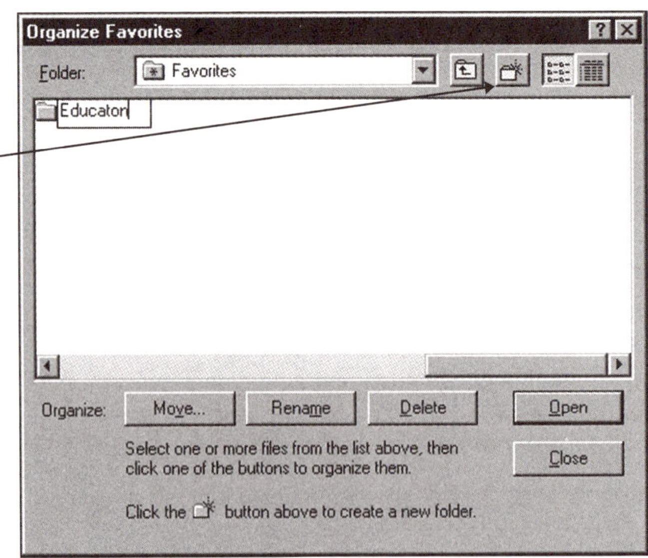

17. Select Organize Favorites from the Favorites menu:
    a. Hold down the Ctrl key while you click on these addresses:
        – **Home Page American Memory from the Library of Congress**
        – **American Memory Collections Search**
    b. Release the Ctrl key, point to one of the highlighted addresses, click, and drag to the Education folder. Release the mouse when the Education folder is highlighted.
    c. Click Close to close the Organize Favorites dialog box.

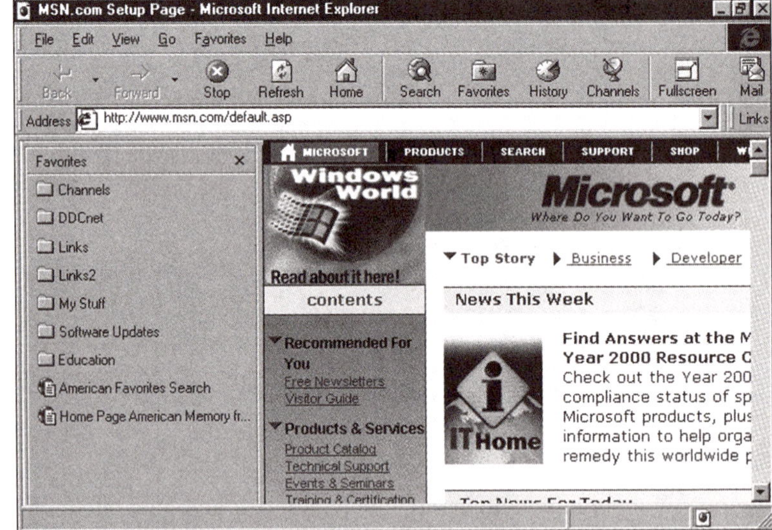

18. Click the Favorites button to open the Explorer bar and do the following:
    a. Open the **DDCnet** folder and click the link to the <u>Smithsonian Institution</u>.

    ➲ *The Smithsonian home page will open in the right side of the browser window.*

    b. Open the Education folder and right-click on the link to <u>American Memory Collections Search</u>.
    c. Select Delete from the shortcut menu that appears. Click Yes to send it to the Recycle Bin.

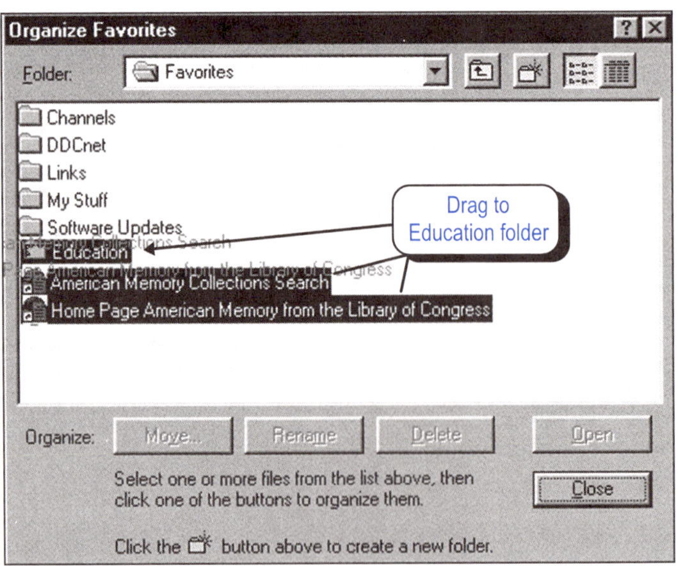

19. Continue on to the next exercise

    OR

    Exit from the simulation.

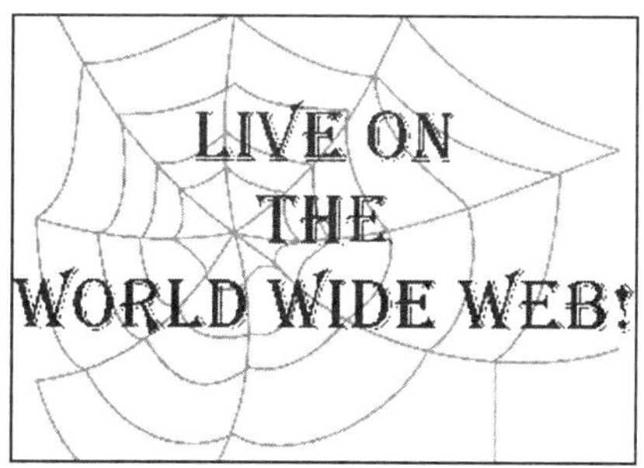

The White House Home Page
http://www.whitehouse.gov

The NASA Home Page
http://nasa.gov

The Nine Planets
http://seds.lpl.arizona.edu/nineplanets/nineplanets/

NEXT LESSON

Lesson 2: Netscape Navigator

Exercise 1

- About Netscape Navigator
- Start Netscape Navigator
- The Home Page
- The Navigator Screen
- Netscape Help
- Hypertext Links
- Image Maps
- Exit Netscape Navigator

Exercise 2

- The Navigation Toolbar
- Open World Wide Web Sites
- Stop a Load or Search
- Status Bar
- Return to the Home Page
- Change the Default Home Page

Exercise 3

- History List
- Bookmarks
- Bookmarks Window
- Add Bookmarks
- Open a Bookmarked Web Site
- Delete Bookmarks
- Create Bookmarks from the History List

Exercise 4

- Netscape Navigator Main Search Page
- Start Search from Location Field

Exercise 1

- About Netscape Navigator
- Start Netscape Navigator
- The Home Page
- The Navigator Screen
- Netscape Help
- Hypertext Links
- Image Maps
- Exit Netscape Navigator

NOTES

About Netscape Navigator

- Netscape Navigator 4.0 is the Internet browser component of Netscape Communicator, a suite of Internet tools that allows you to browse the Web, send and receive e-mail, access newsgroups, publish Web pages, and more. This lesson will focus on the Netscape Navigator browser; Netscape Messenger, the e-mail portion of Netscape Communicator, will be introduced in Lesson 4.
- Netscape Navigator, like other Internet browsers, is a software program that enables you to navigate the Internet to locate data, view Web sites, and access interlinked text, graphic, audio, and video files from around the world.
- Navigator has several built-in programs. One of these is called File Transfer Protocol (FTP). File Transfer Protocol is one of the ways in which files are sent and received from remote computers on the Internet.
- Navigator also uses multimedia software called plug-ins, which allow you to view many different graphic, animation, and audio files on the Internet.
- Netscape works with several search sites that allow you to search for topics of interest. A *search site*, such as the Netscape Net Search page, is a Web site that uses a search engine to build a catalog of Web resources based on key words. A *search engine* is a software program that catalogs Web sites based on words found in the sites. Many search engines, such as Yahoo, Alta Vista, Excite, Lycos, and InfoSeek, also host their own search sites. Search sites will be introduced in Lesson 3.

Start Netscape Navigator

To start Netscape Navigator (Windows 95):

- Click Start on the Windows 95 taskbar.
- Click Programs, Netscape Communicator, Netscape Navigator.

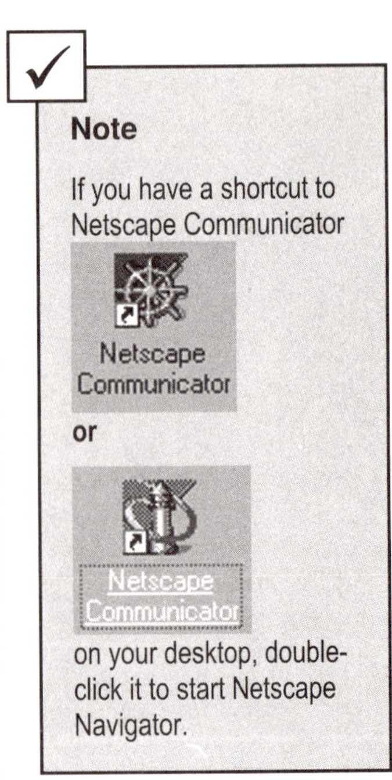

Note

If you have a shortcut to Netscape Communicator

or

on your desktop, double-click it to start Netscape Navigator.

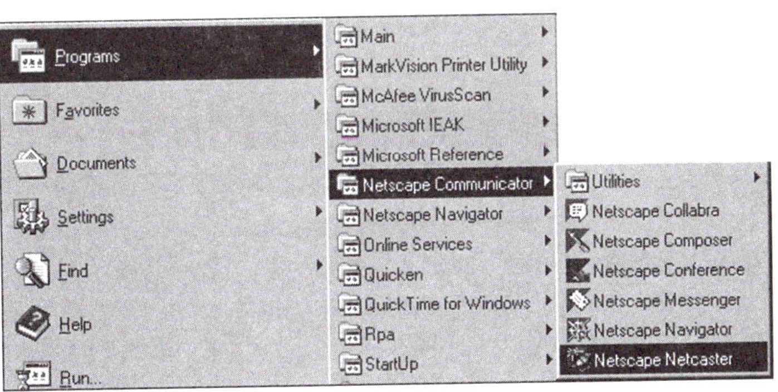

> **Note**
> The first time you start Netscape Communicator, the New Profile Setup dialog box appears. Enter information about your e-mail name and service provider in the dialog boxes that appear. If you do not know the information, you can fill it in later.

The Home Page

- After you start Navigator, you must connect to an Internet service provider (ISP) to establish a connection to the Internet. The procedure for connecting varies depending on your service provider. Once you're connected, you can start to browse the Web.
- When you connect to the World Wide Web, the first screen that displays is called a Home or Start page. Think of the Home/Start page as your launch point to the Web. The default Home page in Netscape Navigator is the Netscape Communications, Inc. Web site, but you can choose any site to be your Home page (see Exercise 2 for details).

> **Note**
> An Internet service provider is a company that provides Internet access, such as Sprynet, World Wide Access, and Prodigy.

The Navigator Screen

- The Netscape Navigator screen contains features that help you explore the Internet. Some of these features remain constant and others change depending on the Web site you visit or the task you want to complete. Note the description of each screen part below and on the following pages.

Navigator Screen

① Title bar
② Menu bar
③ Navigation toolbar
④ Location toolbar
⑤ Personal toolbar
⑥ Netscape Status Indicator moves to indicate action.
⑦ Status bar
⑧ Component toolbar
Bookmarks QuickFile button
Location field
Location icon
Scroll bar
Shortcuts to other sites
Security information
Navigator
Messenger Mailbox
Collabra Discussion Groups
Composer

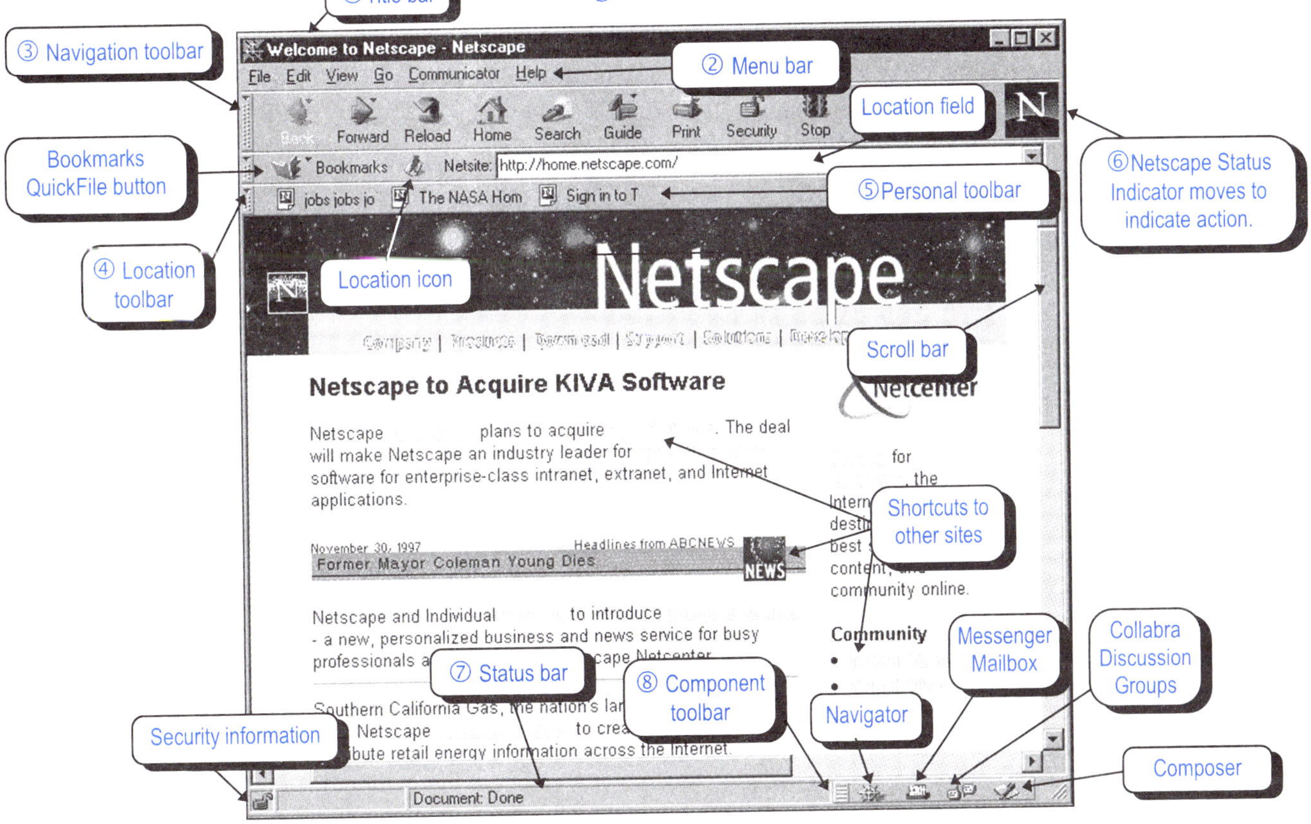

① **Title bar**

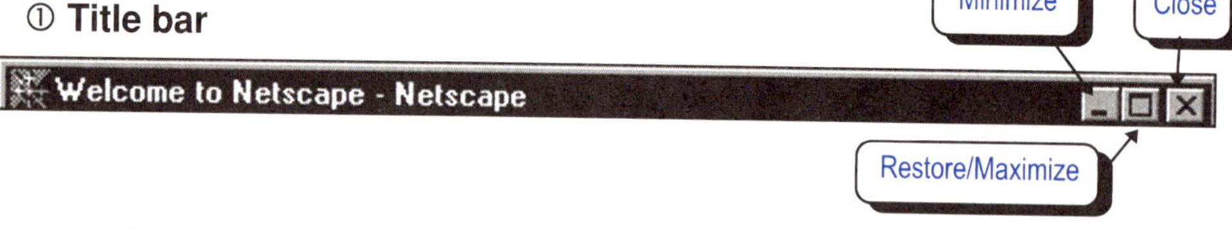

Displays the name of the program (Netscape) and the current Web page, in this case, Welcome to Netscape. Note that there are three buttons on the far right of the Title bar. Use these standard Windows features to minimize, maximize/restore, or close the Navigator window.

② **Menu bar**

Displays the menus that are currently available, which provide drop-down menus of commands for executing Netscape tasks.

③ **Navigation toolbar**

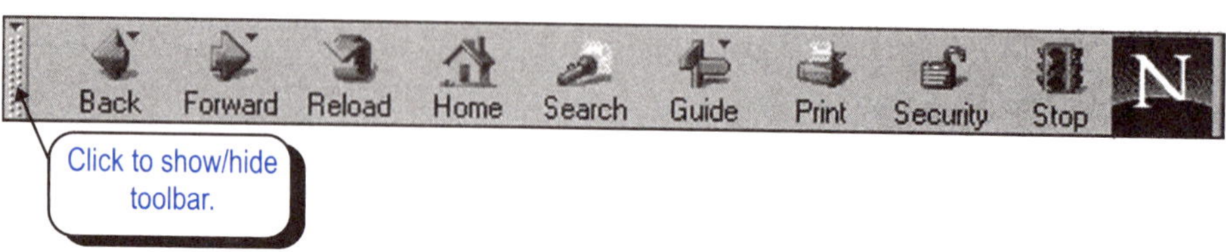

Contains buttons for loading, moving between, and printing Web pages. Each of the buttons display a name and an icon indicating its command. You can access these commands quickly and easily by clicking the mouse on the desired button.

✓ *If the toolbar buttons are not visible, open the View menu and select Show Navigation Toolbar.*

✓ *To hide the Navigation toolbar, click the Show/Hide button on the left edge of the toolbar. Click the button again to redisplay the toolbar.*

④ **Location toolbar**

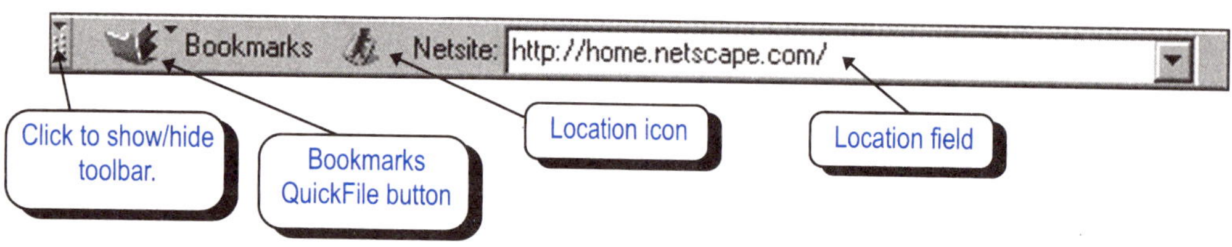

Displays the electronic address of the currently displayed Web page in the Location field. You can type a Web page address in the Location field and press Enter to access it. A Web site address is called a Uniform Resource Locator (URL).

– The Bookmarks QuickFile button Bookmarks on the Location toolbar contains sites that you have bookmarked for quick access. To add a bookmark, display the desired Web site, click this button, and select Add Bookmark from the drop-down menu. For more on bookmarks, see Exercises 3 and 4 of this lesson.

Note

To gain more space on screen, you may want to hide selected toolbars. Go to the View menu and select the desired hide/show options. Or, click the Show/Hide button on the left end of the desired toolbar.

Note

The Security button lets you verify the security level of the document displayed. For example, if you click on the Security button while displaying the Netscape Home page, you will see a message saying that the site is not encrypted (protected) and that the displayed information can be observed by a third party. Because security of files and personal information sent over the Internet is a continuing concern, technology to secure information continues to develop.

– The Location icon on the Location toolbar displays the word *Netsite* if the current Web site uses Netscape software. The word *Location* will replace Netsite if the site does not utilize Netscape as its primary software. However, in most cases, you will still have full viewing capabilities. Drag this icon to the Bookmarks QuickFile button to add the displayed Web site to your Bookmark file instantly.

✓ *If the Location toolbar is not visible, open the View menu and click Show Location Toolbar.*

✓ *To hide the Location toolbar, click the Show/Hide button on the left edge of the toolbar. Click the button again to redisplay the toolbar.*

⑤ Personal Toolbar

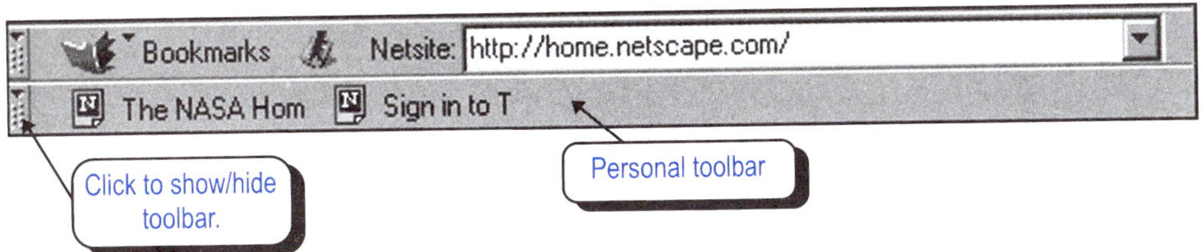

Contains buttons that you add to connect to your favorite sites. The Internet, New and Cool, and Lookup buttons are on the Personal toolbar by default when you install Netscape Communicator. You can add your own buttons to the Personal toolbar by displaying the desired Web site and dragging the Location icon onto the Personal toolbar.

✓ *If the Personal toolbar is not visible, open the View menu and click Show Personal Toolbar.*

✓ *To hide the Personal toolbar, click the Show/Hide button on the left edge of the toolbar. Click the button again to redisplay the toolbar.*

⑥ Netscape Status Indicator

Netscape's icon pulses when an action is being performed. Click on this icon to return immediately to Netscape's Home page.

⑦ Status bar

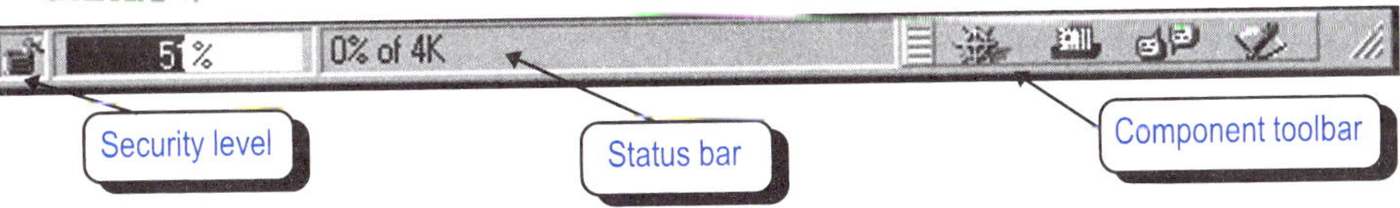

When a Web page is opening, the Status bar indicates the loading progress by a percentage displayed in the center, and the security level of the page by a lock in the far-left corner. When you place the cursor over a hyperlink, the Status bar displays its URL. See Netscape Help for more information on security levels.

⑧ Component toolbar

The icons on this toolbar are links to other Communicator components: Navigator, (Messenger) Mailbox, (Collabra) Discussion Groups, and (Web Page) Composer.

Netscape Help

- You can get help from a variety of sources in Netscape Navigator, which are listed on the Help menu.

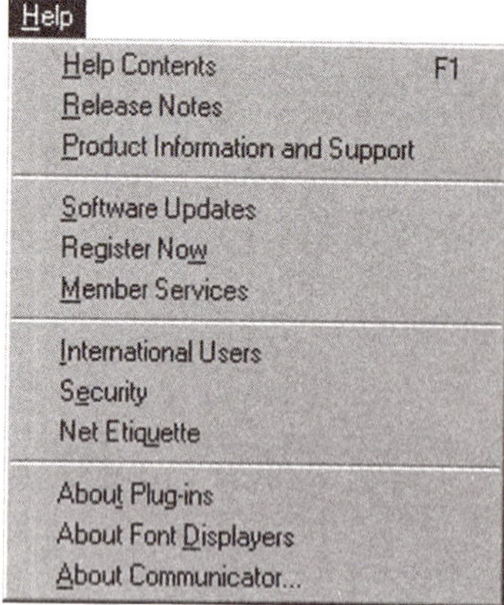

Help Contents

- Select Help Contents to access how-to information organized into chapters according to Netscape task: browsing the Web, sending and receiving e-mail, using discussion groups, composing and editing Web pages, etc.
- In the Netscape NetHelp window that opens, click on the Navigator Help icon at the top of the window, or click the Browsing the Web hyperlink. For help with other Communicator components, click the appropriate icon at the top of the window.

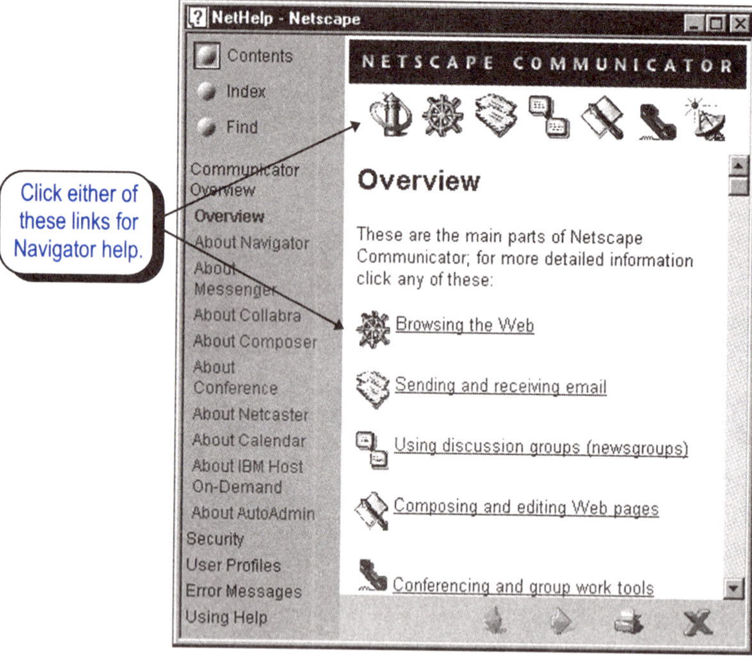

- The Navigator help chapter opens in the right-hand panel, with topic headings listed in the left-hand panel. Scroll through the chapter to find topics of interest or click on the topic you want information on in the left-hand panel to display a list of its subtopics. Then click on a subtopic to display its contents in the right-hand panel.

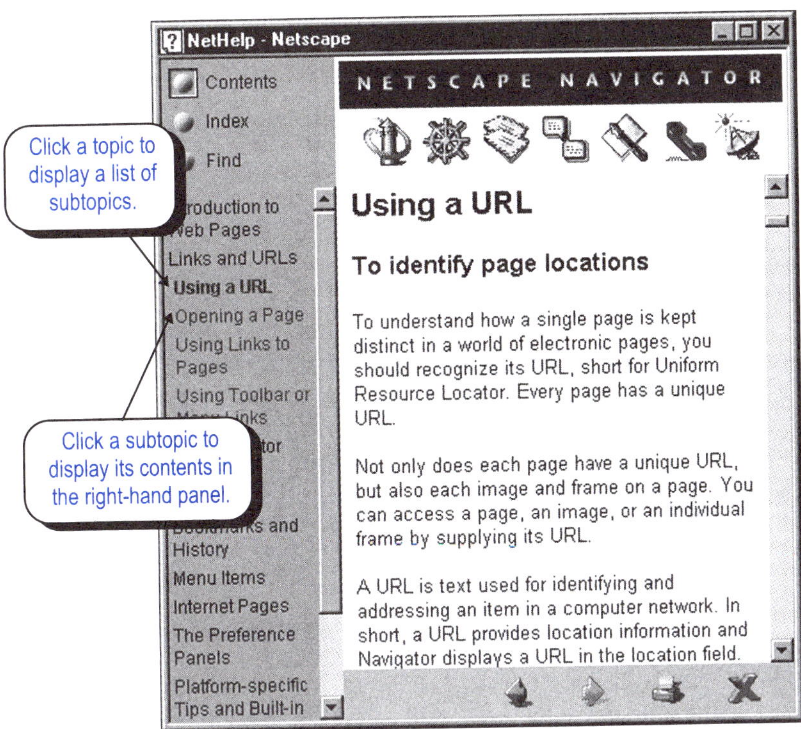

Help Index

- You can search the entire Help database for a topic, rather than searching within specific chapters by clicking the Index hyperlink in the left-hand panel of the NetHelp window. A search text box displays in the left-hand panel, along with an alphabetical listing of all of the help topics contained in the Help database.
- Enter a keyword in the search text box, and the closest matches will display in the left-hand panel. When you find the topic you want information on, click it, and a list of subtopic hyperlinks will display in the right-hand panel. Click on a link to view its help contents.

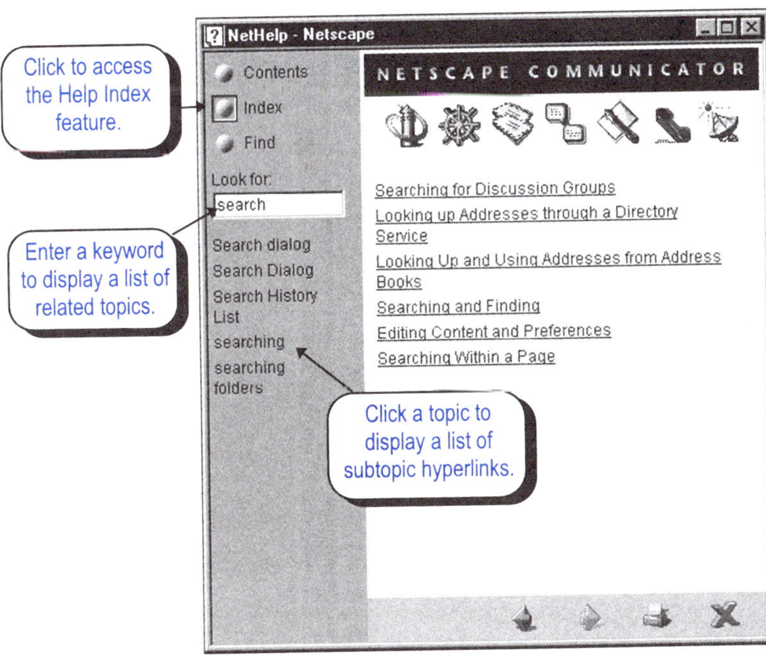

Find

- The Find option works just like the Index option, except that it searches only the current Help document, rather than the entire Help database. Click the Find hyperlink in the upper left corner of the NetHelp window, enter a keyword in the Find dialog box that displays, and click Find Next. The help document automatically scrolls to the next occurrence of the keyword and highlights it.

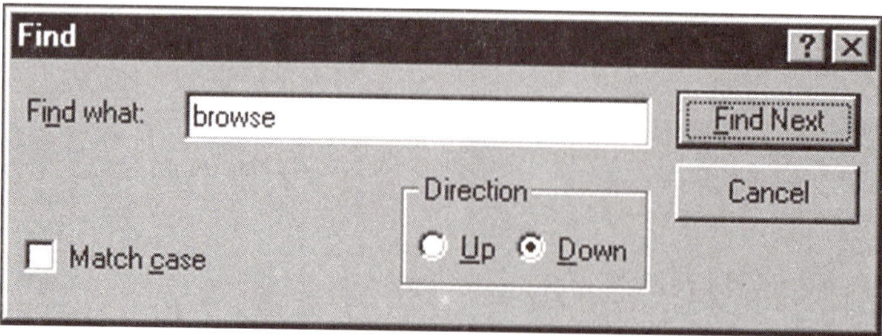

- Use the icons at the bottom of the NetHelp window to navigate through or print Help pages.

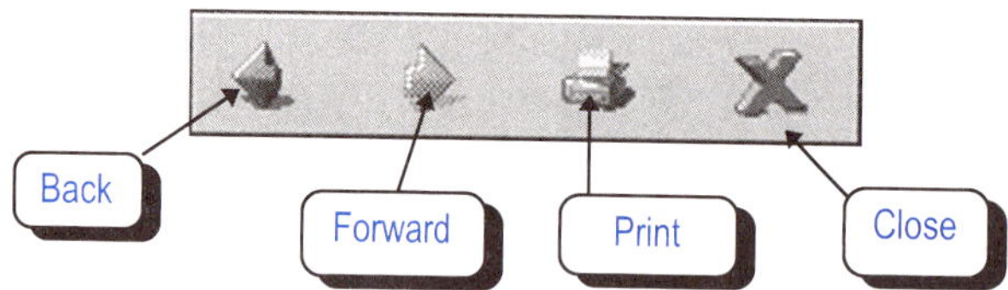

- Click the Close icon at the bottom of the NetHelp window or the Close button (x) in the upper right-hand corner of the window to exit Help.

Online Help

- There are also several online help options available on the Help menu that connect you to Netscape help sites, where you can access up-to-date information. For example, click Release Notes to link to a site containing updates on known problems and solutions in your version of Communicator. Click Product Information and Support to link to the Netscape Tech Support site. Click Software Updates to find information on Communicator software upgrades and enhancement software. You can also click on Net Etiquette and access Usenet sites to learn proper Internet Etiquette.

✓ *Help is also available from the Netscape Home page.*

Hypertext Links

- Hypertext links are words that usually appear in a different **color**, underlined, or **both**. When you click on a link, you'll jump to other information within a site or on another Web site. After you have visited a link, notice that the color of the link changes. This helps you remember which links you've visited.

Image Maps

- The Web is becoming more colorful because of the increased use of graphics and illustrations. Links are generally colored text, but some Web graphics are designed with hidden links as well. These images, called image maps, can also take you to different places on the Web. You know that you are pointing to a link (text or graphic) when the pointer changes to a hand . When that hand appears, click on it to go to another location.

Exit Netscape Navigator

- Exiting Netscape Navigator and disconnecting from your Internet service provider (ISP) are two separate steps. You can actually disconnect from your service provider and still have Netscape Navigator open. In this case you cannot access new Web sites because you are no longer connected to the Web. (Remember that you must first establish a connection to the Internet via your ISP in order to use Netscape to go live on the Web.) You can also disconnect from Navigator and still have your ISP open.
- There are times when you may want to keep Netscape open: to read information obtained from the Web, access information stored on your hard disk using Netscape, or to compose e-mail to send later. If you don't disconnect from your ISP and you pay an hourly rate, you will continue incurring charges.
- To exit Netscape Navigator, select Close from the File menu or click the Close button (X) located in the upper right corner of the Navigator window.

CAUTION

When you exit Netscape, you do not necessarily exit from your Internet service provider. Be sure to check the disconnect procedure from your ISP so that you will not continue to be charged for time online. Most services disconnect when a certain amount of time passes with no activity.

Note

Once you disconnect from your ISP, you can no longer access new Web information using Netscape Communicator. Remember: Netscape Navigator is a browser used to pilot the Internet. It is not an Internet connection.

In this exercise, you will start Netscape Communicator, examine menus and other elements on your home page, and explore the Help feature.

EXERCISE DIRECTIONS

1. Connect to your Internet service provider and start Netscape Navigator by double-clicking the Communicator icon. Or, click **Start**, select Programs, and click on the Communicator program and Netscape Navigator.

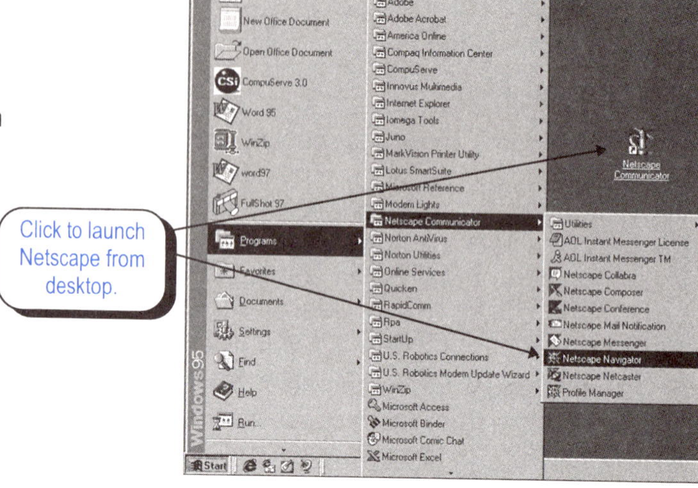

2. Use the scroll bar to move up and down the current Web page.
3. Point to the File menu and click once to open it.
4. Notice the options available on the File menu.
5. Click on each of the menus and note the options available.
6. Press Esc to close any open menu.
7. Move your pointer over several objects on screen. Note that the pointer turns to a hand when it moves over certain locations.
8. Click Go on the Menu bar. You will see options that are also available on the Navigation toolbar, such as Back, Forward, and Home. Below these features notice that the current Web page is listed.
9. Click Communicator on the Menu bar. You will see listed components of the Communicator suite.

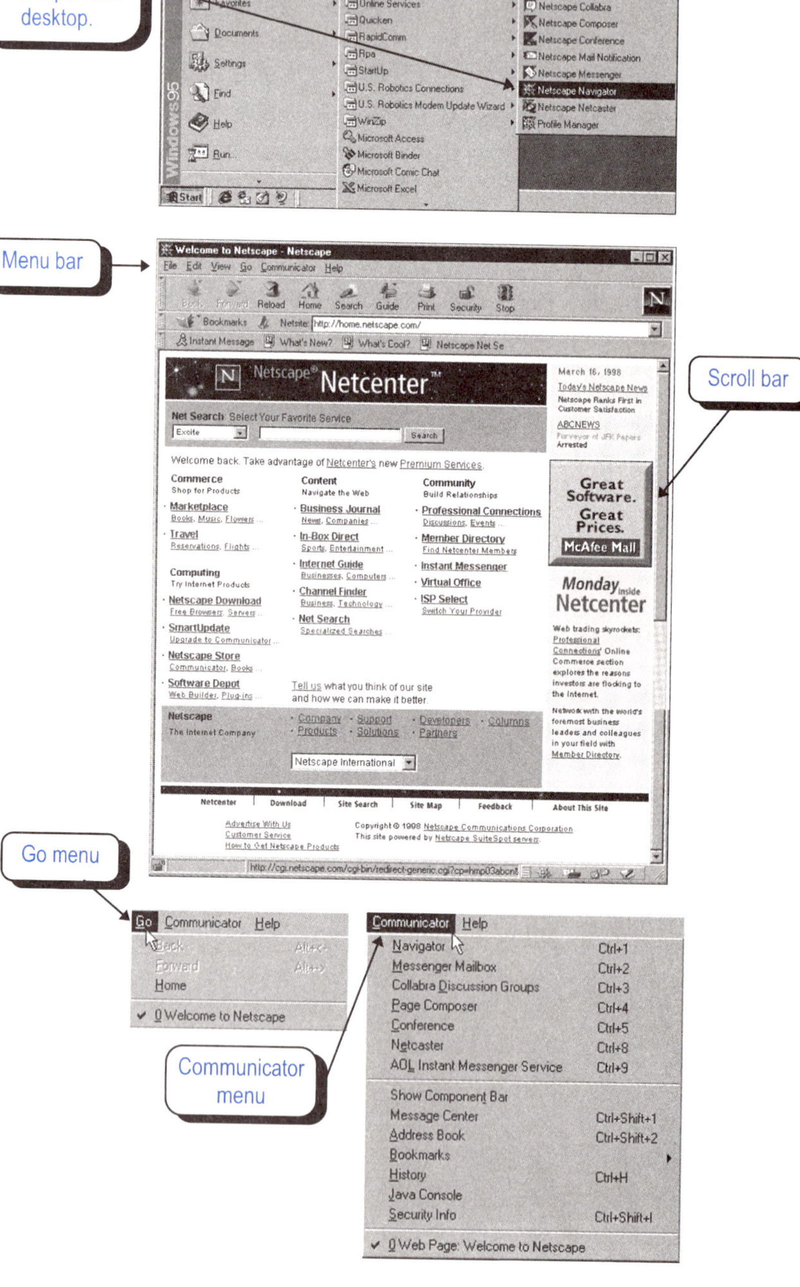

10. Click on the Help menu, click Help Contents and do the following:
    a. Click on Browsing the Web.
    ✓ *Note that Browsing the Web is in color and underlined, indicating that this is a link to another location.*
    b. Click on Links and URLs from the side bar on the left side of the NetHelp window.

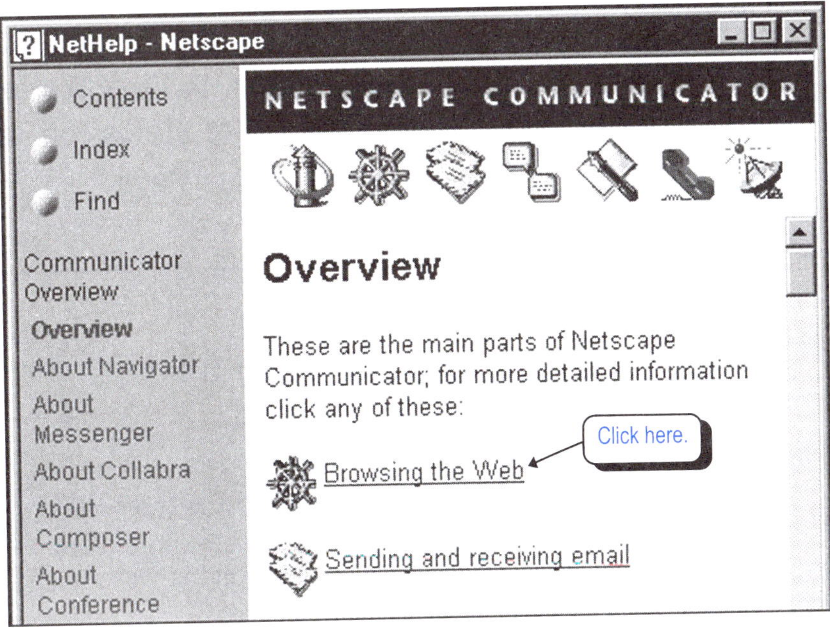

    c. Under Links and URLs click Using a URL to get details about Web addresses.
    Scroll down the listed information to learn more about viewing a Web page.
    d. Click the Back button at the bottom of the NetHelp window twice to return to the NetHelp Overview page.
    e. Click the Close button in the upper right corner of the NetHelp window to close Help and return to the Netscape Home page.
11. Continue on to the next exercise.

    OR

    Exit from Netscape and disconnect from your service provider.

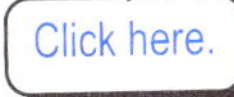

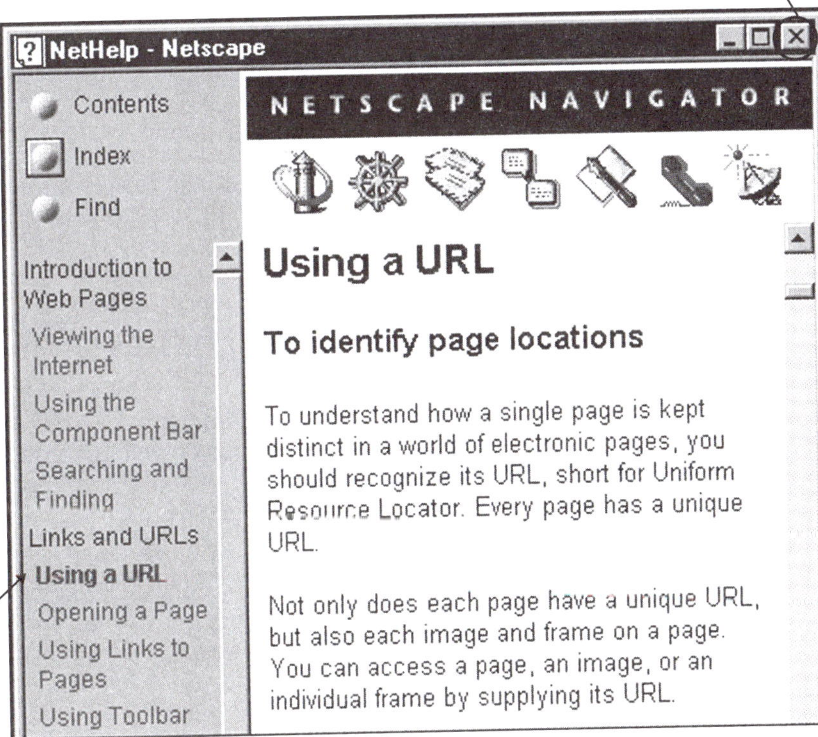

Exercise 2

- The Navigation Toolbar ■ Open World Wide Web Sites
- Stop a Load or Search ■ Status Bar ■ Return to the Home Page
- Change the Default Home Page

NOTES

The Navigation Toolbar

- The Navigation toolbar displays buttons for Netscape's most commonly used commands. Each button contains an icon and a word describing the button's function. Clicking on any of these buttons will activate the indicated task immediately.
- If the Navigation toolbar is not visible, select Show Navigation toolbar from the View menu.

Moves back through pages previously displayed.

✓ *Back is available only if you have moved around among World Wide Web pages in the current Navigator session; otherwise, it is gray.*

Moves forward through pages previously displayed.

✓ *Forward is available only if you have used the Back button; otherwise, it is gray.*

Reloads the currently displayed Web page. Use this button if the current page is taking too long to download, or to update the current page with any changes that may have been made since you first downloaded the page.

Displays your Home page.

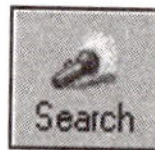

Displays Netscape's Net Search Page.

Displays a drop-down menu with helpful links to Internet sites containing search tools and services.

Prints the displayed page, topic, or article.

Displays security information for the displayed Web page as well as information on Netscape security features.

Stops loading the current Web page.

Note

If the Navigation toolbar is not visible, select Show Navigation Toolbar on the View menu.

Note

If you have explored many sites and would like to see the links that you followed, clicking Back is a good way to review your actions.

Open World Wide Web Sites

- There are several ways to access a World Wide Web site. The most reliable way is to enter the correct URL in the Location field on the Location toolbar.

- If the address you enter is the address of a site you have visited recently or that you have bookmarked, you will notice as you begin to type that Netscape will attempt to complete the address for you. If the address that Netscape suggests is the one you want, press Enter.
- If the address that Netscape suggests is not correct, keep typing to complete the desired address and then press Enter. Or, you can click the down arrow next to the Location field to view a list of other possible matches, select an address, and press Enter.
- You can also enter the URL in the Open Page dialog box to access a Web site. To do so, select Open Page from the File menu, enter the URL in the location line, select Navigator, and click Open.

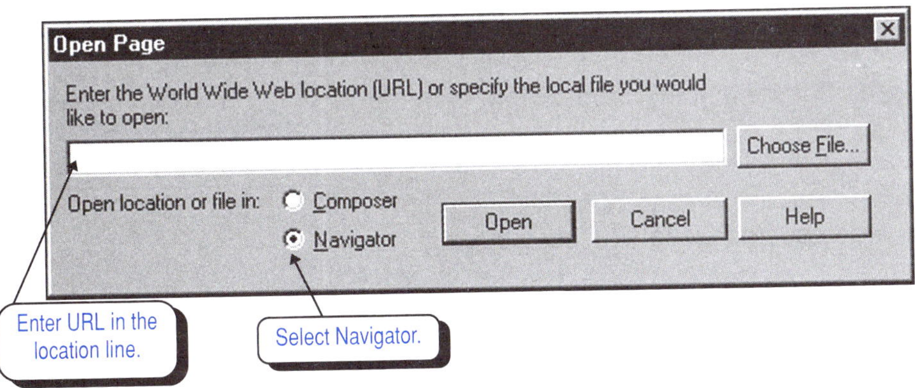

- URLs have several parts. Most Web sites begin with **http://**. This stands for Hypertext Transfer Protocol, a set of standard conventions used to exchange information between computers on the Web.
- This is followed by the address of the computer on which the Web site is stored, for example, www.ddcpub.com. A computer address for a World Wide Web site usually begin with www, indicating that it's located on the World Wide Web, and ends with a domain name, which identifies the kind of organization sponsoring the site.
- A URL usually ends with a domain name and suffix, such as *ddcpub.com*, which identifies the organization sponsoring the site.
- There are seven domain names for worldwide addressing purposes:

com	Commercial enterprise
edu	Educational institution
org	Non commercial organization
mil	U. S. Military location
net	A network that has a gateway to the Internet
gov	Local, state, or federal government location
int	International organization

Note

You can also enter the name of a particular Web site on the location line in the Open Page dialog box to access a Web site. Netscape will return the closest possible matches to the information you enter.

Note

Don't be discouraged if you can't connect to the Web site immediately. The site may be off line temporarily or it may be busy with other users trying to access it. Be sure you've typed the URL accurately. Occasionally, it takes several tries to connect.

- There are a few shortcuts for entering URL addresses. For one, you can omit the http://www. prefix from the Web address. Netscape assumes the **http://** protocol and **www**. If you are trying to connect to a company Web site, entering the company name is generally sufficient. Netscape will assume the **.com** suffix. In the above case, entering **ddcpub** on the location line and pressing Enter would be sufficient to reach http://www.ddcpub.com.

Stop a Load or Search

- Searching for information or loading a Web page can be time-consuming, especially if the Web page has many graphic images, there are many people trying to access the site at the same time, or your modem and computer processor operate at a slow speed. If data is taking a long time to load, you may wish to stop a search or loading process.
- To stop a search or load:
  - Click the Stop button [Stop] on the Navigation toolbar.

    OR

    Right-click anywhere on the screen and choose Stop from the shortcut menu.
- If you decide to continue the load after clicking the Stop button, click the Reload button [Reload] on the Navigation toolbar to redisplay a load that has been interrupted. You can also use the Reload button to reload a page that you think may have been updated since you last loaded it.

Status Bar

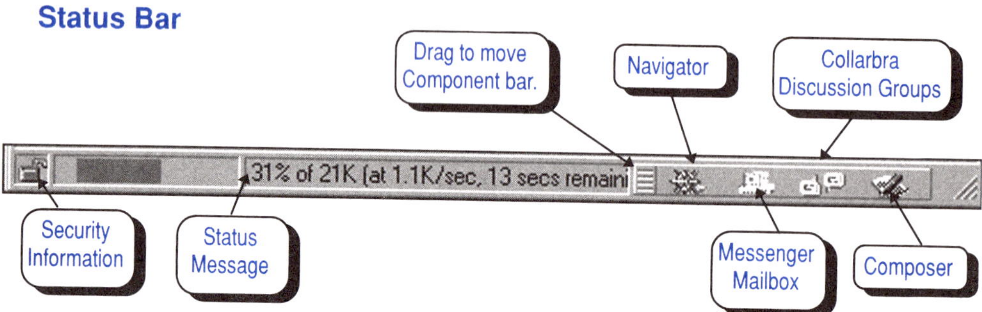

- The Status bar, located at the bottom of the screen, is a helpful indicator of the progress of the loading of a Web page. For example, as you load a Web site, you will see the percentage of the task completed so far and in many cases the remaining time it will take to load the page.
- The Status bar also indicates where specific hyperlinks on the current Web page point, so that when you point to a hyperlink, the URL of the site to which the link is connected displays.
- The padlock icon in the far-left corner of the Status bar indicates the security level of the file in use. An open lock indicates that the displayed document is an insecure document and the information contained in it can be accessed by anyone.
- A closed lock indicates that the displayed information is encrypted (or sent in code) ensuring a higher level of security for information being transmitted. Secured documents are generally used in cases where you can input personal information, such as your home address or credit card

Note

Additional domain names have been proposed to accommodate the rapidly growing number of www sites. Some of the proposed names include:

- .firm - businesses
- .store - businesses selling products or services online
- .web - activities related to the Web
- .arts - cultural and entertainment sites
- .rec - recreational sites
- .info - informational sites
- .nom - sites created by individuals or families

Note

See the Netscape Handbook for more information about security levels.

number. You should never transmit personal information in an unsecured document.

- In the lower-right corner of the Status bar is the Communicator Component bar. The icons are links to Netscape Communicator component programs: Navigator, Messenger (e-mail), Collabra (Discussion Groups), and Composer (Web page composition). You can make the Component bar a floating toolbar by clicking on the far-left button and dragging to the desired location on the screen. To redock the Component bar on the Status bar, click the Close button on the Component bar.

Return to the Home Page

- There are four ways to return to the Home page:
  - Click the Home button on the Navigation toolbar.

    OR

    Click Home on the Go menu.

    OR

    Click the Netscape icon to return to the Netscape Home page.

    OR

    Click Back on the Navigation toolbar to move back through Web links you have visited in the current session until you return to the Home page.

Change the Default Home Page

- By default Netscape Navigator uses the Netscape Communications, Inc. Web site as its Home page. You can, however, assign any Web page you choose to be your default Home page. To do so, open to the Web page you want to use as your Home page and select Preferences from the Edit menu.
- In the Preferences dialog box that follows, click the Use Current Page button and click OK.
- You can also assign a Web page as your default Home page without opening it by opening the Preferences dialog box, entering the URL of the desired page in the Location text box and then clicking OK.

In this exercise, you will open Web sites and use the Navigation toolbar to move from site to site. You will also change and reset your Home page.

Note: To ensure consistent results, this exercise uses simulated sites. The real URLs appear at the end of the exercise.

Web Search

Search for answers to the following questions using the Web sites you will visit in the Web simulation exercise.

1. List the five bulleted links available on the American History museum page.

   ____

2. List the three links available when you click on the arrow next to the Forward button.

   ____

3. List the three rectangular buttons on the left side of the NOAA page.

   ____

EXERCISE DIRECTIONS

1. Launch the Internet simulation. From the Main Menu, select Lesson 2, then select Exercise 2.
2. Open the File menu and select Open Page.
3. On the Address line, type the following URL and press Enter: *http://www.si.edu*

   ➲ *The Home page for the Smithsonian Institution appears.*
4. Move your pointer over the page and note how it changes to a hand when it is over a hyperlink.
5. Find the link to Museums–Organizations and click on it once.

   ➲ *The Museums and Organizations page opens.*
6. Note the new screen.
7. Note that the Back button is now darkened.

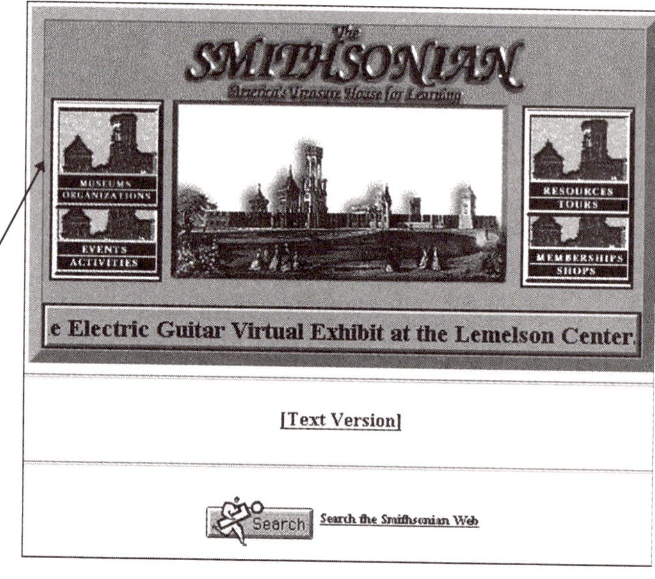

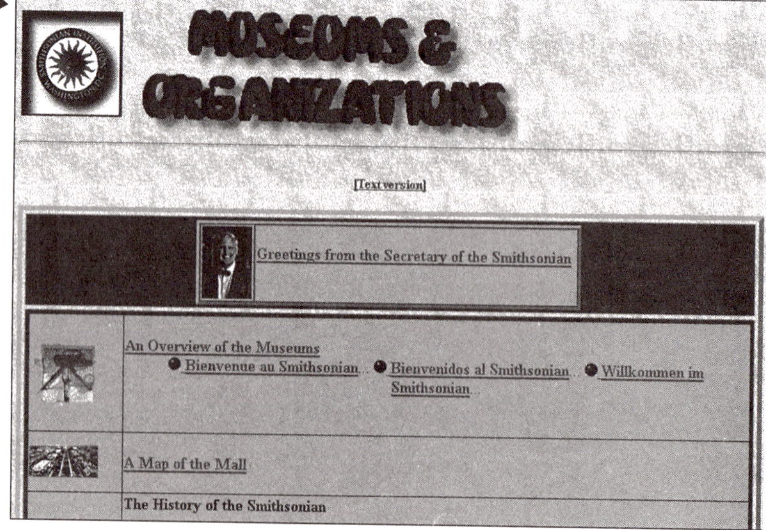

8. Scroll down and click the link to A Map of the Mall and do the following:
   a. Scroll down and click on the American History building.
   b. Click the Back button once to return to the Map of the Mall page.

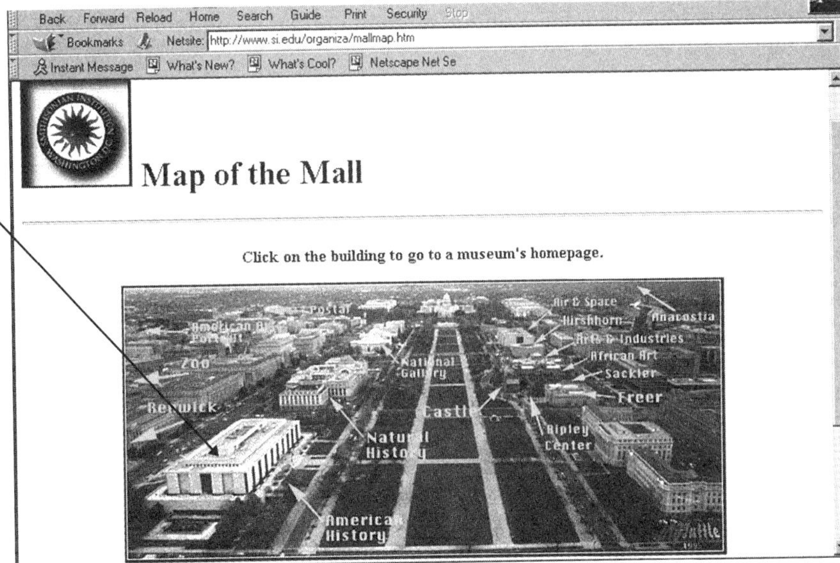

   c. Click the arrow next to the Back button and note the series of links that displays. Click the Smithsonian Institution Home Page.
      ✓ *Note that the Forward button is no longer dimmed.*

   d. Click the arrow next to the Forward button and click on National Museum of History.
      ✓ *Note that the Back button is still available, but the Forward button is now dimmed.*

9. Click the Netscape icon to return to the Netscape Home page.

10. Click once in the Location field. This should automatically highlight the entire address. Start typing the following address: *www.si.edu*.
    ✓ *Netscape should recognize the address as a site you have recently visited and suggest a possible match by finishing the address for you. Since you have just visited this site, the suggested address is probably correct.*

11. Click the down arrow at the end of the Location field to view other recently visited addresses that are possible matches.
12. Accept the **www.si.edu** address by pressing the Enter key.
13. Select Open Page from the File menu and do the following:
    a. Type the following on the Address line and then press Enter: *http://www.noaa.gov/*
    b. Let the page start to load but then click the Stop button before the page is fully loaded.
    c. Note the incomplete graphics.

    ➲ *You may also see the placement symbol that indicates an unloaded graphic.*

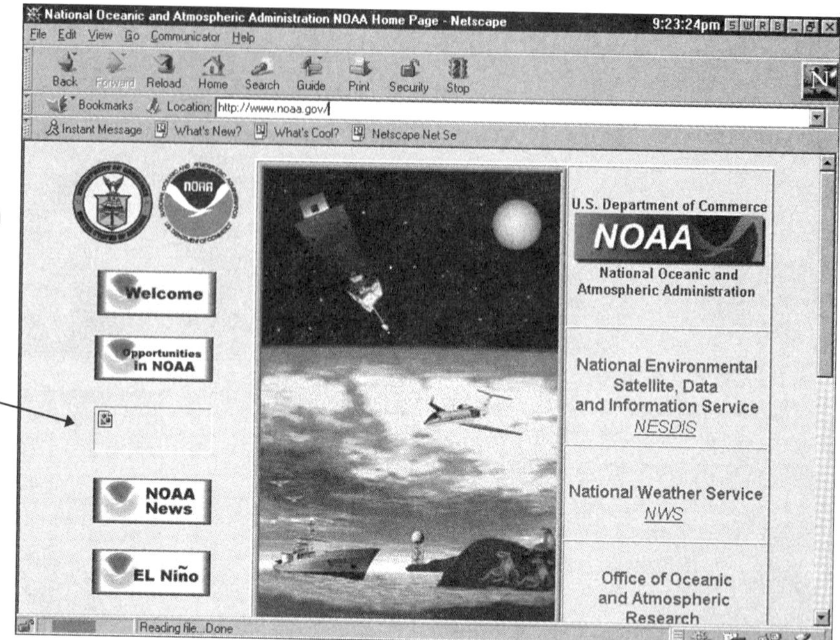

14. Click the Netscape icon to return to the Netscape Home Page.
15. Open the File menu, select Open Page, and enter the following URL: *http://cnn.com/WEATHER/NAmerica/region_map.html*

    ➲ *The CNN North American weather map opens.*

16. Open the Edit menu and select Preferences.

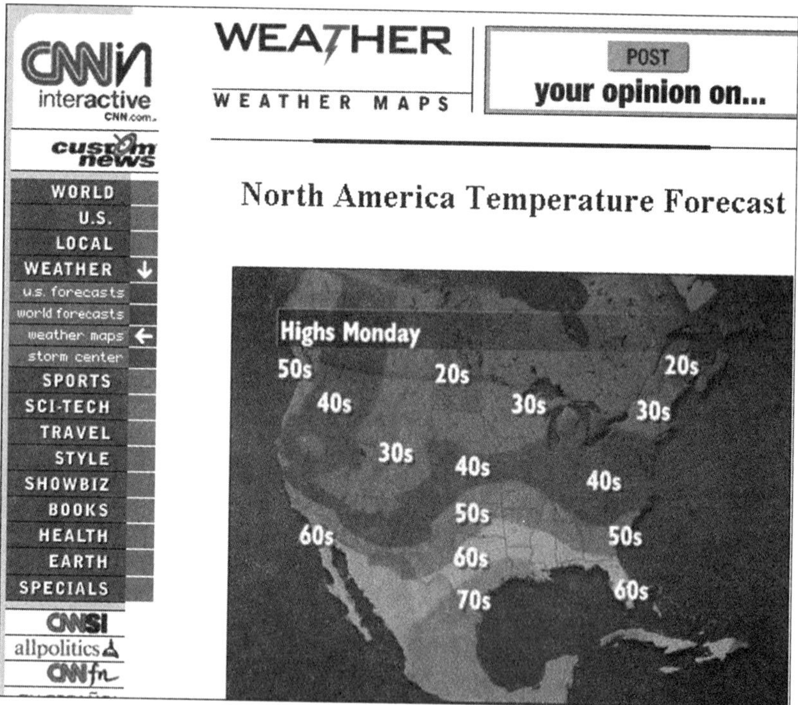

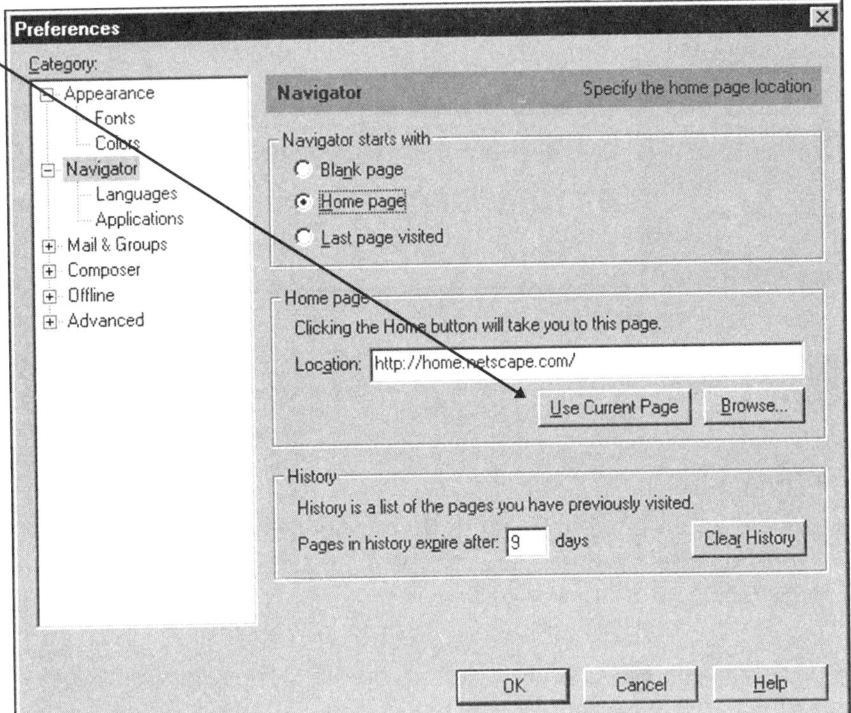

17. Click Use Current Page to make the CNN weather page your new Home page.
    - *The address for the CNN weather page now appears in the Home page Location text box.*
18. Click OK.
19. Click the Back button on the Navigation toolbar twice to return to the NOAA (National Oceanographic and Atmospheric Administration) page.
20. Click Home on the Navigation toolbar to return to your new home page
21. Click the Netscape icon N to return to the Netscape home page.
22. Make it your Home page again by opening the Preference dialog box on the Edit menu and selecting Use Current Page.
23. Click OK to return to Netscape.
24. Continue on to the next exercise.

    OR

    Exit from the simulation.

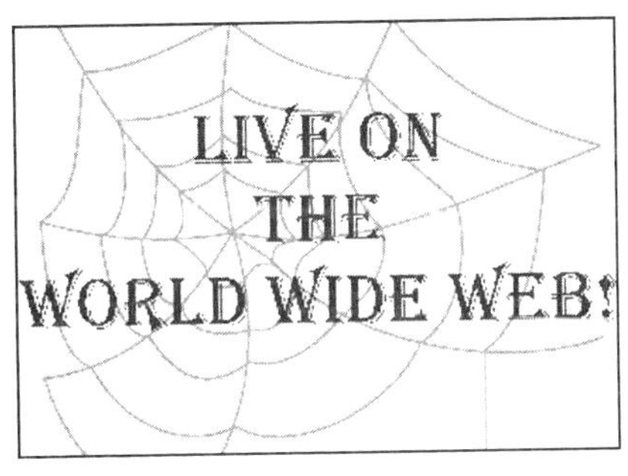

Netscape Navigator's Home Page
http://www.netscape.com

The WeatherChannel Home Page
http://www.weather.com

The Smithsonian Instituition Home Page
http://www.si.edu

DDC Publishing Home Page
http://www.ddcpub.com

Exercise 3

■ History List ■ Bookmarks ■ Bookmarks Window ■ Add Bookmarks
■ Open a Bookmarked Web Site ■ Delete Bookmarks
■ Create Bookmarks from the History List

NOTES

History List

- While you move back and forth among Web sites, Netscape automatically records each of these site locations in a **history** list, which is temporarily stored on your hard drive. You can use the History to track sites you have already visited, or jump to a recently viewed site.
- To view the History, click History on the Communicator menu, or press Ctrl+H. To link to a site listed in History, simply double-click on it.
- Notice that the site title, URL, and the dates of the first and last visit are displayed for each Web page listed. You can also see when Netscape will automatically delete the listing (expiration date) and the number of times you have visited the site by clicking on the Show and Hide columns arrows in the upper right corner of the list (see illustration below).
- By default, History items are listed in the order in which they were viewed, descending from the most recent. You can, however, sort them by title, URL, date of first visit, expiration date, or number of times visited by clicking on the appropriate column heading.

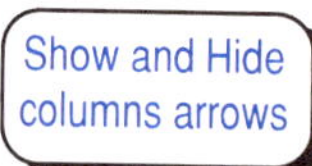

History

File Edit View Communicator Help

Title	Location	First Visit...	Last Visited	Expiration	Visit...
Netscape Navi...	http://home.netsca...	6 days ago	6 days ago	7/12/1997...	2
	http://home.netsca...	6 days ago	6 days ago	7/12/1997...	2
Netscape Navi...	http://home.netsca...	6 days ago	6 days ago	7/12/1997...	2
Helper Applicati...	http://home.netsca...	6 days ago	6 days ago	7/12/1997...	2
Windows Helpe...	http://home.netsca...	6 days ago	6 days ago	7/12/1997...	1
Overview of Pro...	http://home.netsca...	6 days ago	6 days ago	7/12/1997...	1
Netscape Prod...	http://home.netsca...	6 days ago	6 days ago	7/12/1997...	1
Software Downl...	http://home.netsca...	6 days ago	6 days ago	7/12/1997...	1
	http://www.bignet.c...	6/11/1997...	6/11/1997...	7/11/1997...	2
Netscape Navi...	file:///C|/Program F...	6/11/1997...	6/11/1997...	7/11/1997...	1

Note

As you move from one site to another on the Web, you may find yourself asking "How did I get here?" The History list is an easy way to see the path you followed to get to the current location.

- Netscape saves a Web page address in the History for a default time of 9 days. You can change this figure by selecting Preferences from the Edit menu and typing the desired number of days in the Pages in history expire after text box under the History heading.

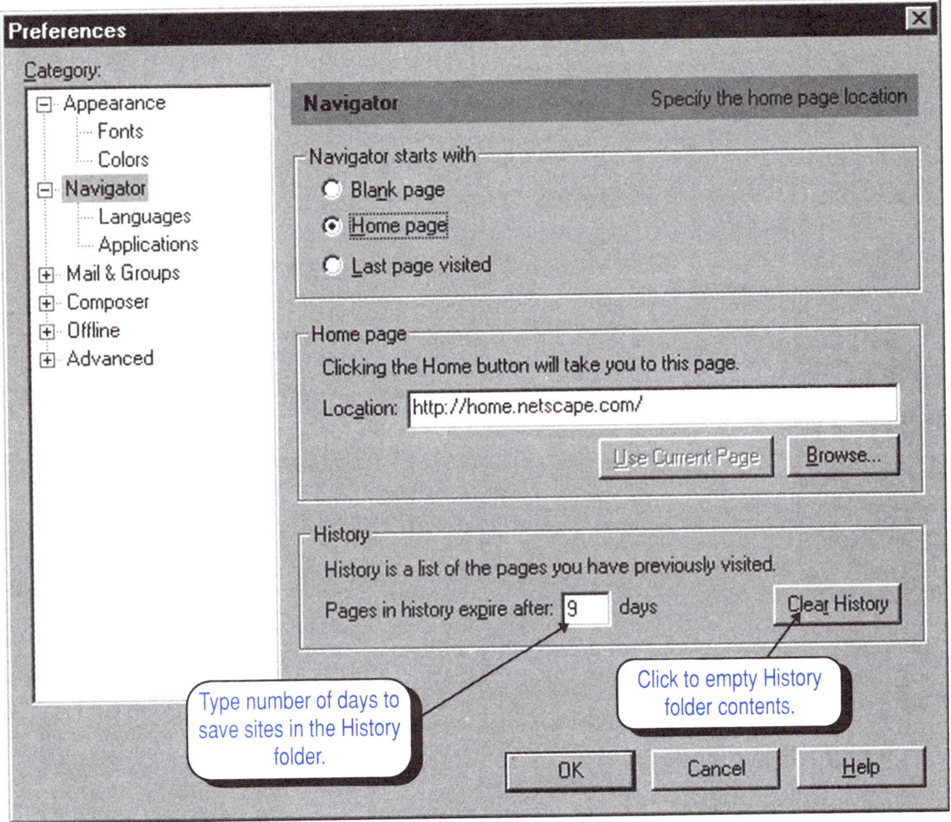

- You can also empty the contents of your History folder in the Preferences dialog box. To do so, click the Clear History button under the History heading.

Bookmarks

- A **bookmark** is a placeholder containing the title and URL of a Web page that, when selected, links directly to that page. If you find a Web site that you like and you want to revisit, you can create a bookmark to record its location. (See Add Bookmarks, on the following page). The Netscape bookmark feature maintains permanent records of the Web sites in your bookmark files so that you can return to them easily.
- You can view the Bookmarks menu by selecting Bookmarks from the Communicator menu or by clicking on the Bookmarks QuickFile button on the Location toolbar.

Bookmarks Window

- Bookmarks are stored in a separate bookmark.htm file on your hard drive. This file can be accessed by selecting Bookmarks, Edit Bookmarks from the Communicator menu. You can edit and organize bookmarks from the bookmark.htm window that displays.

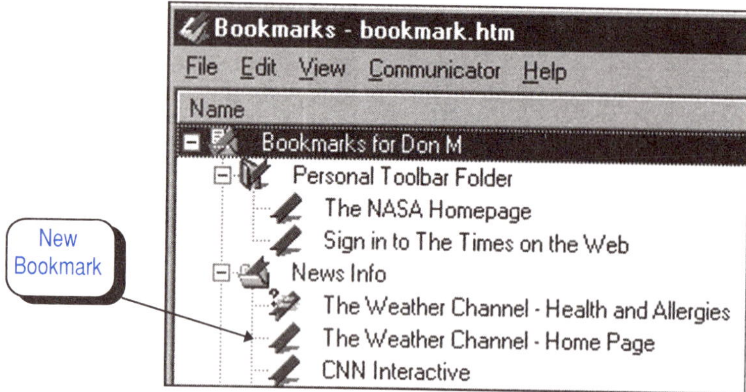

✓ *Bookmark.htm files are automatically saved when you close the Bookmarks window. It is not recommended that you do a Save As to the file unless you wish to create more than one bookmark.htm file. This would be necessary, for example, if you wanted to have only certain bookmarks appear under your Bookmarks menu, but would like to retain additional bookmarks in a separate bookmark file.*

Add Bookmarks

- There are several ways to bookmark a Web site.
  - Display the Web page to add, go to Bookmarks on the Communicator menu and click Add Bookmark.

OR

Display the Web page to add, click the Bookmarks QuickFile button on the Location toolbar, and click Add Bookmark.

OR

Display the Web page to add, right-click and select Add Bookmark from the shortcut menu.

OR

Point to a hyperlink that connects to the page you want to bookmark, right-click and select Add Bookmark.

OR

Display the Web page to add and click and drag the Location icon onto the Bookmarks QuickFile button on the Location toolbar. The Bookmark menu displays, and the mouse pointer changes to a chain link shape. Drag the link and insert it anywhere on the Bookmark listing.

Note

You can create bookmarks from addresses in the History folder. Click Communicator, History and select the listing to bookmark. Right-click on it and choose Add to Bookmarks from the menu.

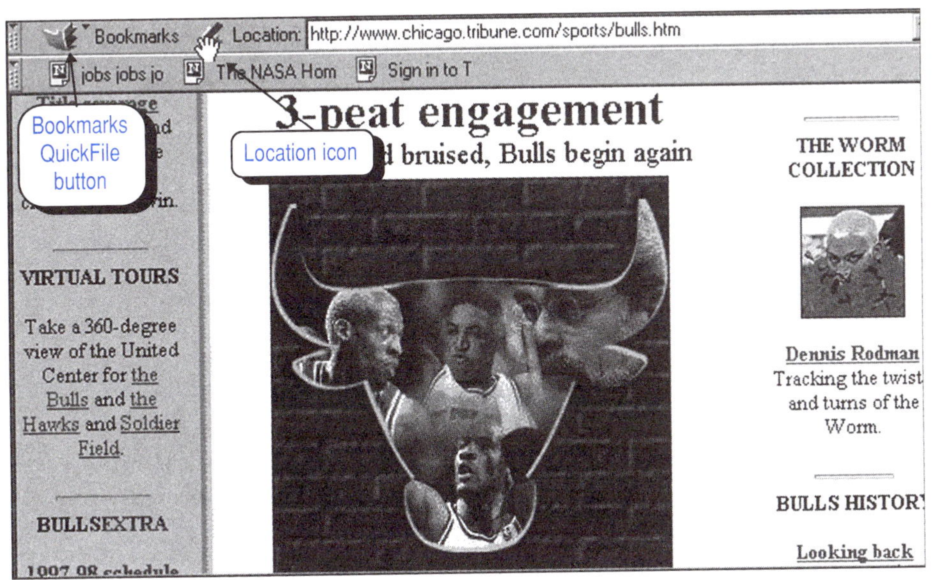

- There is no confirmation box to confirm that a bookmark has been added to the file. It will be automatically added to your bookmark list.

Open a Bookmarked Web Site

- Opening a bookmarked Web site is quick and easy.

  Click on the Bookmarks QuickFile button on the Location toolbar.

  OR

  Select Bookmarks from the Communicator menu.

  Select the bookmark to open from the drop-down menu.

  OR

  Select the folder containing the desired bookmark and then select a bookmark from the submenu that displays.

Delete Bookmarks

- Bookmarks may be deleted at anytime. For example, you may wish to delete a bookmark if a Web site no longer exists or remove one that is no longer of interest to you.
- To delete a bookmark do the following:
  - Click the Communicator menu.
  - Click Bookmarks.
  - Click Edit Bookmarks.
  - In the Bookmarks window, select the bookmark you want to delete by clicking on it from the bookmark list.
  - Press the Delete key.

    OR

    Right-click after selecting the bookmark to delete and choose Delete Bookmark from the shortcut menu.

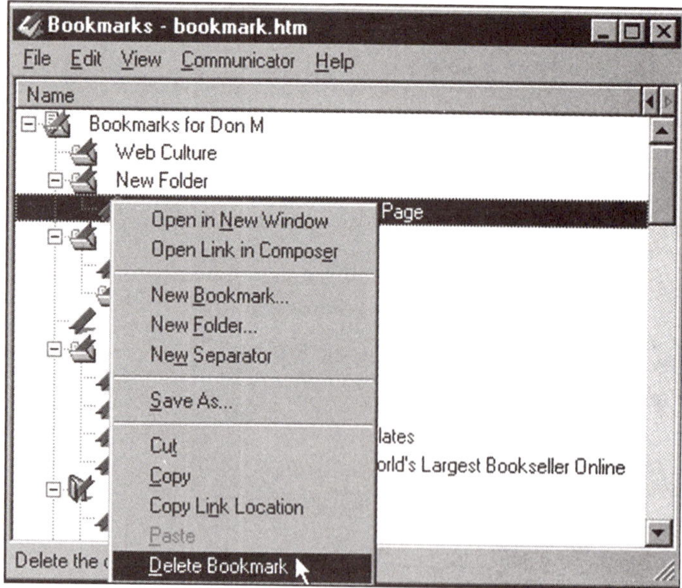

✓ *The bookmark is deleted. There is no confirmation box. If you change your mind, you will have to restore the bookmark manually by choosing File, New Bookmark in the Bookmark Properties dialog box and entering the bookmark name and URL in the appropriate text boxes. You can also revisit the site and add the site to the bookmarks list from there.*

Create Bookmarks from the History List

- You can also bookmark a Web site in the History list.
  - Open the Communicator menu and select History.

  ✓ *The History window displays.*
  - Click to select the History item that you want to bookmark.
  - Click Add To Bookmarks from the File menu.

  OR

  Right-click on the item and select Add To Bookmarks.

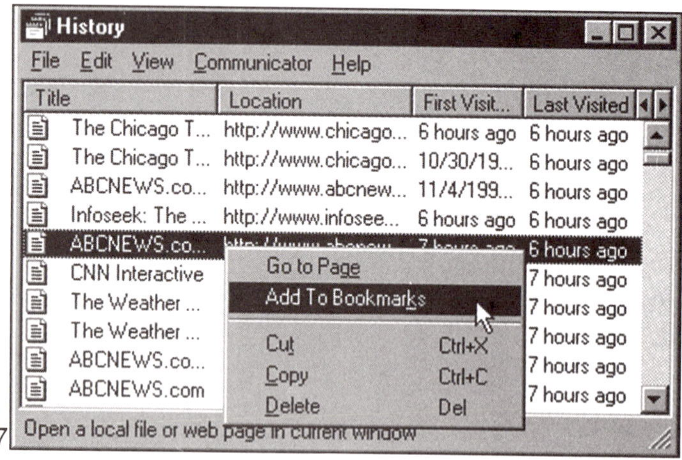

- Click the Close button (X) to exit the History window.

✓ *The bookmark will be added to your bookmark list.*

Note

To bookmark several History items at once, hold down the Ctrl key, click on the desired sites, right-click and select Add To Bookmarks.

In this exercise, you will add and delete Bookmarks and work within the Bookmarks window.

Note: *To ensure consistent results, this exercise uses simulated sites. The real URLs appear at the end of the exercise.*

Web Search

Search for answers to the following questions using the Web sites you will visit in the Web simulation exercise.

1. What type of collections are available from the American Memory home page?

   ____

2. What options appear when you right-click on an address in the History window?

   ____

EXERCISE DIRECTIONS

1. Launch the Internet simulation. From the Main Menu, select Lesson 2, then select Exercise 3.
2. Click in the Location field and type the URL for The Library of Congress and press Enter: *http://www.loc.gov/*
   - ➲ *The Home page of the Library of Congress opens.*
3. Click the link to American Memory.
   - ➲ *The Home page for The American Memory from the Library of Congress opens.*
4. Click the Bookmarks QuickFile button on the Location bar.
5. Click Add Bookmark.
6. Click on the Bookmarks QuickFile button again
   - ➲ *You should see a listing for the Amercian Memory from the Library of Congress at the bottom of the menu.*

   Home Page: American M...e Library of Congress

7. Right-click on the American Memory page and select **Add Bookmark** to add it a second time.
   - ➲ *When you click on the Bookmark QuickFile menu again, you should see two listings for The American Memory Home Page at the bottom of the menu.*

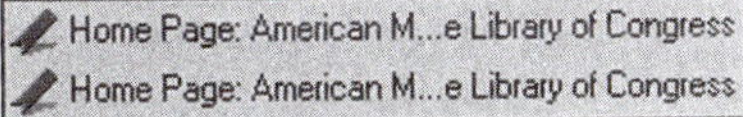

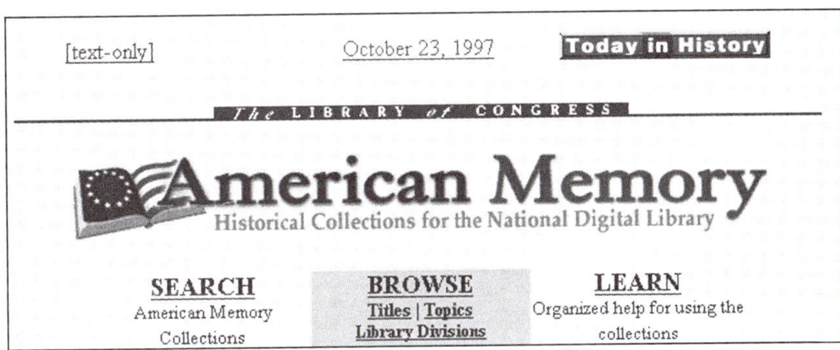

8. Click to display the Bookmark QuickFile menu. To delete the second listing for The American Memory page, click **Edit Bookmarks**.

   ➲ *The Bookmarks window will open.*

9. Right-click on the second occurrence of **The American Memory from the Library of Congress** bookmark and select **Delete Bookmark**.
10. Close the Bookmark.htm window.
11. Click Communicator, History.
12. Click the listing for **The Smithsonian Institution** to select it and right-click on the selected listing.
13. Click **Add To Bookmarks** to add the listing to your Bookmark file and close the History window.
14. Click the Bookmarks QuickFile button [Bookmarks] on the Location toolbar to see the new bookmark at the bottom of the Bookmark list.
15. Press the Esc key to close the Bookmark listing.
16. Continue on to the next exercise.

    OR

    Exit from the simulation.

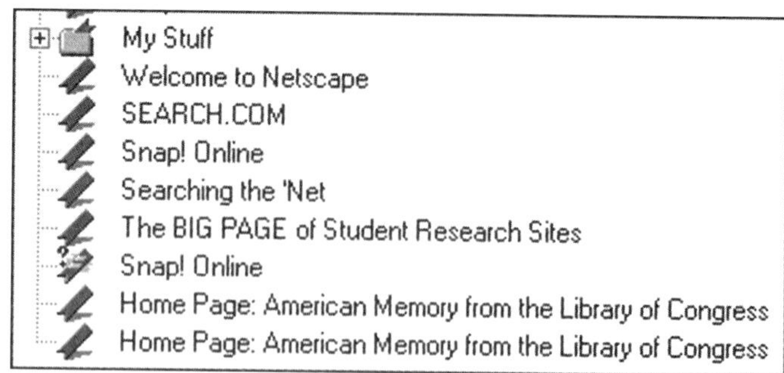

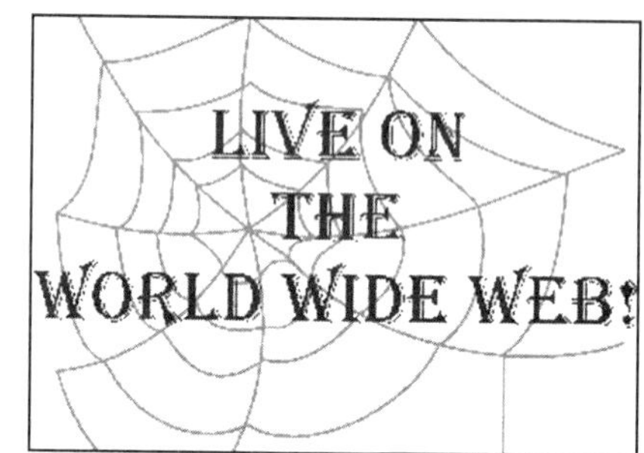

The White House
http://www.whitehouse.gov/WH/Welcome.html

The Chicago Tribune Home Page
http://www.chicago.tribune.com

CNN Interactive
http://www.cnn.com

The Discovery Channel Online
http://www.discovery.com/

NEXT EXERCISE

Exercise

4

- Netscape Navigator Main Search Page
- Start Search from Location Field

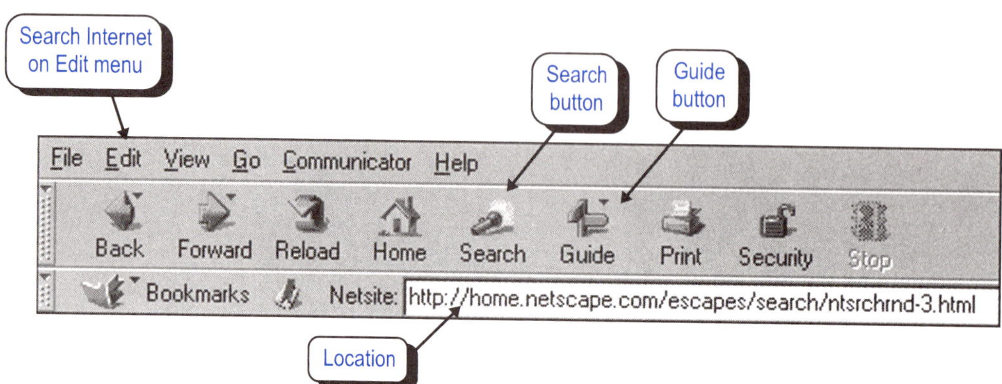

NOTES

Netscape Navigator Main Search Page

- Any Internet browser program offers a variety of search options. You may already be familiar with search engines or directories, such as Yahoo, Lycos, and AltaVista. These providers catalogue, classify, and organize information on the Internet and make it accessible to users. Although you will learn how to conduct effective searches in Lesson 3, it is helpful to first understand the search options that are available in Netscape Navigator.

- Click the Search button [Search] on the Navigation toolbar or select Search Internet from the Edit menu to access Netscape Navigator's Net Search page, where you can conduct a search using one of several search providers. The Netscape Net Search page opens with a search provider, such as Lycos, Excite or Yahoo!, already selected.

Netscape Net Search Page

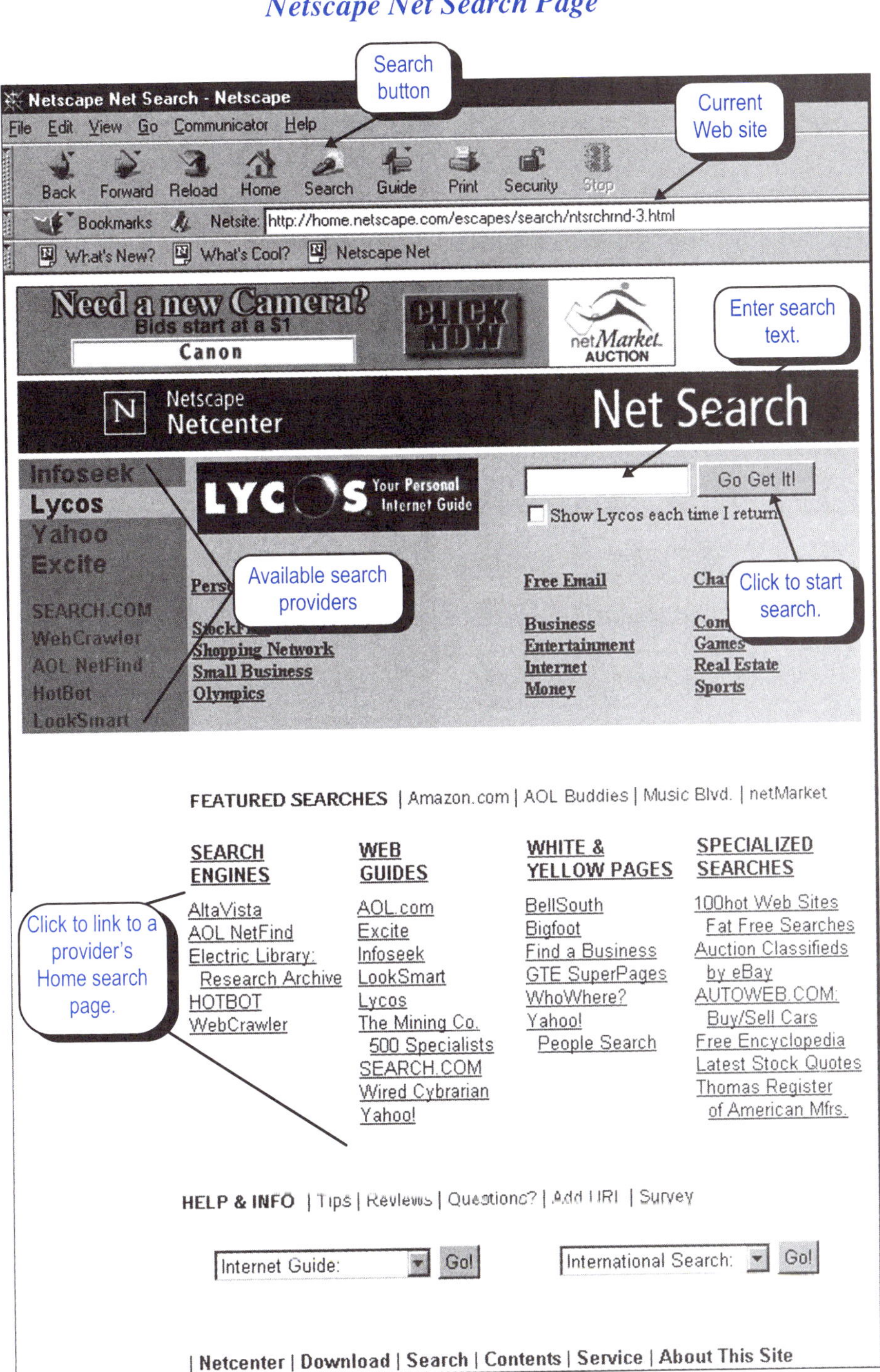

- You can choose a different search provider by clicking on one of the search provider names located on the upper left side of the Net Search window. The new provider will display with a search text box at the center of the Netscape Net Search screen, as in the illustration above.

- Once you have selected a search provider, you can enter a search topic in the textbox and click the appropriate button (*Find, Seek, Go Get It, Search, etc. Search providers will use different words*). The results of the search will display in the Navigator window, replacing the Net Search page. Note the illustration below. Click on a hyperlink to go to one of the Web sites listed in your search results. Click the Back button to return to the Netscape Net Search page.

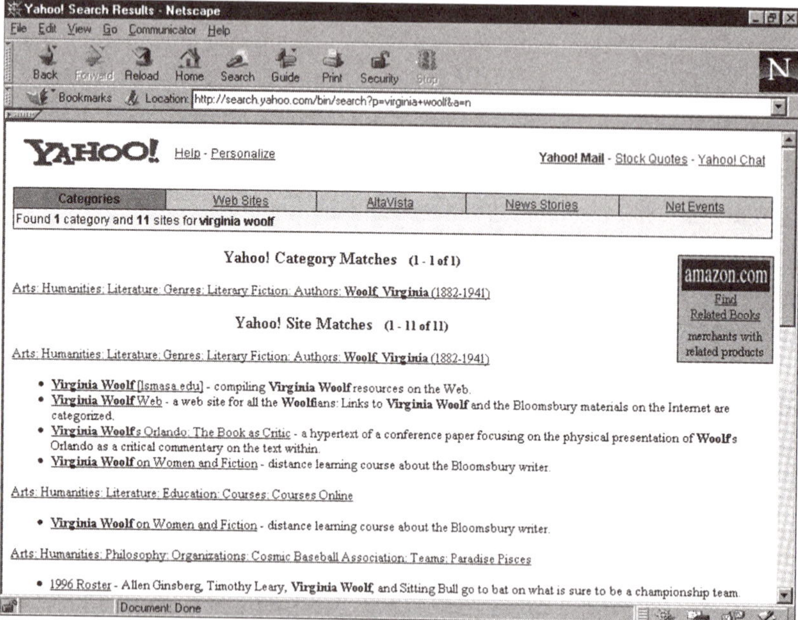

- Listed in the bottom half of the Netscape Net Search screen under the "Search Engines" and "Web Guides" headings are hyperlinks to several search providers' Home search pages. When you select one of these links, the selected provider's search page will open, replacing the Netscape Net Search page. Below, for example, is the search page that opens when the Lycos link is selected. Enter your search text in the appropriate box and click Search (or Find, Go Get It, Submit, etc.).

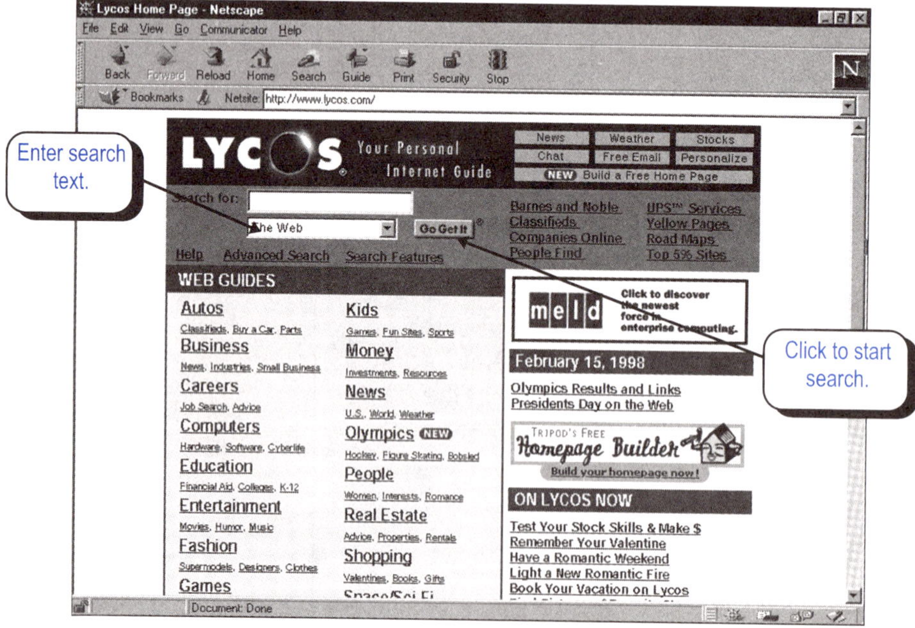

- Netscape Net Search also links to several specialized search providers, such as address directories and classified ad collections. Clicking one of these links will take you to the selected provider's own search page, where you can enter a name or keyword that you want to find. Illustrated below, for example, is the search page for a service that catalogs automobiles for sale around the country.

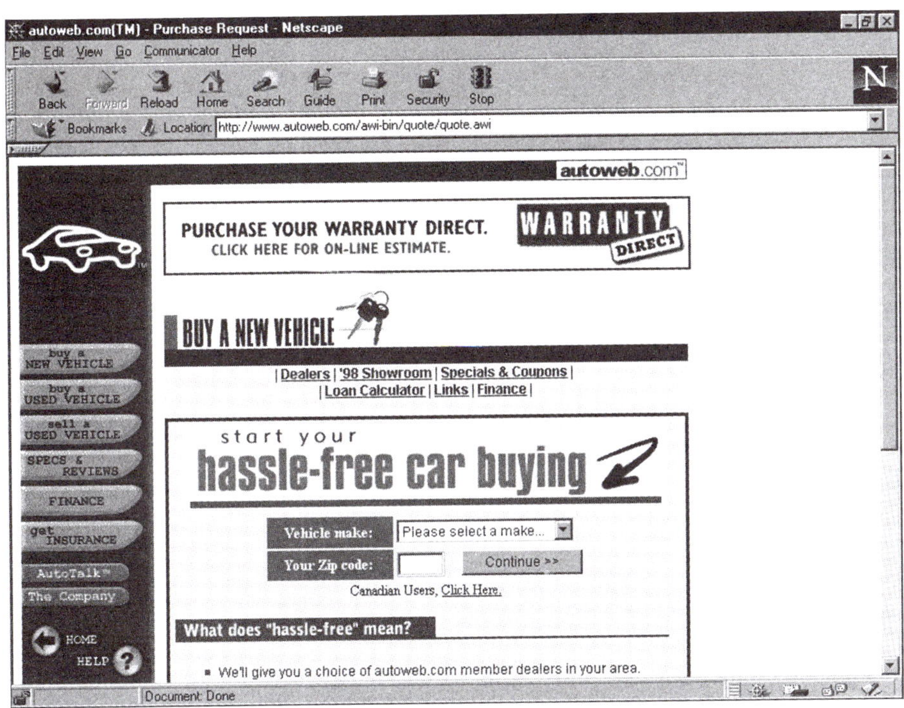

Start Search from Location Field

- In addition to displaying and entering addresses in the Location field, you can also use it to perform a quick search from wherever you are on the Web.

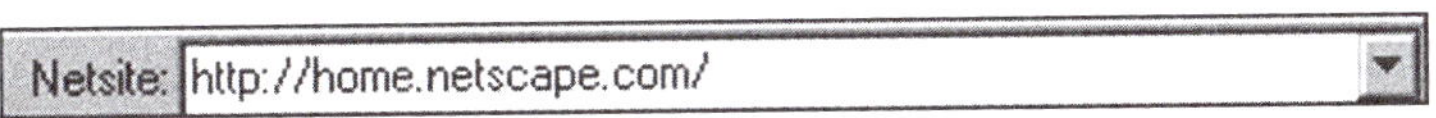

Click once in the Location field and type **go**, **find**, or **?** and press the spacebar once. Enter the word or phrase you want to find and press Enter. For example, if you want to search for information about the year 2000, type "find the year 2000" and press Enter.

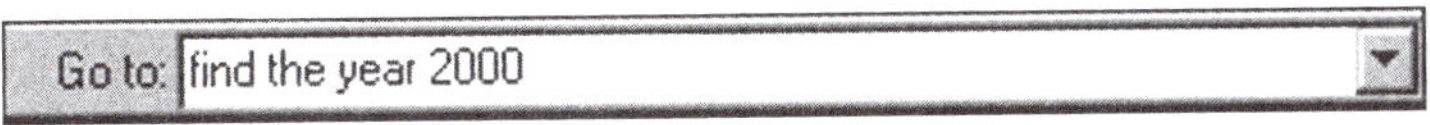

The Status bar will display the message "Connect: Contacting Host…" indicating that it is connecting to a search provider, which will perform your search. In a few moments, the results of your search display.

- Searching from the Location field uses only one search provider. If you want to refine your search or see if other search providers will give you different results, click the Search button on the Navigation toolbar and select a search provider from the links listed on the left side or bottom half of the Netscape Net Search screen.

In this exercise, you will conduct a search using the Location field and the Netscape Net Search page to find information about skiing and accommodations in a Colorado ski area.

Note: To ensure consistent results, this exercise uses simulated sites. The real URLs appear at the end of the exercise.

Web Search

Search for answers to the following questions using the Web sites you will visit in the Web simulation exercise.

1. How many matches are there to the search topic lodging+breckenridge+lodging?

____

2. How many guest rooms are there at The Wellington Inn?

____

EXERCISE DIRECTIONS

1. Launch the Internet simulation. From the Main Menu, select Lesson 2, then select Exercise 4.
2. Click the Search button on the Navigation toolbar to open the Netscape Net Search page.
3. Select Excite as the provider from the list of links on the left side of the window.
4. Type the following in the Search textbox and press Enter: *lodging+breckenridge+lodging.*

   ✓ *Be sure to use the plus signs with no spaces when you enter the search topic. This tells the search engine to display only those sites that include all of the search items.*

   ➲ *Excite displays ten search results at a time in decreasing order of confidence rating. A result rated close to 100% has a good chance of being what you want.*

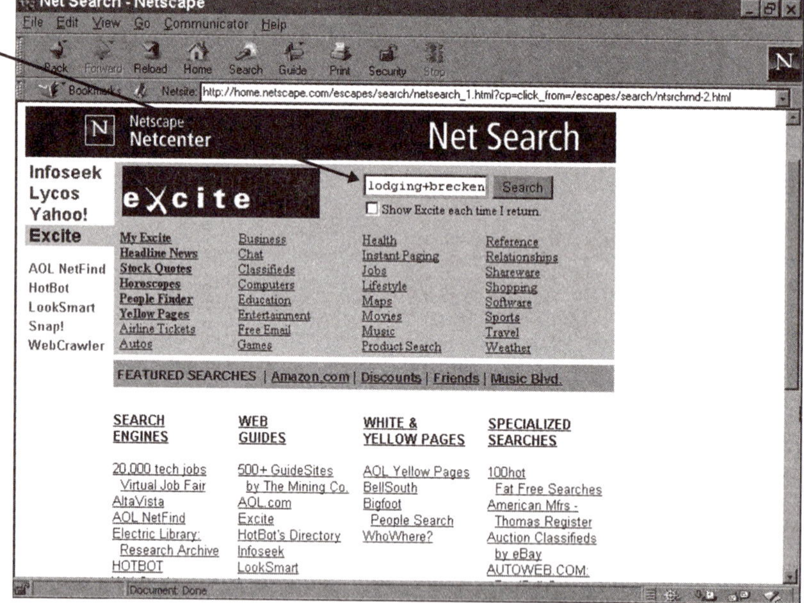

5. Click on the Summit County Lodging Guide–Colorado Resort Net link.

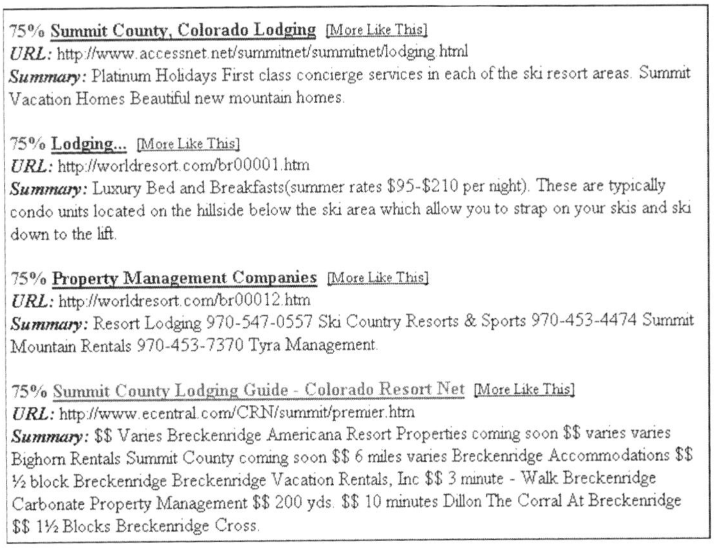

75% **Summit County, Colorado Lodging** [More Like This]
URL: http://www.accessnet.net/summitnet/summitnet/lodging.html
Summary: Platinum Holidays First class concierge services in each of the ski resort areas. Summit Vacation Homes Beautiful new mountain homes.

75% **Lodging...** [More Like This]
URL: http://worldresort.com/br00001.htm
Summary: Luxury Bed and Breakfasts(summer rates $95-$210 per night). These are typically condo units located on the hillside below the ski area which allow you to strap on your skis and ski down to the lift.

75% **Property Management Companies** [More Like This]
URL: http://worldresort.com/br00012.htm
Summary: Resort Lodging 970-547-0557 Ski Country Resorts & Sports 970-453-4474 Summit Mountain Rentals 970-453-7370 Tyra Management.

75% Summit County Lodging Guide - Colorado Resort Net [More Like This]
URL: http://www.ecentral.com/CRN/summit/premier.htm
Summary: $$ Varies Breckenridge Americana Resort Properties coming soon $$ varies varies Bighorn Rentals Summit County coming soon $$ 6 miles varies Breckenridge Accommodations $$ ½ block Breckenridge Breckenridge Vacation Rentals, Inc $$ 3 minute - Walk Breckenridge Carbonate Property Management $$ 200 yds. $$ 10 minutes Dillon The Corral At Breckenridge $$ 1½ Blocks Breckenridge Cross.

➲ *The Summit County Lodging Guide Home page opens.*

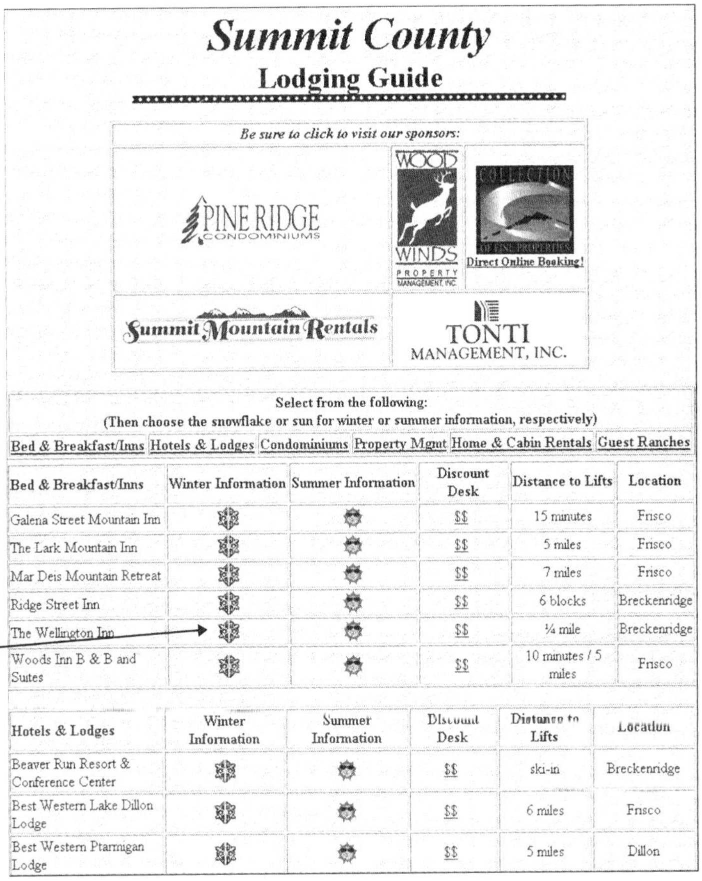

Summit County

Lodging Guide

Be sure to click to visit our sponsors:

PINE RIDGE CONDOMINIUMS

WOOD WINDS PROPERTY MANAGEMENT, INC.

COLLECTION OF FINE PROPERTIES

Direct Online Booking!

Summit Mountain Rentals

TONTI MANAGEMENT, INC.

Select from the following:
(Then choose the snowflake or sun for winter or summer information, respectively)

Bed & Breakfast/Inns | Hotels & Lodges | Condominiums | Property Mgmt | Home & Cabin Rentals | Guest Ranches

Bed & Breakfast/Inns	Winter Information	Summer Information	Discount Desk	Distance to Lifts	Location
Galena Street Mountain Inn			$$	15 minutes	Frisco
The Lark Mountain Inn			$$	5 miles	Frisco
Mar Deis Mountain Retreat			$$	7 miles	Frisco
Ridge Street Inn			$$	6 blocks	Breckenridge
The Wellington Inn			$$	¼ mile	Breckenridge
Woods Inn B & B and Suites			$$	10 minutes / 5 miles	Frisco

6. Scroll down and note the number of lodging possibilities in the Breckenridge area.
7. Find the link to **Winter information** about the Wellington Inn and click it oncc.
8. Continue on to the next exercise

   OR

   Exit from the simulation.

Hotels & Lodges	Winter Information	Summer Information	Discount Desk	Distance to Lifts	Location
Beaver Run Resort & Conference Center			$$	ski-in	Breckenridge
Best Western Lake Dillon Lodge			$$	6 miles	Frisco
Best Western Ptarmigan Lodge			$$	5 miles	Dillon

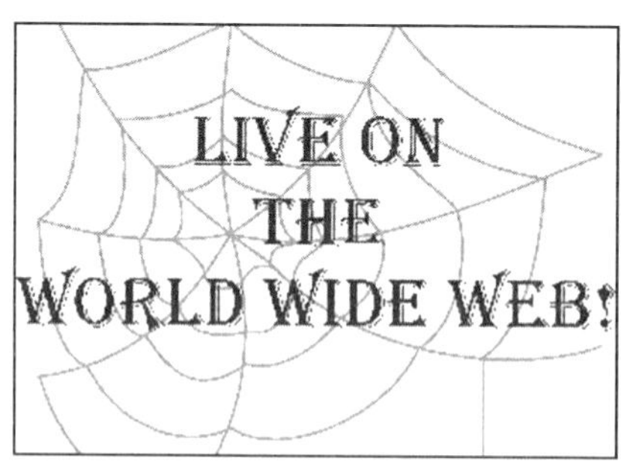

Great Outdoors Recreation Pages
http://www.gorp.com/

Colorado Ski Museum & Ski Hall of Fame
http://www.vailsoft.com/museum/

Arthur Frommer's Outspoken Encyclopedia of Travel
http://www.frommers.com/

CNN Financial News - Currencies Market
http://cnnfn.com/markets/currencies.html

Lesson 3:
Search Engines and Search Sites

Exercise 1

- Searching vs. Surfing
- Search Sites
- Search Basics

Exercise 2

- Keyword Searches
- Refine a Search
- Get Help
- Yahoo! and AltaVista Alliance

Exercise 3

- Operators
- Boolean Operators
- Grouping Operators
- Case Sensitive Searches
- Major Search Engines and Operators

Exercise 1

■ Searching vs. Surfing ■ Search Sites ■ Search Basics

NOTES

Searching vs. Surfing

- Finding a direct route to the information you want on the Web can be a challenge since there is no centralized index or uniform tracking system for the contents of the Internet. Initially, it seems very easy to find information on the Web—you just connect to a relevant site and then start clicking on links to related sites. This random method of searching the Internet is called **surfing**.
- Although surfing can be entertaining, it can also be slow, inefficient, and can lead you to unrelated sites.
- If you want a more direct and organized way of locating information, you can **search** the Web via search sites that track, catalog, and index information on the Internet. This method is more efficient and usually yields more specific results.

Search Sites

- **Search sites**, or search providers, catalog Web sites into databases that you can search to find information of interest.
- Most search sites build their catalogs using software programs, often called crawlers, spiders, robots, or worms. These programs seek new Web sites and catalog them, usually by downloading their Home pages or saving their text.
- Search sites differ in how they sort and catalog Web sites and in how they allow you to search their databases. The three most common types of search sites are search engines, search directories, and multi-threaded search engines. A description of each follows.

Search Engines

- A search engine sorts Web sites by key text and allows you to search the database by keyword(s). When you enter a keyword(s) in the search form, the search engine looks for sites in its database containing the keyword(s) and then displays a list of matches. Search engines usually yield the most comprehensive list of results. However, you often have to wade through numerous sites that may contain your keyword but are not relevant to your search topic.

- Major search engines include: AltaVista, HotBot, Infoseek, Excite, Lycos, Northern Light, Cyberhound, and Open Text. Each engine uses different search methods, which yield varying search results. It is a good idea to experiment with several engines to find the ones that work best for you.

HotBot Opening Search Page

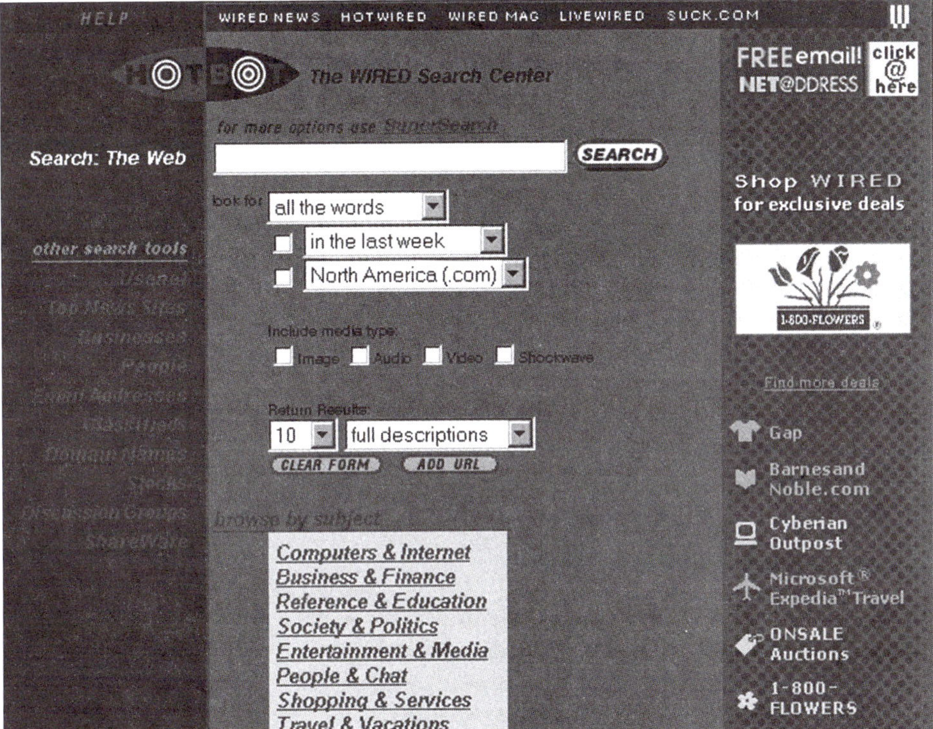

Directories

- A directory sorts Web sites by topic and arranges the topics into hierarchical menus that you can browse level by level. When you click on a topic, a list of subtopics displays. When you click on a subtopic, a list of sub-subtopics displays, and so on until you find a list of Web sites covering a narrowly defined topic of your choice.
- Since directory catalogs are usually organized by humans who discard irrelevant Web sites, the Web sites that turn up are often more likely to be relevant than those you might find using a search engine. This can save you the time and frustration of sorting through dozens of unrelated sites. Although search directories may be better organized and more selective, the human factor can also slow down the cataloging process, making directories less comprehensive and up-to-date than the search engines.

- Yahoo!, the oldest search service on the World Wide Web is the best example of an Internet search directory. Other major search directories are: LookSmart, Infohiway, and Magellan.

Yahoo Opening Search Page

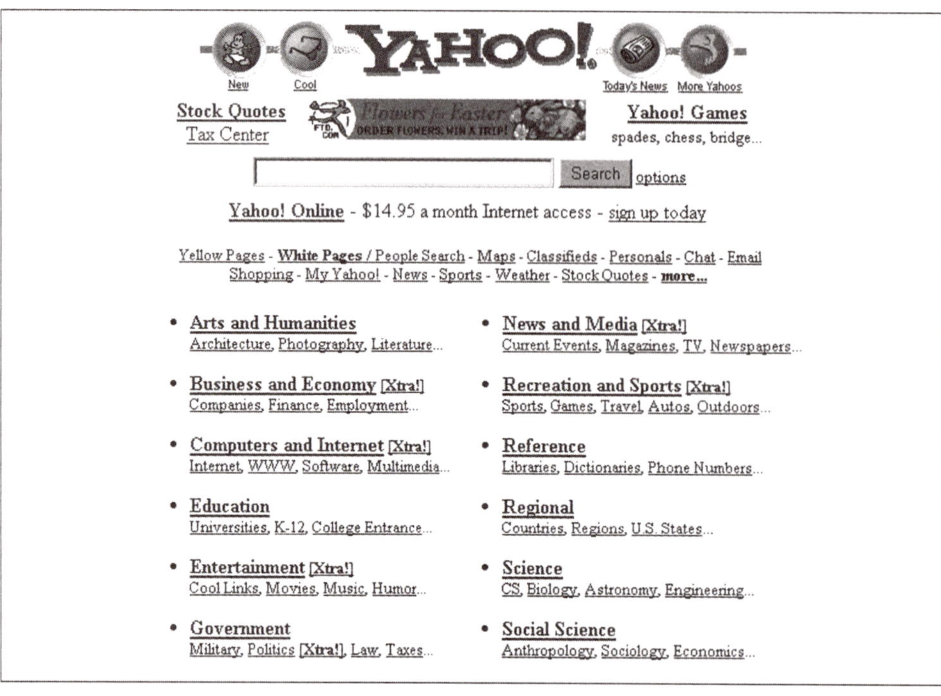

- The distinction between directories and search engines can be hard to detect these days, since most directories now contain a search engine component that allows you to search by keyword, and most search engines now include a directory of topics that you can browse. The important thing to remember is that you will come up with different results depending on the type of search site you use. A directory will yield fewer and more targeted results, while a search engine will yield greater results that will be less targeted, but will likely include some useful sites not yet cataloged by a directory.

Multi-threaded Search Engines

- Another type of search site, called a **multi-threaded** search engine, searches other search sites and gathers the results of these searches for your use.
- Because they search the catalogs of other search sites, multi-threaded search sites do not maintain their own catalogs. These search sites provide more search options than regular search engines and directories and typically return more specific information. However, multi-threaded search sites take much longer to return search results than regular search engines and directories.

- Multi-threaded search sites include SavvySearch, search.onramp, Metacrawler, JavaSearch, and Internet Sleuth.

Internet Sleuth Opening Page

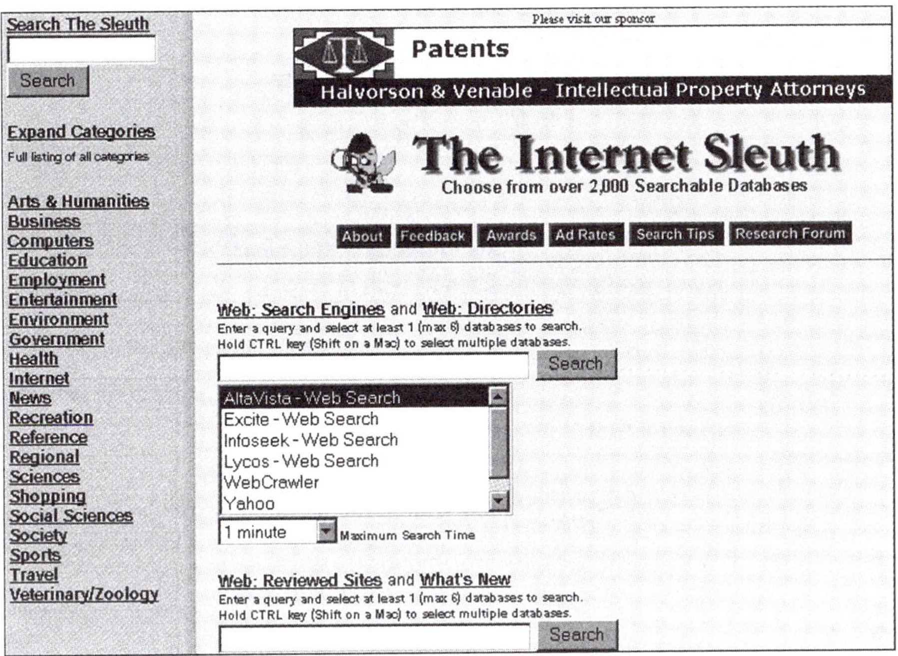

Search Basics

- To access a search site, you can click on the search button on your browser's toolbar, or enter the URL for the search site into the Address line and press Enter. Below are the URLs for several of the most popular search sites.

SITE	URL
Yahoo!	http://www.yahoo.com
AltaVista	http://www. altavista.digital.com
Excite	http://www.excite.com
HotBot	http://www.hotbot.com
Infoseek	http://www.infoseek.com
Lycos	http://www.lycos.com
Northern Light	http://www.nlsearch.com
LookSmart	http://www.looksmart.com
Infohiway	http://www.infohiway.com
Internet Sleuth	http://www.isleuth.com
Metacrawler	http://www.metacrawler.com

- When you connect to a search site, its Home page displays your search options. Most search sites contain a text box for typing the keywords you want to use in your search. Below is an illustration of search text box from the Home page of the AltaVista search site.

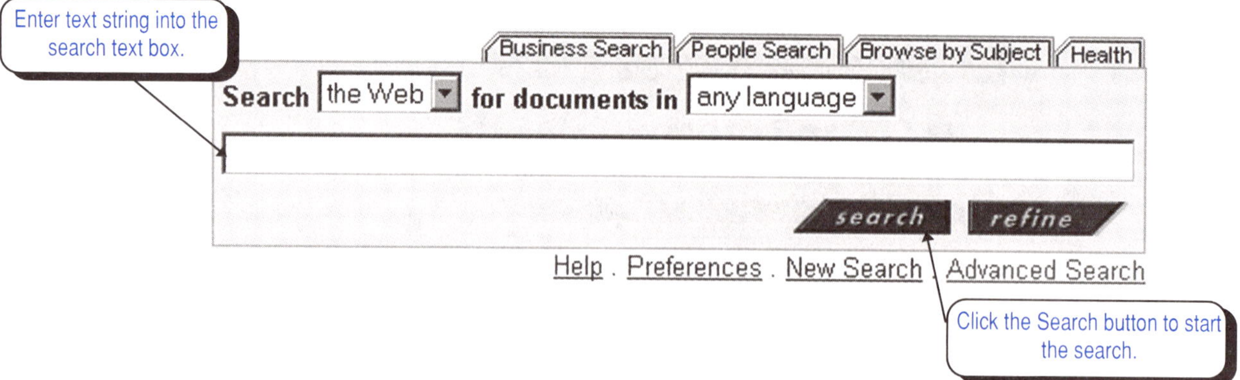

- The keywords you enter are called a **text string**. The text string may be a single word or phrase, or it may be a complex string including operators to modify the search. Operators are words (AND, NOT) or symbols (+, -) that help narrow a search (*see Exercises 3 and 2, for more information on using operators*).
- Once you have entered a text string, you can start the search by either pressing the Enter key or by clicking on the search button. The search provider will then list sites containing the text string you entered or list sites covering the related topic.
- For the best search results:
  - Always check for misspelled words and typing errors.
  - Use descriptive words and phrases.
  - Use synonyms and variations of words.
  - Find and follow the instructions that the search site suggests for constructing a good search.
  - Eliminate unnecessary words (the, a, an, etc.) from the search string.
  - Concentrate on keywords and phrases.
  - Test your search string on several different search sites.
  - Explore some of the sites that appear on your initial search and locate terms that would help you refine your search string.

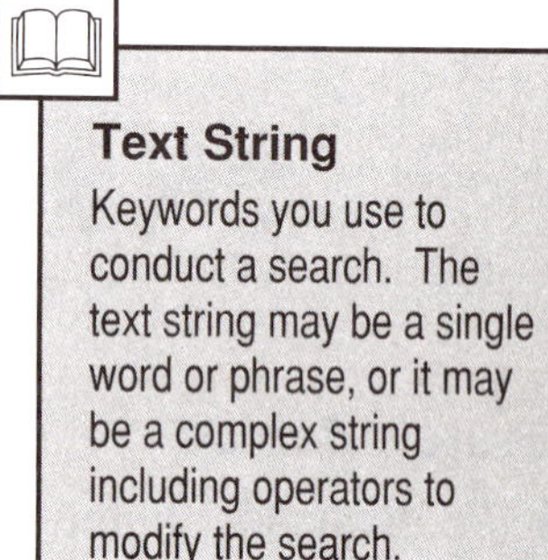

Text String
Keywords you use to conduct a search. The text string may be a single word or phrase, or it may be a complex string including operators to modify the search.

In this exercise you will find information and an illustration of flight Apollo 13 by following links on Yahoo!

Note: To ensure consistent results, this exercise uses simulated sites. The real URLs appear at the end of the exercise.

Web Search

Search for answers to the following questions using the Web sites you will visit in the Web simulation exercise.

1. Name at least five of the categories listed on the Yahoo! home page.

 ____

2. What was the date of Apollo 13's launch?

 ____

EXERCISE DIRECTIONS

1. Launch the Internet simulation. From the Main Menu, select Lesson 3, then select Exercise 1.
2. On the address line of your browser, type and press Enter: *www.yahoo.com.*

   ➲ *The Yahoo! Home page opens.*
3. Scroll down and click the link to Science.

   ➲ *The page containing categories of links related to science opens.*
4. Scroll down and click the link to Space on this page.

   ➲ *The page that displays contains categories of links pertaining to Space.*
5. Click in the Search box and type *Apollo 13*, then click the Search button.

- Bibliographies *(5)* NEW!
- Biology *(9221)* NEW!
- Books@ NEW!
- Chat *(6)*
- Chemistry *(1026)* NEW!
- Cognitive Science *(88)* NEW!
- Complex Systems *(18)*
- Computer Science *(1410)* NEW!
- Dictionaries *(15)*
- Earth Sciences *(2619)* NEW!
- Ecology *(395)* NEW!
- Education *(404)* NEW!
- Employment *(37)*
- Energy *(481)* NEW!
- Engineering *(4288)* NEW!
- Events *(31)*
- Forensics *(44)*
- Geography *(467)* NEW!
- Geology and Geophysics@
- Mathematics *(1569)* NEW!
- Medicine@
- Meteorology@
- Museums and Exhibits *(115)* NEW!
- Nanotechnology *(23)*
- News and Media *(21)* NEW!
- Oceanography@
- Organizations *(172)* NEW!
- Paleontology@
- Paradoxes *(5)*
- Physics *(1291)* NEW!
- Psychology@
- Religion and Science@
- Research *(137)* NEW!
- Space *(838)* NEW!
- Sports@
- Television@
- Weights and Measures *(94)*
- Indices *(46)*

6. Scroll down and click the link to Apollo 13 [gsfc. nasa.gov].

Help - Personalize | Yahoo! Mail - Stock Quotes - Yahoo! Chat

Categories	Web Sites	AltaVista	News Stories	Net Events

Found 2 categories and 15 sites for Apollo 13

Yahoo! Category Matches (1 - 2 of 2)

Entertainment: Movies and Film: Titles: Drama: Apollo 13

Science: Space: Exploration: Missions: Moon: Apollo Project: Apollo 13

amazon.com
Find Related Books
merchants with related products

Yahoo! Site Matches (1 - 15 of 15)

Entertainment: Movies and Film: Titles: Drama: Apollo 13

- Apollo 13 [Film.com Review]
- Apollo 13 [movieweb]
- Apollo 13: The Movie - with screen captures and links.
- James's Apollo 13 Page
- Apollo 13 [mca.com]

Science: Space: Exploration: Missions: Moon: Apollo Project: Apollo 13

- Apollo-13 - James A. Lovell, Jr., John L. Swigert, Jr., Fred W. Haise, Jr.
- Apollo 13 Mission - mission pictures, information, and summary of facts.
- Apollo 13 Lunar Surface Journal
- Apollo 13 [gsfc.nasa.gov]
- Apollo 13 [geocities.com]

7. Scroll down and click the link to Malfunction.

➲ *A detailed account of the explosion on Apollo 13 opens.*

8. Click directly on the image of the space craft.

The Apollo 13 Accident

The picture above shows the Apollo 13 Service Module after it was released from the Command Module and set adrift in space about 4 hours before re-entry of the CM into the Earth's atmosphere. "There's one whole side of that spacecraft missing", Jim Lovell said as the Apollo 13 astronauts got their first view of the damage that had been caused by the explosion. This blurry photo taken by the astronauts shows the extent of the injury to the Apollo 13 spacecraft, which exposed most of the inside of the service module to space. The Service Module was towed all the way back to Earth after the explosion in order to protect the Command Module heat shield. Another view is shown below.

The Apollo 13 malfunction was caused by an explosion and rupture of oxygen tank no. 2 in the service module. The explosion ruptured a line or damaged a valve in the no. 1 oxygen tank, causing it to lose oxygen rapidly. The service module bay no.4 cover was blown off. All oxygen stores were lost within about 3 hours, along with loss of water, electrical power, and use of the propulsion system.

➲ *A close up view of the damaged service module displays.*

9. Click Home on your Internet browser toolbar.
10. Continue on to the next exercise

OR

Exit from the simulation.

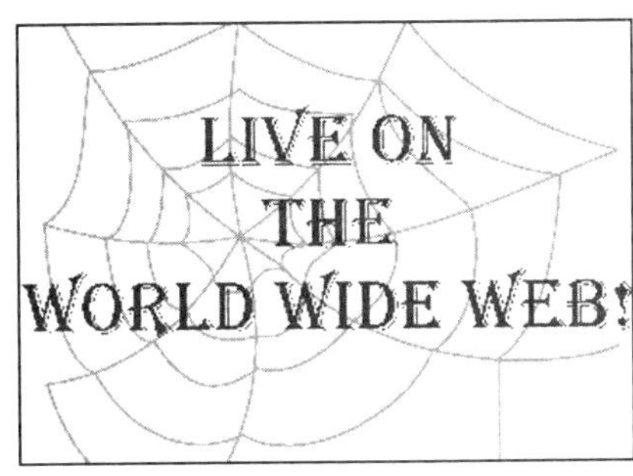

NASA home page
http://www.nasa.gov/

The Aurora Page
http://www.geo.mtu.edu/weather/aurora/

Asteroid and Comet Impact Hazards
http://impact.arc.nasa.gov/index.html

1908 Siberian Explosion
http://www.psi.edu/projects/siberia/siberia.html

The Columbus Optical SETI Observatory
http://www.coseti.org/

Exercise 2

- Keyword Searches ■ Refine a Search ■ Get Help
- Yahoo! and AltaVista Alliance

NOTES

Keyword Searches

- A **keyword search** uses a text string, usually one or two key terms, to search for matches in a search engine's catalog. When you start a keyword search, the search site searches its catalog for occurrences of your text string and then displays the results in decreasing relevance. Note the illustration below of the search results for the keyword *chicago* in Excite.

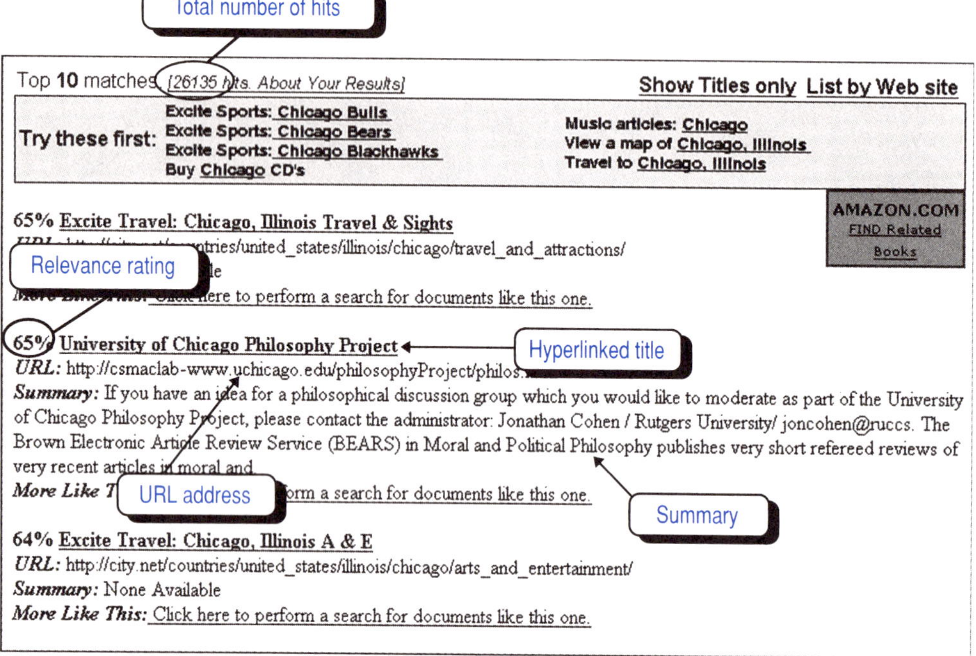

- The information displayed on the results page will vary, but most sites will display the following:
  - A title for the Web page. The title is formatted as a hyperlink in underlined and colored text, which you can click to go to the site.
  - The URL of the site.
  - A summary. This may be the first few lines of the Web page, the Web page title, a review, a summary, or keywords.

Note

There may be thousands of matches that contain your text string. The matches display a page at a time. You can view the next page by clicking on the "next page" link provided by the site at the bottom of each search results page.

- A relevance rating. Most sites indicate the estimated relevance of each site by a number or percentage. This rating may be based on the number of times the specified keyword(s) appears in the document or whether the word appears in the document title or URL.

- You can scan the displayed results to see if a site contains the information you want. If you see a listing that looks like what you want, click on it to connect to that site. You can always return to the search site by clicking the Back button on your browser toolbar; then choose a different site to visit or do another search.
- Most sites list the total number of hits generated by a search at the top of the first results page. This number allows you to gauge the effectiveness of your search. For example, if your text string yields hundreds of thousands of matches, you should refine your search to turn up fewer and more targeted Web sites.

Refine a Search

- To compose searches that return the most relevant matches possible, apply the following search tactics:

Be Precise

- Specific search terms will return fewer matches that have a greater likelihood of being relevant to your topic. For example a search for *dogs* might return nearly 200,000 results, covering everything from tips on obedience training to sites selling cyberpets. A search for *Rottweilers*, on the other hand, might return around 1,500 matches containing sites about Rottweiler training, breeding, merchandise, etc.
- Before entering a keyword, think about *exactly* what kind of information you want. If you take the time to come up with the most specific search string before performing a search, you'll save lots of time and frustration when the results display far fewer and more relevant Web sites.

Add a Keyword

- Sometimes a single keyword may be too vague and return an unwieldy number of hits, many of which are unrelated to the topic of interest. You can often narrow a search topic simply by adding another keyword to the search string.
- For example, suppose you want information on Greek tragedies. If you enter just the word *Greek* you'll get a very large number of results, as illustrated on top of the following page, which run the gamut from fraternities to Greek restaurants.

✓ *These examples use AltaVista to perform the search. Your results may vary with other search tools.*

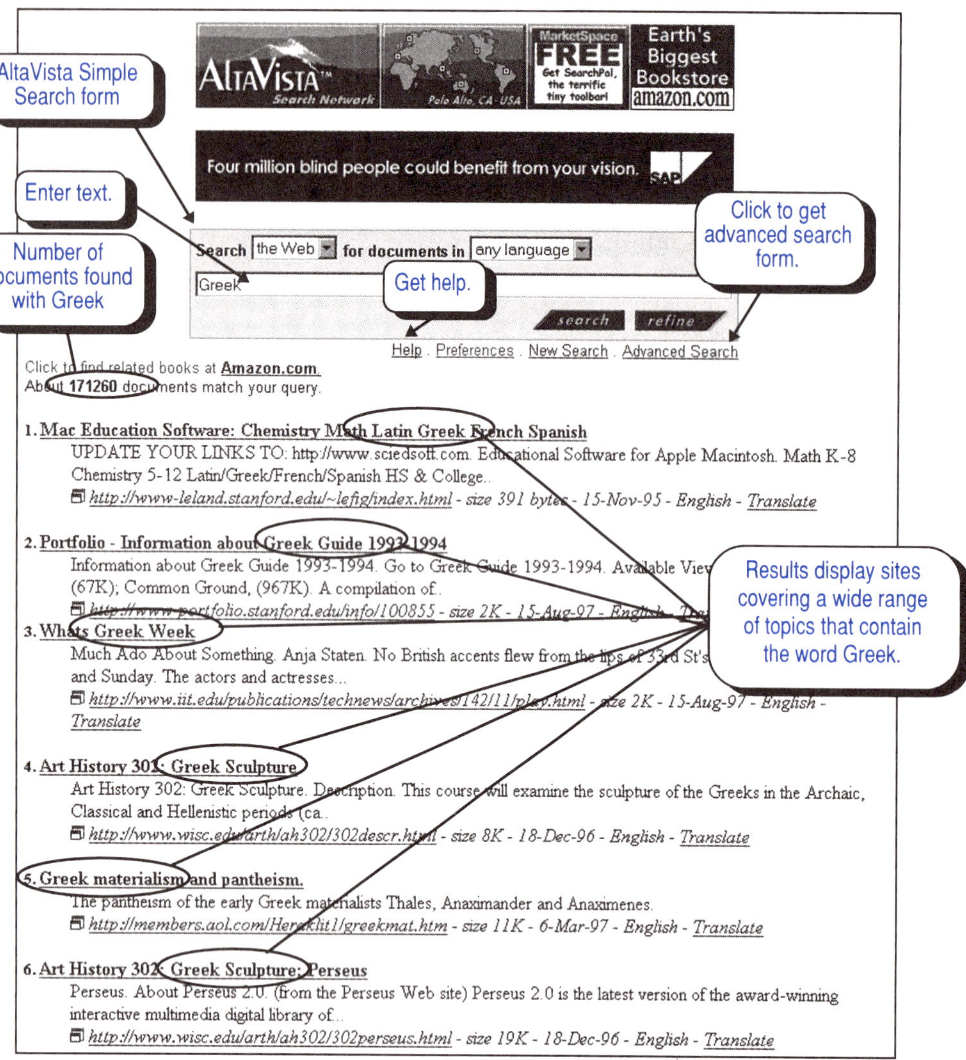

- To yield more focused results, you could replace *Greek* with a more specific term, such as *Euripedes* (a Greek playwright) or *Medea* (a Greek play). If, however, you want to find information on Greek tragedies in general, without limiting yourself to just one playwright or one play, you can refine your search with additional keywords.

Use Operators

- When you include multiple keywords, you'll increase the likelihood of getting relevant hits if you specify that you want to find only sites that contain *all* of the words, and not those that contain *any* one of them.
- For instance, in the current example, the natural inclination would be to enter *tragedies* immediately after the existing keyword, *Greek,* to narrow the search. On some sites, however, this would return *more* sites covering *more* topics, as in the illustration below. This is because many search sites automatically look for sites containing *any* of the keywords, rather than looking only for sites containing *all* of the words. As a result the additional keywords actually widen, rather than narrow, the search topic.

Note

When refining a search, it is important to remember that entering additional keywords is not always a substitute for precision. If entering additional keywords lowers the number of matches, but the matches still cover lots of unrelated topics, you may want to replace your search string with fewer but more precise keywords.

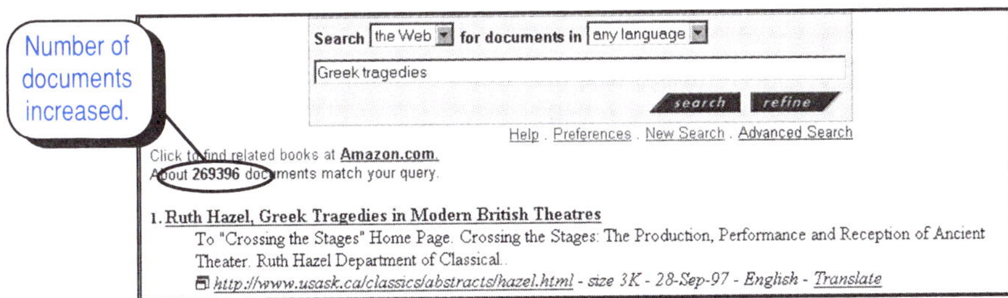

- To ensure that a multiple-word search string will return a shorter list of matches, you need to separate the terms with the **and operator**, which instructs the search provider to look only for sites that contain *all* of the words. The and operator is usually represented by a plus sign (+) or by the word AND spelled out in all capitals.
- For instance, to reduce the number of documents in the current example, you would enter a plus sign (+) immediately before the word *tragedies,* (*Greek +tragedies*) and then click the Search button. Note the diminished results, illustrated below, that display when the plus is added to the search.

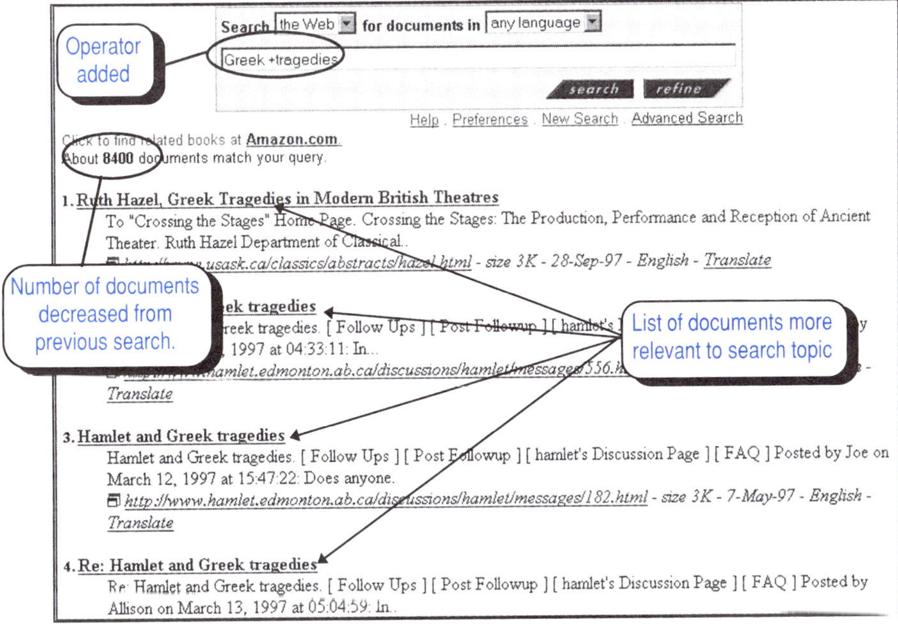

- The number of documents listed is dramatically reduced, and the documents displayed contain information more closely related to the topic of interest.
- You can use the **not operator** to *exclude* words from a search and eliminate unwanted documents from the results. The not operator is usually represented by the minus sign (-) or the word NOT spelled out in all capitals. If, for example, you wanted to find articles about Greek tragedies but not ones that deal with *Hamlet*, you would enter a search string like this: *Greek +tragedies -Hamlet*. Note the different results that display:

Note

Entering several additional keywords can make a search topic so narrow that you get very few or no returns on your search. When this occurs, you'll want to delete some of your keywords or replace them with some broader terms.

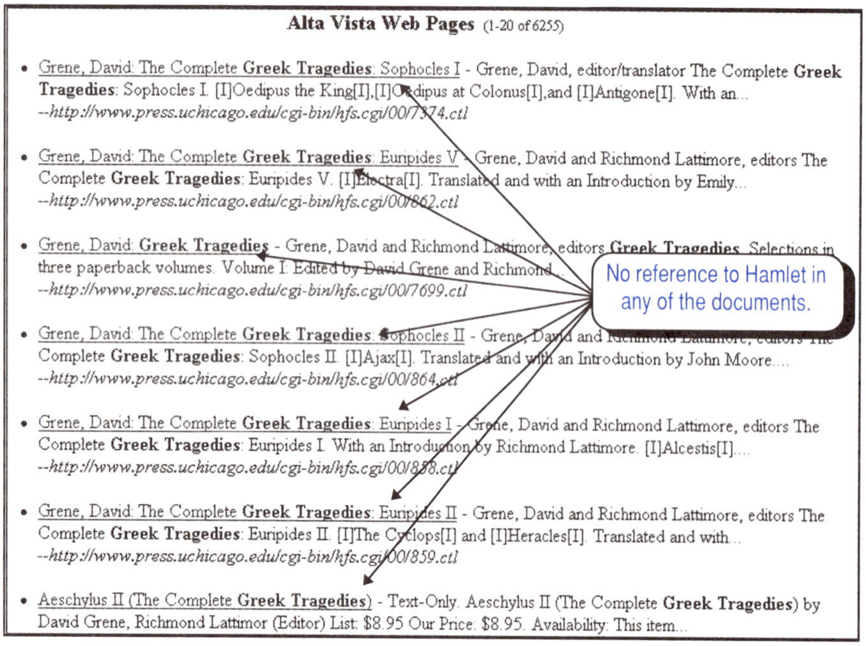

Alta Vista Web Pages (1-20 of 6255)

- Grene, David: The Complete **Greek Tragedies**: Sophocles I - Grene, David, editor/translator The Complete **Greek Tragedies**: Sophocles I. [I]Oedipus the King[I],[I]Oedipus at Colonus[I],and [I]Antigone[I]. With an...
  --http://www.press.uchicago.edu/cgi-bin/hfs.cgi/00/7374.ctl
- Grene, David: The Complete **Greek Tragedies**: Euripides V - Grene, David and Richmond Lattimore, editors The Complete **Greek Tragedies**: Euripides V. [I]Electra[I]. Translated and with an Introduction by Emily...
  --http://www.press.uchicago.edu/cgi-bin/hfs.cgi/00/862.ctl
- Grene, David: **Greek Tragedies** - Grene, David and Richmond Lattimore, editors **Greek Tragedies**. Selections in three paperback volumes. Volume I: Edited by David Grene and Richmond...
  --http://www.press.uchicago.edu/cgi-bin/hfs.cgi/00/7699.ctl
- Grene, David: The Complete **Greek Tragedies**: Sophocles II - Grene, David and Richmond Lattimore, editors The Complete **Greek Tragedies**: Sophocles II. [I]Ajax[I]. Translated and with an Introduction by John Moore....
  --http://www.press.uchicago.edu/cgi-bin/hfs.cgi/00/864.ctl
- Grene, David: The Complete **Greek Tragedies**: Euripides I - Grene, David and Richmond Lattimore, editors The Complete **Greek Tragedies**: Euripides I. With an Introduction by Richmond Lattimore. [I]Alcestis[I]....
  --http://www.press.uchicago.edu/cgi-bin/hfs.cgi/00/858.ctl
- Grene, David: The Complete **Greek Tragedies**: Euripides II - Grene, David and Richmond Lattimore, editors The Complete **Greek Tragedies**: Euripides II. [I]The Cyclops[I] and [I]Heracles[I]. Translated and with...
  --http://www.press.uchicago.edu/cgi-bin/hfs.cgi/00/859.ctl
- Aeschylus II (The Complete **Greek Tragedies**) - Text-Only. Aeschylus II (The Complete **Greek Tragedies**) by David Grene, Richmond Lattimor (Editor) List: $8.95 Our Price: $8.95. Availability: This item...

No reference to Hamlet in any of the documents.

- Different search sites use different words or symbols to represent operators, so be sure to check the help section of the search site to find out what operators you can use. You will learn more about operators in Exercise 3.

Get Help

- There are no standards governing search options and procedures, so search sites develop their own. You'll get better results if you check the search site's Help section to find out what options are available before performing a search. For example, some search sites, such as AltaVista and Yahoo!, allow you to enter quotation marks around a text string to indicate that you want to find sites containing that exact phrase. Or, some sites will recognize the plus sign (+) as the and operator, while others require you to enter the word AND spelled in all capitals, while still others do not accept operators at all.
- You will usually find a link to a search site's help page located below the search text box on the site's main search page. The link might be called Search Tips, Search Options, or Help. Illustrated on top of the next page are help samples from AltaVista and Yahoo!

  ✓ *Most sites also offer tips for performing a complex search, often called an advanced or "power" search. You'll learn about complex searches in Exercise 3.*

AltaVista Help for Simple Searches

Simple Search

Natural Language queries: (always try this first)

Type a word or phrase or a question (for example, **weather Boston** or **what is the weather in Boston?**), then click Search (or press the Enter key). If the information you want from this sort of query isn't on the first couple of pages, try adding a few more specific words.

Requiring/Excluding Words:

Often you will know a word that will be guaranteed to appear in a document for which you are searching. If this is the case, require that the word appear in all of the results by attaching a "+" to the beginning of the word (for example, to find an article on pet care, you might try the query **dog cat pet +care**). You may also find that when you search on a vague topic, you get a very broad set of results. You can quickly reject results by adding a term that appears often in unwanted articles with a "-" before it (for example, to find a recipe for oatmeal raisin cookies without nuts try **oatmeal raisin cookie -nut* -walnut***).

Exact Phrases:

If you know that a certain phrase will appear on the page you are looking for, put the phrase in quotes. (for example, try entering song lyrics such as **"you ain't nothing but a hound dog"**)

Yahoo! Help for Simple Searches

Tips for Better Searching

- **Use Double Quotes Around Words that are Part of a Phrase**

  example "great barrier reef" Search

- **Specify Words that Must Appear in the Results**
  Attach a + in front words that *must* appear in result documents.

  example: sting +police Search

- **Specify Words that Should Not Appear in the Results**
  Attach a – in front of words that *must not* appear in result documents.

  example: python -monty Search

Yahoo! and AltaVista Alliance

- In 1996 Yahoo! (a search directory) agreed to make AltaVista (a search engine) its preferred search engine. This means that when Yahoo! can't locate any categories or sites to match your search string in its own catalog, it will automatically search AltaVista's database. For example, Yahoo! did not find any matches for *Greek tragedies* in its own catalog, so it automatically searched using AltaVista to find the following:

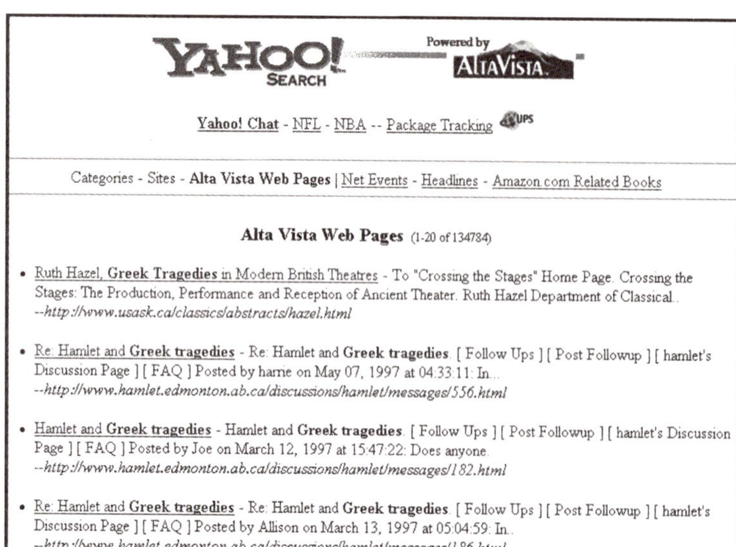

- Now look at the results of a search for *Greek restaurants* using Yahoo!. Since Yahoo! has categories containing links to Greek restaurants, it displays the matches available in Yahoo!'s directory.

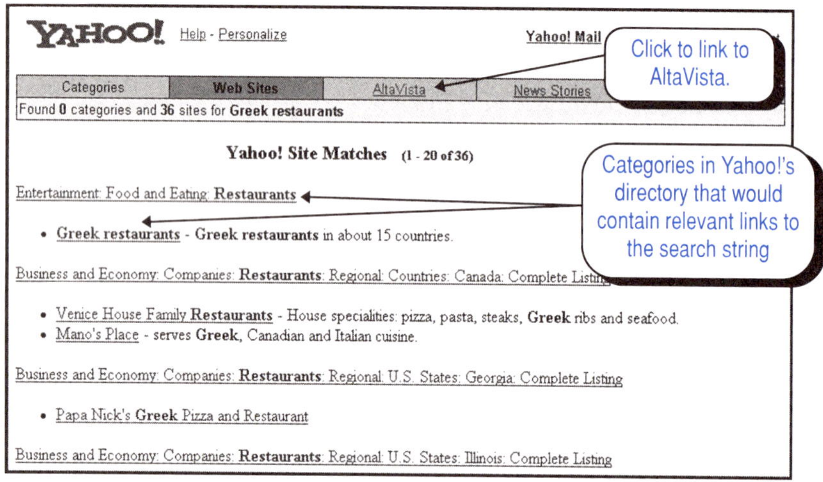

- You can also click on the link to AltaVista to view the documents that AltaVista found to match your search string:

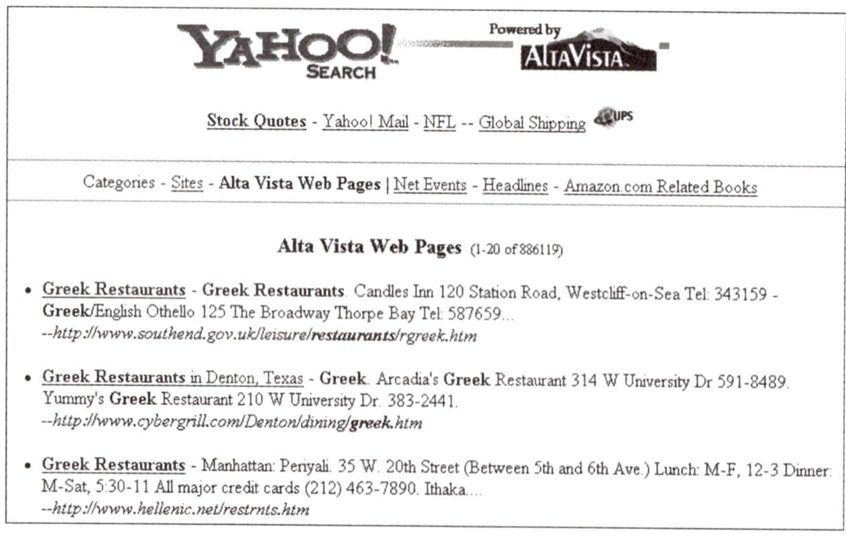

In this exercise, you will see if you can locate Pliny the Younger's eyewitness account of the eruption of Mt. Vesuvius near Pompeii in 79AD. When you have located the information, you will paste it into a WordPad document and send it to the printer. You will also locate, copy, and print a translation of one of the letters describing what he saw.

Note: *To ensure consistent results, this exercise uses simulated sites. The real URLs appear at the end of the exercise.*

Web Search

Search for answers to the following questions using the Web sites you will visit in the Web simulation exercise.

1. How many sites match the search topic Volcanoes?

 ____

2. How many sites match the search topic Volcanoes +Vesuvius?

 ____

3. What are the directions for using exact phrases in your search string

 ____

4. How many sites match the search topic Volcanoes +Vesuvius +Pompeii +"Pliny the Younger"?

 ____

EXERCISE DIRECTIONS

1. Launch the Internet simulation. From the Main Menu, select Lesson 3, then select Exercise 2.
2. On the address line of your browser, type and press Enter: *www.altavista.digital.com*

 ➲ *The AltaVista Home page opens.*
3. Click in the search box and type *volcanoes.* Then click search.
4. When the results of your search display, scroll down and note the types of links listed. Note the number of sites that match your search topic.

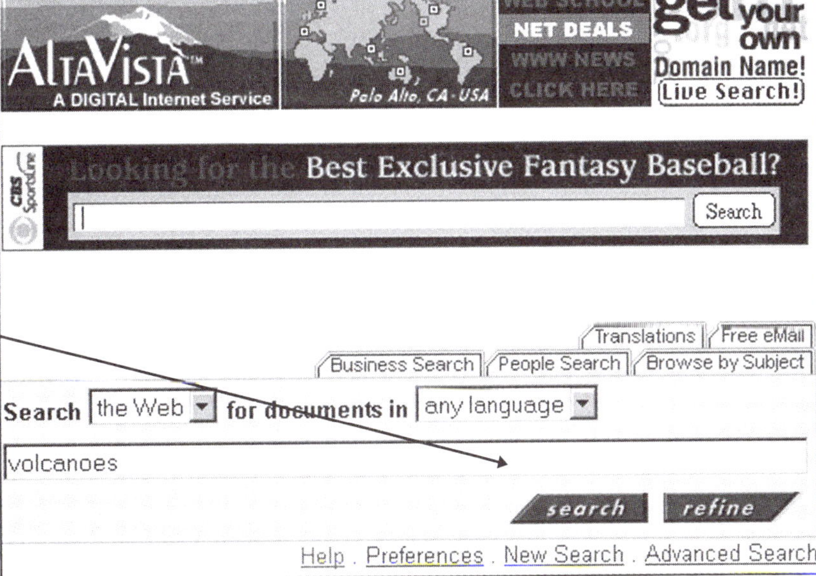

5. Click in the search box, and just after the word *volcanoes*, press the spacebar once and add the following: *+Vesuvius.*

   The search topic should now read as illustrated on the right.

   Click search.

   ✓ *Note that the number of matches has decreased.*

6. Scroll down and note the types of links listed.
7. Click in the search box after the word Vesuvius, press the spacebar, and type: *+Pompeii.*

   Click search.

8. Note that the number of matches has again decreased. Examine the links now listed.
9. Click Help below the search box.
10. Scroll down and read the directions for using Exact phrases in your search string.
11. Click Back on your browser toolbar to return to the AltaVista search page.

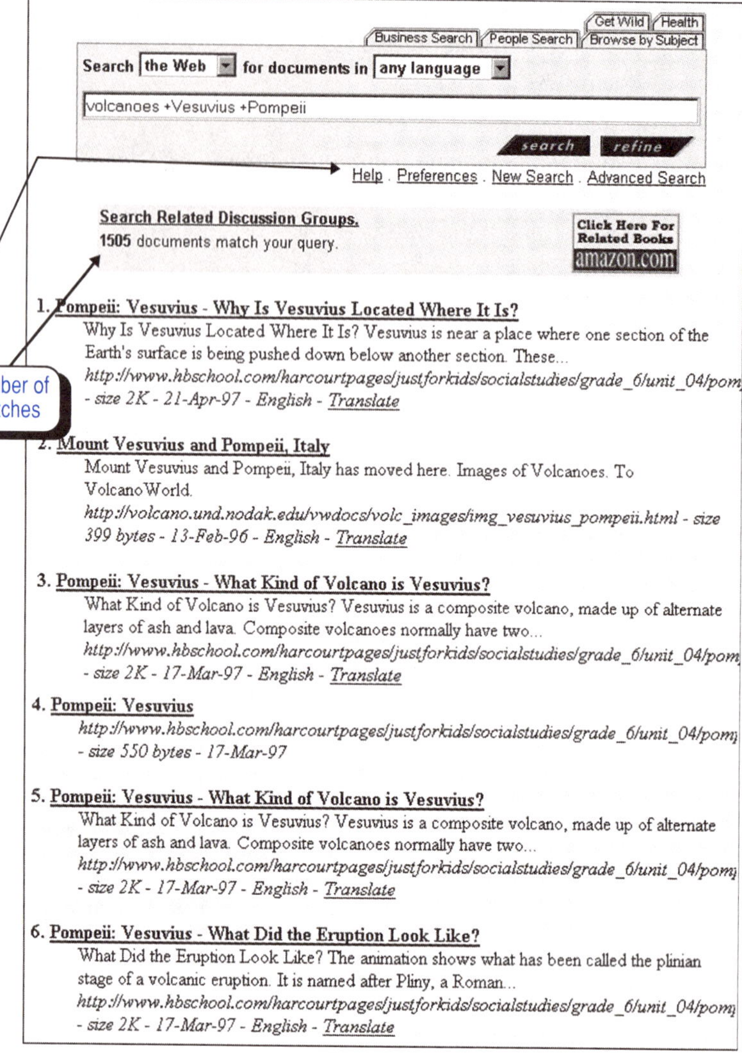

12. Click in the search box after the word Pompeii, press the spacebar, add the following: *+"Pliny the Younger"*
    Be sure to include the quotation marks. Click search.

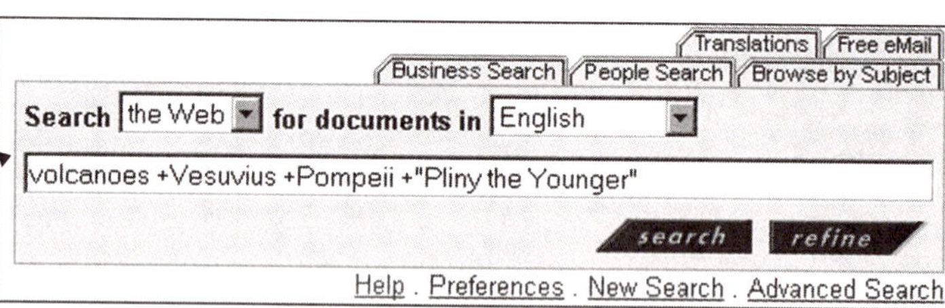

13. The number of matches drops to 71. Scroll down and click the link to: SCALING NEW HEIGHT ON VESUVIUS.

6. Untitled
ART 349. "FIRST-STYLE" WALL PAINTING IN ITALY AND IN THE HELLENISTIC EAST; EARLY "SECOND-STYLE" ROMAN WALL PAINTING. © 1997 Ann...
http://www.willamette.edu/~amcgors/art349/firststyle.html - size 5K - 16-Apr-97 - English - Translate

7. ANTIQUITY: INDEX to volumes 1-70 (1927-1996)
INDEX to volumes 1-70 (1927-1996) A B C D E F G H I J K L M N O P Q R S T U V W X Y Z. The collected Antiquity index of which this is one letter's section.
http://intarch.ac.uk/antiquity/listing/p.htm - size 102K - 14-Mar-97 - English - Translate

8. Earth Sciences 240A
Earth Sciences 240A Homepage. Title: Violent Events in Earth History Earth Sciences 240A. Aim of Course: To introduce students to the sudden and...
http://www.uwo.ca/earth/ugrad/240a/es240a.htm - size 113K - 21-Nov-97 - English - Translate

9. SCALING NEW HEIGHT ON VESUVIUS
European Space Agency Press Information Note No. 07-95 Paris, France 27 March 1995. SCALING NEW HEIGHT ON VESUVIUS. The earthquake that hit Japan in...
http://volcano.und.nodak.edu/vwdocs/vw_news/vesuvius.html - size 11K - 3-Jan-96 - English - Translate

10. 1996 GOALS
1996 GOALS. Advance Existing Aspects of the Project. The CAD Model. The development of a CAD model for the forum remains the central component of the...
http://jefferson.village.virginia.edu/pompeii/ann-rpts/96/gen-intro.html - size 10K - 29-Jan-98 - English - Translate

14. To find if Pliny the Younger is mentioned on this site, do the following:
- Open the Edit menu.
- Select Find (on this page)
- Enter *Pliny the Younger* in Find what box.
- Click Find Next.

15. Click Cancel to close the Find dialog box.

➲ *You have now located links containing references to Pliny the Younger witnessing the eruption of Mt. Vesuvius.*

European Space Agency
Press Information Note No. 07-95
Paris, France 27 March 1995

SCALING NEW HEIGHT ON VESUVIUS

The earthquake that hit Japan in January 1995 reducing parts of the densely populated area around Kobe and Osaka to rubble clearly showed once again how defenseless our civilization with all its advanced technology is when the forces of nature are unleashed. The Japanese were wel ... ey could defy it by resorting to measures such as earthquake-resis ... must have reigned when, on 24 August 79 BC, VESUVIUS erupte ... lava, showers of ash, and clouds of smoke, steam and toxic g ... lying on the southern flank of the almost 1300- meter high volcar ... subsequent generations of archaeologists and historians.

Find
Find what: Pliny the Younger
Find Next
Cancel
Match whole word only
Match case
Direction
Up
Down

Although the eruption of Vesuvius over 1900 years ago is probably the best known example of such a phenomenon, mainly because of the description of it by Pliny the Younger, it was by no means the most violent or caused the most damage. When the Tambora volcano erupted on the Indonesian island of Sumbawa east of Java in April 1815, falling stones and ash killed about 12 000 people and on 8 May 1902, the hot cloud of gas and rivers of lava that raced down the slopes following the "explosion" of Mount Pele, in the north-west of the Carribean island of Martinique, wiped out almost the entire population -- about 38 000 -- of the town of St. Pierre. The only survivor was a prisoner who had been held in an underground cell. But the most violent volcanic eruption in recent times took place on 27 August 1883 on the island of Krakatoa, between Sumatra and Java. The equivalent of about 21 cubic kilometres of stone exploded into the air and for two and a half days the skies were darkened by volcanic ash, which, when it fell, covered an area 800 kilometers square (as large as France and Great Britain put together). The force of the eruption was twenty-five times that of the most powerful H-bomb ever exploded and destroyed all

16. Click the Minimize button.

17. Start WordPad by doing the following:
  a. Click **Start**.
  b. Click Programs, Accessories, WordPad.
  c. Minimize WordPad.

18. Maximize your browser program.

19. Click in the address line of your browser and enter the following URL: **www.excite.com**
Press Enter.

✓ *The opening page of the Excite search site opens.*

20. Click in the search box and enter the following search string: *volcanoes +Vesuvius +Pompeii*
Click Search when you have entered the phrase exactly as illustrated.

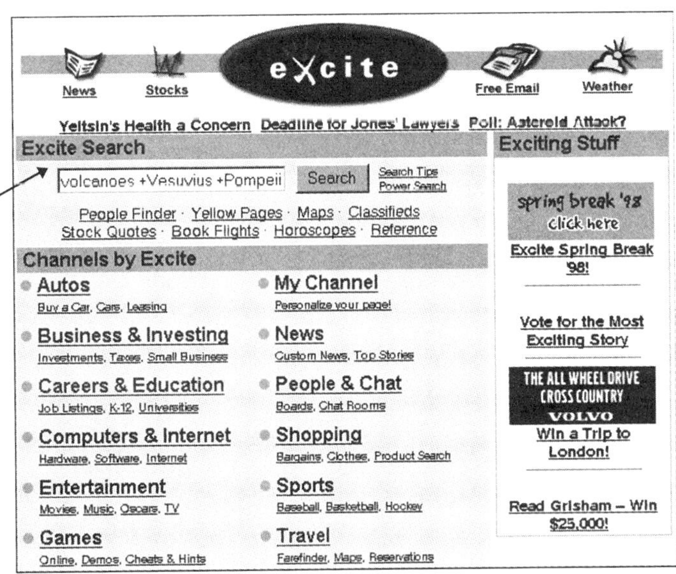

21. When the results of your search display, scroll down and note the types of links listed.
22. Click the link to Content 7.
23. On the page that opens, scroll down and click the link to Extensive Pliny.

87% Vesuvius, Italy
URL: http://www.ku-eichstaett.de/SLF/Klassphil/plinius/vdummy.htm
Summary: Vesuvius has erupted about three dozen times since 79 A.D., most recently from 1913-1944. Vesuvius 2000 presents new ideas about facing the risk of living on or near an active volcano.
More Like This: Click here to perform a search for documents like this one.

86% Content7
URL: http://volcano.und.nodak.edu/vwdocs/vwlessons/lessons/Ch3CM/Content7.html
Summary: The people were used to earthquakes and didn't pay much attention to the numerous quakes that had been rattling their bowls and plates prior to the eruption. What they didn't know would kill thousands of people that beautiful August day in 79 A.D. Vesuvius was awakening from its long slumber.
More Like This: Click here to perform a search for documents like this one.

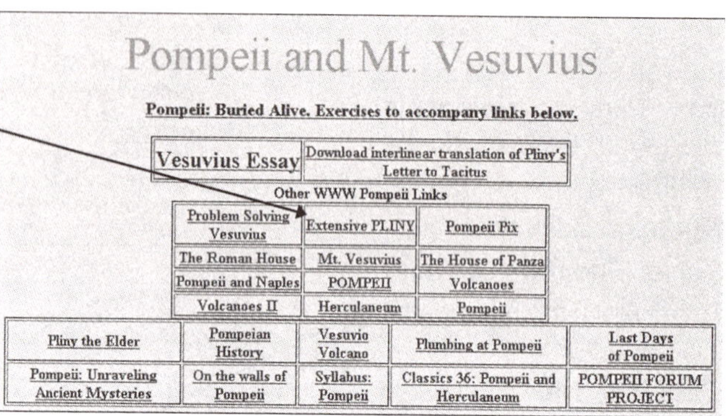
Pompeii and Mt. Vesuvius

Pompeii: Buried Alive. Exercises to accompany links below.

Vesuvius Essay	Download interlinear translation of Pliny's Letter to Tacitus

Other WWW Pompeii Links

Problem Solving Vesuvius	Extensive PLINY	Pompeii Pix
The Roman House	Mt. Vesuvius	The House of Panza
Pompeii and Naples	POMPEII	Volcanoes
Volcanoes II	Herculaneum	Pompeii

Pliny the Elder	Pompeian History	Vesuvio Volcano	Plumbing at Pompeii	Last Days of Pompeii
Pompeii: Unraveling Ancient Mysteries	On the walls of Pompeii	Syllabus: Pompeii	Classics 36: Pompeii and Herculaneum	POMPEII FORUM PROJECT

24. Right-click in the picture and select Copy.
25. Switch to WordPad. Press Ctrl+V to paste the picture into the WordPad document. Scroll down and click below the picture and add the following in the WordPad document:
Photo courtesy, Chalice Yehling CyberLatin.
Then minimize WordPad.
26. Click in the address line and start to type *www.excite.com*. The AutoComplete is turned on, so the browser will complete the address for you. Press Enter.
27. Enter the following search string in the Excite search box:
Pliny +the +Younger +Vesuvius +letter
Then click the Search button.
28. Click the link to Eye Witness to the Eruption of A.D. 79!.

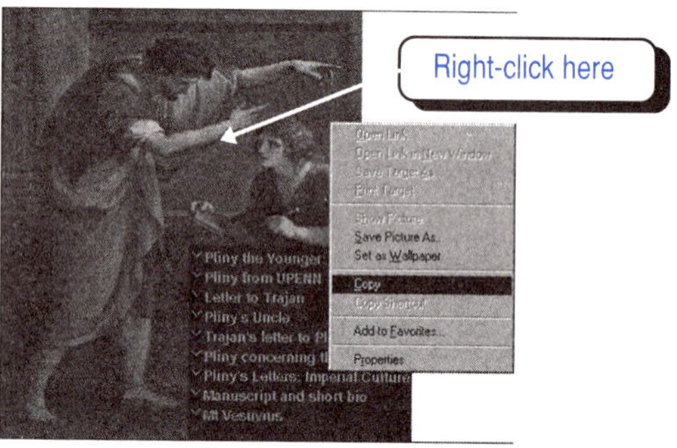

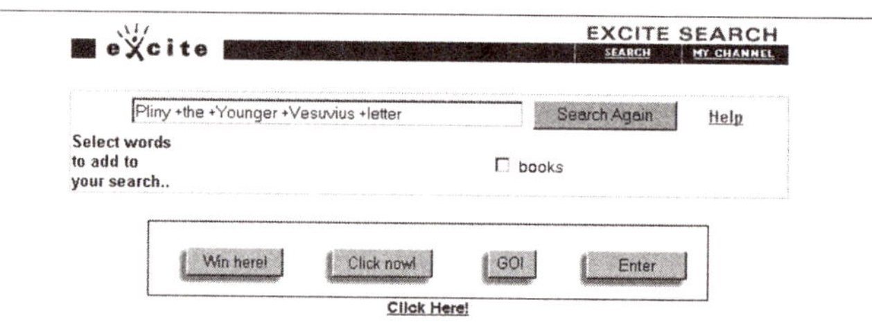

Top **10** matches. *[30 hits. About Your Results]* **Show Titles only** **List by Web site**

91% Eye Witness to the Eruption of A.D 79!
URL: http://pompeii.virginia.edu/pompeii/pliny.html
Summary: Vesuvius in A.D. 79 the Roman fleet under the command of Pliny the Elder was stationed across the Bay of Naples at Misenum. Based on this information Pliny the Younger wrote two letters to the historian Tacitus that recount the events surrounding the eruption of Vesuvius and the death of Pliny the Elder.
More Like This: Click here to perform a search for documents like this one.

91% Pliny the Younger, 61-105 A. D.
URL: http://www.columbia.edu/acis/bartleby/bartlett/492.html
Summary: Well, then, write and let me know just this,--that there is nothing to write about; or tell me in the good old style if you are well ... We put off from time to time going and seeing what we know we have an opportunity of seeing when we please.
More Like This: Click here to perform a search for documents like this one.

90% Where can I find the description of the Vesuvius eruption by Pliny the...
URL: http://volcano.und.nodak.edu/vwdocs/frequent_questions/grp10/question1995.html
Summary: Hi Lobb, Where can I find the description of the Vesuvius eruption by Pliny the Younger? A specific reference: "Pompeii and Herculeneum: The Glory and the Grief" by Marcel Brion Also, Bullard's book Volcanoes has a short passage from the long letter.
More Like This: Click here to perform a search for documents like this one.

90% 79 A.D. Home Page
URL: http://www.isu.edu/~kingkath/ad79.htm
Summary: Ancient Medicine/Medicina Antiqua: Hypertexts:Galen, On the Natural Faculties -- This and the next two are medical texts by the Roman physician Galen. Ancient Medicine/Medicina Antiqua: Galen:Biography -- Biography of Roman physician Galen.
More Like This: Click here to perform a search for documents like this one.

86% Art 215: Roman Painting
URL: http://www.willamette.edu/~arscgors/art215/romanptg.html

29. Scroll down and click the link to Pliny Letter VI.16.

    ➲ *The page on the right displays.*

30. Press **Ctrl+A** to select all the text. Right-click on the highlighted page and click **Copy**.
31. Switch back to the WordPad document. Press Enter. Press **Ctrl+V** to paste the letter into the WordPad document.
32. Add the following at the end of the letter.
    Translation by Professor Cynthia Damon of Amherst College. Used here with Professor Damon's permission.
33. Send the WordPad document to the printer.
34. Continue on to the next exercise

    OR

    Exit from the simulation.

Eye Witness to the Eruption of A.D. 79!

At the time of the eruption of Mt. Vesuvius in A.D. 79 the Roman fleet under the command of Pliny the Elder was stationed across the Bay of Naples at Misenum. Pliny launched ships and sailed toward the erupting volcano for closer observation and to attempt a rescue. No rescue was possible and Pliny himself died during the eruption, not in the streets of Pompeii, but across the bay at Stabiae.

Pliny's nephew, whom we know as Pliny the Younger, was with him at Misenum, but did not venture out on the ships with his uncle. He stayed back at Misenum and observed the events from there. He also received first-hand reports from those who had been with his uncle at his death. Based on this information Pliny the Younger wrote two letters to the historian Tacitus that recount the events surrounding the eruption of Vesuvius and the death of Pliny the Elder. The letters survive and provide a vivid account of the events.

Provided below are links to the two letters. They are translated by Professor Cynthia Damon of Amherst College and are part of her Web site for Classics 36 Pompeii and Herculaneum. The letters are used here with Professor Damon's permission.

Pliny Letter VI.16

Pliny Letter VI.20

1. Pliny Letter 6.16

My dear Tacitus,

You ask me to write you something about the death of my uncle so that the account you transmit to posterity is as reliable as possible. I am grateful to you, for I see that his death will be remembered forever if you treat it [sc. in your Histories]. He perished in a devastation of the loveliest of lands, in a memorable disaster shared by peoples and cities, but this will be a kind of eternal life for him. Although he wrote a great number of enduring works himself, the imperishable nature of your writings will add a great deal to his survival. Happy are they, in my opinion, to whom it is given either to do something worth writing about, or to write something worth reading; most happy, of course, those who do both. With his own books and yours, my uncle will be counted among the latter. It is therefore with great pleasure that I take up, or rather take upon myself the task you have set me.

He was at Misenum in his capacity as commander of the fleet on the 24th of August [sc. in 79 AD], when between 2 and 3 in the afternoon my mother drew his attention to a cloud of unusual size and appearance. He had had a sunbath, then a cold bath, and was reclining after dinner with his books. He called for his shoes and climbed up to where he could get the best view of the phenomenon. The cloud was rising from a mountain-at such a distance we couldn't tell which, but afterwards learned that it was Vesuvius. I can best describe its shape by likening it to a pine tree. It rose into the sky on a very long "trunk" from which spread some "branches." I imagine it had been raised by a sudden blast, which then weakened, leaving the cloud unsupported so that its own weight caused it to spread sideways. Some of the cloud was white, in other parts there were dark patches of dirt and ash. The sight of it made the scientist in my uncle determined to see it from closer at hand.

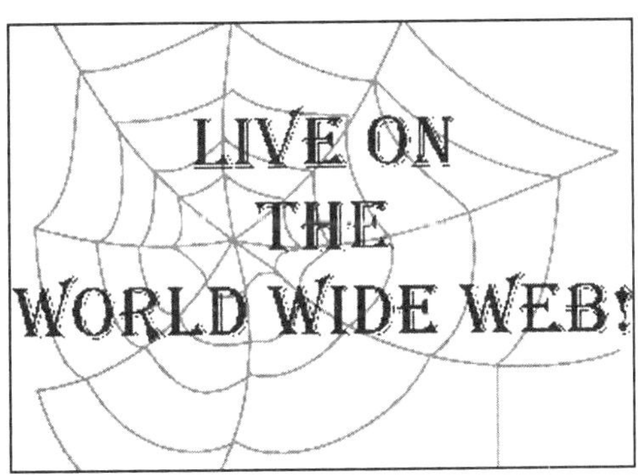

Volcanoes.com
http://www.volcanoes.com/

Volcanoes of the World
_http://volcano.und.nodak.edu/volc_of_world.html_

Hawaii Volcanoes National Park
http://www.nps.gov/havo/

Exercise 3

■ Operators ■ Boolean Operators ■ Grouping Operators
■ Case Sensitive Searches ■ Major Search Engines and Operators

NOTES

- Not all search topics can be described by a single, precise keyword. It is often necessary to use two or more keywords separated by operators that tell the search site how to deal with those keywords. By using additional types of operators and other advanced search features you can target your searches even more precisely.

Operators

- Operators are words or symbols that modify your search string. In addition to the *and* and *not* operator, you can use a number of operators to narrow or widen a search. What follows are descriptions of some of the most commonly used operators and how they are used.

Boolean Operators

- **Boolean operators** specify required words, excluded words, and complex combinations of words to be found during a search. Depending on the search site you're using, Boolean operators may be represented by words or symbols. The table on the following page outlines the most common Boolean operators.

Operator:	Symbol:	Function:	Use to:
AND	Represented by the word AND spelled in all capitals, or by the plus sign (+) placed immediately in front of a word (without a space).	The documents found in the search must contain *all words* joined by the AND operator.	Narrow a search that's returning too many unrelated sites.

For example, if you want information on Microsoft's Internet Explorer browser, a search for Microsoft AND Internet AND Explorer (or Microsoft +Internet +Explorer) will find sites that contain all three words (Microsoft, Internet, and Explorer). This will reduce the number of results by omitting sites about other Microsoft products, other Internet topics, and other explorers.

OR	Represented by the word OR spelled in all capitals or by a vertical line symbol (|) placed immediately in front of a word (without a space).	The documents found in the search must contain *at least one of the words* joined by the OR operator. The documents may contain both, but this is not required.	Broaden a search that's not returning enough results or get the most comprehensive results possible.

For example, if you want information about the Internet, a search for Web OR Internet (or Web/Internet) will increase your results by finding sites that contain either the word Web or the word Internet, in addition to sites that contain both.

NOT	Represented by the words AND NOT spelled in all capitals or by the minus sign (-) placed immediately in front of a word (without a space).	The documents found in the search must *not* contain the word following the NOT operator.	Narrow a search when you're looking for a term that you know is often associated with a topic that is totally unrelated to your search goal.

For example, if you want information on the state of Washington, a search for Washington NOT DC (or Washington -DC) will find sites that contain the word Washington but none that contain Washington DC.

NEAR	Represented by the word NEAR spelled in all capitals or by a tilde symbol (~) placed immediately in front of a word (without a space).	The documents found in the search must contain the words joined by the NEAR operator within ten words of each other.	Narrow a search that's returning too many results or that is often associated with topics unrelated to your search goal.

For example, if you want information about computer memory, the search string, RAM NEAR memory (or RAM ~memory) will find sites with the word RAM and the word memory within ten words of each other. This would reduce your results by omitting unrelated sites about human memory.

Grouping Operators

- **Grouping operators** join words and phrases together to be treated as a single unit or determine the order in which Boolean operators are applied.

  The most common grouping operators are:

  Double quotes

  The documents found in the search must contain the words inside double quotes exactly as entered.

  For example, a search for "*World Wide Web*" will find sites containing the phrase *World Wide Web*, not the individual words separated by other words or the same words uncapitalized.

  Parentheses

  Just as in a mathematical equation, parentheses group words and operators in a search string to define the order in which Boolean operators should be applied. This is useful when you're using several operators at once.

  For example, if you want to find information about a browser, you might enter the following search string: *browser AND* (*Internet OR Web*). This string will find sites that contain either the words *Internet* and *browser* or the words *Web* and *browser*. (Note that this is *not* the same search as *Internet* OR *Web AND browser*, which finds sites that contain either the word *Internet* or both of the words *Web* and *browser.)*

Case Sensitive Searches

- Most search engines are not case sensitive, meaning that if you enter a word starting with a lowercase letter, such as *hamlet,* most search engines will automatically look for the capitalized version of the word *(Hamlet)* in addition to the lowercase version of the word. If, however, you capitalize the first letter of a search word *(Hamlet)*, most search engines will look only for the uppercase version.

Major Search Engines and Operators

- The types of operators you can use and their respective symbols vary from search site to search site. Below is a table of the major search sites and how they use some of the search operators. Search sites are constantly updating and improving their sites in response to users' needs, so it's important to check out search tips and help sections to see the most current search options.

Search Tool	Boolean operators	+/–	Grouping Operators	Case Sensitivity
AltaVista	✗	✗	✗	✗
AOL NetFind	✗	✗		
Excite	✗	✗	✗	
HotBot	✗	✗	✗	✗
Infoseek		✗	✗	✗
Lycos		✗	✗	
SavvySearch		✗	✗	
Yahoo!	✗	✗	✗	✗

In this exercise, you will use a variety of operators to reduce the number of matches returned by a search for Saturn cars and the planet Saturn.

Note: *To ensure consistent results, this exercise uses simulated sites. The real URLs appear at the end of the exercise.*

Web Search

Search for answers to the following questions using the Web sites you will visit in the Web simulation exercise.

1. How many sites match the search topic Saturn?

____

2. How many sites match the search string Saturn AND (cars OR automobiles) AND UAW?

____

EXERCISE DIRECTIONS

1. Launch the Internet simulation. From the Main Menu, select Lesson 3, then select Exercise 3.
2. Click in the Address line and type the following and press Enter: *www.excite.com.*
   - ➲ *The home page for the Excite search site displays.*
3. In the search box, type the word *Saturn* then click Search.
   - ➲ *Excite searches its database and displays matches that include sites about cars, the planet Saturn, and electronic games.*
   - ➲ *Excite also suggests words that you could add to your search string to locate a more relevant list of matches.*

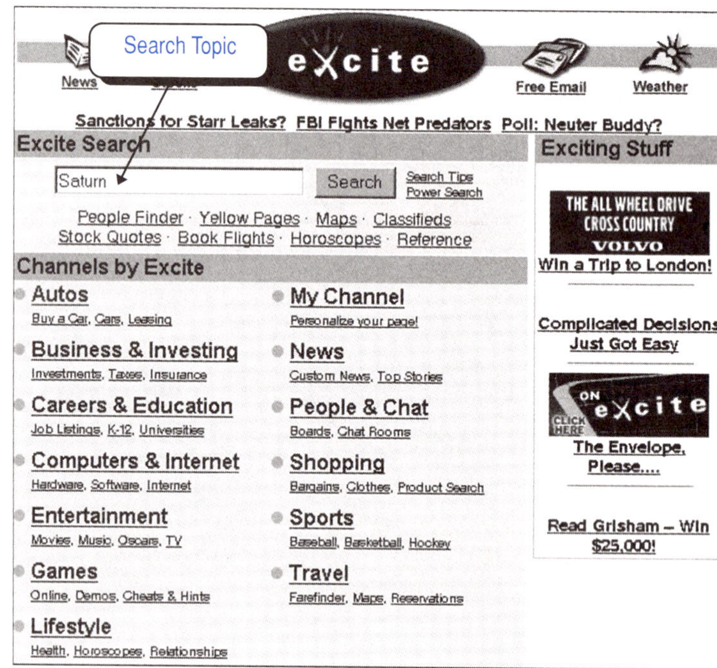

✓ *Note the large number of matches that Excite has located.*

4. Click in the search box after the word *Saturn*, press the spacebar, and add the following: *AND (cars OR automobiles)* Be sure to use uppercase as indicated. Click the Search Again button.

EXCITE SEARCH
excite SEARCH MY CHANNEL

Saturn | Search Again | Help

Select words to add to your search.. ☐ sega ☐ tethys ☐ dione ☐ moons ☐ rings ☐ mimas ☐ cassini ☐ playstation ☐ fainter ☐ rhea

Number of Matches

Click Here

Top 10 matches (6520) hits. About Your Results] Show Titles only List by Web site

Try these first: Web sites about... Web sites about...

Planet

amazon.com FIND RELATED BOOKS

69% Saturn Events
URL: http://www.isc.tamu.edu/~astro/saturn.html
Summary: Last updated on July 5, 1997 [Mars Events | Jupiter Events | Saturn Events]. How to Find Saturn in the Sky. Eclipses, Shadows, Transits, Occultations 1993 to 1999.
More Like This: Click here to perform a search for documents like this one.

68% Sega Online: Support: Repair Costs
URL: http://www.sega.com/support/repaircosts/saturn.html
Summary: None Available
More Like This: Click here to perform a search for documents like this one.

Games

66% Sega Saturn Links
URL: http://www.mcn.net/~montanasites/Saturnlinks.html
Summary: Here is a huge list of Sega Sautrn Links,The Best Video Game System in the World! Poom's Sega Saturn Stop - Your quick stop for all the latest Sega Saturn news, reviews, screenshots, and links!
More Like This: Click here to perform a search for documents like this one.

66% Sega Online: Support: Strategy Guides
URL: http://www.sega.com/support/strategy/strategy01.html
Summary: Game Title Platform Model # Pages Price Amok Saturn 81064 25 $8.00 Astal Saturn 81019 9 $5.00 Baku Baku Saturn 81501 7 $5.00 Blackfire Saturn 81003 22 $8.00 Blazing Heroes Saturn 81300 62 $12.00 Bug Too! Saturn 81040 33 $10.00 Christmas NiGHTS Saturn CN 10 $5.00 Clockwork Knight 2 Saturn 81036 14 $6.00 Clockwork Knight Saturn 81007 11 $6.00 Congo Saturn 81010 13 $6.00 Cyber Speedway Saturn.
More Like This: Click here to perform a search for documents like this one.

➲ *Note that the number of matches decreases. The suggested list of words has decreased and relate only to automobiles.*

5. Click in the search box after the parentheses, press the spacebar, and add the following to the search string (Be sure to use the uppercase): *AND UAW.* Click Search Again.

➲ *The number of matches dramatically decreases.*

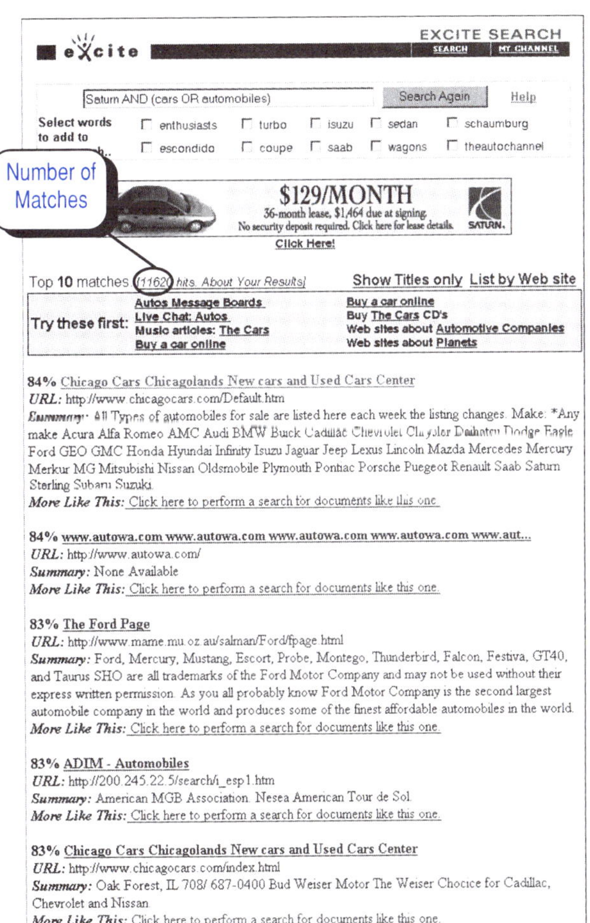
EXCITE SEARCH
excite SEARCH MY CHANNEL

Saturn AND (cars OR automobiles) | Search Again | Help

Select words to add to ... ☐ enthusiasts ☐ turbo ☐ isuzu ☐ sedan ☐ schaumburg ☐ escondido ☐ coupe ☐ saab ☐ wagons ☐ theautochannel

Number of Matches

Click Here!

Top 10 matches (11620) hits. About Your Results] Show Titles only List by Web site

Try these first: Autos Message Boards, Live Chat: Autos, Music articles: The Cars, Buy a car online, Buy a car online, Buy The Cars CD's, Web sites about Automotive Companies, Web sites about Planets

84% Chicago Cars Chicagolands New cars and Used Cars Center
URL: http://www.chicagocars.com/Default.htm
Summary: All Types of automobiles for sale are listed here each week the listing changes. Make: *Any make Acura Alfa Romeo AMC Audi BMW Buick Cadillac Chevrolet Chrysler Daihatsu Dodge Eagle Ford GEO GMC Honda Hyundai Infinity Isuzu Jaguar Jeep Lexus Lincoln Mazda Mercedes Mercury Merkur MG Mitsubishi Nissan Oldsmobile Plymouth Pontiac Porsche Puegeot Renault Saab Saturn Sterling Subaru Suzuki.
More Like This: Click here to perform a search for documents like this one.

84% www.autowa.com www.autowa.com www.autowa.com www.autowa.com www.aut...
URL: http://www.autowa.com/
Summary: None Available
More Like This: Click here to perform a search for documents like this one.

83% The Ford Page
URL: http://www.mame.mu.oz.au/salman/Ford/fpage.html
Summary: Ford, Mercury, Mustang, Escort, Probe, Montego, Thunderbird, Falcon, Festiva, GT40, and Taurus SHO are all trademarks of the Ford Motor Company and may not be used without their express written permission. As you all probably know Ford Motor Company is the second largest automobile company in the world and produces some of the finest affordable automobiles in the world.
More Like This: Click here to perform a search for documents like this one.

83% ADIM - Automobiles
URL: http://200.245.22.5/search/i_esp1.htm
Summary: American MGB Association. Nesea American Tour de Sol.
More Like This: Click here to perform a search for documents like this one.

83% Chicago Cars Chicagolands New cars and Used Cars Center
URL: http://www.chicagocars.com/index.html
Summary: Oak Forest, IL 708/ 687-0400 Bud Weiser Motor The Weiser Chocice for Cadillac, Chevrolet and Nissan
More Like This: Click here to perform a search for documents like this one.

6. Click in the search box, delete the current search string and enter the following:
Saturn AND rings AND NOT (cars OR automobiles)
Click Search Again when you have completed the phrase.

✓ *The matches now point to sites that contain information about the planet Saturn.*

✓ *Note that Excite now suggests words relevant to astronomy, not automobiles.*

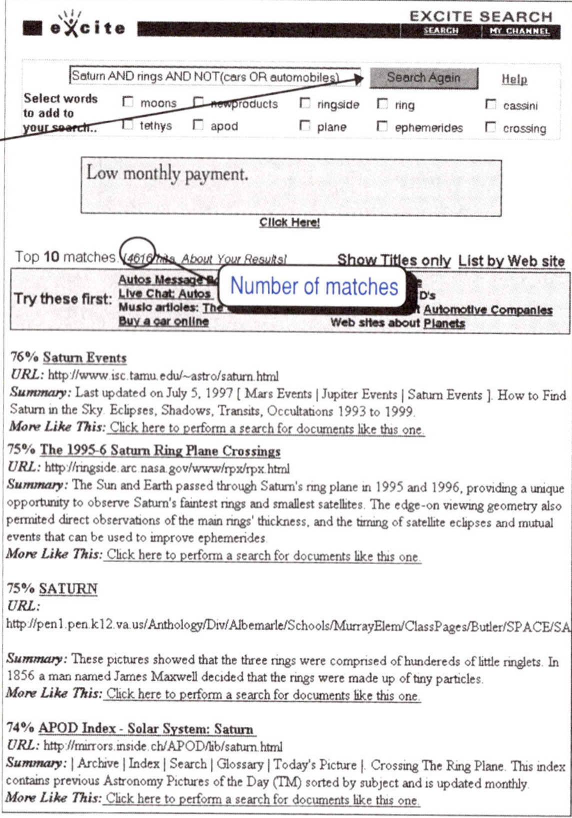

7. Click in the Search box after the parentheses, press the spacebar, and enter the following:
AND Cassini. (Cassini is one of the words that Excite has suggested.)
Click Search Again.

✓ *Excite now displays fewer matches and the word Cassini is no longer in the list of suggested words.*

8. Scroll down and click the link to Saturn Events.

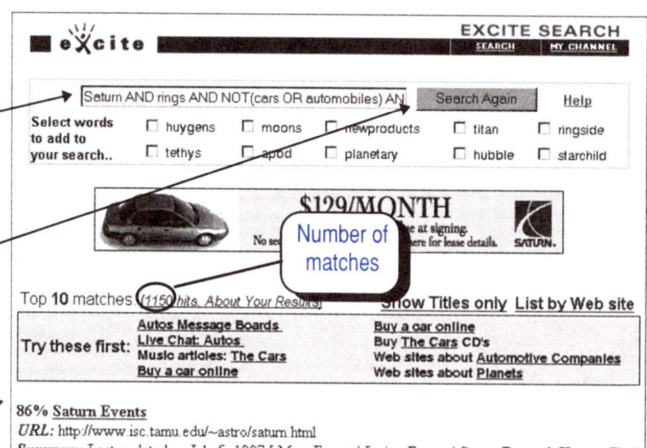

86% Saturn Events
URL: http://www.isc.tamu.edu/~astro/saturn.html
Summary: Last updated on July 5, 1997 [Mars Events | Jupiter Events | Saturn Events]. How to Find Saturn in the Sky. Eclipses, Shadows, Transits, Occultations 1993 to 1999.
More Like This: Click here to perform a search for documents like this one.

86% To Saturn We'll Go...
URL: http://www.windows.umich.edu/headline_universe/cassini.html
Summary: NASA, the European Space Agency, and the Italian Space Agency are all working together to make the Cassini mission a success. The Cassini mission is a joint project of NASA, the European Space Agency, and the Italian Space Agency.
More Like This: Click here to perform a search for documents like this one.

86% Cassini project
URL: http://www.gallaudet.edu/~mssdsci/cassini.html
Summary: Cassini will orbit Saturn for four years, gathering data on Saturn, its rings, magnetic environment, and moons. Your signature will be scanned and stored on a CD-ROM, placed inside the Cassini spacecraft, and flown on a deep-space journey to Saturn.
More Like This: Click here to perform a search for documents like this one.

85% Cassini's mission to Saturn
URL: http://www.fiu.edu/~ron/cassini.html
Summary: Cassini, scheduled for launch on October 6, 1997, is a joint mission of NASA, the European Space Agency (ESA), and the Italian Space Agency (ASI). The Cassini spacecraft will orbit Saturn for four years, gathering data on Saturn, its rings, magnetic environment and moons.
More Like This: Click here to perform a search for documents like this one.

85% exoScience - Cassini's Ring Objectives
URL: http://exosci.com/probes/cassini/5.html
Summary: None Available
More Like This: Click here to perform a search for documents like this one.

[Mars Events | Jupiter Events | Saturn Events]

9. Scroll down and click the link to Cassini: Voyage to Saturn.

How to Find Saturn in the Sky

- Sky at a Glance - general location
- Solar System Live - here are the coordinates
- Saturn PC Software - relative positions of Saturn's moons

Saturn Home Pages

- SEDS - "The Nine Planets"
- Cassini: Voyage to Saturn
- NASA - "Planetary Data System Rings Node"

10. Click the link to Mission located on the picture.

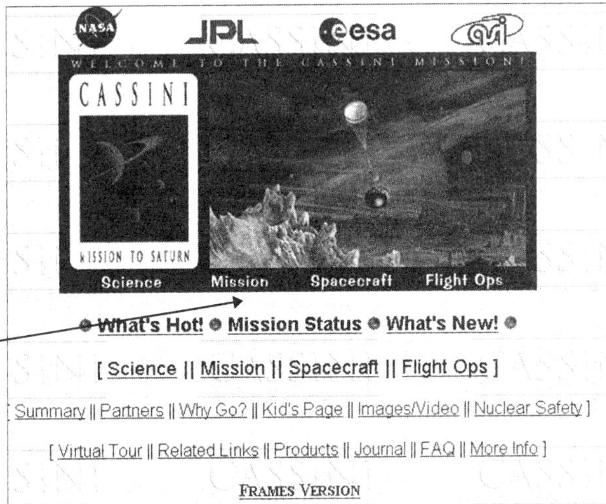

11. Use Find on this Page to locate "Saturn," "rings," and "Cassini."
12. Click Cancel to close the Find dialog box.
13. Continue on to the next exercise

OR

Exit from the simulation.

NEXT LESSON

Lesson 4: E-mail

Exercise 1

- About Electronic Mail
- Launch Outlook Express
- Configure Outlook Express to Send and Receive Mail

Exercise 2

- Outlook Express Main Window
- Compose New Messages
- Send Messages
- New Message Toolbar

Exercise 3

- Retrieve New Messages
- The Mail Window
- Read Messages
- Delete a Message
- File a Message
- Save a Message
- Print a Message
- Reply to a Message
- Forward a Message

Exercise 4

- Launch Netscape Messenger
- Configure Messenger to Send and Receive E-mail

Exercise 5

- The Message List Window
- Compose New Messages
- Send Messages
- Message Composition Toolbar

Exercise 6

- Get New Messages
- Read Messages
- Delete a Message
- File a Message
- Bookmark a Message
- Save a Message
- Print a Message
- Reply to Mail
- Forward Mail

Exercise 1

- About Electronic Mail
- Launch Outlook Express
- Configure Outlook Express to Send and Receive Mail

NOTES

About Electronic Mail (E-mail)

- Electronic mail (e-mail) is a method of sending information from one point to another across the Internet.
- Due to its speed, convenience, and low cost, sending e-mail is one of the most popular uses of the Internet.

What E-mail Is Used For

- E-mail is used for sending electronic messages—business and personal correspondence—to anyone with an e-mail address anywhere in the world.
- E-mail is also used for sending files. Files can be sent as part of the e-mail message or they can be added as **attachments** and "ride" along with the e-mail. Using the Internet Explorer e-mail program, Outlook Express, you can send and receive text files, graphic files, program files, application data files, or virtually any type of file you wish.

How E-mail Works

- When you send e-mail to someone, Outlook Express uses Simple Mail Transfer Protocol (SMTP) to send your e-mail to your Internet service provider's mail server, which in turn uses SMTP to send your e-mail to the recipient's mail server. Once mail is saved on your Internet service provider's mail server, you can use Outlook Express to retrieve it to your computer, where you can read it.
- On some networked systems, when e-mail arrives on the mail server it is immediately available to the user.
- On other networked systems and on systems that use an Internet service provider (including most "home" Internet accounts), e-mail messages are held on the server until it is called by the user. This transaction is governed by another protocol, called **Post Office Protocol (POP)**.

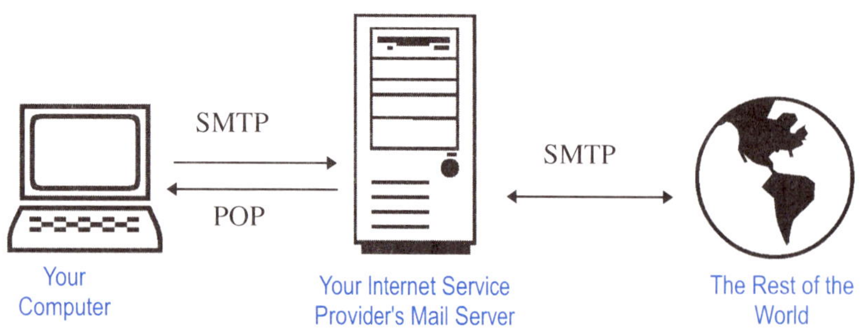

SMTP (Simple Mail Transfer Protocol) The standard communications protocol for routing e-mail between Internet hosts.

POP (Post Office Protocol) A communications protocol used to transfer incoming messages from e-mail servers to your system.

E-mail Addresses

- Each user who wants to send or receive e-mail must have an e-mail account on a mail server. E-mail service is usually supplied by your Internet service provider (ISP) as part of your regular service.
- Each user with a mail account is uniquely identified by an **e-mail address**.
- An e-mail address consists of a user name, a mail server name, and a domain. For example: **username@servername.domain** or **archie@sprynet.com**
- The **user name** identifies the e-mail account holder. The user name is always unique among the users of a particular mail server and can consist of any combination of letters and numbers.
- The @ symbol ("at") separates the user name from the server name.
- The **server name** identifies the mail server at the user's Internet service provider, company, or organization. The server name can consist of any combination of letters and numbers.
- Sometimes the mail server address can be more complex and may require several parts to identify its location. For example: username@server.subserver.domain
- A period separates the mail server name from its domain.
- The **domain** identifies the kind of organization that hosts the mail server. The most common organizations are:
  - **.com** for companies
  - **.edu** for educational institutions
  - **.net** for networking companies
  - **.mil** for military organizations
  - **.gov** for government departments and groups
  - **.org** for non-profit organizations or other groups
- E-mail addresses outside the United States typically have a two-letter suffix designating the country the mail server is in. For example:
  - **.ca** for Canada
  - **.uk** for the United Kingdom
  - .**de** for Germany ("Deutschland")
  - **.au** for Australia
  - **.jp** for Japan

Launch Microsoft Outlook Express

- Included in the Internet Explorer 4 browser suite is a comprehensive e-mail program called Outlook Express, which allows you to send, receive, save, and print e-mail messages and attachments.

  To launch Outlook Express:

  - Click the Mail icon from the Explorer component toolbar.

    OR

    Click **Start** on the Windows taskbar and select Programs, Internet Explorer, Outlook Express.

    OR

    Select Go, Mail in the Internet Explorer window.

    OR

    Click the Mail button on the Explorer toolbar and select Read Mail.

- If you are not already connected to the Internet when you launch Outlook Express, it will automatically begin connecting to your ISP.

Configure Outlook Express to Send and Receive Mail

✓ *The notes in this section presume that you have already set up an e-mail account with a service provider. What follows are steps that will get you connected, but some of the information may have to be supplied by your Internet service provider. Calling for help will save you time and frustration.*

- Before you can use Outlook Express to send and receive e-mail, you must configure the program with your e-mail account information (user name, e-mail address, and mail server names). You may have already filled in this information if you completed the Internet Connection Wizard when you started Internet Explorer for the first time. If not, you can enter the information by running the Internet Connection Wizard again.

Run the Internet Connection Wizard

- Launch Outlook Express. Open the Tools menu, select Accounts and click the Mail tab. In the Internet Accounts dialog box that follows, click the Add button and select Mail to start the Connection Wizard. The Internet Connection Wizard will ask for information necessary to set up or add an e-mail account.

Note

There is a chance that clicking the Mail icon from the Explorer main window will take you to the Microsoft Outlook organizational program. To use the more compact Outlook Express as your default mail program, click View, Internet Options from the Explorer main window. Click the Programs tab and choose Outlook Express from the the Mail pull-down menu.

Internet Accounts Dialog Box

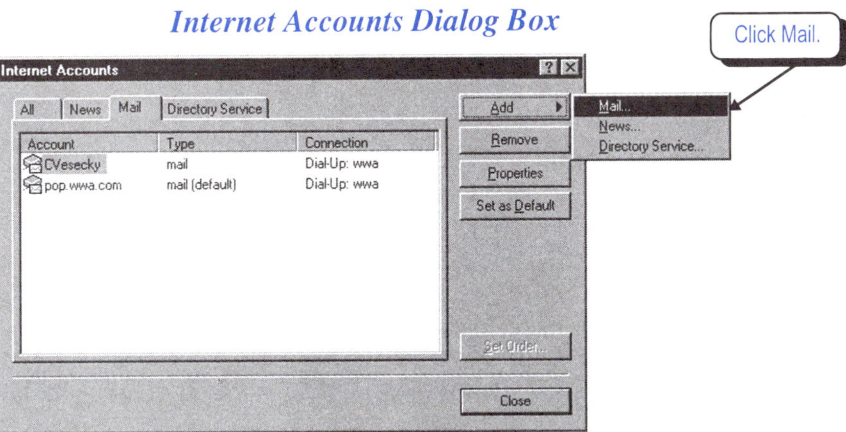

- In the first Internet Connection Wizard dialog box that appears, enter the name you want to appear on the "From" line in your outgoing messages. Click Next.

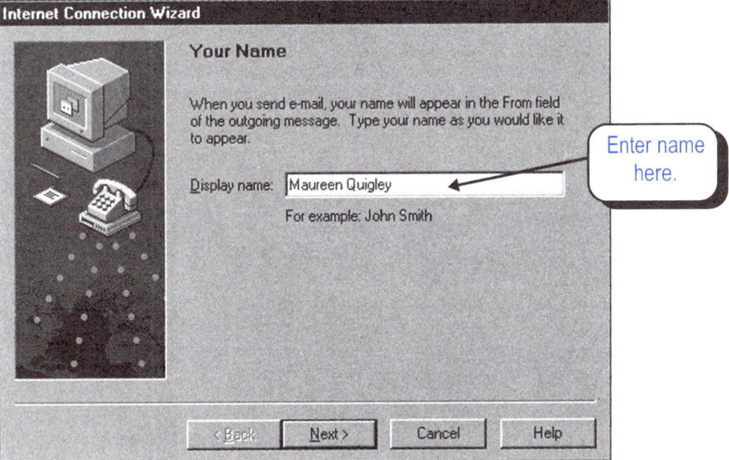

- Type your e-mail address. This is the address that people use to send mail to you. You usually get to create the first part of the address (the portion in front of the @ sign); the rest is assigned by your Internet service provider. (If you are not sure about what server name or domain you should use, contact your ISP.) Click Next.

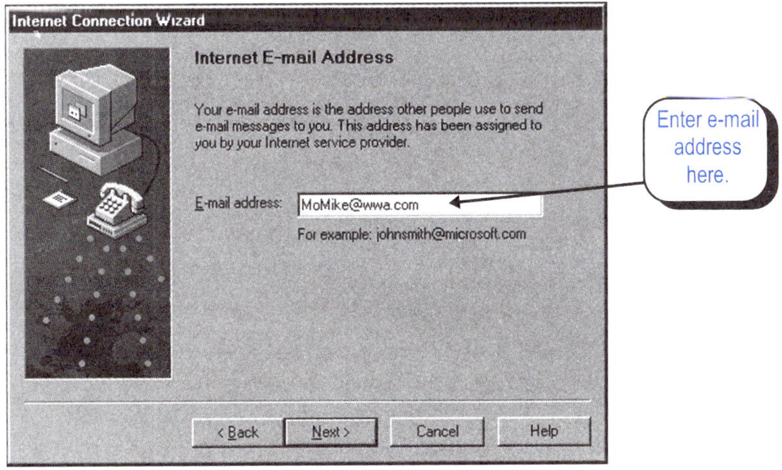

- Enter the names of your incoming and outgoing mail servers. Check with your Internet service provider if you do not know what they are. Click Next.

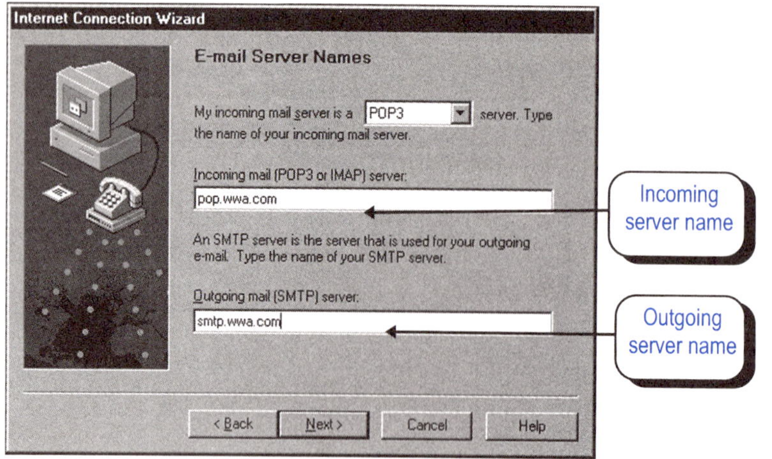

- If your ISP requires you to use Secure Password Authentication (SPA) to access your e-mail, select the Log on using Secure Password Authentication (SPA) option (check with your ISP if you are not sure whether this option applies to you).

  OR

  If your ISP requires you to enter a password before you can access your e-mail account, select the Log on using option and enter the name of your e-mail account in the POP account name text box. If you would like Outlook Express to save your password so that you will not have to enter it manually each time you access your e-mail, enter the password in the Password text box. The password will appear as asterisks (******) to prevent others from knowing it.
- If, however, you would prefer to have a prompt display each time you attempt to access your e-mail requiring you to enter your password leave the Password text box blank. You might want to do this, for example, if others frequently use your computer and you want to ensure that they cannot access your E-mail.
- Click Next when you are finished.

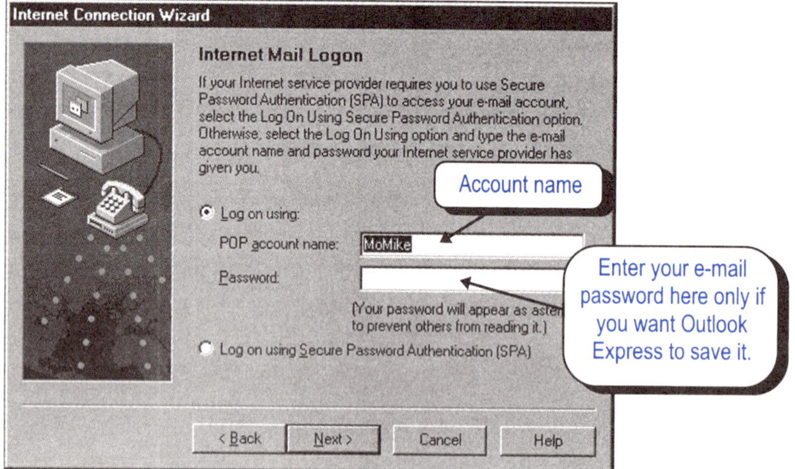

- Enter the name of the account that will appear when you open the Accounts list on the Tools menu in Outlook Express. It can be any name that you choose. Click Next when have finished.

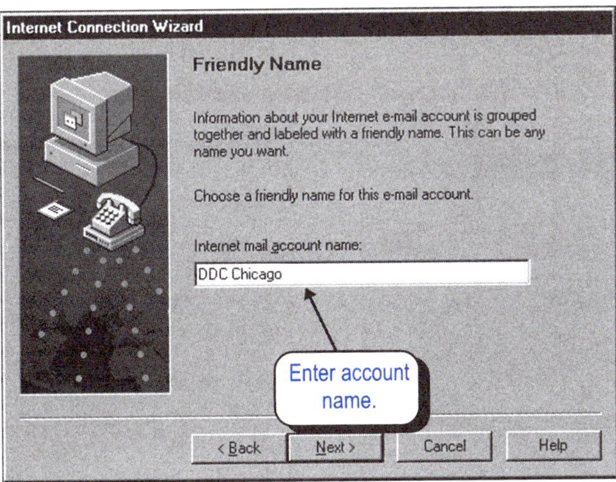

- Select the type of connection that you are using to reach the Internet. Click Next.

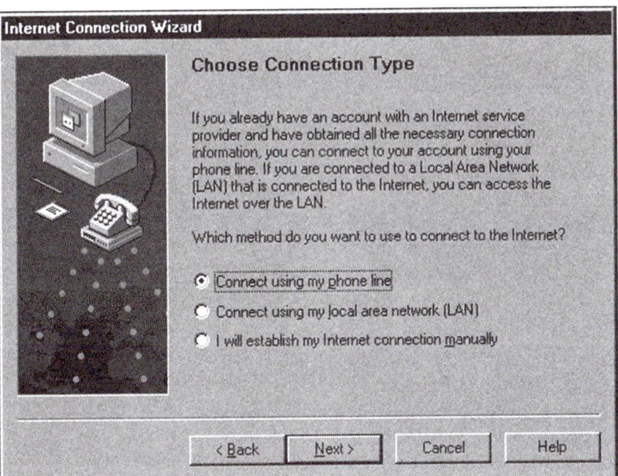

- If you are connecting through a phone line, the following dialog box will appear for you to select a dial-up connection or create a new one. (The dial-up connection contains the phone number your computer will dial to connect to your ISP mail server.) Select an existing dial-up connection, or select Create a new dial-up connection and click Next.

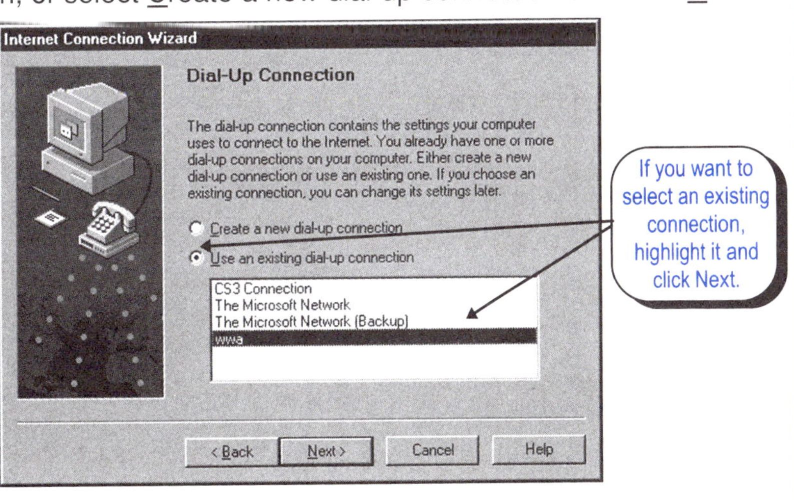

- If you chose the Create a new dial-up connection option, the following dialog box opens. Enter the appropriate phone number and country code for your ISP mail server (contact your ISP if you're not sure about this information). Then click Next.

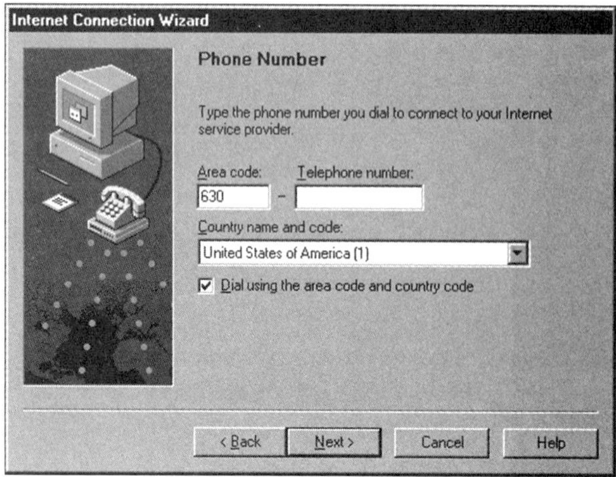

- When you reach the final Internet Connection Wizard dialog box, click Finish to save your e-mail configuration settings. You should then be able to launch Outlook Express and send and receive mail and attachments.

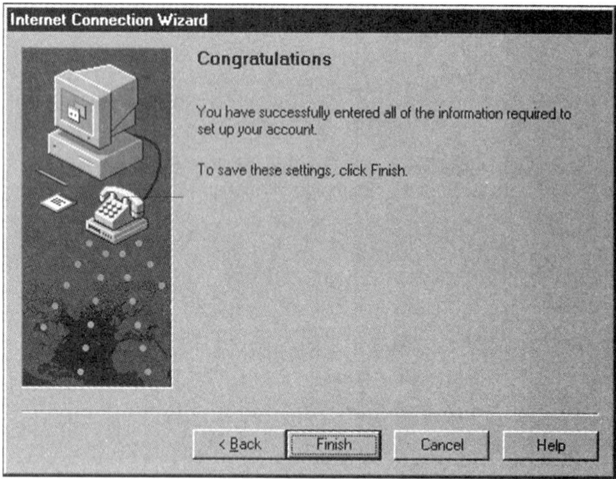

CAUTION: The exercise directions below presume that you have already set up a mail account with a service provider. If you are not set up with Internet mail, contact your service provider.

In Part I of this exercise, you will enter (or verify) information that establishes a connection with your mail server. In Part II, you will customize the way you send and receive mail.

EXERCISE DIRECTIONS

Part I

1. Connect to your Internet service provider.
2. Launch Outlook Express from the Programs menu on the Start menu.

   OR

   Click the Outlook Express button on the Quick Launch toolbar on the Windows 95 desktop.
3. Click Tools, Accounts to open the Internet Accounts dialog box.
4. Click Add, Mail to access the Internet Connection Wizard.

   ➲ *The Internet Connection Wizard opens.*

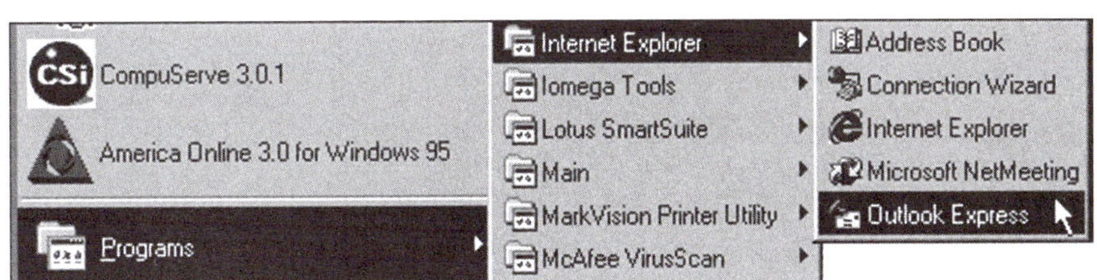

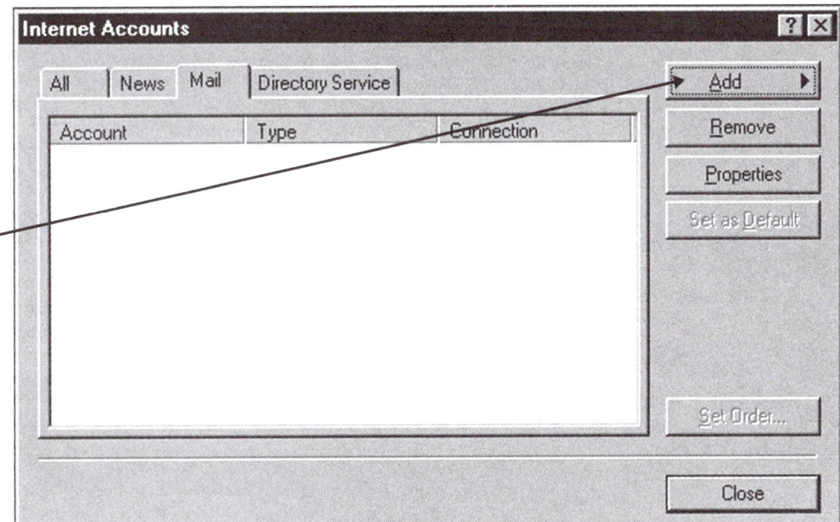

5. Enter your name as you want it to appear on e-mail messages. Click Next.

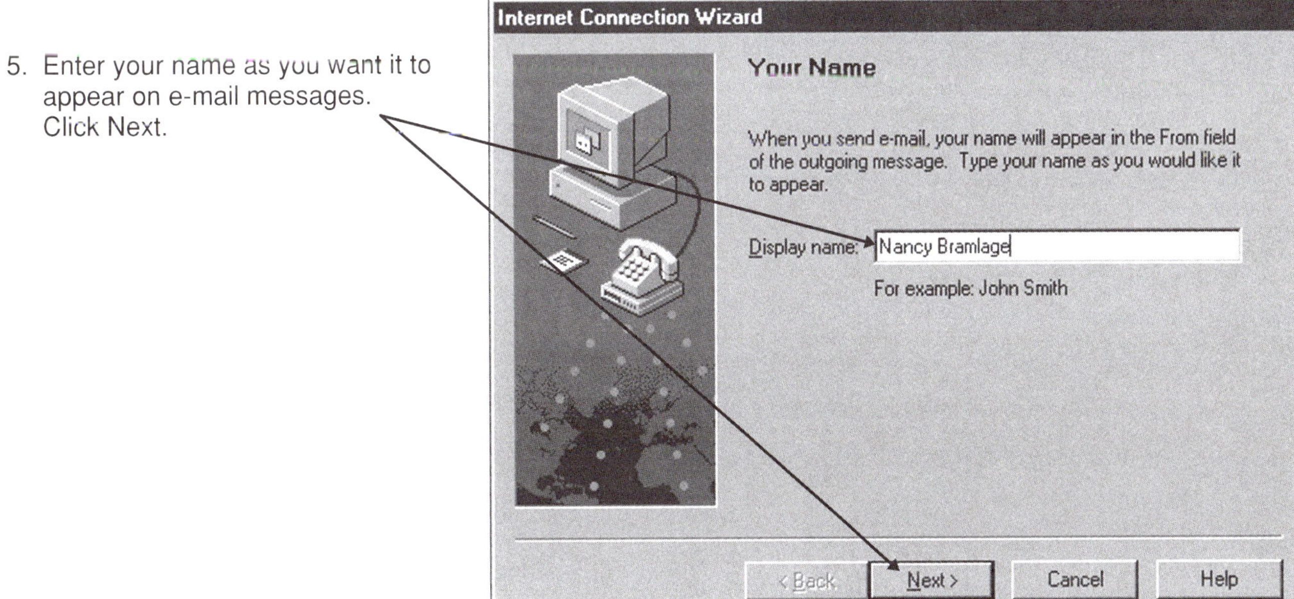

6. Enter your entire e-mail address (**username@servername.domain**). Click Next.

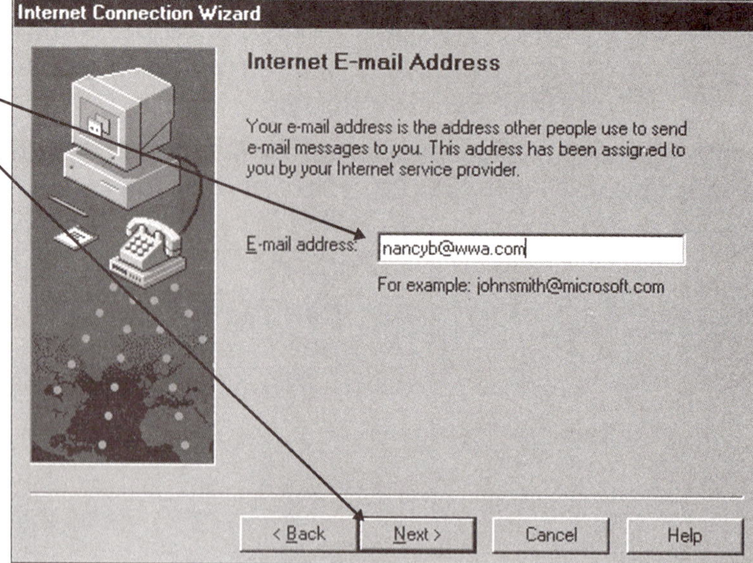

7. Enter mail server information for your incoming and outgoing mail. Click Next.

   ✓ *Your Internet service provider or system administrator can provide this information.*

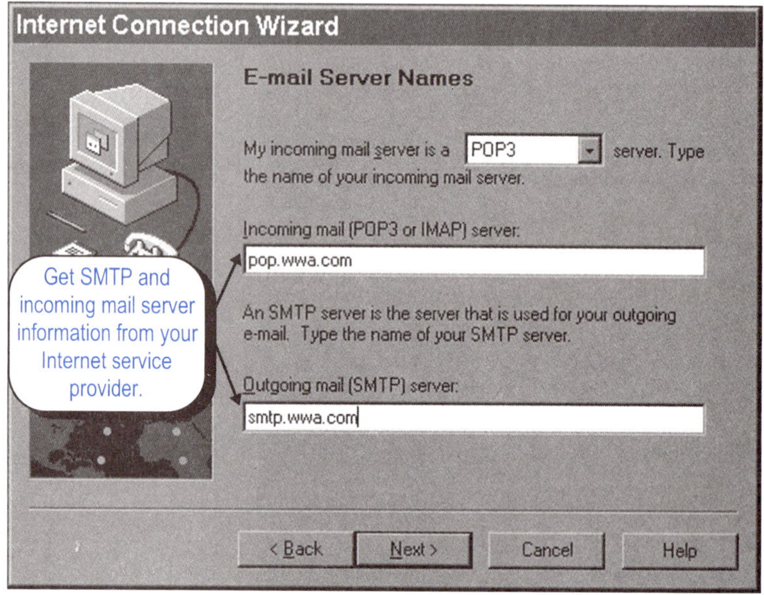

8. Enter the log on name and password that your Internet service provider requires you to use to log on to their server. Or, if your Internet service provider requires you to use Secure Password Authentication to access your e-mail account, select the second option. Click Next.

9. Enter a name that will distinguish your mailbox from other users on the same system. Click Next.

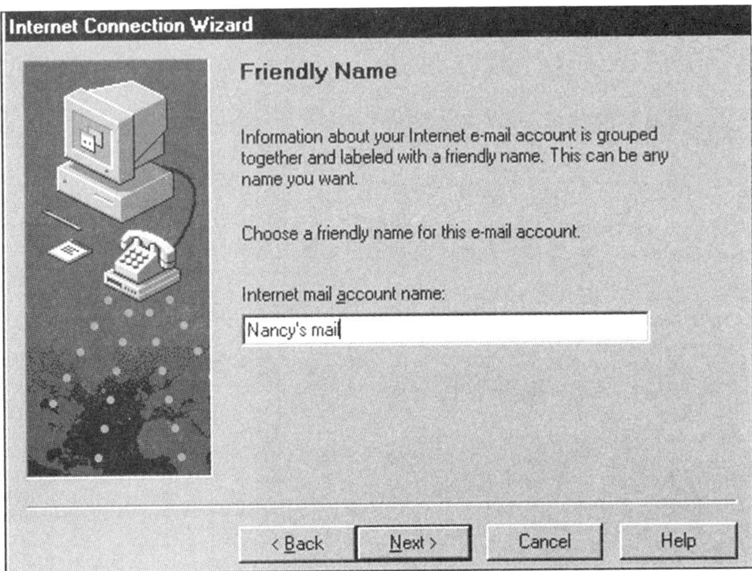

10. Select the way you want to connect to the Internet in the Choose Connection Type box and click Next.
    - ✓ *If you are using a modem, select Connect using my phone line.*
    - ✓ *If you are on a network, check with your network administrator to establish a connection.*

Internet Connection Wizard

Choose Connection Type

If you already have an account with an Internet service provider and have obtained all the necessary connection information, you can connect to your account using your phone line. If you are connected to a Local Area Network (LAN) that is connected to the Internet, you can access the Internet over the LAN.

Which method do you want to use to connect to the Internet?

Connect using my phone line

Connect using my local area network (LAN)

I will establish my Internet connection manually

< Back | Next > | Cancel | Help

11. If you already have an existing connection, select the one that you want to use for this mailbox and click Next. If you want to create a new connection, select Create a new dial-up connection, click Next, and follow the steps in the Internet Connection Wizard.
    - ✓ *If you are connecting using a local area network, you will not see this dialog box.*

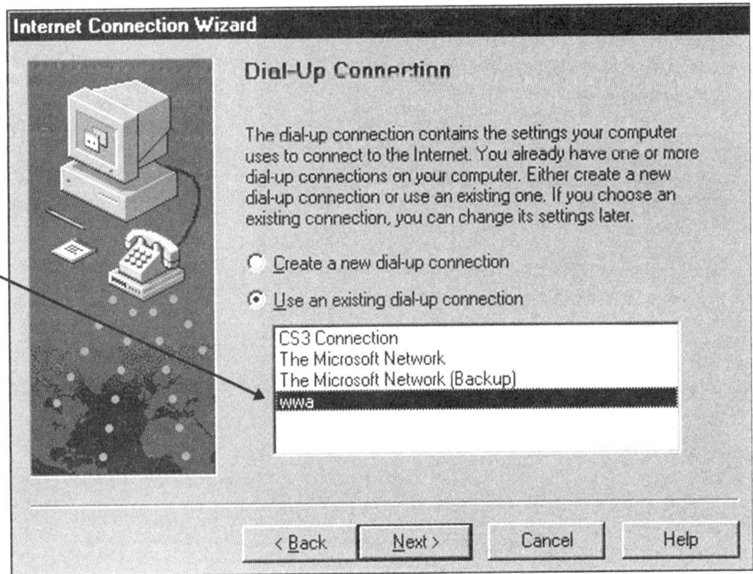

12. Click Finish.
13. When you have finished the Internet Connection procedure, your new account will appear in the Internet Accounts list. Click Close to return to Outlook Express.

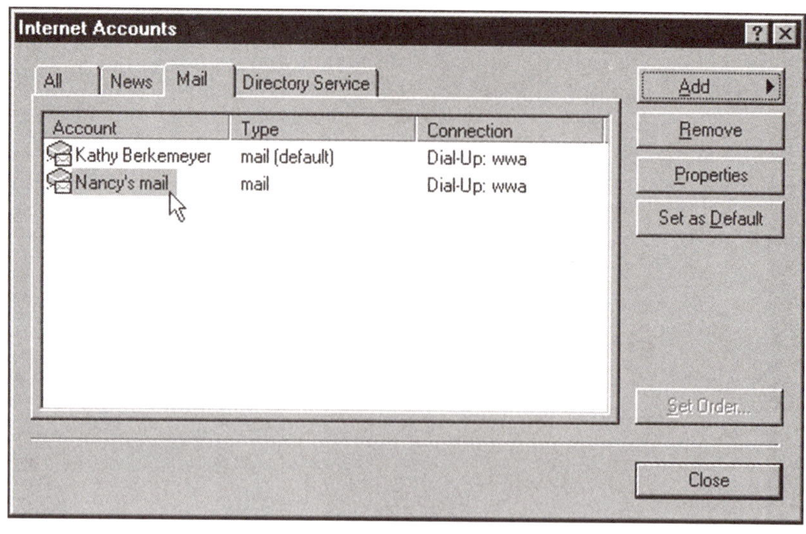

Part II

1. After configuring Outlook Express, select Tools, Options, and click the **General** tab.
   - Select or deselect the options that you want.
   - Be sure that Check for new Messages is set to every 30 minutes.

   ✓ *If you expect to receive mail frequently, you can change this option so that Outlook Express will check for messages more frequently.*
   - If Outlook will be your primary e-mail program, select Make Outlook Express my default e-mail program.

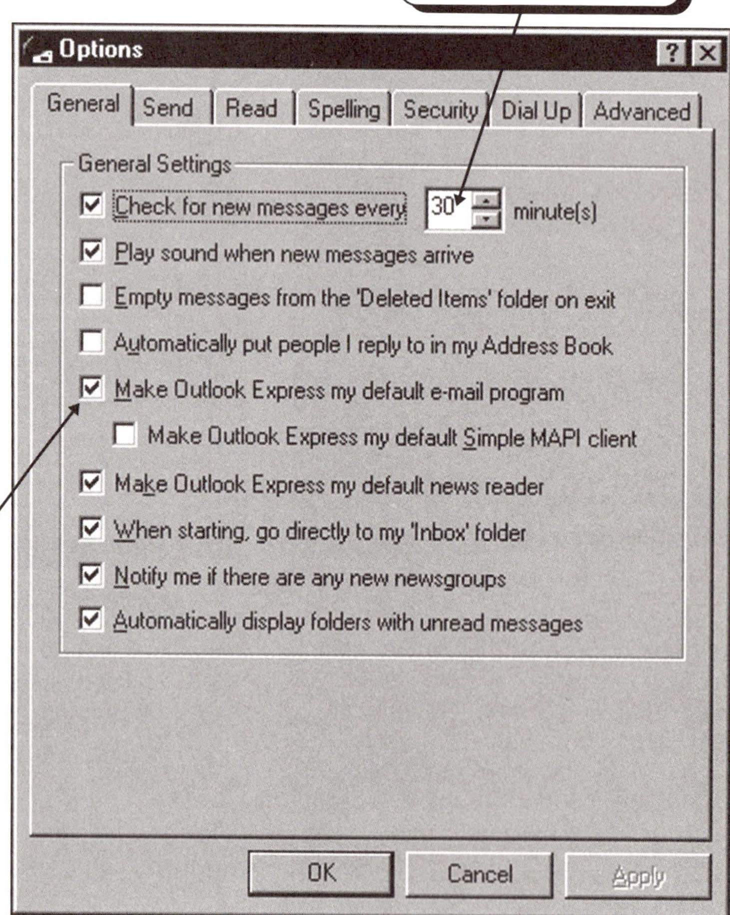

2. Click the **Send** tab. Make sure HTML is selected under the Mail sending format heading.

   ✓ *Most browsers will accept HTML or Rich Text messages. Some mail servers will display HTML formatted messages as a separate file.*

3. Click Settings next to the HTML button.

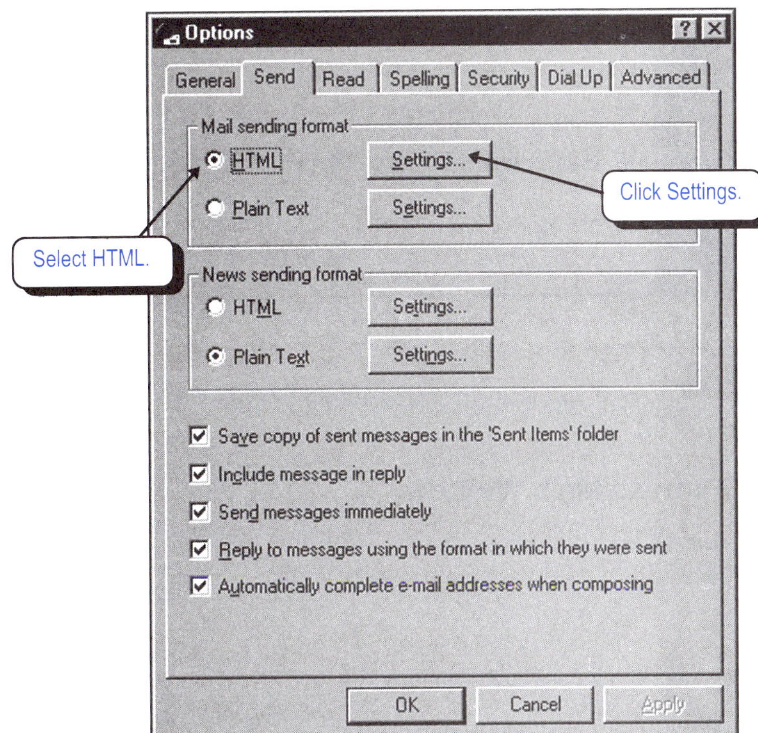

4. Select Send pictures with messages, then click OK.

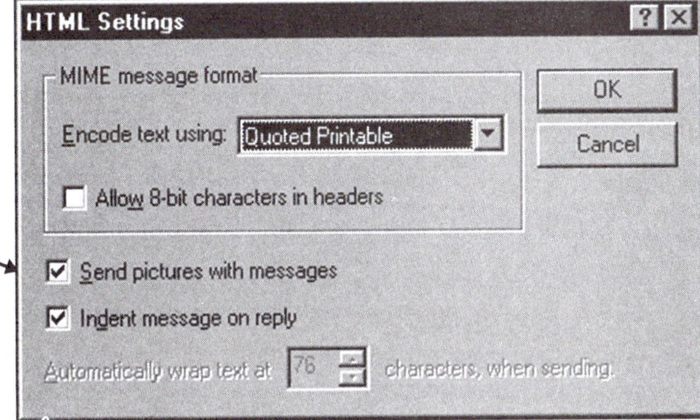

5. Click the **Spelling** tab.
6. Make sure that the Always suggest replacements for misspelled words and Always check spelling before sending under the General options category are selected. Click OK.
7. Continue on to the next exercise.

   OR

   Exit Outlook Express and disconnect from your service provider.

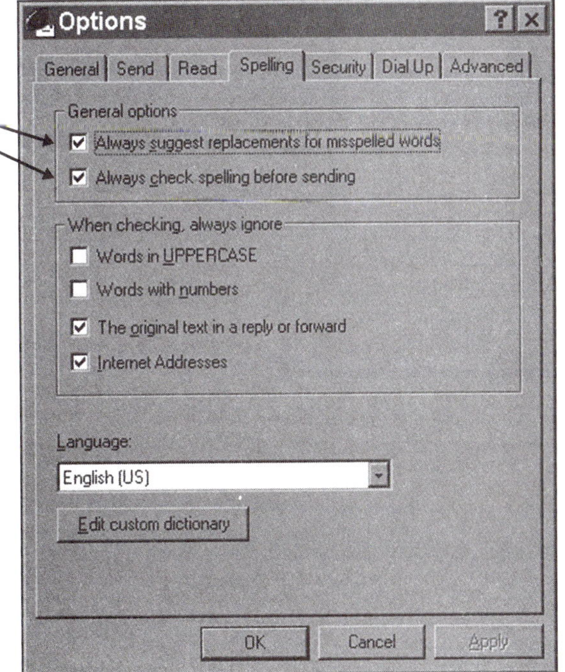

Exercise

2

■ Outlook Express Main Window ■ Compose New Messages
■ Send Messages ■ New Message Toolbar

NOTES

Outlook Express Main Window

- After you launch Outlook Express, the main Outlook Express window opens by default. You can access any e-mail function from this window.

Outlook Express Main Window

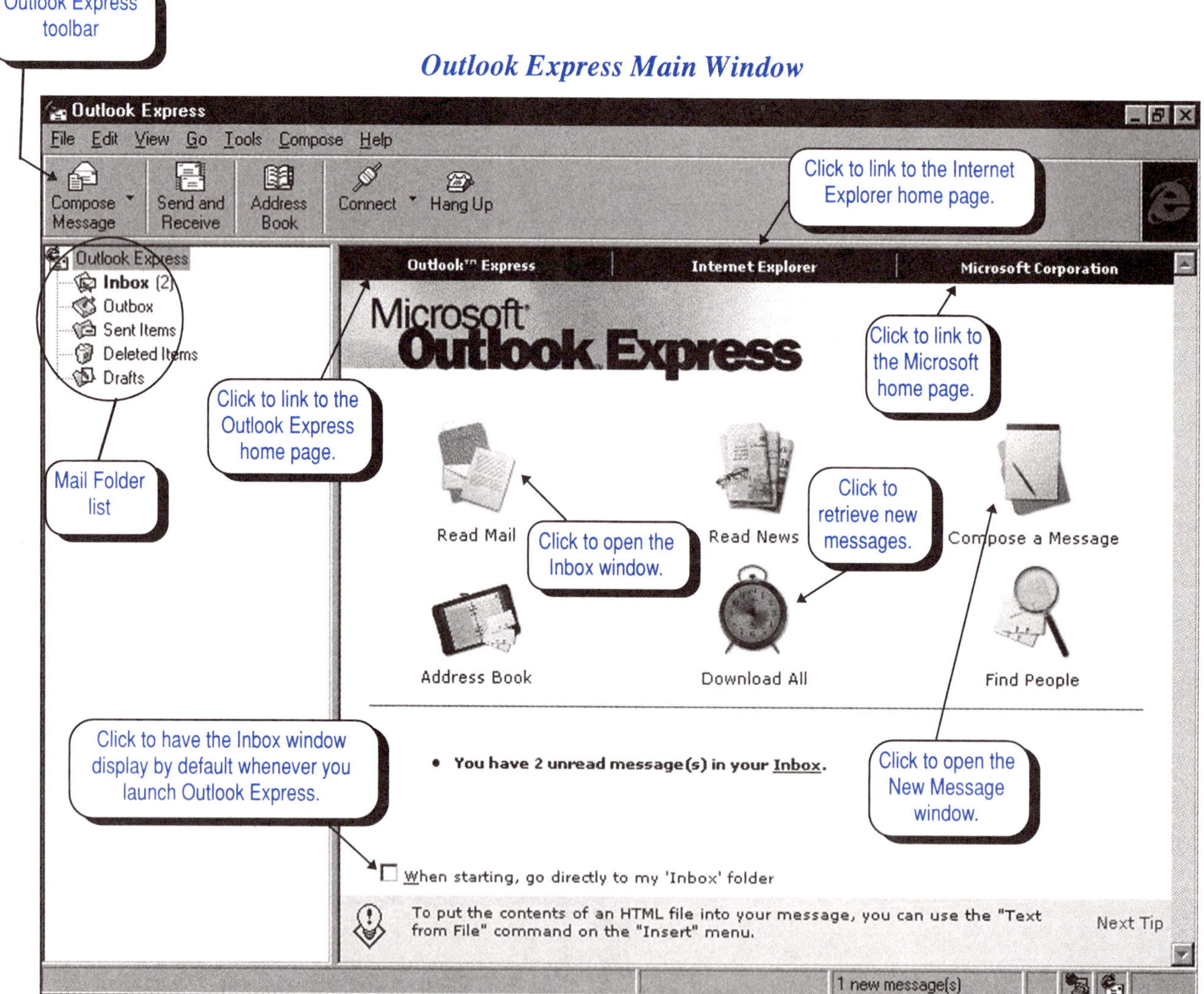

- Descriptions of items in the main window follow below:
  - The **Mail Folder list** displays in the left column of the window, with the Outlook Express main folder selected. To view the contents of a different folder, click on the desired folder in the folder list.
  - **Shortcuts** to different e-mail functions are located in the center of the window. These shortcuts work like toolbar buttons: click once on a shortcut to access the indicated task or feature.
  - **Hyperlinks** to Microsoft home pages are located at the top of the window. Click once to connect to the indicated home page.
  - The **Outlook Express toolbar** displays buttons for commonly used commands. Note that each button contains an image and text that describes the button function. Click any of these buttons to activate the indicated task immediately.

Outlook Express Toolbar Buttons and Functions

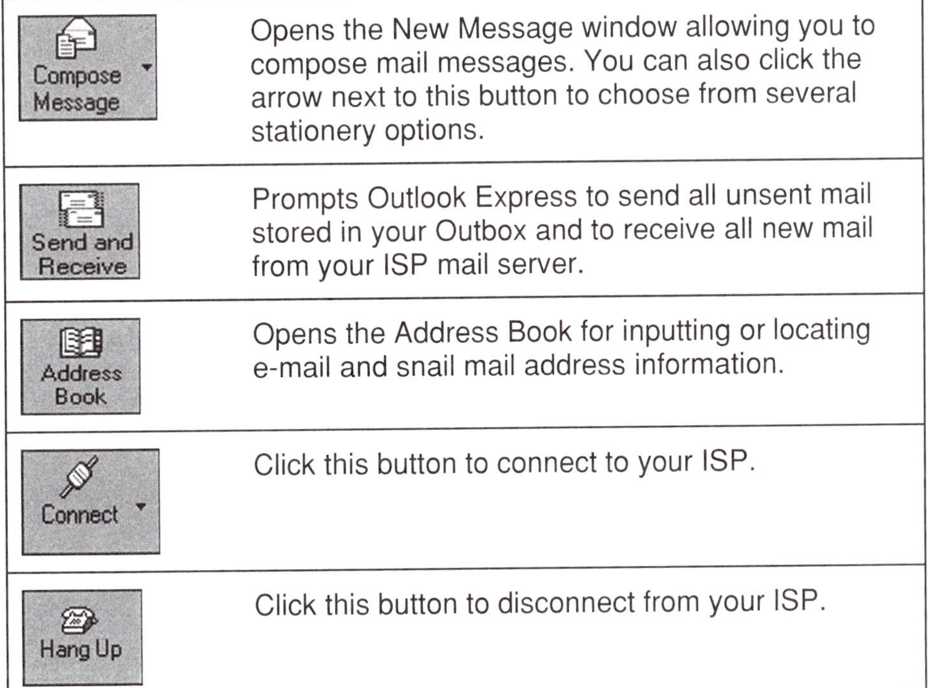

Button	Function
Compose Message	Opens the New Message window allowing you to compose mail messages. You can also click the arrow next to this button to choose from several stationery options.
Send and Receive	Prompts Outlook Express to send all unsent mail stored in your Outbox and to receive all new mail from your ISP mail server.
Address Book	Opens the Address Book for inputting or locating e-mail and snail mail address information.
Connect	Click this button to connect to your ISP.
Hang Up	Click this button to disconnect from your ISP.

Snail Mail
Mail sent by the U.S. Postal Service.

- If you prefer, you can change the default opening window from the main window to the Mail window, with the contents of the Inbox displayed. To do so, select the When starting, go directly to my 'Inbox' folder check box at the bottom of the main window.

Compose New Messages

- You can compose an e-mail message in Outlook Express while you are connected to the Internet or while you are offline. When composing an e-mail message online, you can send the message immediately after creating it. When composing a message offline (which is considered proper Netiquette), you will need to reconnect to the Internet to send the message, or else store the message in your Outbox folder for delivery later when you are online.
- To create a message, you first need to open the New Message window. To do so:
  - Click the Compose Message button  on the Outlook Express toolbar.

    OR

    Select New Message from the Compose menu.

    OR

    Click the Compose a Message shortcut 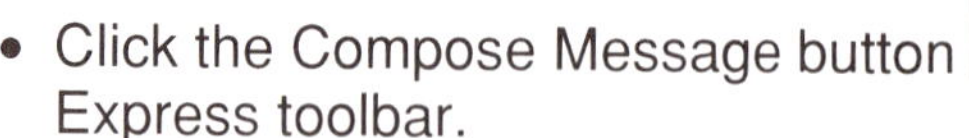 in the Outlook Express main window.

✓ *The New Message window displays.*

New Message Window

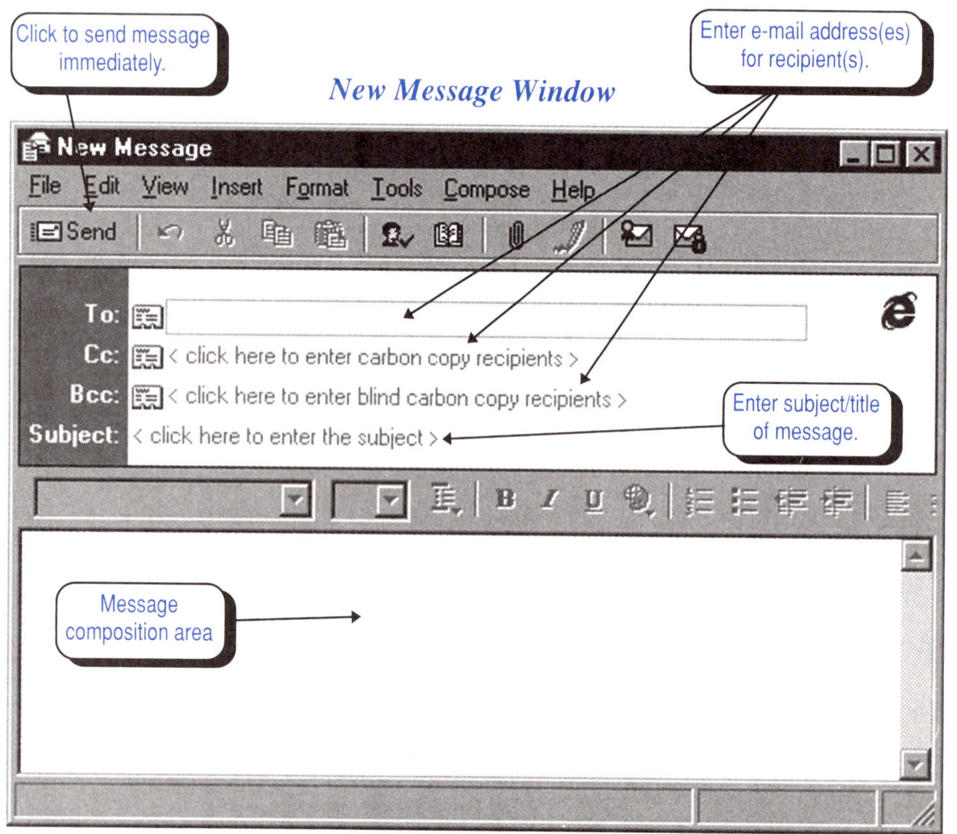

Netiquette
The Network equivalent of respectfulness and civility when dealing with people and organiztions.

WARNING
Before including any published work in an e-mail message, obtain permission from the copyright holder.

Note
You can hide any toolbar in the New Message window by going to the View menu and deselecting Toolbar, Formatting Toolbar, or Status Bar.

- In the New Message window, type the e-mail address(es) of the message recipient(s) in the To field.

  OR

  Click the index card icon in the To field or the Address Book button on the New Message toolbar to select an address from the Address Book or an online directory.

  ✓ *If you are sending the message to multiple recipients, insert a comma or semicolon between each recipient's address.*

- After inserting the address(es) in the To field, click in either or both of the following fields and enter the recipient information indicated as desired.

Cc (Carbon Copy)	The e-mail addresses of people who will receive copies of the message.
Bcc (Blind Carbon Copy)	Same as Cc, except these names will not appear anywhere in the message, so other recipients will not know that the person(s) listed in the Bcc field received a copy.

- Click in the Subject field and type the subject of the message.
- Click in the blank composition area below the Subject field and type the body of your message. Word-wrap occurs automatically, and you can cut and paste quotes from other messages or text from other programs. You can also check the spelling of your message by selecting Spelling from the Tools menu in the New Message window and responding to the dialog prompts that follow.
- You can also include images, hyperlinks, and formatted text in an e-mail message.

Send Messages

- Once you have created a message, you have three choices:
  - to send the message immediately
  - to store the message in the Outbox folder to be sent later
  - to save the message in the Drafts folder to be edited and sent later

  To send a message immediately:

  - Click the Send button on the New Message toolbar.

    OR

    Click File, Send Message in the New Message window.

- Outlook Express connects to your ISP's mail server and sends out the new message. If the connection to the mail server is successful, the Sending Mail icon displays in the lower-right corner of the Status bar until the transmittal is complete.

Status Bar

Sending Mail icon

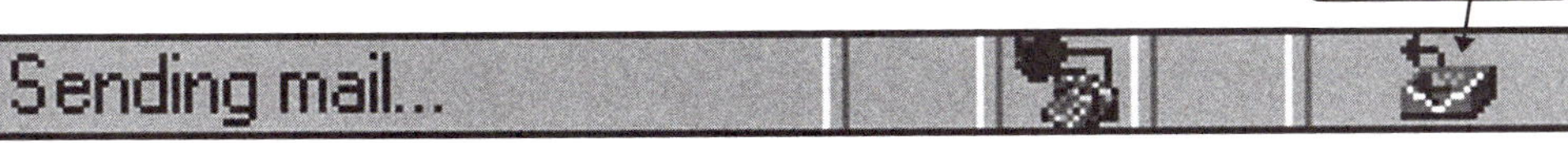

Note

If you do not know the recipient's address, you can look it up and insert it from your Address Book or an online directory.

Note

If you type the first few characters of a name or e-mail address that is saved in your Address Book, Outlook Express will automatically complete it for you.

Note

To be able to send messages immediately, you must first select Options from the Tools menu in the Outlook Express main window. Then click on the Send tab and select the Send messages immediately check box and click OK. If this option is **not** selected, clicking the Send button will send the message to your Outbox where it will remain until you perform the Send and Receive task.

- Sometimes, however, Outlook Express cannot immediately connect to the mail server and instead has to store the new message in the Outbox for later delivery. When this happens, the sending mail icon does not appear, and the number next to your Outbox folder **Outbox** (1) increases by one.
- Outlook Express does not automatically reattempt to send a message after a failed connection. Instead, you need to manually send the message from the Outbox.

To store a message in your Outbox folder for later delivery:

- Select File, Send Later in the New Message window.
- The Send Mail prompt will display. Click OK.

- The message is saved in the Outbox.

To send messages from your Outbox folder:

- Click on the Send and Receive button Send and Receive on the toolbar.

  OR

  Click Tools, Send and Receive.

To save a message to your Drafts folder:

- Click File, Save.
- The Saved Message prompt displays. Click OK.

Note

If you are offline when you select the Send and Receive Command, Outlook Express will automatically begin connecting to the Internet, or will display a dialog box where you can click Yes to connect.

Note

When you use the Send and Receive command, Outlook Express sends out **all** messages stored in the Outbox and automatically downloads any new mail messages from the mail server. If you have not saved your e-mail password or entered it during the current Internet session, you may be prompted to enter it before Outlook Express will check your mailbox for new messages.

To edit and send message drafts:

- Click on the Drafts folder Drafts (1) in the Mail Folder list.
- Double-click on the desired message from the message list that appears on the right.
- In the New Message window that appears, edit your message as necessary. When you are finished, select File, Send Message to send the message immediately, or File, Send Later to store it in the Outbox folder for later delivery.

■ Outlook Express automatically saves all sent messages in the Sent Items folder. To view a list of the messages you have sent, select the Sent Items folder Sent Items from the Mail Folder list. The contents will display in the message list.

New Message Toolbar

■ The New Message window has several toolbar features that are specific to composing and editing messages.

■ Also provided is a Formatting toolbar that contains commands for applying styles, fonts, font size, bulleted lists, and for inserting objects.

■ Below are descriptions of the New Message toolbar button functions.

New Message Toolbar

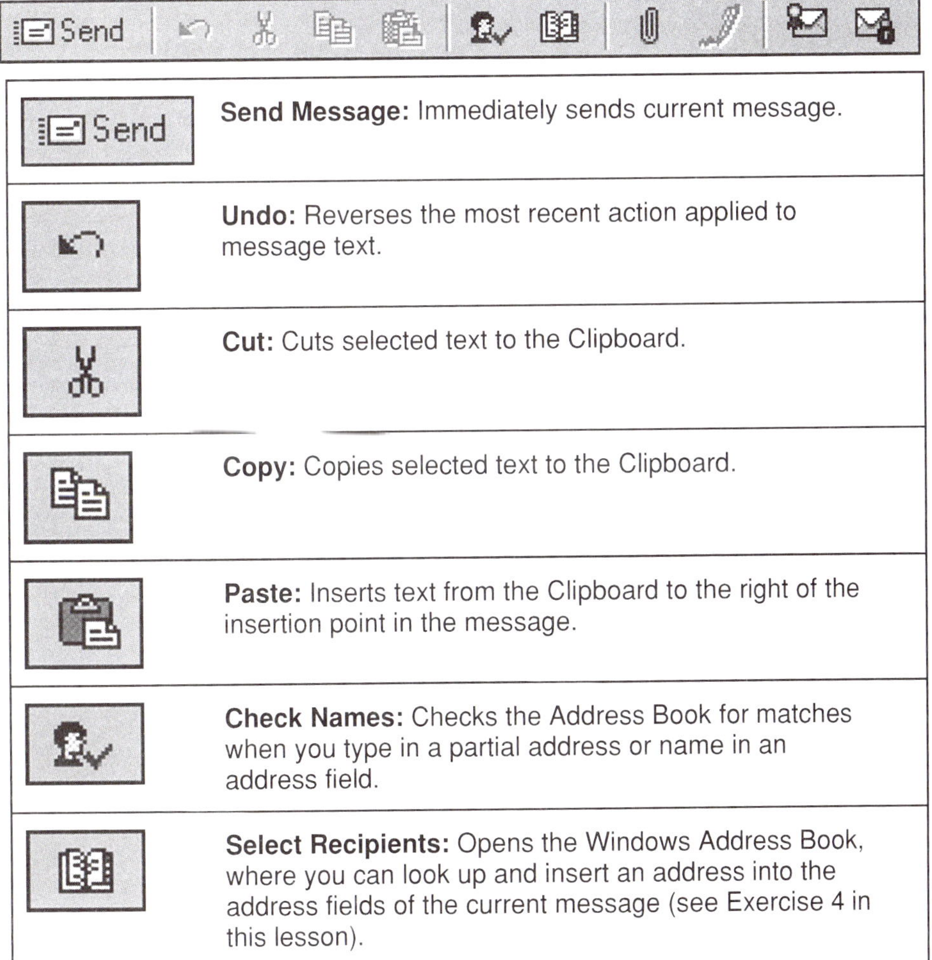

Button	Description
Send	**Send Message:** Immediately sends current message.
	Undo: Reverses the most recent action applied to message text.
	Cut: Cuts selected text to the Clipboard.
	Copy: Copies selected text to the Clipboard.
	Paste: Inserts text from the Clipboard to the right of the insertion point in the message.
	Check Names: Checks the Address Book for matches when you type in a partial address or name in an address field.
	Select Recipients: Opens the Windows Address Book, where you can look up and insert an address into the address fields of the current message (see Exercise 4 in this lesson).

	**Insert File:** Opens the Insert Attachment dialog box, where you can select a file to attach to the current e-mail message (see Exercise 5 in this lesson).
	**Insert Signature:** Inserts your textual signature (personal tag line) at the end of the current message. This button will be dimmed (unavailable) if you have not created your own signature. (See Outlook Express Help for more information on textual signatures.)
	**Digitally Sign Message:** Sends your digital signature with the current message, so the recipient knows the message came from you and has not been tampered with. (See Outlook Express Help for more information on digital signatures and other security features.)
	**Encrypt Message:** Encrypts the current message in a code for security. (See Outlook Express Help for more information on encryption and other security features.)

In this exercise, you will compose and send two e-mail messages using Outlook Express.

EXERCISE DIRECTIONS

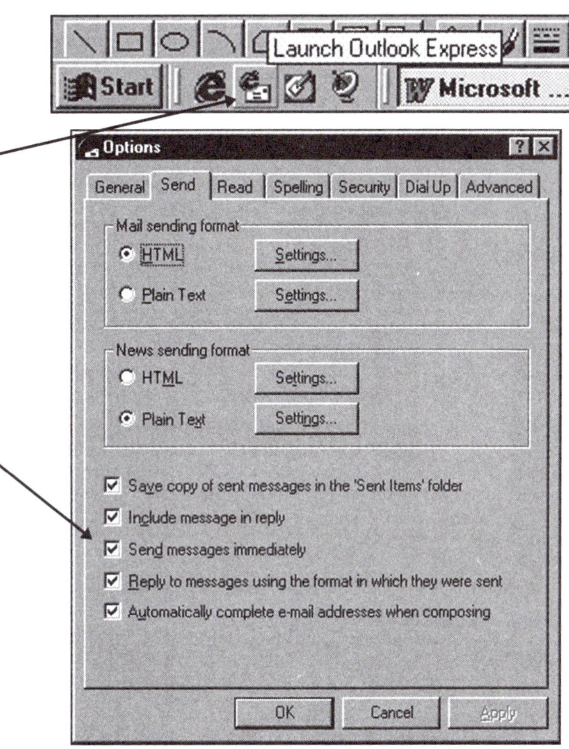

1. If you are already connected to your service provider and Outlook Express is open, go to step 2.

   OR

   Connect to your service provider and launch Outlook Express.
2. Select Tools, Options on the Outlook Express main menu and be sure that Send messages immediately is selected on the **Send** tab.
3. Click OK.
4. Click the Compose Message button  on the Outlook Express toolbar.
5. In the New Message composition window, fill in these headers as follows:

To:	learn@ddcpub.com
Subject:	e-mail test
Body:	This is an e-mail test. Send me a message.

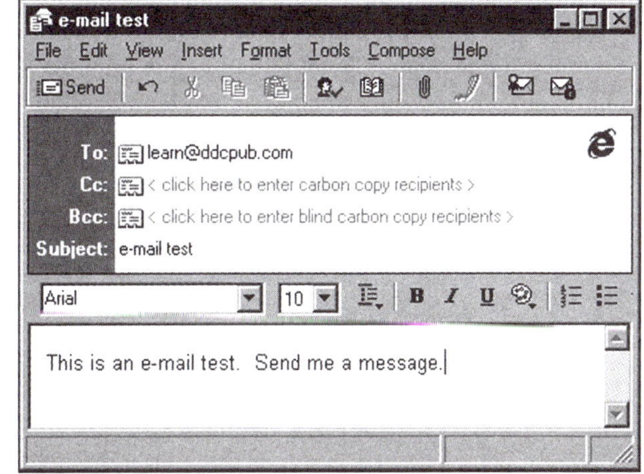

6. Click the Send button **Send** on the New Message toolbar.
7. Disconnect from your Internet service provider but keep Outlook Express open.

   ✓ *You can read and write responses to e-mail messages offline.*
8. Select the Sent Items folder from the folders list on the left side of the Outlook Express screen.

   ➲ *The message you just sent should be listed in the Sent mail message window.*

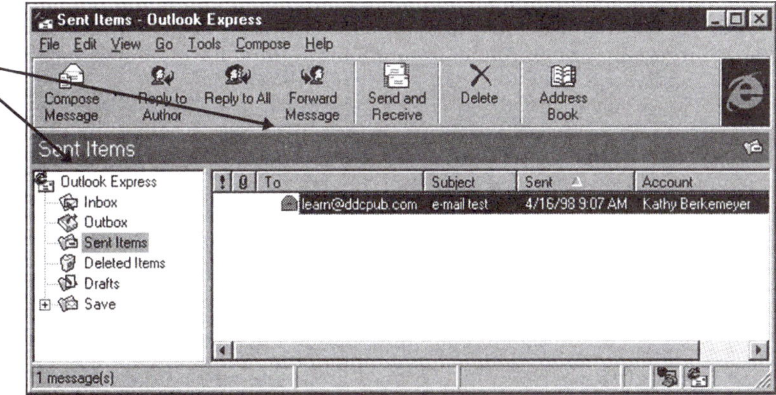

9. Click the Compose Message button Compose Message on the Outlook Express toolbar.
10. In the New Message composition window, enter your own e-mail address in the To field. In the Subject field, enter the following: *e-mail test*.
11. In the Message composition area enter the following: *I'm sending this to myself.*
12. Click File, Send Later. Click OK.

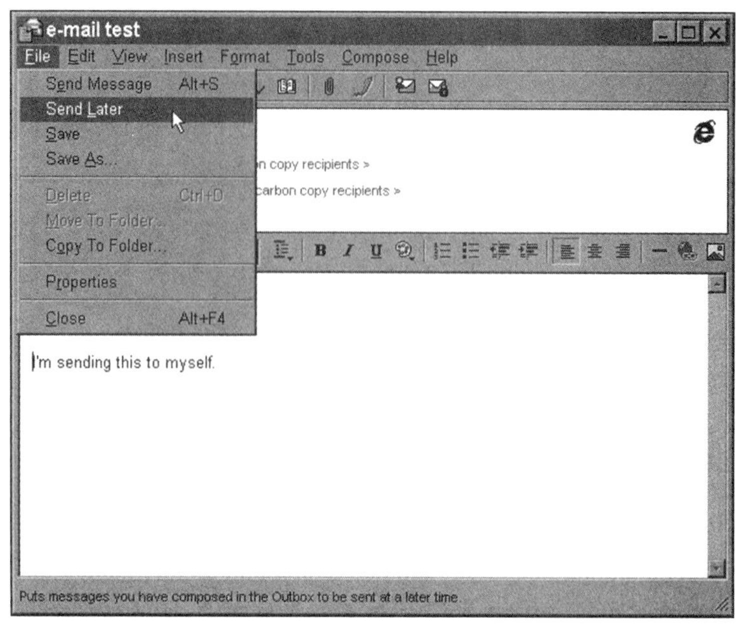

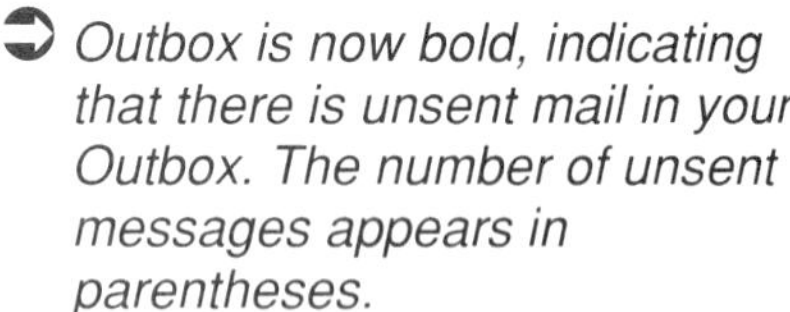

➲ *Outbox is now bold, indicating that there is unsent mail in your Outbox. The number of unsent messages appears in parentheses.*

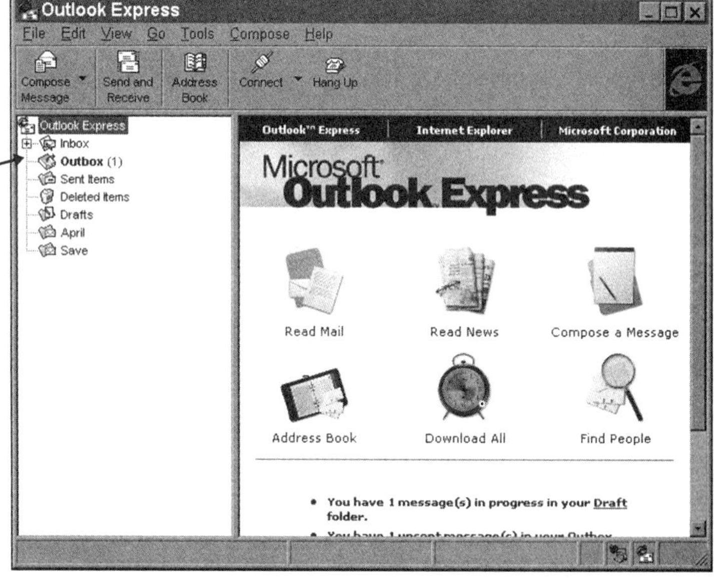

13. Click Connect Connect on the Outlook Express toolbar to reconnect to your service provider.

14. Click the Send and Receive button Send and Receive on the Outlook Express toolbar.

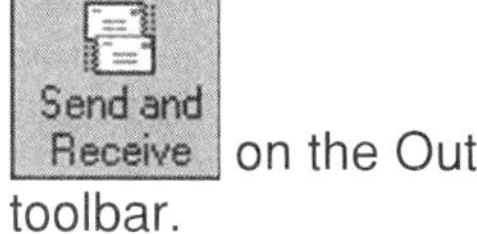

➲ *Both messages that you sent now appear in the Sent Items folder. Your Inbox should now be bolded, indicating that you have received new mail.*

15. Continue on to the next exercise.

OR

Exit from Outlook Express and disconnect from your service provider.

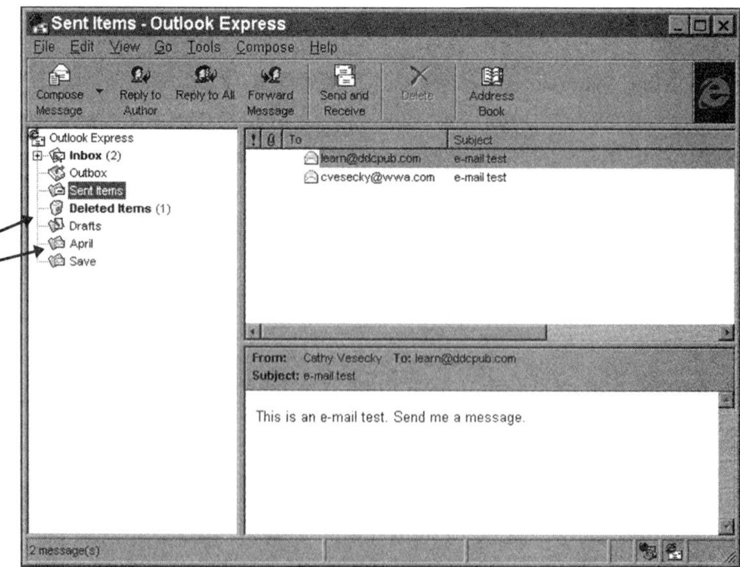

NEXT EXERCISE

Exercise 3

■ Retrieve New Messages ■ The Mail Window ■ Read Messages ■ Delete a Message ■ File a Message ■ Save a Message ■ Print a Message ■ Reply to a Message ■ Forward a Message

NOTES

Retrieve New Messages

- New e-mail messages are stored on a remote ISP mail server. Before you can read them, Outlook Express must first connect to the mail server and then download the messages onto your computer.
- You can access the retrieve new mail command from any Outlook Express window. To do so:
  - Click the Send and Receive button (Send and Receive) on the toolbar.

    OR

    Click Tools, Send and Receive.
- If you are not already connected to the Internet before you retrieve new messages, Outlook Express will automatically begin connecting to your ISP or will display a dialog box where you can click Yes to connect. The connection box will then display the connection status.

- Once you are connected to the Internet, Outlook Express will attempt to connect to your ISP mail server. If you entered your e-mail account password in the Internet Connection Wizard when you configured the program, Outlook Express will be able to access your ISP mail server automatically and begin downloading new messages. A dialog box displays the status of the transmittal.

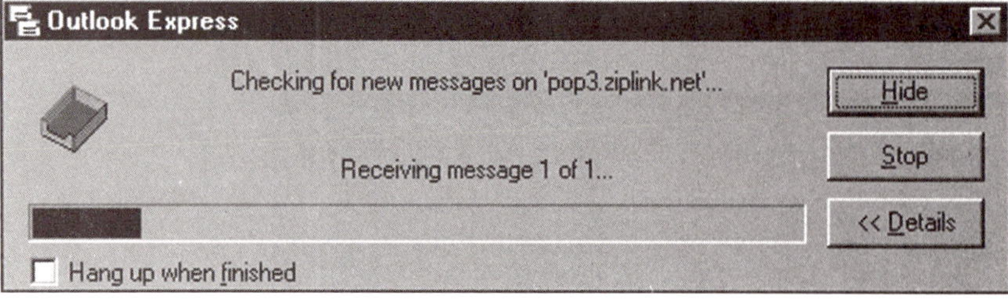

- If, however, you did not enter a password for your e-mail account in the Internet Connection Wizard when you configured Outlook Express, the following connection dialog box will display.

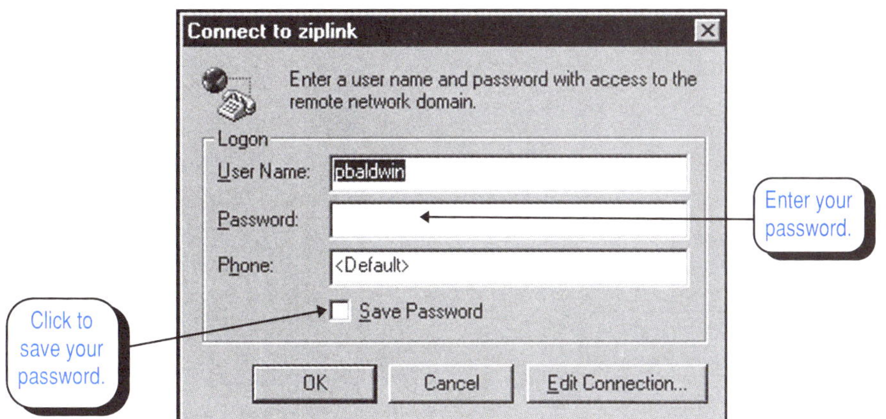

- Enter your password in the Password text box and click OK. (If you do not know your password, contact your ISP.) Outlook Express will send this information to your ISP mail server in order to make a connection and begin downloading new messages.
- Outlook Express will automatically save your password for the rest of the current Internet session. You must re-enter your password, however, each time you reconnect to the Internet or retrieve new mail, unless you set Outlook Express to save your password permanently. To do so, select the Save Password check box in the connection dialog box and click OK.

Note
You can set Outlook Express to check the mail server automatically for new mail whenever you launch Outlook Express and at periodic intervals during an Internet session. To do so, select Tools, Options and click on the General tab in the dialog box that appears. Select the Check for new messages every... check box, enter the desired number of minutes between mail checks, and click OK.

The Mail Window

- After retrieving new messages, Outlook Express stores them in the Inbox folder.
- To view your new messages, you must open the Mail window and display the contents of the Inbox folder. To do so:
  - Click on the Inbox Folder [Inbox] in the Mail Folders list.

  OR

  Click Read Mail [Read Mail] in the Outlook Express main window.

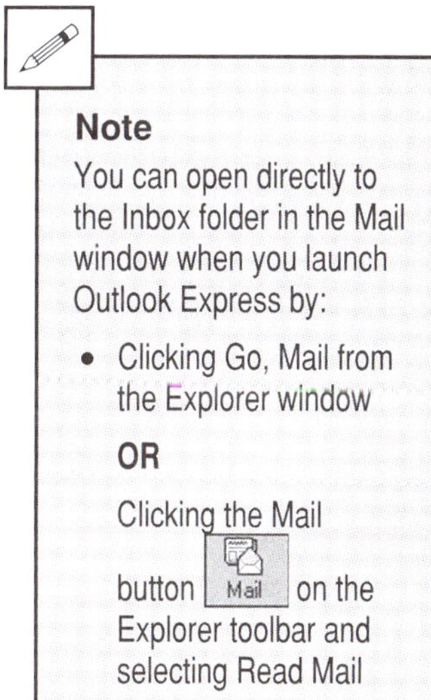

Note
You can open directly to the Inbox folder in the Mail window when you launch Outlook Express by:

- Clicking Go, Mail from the Explorer window

  OR

  Clicking the Mail button [Mail] on the Explorer toolbar and selecting Read Mail

- The Mail window opens with the Inbox folder displayed. A description of the items in the Mail window appears below.

Mail Window with Inbox Folder Displayed

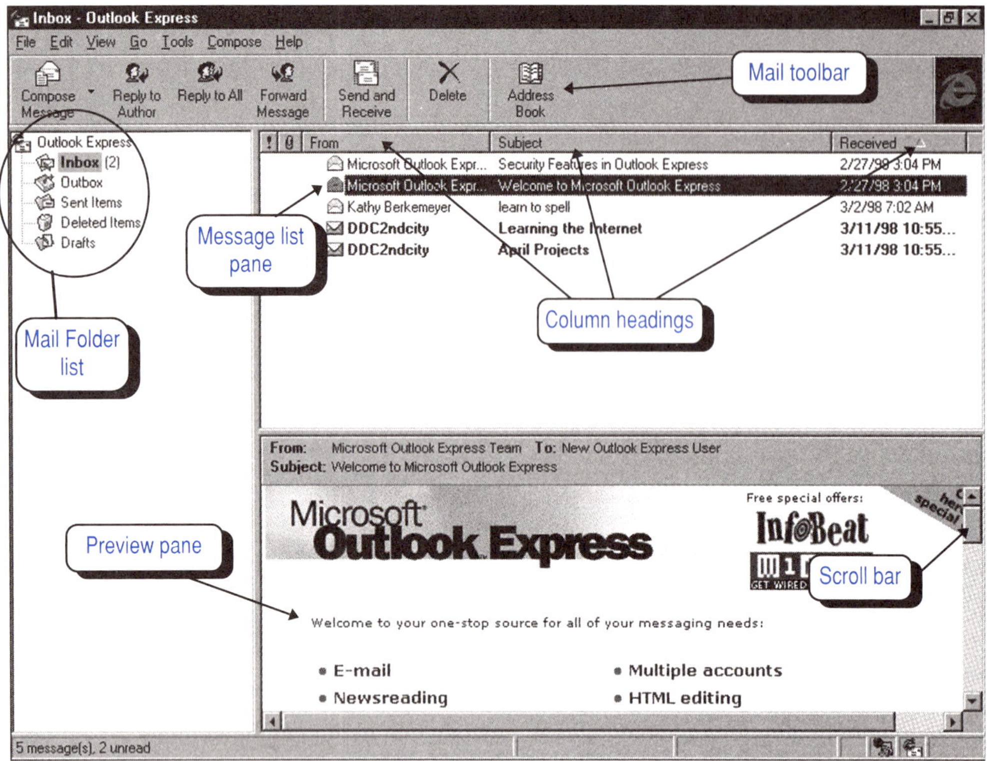

- The **Mail Folder list** displays a list of available message folders. The currently selected message folder is highlighted and its contents are displayed in the message list. Click on another folder to display its contents in the message list.
- The **message list** displays a header for each of the messages contained in the currently selected mail folder.
- **Column headings** list the categories of information included in each message header, such as Subject, From, and Date Received.
- The **preview pane** displays the content of the message currently selected from the message list.

Note

In the message list, unread messages are displayed in bold text with a sealed envelope icon to the left of the header.

Messages that have been read are listed in regular text with an open envelope icon to the left of the header.

Note

You can customize the display of the header columns in a number of ways:

- Resize column widths by placing the mouse pointer over the right border of a column heading until the pointer changes to a double arrow and then dragging the border to the desired size.
- Rearrange the order of the columns by clicking and dragging a column heading to a new location in the series.

Note

You can show/hide the preview pane by selecting View, Layout and clicking on the Use preview pane check box at the bottom of the dialog box. You can resize the preview pane or the message list pane by placing the pointer over the border between the two panes until the pointer changes to a double arrow and then dragging the border up or down to the desired size.

- The **Mail toolbar** displays command buttons for working with messages. These commands vary depending on the message folder currently displayed (Inbox, Sent, Outbox, etc.). Below are the buttons contained on the Mail toolbar when the Inbox folder is displayed. Note that each button contains an image and text describing the function. Clicking any of these buttons will activate the indicated task immediately.

Mail Toolbar Buttons and Functions

Button	Function
	Opens the New Message window allowing you to compose mail messages.
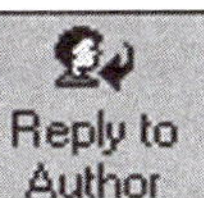	Allows you to reply to the sender of an e-mail message.
	Allows you to reply to the sender and all other recipients of an e-mail message.
	Forwards a message you have received to another address.
	Prompts Outlook Express to send all unsent mail stored in your Outbox and to receive all new mail from your ISP mail server.
	Deletes the selected message.
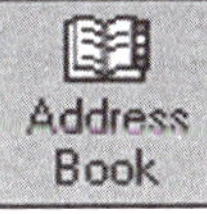	Opens the Address Book where you can add or locate an address.

Read Messages

- To read a message, you must first click on the mail folder containing the message to read so that its contents display in the message list pane.

Message List Window

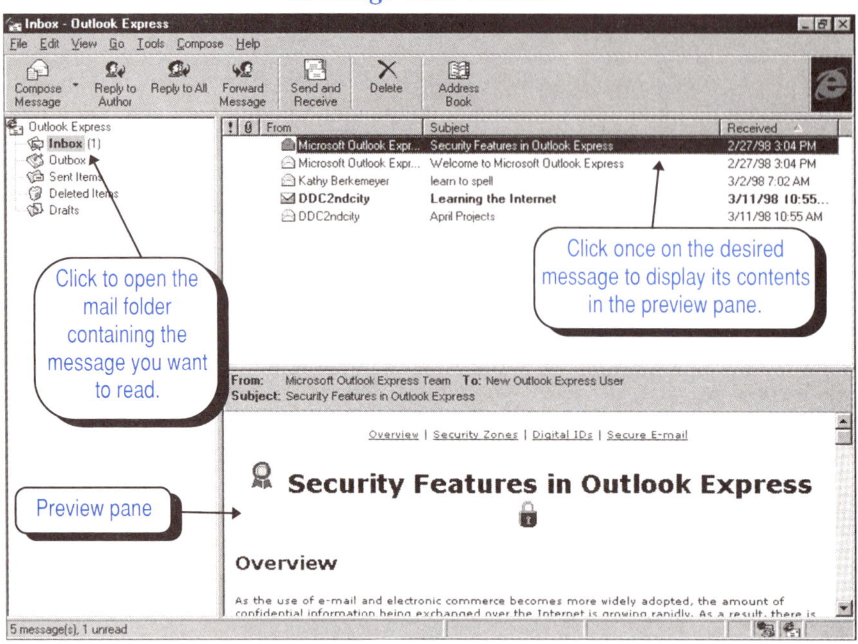

- You can read a message in the preview pane of the Mail window, or in a separate window.
- To read a message in the preview pane, click on the desired message in the message list. The message contents display in the lower half of the Mail window (see illustration above).
- To open and read a message in a separate window, double-click on the desired message in the message list.

  ✓ *The Message window opens displaying the Message toolbar and the contents of the selected message.*

Message Window

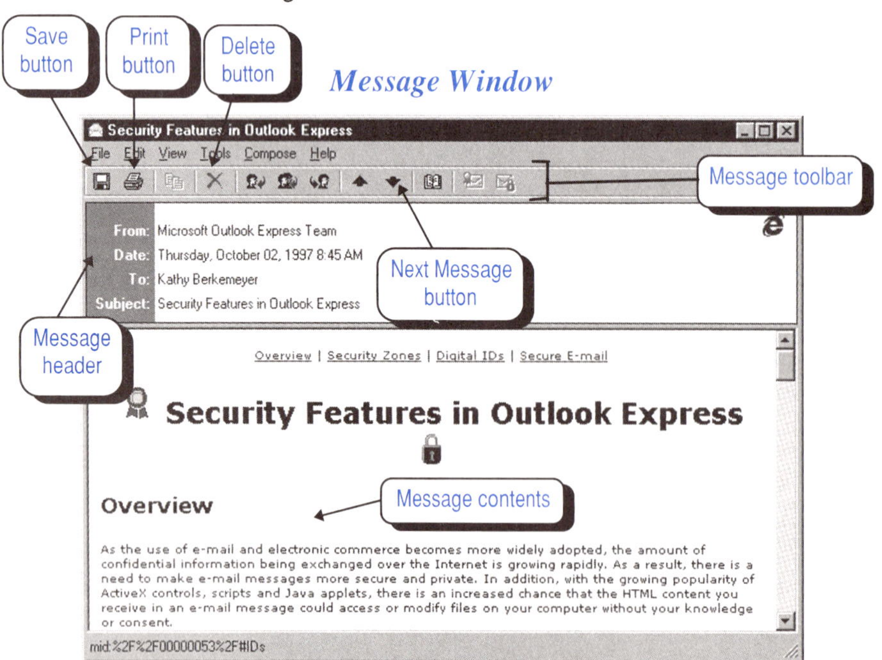

Note

You do not have to be online to read e-mail. You can reduce your online charges if you disconnect from your ISP after retrieving your messages and read them offline.

Note

If the message does not appear in the preview pane, select View, Layout. In the dialog box that follows, select Use preview pane and click OK.

- You can close the Message window after reading a message by clicking File, Close or by clicking on the Close button (X) in the upper-right corner of the window.
- Use the scroll bars in the Message window or the preview pane to view hidden parts of a displayed message. Or, press the spacebar to scroll down through the message.

To read the next unread message:

- Select View, Next, Next Unread Message.

  OR

  Press Ctrl+U.

  ✓ *If you have no unread messages, nothing will happen.*

  OR

  Click on the header for the next unread message in the message list.

  OR

  If you are viewing a message in the Message window, click the Next Message button on the Message toolbar.

- Once you have read a message, it remains stored in the Inbox folder until you delete it or file it in another folder.

Delete a Message

To delete a message:

- Select the desired message from the message list in the Mail window.

  Then click the Delete button in the Mail toolbar or select Edit, Delete.

  OR

  Open the desired message in the Message window and click the Delete button on the Message toolbar.

- When you delete a message, it is not immediately removed from your hard drive. Instead, if you use a POP3 (Post Office Protocol) incoming mail server, Outlook Express moves deleted messages to the Deleted Items folder, where they are stored until you delete them from there. To do so, click on the Deleted Items folder Deleted Items in the Mail Folder list. The contents of the Deleted Items folder display in the Mail window. Select the messages to delete permanently, or, to delete all items in the folder, select Edit, Select All. Then click the Delete button in the Mail toolbar. A dialog box will display asking you to confirm the deletion. Click Yes.
- If you use an IMAP (Internet Message Access Protocol) incoming mail server, Outlook Express marks deleted messages for deletion, leaving them in their message folder until you select Clear Deleted Messages from the File menu.

Note

To select more than one message to delete, press the Ctrl button while you click each message header.

Note

To find out what kind of mail server you have, click Tools, Accounts. In the dialog box that follows, click the Mail tab and click on the Properties button. In the Properties dialog box that opens, click the Servers tab and check to see whether POP3 or IMAP is entered in the My incoming mail server is text box.

File a Message

- After you read a message, it will remain in the Inbox until you delete it. Or you can file it in another message folder for future reference. To do so:
  - Double-click the desired message in the message list to open it in its own message window.
  - Select File, Move To Folder.

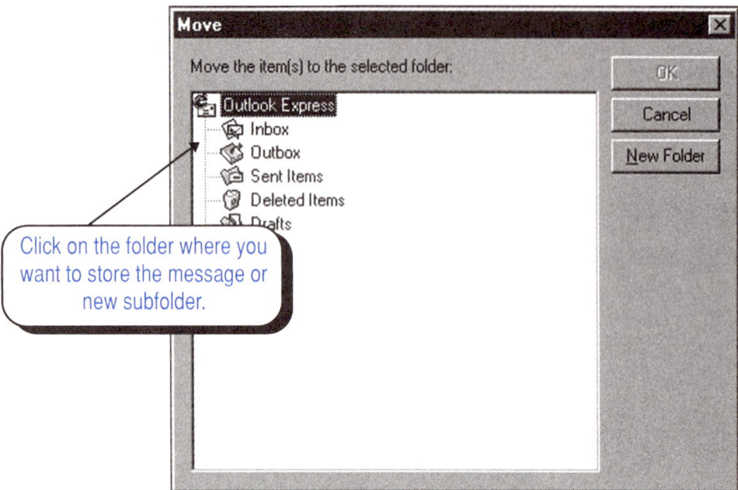

  - In the Move dialog box that follows, click on the folder in which to store the message and click OK.

  OR

  To create a new folder in which to store the message:

  - Highlight the Outlook Express folder or other folder in which to create the subfolder.
  - Click the New Folder button.
  - In the New Folder dialog box that displays, enter a name for the new folder and click OK to return to the Move dialog box.
  - Select the new folder from the list in the Move dialog box and click OK. The message will be moved to the new folder.

Save a Message

- To save a message to your hard drive:
  - Select the desired message from the message list in the Mail window and click File, Save As.

    OR

    Open the desired message in its own message window and click the Save button on the Message toolbar.
  - In the Save Message As dialog box that opens, click the Save in drop-down list box and select the drive and folder(s) in which to store the message file.

Save Messages As Dialog Box

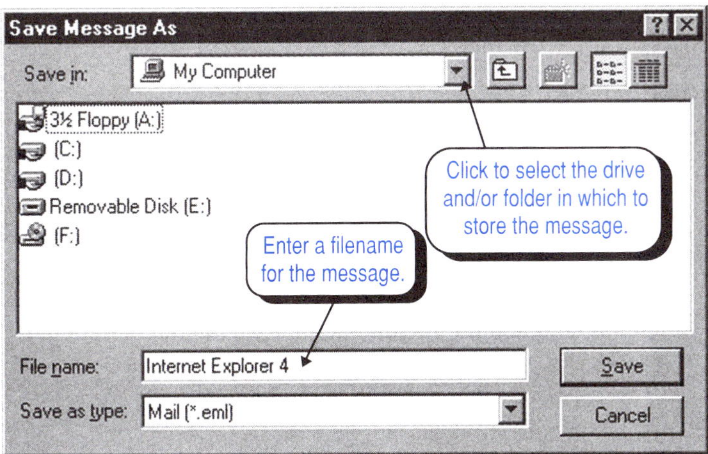

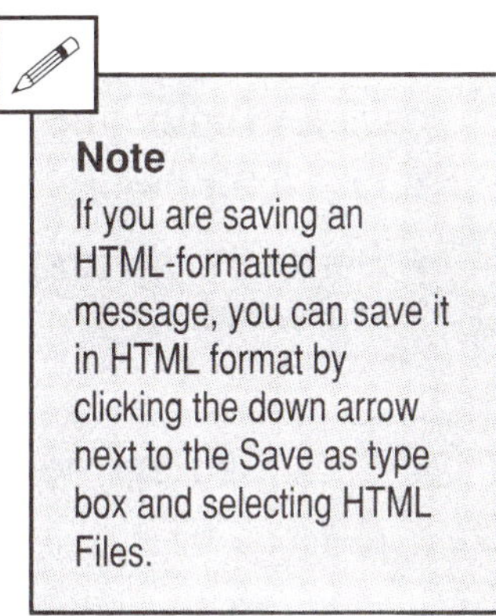

Note
If you are saving an HTML-formatted message, you can save it in HTML format by clicking the down arrow next to the Save as type box and selecting HTML Files.

- Click in the File name box and enter a name for the message.
- Click Save.

✓ *This procedure will save your message as a Plain Text file, which you can open in Notepad, Microsoft Word, or any word processing or text editor program.*

Print a Message

■ To print a message:

- Select the message you want to print from the message list in the Mail window or double-click on the message to open it in its own message window.
- Select Print from the File menu.
- In the Print dialog box that opens, select the desired print options and click OK.

Print Dialog Box

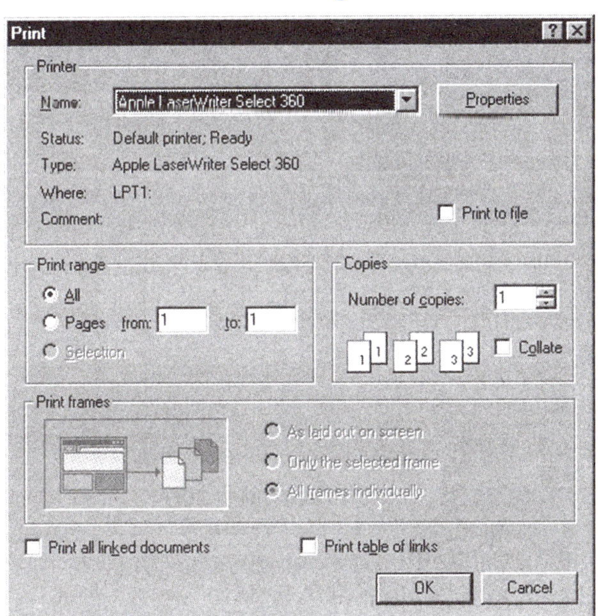

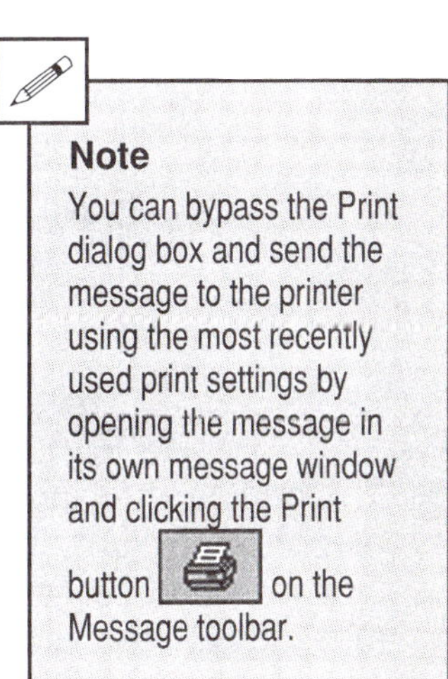

Note
You can bypass the Print dialog box and send the message to the printer using the most recently used print settings by opening the message in its own message window and clicking the Print button on the Message toolbar.

Reply to a Message

- In Outlook Express, you can reply to a message automatically without having to enter the recipient's name or e-mail address.

  To reply to the author and all recipients:

  - Select the message you want to reply to from the message list in the Mail window.
  - Click the Reply to All button 

 on the Mail toolbar.

    OR

    Right-click on the message in the message list and select Reply to All.

  To reply to the author only:

  - Click the Reply to Author button 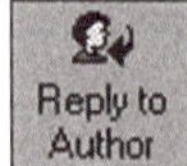

 on the Mail toolbar.

    OR

    Right-click on the message in the message list and select Reply to Author.

- Once you have selected a reply command, the New Message window opens with the address fields and the Subject filled in for you.

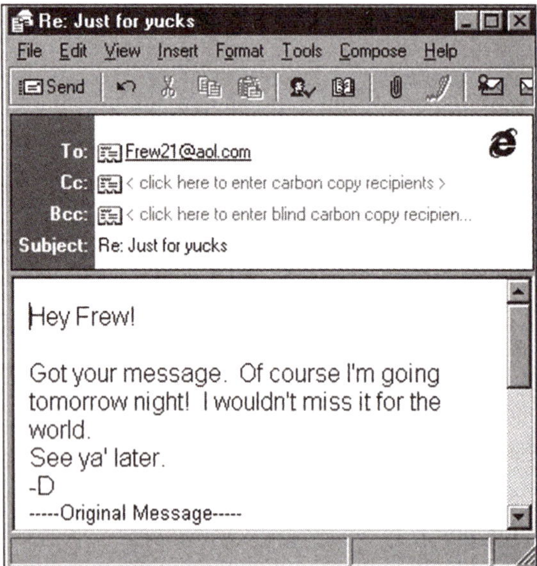

- The original message is automatically included in the body of your response. To turn off this default insertion, go to the Mail window, select Options from the Tools menu, click on the Send tab, deselect the Include message in reply check box, and click OK.
- To compose your reply, click in the composition area and type your text as you would in a new message.
- When you are done, click the Send button on the New Message toolbar to send the message immediately. Or select Send Later from the File menu to store the message in the Outbox folder for later delivery. To save the reply as a draft to be edited and sent later, select File, Save.

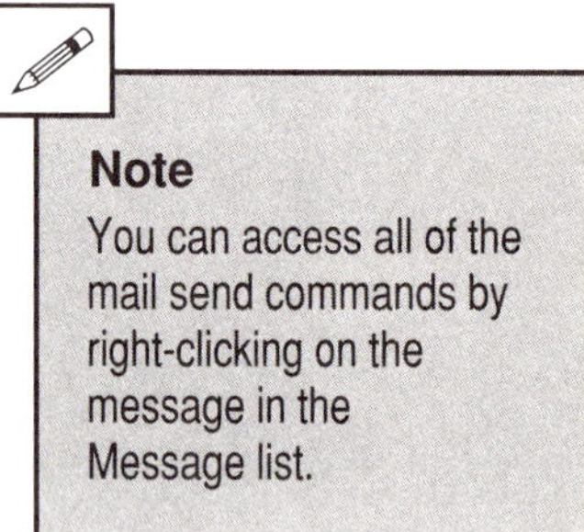

Note

You can access all of the mail send commands by right-clicking on the message in the Message list.

Forward a Message

- To forward a message automatically without having to enter the message subject:
  - Select the message to forward from the message list in the Mail window.
  - Click the Forward Message button on the Mail toolbar.

    OR

    Right-click on the selected message in the message list and choose Forward from the shortcut menu.

    ✓ *The New Message window opens with the original message displayed and the Subject field filled in for you.*

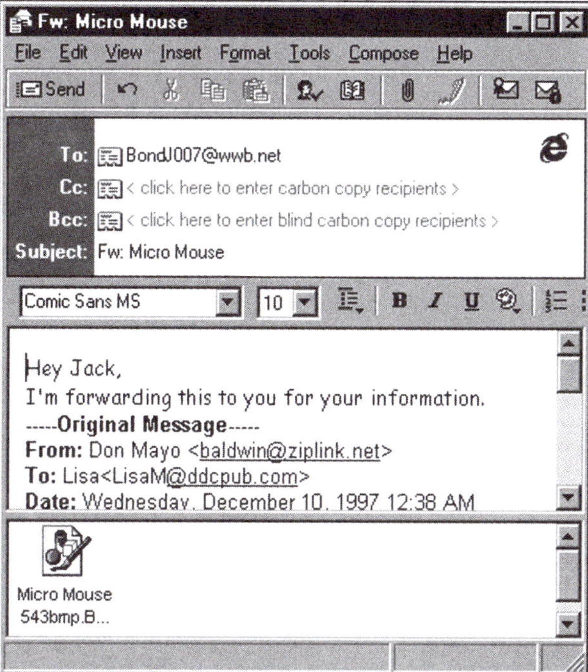

  - Fill in the e-mail address information by either typing each address or selecting the recipients from the Address Book. (See Exercise 4 of this lesson for more information on using the Address Book.)

    ✓ *If you are forwarding the message to multiple recipients, insert a comma or semicolon between each recipient's address.*

  - Click in the composition area and type any text you wish to send with the forwarded message.
  - When you are done, click the Send button on the New Message toolbar to send the message immediately. Or select Send Later from the File menu to store the message in the Outbox folder for later delivery. To save the reply as a draft to be edited and sent later, select Save from the File menu.

In this exercise, you will retrieve, read, and reply to new messages. You will also print a message and then send it to the Deleted Items folder.

EXERCISE DIRECTIONS

1. If you are already connected to your service provider and Outlook Express is open, go to step 2.

   OR

   Connect to your service provider and launch Outlook Express.

2. Open the Tools menu, select Options and deselect Empty messages from the Deleted Items folder on exit. Click OK.

   ✓ *You can reset and change any of these options when you complete the exercise.*

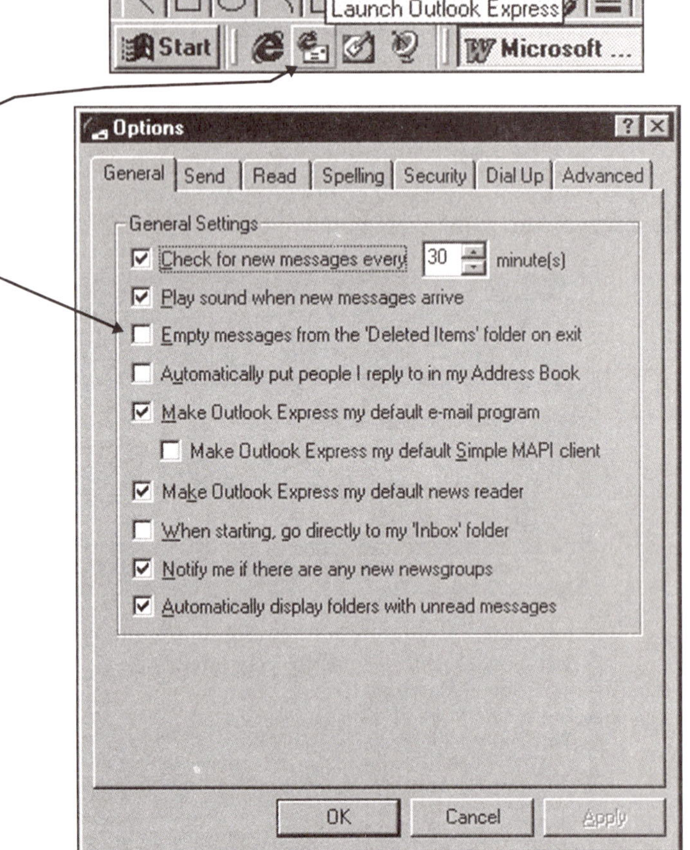

3. Check for incoming mail by clicking the Send and Receive button [Send and Receive] on the Outlook Express toolbar and enter your e-mail password, if necessary.

4. After Outlook Express connects to your mail server and retrieves any new messages into your Inbox, go offline by disconnecting from your ISP. Keep Outlook Express open.

5. Select the Inbox folder from the Outlook Express folder list.

   ➲ *You should see two messages in your Inbox folder: a response from DDC Publishing to the test mail you sent and the message you sent to yourself.*

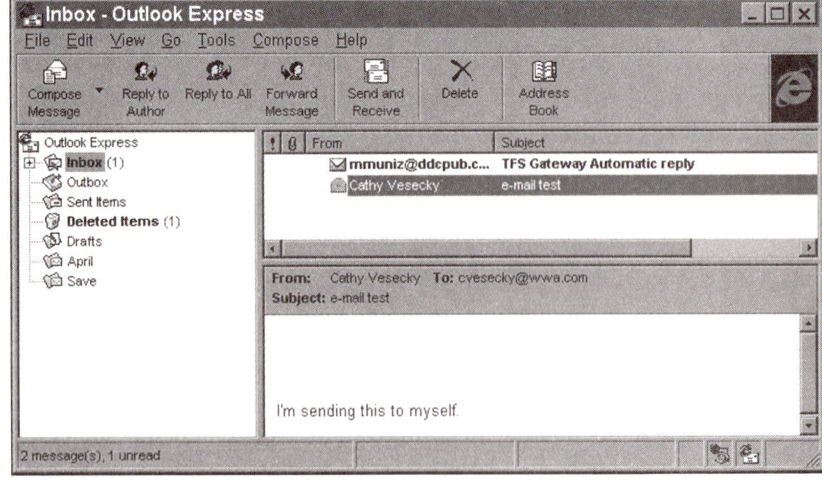

✓ *If the messages are no longer in your Inbox folder, you may need to repeat the steps from Exercise 2.*

6. Double-click on the message from ddcpub.com to open it.
7. Click the Print button to send the message from ddcpub.com to the printer.

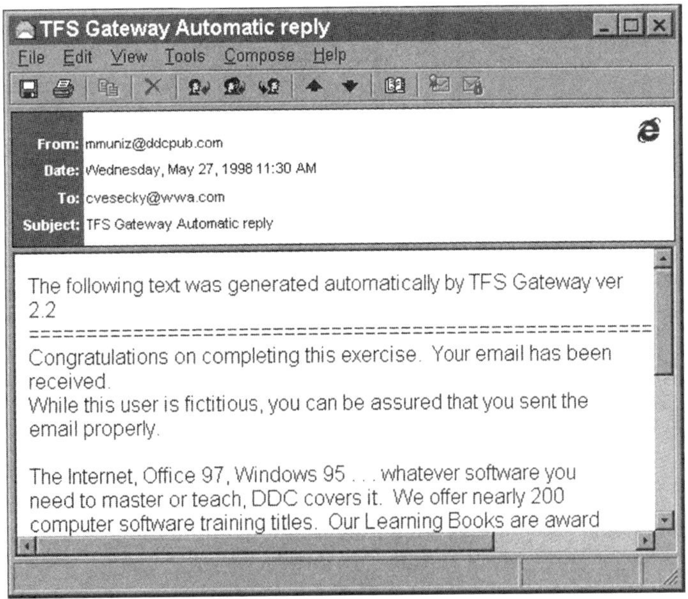

8. Click the Previous or Next button on the Outlook Express toolbar until you see the message that you sent to yourself.
9. Click the Reply to Author button on the toolbar to reply to your own message.

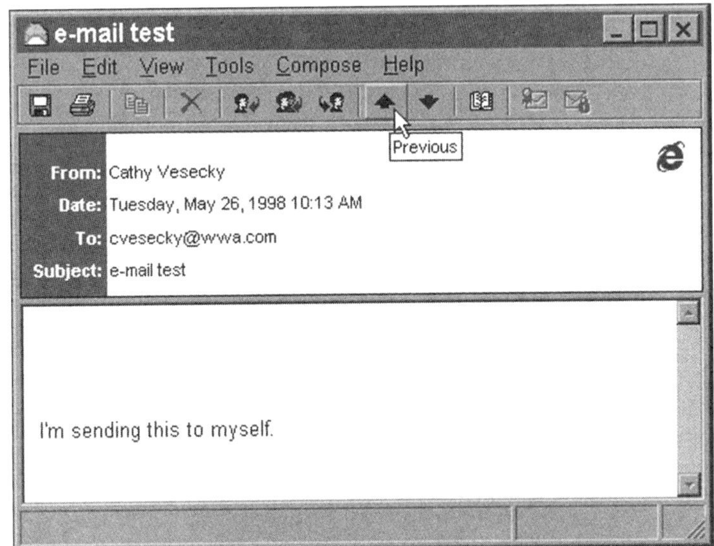

10. In the Message reply window above the original message, type the following: *I'm replying to myself.*
11. Select File, Send Later to store the message in your Outbox folder. Click OK.
12. Click the Send and Receive button on the toolbar to go online and send the reply.
13. Click on the message from ddcpub.com in the message list and click the Delete button on the Outlook Express toolbar.
14. Continue on to the next exercise.

    OR

    Exit from Outlook Express and disconnect from your service provider.

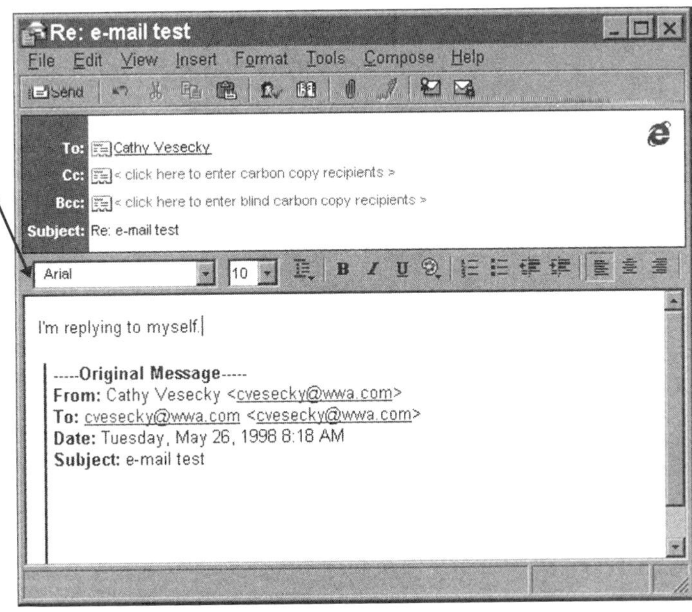

Exercise 4

- Launch Netscape Messenger
- Configure Messenger to Send and Receive E-mail

NOTES

Launch Netscape Messenger

- The Netscape Communicator browser suite includes a comprehensive e-mail program called Netscape Messenger, which allows you to send, receive, save, and print e-mail messages and attachments.

To launch Netscape Messenger:

- Click **Start** on the Windows 95 taskbar and select Programs, Netscape Communicator, Netscape Messenger.

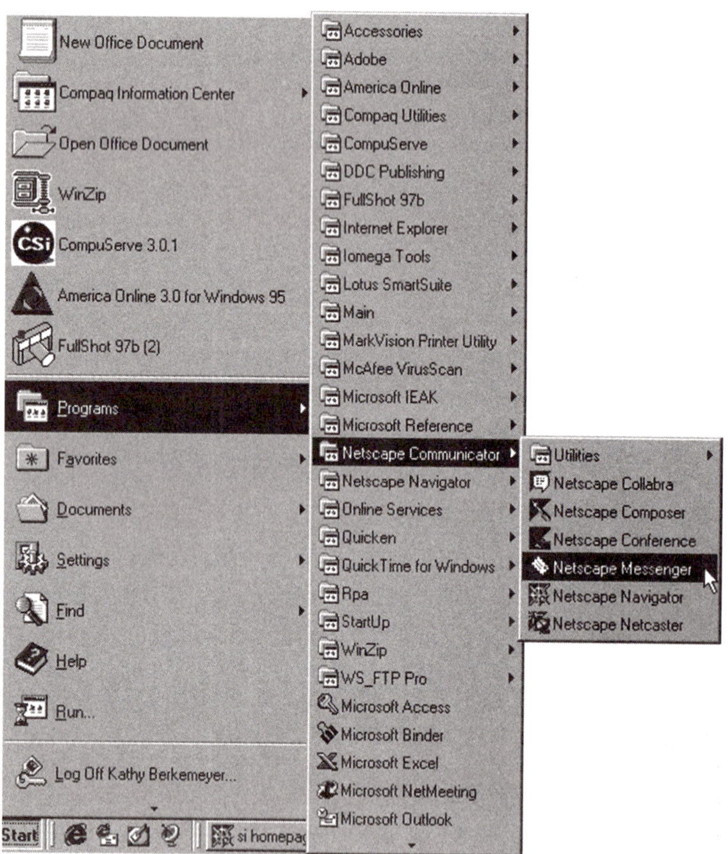

OR

If Netscape Navigator is running:

- Click the Mailbox icon in the Component bar in the Navigator window.

OR

Click Communicator, Messenger Mailbox in the Navigator window.

OR

Press Ctrl+2.

Configure Messenger to Send and Receive E-mail

✓ *The notes in this section presume that you have already set up an e-mail account with a service provider. What follows are steps that will get you connected, but some information may have to be supplied by your ISP. Calling for help will save you time and frustration.*

- Before you can use Messenger to send and receive e-mail, you must configure the program with your e-mail account information (user name, e-mail address, and mail server names). You may have already filled in this information if you completed the New Profile Setup Wizard when you installed Netscape Communicator. If not, you can perform the following steps to get connected. You can also use these steps to update and change settings to your e-mail account.
  - Open the Edit menu in the Netscape Navigator or Netscape Messenger window and select Preferences. Click on the plus sign next to Mail & Groups in the Category list. In the subcategory list that displays, click on Identity.

Preferences Dialog Box

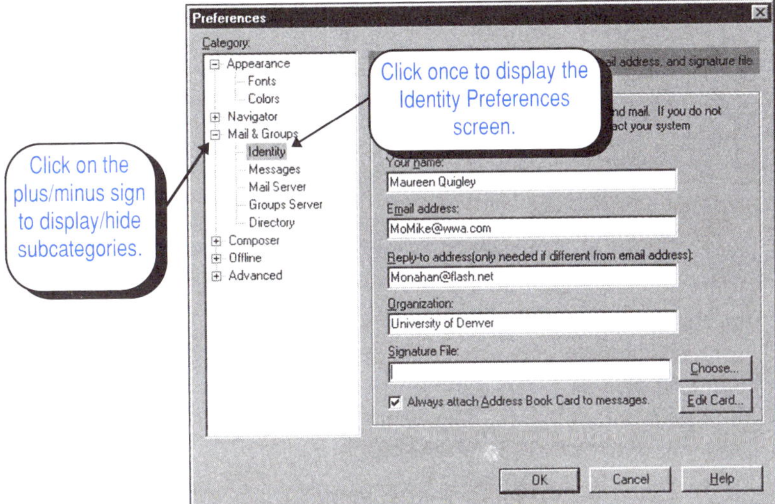

  - In the Identity Preferences screen that follows, enter your name in the first box and your e-mail address in the second box. This is the address that people use to send mail to you. You usually get to create the first part of the address (the portion in front of the @ sign); the rest is assigned by your ISP. Contact your ISP if you are not sure what your e-mail address is. Enter any other optional information in the Identity dialog box.
  - Next click the Mail Server Mail Server subcategory under Mail & Groups to configure your mailbox to send and receive mail.

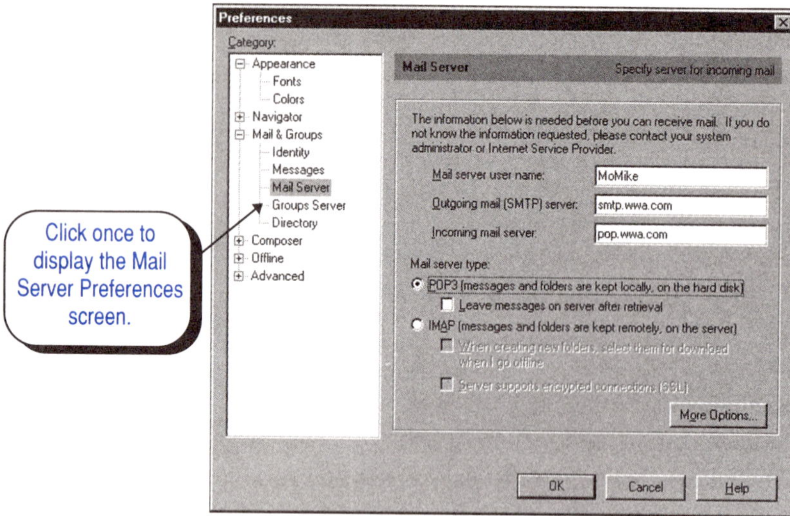

- In the Mail Server Preferences screen that follows, enter your Mail server user name in the first box. This is usually the part of your e-mail address that appears in front of the @ sign.
- Enter your Outgoing and Incoming mail server names in the appropriate boxes. Check with your ISP if you are not sure what these settings are.
- Click OK to save and close the Preference settings. You should now be able to send and receive e-mail messages and/or files.

CAUTION: The exercise directions below presume that you have already set up a mail account with a service provider. If you are not set up with Internet mail, contact your service provider.

In this exercise, you will enter (or verify) information that establishes a connection with your mail server. Then, you will customize the way you send and receive mail.

EXERCISE DIRECTIONS

1. Connect to your Internet service provider.
2. Launch Netscape Messenger from the Netscape Communicator menu on the Start menu.

   OR

   Click the Netscape Communicator icon from your desktop, and press Ctrl + 2.
3. Select Edit, Preferences from the Messenger main screen.
4. Select Mail Server under the Mail & Groups category to display the Mail Server screen.
5. Enter Mail server information for your Incoming and Outgoing mail.

   ✓ *Contact your ISP or system administrator for this information and how to set up Netscape Messenger for e-mail.*

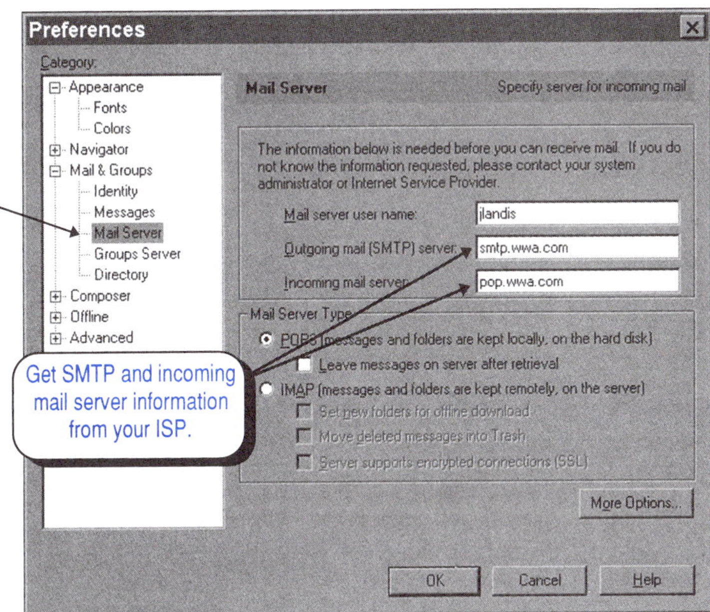

6. Click the More Options button.
7. Enter 25 minutes in the Check for Mail minutes box.

   ✓ *Messenger will check for new mail messages every 25 minutes.*
8. Accept all other default settings by clicking OK.

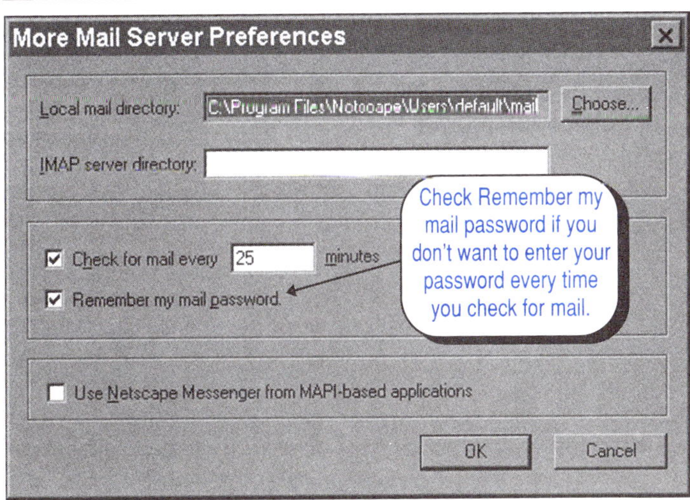

9. Select the **Identity** tab under the Mail & Groups category.
10. Supply the following information:

Your Name	Enter your name as you want it to appear on mail messages.
Your E-mail	Enter your entire e-mail address. (**username@servername.domain)**
Reply-to Address	Enter an address in this field only if you want replies to your e-mail sent to an address other than the e-mail address you entered above. In most cases this field should be left blank.
Your Organization	Enter your company name, if applicable.
Signature File	If desired, enter the path of a file or click the Browse button to locate the file containing the signature you want to include at the end of your e-mail messages.
Address Book Card	If desired, check the Always attach Address Book card box to include a personal address card with every message.

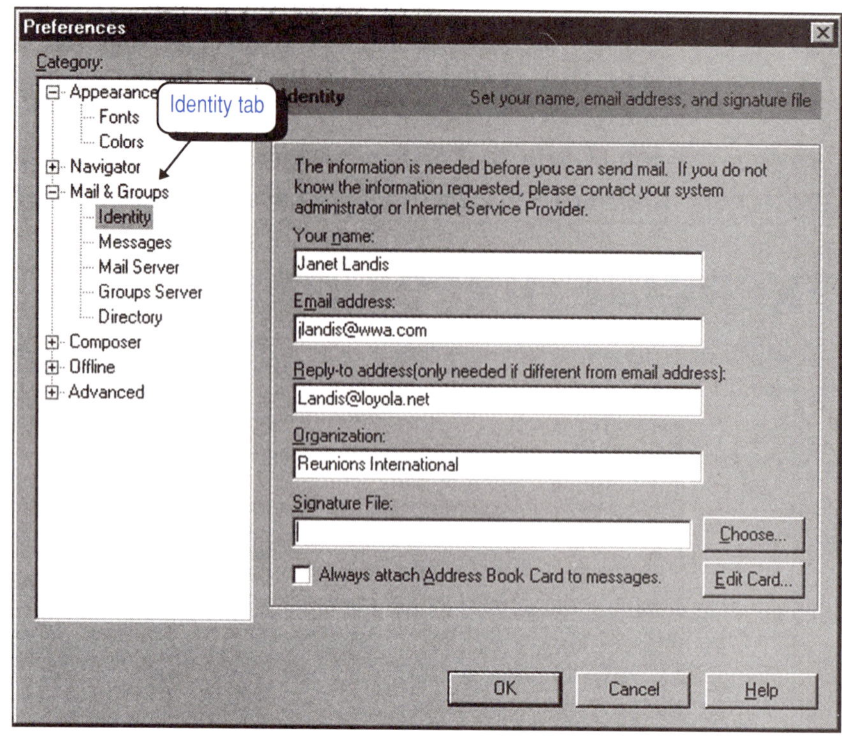

11. Select Messages under the Mail & Groups category and do the following:

In messages properties area:

a. Check the By default, send HTML messages check box.
b. Check the Automatically quote original message when replying box. This will insert the original message into the message body whenever you reply to a message.
c. Wrap long lines at 72 characters.

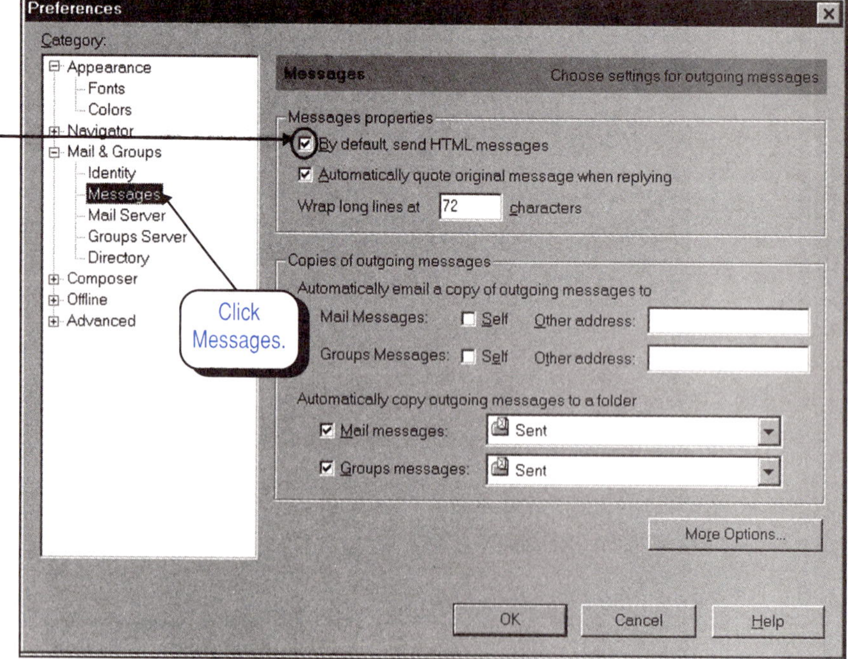

In automatically email a copy of outgoing messages area:

a. Mail Messages: To receive a copy of every message you send, check the Self box. If you wish to send a copy of every message to someone else, enter that e-mail address in the Other address box.

b. To receive or send copies of Newsgroup postings, check the Self box and/or enter another e-mail address in the Other box.

✓ *We don't discuss Newsgroups in this book. Consult Netscape Messenger Help for more information.*

In automatically copy outgoing messages to a folder:

a. Mail Messages: Send a copy of all messages to the Sent folder.

✓ *Selecting this option automatically stores a copy of every sent message in the Sent folder. Later you may want to select a different folder from the pull-down menu or create a new folder for this purpose.* (see Exercise 3).

b. Groups Messages: Send a copy of all Newsgroup postings to the Sent folder.

✓ *Selecting this option automatically sends a copy of every sent newsgroup posting to the Sent folder. Again, you may want to select a different folder from the pull-down menu or create a new folder for this purpose.*

12. Click the More Options button. Leave all default settings checked.
13. Click OK.

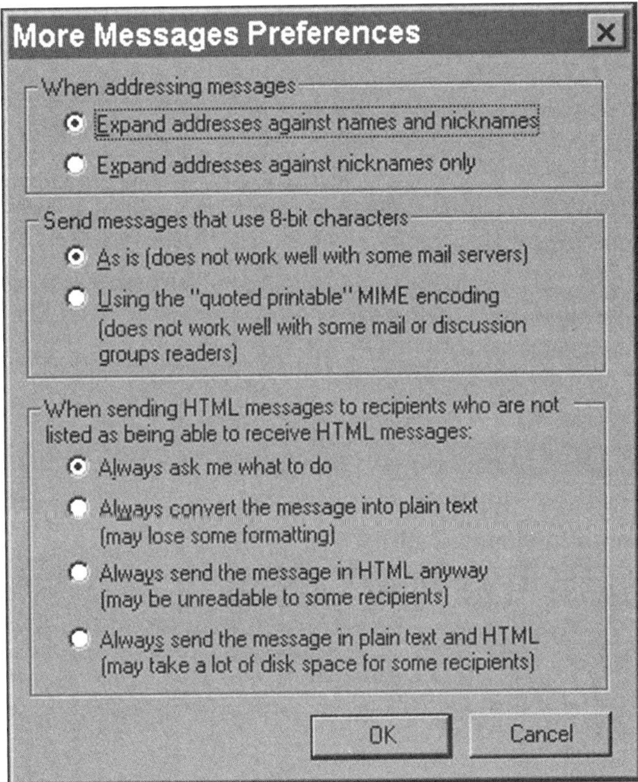

14. Click Mail & Groups to display the Change appearance settings for Mail & Groups screen.
15. Make sure the following options are selected. Use the scroll arrows to see additional options under each heading.

    Plain quoted text beginning with ">" is displayed with:

    - Text Style – **Italic**
    - Text Size – **Regular**
    - Text color – **Black**

    ✓ *You can click on the color box to choose an alternate text color from the Netscape color pallet.*

    Display messages and articles with:

    - Variable Width Font (*All text appears in variable-width characters)*
16. Be sure all the options at the bottom of the dialog box are selected.

    - Reuse message list (thread) window

    (All message lists appear in the same window)

    - Reuse message window

    (All messages appear in the same window)

    - Enable sound alert when messages arrive.
17. Click OK to save your mail preferences.
18. Continue on to the next exercise.

    OR

    Exit from Messenger and disconnect from your service provider.

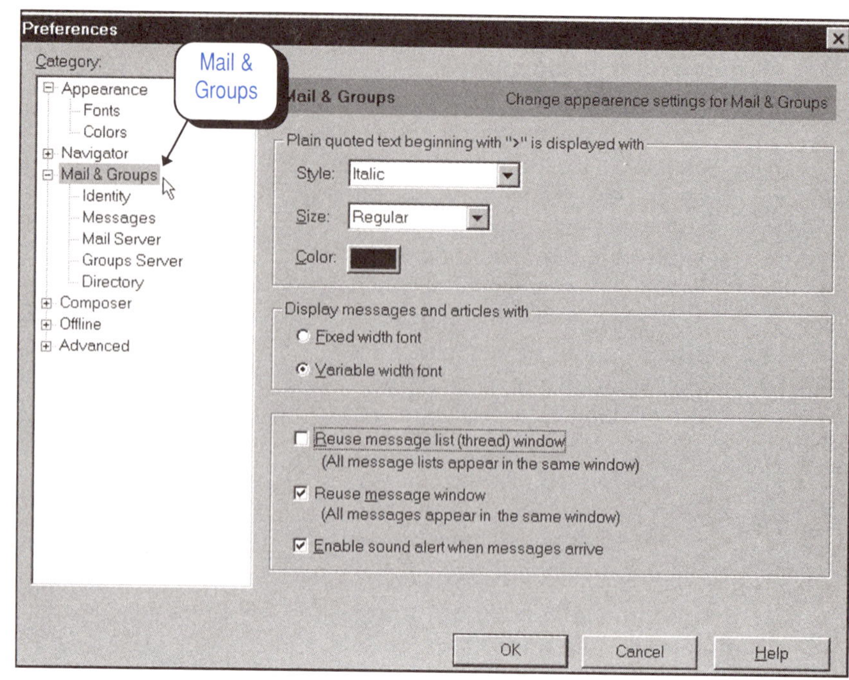

NEXT EXERCISE

Exercise 5

- The Message List Window
- Compose New Messages
- Send Messages
- Message Composition Toolbar

NOTES

The Message List Window

- After you launch Messenger, the Message List window will open, displaying the contents of the e-mail Inbox folder. You can retrieve, read, forward, and reply to messages from this window.

Message List Window

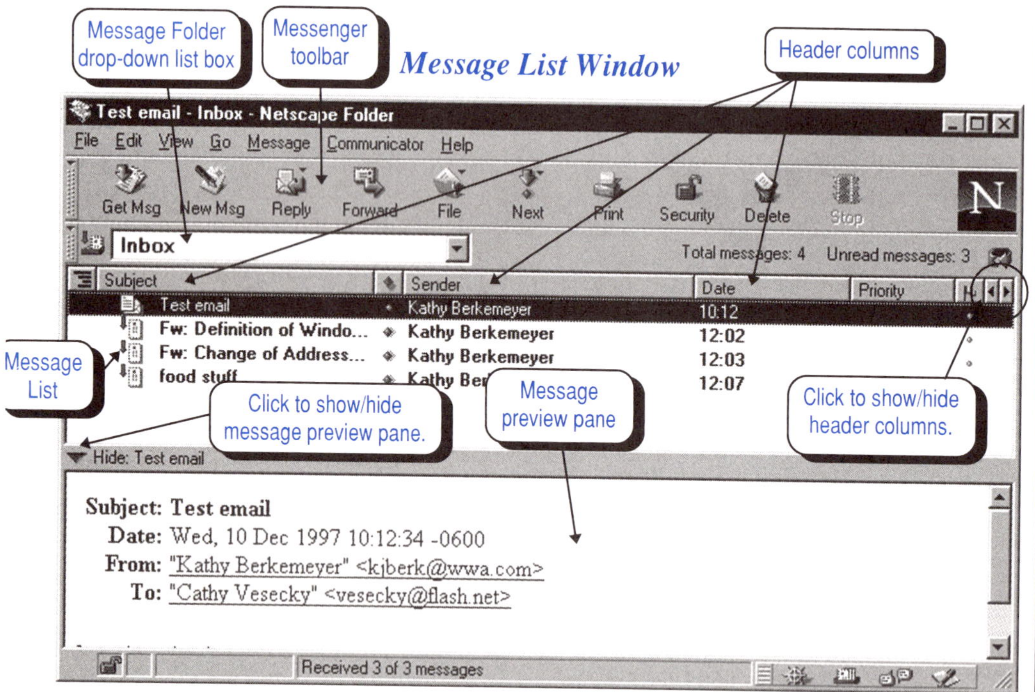

- A description of the items in the message list window appears below:
  - The **Message Folder drop-down list box** displays the currently selected message folder, the contents of which are displayed in the message list. Click the down arrow to select a different message folder and display its contents in the message list area.
  - The **message list** displays a header for each of the messages contained in the currently selected message folder.
  - **Header columns** list the categories of information available for each message, such as subject, sender, and date. You can customize the display of the header columns in a number of ways:

Note

If text in a message header is cut off so that you cannot read it all, position the mouse pointer on the header in the column containing the cropped text. A small box will display the complete text for that column of the header. For example:

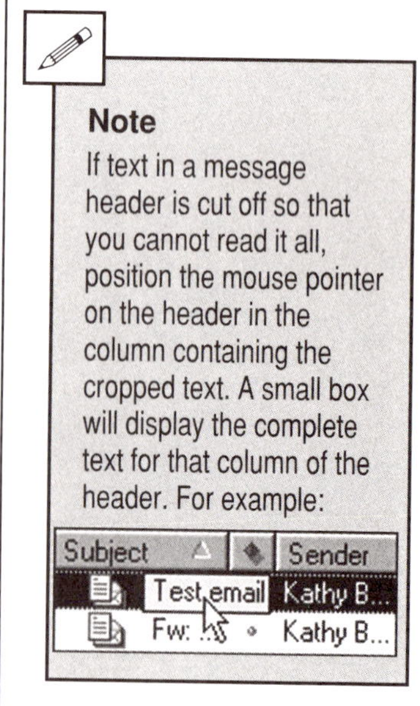

- Resize column widths by placing the mouse pointer over the right border of a column until the pointer changes to a double arrow and then dragging the border to the desired size.
- Rearrange the order of the columns by clicking and dragging a header to a new location in the series.
- Show/hide different columns by clicking the arrow buttons on the upper-right side of the message list window.

- The **message preview pane** displays the content of the message currently selected from the message list. You can show/hide the preview pane by clicking on the blue triangle icon in the bottom left corner of the message list pane. You can resize the preview pane and message list pane by placing the pointer over the border between the two panes until the pointer changes to a double arrow and then dragging the border up or down to the desired size.
- The **Messenger toolbar** displays buttons for activating Netscape Messenger's most commonly used commands. Note that each button contains an image and a word describing the function. Choose any of these buttons to activate the indicated task.

Messenger Toolbar Buttons and Functions

Button	Function
Get Msg	Retrieves new mail from your Internet mail server and loads it into the Inbox message folder.
New Msg	Opens the Message Composition window, allowing you to compose new mail messages.
Reply	Allows you to reply to the sender of an e-mail message or to the sender and all other recipients of the e-mail message.
Forward	Forwards a message you have received to another address.
File	Stores the current message in one of six Messenger default file folders or in a new folder that you create.
Next	Selects and displays the next of the unread messages in your Inbox.
Print	Prints the displayed message.
Security	Displays the security status of a message.
Delete	Deletes the selected message.
Stop	Stops the current message transfer.

Compose New Messages

- You can compose an e-mail message in Netscape Messenger while you are connected to the Internet, or while you are offline. When composing an e-mail message online, you can send the message immediately after creating it. When composing a message offline (which is considered proper Netiquette), you will need to reconnect to the Internet to send the message, or store the message in your Unsent Messages folder until you are online and can send it.
- To create a message, your first need to open Messenger's Message Composition window. To do so:
  - Click the New Message button on the toolbar in the Message List window.

    OR

    Click File, New, Message in the Message List window.

    OR

    Press Ctrl+M.

    ✓ *The Message Composition window displays.*

Netscape Message Composition Window

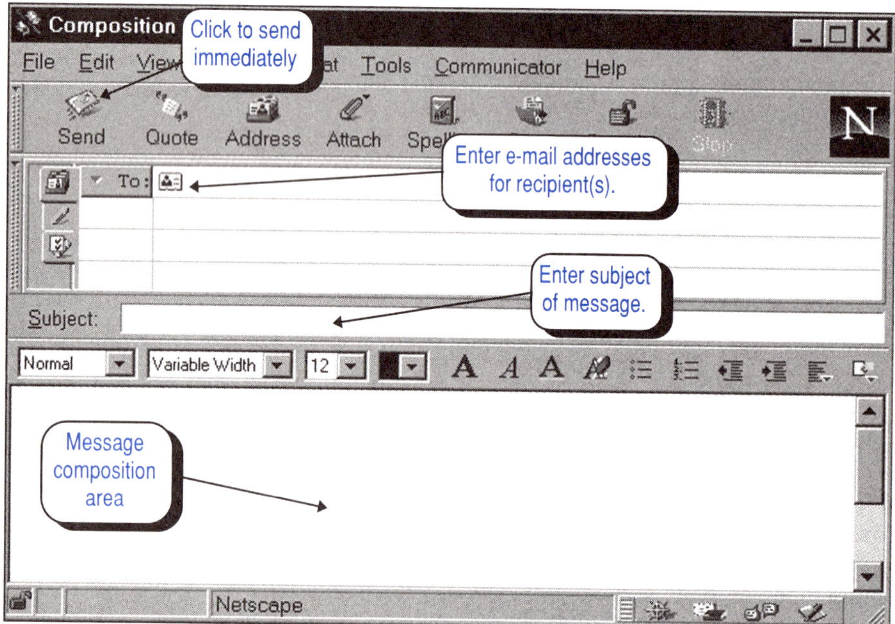

- In the Message Composition window, type the Internet address(es) of the message recipient(s) in the To field. Or, click the Address button on the Message Composition toolbar and select an address to insert.

  ✓ *If you are sending the message to multiple recipients, press Enter after typing each recipient's address.*

Netiquette

The Network equivalent of respectfulness and civility when dealing with people and organiztions.

WARNING

Before including any published work in an e-mail message, obtain permission from the copyright holder.

Note

You can hide any toolbar in the Message Composition window by going to View, Hide Message Toolbar or Hide Formatting Toolbar.

Note

If you do not know the recipient's address, you can look it up and insert it from your personal address book or an online directory.

- After inserting the address(es) in the To field, press Enter and click the To icon [To:] to display a drop-down menu of other addressee options. Select any of the following options from the drop-down menu and enter the recipient information indicated. Repeat this procedure as necessary to fill in all the address fields that you want to use.

Cc (Carbon Copy)	The e-mail addresses of people who will receive copies of the message.
Bcc (Blind Carbon Copy)	Same as Cc, except these names will not appear anywhere in the message, so other recipients will not know that the person(s) listed in the Bcc field received a copy.
Group	Names of newsgroups that will receive this message (similar to Mail To).
Reply-To	The e-mail address to which replies should be sent.
Followup-To	Another newsgroup heading; used to identify newsgroups to which comments should be posted (similar to Reply To).

- Click in the Subject field and type the subject of the message.
- Type the body of your message in the blank composition area below the Subject field. Word-wrap occurs automatically. You can cut and paste quotes from other messages or text from other programs. You can also check the spelling of your message by clicking on the Spelling button [Spelling] on the Message Composition toolbar and responding to the dialog prompts that follow.
- You can also include images, hyperlinks, and formatted text in an e-mail message.

Send Messages

- Once you have created a message, you have three choices:
  - to send the message immediately
  - to store the message in the Unsent Messages folder to be sent later
  - to save the message in the Drafts folder to be edited and sent later

To send a message immediately:

- Click the Send button [Send] on the Message Composition toolbar.
- If you are currently online, Messenger contacts your ISP mail server, and the Sending Message box displays the status of the transmittal.

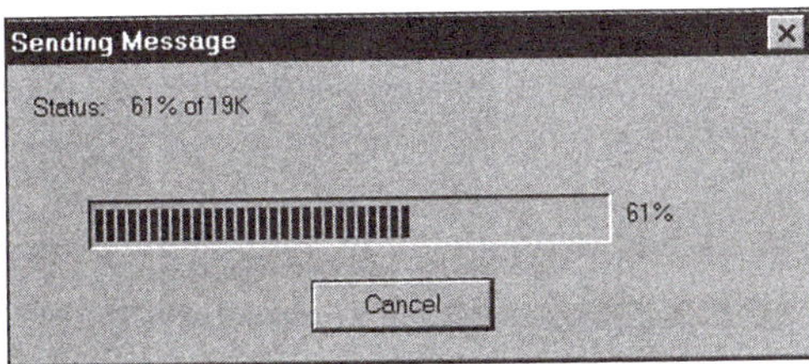

- If you are offline when you click the Send button, your message will not be sent immediately, but will be stored in the Unsent Messages folder for later delivery.

- You can also send a new message by clicking File, Send Now. If you are offline when you select this command, Messenger will automatically begin connecting to your ISP. Once you are connected to the Internet, Messenger will contact your ISP mail server, and the Sending Message box will display the status of the transfer.

To store a message in your Unsent Messages folder for later delivery:

- Select File, Send Later in the Message Composition window.

To send messages from your Unsent Messages folder:

- Select File, Send Unsent Messages (you can perform this task from any Netscape Messenger window).

✓ *If you are offline when you select this command, Messenger will automatically begin connecting to your ISP.*

To save a message to your Drafts folder:

- Click File, Save Draft.

  OR

  Click the Save button [Save] on the Message Composition toolbar.

  OR

  Press Ctrl+S.

To edit and send message drafts:

- In the Message List window, click in the Message Folder drop-down arrow and select the Drafts folder.

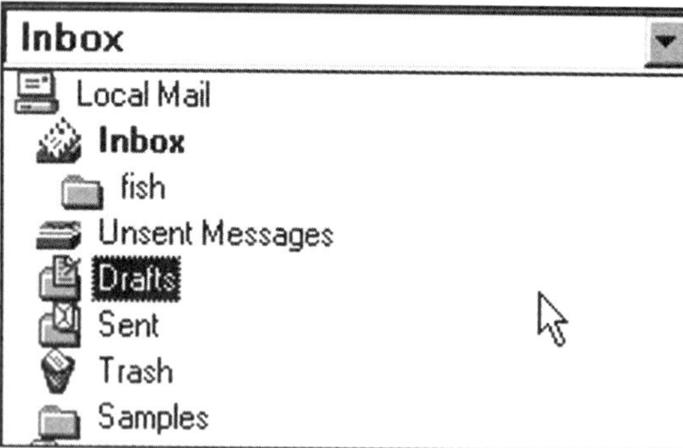

- Select the desired message from the message list and select Edit Message from the File menu.
- In the Message Composition window that appears, edit the message as necessary. When you are finished, select File, Send Now to send the message immediately, or select File, Send Later to store the message in the Unsent Messages folder for later delivery.

■ Messenger automatically saves all sent messages in the Sent folder. To view a list of the messages you have sent, click the Message Folder drop-down arrow in the Message List window and select the Sent folder. The contents will display in the message list.

Message Composition Toolbar

- The Message Composition window has several toolbar features that are specific to composing and editing messages.
- Also provided is a formatting toolbar that contains commands for applying styles, fonts, font size, bulleted lists, and inserting objects.
- Below are descriptions of the Message Composition toolbar button functions.

Message Composition Toolbar

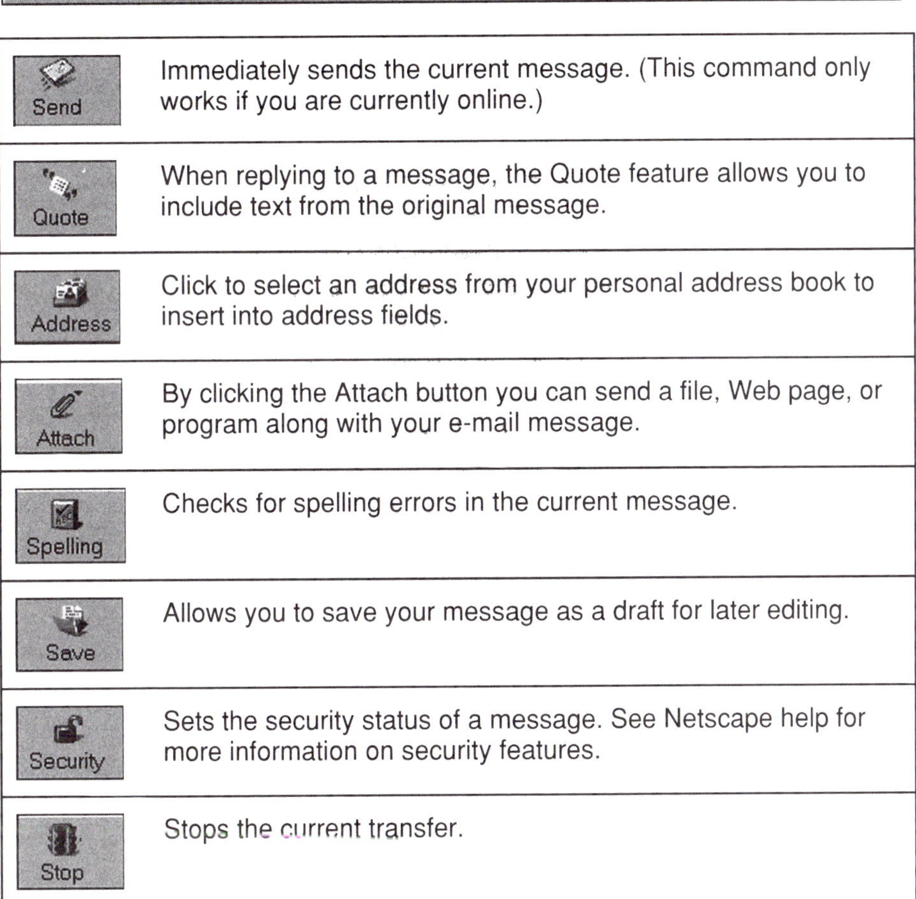

Button	Description
Send	Immediately sends the current message. (This command only works if you are currently online.)
Quote	When replying to a message, the Quote feature allows you to include text from the original message.
Address	Click to select an address from your personal address book to insert into address fields.
Attach	By clicking the Attach button you can send a file, Web page, or program along with your e-mail message.
Spelling	Checks for spelling errors in the current message.
Save	Allows you to save your message as a draft for later editing.
Security	Sets the security status of a message. See Netscape help for more information on security features.
Stop	Stops the current transfer.

In this exercise, you will compose and send two e-mail messages using Netscape Messenger.

EXERCISE DIRECTIONS

1. If you are already connected to your service provider and Netscape Messenger is open, go to step 2.

   OR

   Connect to your service provider and open Netscape Messenger.

2. Click the New Message button 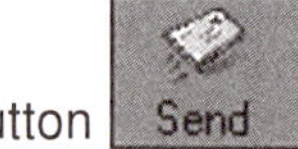

on the Messenger toolbar.

3. In the Message Composition window, fill in these headers as follows:

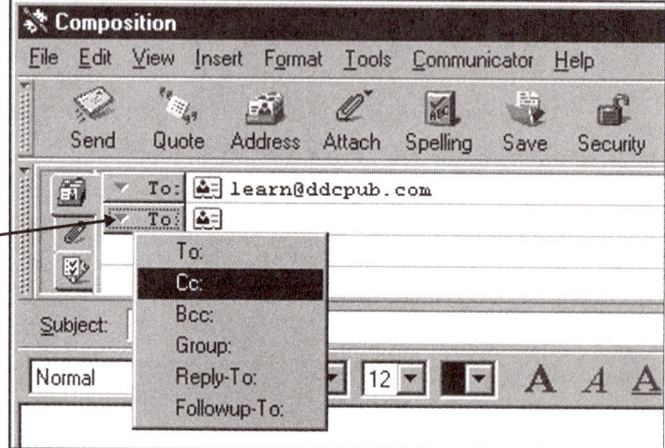

To:	learn@ddcpub.com
Cc:	Press Return. Then clik the To: icon to display addressee options. Select Cc: to carbon copy the message and add the address of a friend, business associate or, if you like, to your own address.
Subject:	This is an e-mail test
Body:	This is just a test.

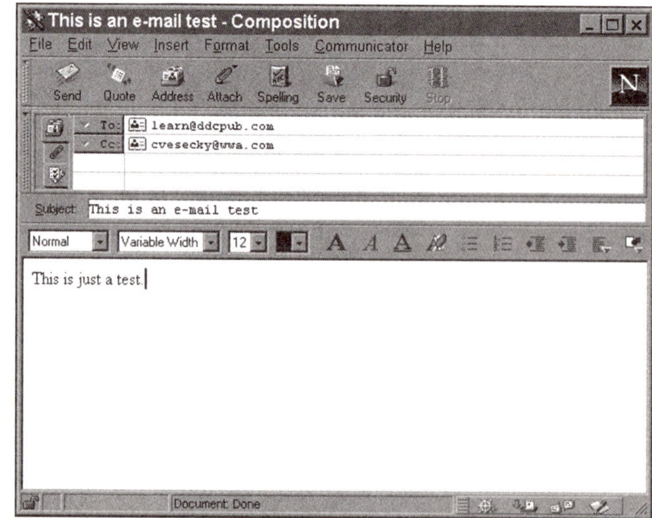

4. Click the Send button

.

5. After the message has been sent, disconnect from your ISP but keep Messenger open.

   ✓ *You can read and write responses to e-mail messages offline.*

6. With the Netscape Message List window open, select the Sent folder from the pull-down menu. The message you just sent should be listed in the Sent mail message window.
7. Click the New Message button New Msg on the Messenger toolbar.

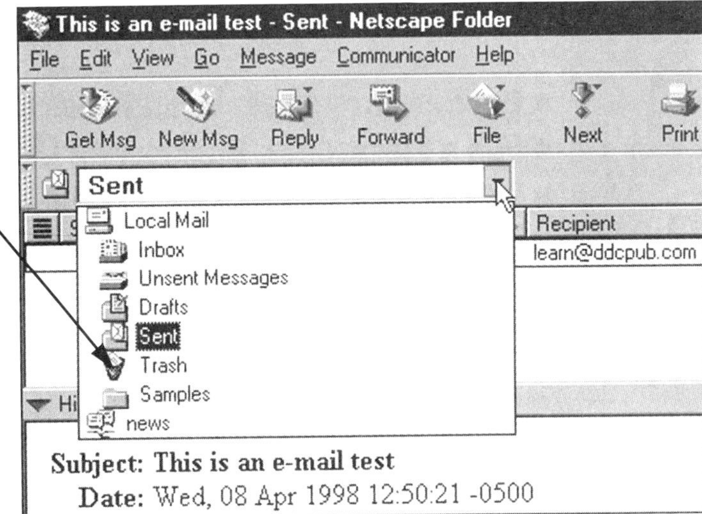

8. In the Composition window, enter your own e-mail address in the To field. Type *e-mail test* in the Subject field.
9. In the message composition area, type: *This is only a test.*
10. Click File, Send Later to store the message in your Unsent Messages folder.
11. Reconnect to your service provider.
12. Click File, Send Unsent Messages to send the message in your Unsent Messages folder.
13. Continue on to the next exercise.

    OR

    Exit from Messenger and disconnect from your service provider.

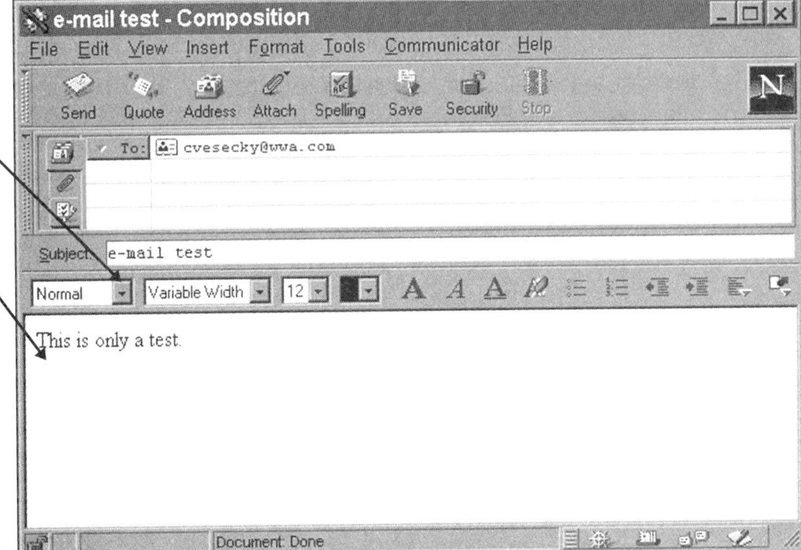

Exercise 6

- Get New Messages ■ Read Messages ■ Delete a Message
- File a Message ■ Bookmark a Message ■ Save a Message
- Print a Message ■ Reply to Mail ■ Forward Mail

NOTES

Get New Mail

- New e-mail messages are stored on a remote ISP mail server. Before you can read them, Messenger must first connect to the mail server and then download the messages onto your computer.
- To retrieve new messages to your computer, display the Message List window and do the following:
  - Click the Get Message button Get Msg on the Messenger toolbar.

    OR

    Select File, Get Messages, New.

    OR

    Press Ctrl+T.
- If you are not already connected to the Internet before you retrieve new messages, Messenger will automatically begin connecting to your ISP. The Dialing Progress box appears, displaying the status of the connection.

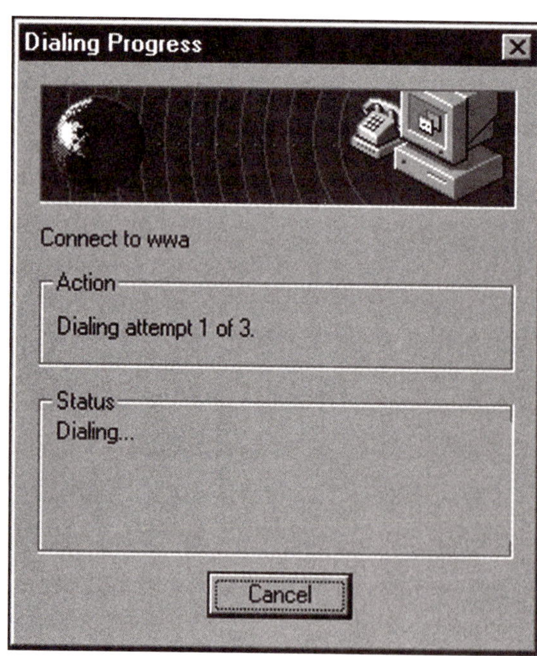

Note

Messenger will save your password for the rest of the current Messenger session. You must re-enter it the first time you retrieve new mail in each Messenger session. You can, however, set the program to save your password permanently. To do so:

- Click Edit, Preferences.
- Click on the plus sign next to Mail & Groups in the Category list to display its subcategory.
- Click once on the Mail Server subcategory.
- Click the More Options button.
- Select the Remember my mail password check box and click OK twice.

- Once you are connected to the Internet, Messenger will attempt to connect to your ISP mail server. When the connection is made, the Password Entry dialog box displays, prompting you to enter your e-mail password. If you do not know your e-mail password, contact your ISP. Click OK when you are finished.

Password Entry Dialog Box

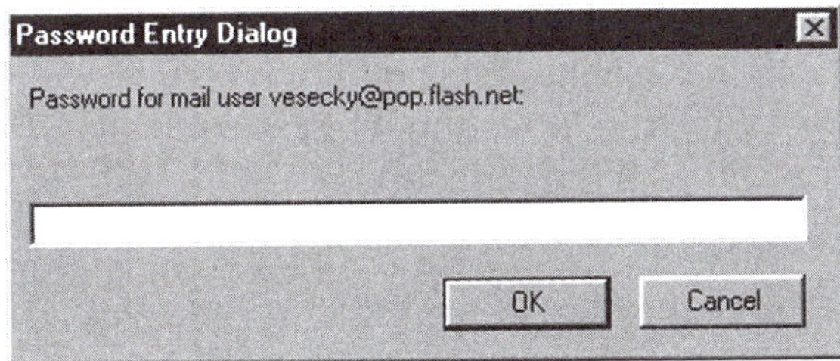

- Messenger will send the information to your ISP mail server and then will begin downloading new messages. The Getting New Messages box will display the status of your message retrieval.

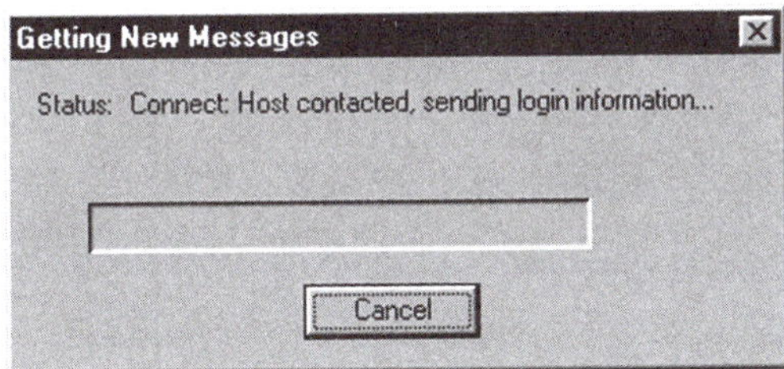

- Once your new messages are retrieved, Messenger stores them in the Inbox folder.

Read Messages

- To read a message, you must first open the folder containing the desired message in the Message List window. To do so, click the down arrow next to the Message Folder drop-down list box and select the desired folder. If you want to read a new message, select the Inbox folder.

Message List Window

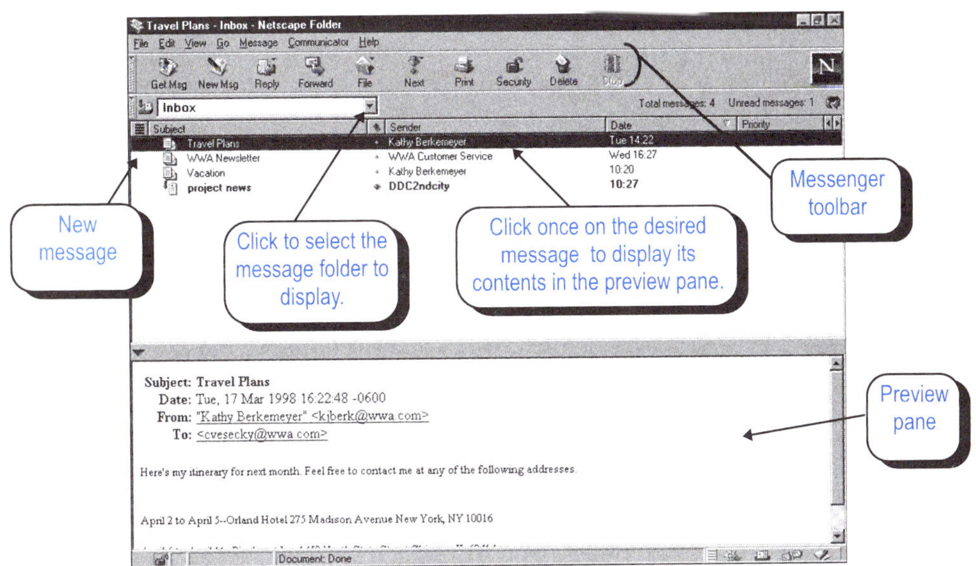

Note

You can set Messenger to check the mail server for new mail automatically at periodic intervals.

To do so:

- Select Edit, Preferences and click the plus sign next to the Mail & Groups category to display its contents.
- Click the Mail Server subcategory once.
- Click the More Options button and select the Check for mail every... check box.
- Enter the desired number of minutes between mail checks, and click OK twice.

Note

You do not have to be online to read e-mail. You can reduce your online charges if you disconnect from your ISP after retrieving your messages and read them offline. To do so:

- Select File, Go Offline in any Messenger window.
- In the Download dialog box that follows, select what to download before disconnecting from the Internet and click OK.

- You can read a message in the preview pane of the Message List window, or in a separate window.
    - To read a message in the preview pane, click on the desired message in the message list. The message contents display in the lower half of the Message List window. If the message does not appear, click on the blue triangle icon at the bottom of the Message List window to display the preview pane.
    - To open and read a message in its own window, double-click on the desired message in the message list. The Netscape Message window opens, displaying the message contents along with the Messenger toolbar, as in the illustration below.

Netscape Message Window

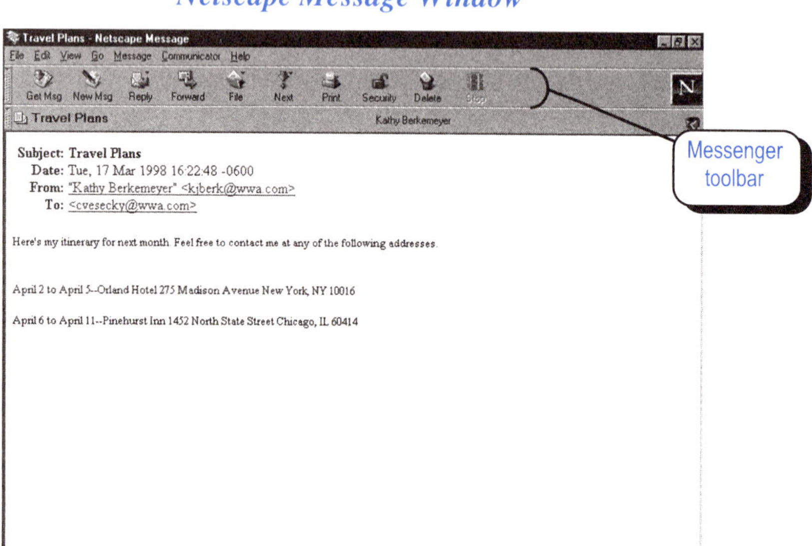

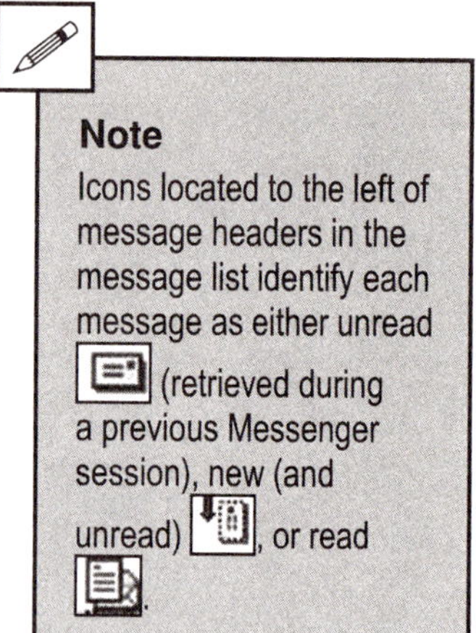

    - You can close a message opened this way by clicking File, Close or by clicking on the Close button (X) in the upper right corner of the window.
- Use the scroll bars to view hidden parts of the displayed message. Or, press the spacebar to scroll down through the message.

To read the next unread message:

- Click the Next button Next on the Messenger toolbar.

  OR

  If you have reached the end of the current message, press the spacebar to proceed to the next unread message.

  OR

  Select Go, Next Unread Message.

- Once you have read a message, it remains stored in the Inbox folder until you delete it or file it in another folder.

Delete a Message

- To delete a message:
  - Open it in the preview pane or in its own window.
  - Click the Delete button Delete in the Messenger toolbar.

    OR

    Select Edit, Delete Message.

    OR

    Press the Delete button.
- When you delete a message, it is not immediately removed from your hard drive. Instead, if you use a POP3 (Post Office Protocol) mail server, Messenger moves deleted messages to the Trash folder, where they are stored until you empty the Trash. To empty the Trash folder, select File, Empty Trash Folder from the Message List window.
- If you use an IMAP (Internet Message Access Protocol) mail server, Messenger marks deleted messages for deletion, leaving them in their message folder until you select Compress Folders from the File menu in the Message List window.
- To find out what kind of mail server you have, click Edit, Preferences from any Messenger window. In the Preferences dialog box that displays, click on the plus sign next to Mail & Groups in the Category list box. In the subcategory list, click on Mail Server. In the Mail Server Preferences screen that displays, check to see whether POP3 or IMAP is selected under Mail Server Type.

File a Message

- After you read a message, it remains in the Inbox folder until you delete it. Or, you can file it in another message folder for future reference. To do so, open the message to file in either the preview pane or its own window and do the following:
  - Click the File button File on the Messenger toolbar and select a file in which to store the message from the drop-down list that appears.

    OR

    Select Message, File Message, and select the folder in which to store the message from the submenu that appears.

Note

To select more than one message to delete, click the Ctrl button while you click each message in the message list.

- There are six default message folders provided by Messenger: Inbox, Unsent Messages, Drafts, Sent, Trash, and Samples. You might find it useful to create additional message folders in which to organize your messages. To do so:
  - Display the Message List window and click File, New Folder.
  - In the New Folder dialog box that follows, enter a name for the new message folder.

New Folder Dialog Box

  - If you want to create the new folder as a subfolder of an existing message folder, click the down arrow and select the folder in which to create the new one.
  - Click OK when you are finished.

Bookmark a Message

- You can add an e-mail message to your Bookmarks folder for easy access from anywhere within the Communicator suite. To bookmark a message:
  - Display the message you want to bookmark in either the preview pane or in its own window.
  - Select Communicator, Bookmarks, Add Bookmark.
- Messenger will add the message to the bottom of your Bookmarks menu.
- You can file a bookmarked message just as you would any bookmark.

Save a Message

- In addition to filing and bookmarking an e-mail message, you can also save a message on your hard drive. To do so:
  - Open the desired message in the preview pane or in its own message window.
  - Select File, Save As.

- In the Save Messages As dialog box that follows, click the down arrow next to the Save in box and select a drive and/or folder in which to store the message.

Save Messages As Dialog Box

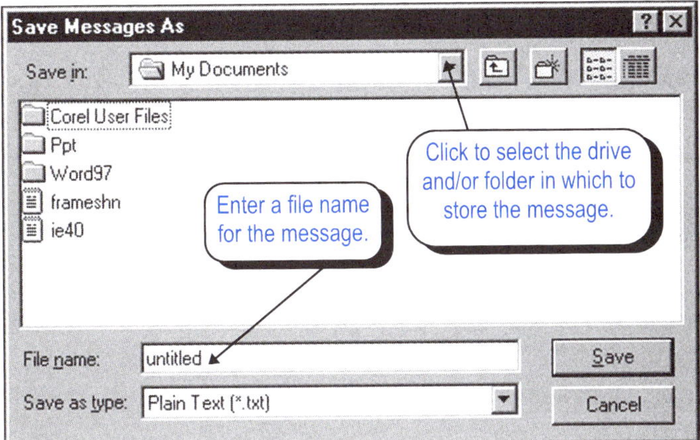

- Click in the File name text box and enter a name for the message and click Save.

✓ *This procedure will save your message as a Plain Text file, which you can open in any word processing or text editor program. If you are saving an HTML-formatted message, click the down arrow next to the Save as type box and select HTML Files.*

Print Messages

- In order to print a message you must first display the message in either the preview pane or in a separate window.
- Once the message is displayed, click File, Print.

  OR

  Click the Print button [Print] on the Messenger toolbar.
- In the Print dialog box that appears, select the desired print options and click OK.

Print Dialog Box

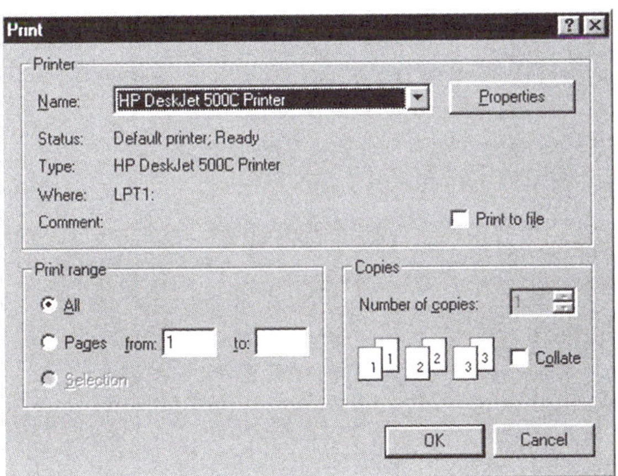

Reply to Mail

- In Netscape Messenger, you can reply to a message automatically, without having to enter the recipient's name or e-mail address.
- To reply to a message, select or open the desired message and click the Reply button Reply on the Messenger toolbar.
- From the submenu that appears, select Reply to Sender to reply to the original sender only, or select Reply to Sender and All Recipients to send a reply to the sender and all other recipients of the original message.

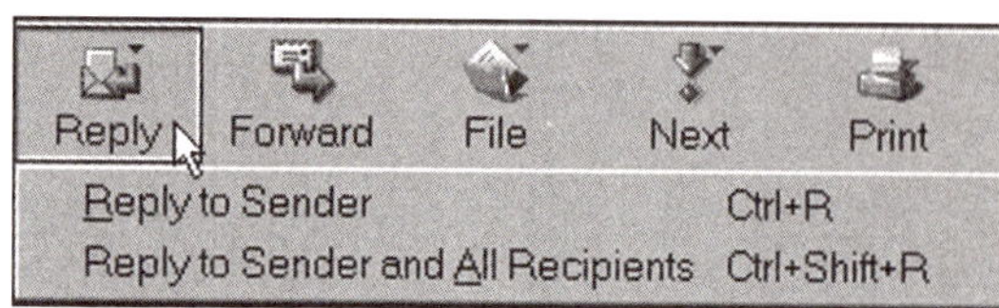

✓ *The Message Composition window opens, with the To, Cc, and Subject fields filled in for you.*

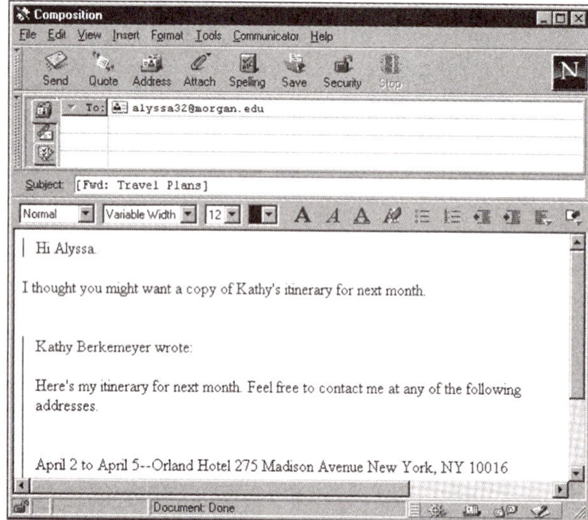

- Compose your reply as you would a new message.
- To include a copy of the original message with your reply, click the Quote button Quote on the Message Composition toolbar. You can edit the original message and header text as you wish.
- When you are done, select File, Send Now to send the message immediately. Or select Send Later from the File menu to store the reply message in the Unsent Messages folder to send later. To save the reply as a draft to be edited and sent later, select Save Draft from the File menu.

Note

You can set Messenger to include the contents of the original message automatically every time you send a reply. To do so:

- Click Edit, Preferences.
- Click on the plus sign next to Mail & Groups in the Category list box to display the subcategory list.
- Click on the Messages subcategory below Mail & Groups.
- Select the Automatically quote original message when replying check box and click OK.

Forward Mail

- To forward a message automatically without having to enter the message subject, first select or open the message to forward. Then click on the Forward button [Forward] on the Messenger toolbar.

  ✓ *The Message Composition window opens, with the Subject field filled in for you.*

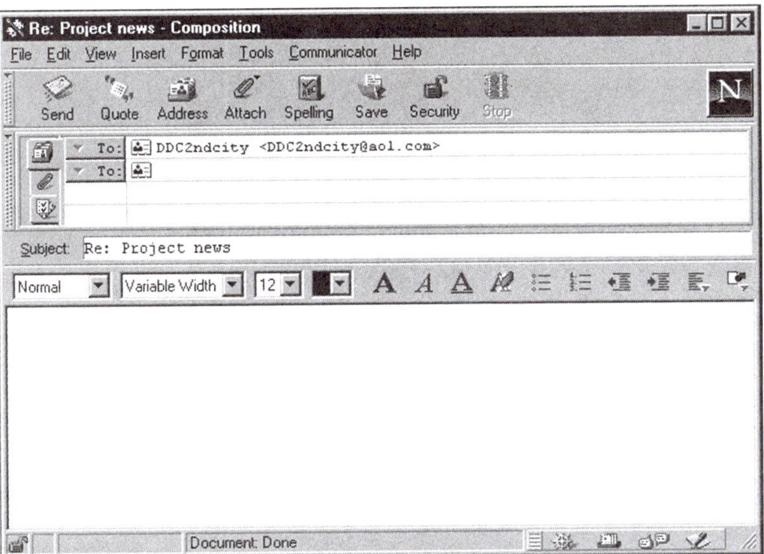

- Type the e-mail address of the new recipient in the To field, or click the Address button [Address] on the Message Composition toolbar and select a name from your address book. (See Exercise 4 of this lesson for more information on using the address book.)
- If the original message does not appear in the composition area, click the Quote button [Quote] on the Message Composition toolbar to insert it.
- Click in the composition area and edit the message as desired. You can also type any additional text you want to include with the forwarded message.
- When you are done, select Send Now from the File menu to send the message immediately. Or, select Send Later from the File menu to store the message in the Unsent Messages folder to be sent later. To save the reply as a draft to be edited and sent later, select Save Draft from the File menu.

In this exercise, you will retrieve, read, print, and reply to new messages. You will also send a message to the Trash folder, open it, and send it to the printer.

EXERCISE DIRECTIONS

1. If you are already connected to your service provider and Netscape Messenger is open, go to step 2.

   OR

   Connect to your service provider and launch Messenger.
2. Check for incoming mail by clicking the Get Message button [Get Msg] on the Messenger toolbar and enter your e-mail password if necessary.
3. After Messenger connects to your mail server and retrieves the messages into your Inbox, disconnect from your ISP. Keep Messenger open.
4. Make sure the Inbox folder is displayed or select it from the Message Folder drop-down list box. In the Message list pane, you should see two messages: a response from DDC Publishing to the test mail you sent as well as the message you sent to yourself.

   ✓ *You can reset and change any of these options when you complete the exercise.*

   ✓ *If the messages are no longer in your Inbox folder, you may need to repeat the steps from Exercise 5*

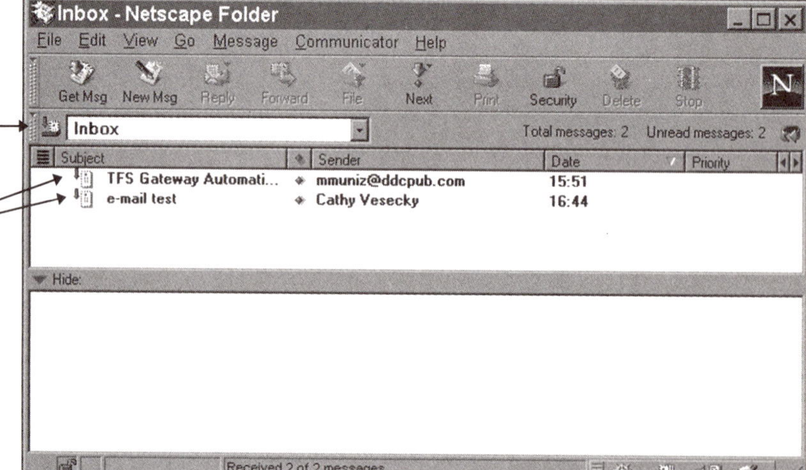

5. Single-click to select the message from mmuniz@ddcpub.com. Notice that the text of the message is displayed in the Messenger preview pane below the message list pane.
   - ✓ *If the preview pane is not visible, click the Show/Hide preview pane icon at the bottom left corner of the Messenger screen.*
6. Close the message pane by clicking the Hide message icon located on the top left corner of the preview message pane.
   - ✓ *Notice that the icon next to the message header you just read has changed from the new message icon to the read message icon.*
7. Now double-click on the header in the Message list pane for the message you just read to open it in its own window.

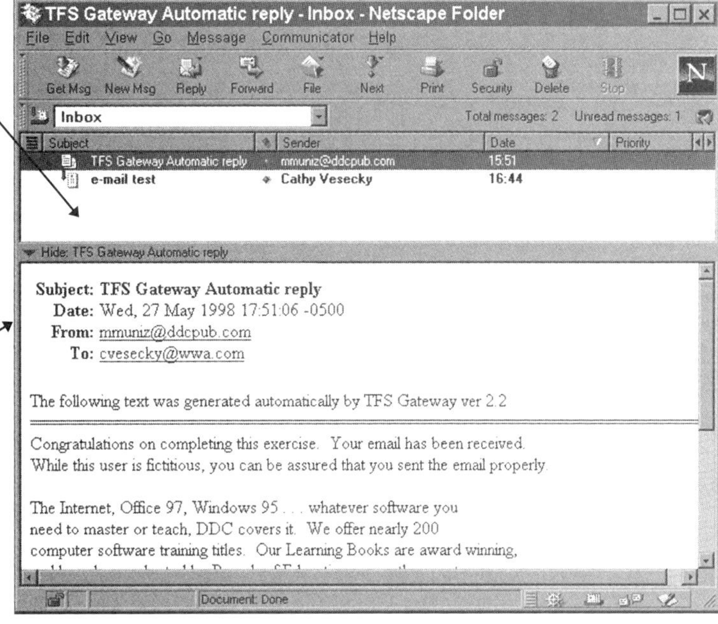

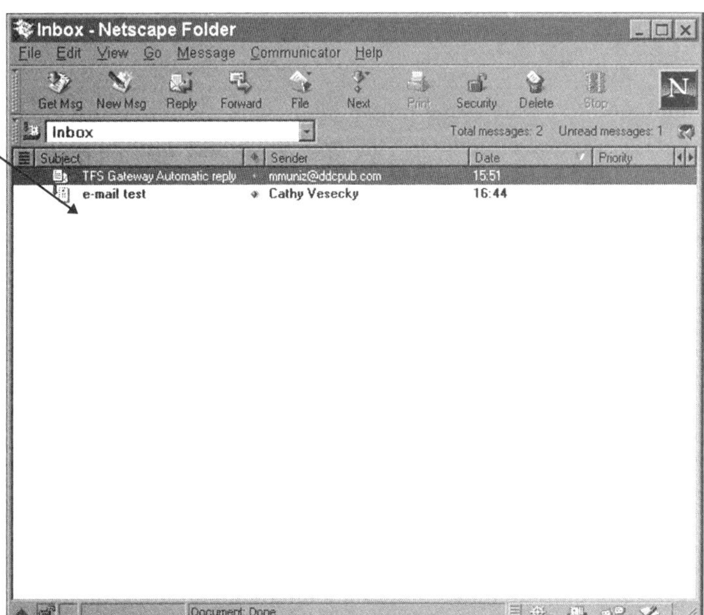

8. Print the message by clicking the Print icon 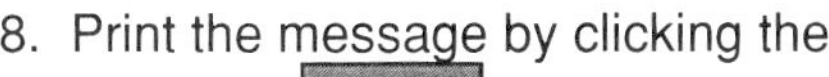 on the toolbar. Click OK when the Print dialog box appears to send the message to the printer.

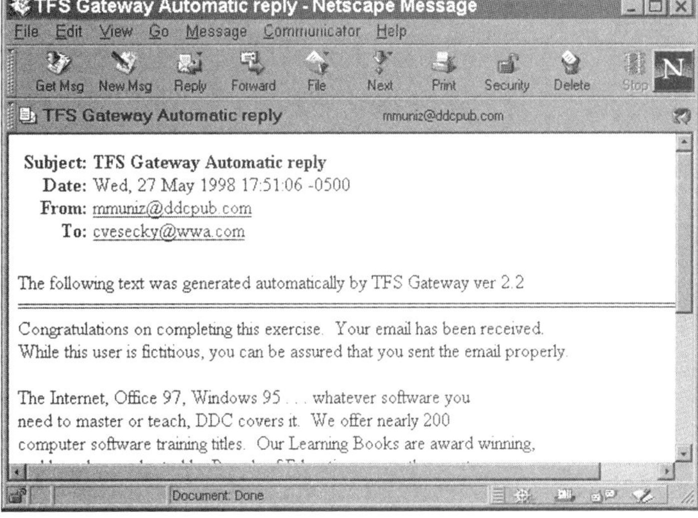

9. Press the spacebar until the next new message appears. This should be the message you sent to yourself titled **e-mail test**.

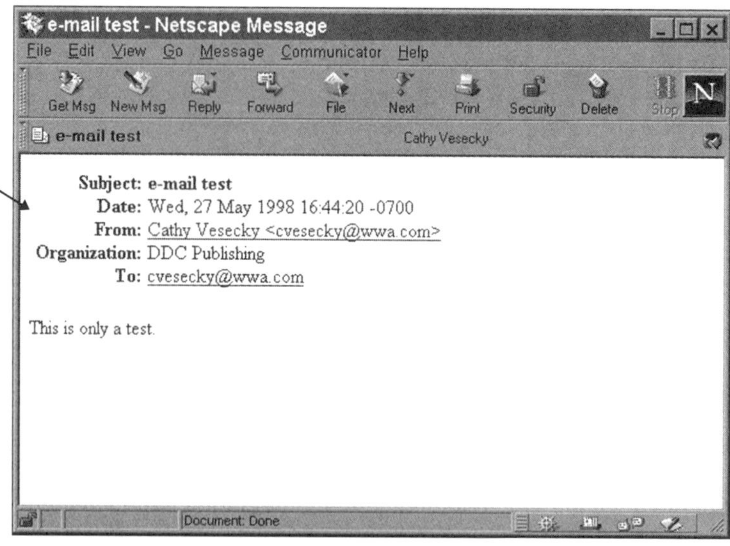

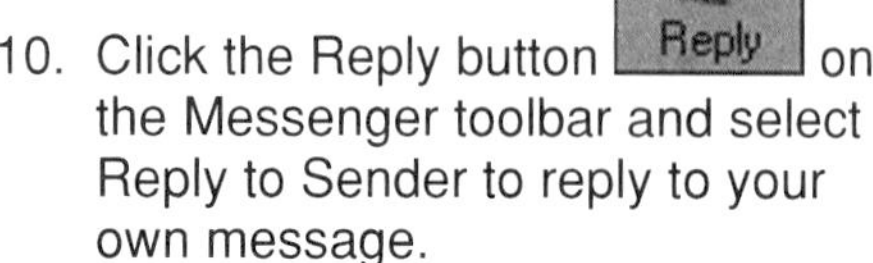

10. Click the Reply button on the Messenger toolbar and select Reply to Sender to reply to your own message.
11. In the Composition window that appears, type the following above the original message: *I'm replying to myself.*
12. Select File, Send Later to store the message in your Unsent Messages folder.
13. Select Send Unsent Messages from the File menu to go online and send the reply.
14. Close the message by clicking File, Close to return to the Message list window.

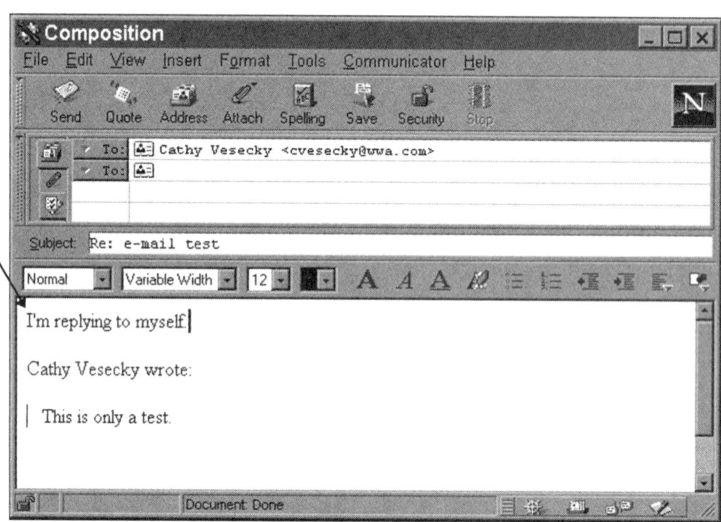

15. Click on either of the two messages you just read from the message list and click the Delete button on the Messenger toolbar. The message is now stored in your Trash folder and will remain there until you empty the folder.

   ✓ *If you are using an IMAP mail server, Messenger will mark the message for deletion, but it will remain in your message folder until you select Compress Folders from the File menu.*

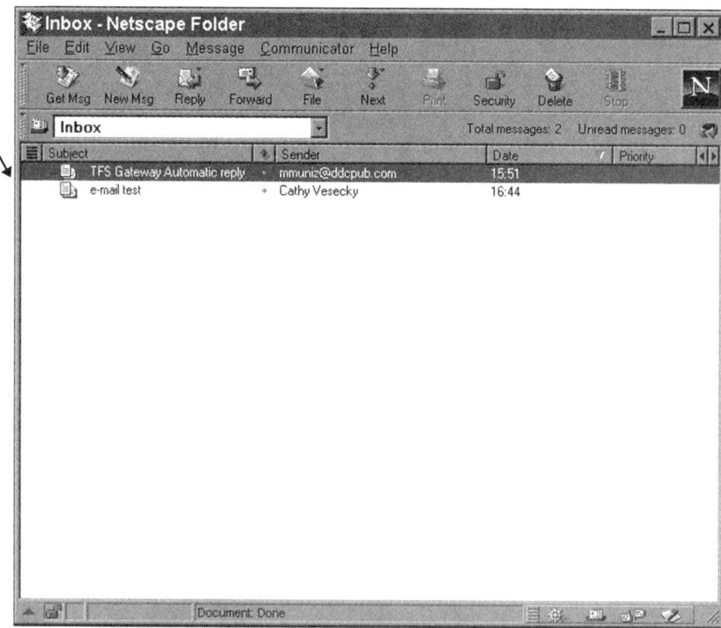

16. Select Trash from the Message Folder drop-down list and open the deleted message in the preview pane.
17. Print the message by clicking the Print icon (Print) from the toolbar. Click OK when the Print dialog box appears to send the message to the printer.
18. Continue on to the next exercise.

    OR

    Exit from Messenger and disconnect from your Internet Service Provider.

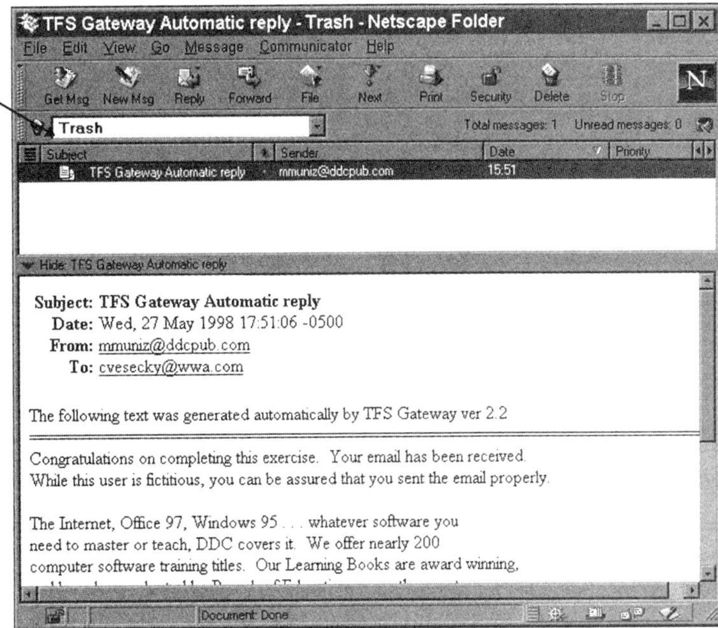

NEXT LESSON

Lesson 5: Finding News and Information

Exercise 1

- Jump Online at AOL.com
- Web Resources at MSN.com
- News and Entertainment at the Pathfinder Network

Exercise 2

- Check Business News with BusinessWeek Online
- Check Business News with Forbes Digital Tool
- Use the NewsHound Push Service

Exercise 3

- Research Investments with Morningstar
- Check Interest Rates with Bank Rate Monitor

Exercise 4

- Find Business Capital with MoneyHunter

Exercise 5

- Find Legal Information at the Legal Information Institute
- Consult OSHA Regulations at the OSHA Web Site
- Find Tax Information with IRS Digital Daily

Exercise 1

- Jump Online at AOL.com ■ Web Resources at MSN.com
- News and Entertainment at the Pathfinder Network

NOTES

Jump Online at AOL.com

- General sites such as AOL.com (America Online) and MSN.com (the Microsoft Network) have become much more than gateways to the World Wide Web. These sites offer a rich source of online content that can eliminate wasteful surfing and searching.
- The AOL Web site isn't just for Internet newcomers and home Web surfers. This site provides a good starting point for any practical Web search. At AOL.com you can find daily news, weather, sports, opinion, special interest features, as well as travel services, entertainment reviews, and other specialty information.

AOL Home Page

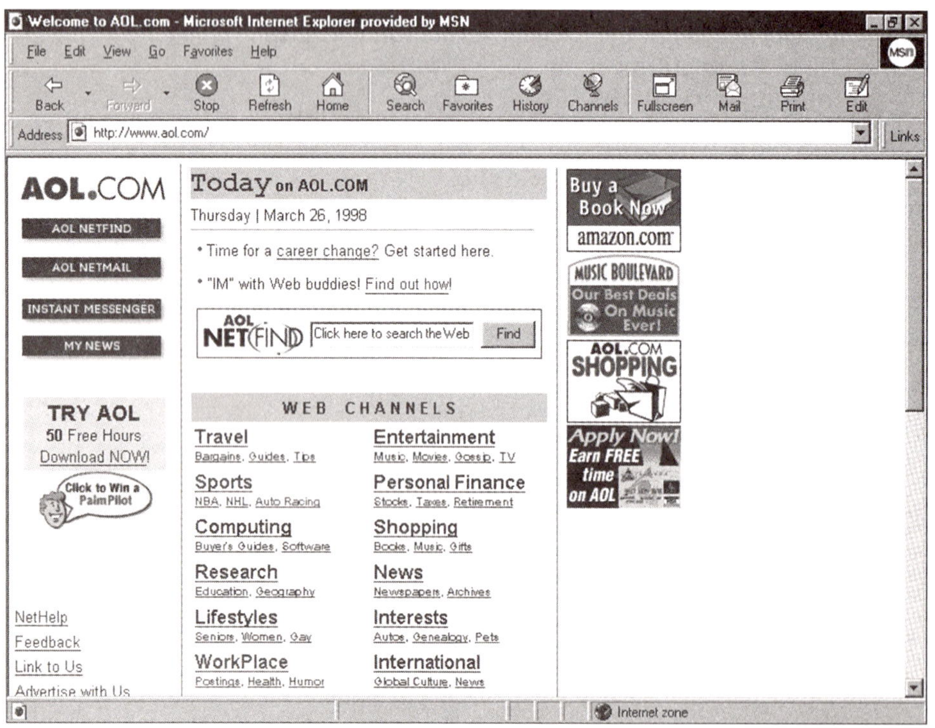

- The AOL site has a comprehensive and well organized Web directory, with access to hundreds of links to the Web's best resources. Just click one of the AOL channels to see links to Web sites that AOL has selected as favorites along with a brief description of each site.

Note

Click the AOL NetFind link to use the Time Savers directory. Here you will find links to Web resources for many common tasks such as Find an Airline or Hotel, Plan a Night Out, Plan a Night In, Manage Your Investments, Your Health, and Your Government.

- Though most of the channels are primarily oriented to a consumer audience, you can click the WorkPlace channel to see a very complete directory of business Web site links and associated site reviews.

AOL WorkPlace Channel

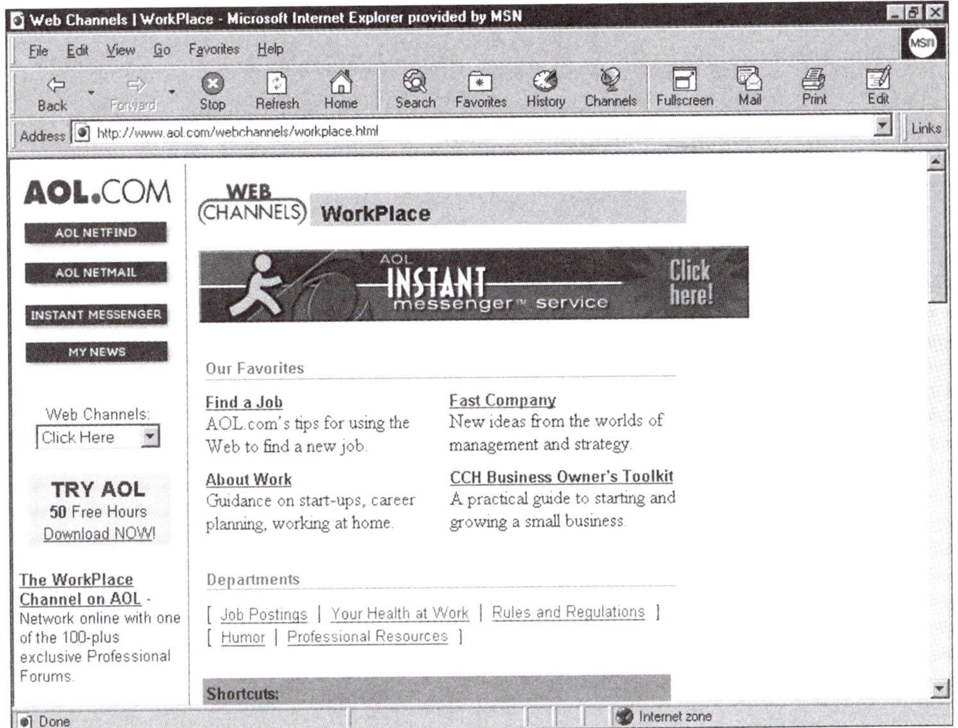

Note

One or two of the selected favorites on each channel may be a link to a service available only to AOL member, but non AOL-members will find many more links to available sites.

- You can find links to AOL Web site reviews on the left side of each channel page. Click one of the review topics that interests you to find more related Web site links.
- The AOL site provides easy access to search engine text boxes, where you can quickly enter a keyword search topic and click to find what you need. Each AOL channel typically showcases two or three Web sites near the top of the channel page by including search engine text boxes for those sites.

Note

Links to AOL services such as NetMail (Web access e-mail) and Instant Messenger are also featured at the AOL site, but you must be an AOL member to use these services.

Web Resources at MSN.com

- The Microsoft Network's (MSN) wide range of consumer and business Web sites make it well worth a stop on each online journey you make. MSN is really a collection of more than two dozen individual Web sites that offer a variety of resources and information.
- From the MSN home page, click Essentials for links to MSN's consumer Web sites, such as Expedia (travel), CarPoint, Plaza (shopping), Music Central, and Cinemania.
- Click Onstage from the home page to see a list of links to MSN's news and entertainment sites, such as MSNBC, MSN Games, Mungo Park (online travel expeditions), and the online edition of the popular Slate magazine, which features news and views on art, entertainment, and popular culture.

- Topping the list of MSN sites is the award-winning Expedia travel service, which you will explore in more detail in Lesson 6. Expedia is an example of how much interactivity and rich content can be delivered on a commercial Web site. Expedia's outstanding travel-booking wizard makes it a fine business and sales resource.
- The Mining Company is a new search site offered by MSN that offers the services of online guides—people who specialize in a particular area and organize the Web so that you can find what you want.

The Mining Company's Business Page

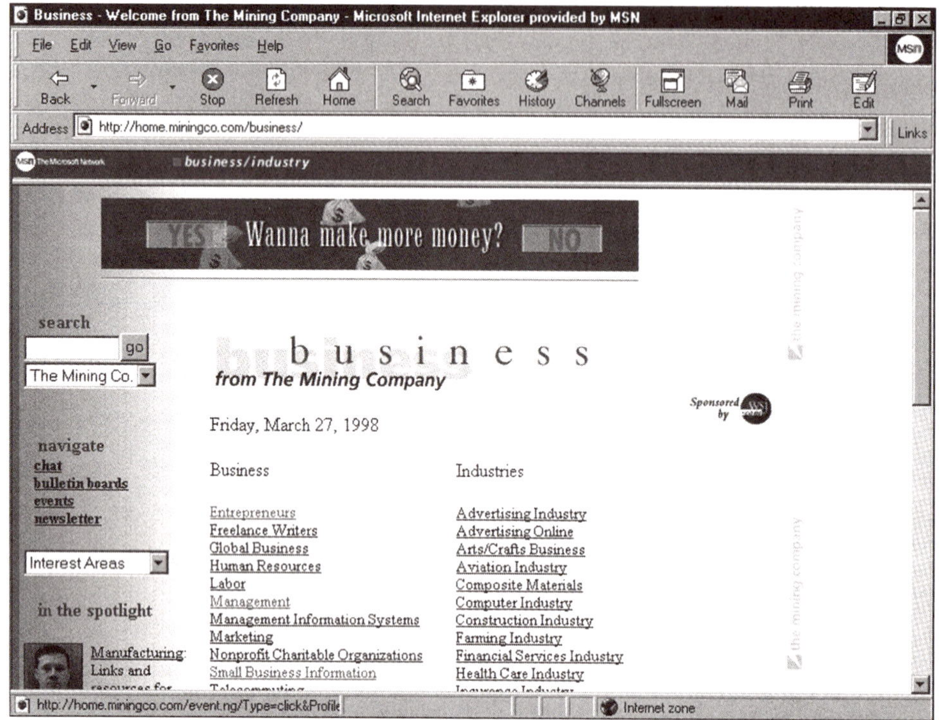

- From The Mining Company home page, click on one of the categories you want to browse or enter a keyword in the search text box.
- Click the Business link to go to a directory page that includes links for management, sales, marketing, small business, finance, and investing, as well as various industry categories. In turn, each of these links leads you to more links to articles and Web sites on the topic.

Note

Click Sidewalk to browse a complete guide to arts and entertainment in nine U.S. cities as well as Sydney, Australia.

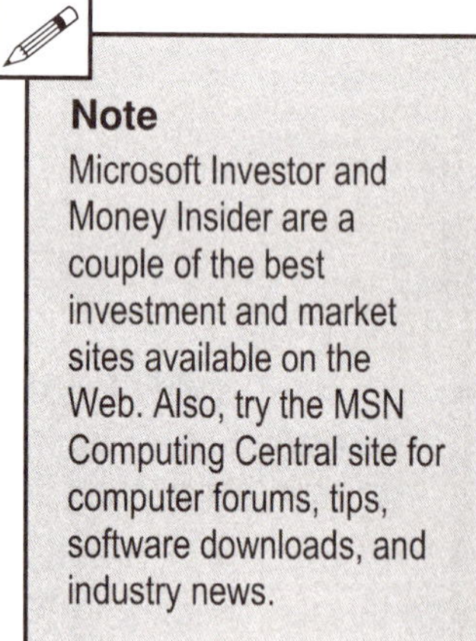

Note

Microsoft Investor and Money Insider are a couple of the best investment and market sites available on the Web. Also, try the MSN Computing Central site for computer forums, tips, software downloads, and industry news.

News and Entertainment at the Pathfinder Network

- The Pathfinder Network Web site brings together news, information, and entertainment content of dozens of Web, magazine, and video properties owned by the Time Warner media conglomerate.
- Pathfinder is a great source for news, sports, politics, and entertainment coverage, offering links to Time, CNN, People, Entertainment Weekly, Variety Netwire, Life, and AllPolitics.

Fortune Home Page at Pathfinder Network

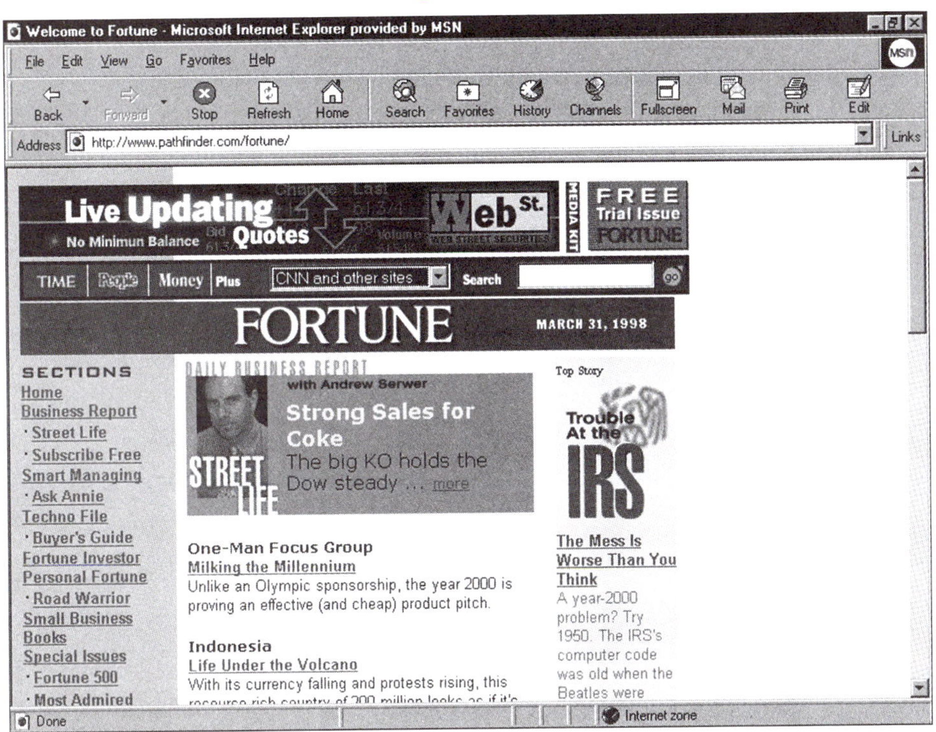

- You can also find business and finance Web sites such as Fortune, Hoover's Business Resources, Money Daily, Money Online, Portfolio Tracker, and Quick Quotes.
- Get travel news and fares at the Travel & Leisure, WebFlyer, PlanetSurfer, and Magellan Maps sites. Net Culture sites feature PC and Web news and information.
- Pathfinder also provides free e-mail service, a financial calculator, community chat sites, a cyberdating service, and an investment portfolio tracker. This wide-ranging collection of sites may in fact be the most comprehensive information source available on the Web.

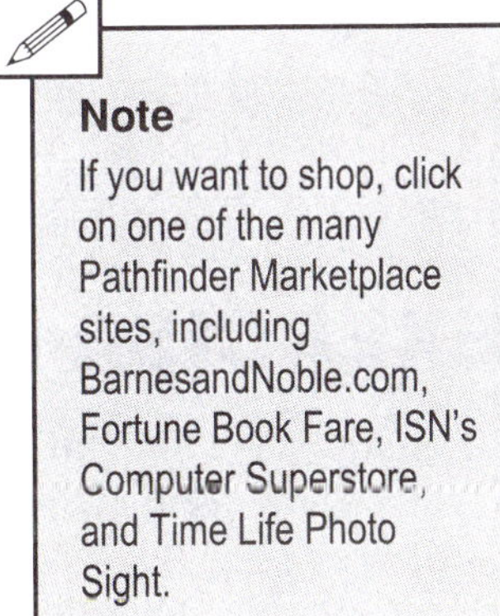

Note

If you want to shop, click on one of the many Pathfinder Marketplace sites, including BarnesandNoble.com, Fortune Book Fare, ISN's Computer Superstore, and Time Life Photo Sight.

In this exercise, you will use AOL.com to find small information at the Fast Company Web site. You will then use MSN.com and the Mining Company to search for more small business tips. Finally, you will use the Pathfinder Network and Fortune magazine to get workplace advice and search the Fortune 500 for company information.

Note: *To ensure consistent results, this exercise uses simulated sites. The real URLs appear at the end of the exercise.*

Web Search

Search for answers to the following questions using the Web sites you will visit in the Web simulation exercise.

1. What is the biggest complaint from bosses about their employees' voice mail messages?

   ____

2. Where does Anne Donellon teach?

   ____

3. For what company does Kerry Shampine work?

   ____

4. According to the Small Business Tips article, from where does profit come?

   ____

5. According to the Ask Annie column, who is the author of *Territorial Games: Understanding and Ending Turf Wars at Work*?

   ____

6. What Fortune 500 company ranks number 13 in profits?

   ____

7. According to the Company Snapshot, what is the current stock price of IBM?

   ____

EXERCISE DIRECTIONS

1. Launch the Internet simulation. From the Main Menu, select Lesson 5, then select Exercise 1.

   ✓ *The examples in the simulation use Internet Explorer. The home page for the simulation is the DDC Web site.*

2. On the Address line, type the following URL and press Enter:

   http://www.aol.com/

   ➲ *The America Online home page opens.*

AOL Home Page

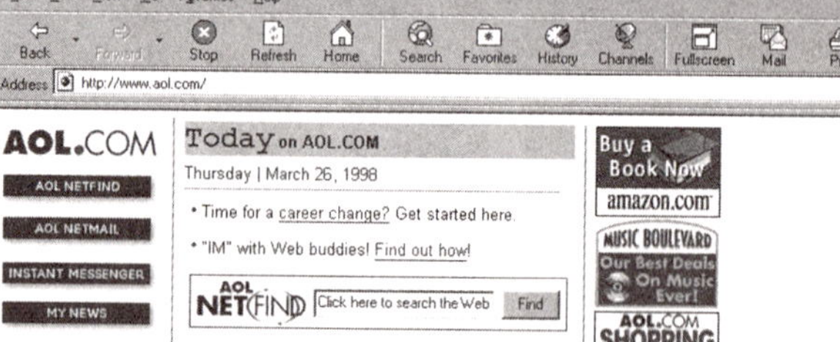

3. Scroll down and click the WorkPlace link.

   ➲ *The AOL WorkPlace page opens.*

4. Scroll down the page and look at the various links this directory lists.

5. Click the Fast Company link.

   ➲ *The Fast Company home page opens.*

AOL WorkPlace Page

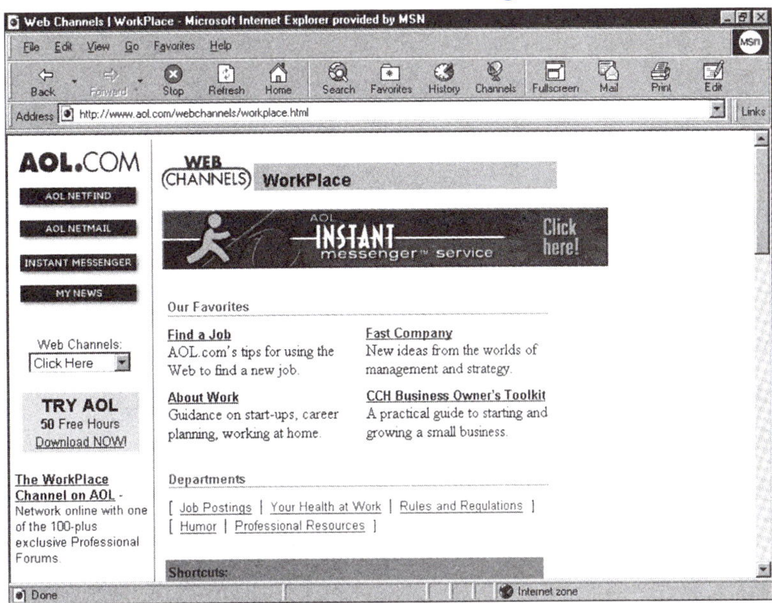

6. Click the magazine link at the top of the page.

   ➲ *The Fast Company Magazine page opens.*

Fast Company Home Page

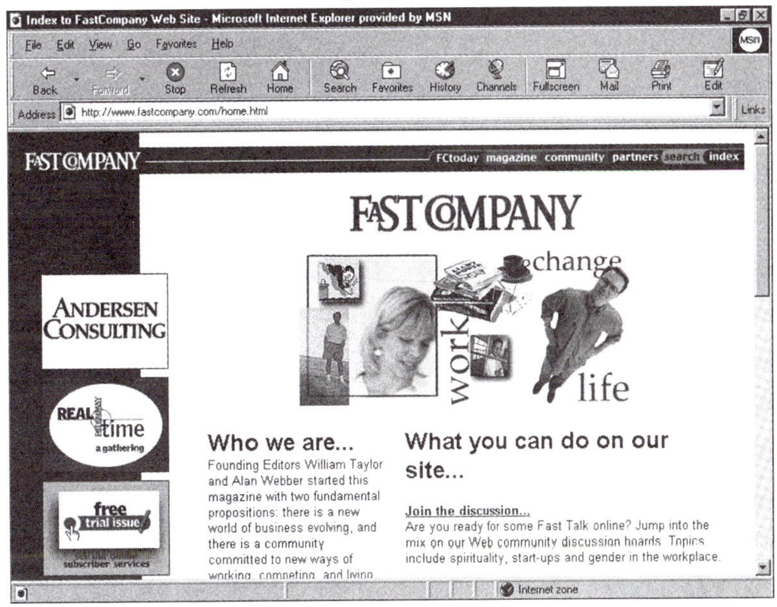

7. Click the Themes and Sections link.

   ➲ *The Themes and Ideas page opens.*

8. Scroll down and click the Power Tools link.

   ➲ *The Power Tools page opens.*

Themes and Ideas Page

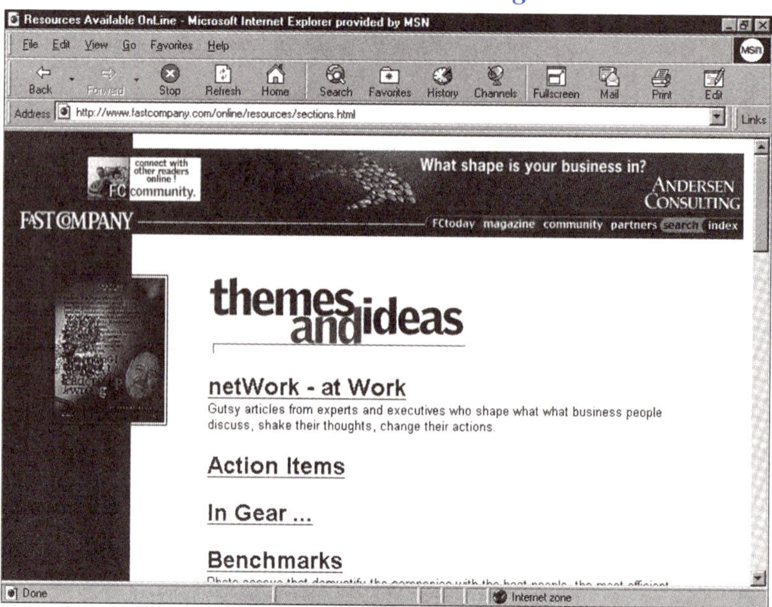

Power Tools Page

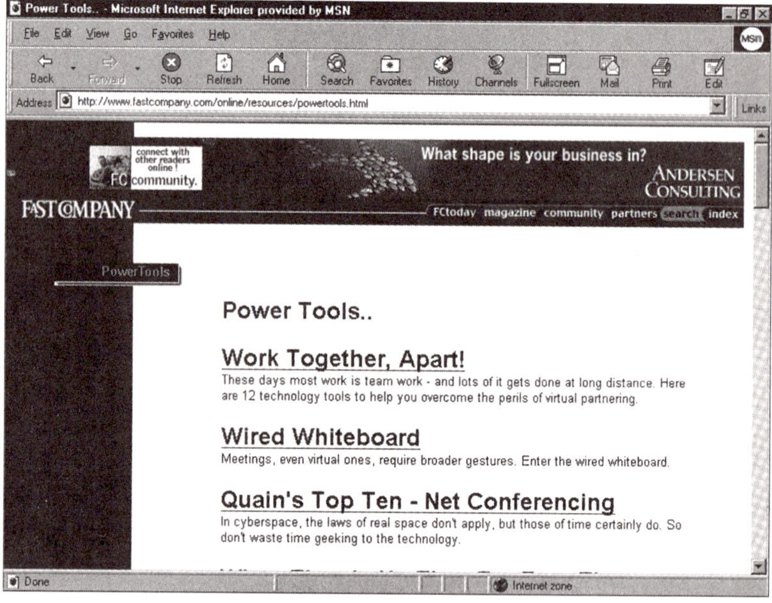

9. Scroll down and click the When There's No Time For Face Time link.

   ➲ *The article opens.*

10. Scroll down and read the article.

    ✓ *Note the techniques for sending effective e-mail and voice mail, and when to use each.*

11. Use your browser's Back button to return to the Power Tools page, then click Congratulations, You're Promoted (now what?) link.

    ➲ *The article opens.*

12. Scroll down and read the article, then click the Never do what you can delegate link.

13. Read the article, then click your browser's Back button. When the main article page opens, click the Nobody likes a know-it-all link.

14. Type the following URL in your browser's Address line and press Enter:

    http://www.msn.com/

    ➲ *The Microsoft Network home page opens.*

Power Tools Article

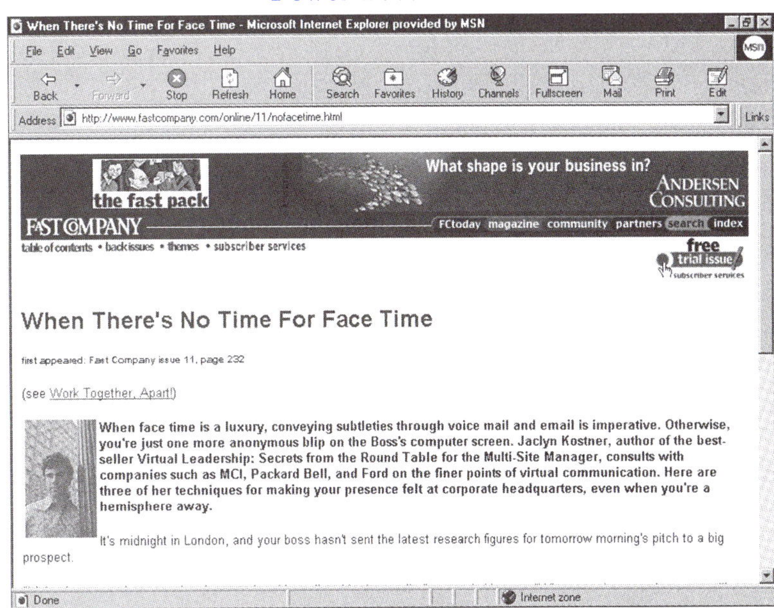

Microsoft Network Home Page

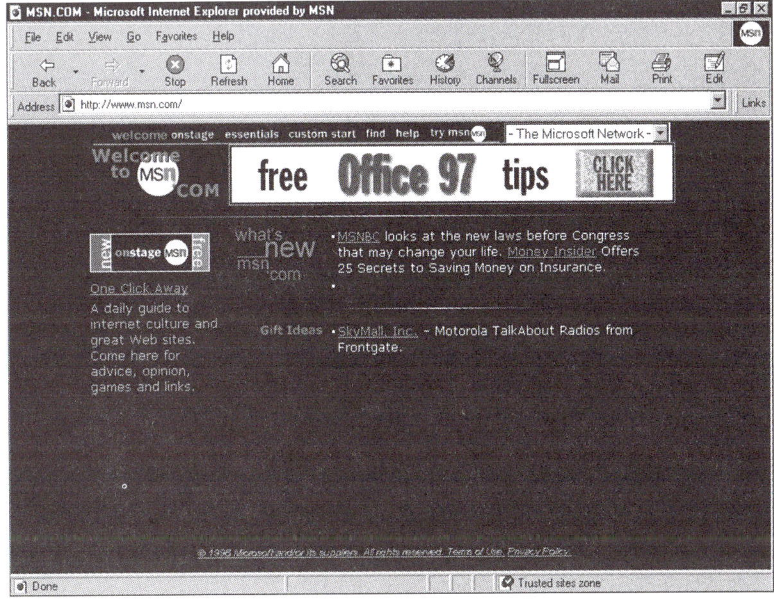

15. Click essentials at the top of the page.
    ➲ *The MSN Essentials page opens.*
16. Click The Mining Company link.
    ➲ *The Mining Company home page opens.*
17. Click the business link.
    ➲ *The Mining Company's Business page opens.*

Mining Company Home Page

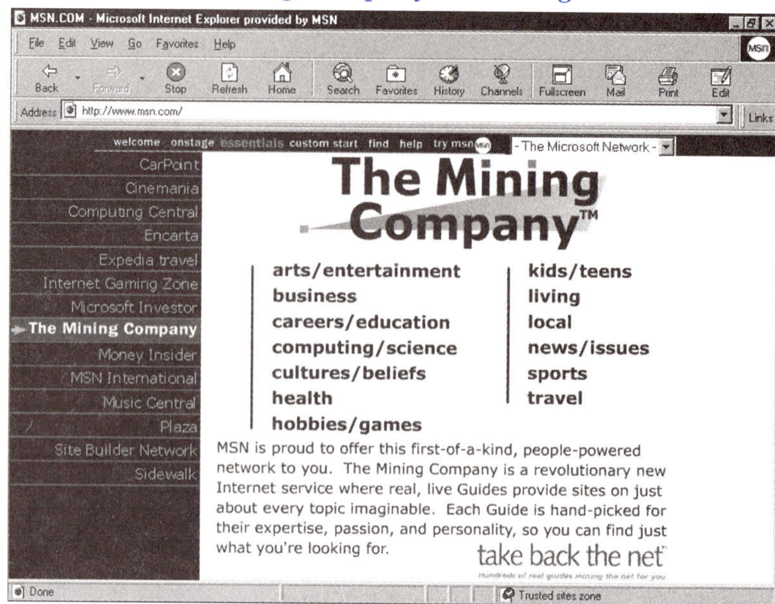

Business from The Mining Company

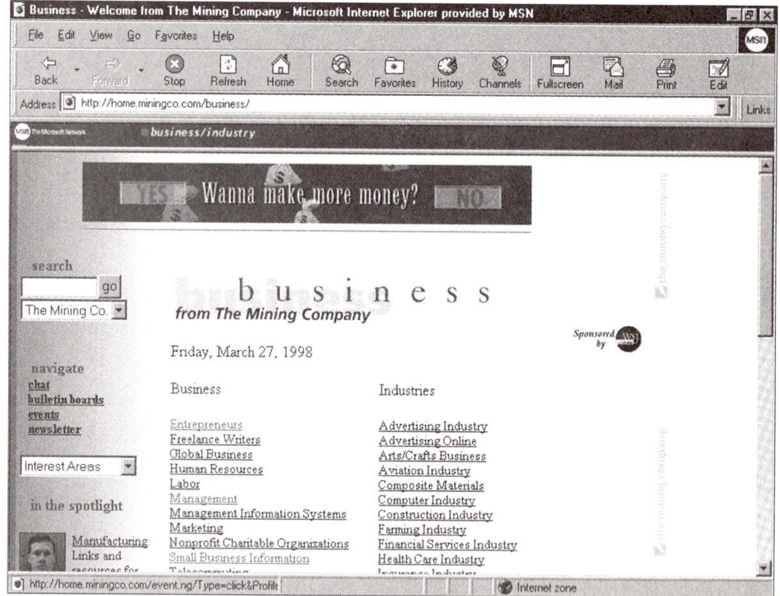

18. Click the Small Business Information link.
    - ➲ *The Small Busines Information page opens.*
19. Click the Tips You Can Use link.
    - ➲ *The Tips to Help Your Small Busines page opens.*

Small Business Information from The Mining Company

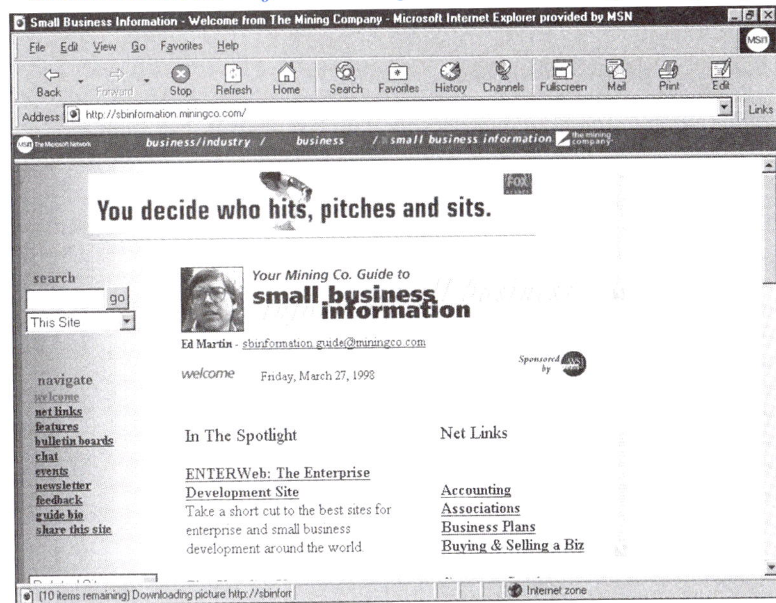

20. Scroll down and click the Tip 32 link.
    - ➲ *The Path To Better Business Is Just 8 Steps Long page opens.*
21. Scroll down and read the article.
    - ✓ *Notice that the foundation of success in business is building long-term relationships with customers based on character and integrity.*

Weekly Small Business Tip

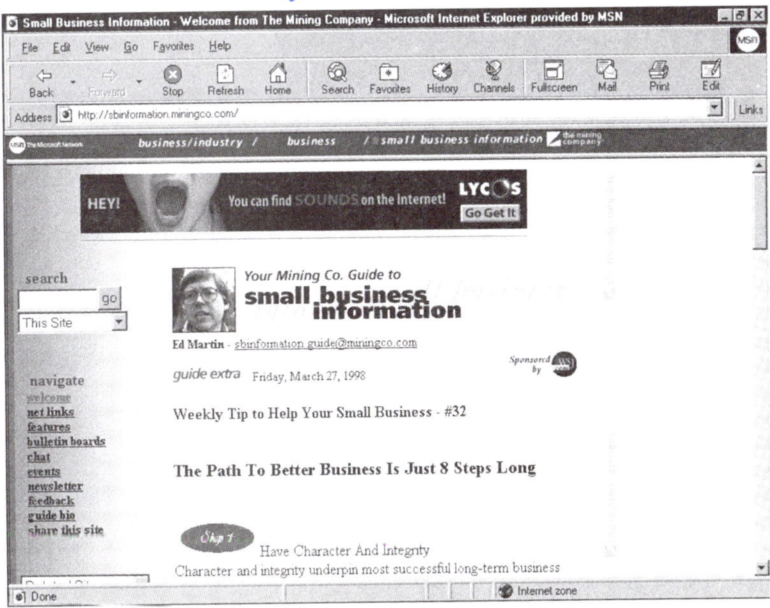

22. Type the following URL in your browser's Address line and press Enter:

    http://www.pathfinder.com/

    ➲ *The Pathfinder home page opens.*

23. Click the FORTUNE link in the bar near the top of the page.

    ➲ *The Fortune magazine home page opens.*

Pathfinder Home Page

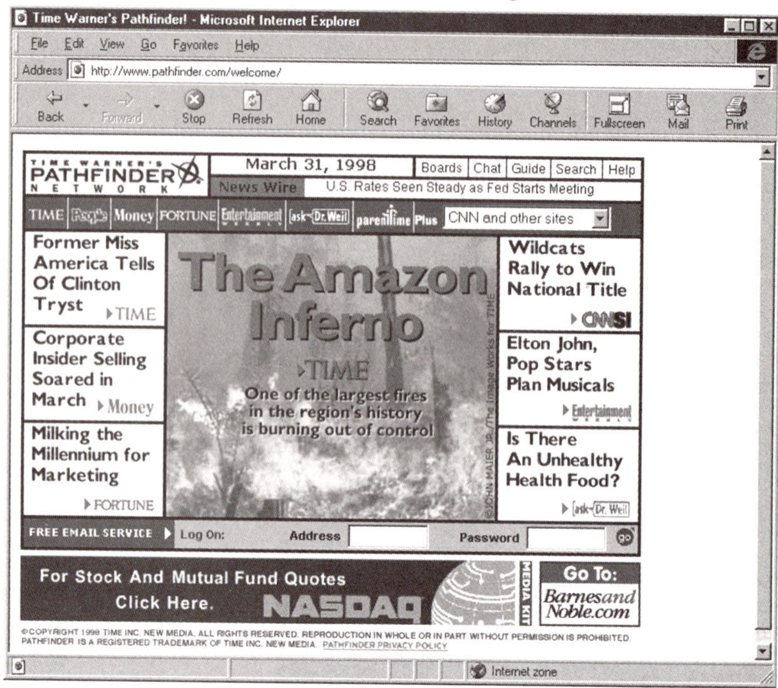

Fortune Home Page

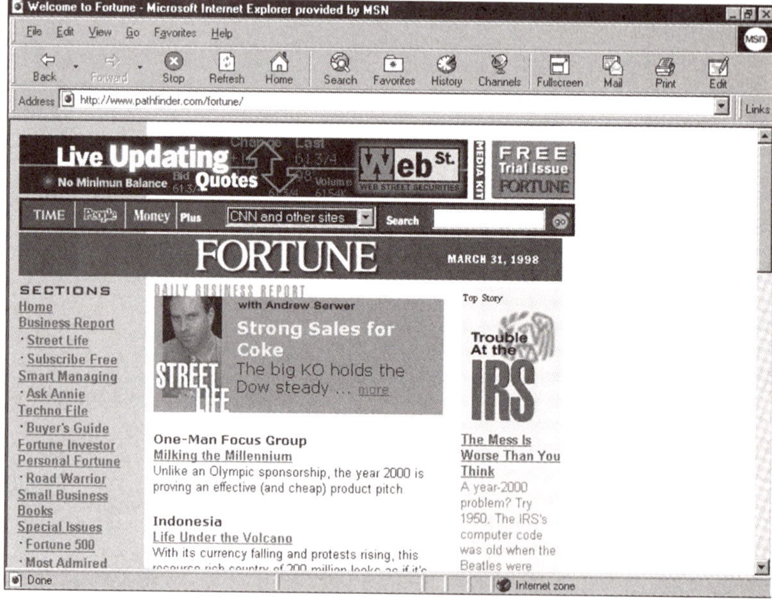

24. Click the Ask Annie link at the left of the page.
    ➲ *The Ask Annie page opens.*
25. Read the columnist's advice about "poison pen" e-mail.
26. Click the Fortune 500 link at the left of the page.
    ➲ *The Fortune 500 page opens.*
27. Click the Top Performers link in the left pane.
    ➲ *The Top Performers page opens.*

Ask Annie Page

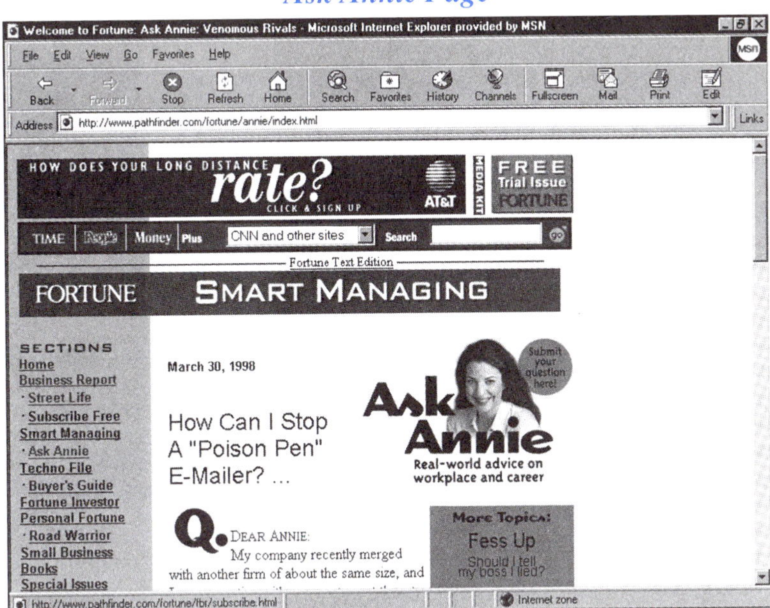

Fortune 500 Page

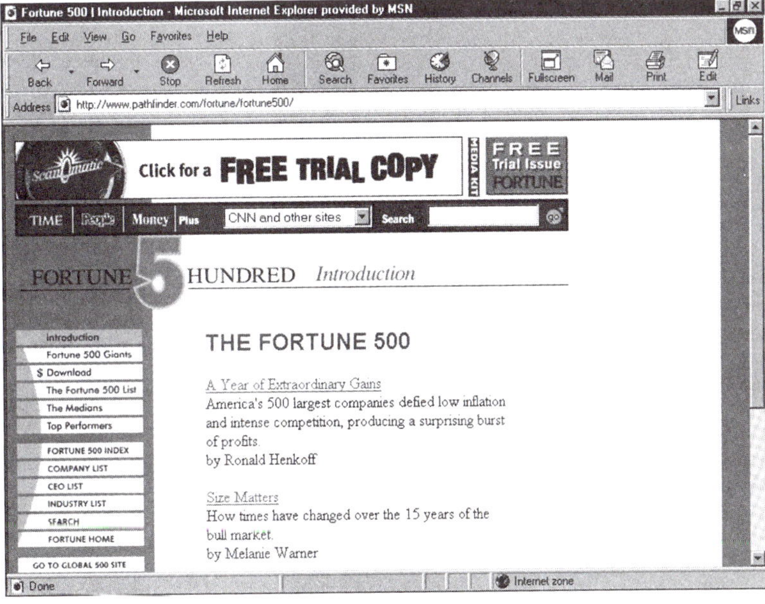

28. Click the Highest Profits link.

   ➲ *A chart ranking Fortune 500 companies by highest profits appears.*

29. Click the link for International Business Machines Corporation.

   ➲ *The Company Snapshot for IBM opens.*

30. Scroll down and review the financial information for IBM.

   ✓ *Note the growth in profits and in earnings per share.*

31. Continue on to the next exercise.

   OR

   Exit from the simulation.

IBM Company Snapshot

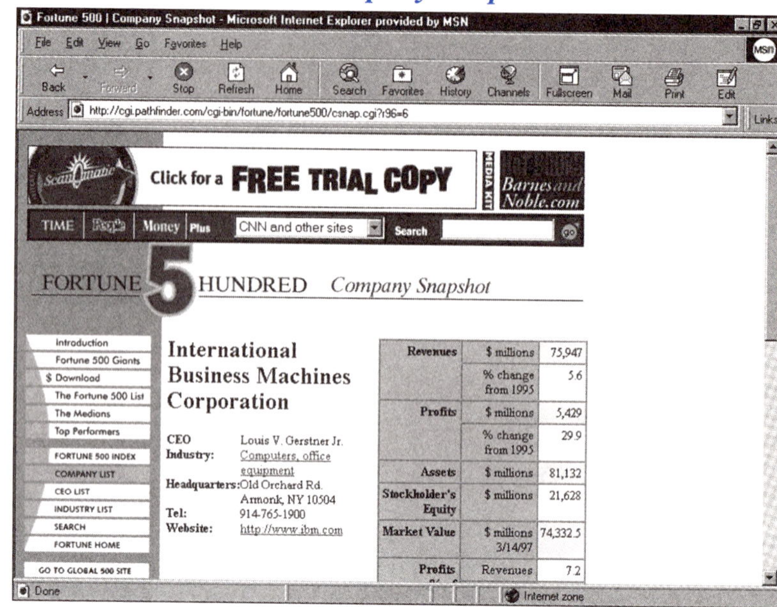

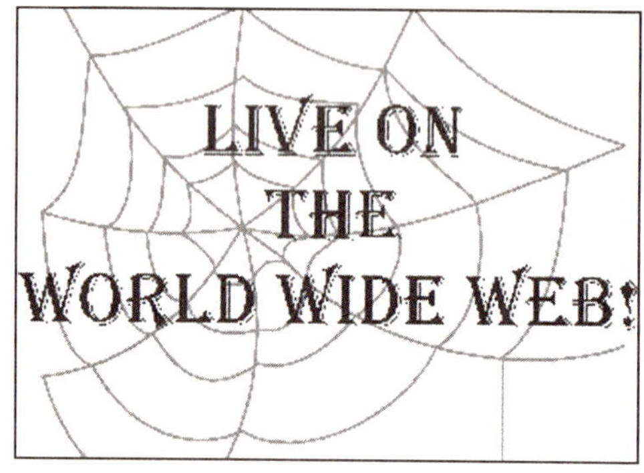

America Online Home Page

   http://www.aol.com/

Fast Company Home Page

   http://www.fastcompany.com/

Microsoft Network Home Page

   http://www.msn.com/

The Mining Company Home Page

   http://www.miningcompany.com/

Pathfinder Network Home Page

   http://www.pathfinder.com/

Fortune Home Page

   http://www.fortune.com/

NEXT EXERCISE

Exercise 2

- Check Business News with BusinessWeek Online
- Check Business News with Forbes Digital Tool
- Use the NewsHound Push Service

NOTES

Check Business News with BusinessWeek Online

- A multitude of Web sites allow you to check business news and monitor business and technology trends. These sites are typically online versions of business magazines, journals, and newspapers, and they feature complete news coverage, timely updates, and in-depth reporting. Columns and opinion pieces provide you with expert analysis to aid in business decision-making.
- BusinessWeek is one such site that is a leading source of information for businesspeople. Its online site delivers all the information you will find in the weekly magazine as well as additional content only available online.

BusinessWeek Online Home Page

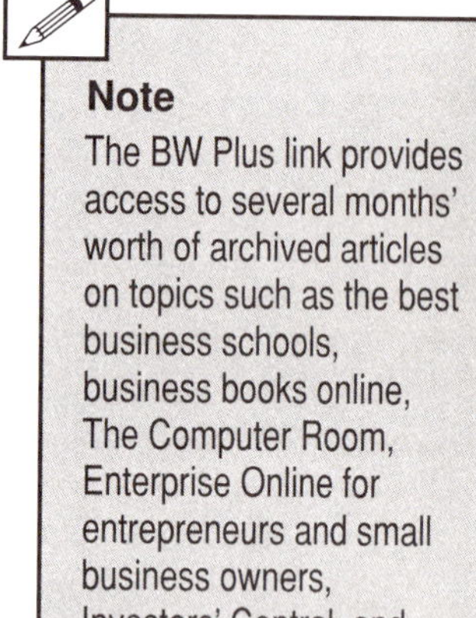

Note

The BW Plus link provides access to several months' worth of archived articles on topics such as the best business schools, business books online, The Computer Room, Enterprise Online for entrepreneurs and small business owners, Investors' Central, and Personal Business.

- The home page features articles from the current week's edition of the magazine. Click the picture of the magazine's cover to see a complete directory of links to the issue's contents.

- Click the BW Daily link to get a complete look at the day's business news with links to numerous in-depth articles produced by BusinessWeek and Standard & Poor's. Click one of the article links to read the complete text of the article and see links to related stories.
- From the BusinessWeek home page, use the Company of the Week link to view detailed financial profiles of companies featured in current and recent issues of BusinessWeek.

Check Business News with Forbes Digital Tool

- Forbes Magazine has long been noted for its irreverent mix of business news reporting, insightful features, and opinionated columns. You can browse the content of five Forbes publications online at the Forbes Digital Tool Web site.

Forbes Digital Tool Home Page

- Publications available at the Digital Tool site include the original Forbes Magazine, Forbes ASAP (articles about the impact of technology on business), Forbes FYI (features, entertainment, and opinion), American Heritage (a lively magazine about American history), and the Gilder Telecosm Series (articles excerpted from the book *Telecosm*, which examines and predicts trends in the online world).
- You can also click on the Toolbox icon to use Forbes' collection of tools, calculators, and databases. Lists include corporations and businesspeople, such as The 500 Largest Private Companies in the US and the World's Richest People. Use the Digital Tool Databases to find things such as a New York dining guide and a fitness guide, download software such as the NBD Daily Rocket Investment Monitor, and use handy financial calculators.

Note

To participate in an active and entertaining online forum, click the On My Mind icon near the bottom of the left frame on the Forbes Digital Toolbox home page.

Use the NewsHound Push Service

- Push technology has received a lot of press coverage touting it as the next, or perhaps first, "killer application" for the World Wide Web. Push Web sites offer you a selection of channels that deliver a steady stream of information and content to your computer's desktop over the Internet.
- Still, there are distinct advantages to tailoring news and information from the Web to fit your needs. Various push Web services deliver information somewhat differently, using more or less intrusive means to give you what you want. Because push channels can cause a drain on system performance, you must be sure to consider your hardware system and your information needs when deciding which push service to use.
- The NewsHound push service provided by the Knight-Ridder newspaper chain tracks and delivers up to five news or information topics for about $8 per month.

NewsHound Home Page

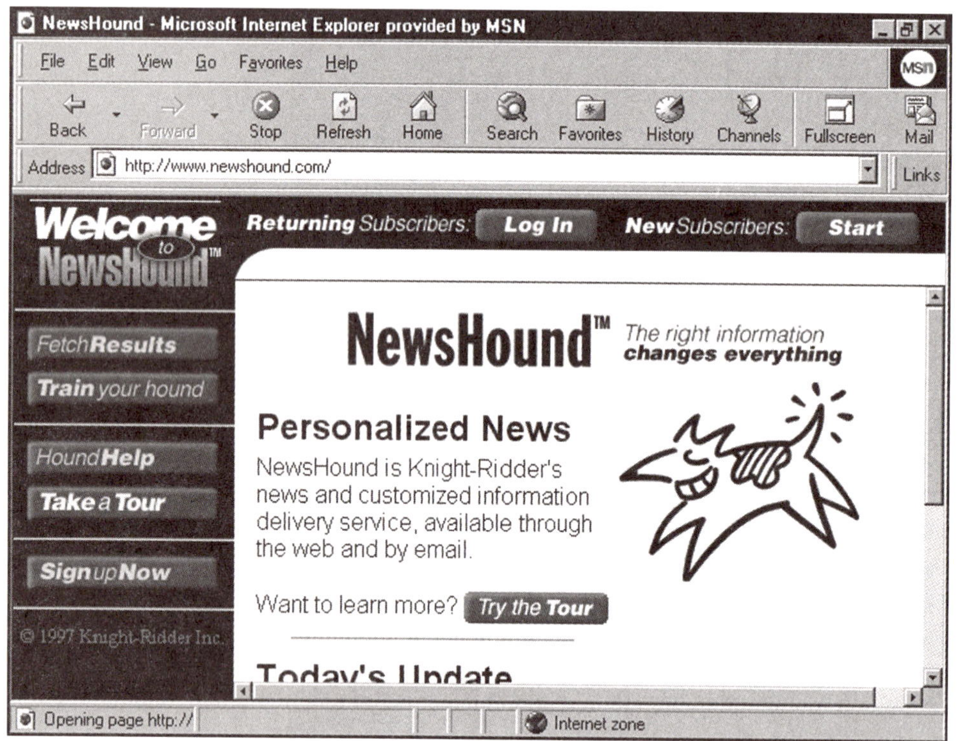

- To use NewsHound, you must first sign up for the basic service, then "train" your NewsHounds to search for the information you want by supplying a personalized search profile.
- The NewsHound service will then keep an eye out for stories and Web information that fit your search profile, gather anything that matches, and send it to your computer in the format you choose.
- NewsHound is a great way to keep tabs on a particular company, market, or developing news or technology story without the intrusiveness of other push services.
- To "train" a "hound" to retrieve news for you, click the Train your hound button on the NewsHound home page. You will be asked to type the name of your new hound (a username) and password in the dialog box that appears and click OK.

Caution

While the idea of having continuously updated and readily available information on your computer about topics of interest may sound appealing, beware of drawbacks. Sending a stream of incoming "live" information over the Internet can slow computers and networks to a crawl.

- Next, use the Train Your Hound page to click on links that enable you to create your search criteria.
  - Click Power Topics to use preselected search criteria such as Editor's Picks, Company Tracking, and Law and Order.
  - Click Terms to enter keywords and phrases as you would in a Web search engine such as Yahoo! or Excite.
  - Click Sources to select the newspapers and newswires for NewsHound to search.
  - Click Delivery Options to select how often and in what form (e-mail, Web pages, or plain text) you want articles delivered.

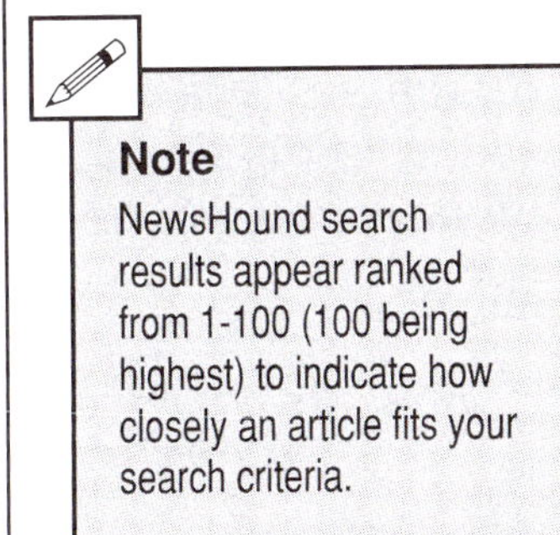

Note
NewsHound search results appear ranked from 1-100 (100 being highest) to indicate how closely an article fits your search criteria.

Select News Hound Search Criteria

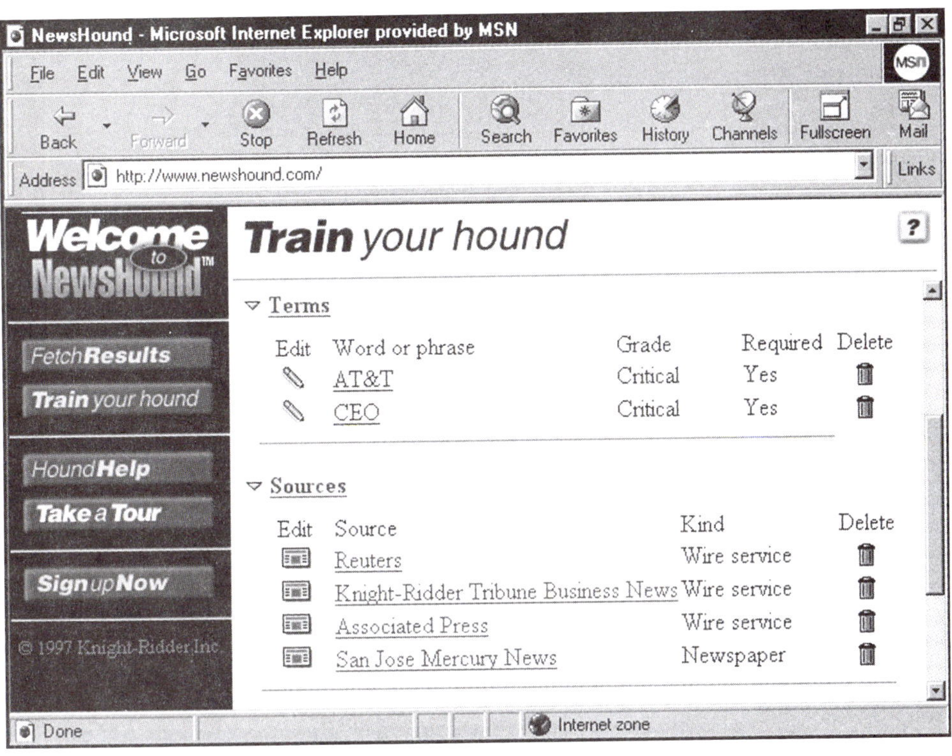

- To retrieve hound search results, click the Fetch Results button and then click a story link to read the complete article.

In this exercise, you will read news stories and check company information using the BusinessWeek Online Web site. You will then scan business news headlines and search a database of the world's richest people at the Forbes Digital Tool Web site. Finally, you will use the NewsHound push service to create a business news search agent.

Note: *To ensure consistent results, this exercise uses simulated sites. The real URLs appear at the end of the exercise.*

Web Search

Search for answers to the following questions using the Web sites you will visit in the Web simulation exercise.

1. How much has Armstrong reduced AT&T's annual costs during his tenure?

   ____

2. How have AT&T stock prices done with Armstrong as CEO?

   ____

3. From the Company of the Week Income Statement, what was AT&T's Gross Profit in December of 1996 (answer in millions)?

   ____

4. How many American Billionaires did Forbes identify last year?

   ____

5. List the people who made their millions in chemicals.

   ____

6. What types of communication services are Reuters, Knight-Ridder Tribune Business News, and San Jose Mercury News?

   ____

EXERCISE DIRECTIONS

1. Launch the Internet simulation. From the Main Menu, select Lesson 5, then select Exercise 2.
2. On the Address line, type the following and press Enter: http://www.businessweek.com

   ➲ *The BusinessWeek Online home page opens.*

BusinessWeek Online Home Page

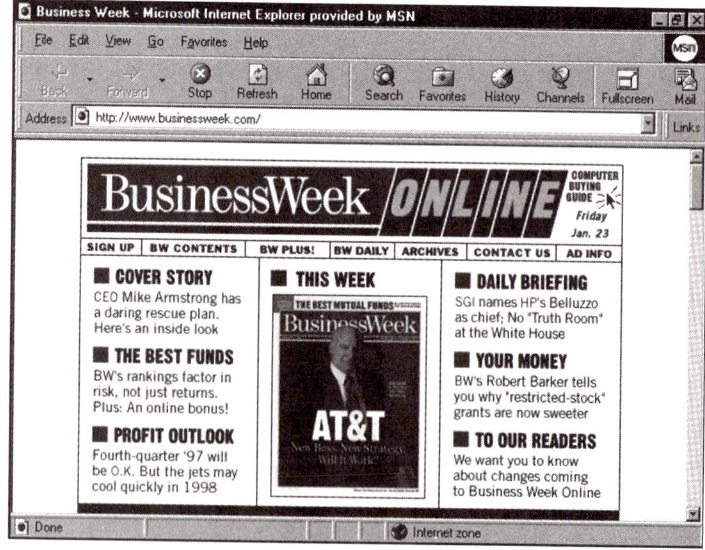

3. Click the COVER STORY link.

   ➲ *The BusinessWeek cover story on AT&T's future opens.*

4. Scroll down the page to read the article regarding AT&T's role in the future of the telecommunications industry.

5. At the bottom of the article, click the CHART: A Better Connection link.

   ➲ *A series of charts showing AT&T's recent performance opens.*

6. Click the BW HOME link to return to the BusinessWeek Online home page.

7. Scroll down the home page and click on the Company of the Week link.

   ➲ *The BusinessWeek Company of the Week page opens.*

8. Scroll down until you see the Financial and market reports heading. The current issue article on AT&T will be highlighted in the first scroll box. In the second scroll box, select **Income Statement** and then click the View The Report button.

   ➲ *A report showing AT&T's income statement for 1992-1996 opens.*

   ✓ *Notice the recent decrease in Sales and the increase in EPS (Earnings per Share) from Operations year over year. EPS from Operations is near the bottom of the report.*

Cover Story on AT&T's Future

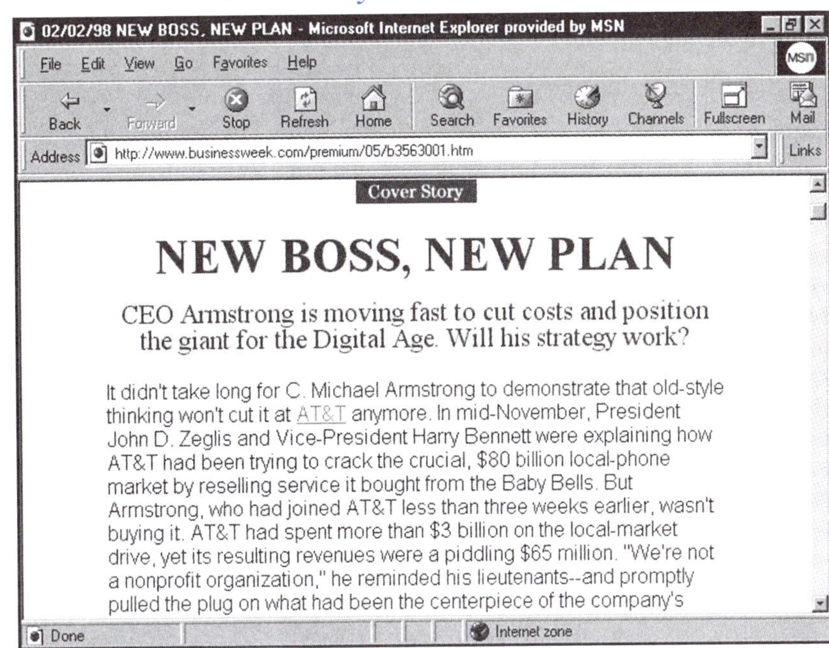

Charts Showing AT&T's Recent Performance

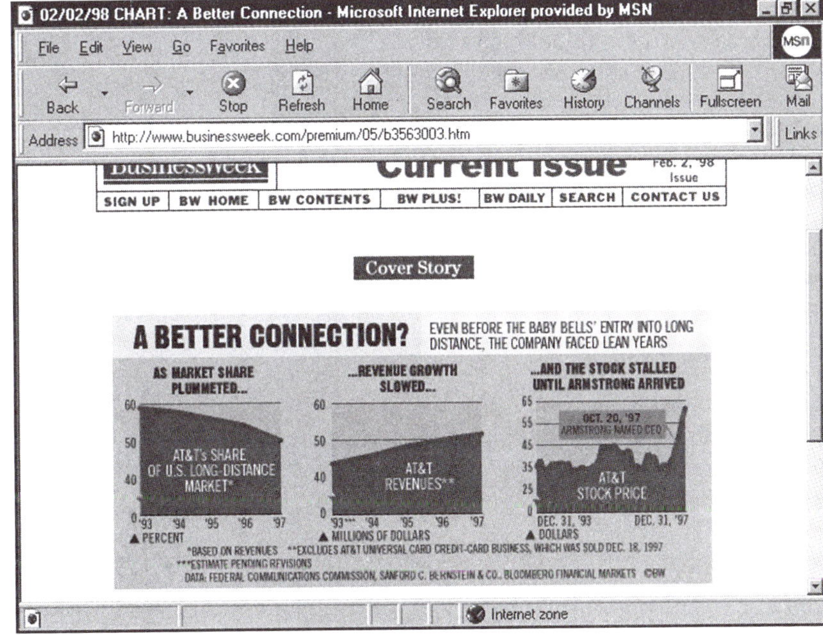

9. Type the following URL in your Web browser's Address box and press Enter:

   http://www.forbes.com

   ➲ *The Forbes Digital Tool home page opens.*

10. Use the scroll box at the right of the page to move down and read the news headlines. Next, click on the TOOLBOX icon near the upper-left corner of the page.

    ➲ *The Forbes Toolbox page opens.*

11. Scroll down and then click the GO link under 1997 World's Richest People.

    ➲ *The Forbes Digital Tool listing of the world's billionaires opens.*

12. Use the scroll bar at right to read the description of this database. Next, click on the Net Worth link to see the listing of billionaires.

13. Scroll down the page to see how many on the list of World's Richest People got their wealth from telecommunications (or telephony). See how many names you recognize on the list.

Forbes Digital Tool Home Page

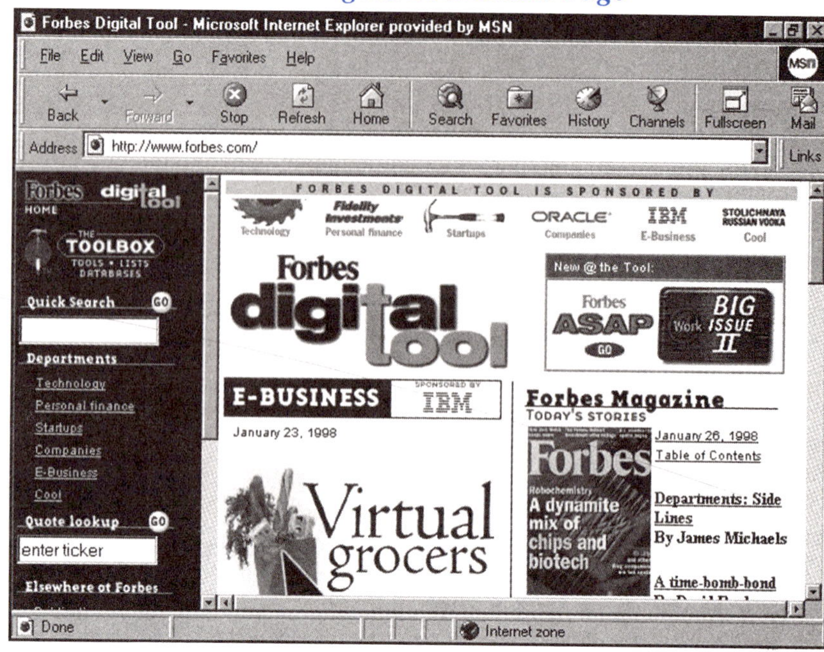

Forbes Database of the World's Richest People

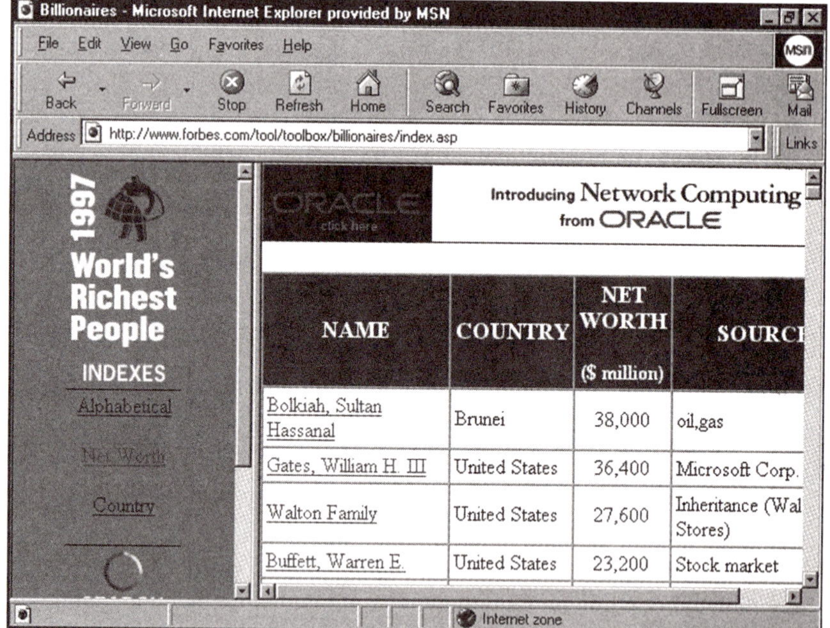

14. Click on the McCaw family link to read about the McCaw fortune.

    Hint: Scroll about one-third of the way down the listing to find the McCaw link.

Description of the McCaw Fortune

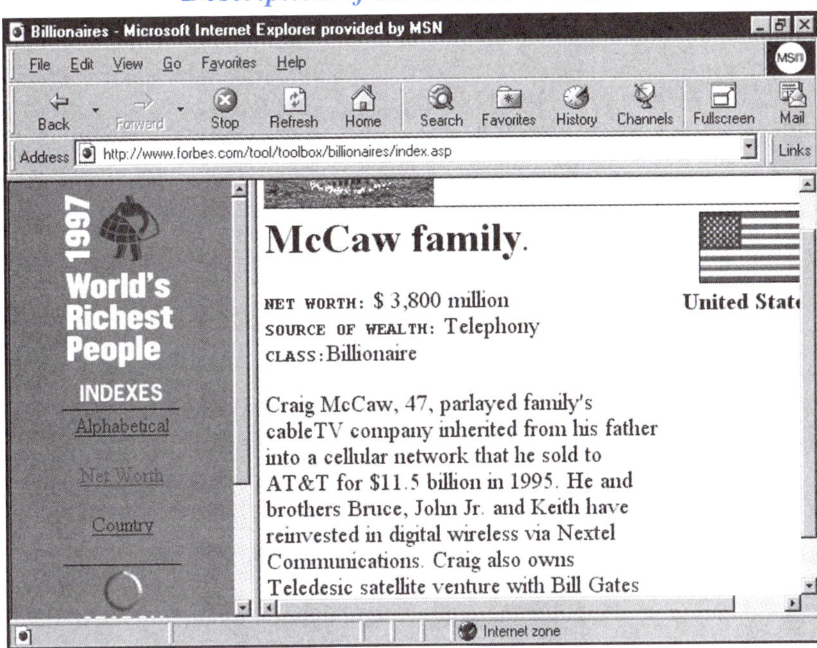

15. Type the following URL in your Web browser's Address box and press Enter:

    http://www.newshound.com

    ➲ *The NewsHound home page opens.*

16. Click the Train your hound button.

    ➲ *The Train your hound page opens.*

17. Click the Create a Hound button.

NewsHound Home Page

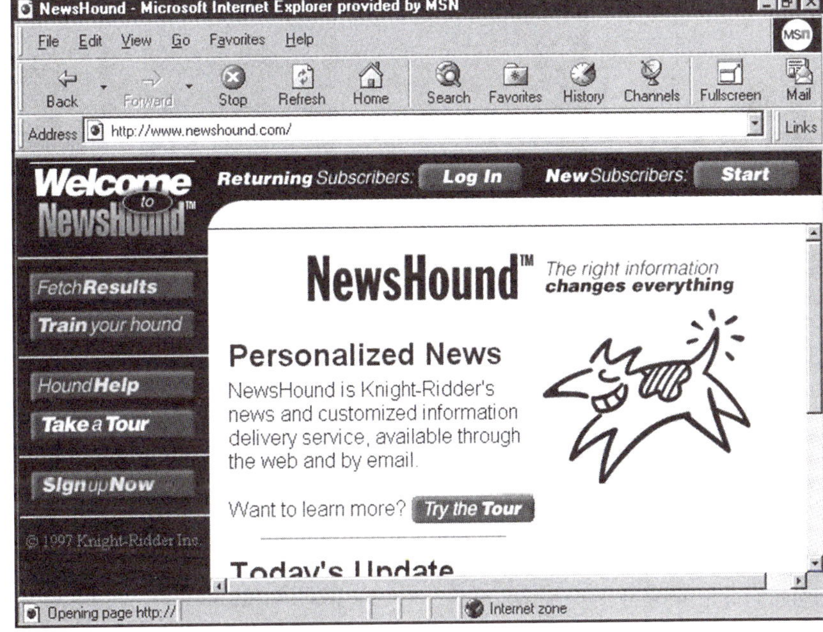

18. Enter the name AT&T in the dialog box that appears.
19. Click OK.
    ➲ *The Train your hound page appears with links to news tracking criteria.*
20. Click the Terms link.
    ➲ *The Train your hound Terms page opens.*
21. Type *AT&T, CEO* in the Term or phrase text box.
22. Click the **Require** check box, then select **Critical** from the Grade drop-down list.
23. Click the Done button.
    ➲ *The search criteria are added to your Hound.*
24. Click the Sources link.
    ➲ *The Train your hound Sources page opens.*
25. Click to select the following sources:

    San Jose Mercury News

    Knight-Ridder Tribune Business News

    Reuters
26. Click the Done button.
    ➲ *The news sources are added to your Hound.*

Give Your Hound a Name

Train Your Hound Page

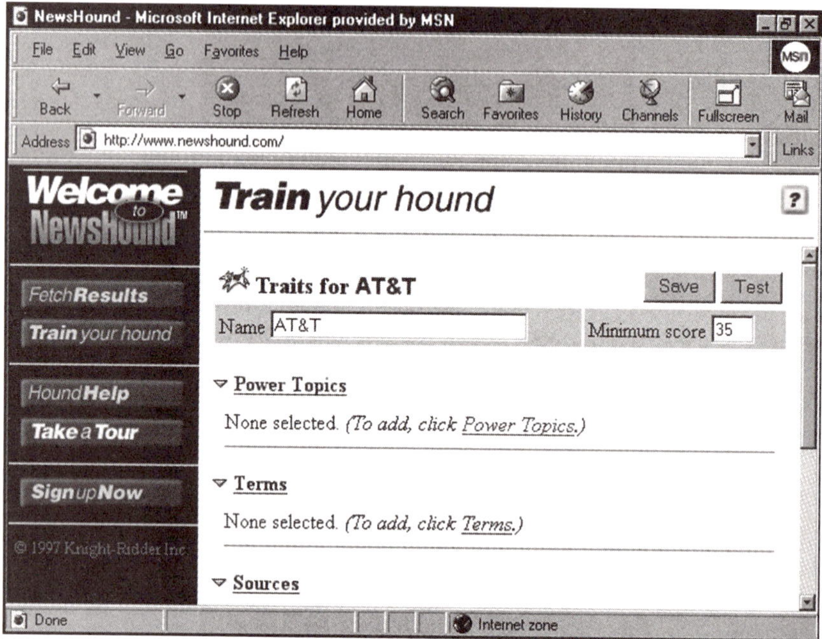

Enter Search Criteria in the Terms Page

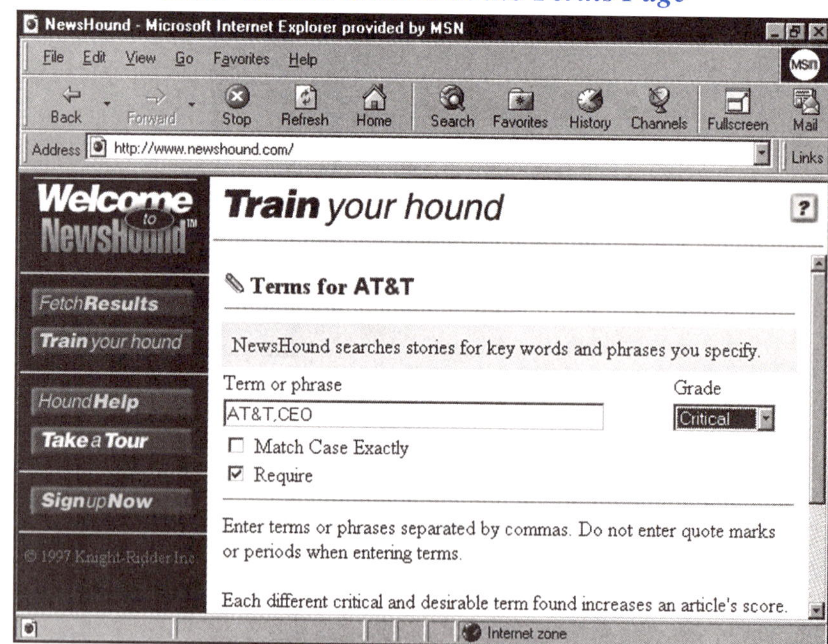

27. Click the Save button near the top of the Train your hound page.
    ➲ *Search criteria for the AT&T hound are saved.*

Select News Sources

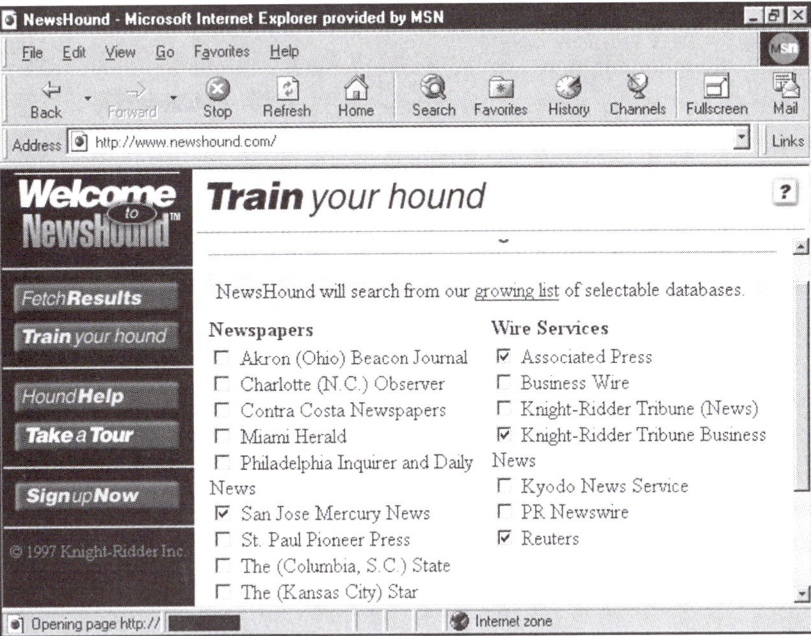

Search Criteria for the AT&T Hound

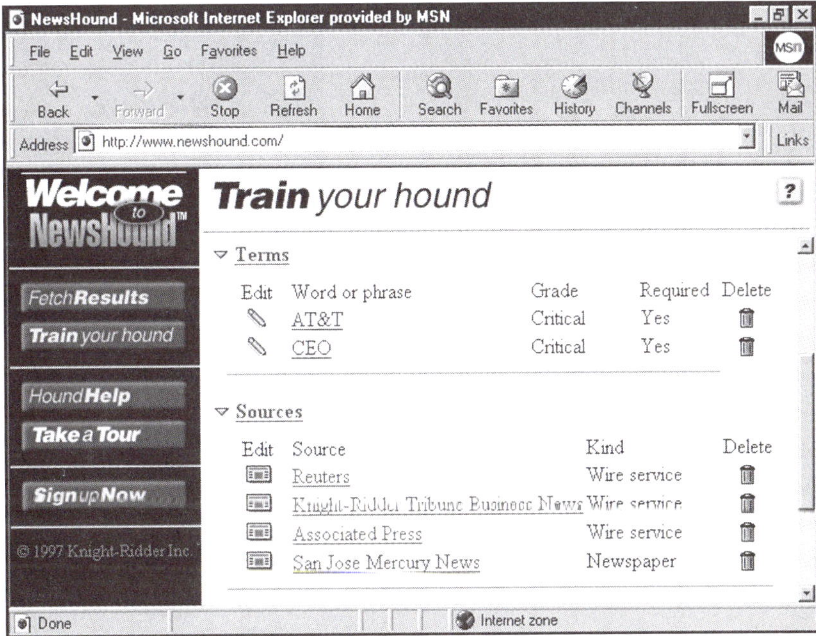

28. Click the Test button near the top of the Train your hound page.

   ➲ *A new window opens showing sample articles from the previous week that your new AT&T hound selects.*

   ✓ *Notice the scores NewsHound assigns to the articles.*

29. Scroll down the TestResults page to read the story summaries, then click the top link on the TestResults page to read the news article.

30. Click the Close button (x) to close the TestResults window and return to the Train your hound page.

31. Continue on to the next exercise.

   OR

   Exit from the simulation.

Sample Search Results for the AT&T Hound

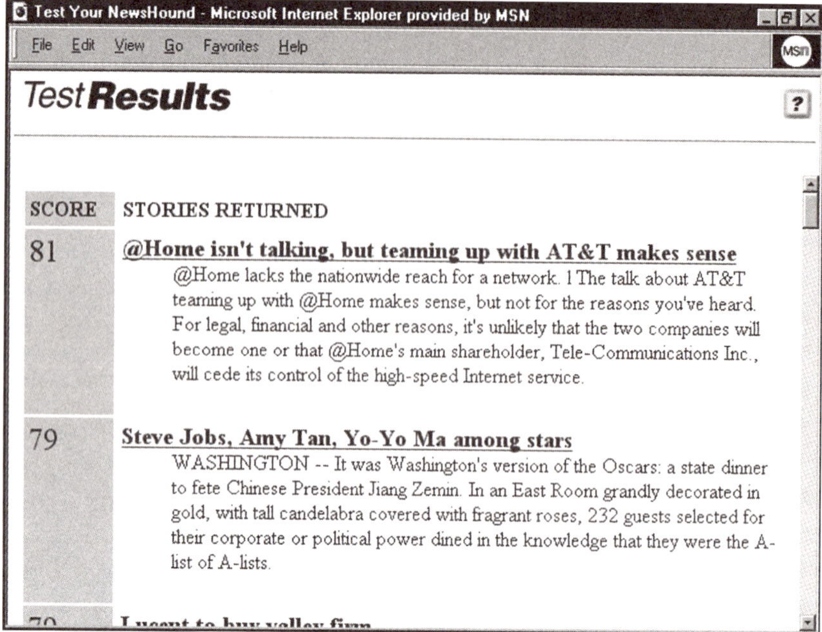

Test Your NewsHound - Microsoft Internet Explorer provided by MSN

File Edit View Go Favorites Help

TestResults

SCORE	STORIES RETURNED
81	**@Home isn't talking, but teaming up with AT&T makes sense** @Home lacks the nationwide reach for a network. 1 The talk about AT&T teaming up with @Home makes sense, but not for the reasons you've heard. For legal, financial and other reasons, it's unlikely that the two companies will become one or that @Home's main shareholder, Tele-Communications Inc., will cede its control of the high-speed Internet service.
79	**Steve Jobs, Amy Tan, Yo-Yo Ma among stars** WASHINGTON -- It was Washington's version of the Oscars: a state dinner to fete Chinese President Jiang Zemin. In an East Room grandly decorated in gold, with tall candelabra covered with fragrant roses, 232 guests selected for their corporate or political power dined in the knowledge that they were the A-list of A-lists.

AT&T Hound News Article

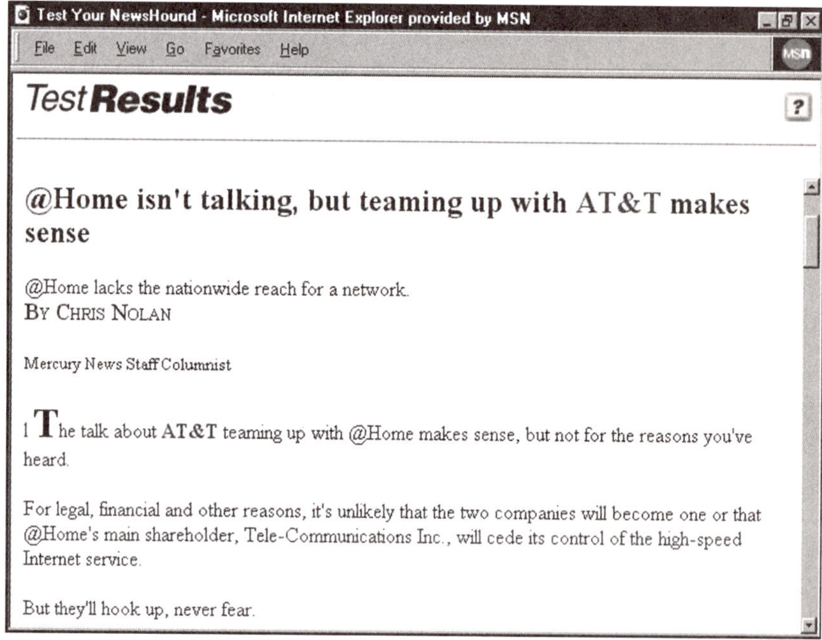

Test Your NewsHound - Microsoft Internet Explorer provided by MSN

File Edit View Go Favorites Help

TestResults

@Home isn't talking, but teaming up with AT&T makes sense

@Home lacks the nationwide reach for a network.
By Chris Nolan

Mercury News Staff Columnist

1 The talk about AT&T teaming up with @Home makes sense, but not for the reasons you've heard.

For legal, financial and other reasons, it's unlikely that the two companies will become one or that @Home's main shareholder, Tele-Communications Inc., will cede its control of the high-speed Internet service.

But they'll hook up, never fear.

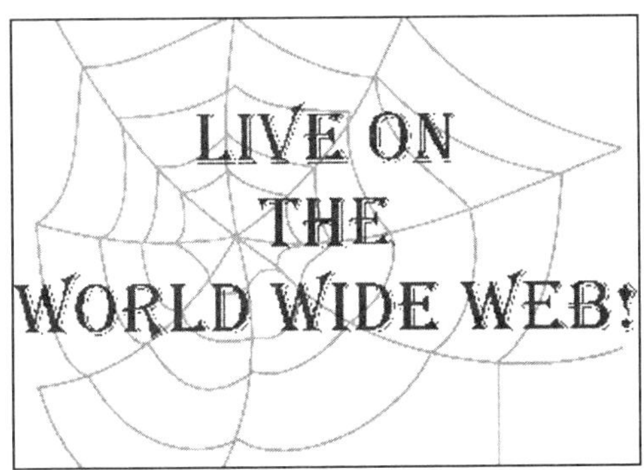

BusinessWeek Online
 http://www.businessweek.com

Forbes Digital Tool
 http://www.forbes.com

NewsHound
 http://www.newshound.com

Exercise 3

- Research Investments with Morningstar
- Check Interest Rates with Bank Rate Monitor

NOTES

Research Investments with Morningstar

- Use online investment research and analysis Web sites to make the best decisions for your investment portfolio. These sites offer market news, expert trader insight, as well as stock and fund comparison and screening tools. Sites include many free research services as well as top-flight portfolio management for subscribers.
- Morningstar has made its name as the top provider of mutual fund data and analysis. You can have free access to a wealth of Morningstar investment research tools at the Morningstar.Net Web site.

Morningstar.Net Home Page

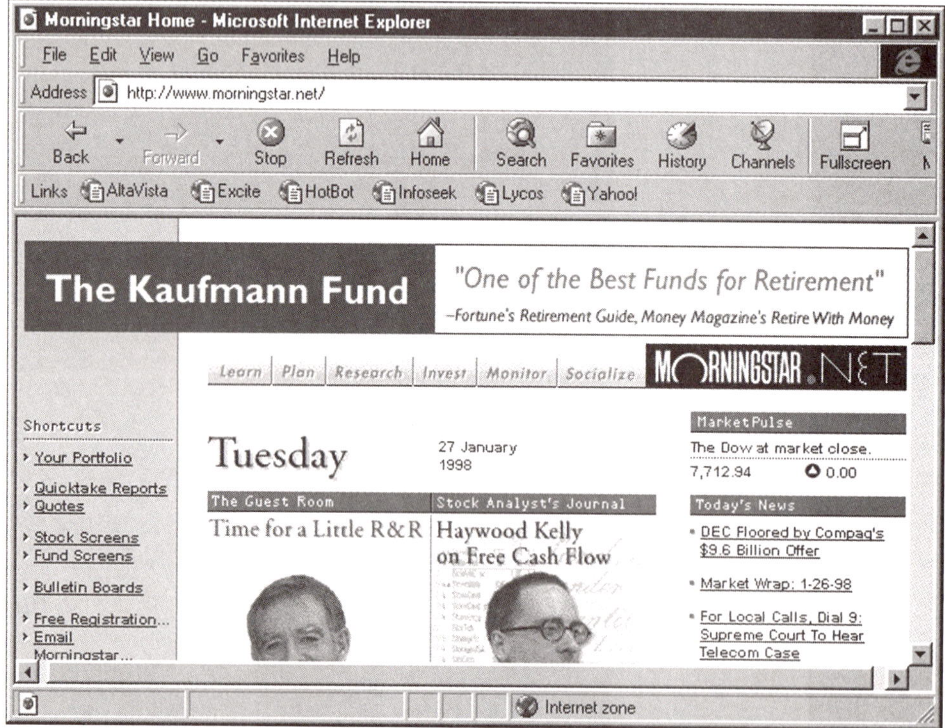

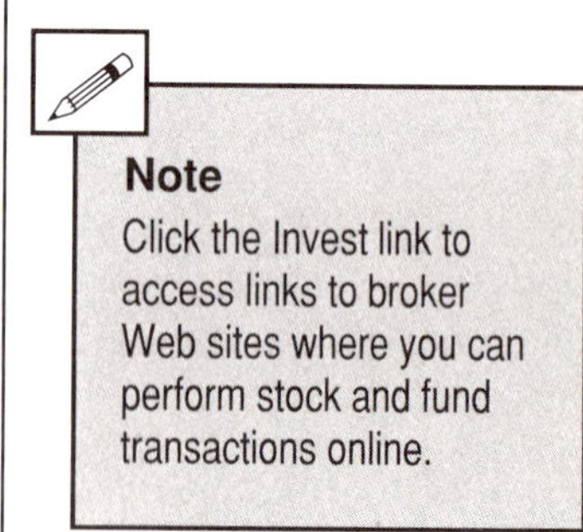

Note

Click the Invest link to access links to broker Web sites where you can perform stock and fund transactions online.

- Morningstar.Net is a complete investing tool. Use the Monitor feature to check fund winners and losers on the current day's trading.
- Click the Plan page to review articles and features on preparing your investment strategy. You can also track up to ten investment portfolios you create using the Morningstar site.

- Use the Learn feature to access links to news, articles, and expert advice on building and managing your own portfolio. Here you can click on articles including Investing 101: Funds, Investing 101: Stocks, or The Guestroom, where featured columnists hold forth.
- Click the Research link to find the most powerful tools available at the Morningstar site. The Data Screen tool enables you to search the vast Morningstar database of stocks and mutual funds for an investment that meets your criteria.
- From the Research page, click on the Stock Screens or Fund Screens link. Next, select a stock sector or fund category from the lists provided, then select a screen. For example, you might want to find the ten best 3-year annualized returns for hybrid funds. Simply select those screening criteria from the drop-down menus and click View Results.

Use Fund Screens to Research Investments

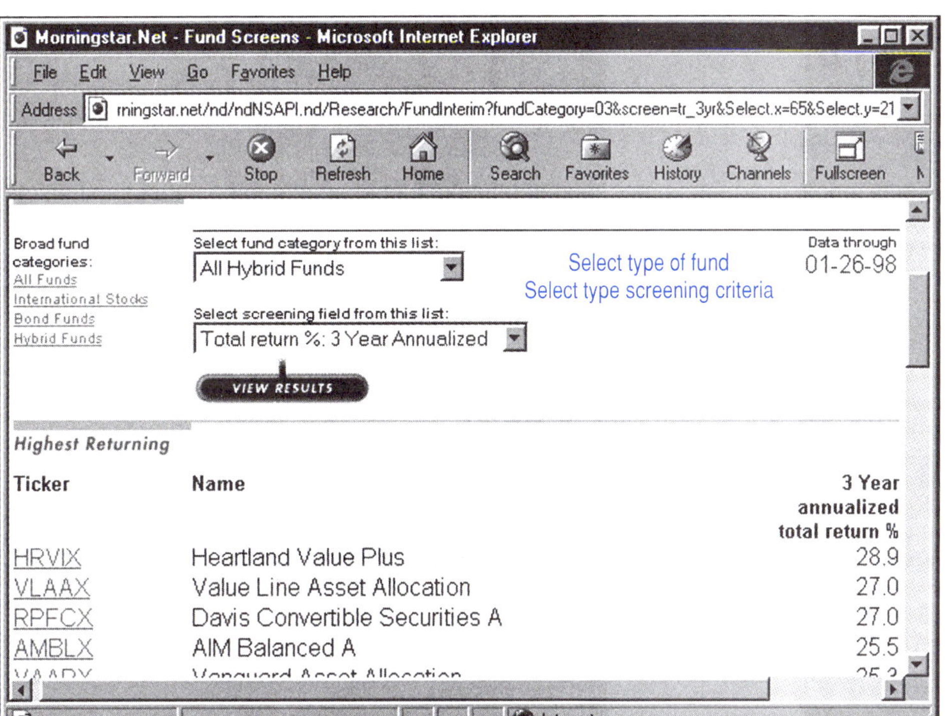

- You can also use Morningstar Reports such as Quicktake, Quote, and Ticker Lookup on the Research page.
  - Click the Quicktake button and enter a company's stock ticker symbol in the text box below to access a report on the company's recent performance.
  - Click the Quote button and enter up to 30 ticker symbols to see a current stock market quote for each company you enter.
  - Click the Ticker Lookup button and enter a company name to find the firm's ticker symbol.

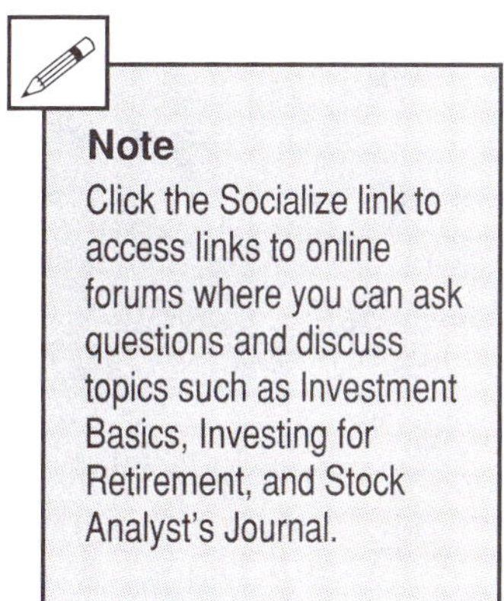

Note

Click the Socialize link to access links to online forums where you can ask questions and discuss topics such as Investment Basics, Investing for Retirement, and Stock Analyst's Journal.

Check Interest Rates with Bank Rate Monitor

- Interest rate monitor Web sites can help you find the best interest rates for bank cards, mortgages, and car loans. Use financial calculators supplied with these sites to weigh investment and loan payment options. Many of these sites also enable you to apply for loans, mortgages, and credit cards online.
- Bank Rate Monitor provides the most complete and easy-to-use interest rate tracking service. You can use Bank Rate Monitor to find the best interest rate for a company credit card, mortgage, or other type of loan.

Bank Rate Monitor Home Page

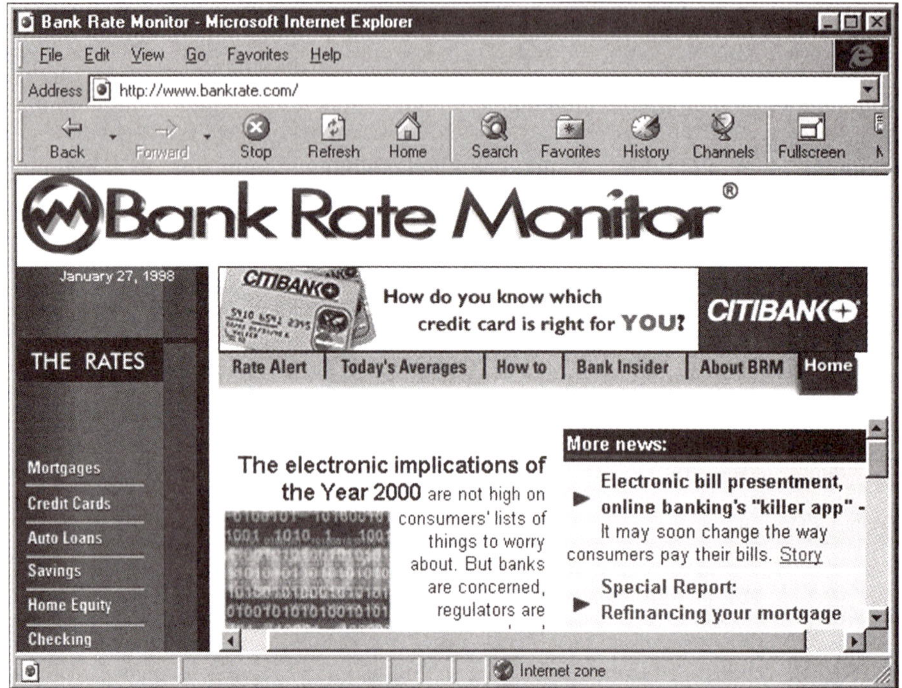

- Click one of the links at the left of the Bank Rate Monitor home page to find the best available interest rates. Links include Mortgages, Credit Cards, Auto Loans, Savings, Home Equity, Checking, ATMs, and Online Banking.
- Click Mortgages to see the Mortgage Watch page, which includes links to mortgage trend information, rates in your area, state and national averages, and loan cost comparison charts.
- Use the Credit Cards link at the left of the home page to go to the Credit Card Watch page. Here you can search for the best available credit card deal. Also included are links you can use to search for gold cards, rebates, and secured cards.
- The Online Banking Watch page includes links to Internet banking deals, online banking fees, as well as a step-by-step guide to banking via the Internet.
- One of Bank Rate Monitor's top tools is the Rate Alert service. Click on the Rate Alert link from the Bank Rate Monitor home page, then submit a form to indicate the type of rates you are interested in tracking. Bank Rate Monitor will send you e-mail to alert you when mortgage interest rates move up or down a tenth of a point or more. You can also follow changes in CD rates and in the Federal Reserve Bank's discount rate.

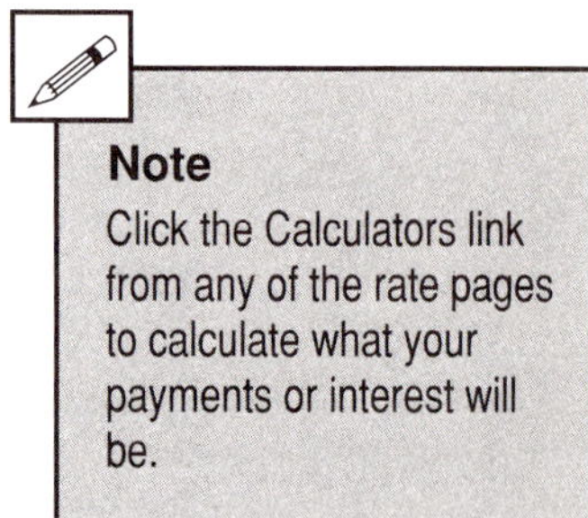

Note

Click the Calculators link from any of the rate pages to calculate what your payments or interest will be.

In this exercise, you will use the Morningstar.Net Web site to check stock market activity, review company financial data, and read an analyst's market commentary. You will also look up a company stock quote and search for mutual funds using the Morningstar database screening tool . Finally, you will check mortgage and credit card interest rates using the Bank Rate Monitor Web site.

Note: *To ensure consistent results, this exercise uses simulated sites. The real URLs appear at the end of the exercise.*

Web Search

Search for answers to the following questions using the Web sites you will visit in the Web simulation exercise.

1. Of the most active stocks on the American Stock Exchange, which one is the least active?

   ____

2. What is the per share price?

   ____

3. What percent of Compaq sales are outside of North America?

   ____

4. How did Nine West stock do in the last six months of 1997?

   ____

5. What percent of Nike's revenue is generated from domestic sales?

   ____

6. According to the Bank Rate Monitor, what is the best credit card for the next twelve months?

   ____

7. What is the interest rate?

   ____

EXERCISE DIRECTIONS

1. Launch the Internet simulation. From the Main Menu, select Lesson 5, then select Exercise 3.
2. On the Address line, type the following and press Enter:

   http://www.morningstar.net

   ➲ *The Morningstar.Net home page opens.*

Morningstar.Net Home Page

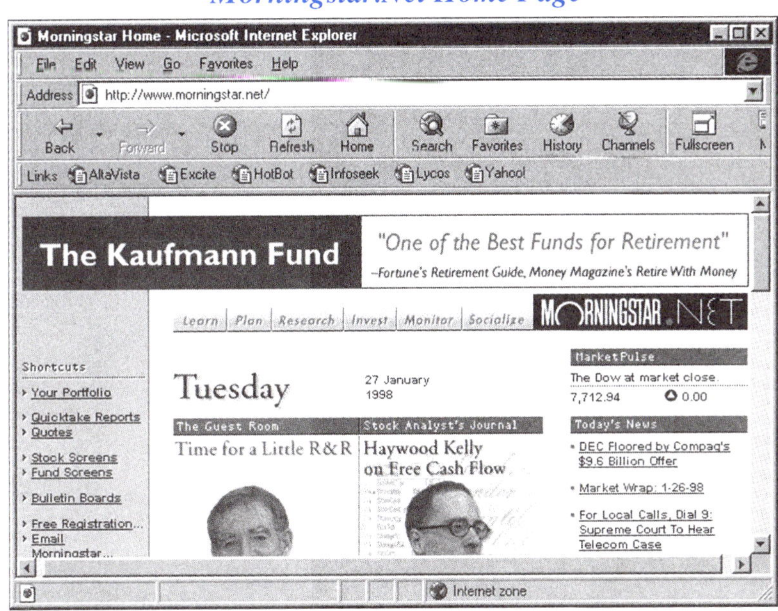

3. Scroll down the home page to read the financial news headlines and feature story summaries.
4. Click the Monitor link at the top of the home page.

   ➲ *The Morningstar.Net Monitor page opens.*
5. Read the update of stock exchange indexes at the right of the page, then click on the Stock Movers icon.

   ➲ *The Market Pulse Stock Movers page opens.*
6. Click on the drop-down list and choose **Most Active Shares**, then click Select.

   ➲ *A listing of most active shares on the New York Stock Exchange, NASDAQ, and American Stock Exhange appears.*
7. Scroll down to review the listing of most active shares, then click on the CPQ link for Compaq Computer Corp.

   ✓ *Notice that the stocks for each index are listed from most active to less active and can be trading up or down at the time of the report.*

   ➲ *A company profile for Compaq opens after you click its link.*
8. Scroll down the page to view the Quicktake company profile for Compaq. Notice the general upward trend for the company's stock over the past several years, the recent downturn, as well as today's change.
9. Also read the description of the company and the descriptions of the various tools Morningstar provides investors to analyze Compaq's performance.
10. At the News section of the Compaq profile, click on the Compaq to Acquire Digital for $9.6 Billion link.

    ➲ *Read about this acquisition, the largest in computer industry history.*

Morningstar.Net Monitor Page

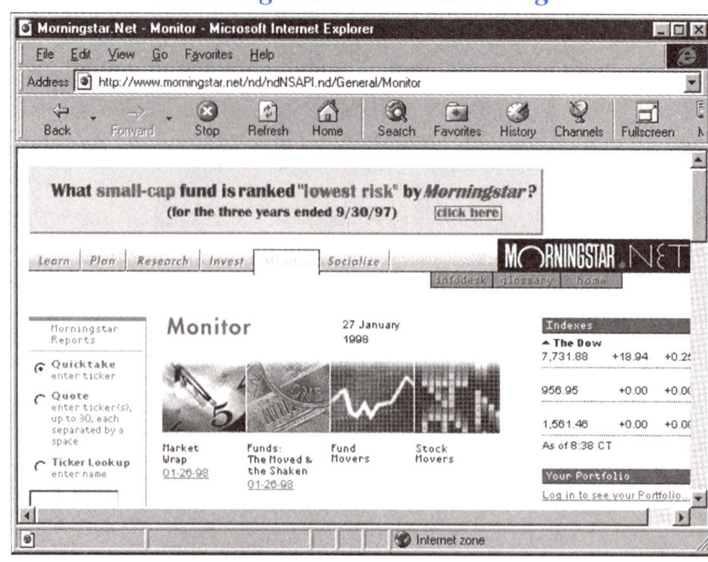

Most Active Shares Search Result

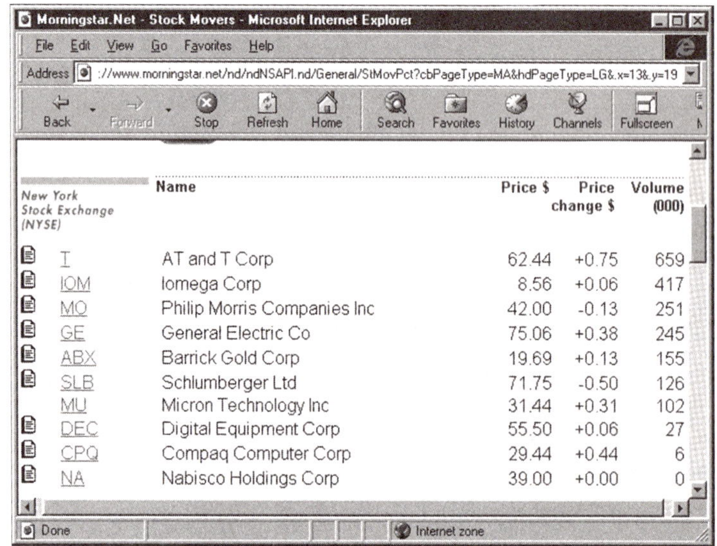

Company Profile for Compaq

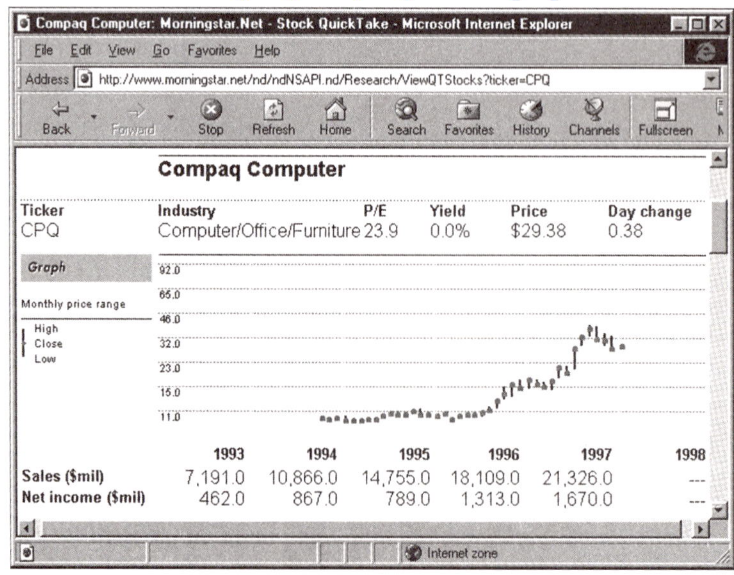

11. Return to the top of the Compaq acquisition news article page and click on the Research link.

   ➲ *The Morningstar.Net Research page opens.*

12. Scroll down the page and click on the link for Catherine Odelbo 01-16-98.

   ➲ *The Stock Analyst's Journal page for Catherine Odelbo opens.*

Morningstar.Net Research Page

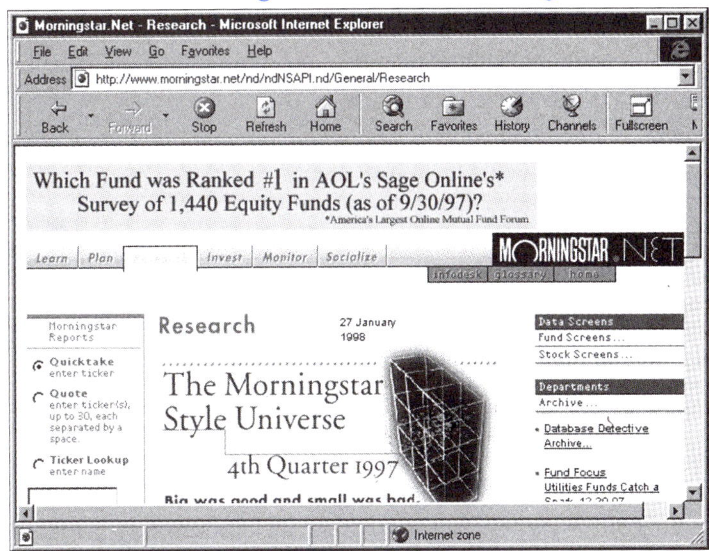

13. Read Catherine's analysis of why Nine West stock appears to be undervalued.

   ✓ *Note also her analysis of how stocks in the footwear industry in general typically perform.*

14. Click your browser's Back button to return to the Research page. Select **Ticker Lookup**, then type *Nike* in the text box underneath it and click GET IT.

   ➲ *The stock symbol NKE is displayed as the closest match for Nike.*

Stock Analyst's Journal Page

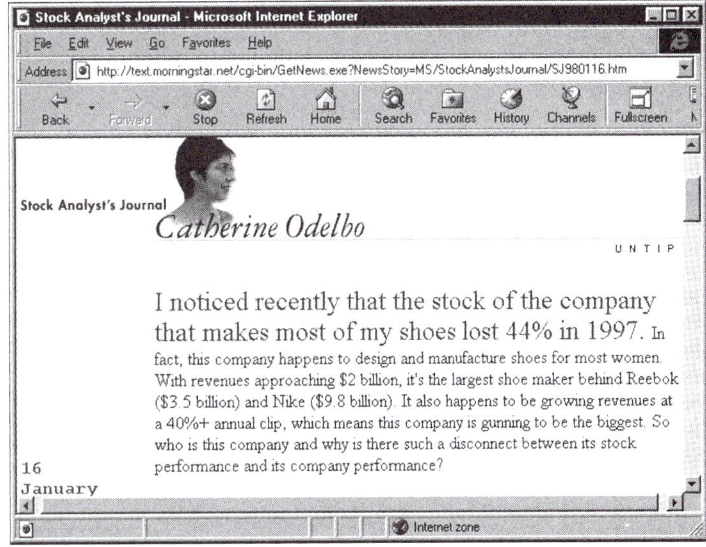

15. Click on the NKE link under Quicktake Report.

   ➲ *The Quicktake company report for Nike appears.*

   ✓ *Notice the graph showing the general trend for Nike stock over the past several years. Does this trend match the analyst's statements about the footwear industry?*

Company Report for Nike

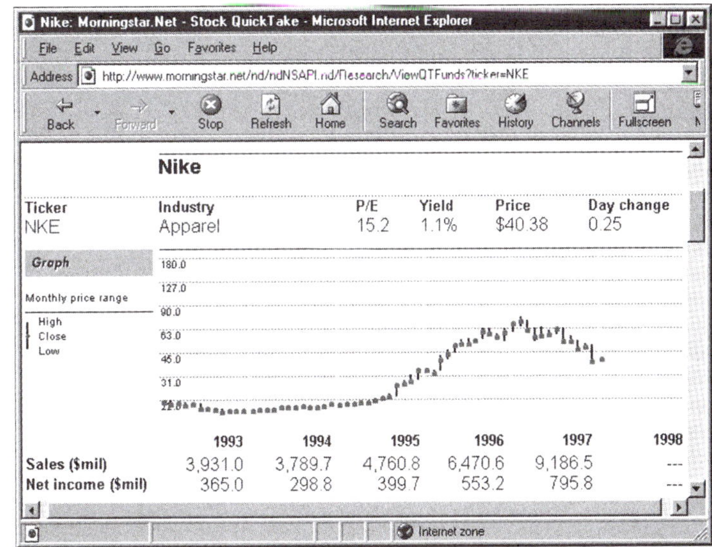

	1993	1994	1995	1996	1997	1998
Sales ($mil)	3,931.0	3,789.7	4,760.8	6,470.6	9,186.5	---
Net income ($mil)	365.0	298.8	399.7	553.2	795.8	---

16. Click the Research link at the top of the Nike company report. On the Morningstar.Net Research page, click the Fund Screens link.

   ➲ *The Fund Screens tool opens.*

17. Select **Hybrid Funds** from the fund category drop-down list.

18. Select **Total Return %: 3 Year Annualized** from the screening field drop-down list. Click VIEW RESULTS.

   ➲ *A list of top-performing funds screened for the criteria you selected appears.*

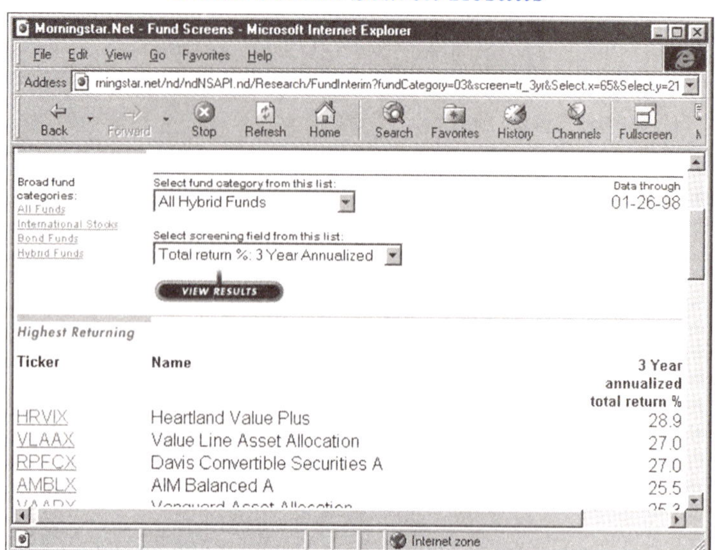

Fund Screen Search Results

19. On your browser's Address line, type the following URL and press Enter:

   http://www.bankrate.com/

   ➲ *The Bank Rate Monitor home page opens.*

20. Click the Today's Averages link.

   ➲ *A page showing the day's national interest rate averages for various types of loans and investments opens.*

21. Scroll down and review the various interest rates.

22. Click the Mortgages link at the left side of the page.

   ➲ *The Mortgage Watch page opens.*

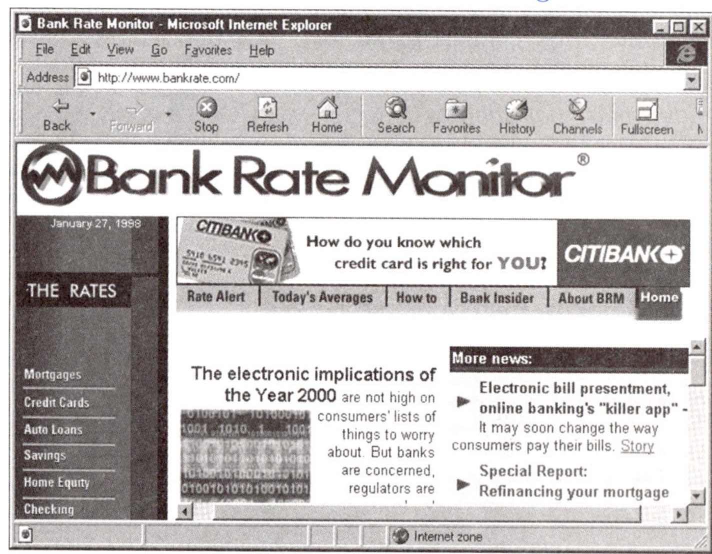

Bank Rate Monitor Home Page

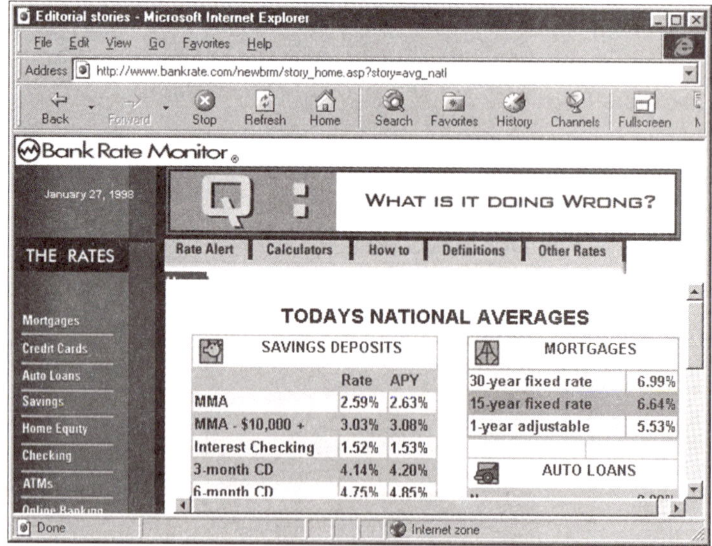

National Average Interest Rates

23. Scroll down and review the table showing high and low 30-year mortgage rates for 1997.
    ✓ *Notice the savings a 1-point decrease in the mortgage interest rate can provide.*
24. Click the Calculators link.
    ➲ *The Bank Rate Monitor calculator page opens.*
25. Enter the following information in the calculator text boxes:

    Loan Term (years): 30

    Annual Interest Rate (%): 7.09

    Loan Amount: 200000

    ✓ *Do not use a comma in the Loan Amount box.*

Mortgage Watch Page

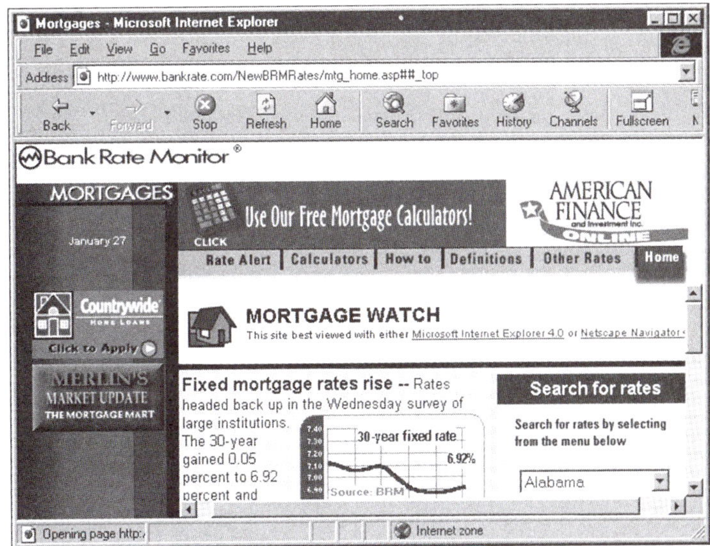

Mortgage Rate Calculator

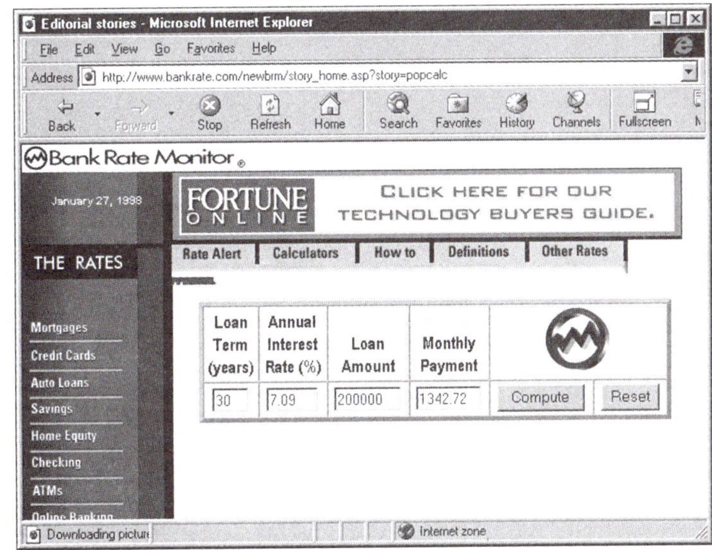

26. Click the Compute button.
    ➲ *The calculator computes the monthly mortgage payment.*

Credit Card Watch

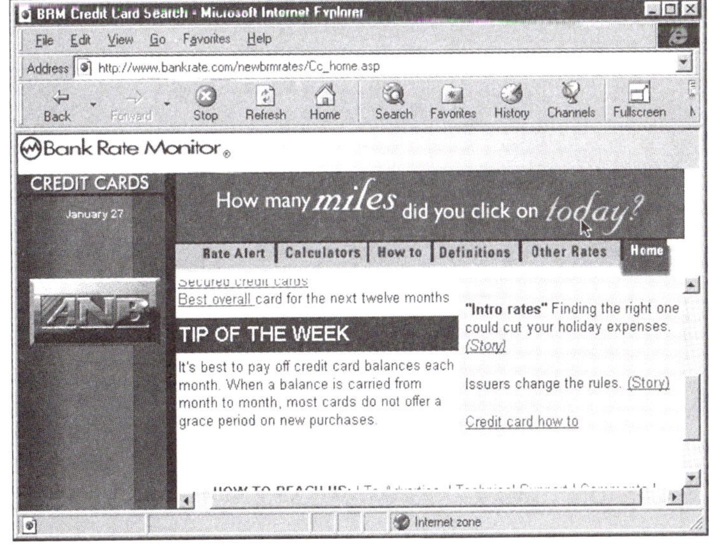

27. Click the Credit Cards link.
    ➲ *The Credit Card Watch page opens.*
28. Scroll down to read the Credit Cards Tip of the Week.

29. Click the Best overall link.

   ➲ *A table showing the best overall credit cards currently available opens.*

   ✓ *Notice the differences in the annual fees caused by the various interest rates.*

30. Continue on to the next exercise.

   OR

   Exit from the simulation.

Best Overall Credit Cards Available

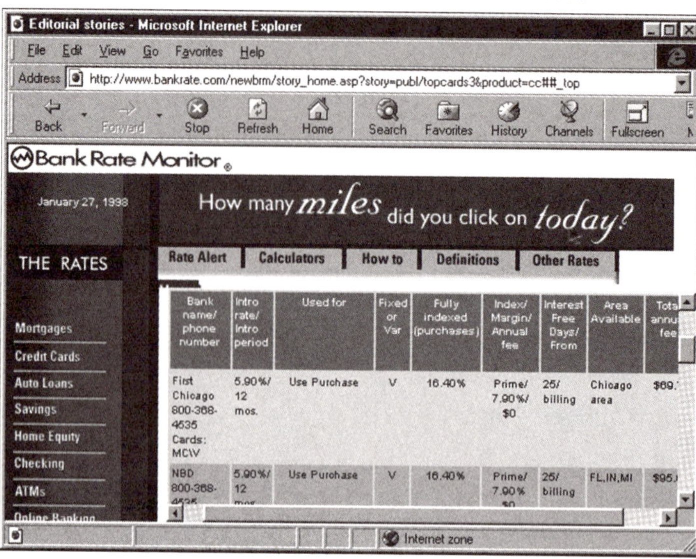

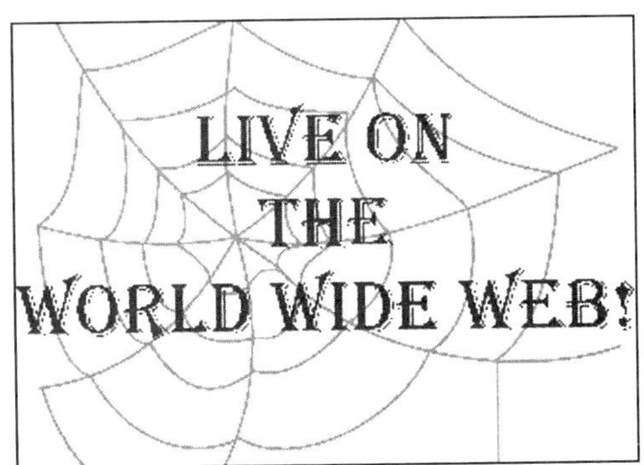

Morningstar.Net
http://www.morningstar.net

Bank Rate Monitor
http://www.bankrate.com/

Exercise 4

■ Find Business Capital with MoneyHunter

NOTES

Find Business Capital with MoneyHunter

- MoneyHunter is the Web site of the popular public television show the MoneyHunt. More than a million people tune into the MoneyHunt each week to see entrepreneurs present their business plans to a panel of financial experts, who either give the plans their approval or offer constructive criticism.
- The show is entertaining but has its serious side—in its first season, 13 of 26 guest entrepreneurs garnered $17 million in capital after presenting their business plans on the air.

MoneyHunter Home Page

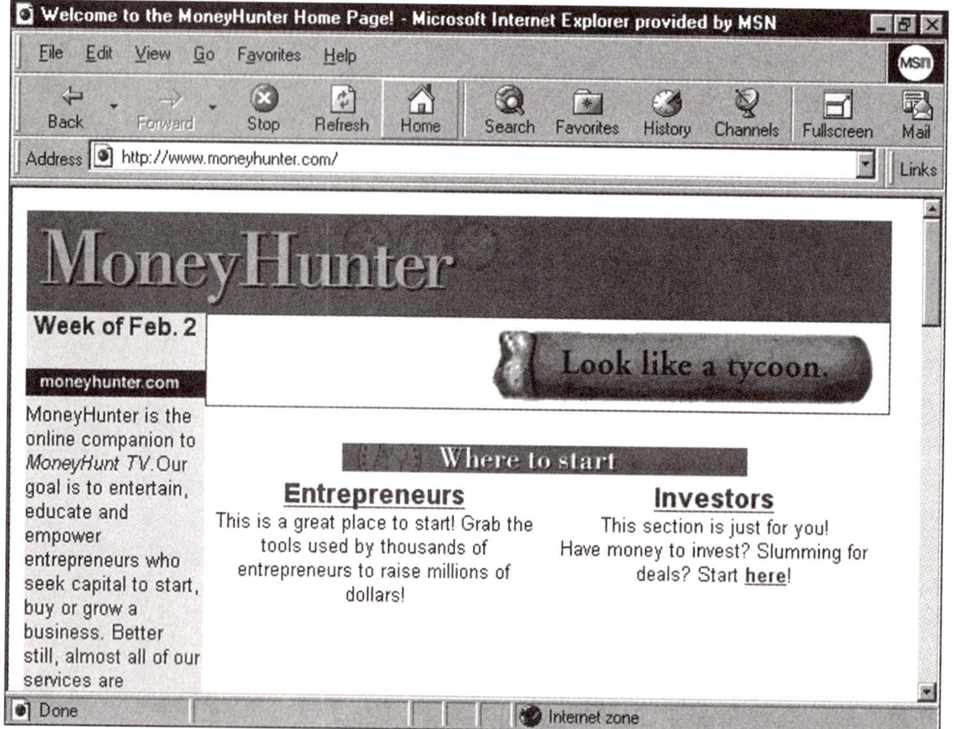

- The MoneyHunter Web site lets you tap into the expertise and exposure showcased on the TV show. If you're looking for investor dollars, click the Entrepreneur link and choose from a menu of outstanding resources.

Note

Click Business Plan Template to access a time-proven blueprint for writing a business plan that you can use to help win capital investment funds. A quarter of a million entrepreneurs have used the plan template to present their businesses to potential investors.

- Click the How to Hunt link to read the advice of a featured MoneyHunter columnist about the best ways to drum up capital.
- Click the Mentors link to see a list of business leaders and venture capital experts who offer their savvy advice free of charge.
- Use Golden Rolodex to search the MoneyHunter database of investors and fellow entrepreneurs. After filling out a Guestbook registration form, you can enter your venture capital search criteria and then click Search for Data. Investor and entrepreneur contacts are provided free of charge.

Note

MoneyHunter is also a great site for investors who are looking for hidden gems. Venture capitalists can search the Golden Rolodex, check out spotlighted companies, and take a peek at the Capital Calendar of upcoming venture capital events in their area.

Enter Criteria to Search the Golden Rolodex

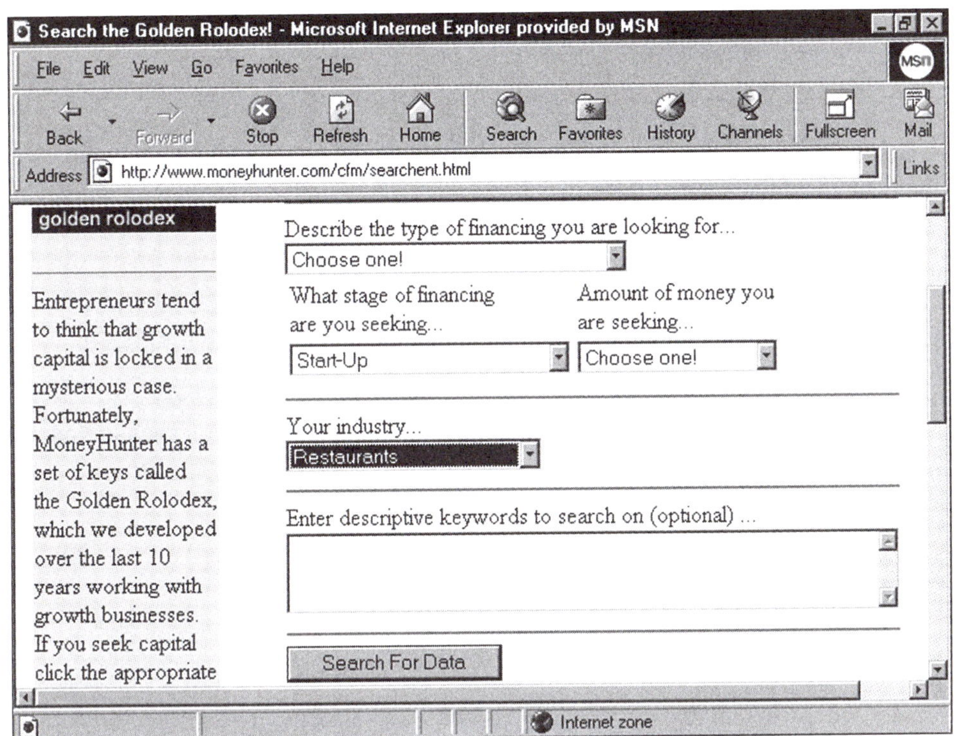

- Click the MoneyHunt TV Show link to find out information about past and upcoming TV shows. Here you can also click the Where Are They Now? link to learn about the success stories of entrepreneurs who have appeared as guests on the show.

Note

You can even click Online Audition to see if you have the right stuff to appear on the MoneyHunt TV show.

In this exercise, you will read the advice of a MoneyHunter columnist and a MoneyHunter mentor on how to find business venture capital. You will then read about a MoneyHunt Show and find out more about guest entrepreneurs who have appeared on the show. Finally, you will search the Golden Rolodex for potential investors.

Note: To ensure consistent results, this exercise uses simulated sites. The real URLs appear at the end of the exercise.

Web Search

Search for answers to the following questions using the Web sites you will visit in the Web simulation exercise.

1. From the How to Hunt column, what character does David Duchovny play in the movie *Beethoven?*

   ____

2. What is the name of the woman who was a recent MoneyHunter mentor?

   ____

3. In the Telltale Signs When Analyzing a Business Opportunity page, does the mentor say an entrepreneur should be "short-term greedy" or "long-term greedy"?

   ____

4. According to Thomas Shattan, what is the most important characteristic of a good management team?

   ____

5. In the Where Are They Now page, how much have the sales of Doctor Bronze Solar Potions increased as a result of being featured on the Money Hunt Show?

   ____

EXERCISE DIRECTIONS

1. Launch the Internet simulation. From the Main Menu, select Lesson 5, then select Exercise 4.
2. On the Address line, type the following and press Enter:

   http://www.moneyhunter.com

   ➲ *The MoneyHunter home page opens.*

MoneyHunter Home Page

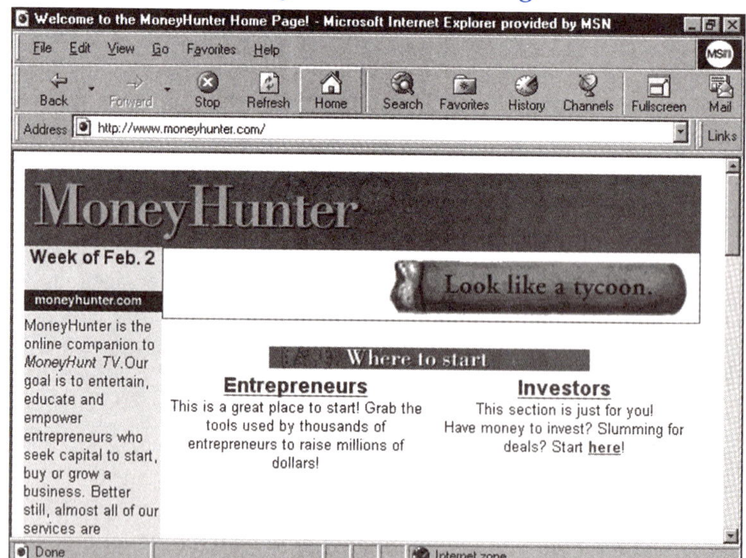

3. Click the Entrepreneurs link.
   ➲ *The MoneyHunter Entreprenur Resources page opens.*
4. Click the How to Hunt Column link. Read the article on this page.
   ✓ *Note the columnist's tips on how to persuade investors of a company's potential for success.*

MoneyHunter's Entrepreneur Resources

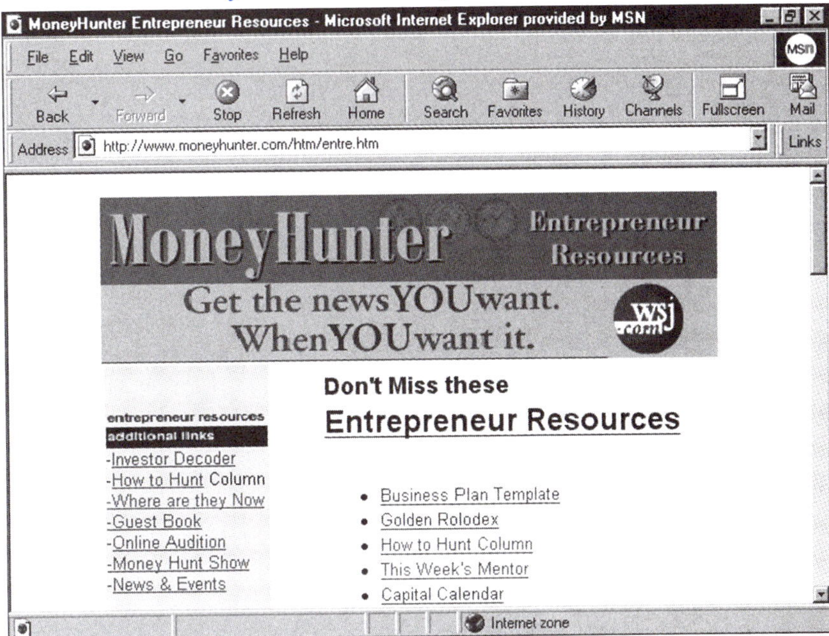

5. Click the Entrepreneurs link at the bottom of the page.
   ➲ *The Entrepreneur Resources page opens again.*
6. Click the This Week's Mentor link.
   ➲ *The MoneyHunter Mentors page opens.*

How to Hunt Column

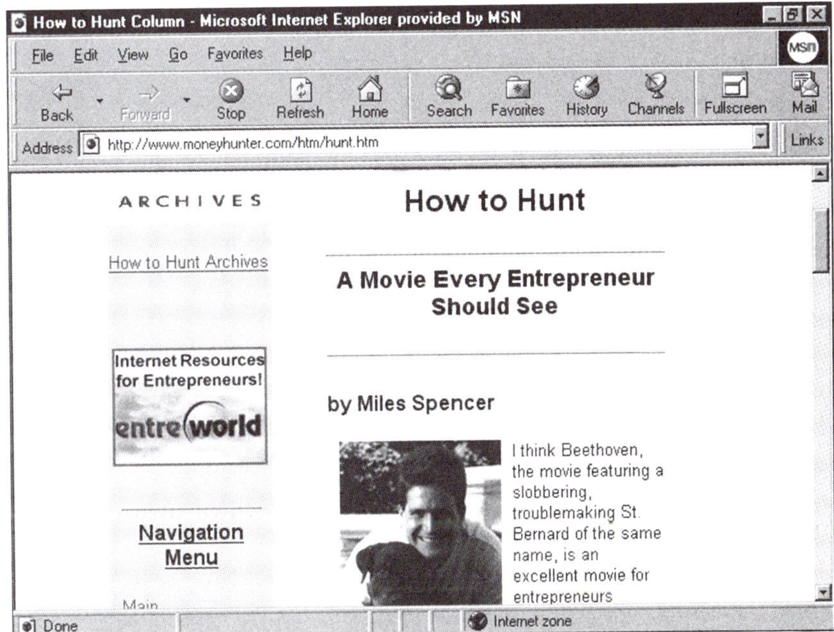

7. Scroll down and read about this month's featured mentor, Thomas Shattan.
8. Click the Telltale Signs link and then read this mentor's advice.

   ✓ *Note the mentor's advice about what to look for in analyzing a business investment opportunity.*

9. Click the Good Management link at the bottom of the page. Read the mentor's advice about what to look for in a good management team.
10. Click the Money Hunt Show link in the Navigation Menu at the top left of the page.

    ➲ *The Money Hunt Show page opens.*

MoneyHunter Featured Mentor

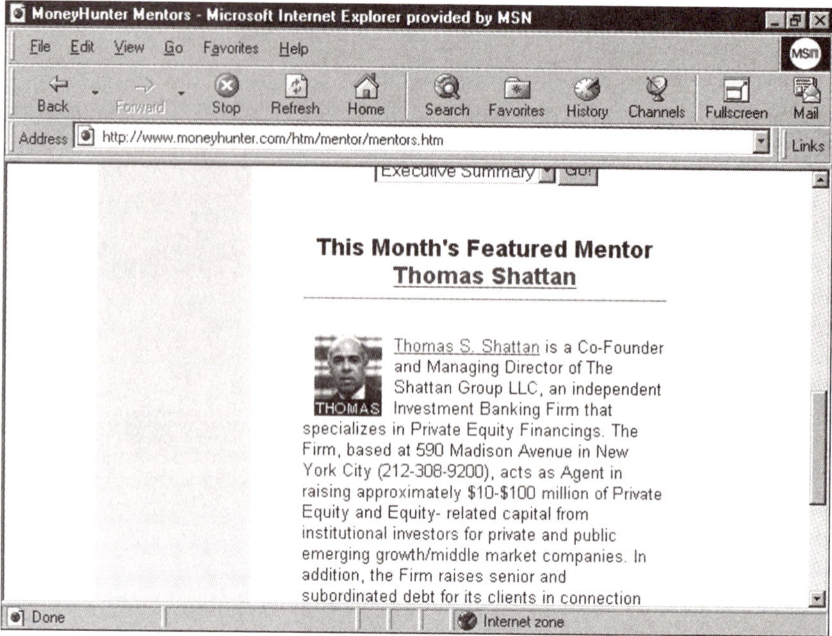

Mentor's Advice

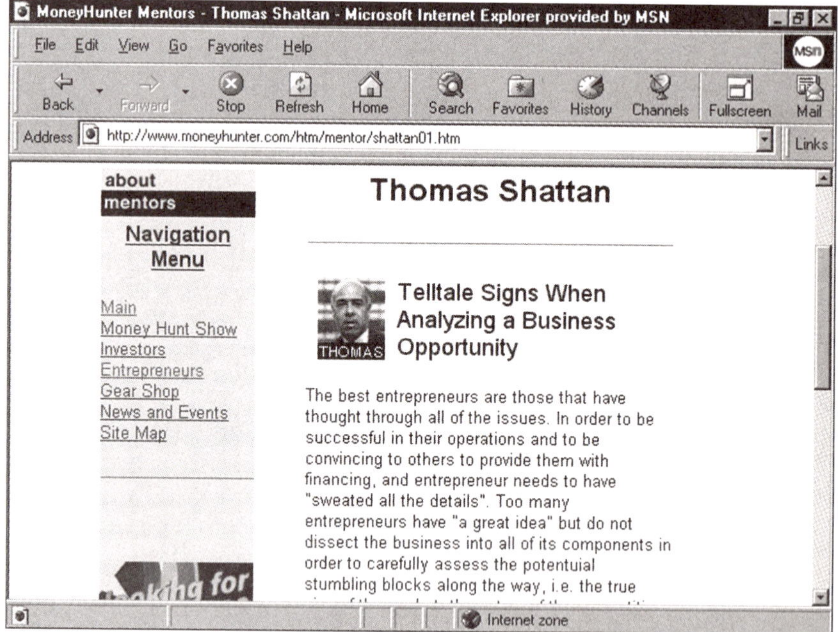

11. Click the This Season link at the left of the page.

➲ *The This Season page opens.*

12. Scroll down and click the Show 1007 link.

13. Read the description of Money Hunt show 1007.

❓ *How successful do you think these MoneyHunters will be in raising capital for their businesses?*

14. Use your browser's Back button to return to the This Season page, then scroll down and click Entrepreneurs on the Navigation Menu.

➲ *The Entrepreneur Resources page opens.*

This Season on Money Hunt

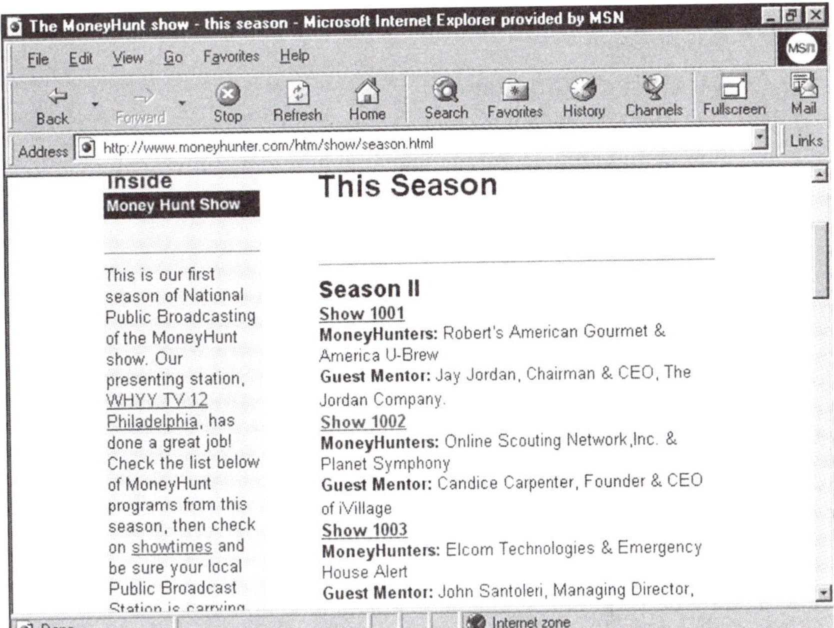

Description of Show 1007

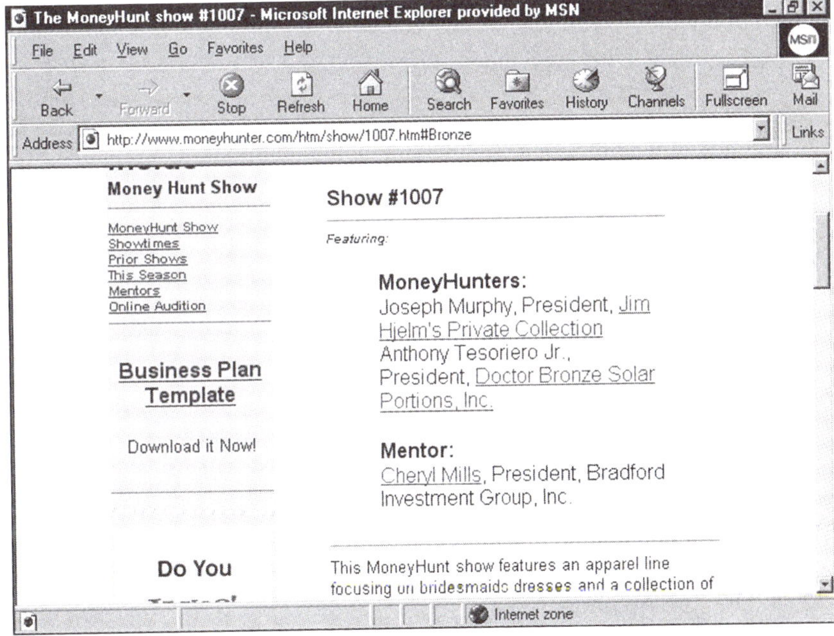

15. Click the Where are they Now link.

   ➲ *The Where Are They Now? page opens.*

16. Click the Anthony Tesoriero - Dr. Bronze Solar Potions link.

Where Are They Now Page

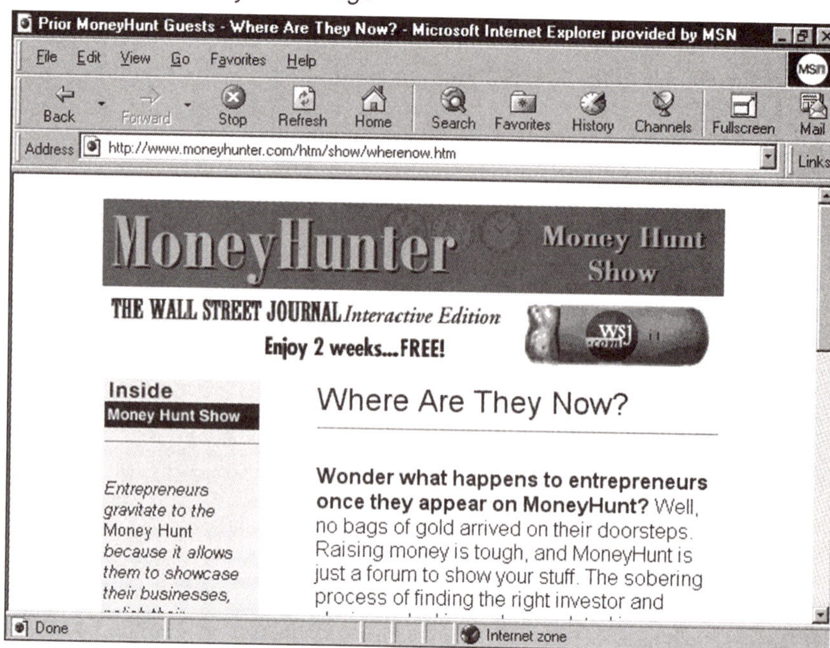

17. Read the page describing Dr. Bronze Solar Potions.

   ❓ *In what ways has appearing on the MoneyHunt TV show helped the company?*

18. Click your browser's Back button to return to the Where Are They Now? page.

19. Click the Doug Bush - Online Scouting Network link.

20. Read the description of Doug's quest for capital since appearing on Money Hunt.

   ❓ *How do you think Doug can improve his chances of gaining financial support for his business?*

21. Click the Entrepreneurs link at the bottom of the page.

   ➲ *The Entrepreneur Resources page opens.*

22. Click the Golden Rolodex link.

Dr. Bronze Solar Potions

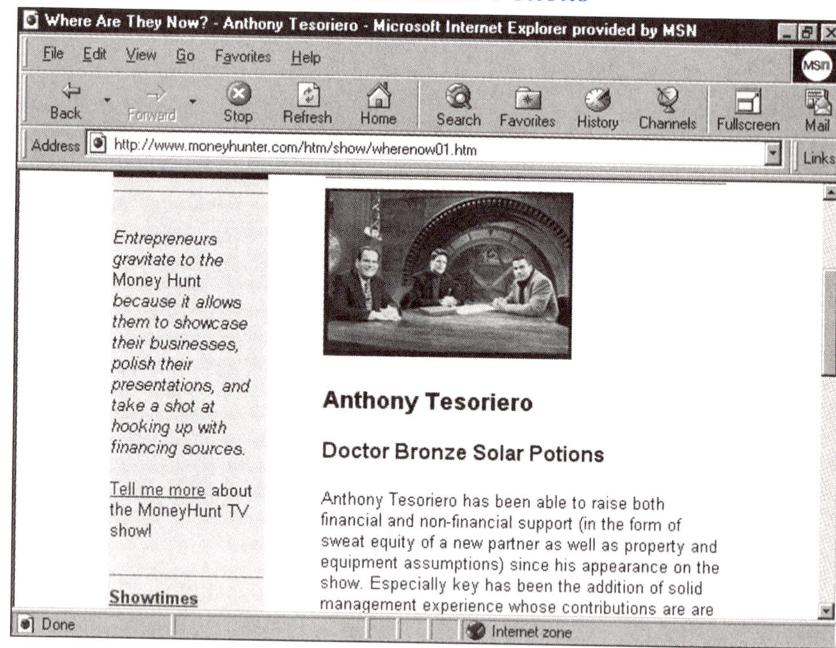

23. Click the entrepreneur link under Search the Golden Rolodex.
    ➲ *The Golden Rolodex search form opens.*
24. Select **Start-Up** from the What stage of financing are you seeking menu, then select **Restaurants** from the Your industry menu.
25. Click the Search For Data button.
    ➲ *MoneyHunter searches for suitable investor matches.*

Enter Search Criteria

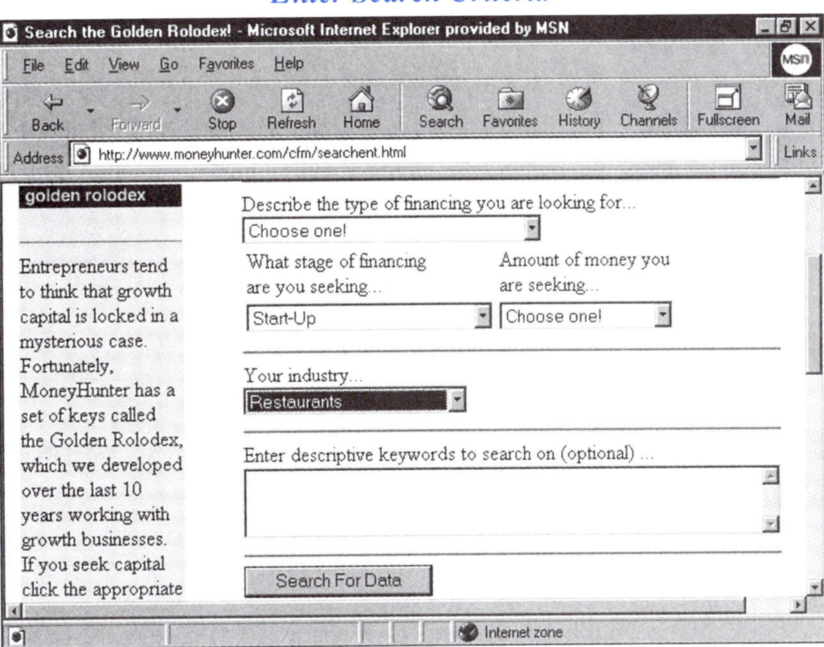

26. Read the search results information and notice the specialties of the matching venture capital firms.
27. Continue on to the next exercise.

    OR

    Exit from the simulation.

Matching Venture Capital Firms

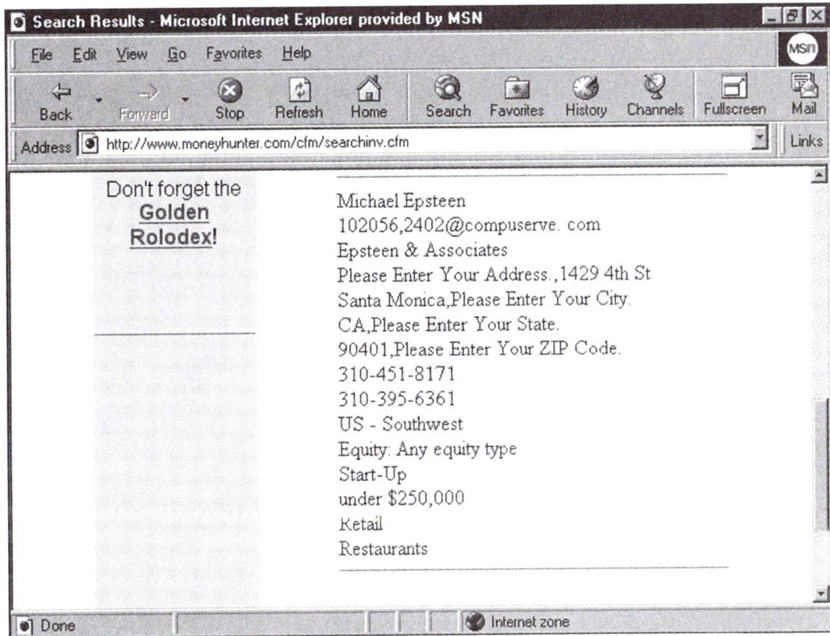

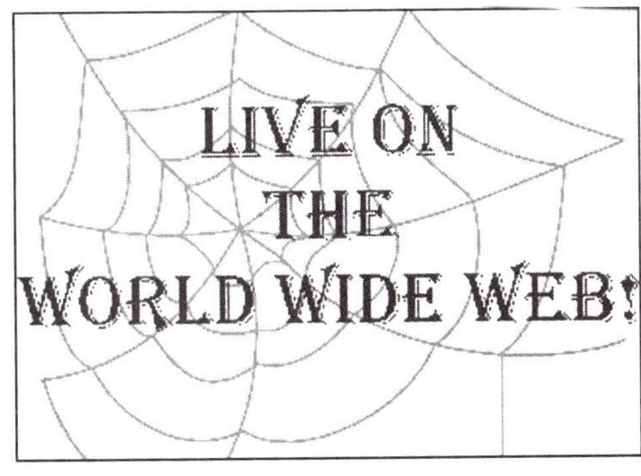

MoneyHunter Home Page

http://www.moneyhunter.com

Exercise 5

- Find Legal Information at the Legal Information Institute
- Consult OSHA Regulations at the OSHA Web Site
- Find Tax Information with IRS Digital Daily

NOTES

Find Legal Information at the Legal Information Institute

- Legal advice can be expensive, unless you find it on the Web. With the help of dozens of legal research Web sites, you can find the answers to your legal questions without consulting an attorney—or at least find the right attorney to consult. Use legal Web sites to consult the actual text of laws and regulations, review court rulings and case precedents, and contact legal advisors.
- Check the Legal Information Institute (LII) Web site for a comprehensive collection of law resources. The Institute is a service of the Cornell University Law School and contains a wide variety of services for finding the legal information you need.

Legal Information Institute Home Page

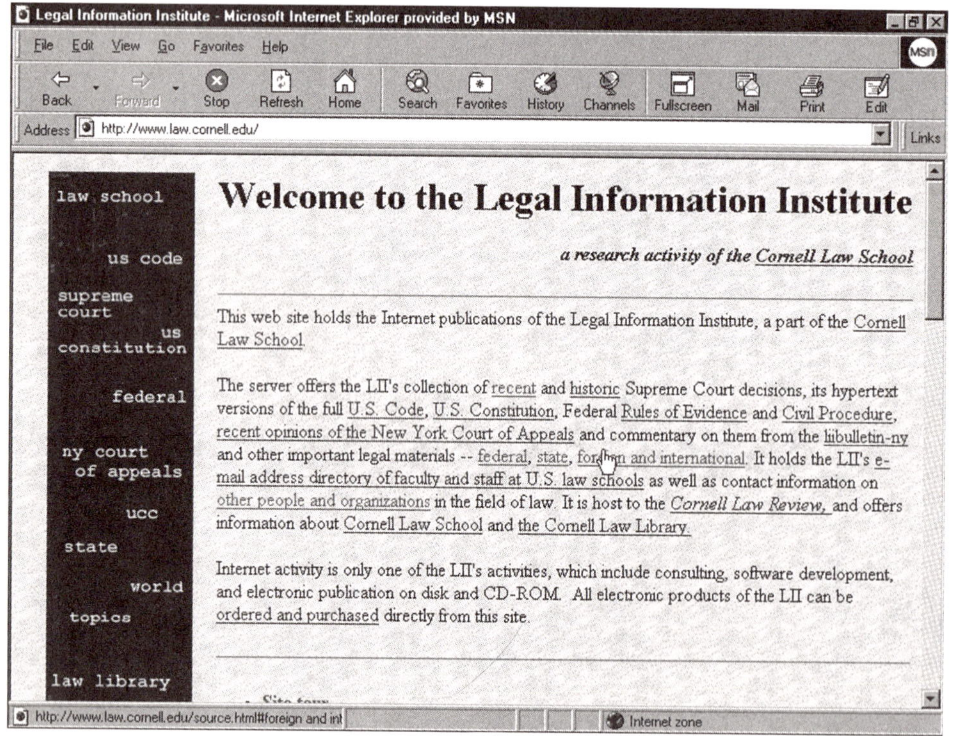

Note

The State link includes legal documents and information from all 50 states. The Federal and World links telescope into topic links in the LII database.

- For example, you can click the LII list of topic summary links to search primary law and regulation source material either via an alphabetical listing of topics or a searchable index.
- Click the Supreme Court link to search summaries of recent and historic decisions. Click the Constitution link to see a hyperlinked version of the complete U.S. Constitution.
- Click the Items of Special Current Interest to track newsworthy legal cases. Click one of the links under the New or Newsworthy heading to see a listing of current cases with links to source information. New or Newsworthy links also include special interest pages such as LII's Amistad page. These special pages can help you trace the development of significant cases and particular areas of the law. The pages contain information describing overriding legal issues and provide links to relevant source documents.

LII's Amistad Page

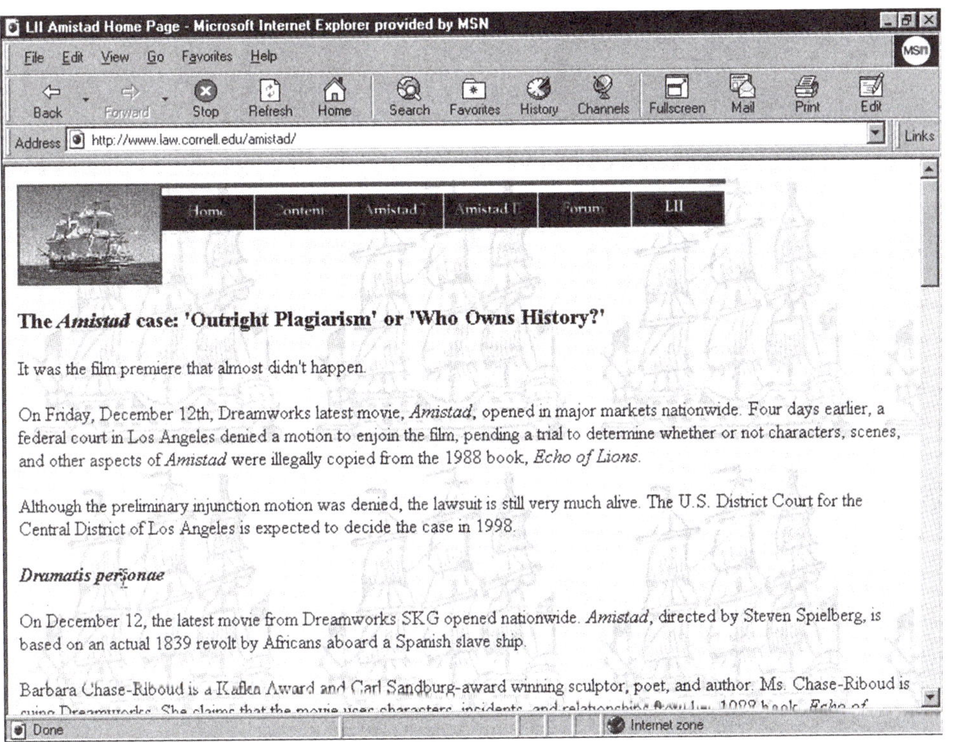

The *Amistad* case: 'Outright Plagiarism' or 'Who Owns History?'

It was the film premiere that almost didn't happen.

On Friday, December 12th, Dreamworks latest movie, *Amistad*, opened in major markets nationwide. Four days earlier, a federal court in Los Angeles denied a motion to enjoin the film, pending a trial to determine whether or not characters, scenes, and other aspects of *Amistad* were illegally copied from the 1988 book, *Echo of Lions*.

Although the preliminary injunction motion was denied, the lawsuit is still very much alive. The U.S. District Court for the Central District of Los Angeles is expected to decide the case in 1998.

Dramatis personae

On December 12, the latest movie from Dreamworks SKG opened nationwide. *Amistad*, directed by Steven Spielberg, is based on an actual 1839 revolt by Africans aboard a Spanish slave ship.

Barbara Chase-Riboud is a Kafka Award and Carl Sandburg-award winning sculptor, poet, and author. Ms. Chase-Riboud is

Consult OSHA Regulations at the OSHA Web Site

- Managers, small business owners, and human resources staff often need to consult the latest updates to OSHA (Occupational Safety and Health Administration) regulations to help determine what decision to make regarding personnel and work safety issues.
- The OSHA Web site is the definitive online source for finding the information you need when you have a question about OSHA programs, regulations, and compliance.

OSHA Web Site Home Page

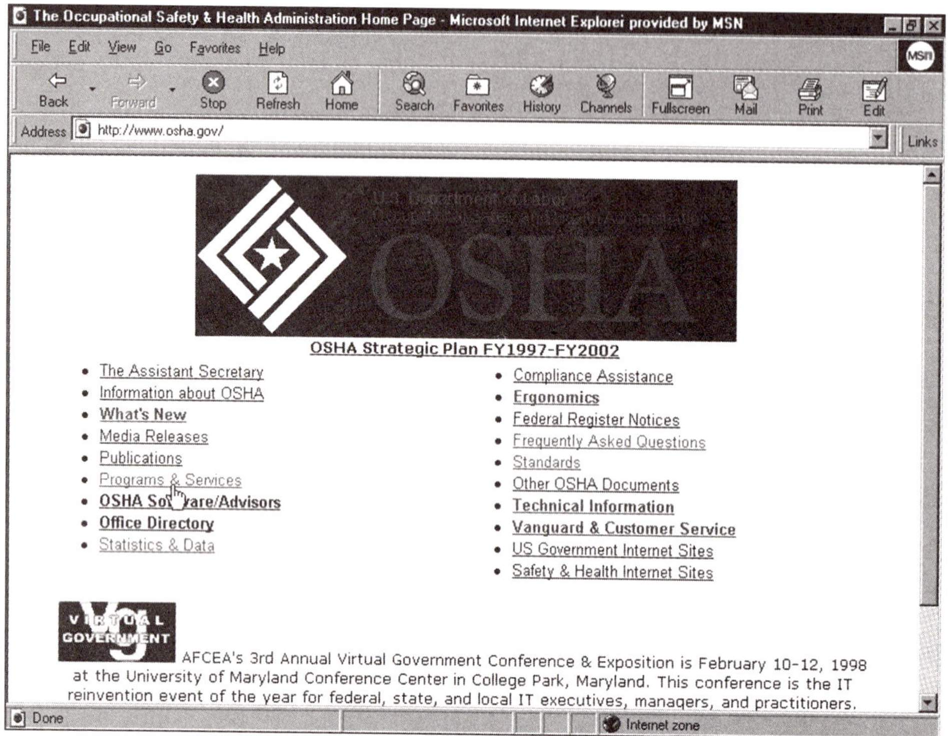

- Check the Frequently Asked Questions link for concise information about the most common OSHA questions you may have.
- Click the Compliance Assistance link to learn what regulations are of most common concern for your industry and size of business. You can use the Most Frequently Violated Standards tool to search by number of employees, federal or state jurisdiciton, and Standard Industrial Classification code (SIC).
- From the OSHA home page, the Ergonomics link takes you to a page describing the science of ergonomics and concerns about repetitive stress injuries (RSIs). Links at the Ergonomics page display statistical information about RSIs and resources for preventing this growing workplace health hazard.
- You can also use the OSHA site to check for updates on Federal Register Notices and Standards as well as information about OSHA programs and services.

Note

You can also find which SIC code has the most violations for a federal or state OSHA standard. Click the Industry Profile for an OSHA Standard link.

Find Tax Information with IRS Digital Daily

- Check the IRS Digital Daily Web site if you prepare your own taxes, prepare returns for your business, or if you need to keep informed about the latest tax legislation updates. You can find tax forms online and even file your return electronically via this official IRS site.

IRS Digital Daily Home Page

- The Digital Daily provides advice for tax professionals that even amateurs who like to file their own returns can use.
- Click the Tax Info for Business link to see a complete directory of links to common business tax topics and questions. One of the most useful services at the Digital Daily site is the Tax Trails for Business troubleshooting service.
- The Tax Trails for Business link presents a list of frequently asked business tax questions. Click a question or topic link and then answer a series of questions that leads you to the correct tax strategy for your business.

Note

Click the Tax Stats link to access statistical reports compiled from IRS taxpayer information. Reports such as Data by Size of Income can provide useful demographics data for marketers.

Tax Trails Troubleshooting Service

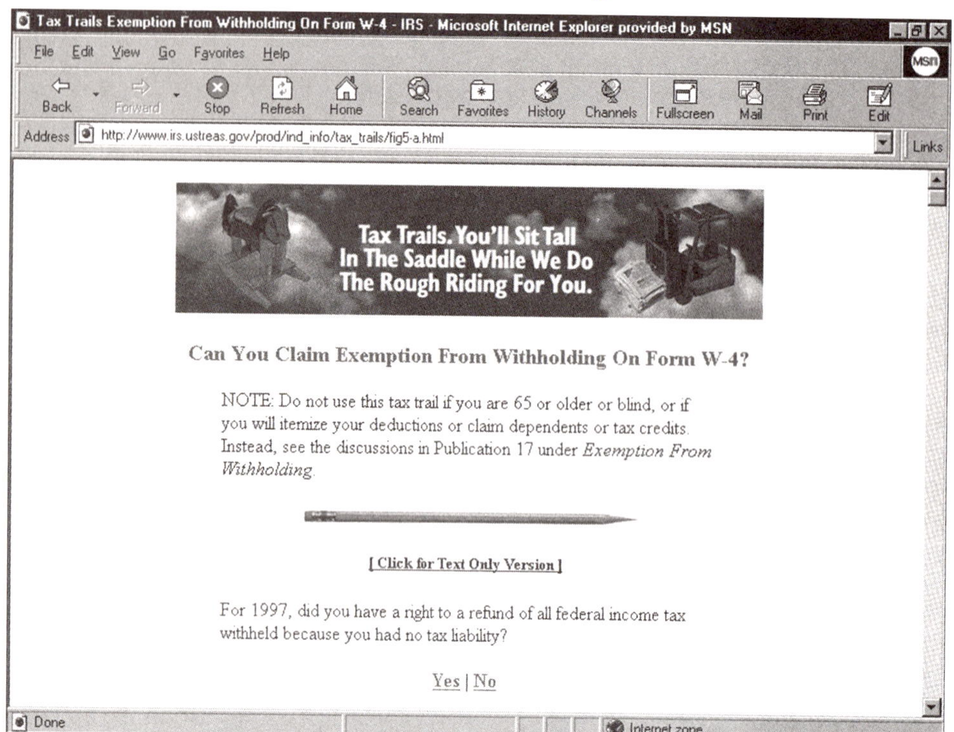

Note

Click the Tax Info for You link and then click Tax Trails to answer your personal tax questions with this interactive troubleshooting service.

- Often, a major last-minute tax preparation snag is not being able to track down the right form or schedule. Now you can click on the Forms and Publications link at The Digital Daily to browse more than twenty IRS publications online. You can then click the Publications or Forms and Instructions link to download the files you want. Use search tools to find the file you need and even locate forms from previous years.
- If you have a problem in your dealings with the IRS, click the Tax Info For You link and then click on the Taxpayer Advocate link. Use this service to find out your rights as a taxpayer or resolve a dispute with an auditor.

In this exercise, you will use the Legal Information Institute Web site to find information on a current legal case and research a legal topic. You will then use the OSHA Web site to further research the regulatory aspects of repetitive stress injuries. Finally, you will use the IRS Digital Daily Web site to find the answer to a common business tax question.

Note: To ensure consistent results, this exercise uses simulated sites. The real URLs appear at the end of the exercise.

Web Search

Search for answers to the following questions using the Web sites you will visit in the Web simulation exercise.

1. According to the second *Amistad* case, what happened on December 8, 1997?

   ____

2. When was the first Amistad case argued before the Supreme Court?

   ____

3. What lawyer and former U.S. president argued before the court that the Africans on the Amistad should be given their freedom?

   ____

4. What is the main statute protecting the health and safety of workers in the workplace?

   ____

5. Who wrote the compliance letter describing the proper recording of occupational strains and sprains?

   ____

EXERCISE DIRECTIONS

1. Launch the Internet simulation. From the Main Menu, select Lesson 5, then select Exercise 5.
2. On the Address line, type the following and press Enter:

   http://www.law.cornell.edu/

   ➲ *The Legal Information Institute home page opens.*

Legal Information Institute Home Page

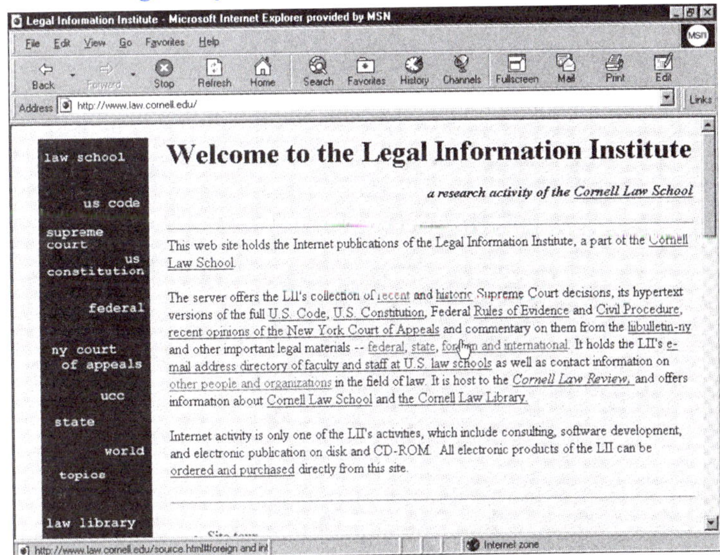

3. Scroll down the page and read about the services offered at the Legal Information Institute.
4. Click The LII's Amistad Site link under the New or Newsworthy heading.

   ➲ *The LII's page on the Amistad copyright infringement case opens.*
5. Scroll down and read about the case between the author of *Echo of Lions* and Dreamworks SKG, producers of the movie *Amistad.*

LII's Amistad Page

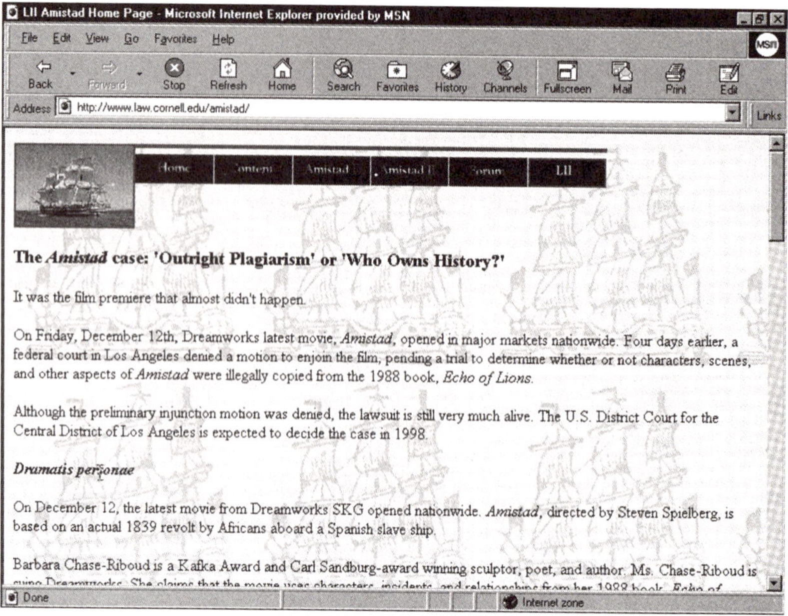

6. Click The second *Amistad* case link.

   ➲ *A description of the Amistad copyright infringement case opens.*
7. Scroll down and read the description of the case.
8. Click your browser's Back button to return to the Amistad page.

The Second Amistad Case

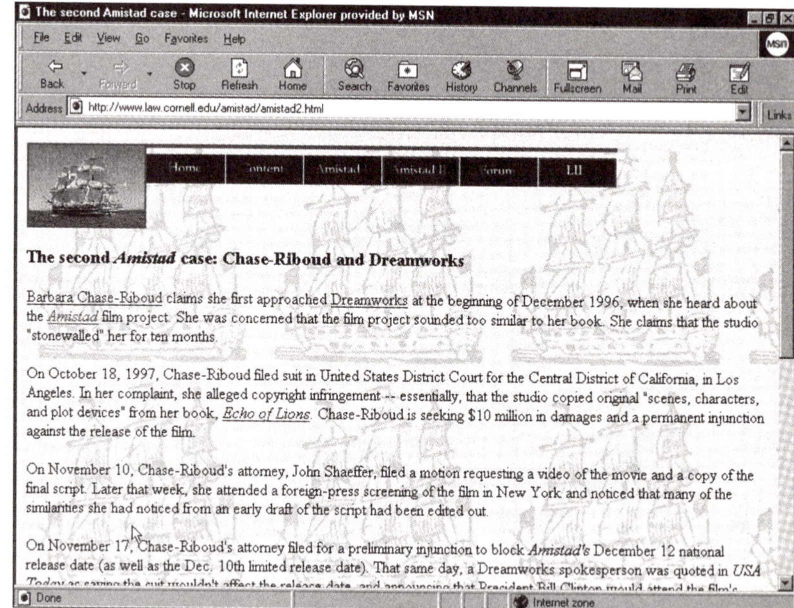

9. Scroll down the Amistad page and click the Copyright law link under the Legal issues – Amistad II heading.

   ➲ *A general description of the U.S. copyright law opens.*

10. Scroll down and read the description of the copyright law.

    ❓ *Why do you think the book author feels her copyright was violated?*

11. Click your browser's Back button to return to the Amistad page.

Description of U.S. Copyright Law

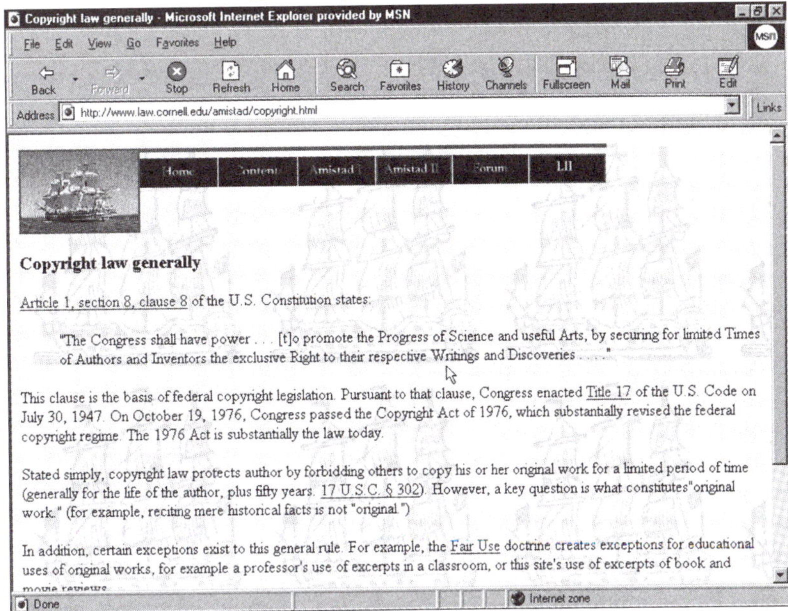

12. Click the Civil procedure: What is a preliminary injunction? Link under Legal issues – Amistad II heading.

    ➲ *A general description of preliminary injunctions opens.*

13. Scroll down and read the description.

    ❓ *Why do you think the book author asked for a preliminary injunction?*

14. Click the LII link at the top of the page.

Description of Preliminary Injunctions

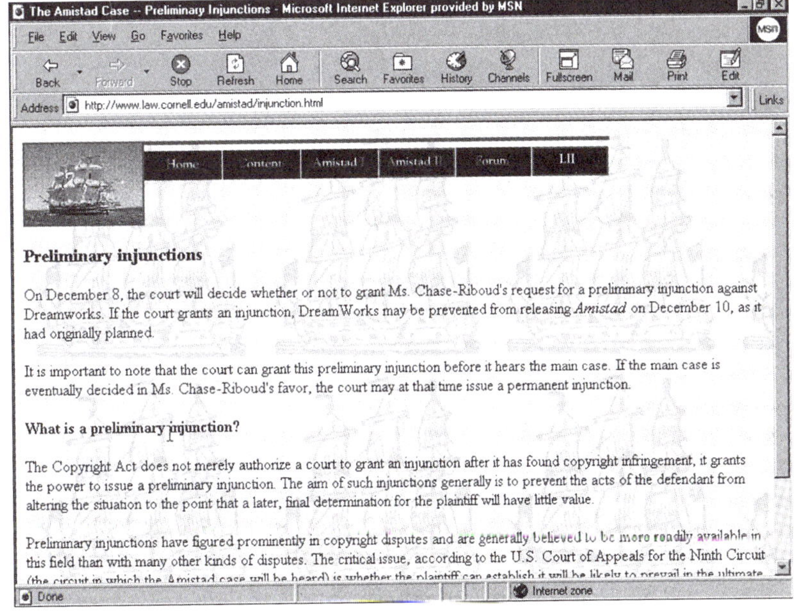

15. Scroll down and type *repetitive stress injury* in the Search text box. Click Search.

    ➲ *LII searches for cases relevant to the topic you entered. Nine documents match your search criteria.*

Enter Legal Search Criteria

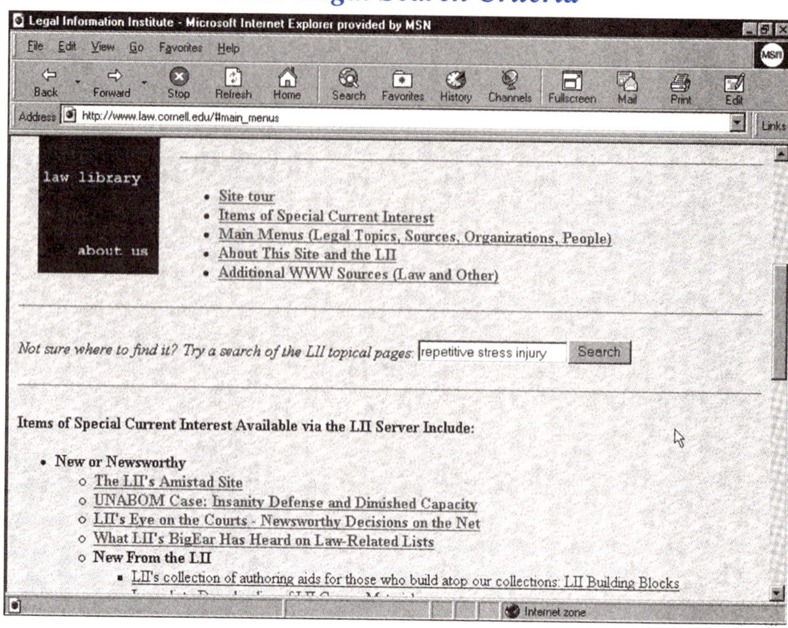

16. Scroll down to read descriptions of the matching documents, then click the U.S. Workplace Safety and Health Law link.

Results of Legal Document Search

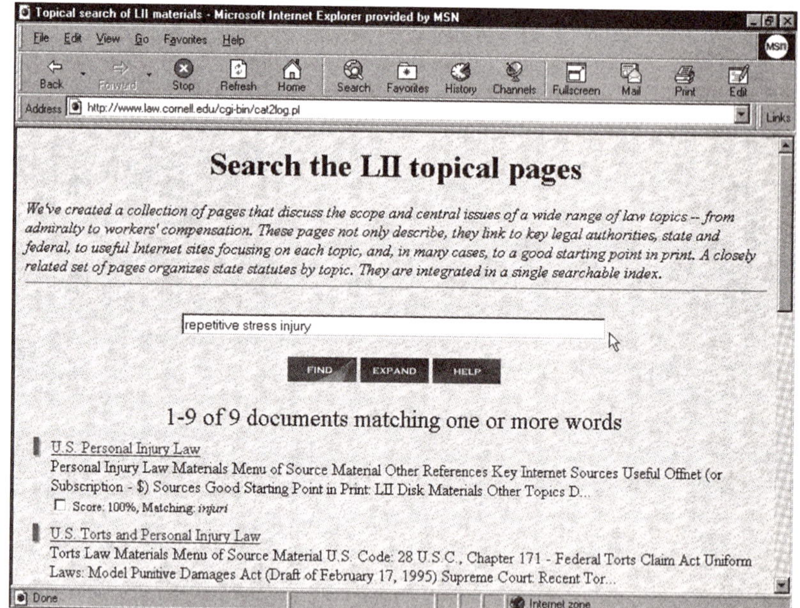

17. Read the Overview description of workplace safety and health law, then click the U.S. Occupational Safety and Health Administration link under the key Internet sources heading.

➲ *The link takes you to the federal government's OSHA Web site.*

18. Click the Ergonomics link.

➲ *The OSHA Ergonomics page opens.*

OSHA Home Page

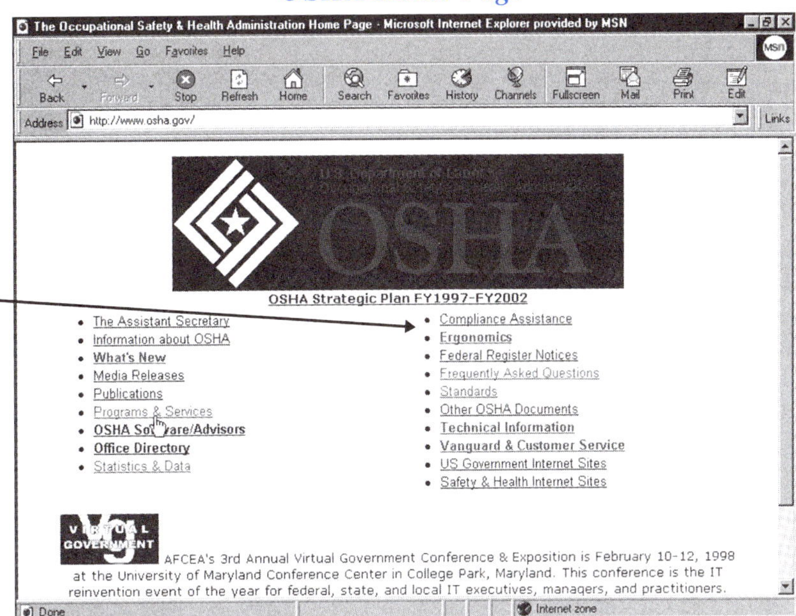

OSHA Ergonomics Page

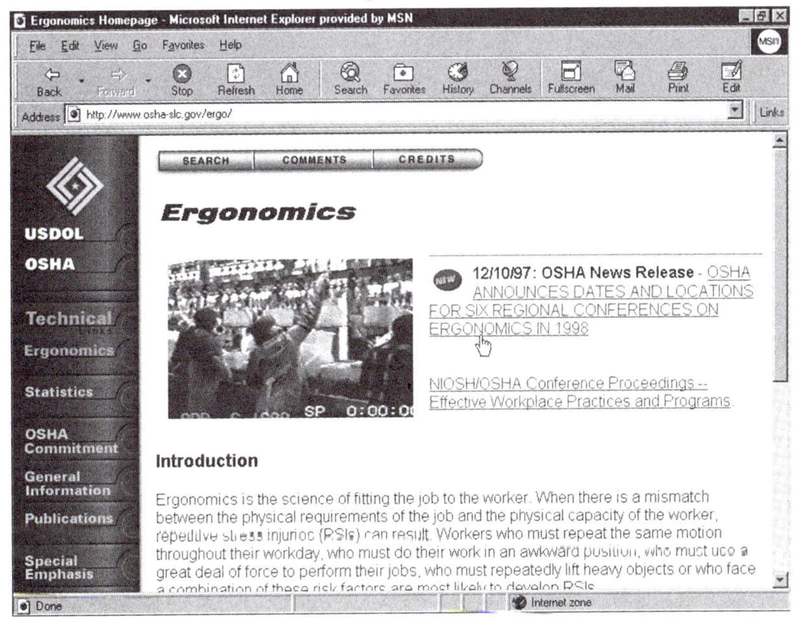

19. Scroll down and read the description of ergonomics, the science of fitting the job to the worker. Also read about repetitive stress injuries, the result of poor ergonomics.

20. Click the Statistics link on the left side of the page.

21. Click the Number of Occupational Illnesses (line chart) link.

   ➲ *A chart showing the rate of occupational illnesses opens. Why do you think repetitive stress injuries have been on the rise?*

22. Click the OSHA link to return to the OSHA home page.
23. Click the Standards link.

Chart Showing Rise in Repetitive Stress Injuries

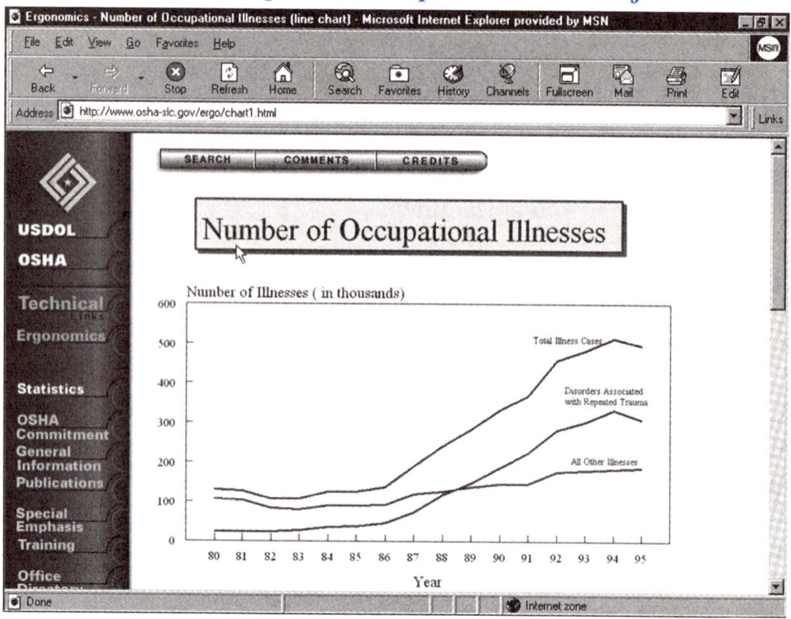

24. Click the Standard Interpretations and Compliance Letters link.
25. Enter the word *Strain* in the search text box, then click Search.

   ➲ *The search engine searches the OSHA database of interpretation and compliance letters for a match. 23 documents match your search keyword.*

26. Click the link for the second document listed in the search results. Read the letter describing the proper recording of occupational strains and sprains.

Standard and Compliance Search Results

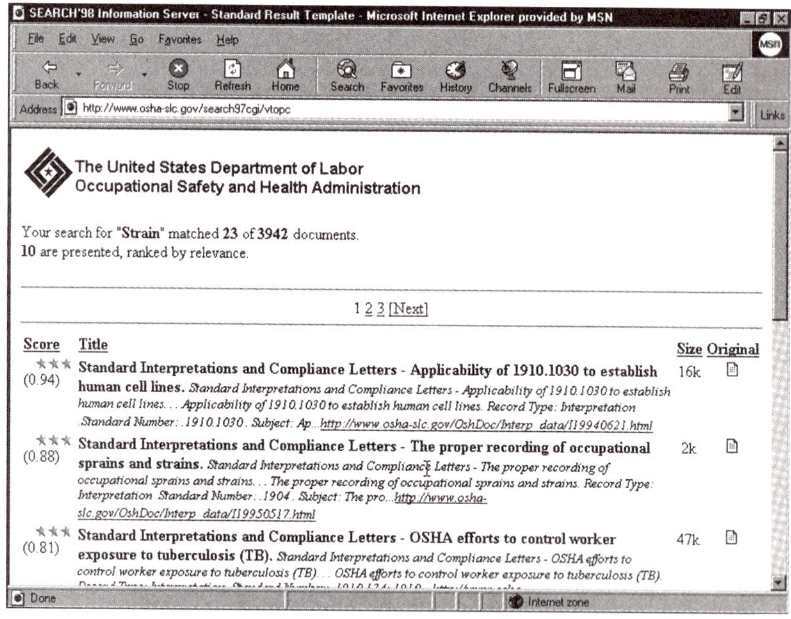

27. On the Address line of your browser, type the following URL and press Enter:

    http://www.irs.ustreas.gov/prod/cover.html

    ➲ *The IRS Digital Daily home page opens.*

28. Scroll to the bottom of the page and click the Tax Info For Business link.

    ➲ *The IRS Tax Info for Business page opens.*

IRS Digital Daily Home Page

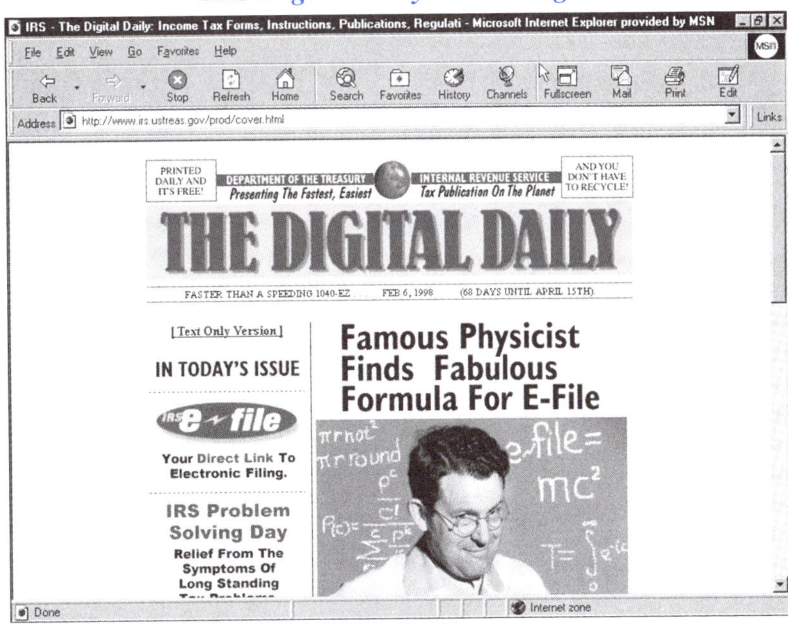

29. Scroll down and read the descriptions of services the IRS offers businesses. Click the Tax Trails for Business link.

30. Click the Can You Deduct Business Use Of The Home Expenses? link.

    ➲ *The Tax Trail for this question opens.*

31. Click Yes in answer to the first Tax Trail question: Is part of your home used in connection with a trade or business?

32. Click Yes in answer to the next Tax Trail question: Are you an employee?

33. Click Yes in answer to the next Tax Trail question: Do you work at home for the convenience of your employer?

34. Click No in answer to the next Tax Trail question: Do you rent part of your home used for business to your employer?

35. Click Yes in answer to the next Tax Trail question: Is the use regular and exclusive?

IRS Tax Info for Business

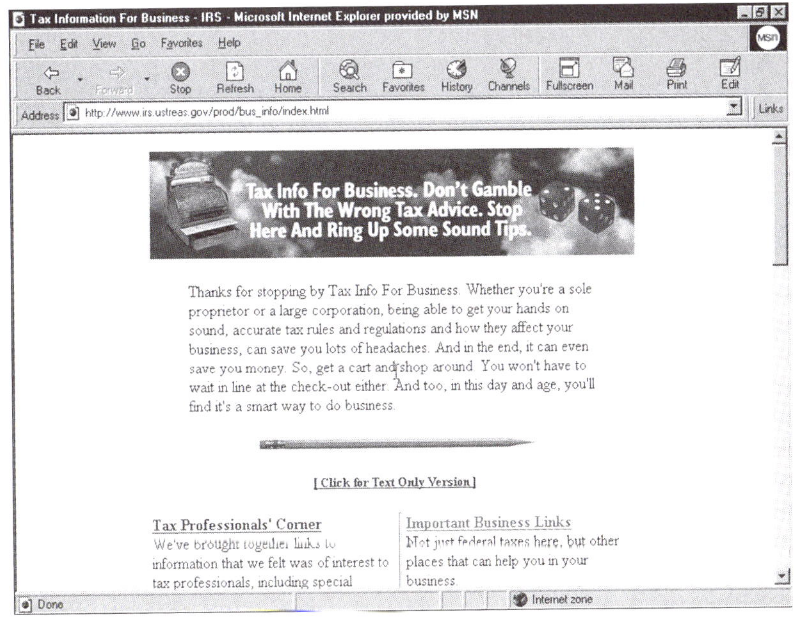

36. Click Yes in answer to the next Tax Trail question: Is it your principal place of business?

    ➲ *The Tax Trail states that in this case the deduction for business use of the home is allowed.*

37. Continue on to the next exercise.

    OR

    Exit from the simulation.

Tax Trail Recommendation

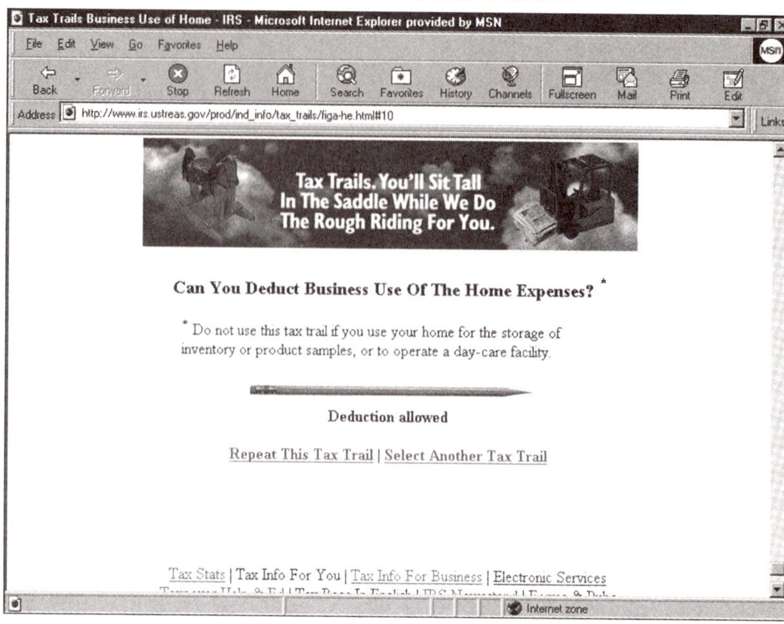

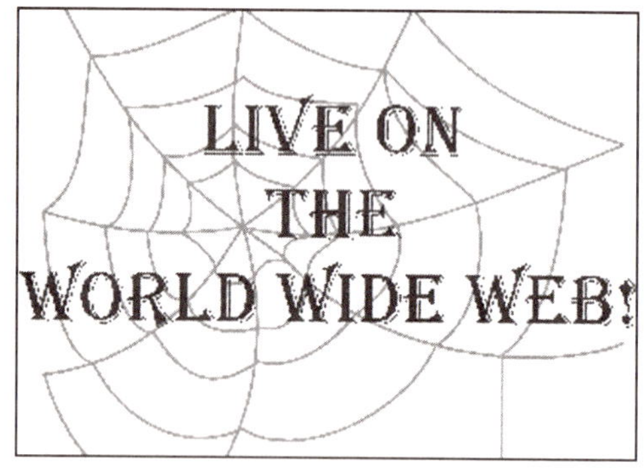

Legal Information Institute
http://www.law.cornell.edu/

OSHA Home Page
http://www.osha.gov/

IRS Digital Daily Home Page
http://www.irs.ustreas.gov/prod/cover.html

Lesson 6: Operations

Exercise 1

- Search for Commercial Real Estate with NetProperties
- Search for Residential Real Estate with HomeScout
- Make Relocation Decisions with HomeBuyer's Fair

Exercise 2

- Hire Employees or Find a Job with America's Job Bank

Exercise 3

- Find Business Resources at the Small Business Administration
- Manage a Small Business with Edge Online Business Tools

Exercise 4

- Research Computer Purchases with CNET
- Purchase a Computer Online
- Troubleshoot Computer Problems with The Tech Support Guy

Exercise 5

- Send and Track Packages with the United States Postal Service
- Cut Your Phone Bill with TRAC

Exercise 6

- Master Common Tasks with Learn2
- Look up Words with Merriam-Webster Online
- Find Historical Documents at the National Archives
- Find the Correct Time for Any City in the World
- Use Financial Calculators

Exercise 7

- Plan Travel with Microsoft Expedia
- Book Travel with Expedia's Travel Agent

Exercise 8

- Find a Restaurant with Zagat Survey
- Get Directions with MapQuest
- Check the Travel Forecast with Intellicast

Exercise 1

- Search for Commercial Real Estate with NetProperties
- Search for Residential Real Estate with HomeScout
- Make Relocation Decisions with HomeBuyer's Fair

NOTES

Search for Commercial Real Estate with NetProperties

- There are literally hundreds of outstanding local real estate Web sites that can help you find commercial or residential property for sale or lease. NetProperties is one of the top nationwide real estate sites.
- The NetProperties Web site offers links to what are essentially two separate sites: HomeNet for residential real estate and CenterNet for commercial real estate.
- From the NetProperties home page, click on CenterNet to use its searchable database of commercial properties available for sale or lease nationwide. At the CenterNet home page, click on the Property Database link to start using the search engine. Click one of the two globe icons to select properties for lease or for sale.

Note

Other resources available at the CenterNet site include links to news, real estate companies, associated products and services, trade journals, and associations. You can also list your company at CenterNet.

NetProperties Home Page

- You can enter a number of search criteria at the Properties for Sale and Properties for Lease pages, including property type, year built range, minimum and maximum prices, minimum and maximum square feet, and location. You can then click on property listings from the search results page.
- From the NetProperties home page, click on HomeNet to search residential listings nationwide. At the HomeNet home page, click on the U.S. Real Estate Directory link to start your search, then click on a state to narrow the search location.
- Also available on the HomeNet site are links to various services such as census data, a mortgage calculator, and lenders.

Note

Click the Real Estate Company Directory to see a listing of links by county to real estate agency sites. From here you can search the agency sites for many more listings than you will find on the HomeNet properties residential database.

Search for Residential Real Estate with HomeScout

- HomeScout is a top residential real estate search Web site. This site searches a nationwide database of properties from hundreds of independent listing Web sites.
- Use the Power Search form available on the HomeScout home page to enter your search criteria. Enter the city, state, mile radius, type of property, and minimum and maximum price. If you like, select the number of bedrooms for the property. Click Go Get It to start the search.

HomeScout Power Search

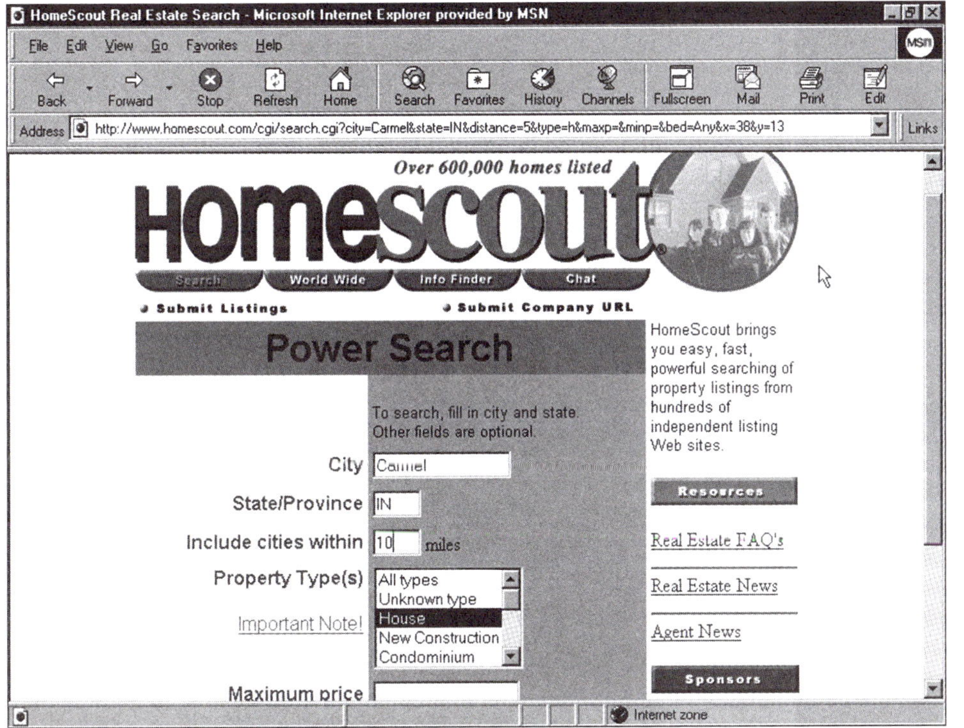

Note

Click the Real Estate FAQ's link to find the answers to hundreds of commonly asked real estate questions.

- Search results are displayed in a table listing the city, price, number of beds and baths, the neighborhood, and the source of the listing. Click the city name link for a house to see a page with the complete listing. Click the source link to go to the original listing Web page.

HomeScout Power Search Listing

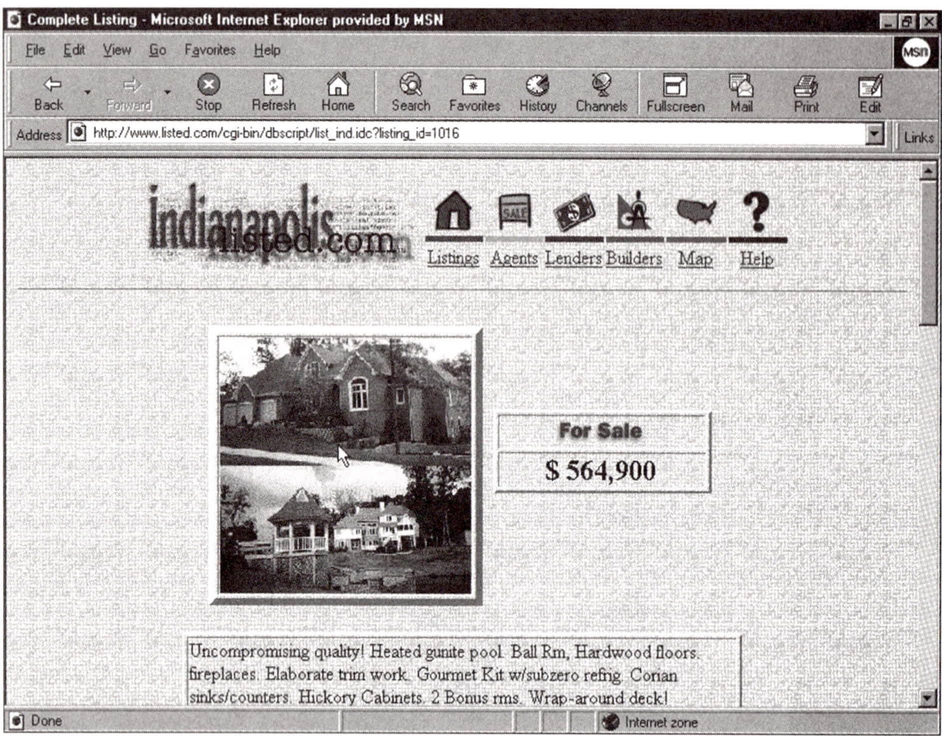

Make Relocation Decisions with Homebuyer's Fair

- Use Homebuyer's Fair to consider all the angles when you relocate. This popular site includes numerous interactive tools to help you decide where you want to buy and how best to do it.
- The most useful tool for considering a possible relocation is the Salary Calculator. Use the calculator to see how much you have to make in a new city to match your current salary. The results can be surprising—this is a good check to use before making the decision to go somewhere new.

Homebuyer's Fair Salary Calculator

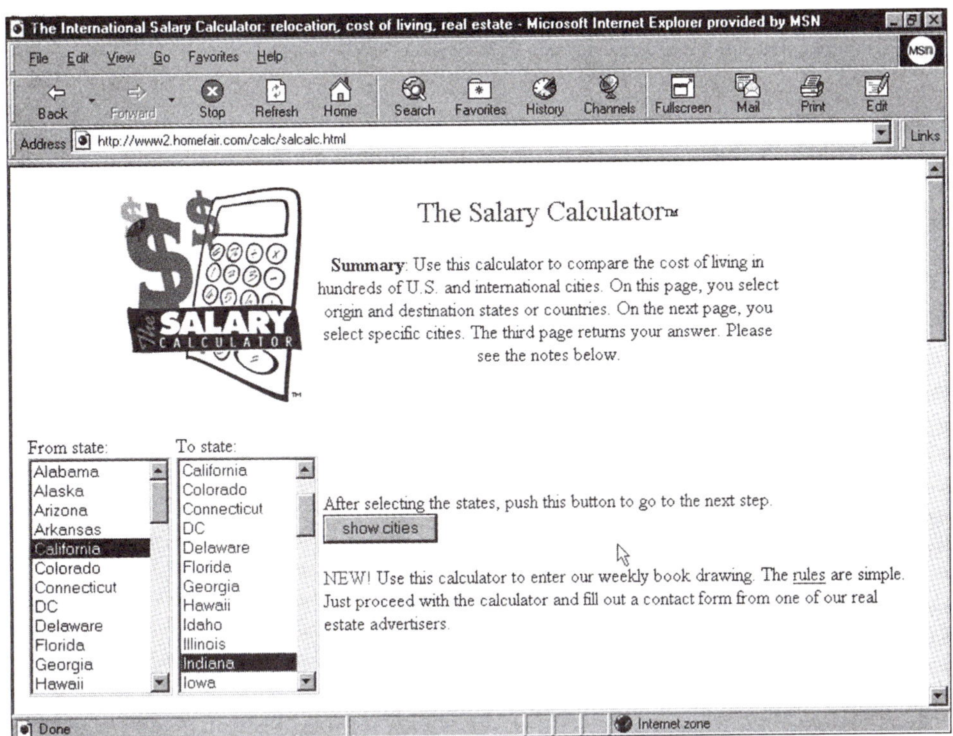

- The Lifestyle Optimizer enables you to search for a city that matches the kind of lifestyle you want. Enter search criteria such as size of city, average income, housing cost, and climate, then click Search to see a listing of city descriptions that fit your criteria.
- You can also use the School Information Service to compare school districts for counties that you select.
- Use the Relocation Wizard to create a customized timeline of tasks for making a smooth move. The resulting to-do list can be a handy way to get organized for the day of the move. The Moving Calculator can help you estimate the cost of the move.
- Click the Buying Your First Home link to use calculators such as Mortgage Qualification, Rent-vs.-Buy, and Annual Percentage Rate.

Note

Try the Relocation Crime Lab to compare crime rates between cities. This is an interesting tool to look up the crime rate in your city and see how it compares to others even if you're not considering a move.

In this exercise, you will search for commercial real estate using the NetProperties Web site, then search for residential real estate using the HomeScout Web site. Next, you will use tools available at Homebuyer's Fair to consider relocation options such as cost of living, lifestyle, schools, and moving expense.

Note: To ensure consistent results, this exercise uses simulated sites. The real URLs appear at the end of the exercise.

Web Search

Search for answers to the following questions using the Web sites you will visit in the Web simulation exercise.

1. What is the name of the restaurant near the Allison Pointe/Lake Pointe Center 4 office space?

   ____

2. What is the name of the realtor showing the office property?

   ____

3. In what town is the 15th house in the Home Scout Power Search results located?

   ____

4. How many square feet does the house in Zionsville have?

   ____

5. What is the average composite SAT score for children in the Carmel Clay school district?

   ____

EXERCISE DIRECTIONS

1. Launch the Internet simulation. From the Main Menu, select Lesson 6, then select Exercise 1.
2. On the Address line, type the following and press Enter:

   http://www.netprop.com/

   ➲ *The Net Properties home page opens.*

NetProperties Home Page

3. Click the CenterNet icon.

   ➲ *The CenterNet home page opens.*

4. Click the PROPERTY DATABASE link.

5. Click the Properties for Lease globe.

   ➲ *The CenterNet property database search form opens.*

6. Choose **Office** from the Property Type menu.

CenterNet Home Page

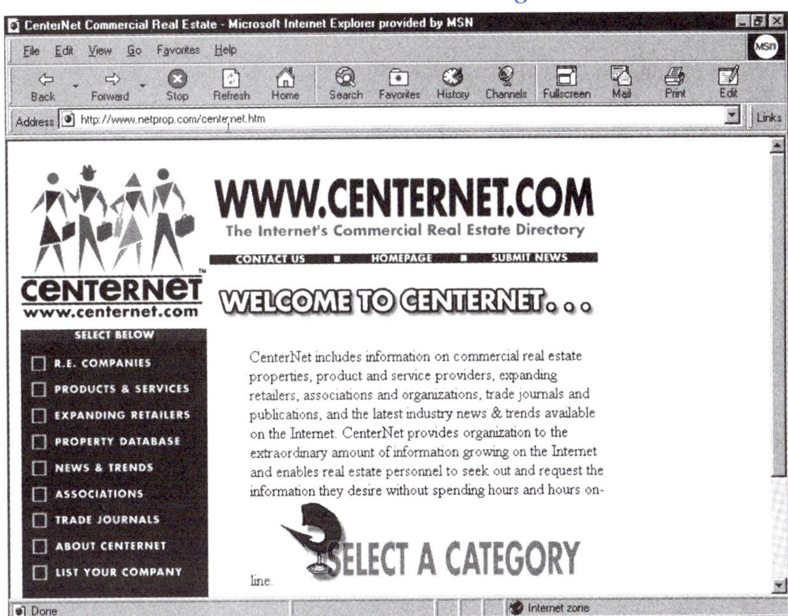

7. Enter the following search criteria into the form's text boxes:

   Min. Lease Rate: $10

   Max. Lease Rate: $15

   City: Indianapolis

   County: Marion

   State: Indiana

   Min. Avail. Sq. Ft.>: 25,000

   ✓ *Leave other search form text boxes blank.*

8. Click Begin Property Search.

   ➲ *The search engine locates properties for lease that fit your criteria in the CenterNet database.*

   ✓ *Only properties listed for more than 7 days are shown.*

Enter Commercial Real Estate Search Criteria

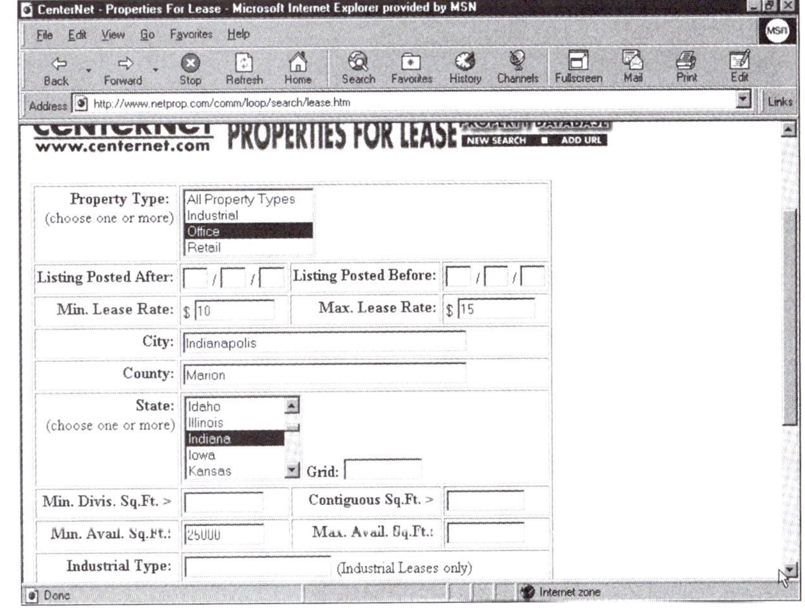

9. Click the Allison Pointe / Lake Pointe Center 4 link.

   ➲ *An overview of the property appears.*

Commercial Real Estate Search Results

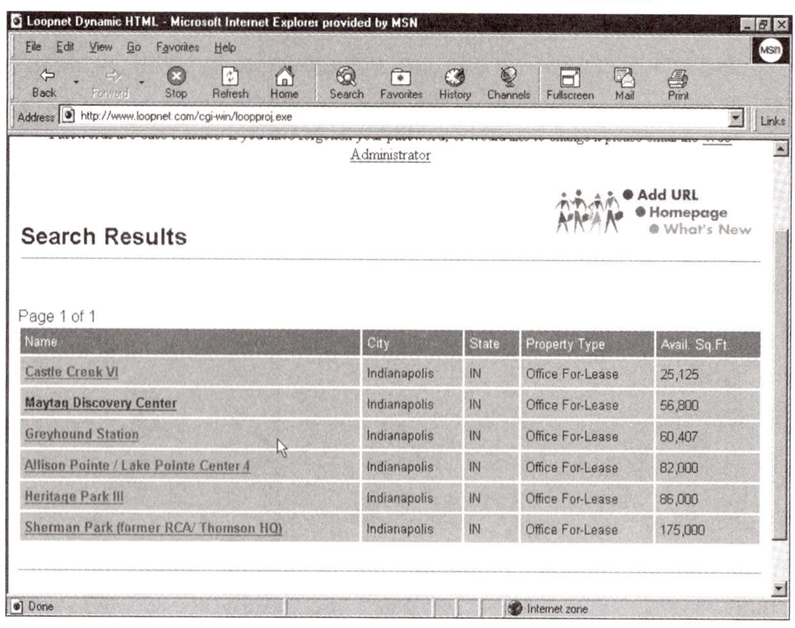

10. On the Address line of your browser, type the following URL and press Enter:

    http://www.homescout.com/

    ➲ *The HomeScout home page opens.*

Overview of Commercial Property

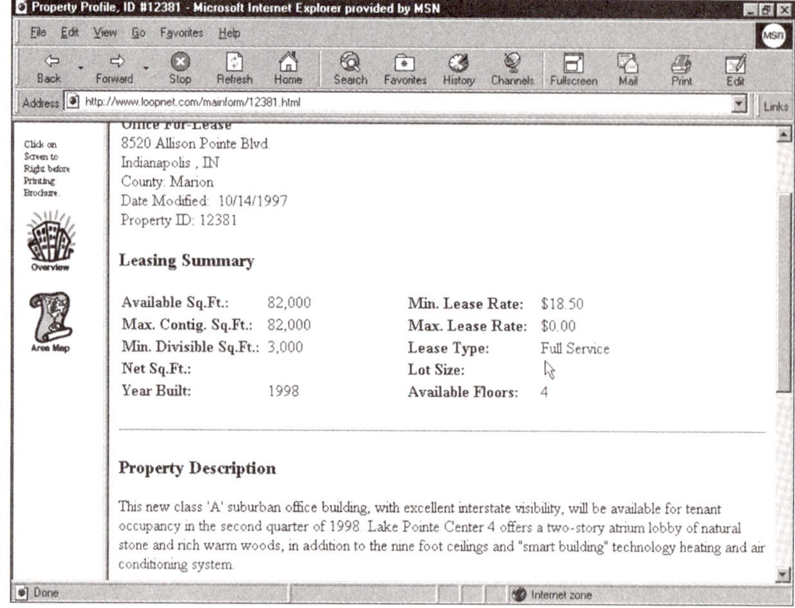

11. Enter the following information in the Power Search form:

    City: Carmel

    State: IN

    Include cities within 10 miles.

    Property Type(s): House

HomeScout Home Page with Search Criteria

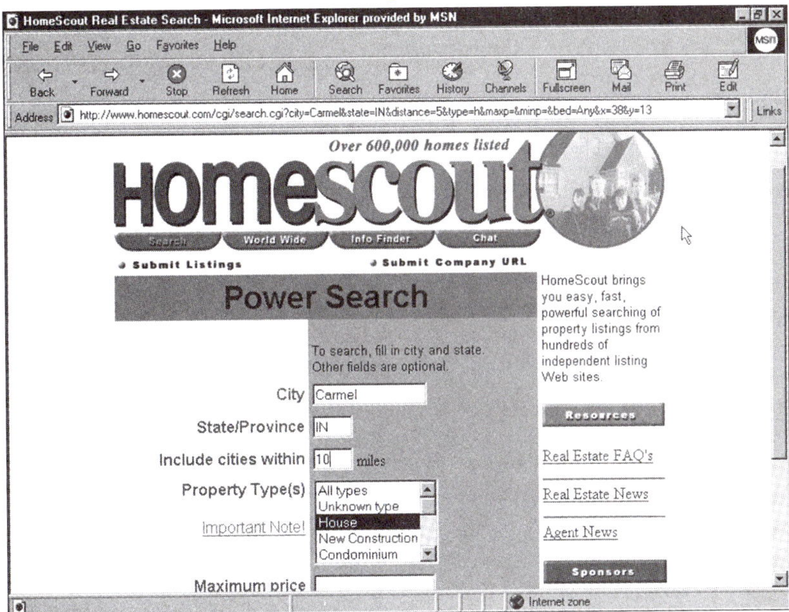

12. Click Go Get It.

    ➲ *HomeScout searches its database for homes matching your search criteria in Carmel, a suburb of Indianapolis. 136 matches are found.*

HomeScout Search Results

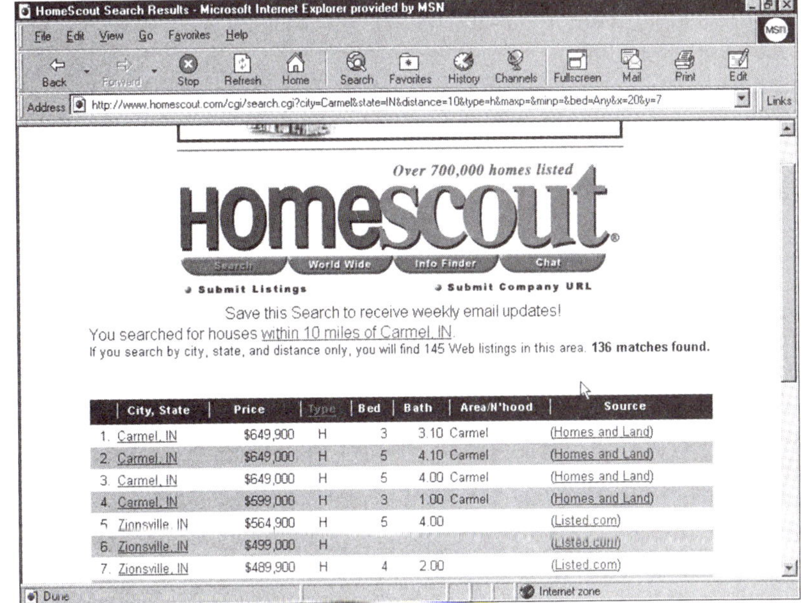

13. Click the fifth link from the top of the list, Zionsville, IN.

    ➲ *The real estate listing for this house opens.*

14. Scroll down to read about the house.

HomeScout Real Estate Listing

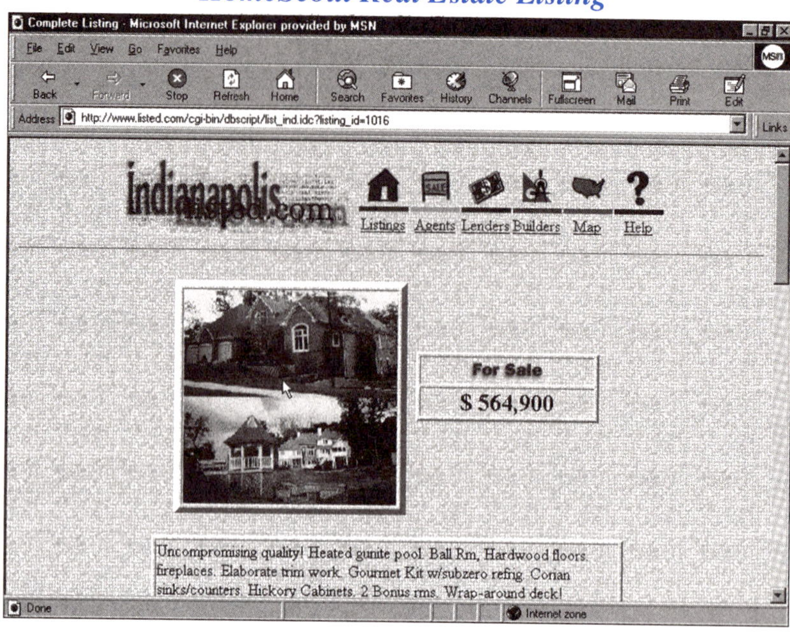

15. On the Address line of your browser, type the following URL and press Enter:

    http://www.homefair.com/

    ➲ *The Homebuyer's Fair home page opens.*

16. Scroll down and click the Choose the Best Cities to Live link in the Announcements section of the home page.

    ➲ *The Homefair.com Life Style Optimizer opens.*

Homebuyer's Fair Home Page

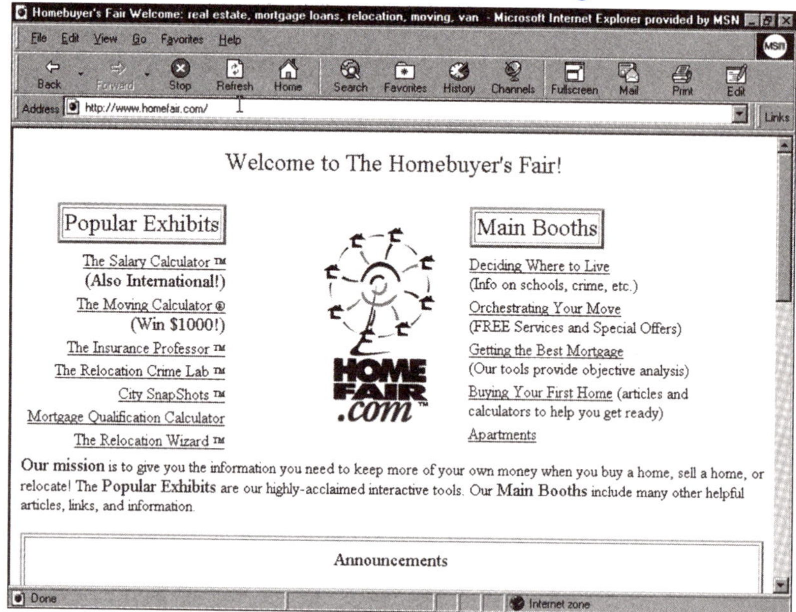

17. Select the following search criteria from the Optimizer form's menus:

    Select the number of cities to return: 20

    Median Household Disposable Income: High (greater than $45,000)

    4 BR House Price Range: Medium (between $150,000 and $300,000)

    ✓ *Leave other search form menus as is.*

18. Click Search.

    ➲ *Homefair searches for cities that match your criteria. 20 cities are displayed.*

19. Click the link for Carmel, Indiana. Read the description of the city.

20. At the bottom of the page, select **Salary Calculator** from the Popular Attractions menu, then click Go!.

    ➲ *The Homefair.com Salary Calculator page opens.*

Enter Life Style Optimizer Search Criteria

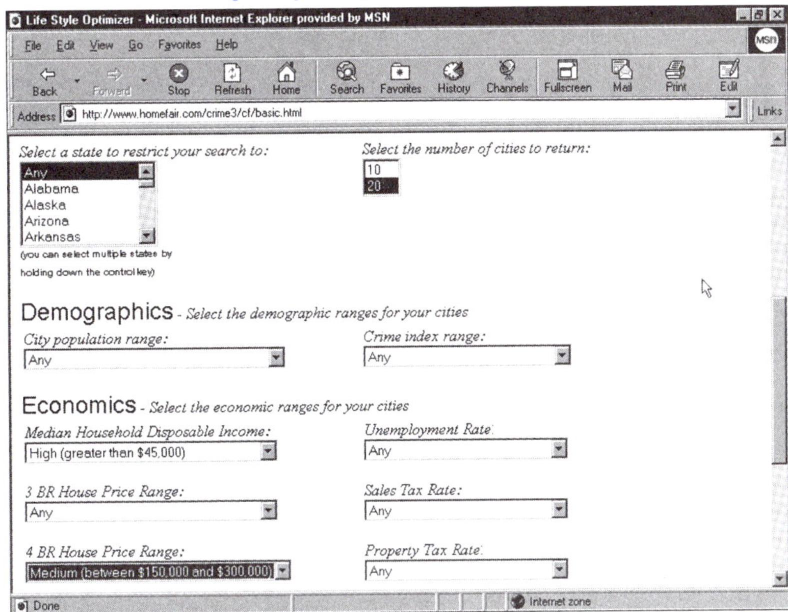

City Description

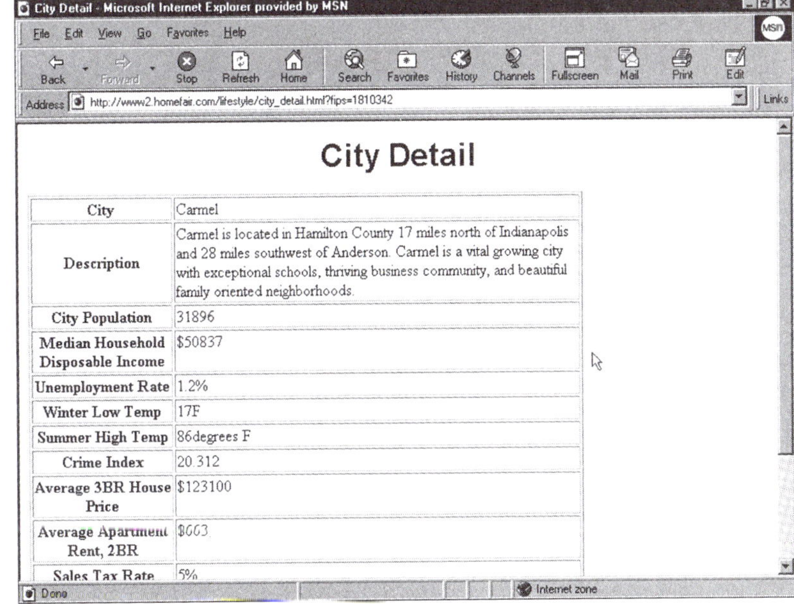

21. Select **California** in the From state menu. Select **Indiana** in the To state menu. Click show cities.

Homebuyer's Fair Salary Calculator

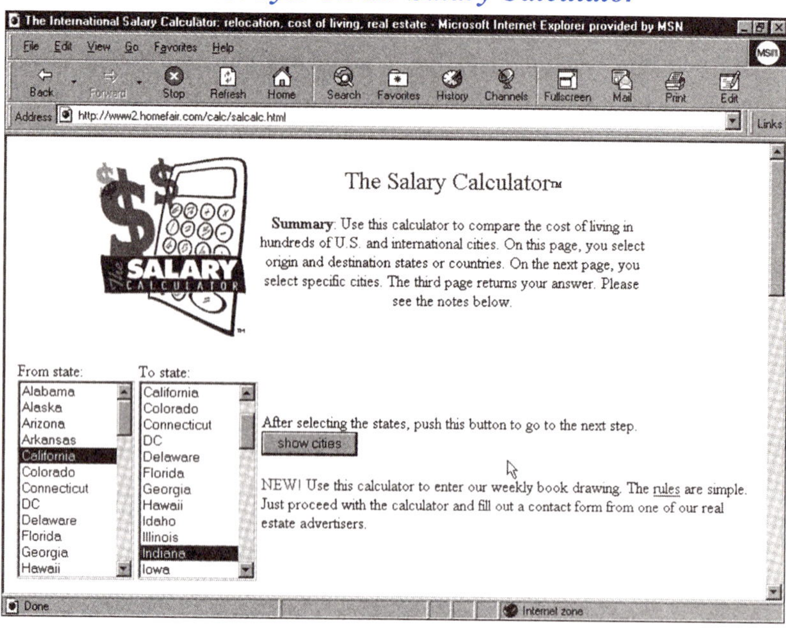

22. Enter *35000* as your current salary. Select **Westlake Village** in the City moving from menu, then select **Carmel** in the City moving to menu.

    ✓ *Don't use commas in the salary text box. You will have to scroll down the City moving from menu to find Westlake Village.*

23. Click calculate salary.

    ➲ *The Salary Calculator shows that you would only need to make $24,774 in Carmel to maintain the same standard of living as in Westlake Village. The cost of living in Carmel is lower.*

24. Select **Deciding Where to Live** from the Main Booths menu and then click Go!.

    ➲ *The Homefair.com Deciding Where to Live page opens.*

25. Click the School Information link.

26. Select **Indiana** from the Select a State menu on the School Information Service page, then click Go.

Enter Salary and Relocation Cities

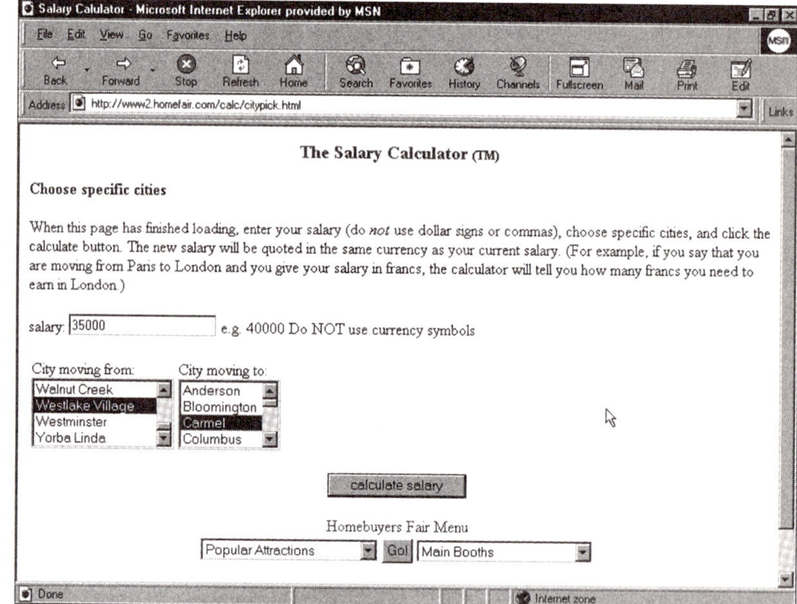

27. Select **Hamilton** from the Select a County in Indina menu, then click Go.

   ➲ *A table comapring school districts within Hamilton County, Indiana opens. Note the difference in SAT scores among the various districts.*

Select a County for School Information

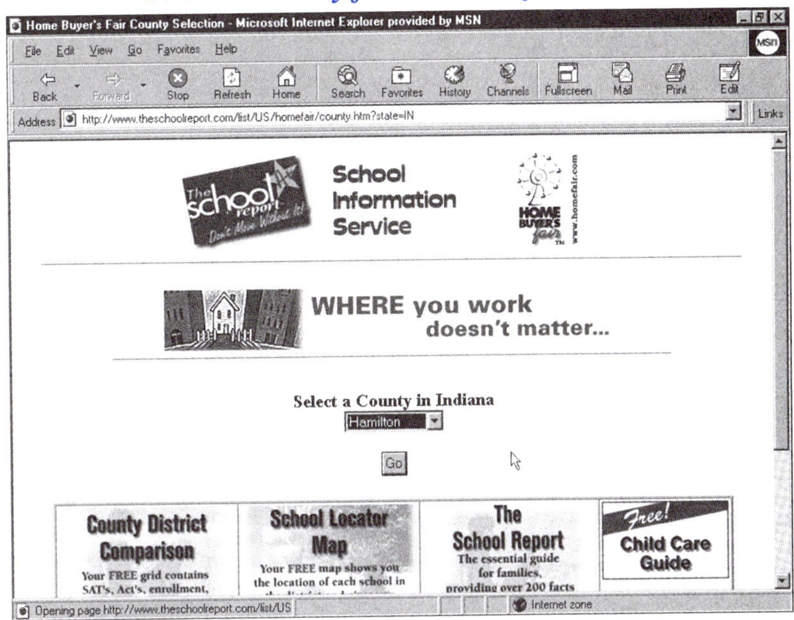

School District Comparison for Hamilton County

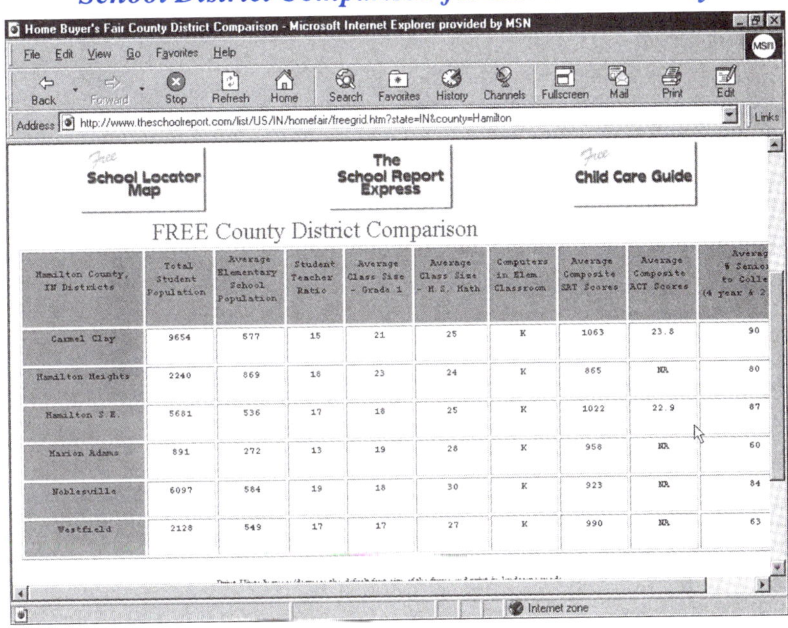

FREE County District Comparison

Hamilton County, IN Districts	Total Student Population	Average Elementary School Population	Student Teacher Ratio	Average Class Size - Grade 1	Average Class Size - H.S. Math	Computers in Elem. Classroom	Average Composite SAT Scores	Average Composite ACT Scores	Averag % Senio to Colle (4 year & 2
Carmel Clay	9654	577	15	21	25	K	1063	23.8	90
Hamilton Heights	2240	869	18	23	24	K	865	NR	80
Hamilton S.E.	5681	536	17	18	25	K	1022	22.9	87
Marion Adams	891	272	13	19	28	K	958	NR	60
Noblesville	6097	584	19	18	30	K	923	NR	84
Westfield	2128	549	17	17	27	K	990	NR	63

28. Select **Moving Calculator** from the Popular Attractions menu at the bottom of the page. Click Go!.

   ➲ *The Homefair.com Moving Calculator opens.*

29. Enter the following information in Moving Calculator for:

    County moving from:
    Ventura

    City and State moving from:
    Westlake Village, Ca

    City and State moving to:
    Carmel, In

    Number of bedrooms:
    Four

    Click to check the following rooms that have furniture:
    kitchen, living room, dining room, den, play room, office, patio, shed

    Click to check the following boxes:
    family has more than 3 members, been in your current residence more than five years

30. Click <u>Calculate</u>.

    ✓ *The calculator can't match the two locations you entered, so you will have to estimate the mileage between cities. The distance is approximately 2080 miles.*

31. Enter 2080 in the distance in miles text box, then click <u>Calculate</u>.

    ➲ *The Moving Calculator provides a lower estimate of $10,924 and an upper estimate of $13,656 for your moving expense.*

32. Continue on to the next exercise.

    OR

    Exit from the simulation.

Enter Moving Calculator Information

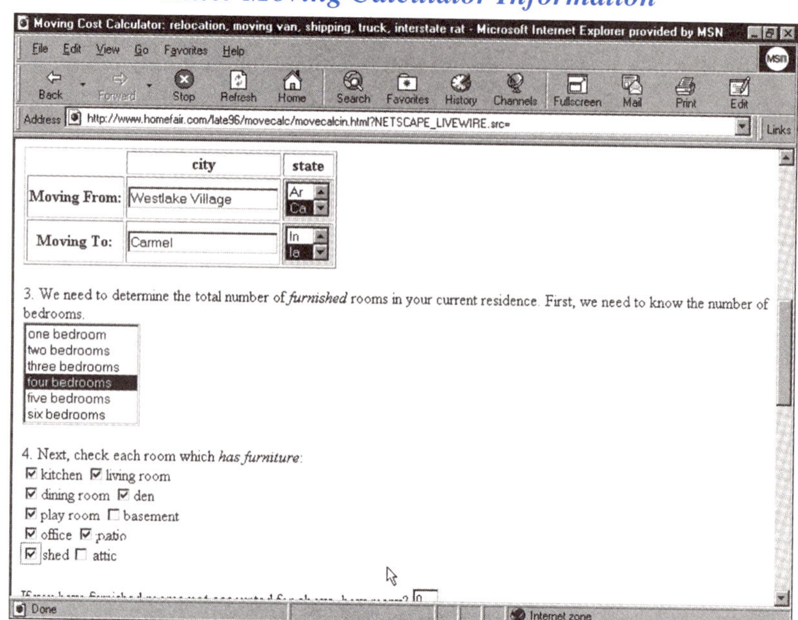

Moving Calculator Results

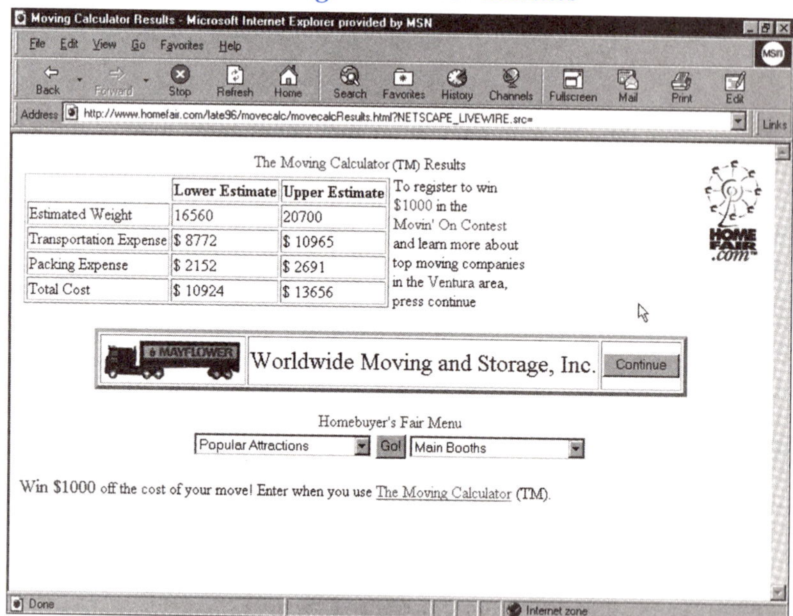

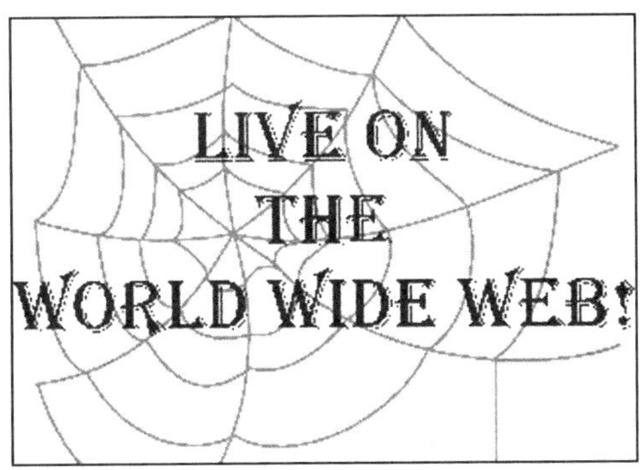

Net Properties Home Page
http://www.netprop.com/

HomeScout Home Page
http://www.homescout.com/

Homebuyer's Fair Home Page
http://www.homefair.com/

Exercise 2

Hire Employees or Find a Job with America's Job Bank

NOTES

Hire Employees or Find a Job with America's Job Bank

- Avoid the high cost of hiring through recruiters by checking the America's Job Bank Web site. If you're looking for a career change, you can search extensive databases of job openings at this site free of charge. You can also check into career planning resources and find links to employer Web sites.

America's Job Bank Search Results

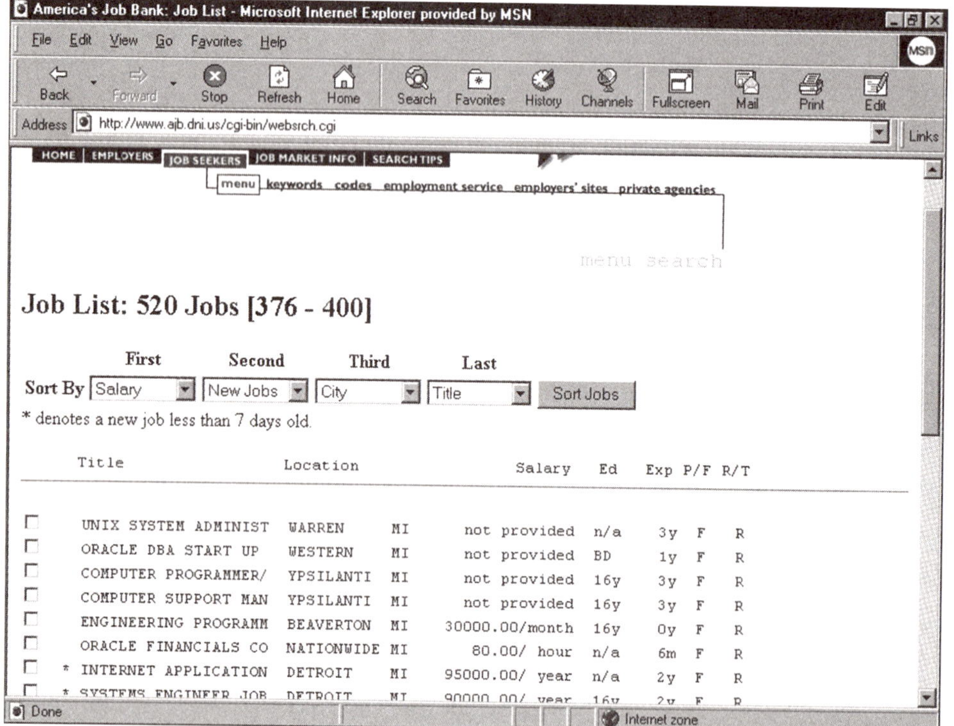

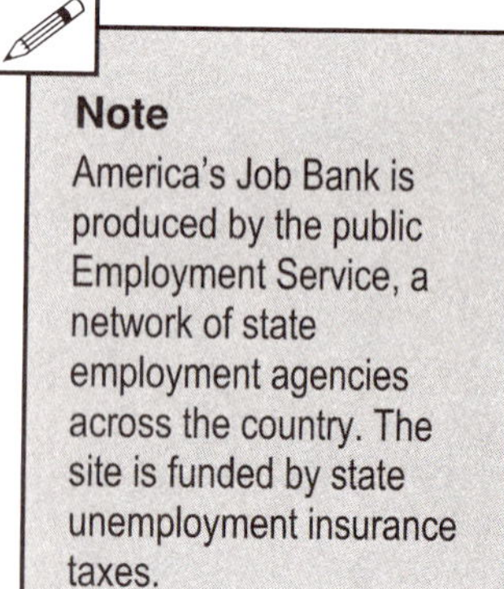

Note

America's Job Bank is produced by the public Employment Service, a network of state employment agencies across the country. The site is funded by state unemployment insurance taxes.

- Employers can post job openings at America's Job Bank (AJB) free of charge. To post a job, click the Employers link at the home page, then click the Post link. You must fill out a brief registration form to use the employers service, but after doing so you can post jobs, link your Web site to the America's Job Bank site, use recruiting services, and use an automatic job posting service.
- If you're looking for a job, click the Job Seekers link from the home page. You can search using either a drop-down list of occupations and locations, a keyword search, or federal and military job codes. Click the employers' sites link to see an alphabetical index of more than 2,000 company Web sites.
- Click on the Job Market Info link to see career development information, including profiles of state job markets, job search resources, and an interesting list of career trends showing what jobs and fields are expected to grow in the next ten years.

In this exercise, you will post a job at America's Job Bank. You will then check job market information for the fastest growing and highest paying careers. Finally, you will search for a job as a systems analyst, sorting search results by salary and location.

Note: *To ensure consistent results, this exercise uses simulated sites. The real URLs appear at the end of the exercise.*

Web Search

Search for answers to the following questions using the Web sites you will visit in the Web simulation exercise.

1. According to the Fastest Growing Occupations Web page, what is the projected percent employment change for secondary school teachers?

   ____

2. How many jobs are projected through 2005 for Recreation Workers?

   ____

3. What is the median weekly earnings for speech therapists?

   ____

4. Name 3 of the 5 degrees listed as typical requirements for becoming a systems analyst.

   ____

5. What is the salary for the SAP Software Consultant position in Holland, MI?

   ____

6. What is the reference number for the SAP Software Consultant job?

   ____

EXERCISE DIRECTIONS

1. Launch the Internet simulation. From the Main Menu, select Lesson 6, then select Exercise 2.
2. On the Address line, type the following URL and press Enter:

   http://www.ajb.dni.us/

   ➲ *The America's Job Bank (AJB) home page opens.*

America's Job Bank Home Page

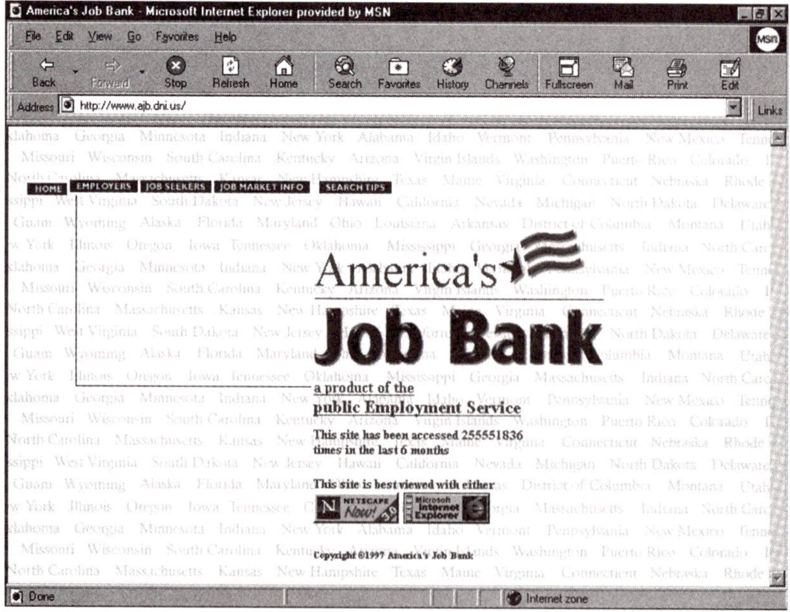

3. Click the EMPLOYERS link.
   - ➲ *The AJB Employers page opens.*
4. Click the Post link.
   - ✓ *If you were live online, you would need to register and enter a network password to continue.*
   - ➲ *The Post Job Referral Information page opens. The information on the form will already be filled in for you.*
5. Scroll down and click the **E-Mail** check box to select it, then click the Move Forward button.
   - ➲ *The Job Order Entry page opens.*

America's Job Bank Employers Page

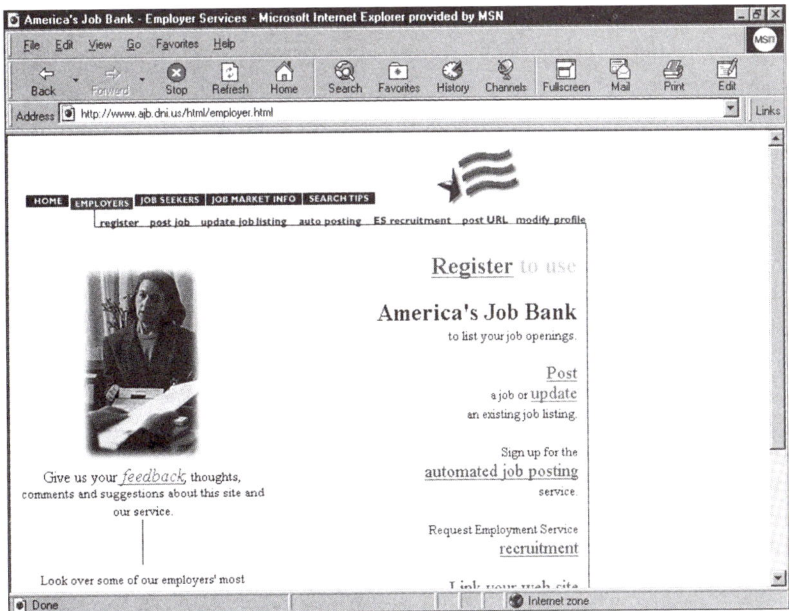

Employers Referral Information

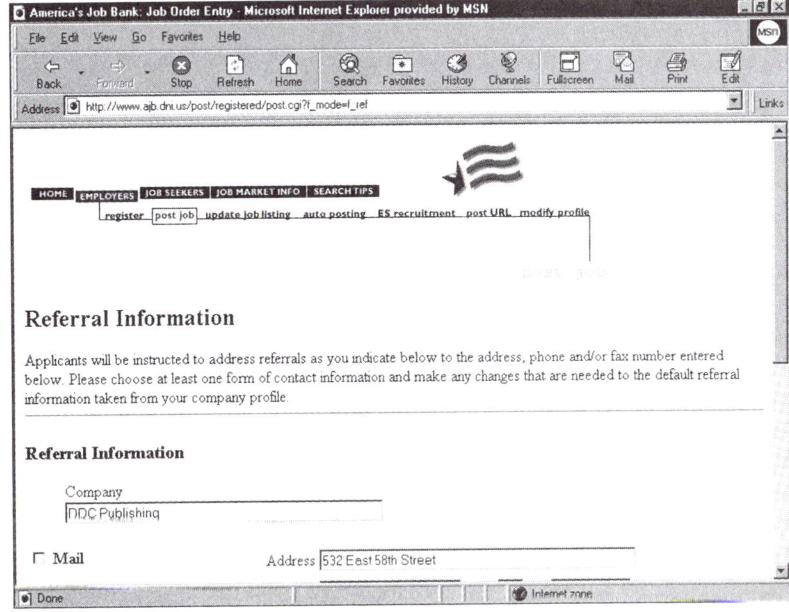

6. Type the following information into the appropriate text boxes:

   Title: Editorial Assistant

   City: New York

   State: NY

   Zip Code: 10016

   Number of positions available: 1

   Number of hours per week: 40

   Months of Experience Required: 12

   What level of education do you require: Bachelors Degree

   ✓ *Leave all other text boxes blank.*

7. Enter the following text in the Job Description text box:

   Our Editorial Assistant will be responsible for copy editing and proofreading book manuscripts as well as updating our book production schedule. Requires an eagle eye for detail, strong language skills, and excellent organizational skills. Knowledge of computer applications is helpful.

8. Click the Submit to AJB button.

   ➲ *The Entry Complete page appears, confirming the job order.*

Enter Job Description

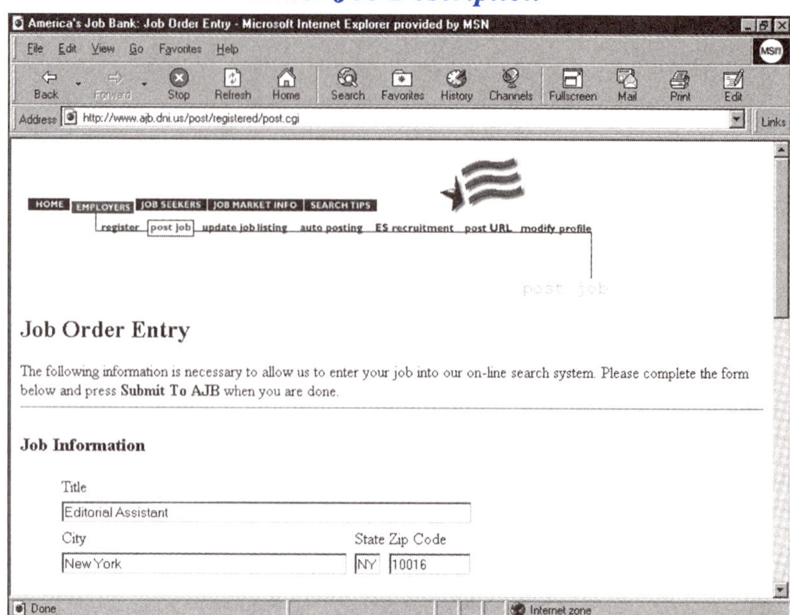

Confirmation of Job Posting

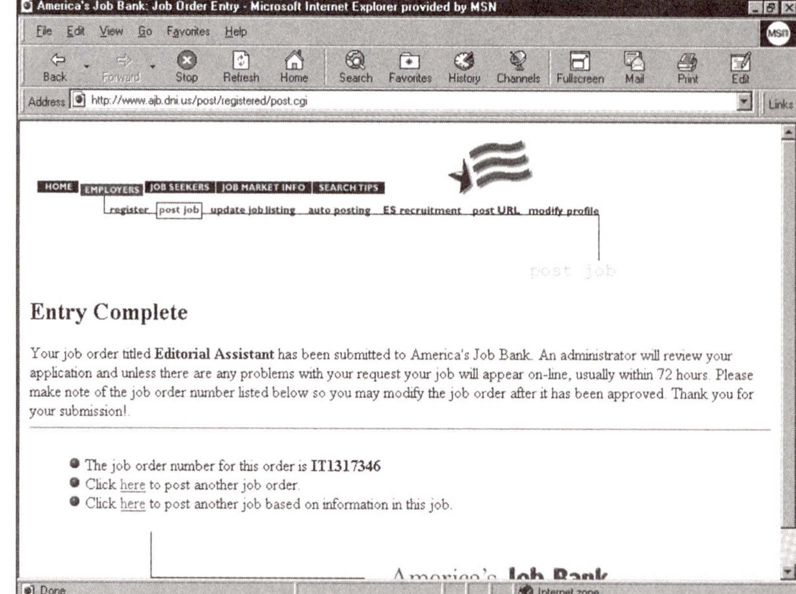

9. Click the Job Market Info link at the top of the page.

   ➲ *The America's Career InfoNet page opens.*

10. Scroll down and click the Trends link.

    ➲ *The Trends in the U.S. Job Market page opens.*

11. Under the What are the fastest growing occupations.... heading, click the requiring a bachelor's degree or higher? link.

    ➲ *A page opens listing employment projections for the fastest growing occupations requiring a bachelor's degree or higher.*

    ✓ *Note that Systems Analysts, Electronic Data Processing is projected to have the largest percentage increase.*

Job Market Information Page

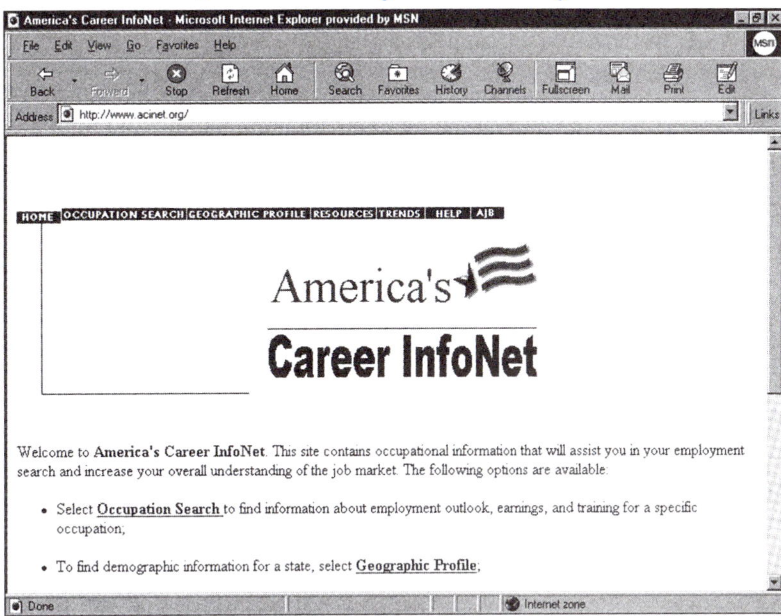

Fastest Growing Occupations for College Grads

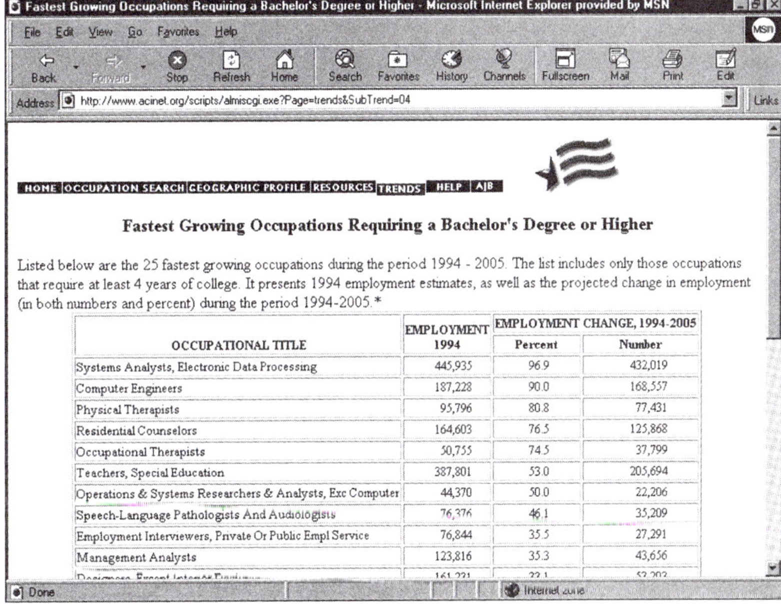

Fastest Growing Occupations Requiring a Bachelor's Degree or Higher

Listed below are the 25 fastest growing occupations during the period 1994 - 2005. The list includes only those occupations that require at least 4 years of college. It presents 1994 employment estimates, as well as the projected change in employment (in both numbers and percent) during the period 1994-2005.*

OCCUPATIONAL TITLE	EMPLOYMENT 1994	EMPLOYMENT CHANGE, 1994-2005	
		Percent	Number
Systems Analysts, Electronic Data Processing	445,935	96.9	432,019
Computer Engineers	187,228	90.0	168,557
Physical Therapists	95,796	80.8	77,431
Residential Counselors	164,603	76.5	125,868
Occupational Therapists	50,755	74.5	37,799
Teachers, Special Education	387,801	53.0	205,694
Operations & Systems Researchers & Analysts, Exc Computer	44,370	50.0	22,206
Speech-Language Pathologists And Audiologists	76,376	46.1	35,209
Employment Interviewers, Private Or Public Empl Service	76,844	35.5	27,291
Management Analysts	123,816	35.3	43,656

12. Click the Back button at the bottom of the page.
13. Under the What occupations will have the most openings .... heading, click the requiring a bachelor's degree or higher? link.

   ➲ *A page opens listing occupations projected to have the most openings for college grads.*

   ✓ *Note that Systems Analysts, Electronic Data Processing ranks fourth on the list.*

14. Click the Back button at the bottom of the page.
15. Scroll down the page and click the requiring a bachelor's degree or higher? link under the What are the highest paying occupations.... heading.

   ➲ *A page opens listing the 25 occupations with the highest earnings for college grads.*

   ✓ *Note that Computer Systems Analysts and Scientists ranks tenth on the list.*

Occupations with the Most Openings for College Grads

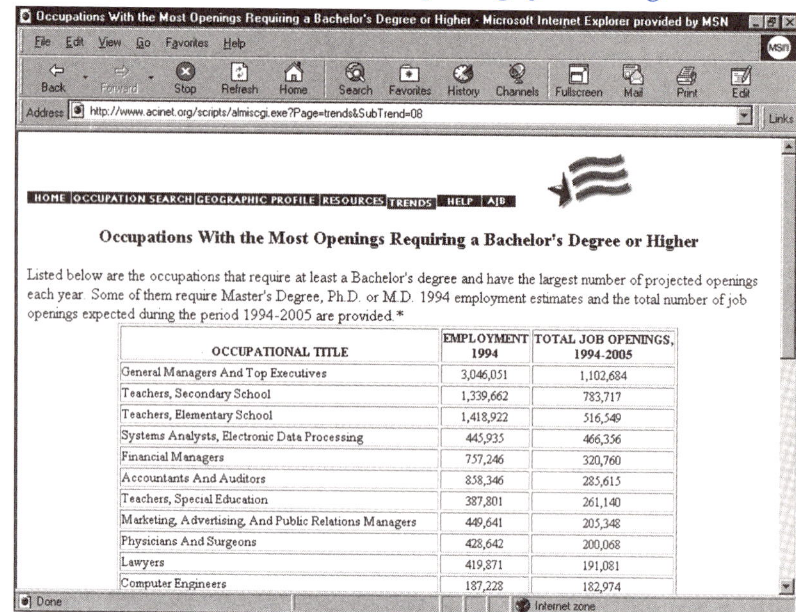

Occupations With the Most Openings Requiring a Bachelor's Degree or Higher

Listed below are the occupations that require at least a Bachelor's degree and have the largest number of projected openings each year. Some of them require Master's Degree, Ph.D. or M.D. 1994 employment estimates and the total number of job openings expected during the period 1994-2005 are provided.*

OCCUPATIONAL TITLE	EMPLOYMENT 1994	TOTAL JOB OPENINGS, 1994-2005
General Managers And Top Executives	3,046,051	1,102,684
Teachers, Secondary School	1,339,662	783,717
Teachers, Elementary School	1,418,922	516,549
Systems Analysts, Electronic Data Processing	445,935	466,356
Financial Managers	757,246	320,760
Accountants And Auditors	858,346	285,615
Teachers, Special Education	387,801	261,140
Marketing, Advertising, And Public Relations Managers	449,641	205,348
Physicians And Surgeons	428,642	200,068
Lawyers	419,871	191,081
Computer Engineers	187,228	182,974

Occupations with the Highest Earnings for College Grads

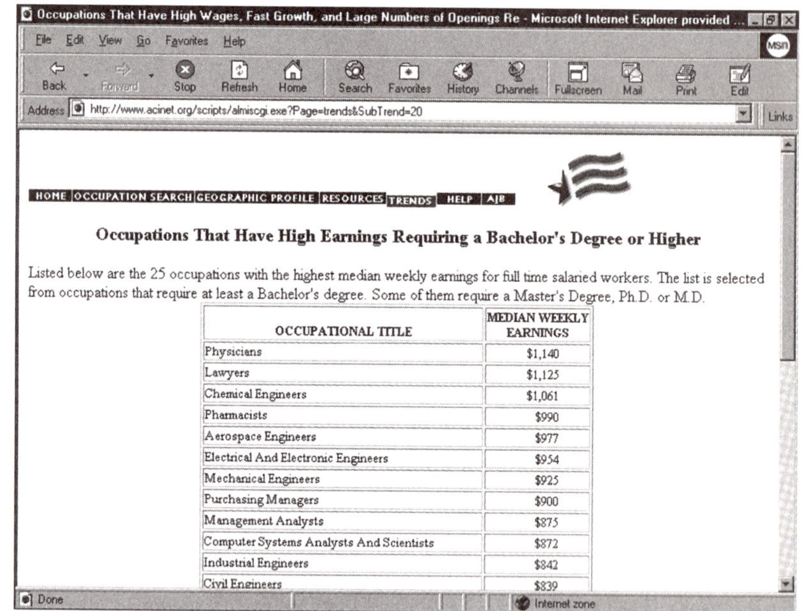

Occupations That Have High Earnings Requiring a Bachelor's Degree or Higher

Listed below are the 25 occupations with the highest median weekly earnings for full time salaried workers. The list is selected from occupations that require at least a Bachelor's degree. Some of them require a Master's Degree, Ph.D. or M.D.

OCCUPATIONAL TITLE	MEDIAN WEEKLY EARNINGS
Physicians	$1,140
Lawyers	$1,125
Chemical Engineers	$1,061
Pharmacists	$990
Aerospace Engineers	$977
Electrical And Electronic Engineers	$954
Mechanical Engineers	$925
Purchasing Managers	$900
Management Analysts	$875
Computer Systems Analysts And Scientists	$872
Industrial Engineers	$842
Civil Engineers	$839

16. Click the Occupation Search link at the top of the page.

    ➲ *The main search page for America's Career InfoNet opens.*

17. Click the Menu link.

    ➲ *The first Menu Search page opens.*

18. Click **Computer/Information Technology** in the Job Families menu, then click Next.

19. Click **Systems Analysts, Electronic Data Processing** in the Code/Occupation menu, then click the Search button.

    ➲ *An Occupation Report summarizing the employment outlook and earnings for systems analysts opens.*

20. Click the Training Requirements button at the bottom of the page.

    ➲ *A page opens listing degrees typically required to become a systems analyst.*

21. Click the AJB link at the top of the page.

    ➲ *The America's Job Bank home page opens.*

Menu Search for Occupations

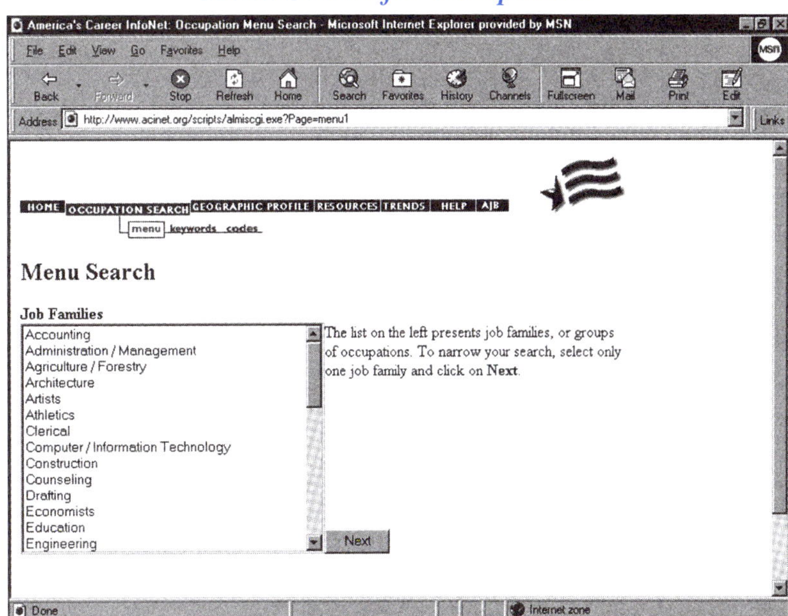

Occupation Report Page

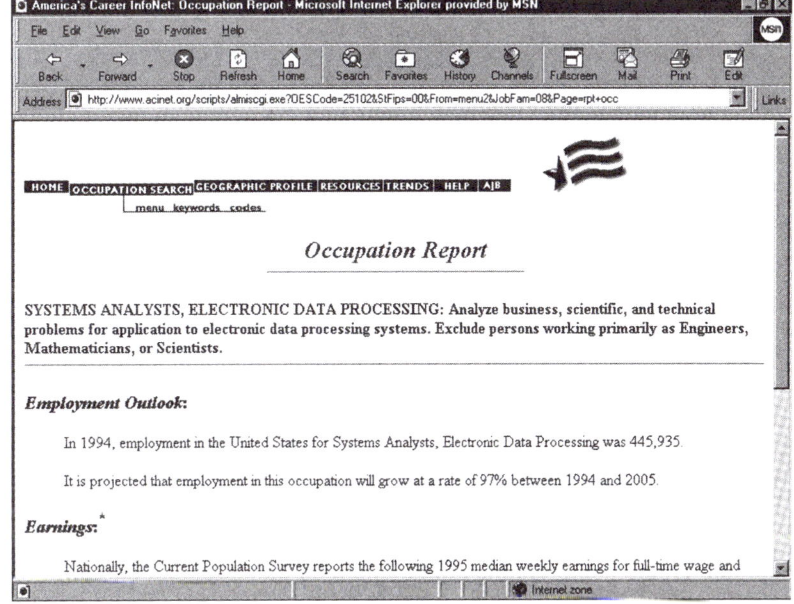

22. Click the Job Seekers link.

    ➲ *The Search America's Job Bank page opens.*

23. Click the Menu link.

    ➲ *The Menu Search page opens.*

24. Click to select **Computer/Information Technology** in the Occupation menu.

25. Click to select **Michigan** in the Location(s) menu, then click the View Jobs Now button.

    ➲ *The search results show a list of 520 systems analyst jobs in the state of Michigan. The first 25 jobs are displayed.*

    ✓ *Jobs are sorted by state and then by city.*

26. Click to select **Salary** from the First menu. Click to select **New Jobs** from the Second menu. Click to select **City** from the Third menu.

27. Click to select **Title** from the Last menu, then click Sort Jobs.

    ✓ *Many job listings do not show salary.*

28. Scroll down and select **376-400** from the menu at the bottom of the page, then click Jump to Jobs.

    ➲ *This page shows the first listings in the search results that include salary information. Jobs are sorted from highest salary to lowest salary.*

29. Click the check box next to the **SAP Software Consultant** job in Holland, MI, then click View Jobs at the bottom of the page.

    ➲ *A description of the job opens.*

30. Scroll down and read the job description.

31. Continue on to the next exercise.

    OR

    Exit from the simulation.

Job Search Results

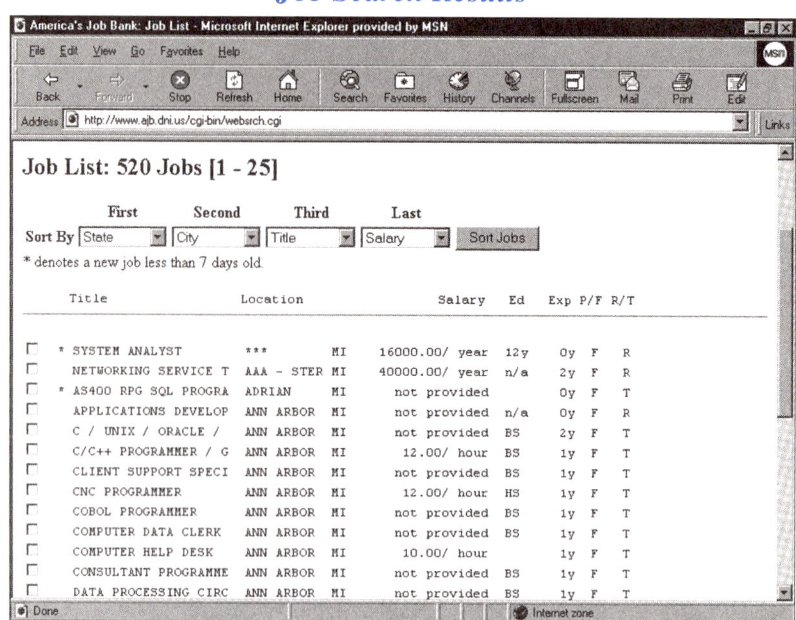

Job Search Results Sorted by Salary

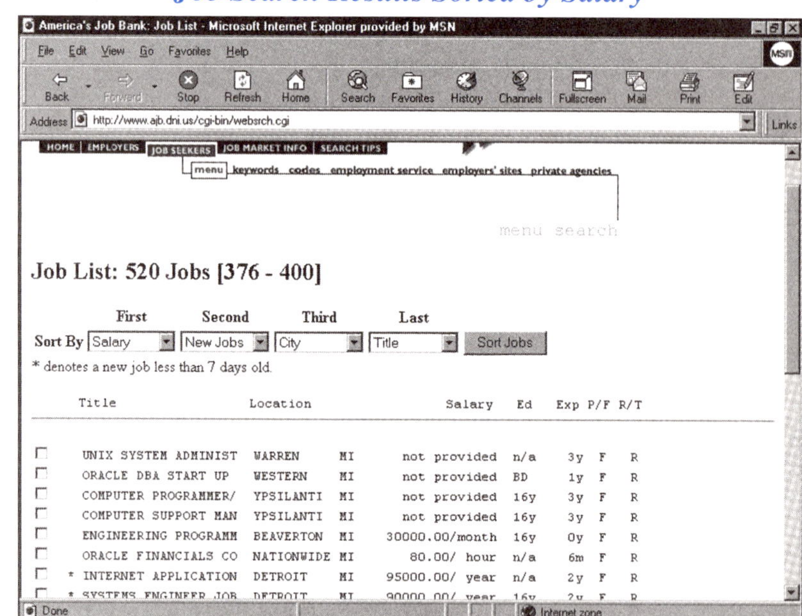

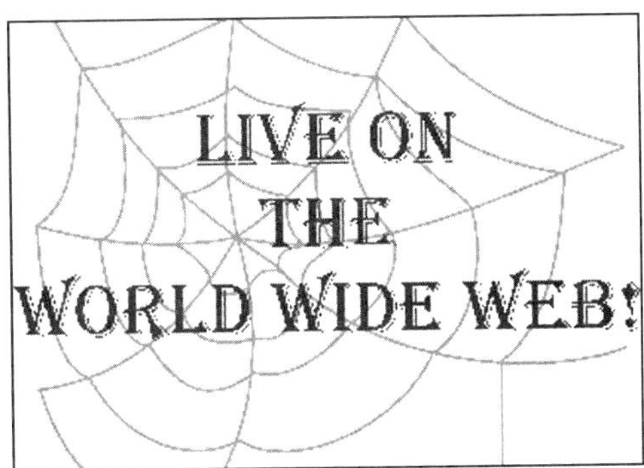

America's Job Bank Home Page
http://www.ajb.dni.us/

Exercise 3

- Find Business Resources at the Small Business Administration
- Manage a Small Business with Edge Online Business Tools

NOTES

Find Business Resources at the Small Business Administration

- Many Web sites focus on tools specifically designed to run a small business. These sites offer free resources, support, services, and information that can make the busy life of an entrepreneur much easier.
- The U.S. government's Small Business Administration (SBA) Web site is the authoritative source for information about small business regulation. The site also contains many links to information that addresses the challenges of small business management and ownership.

Small Business Administration Home Page

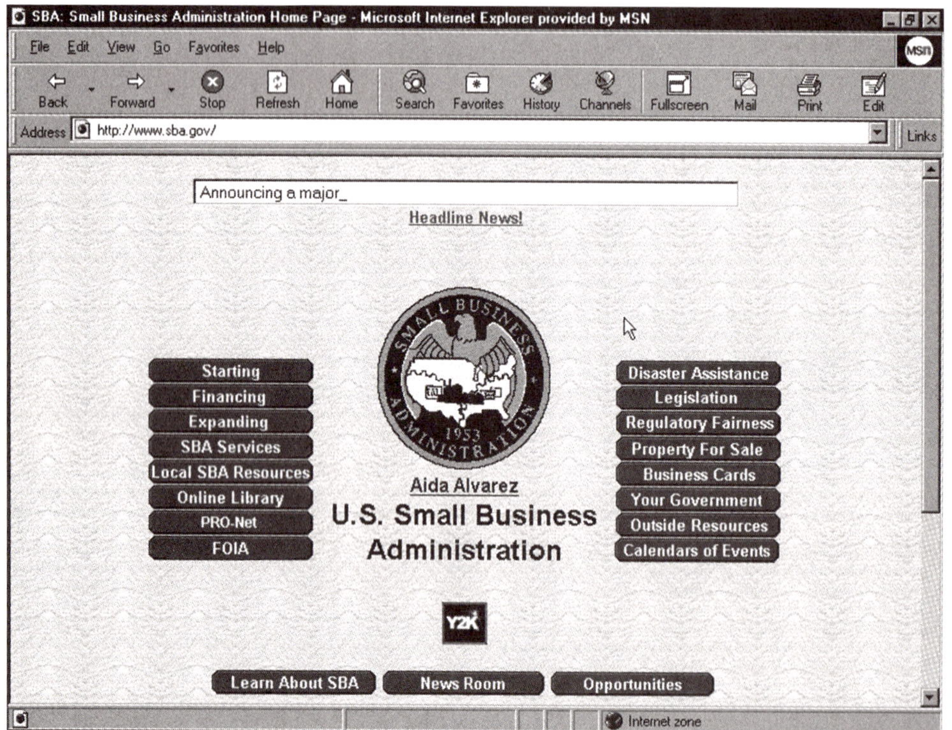

- Click on the Starting link to find resources such as sample business plans, links to more than 500 shareware programs, special assistance and counseling, and patent and trademark information.
- You can also find links to local SBA resrouces, property for sale, financing sources, and a link to SBA's PRO-Net, a searchable database of government procurement information.

Note

Click the Outside Resources link and then click SCORE to access a link to the SCORE Web site. SCORE stands for Service Core of Retired Executives. SCORE executives provide free advice to small business owners.

Manage a Small Business with Edge Online Business Tools

- The Entrepreneurial Edge Online Web site is the digital version of Entrepreneurial Edge magazine. Edge Online includes interactive financial and business management tools at its Business Builders and Interactive Toolbox links that can provide even a large, well-established firm with useful resources.

Edge Online Home Page

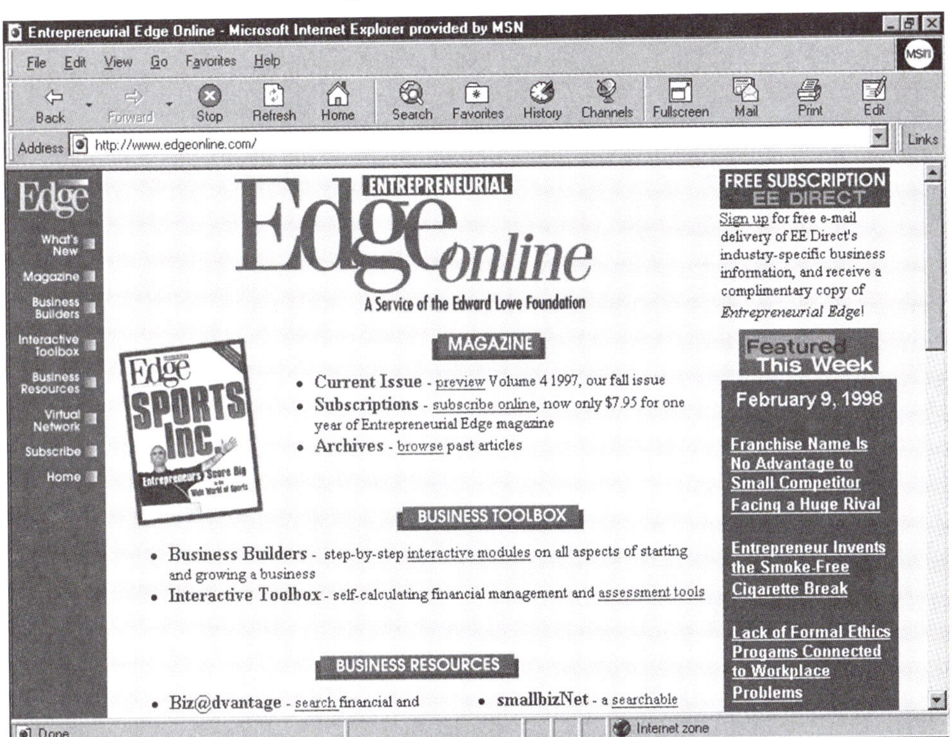

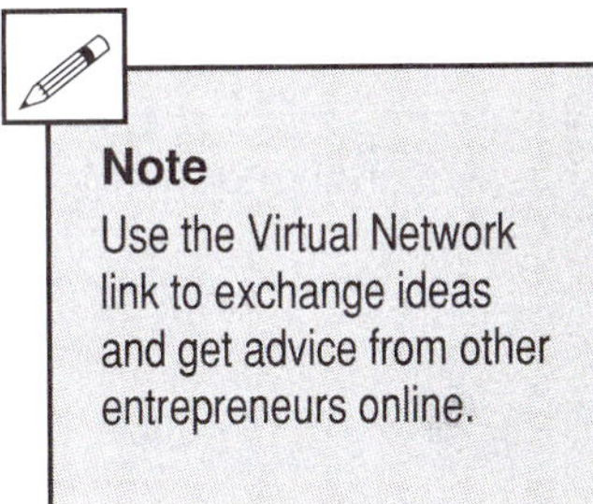

Note

Use the Virtual Network link to exchange ideas and get advice from other entrepreneurs online.

- An example is the interactive Balance Sheet I-Tool, which creates a balance sheet based on data you enter. The I-Tool is accompanied by a Business Builder article titled How to Prepare and Analyze a Balance Sheet.
- Use the I-Tools and the articles that accompany them to learn how to prepare common financial reports. Use the Arthur Andersen Enterprise Group Tools to analyze how your business management stacks up to the best practices recommended by this world-renowned consulting firm.
- Click the Magazine link to view the latest edition of Entrepreneurial Edge. Click What's New to read news that affects small business owners.

In this exercise, you will find information on starting and managing a small business at the Small Business Administration Web site. You will then use the Entrepreneurial Edge Online Web site to gather more small business advice and analyze management of your accounts receivable department.

Note: To ensure consistent results, this exercise uses simulated sites. The real URLs appear at the end of the exercise.

Web Search

Search for answers to the following questions using the Web sites you will visit in the Web simulation exercise.

1. According to SBA, what are the five things you need to start and manage a business?

   ____

2. How many key stages are there to SBA's plan to start a small business?

   ____

3. Name two of the most common reasons for starting a business.

   ____

4. What tip does the small business owner from Delaware offer?

   ____

5. According to the Market Planning article, what are the two kinds of target markets?

   ____

EXERCISE DIRECTIONS

1. Launch the Internet simulation. From the Main Menu, select Lesson 6, then select Exercise 3.
2. On the Address line, type the following and press Enter:

   http://www.sba.gov/

   ➲ *The U.S. Small Business Administration home page opens.*

Small Business Administration Home Page

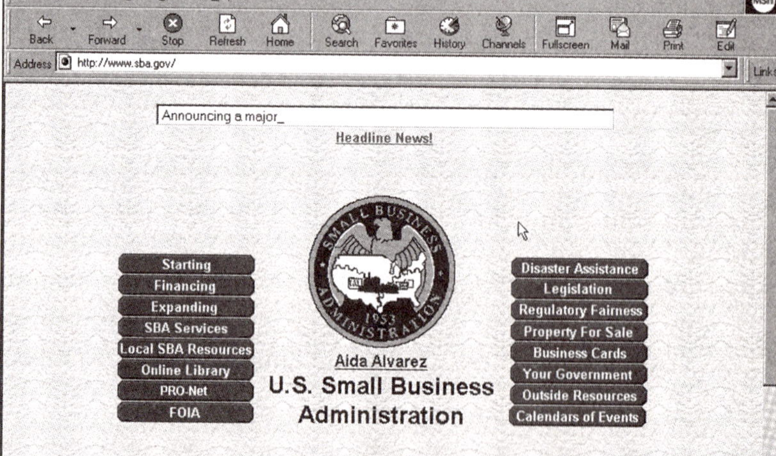

3. Click the Starting link.

   ➲ *The SBA Starting Your Business page opens.*

4. Click the Your First Steps link.

   ➲ *A page with a strategy for starting a new small business opens.*

5. Scroll down the page and read the plan provided by the SBA.

   ❓ *What do you think is the most important step in this plan for starting a successful business?*

6. Click your browser's Back button to return to the Starting Your Business page.

7. Click the Success Series link.

   ➲ *A table with three small business success tools opens.*

SBA Starting Your Business Page

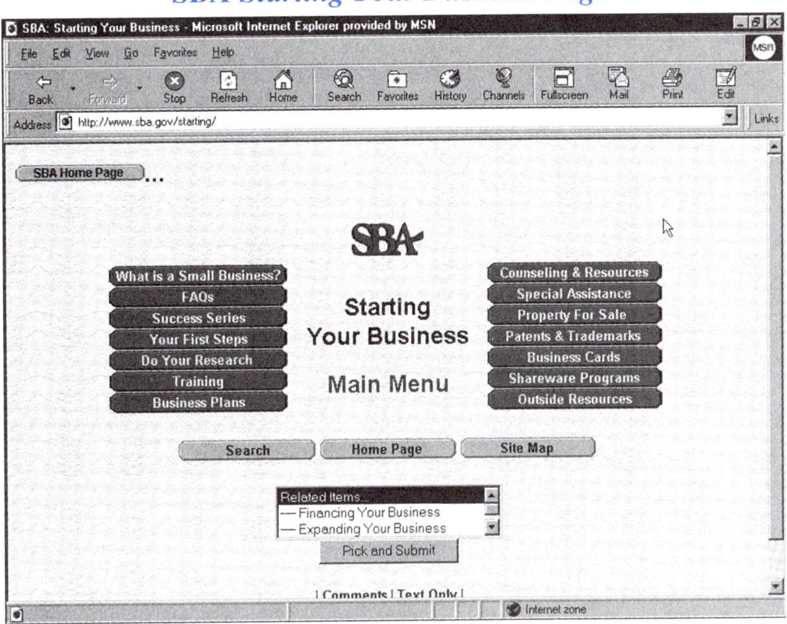

How to Start a Small Business

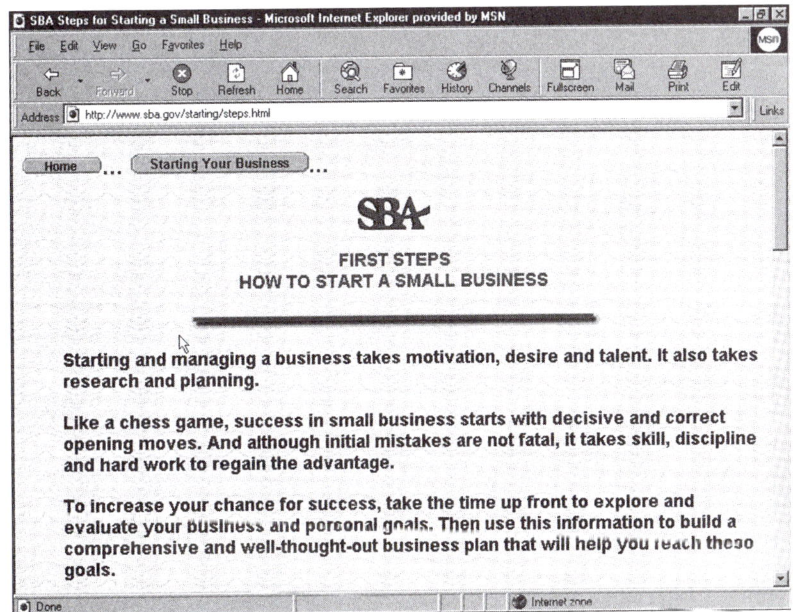

8. Click the Go To dot at the right of the Quiz item.

   ➲ *A page containing a small business success quiz opens.*

9. Scroll down the page and answer each question of the quiz.

   ✓ *Write your answers on a piece of paper.*

10. Check your quiz answers using the key at the bottom of the page. Refer to the quiz questions to see how points have been assigned to each answer.

    ✓ *Note how your score matches up with the business success quotient at the bottom of the page.*

11. Click your browser's Back button to return to the Success page.

12. Click the Go To dot at the right of the Tips item.

    ➲ *A page containing tips from award-winning small business owners opens.*

13. Scroll down the page and read the tips from these successful small business owners.

    ❓ *Imagine yourself starting a small business of your own. Which tip is most helpful to you?*

14. Click your browser's Back button to return to the Success page, then click the Home link at the top of the page.

    ➲ *The SBA home page opens.*

Small Business Success Quiz

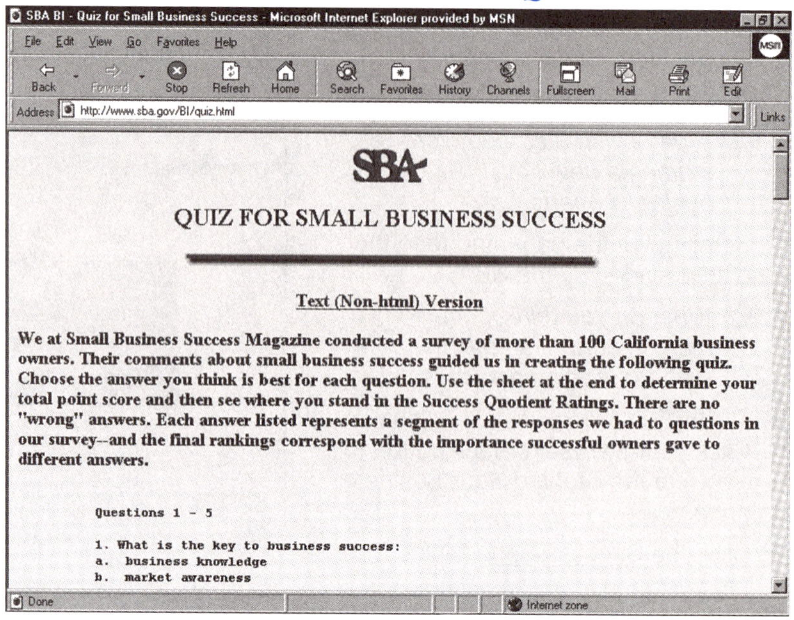

Tips from Small Business Owners

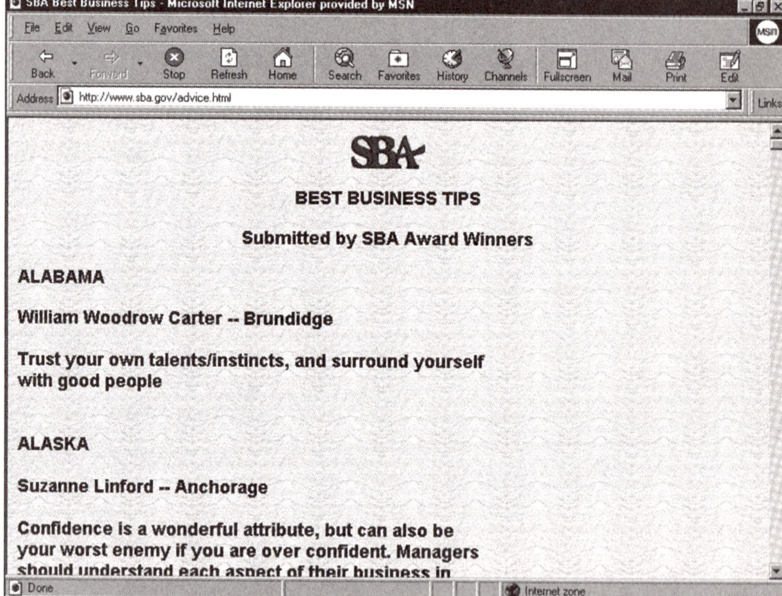

15. Click the Y2K link.

   ➲ *The SBA Year 2000 computer help page opens.*

16. Click the Definition of the Y2K Problem link.

   ➲ *A page opens describing the problem many computer systems will have when the year 2000 arrives.*

17. Scroll down and read the page describing the Y2K problem.

   ❓ *Do you think this problem will have an impact on you or your computer? What steps can you take to counter it?*

SBA Year 2000 Computer Help

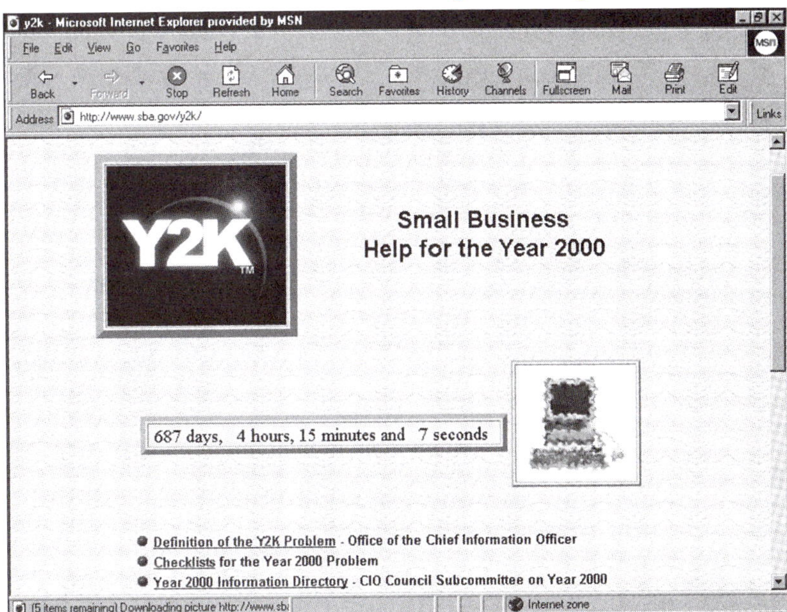

Description of the Year 2000 Computer Problem

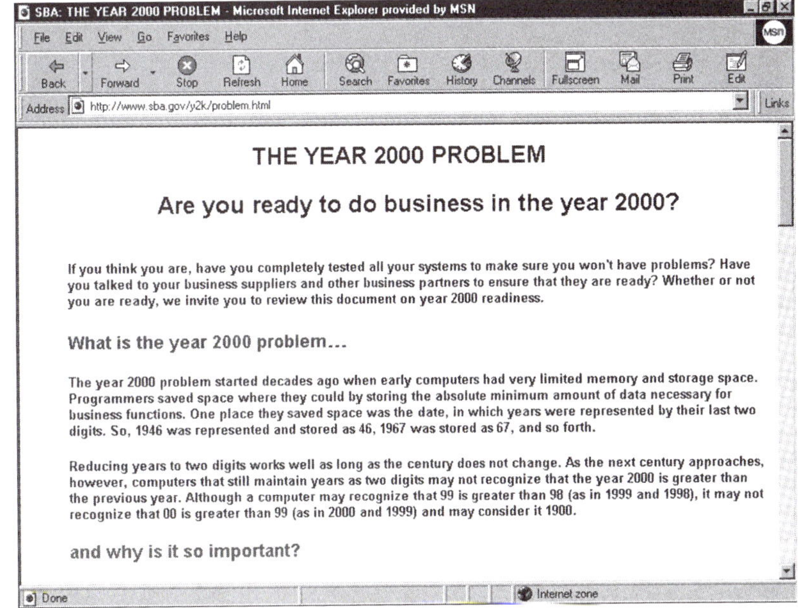

18. On the Address line of your browser, type the following URL and press Enter:

    http://www.edgeonline.com/

    ➲ *The Entrepreneurial Edge Online home page opens.*

19. Click the <u>Business Builders</u> link at the left of the page.

    ➲ *The Edge Online Business Builders page opens.*

Entrepreneurial Edge Online Home Page

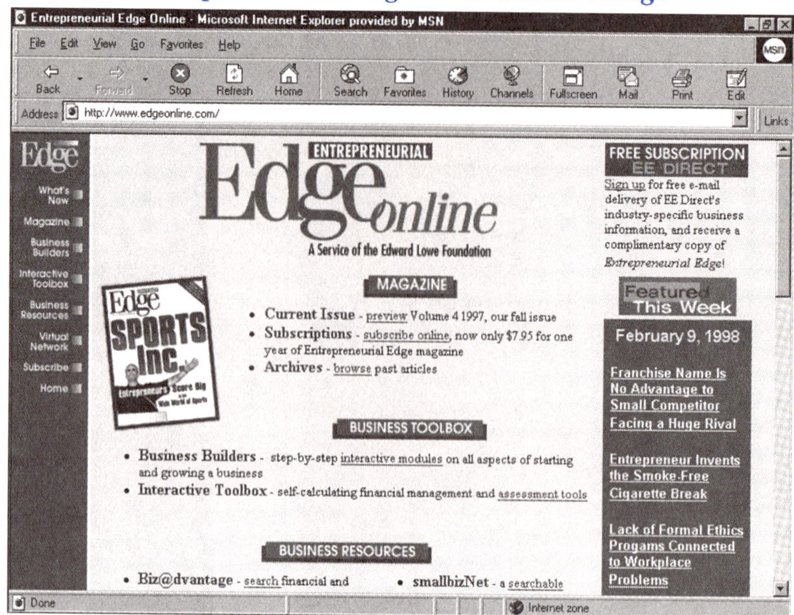

Edge Online Business Builders

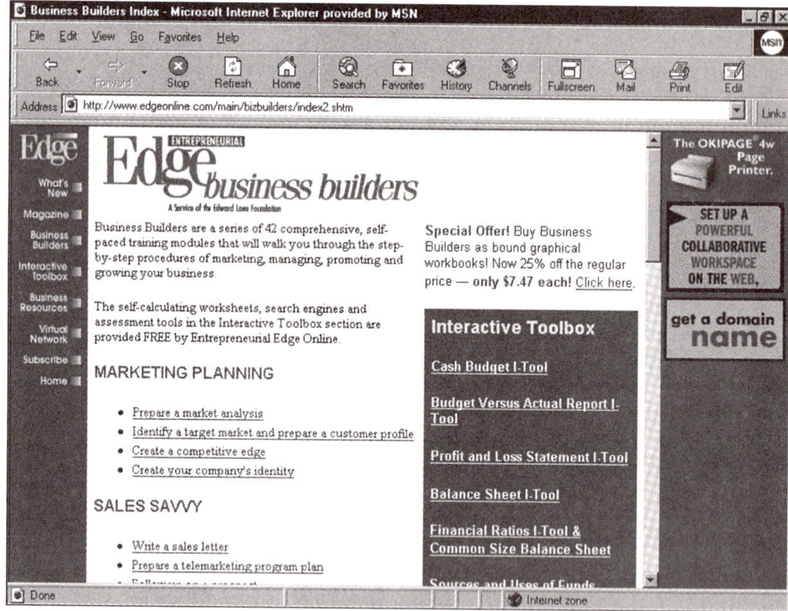

20. Click the Create a competitive edge link.

   ➲ *The How To…Gain a Competitive Edge page opens.*

21. Scroll down to read the article on building a competitive edge.

   Pay particular attention to Section B: What Is Your Target Market? And Section C: How Are Market Opportunities Classified?

   Imagine you are starting your own small business. How would you classify the market for your product or service?

22. Click the Interactive Toolbox link at the left of the page.

   ➲ *The Business Builders page opens with the Interactive Toolbox at right.*

23. Click the Global Best Practices Sales Force Assessment Tool link under the Arthur Andersen Enterprise Group Tools heading.

   ➲ *A questionnaire concerning accounts receivables practices opens.*

24. Click **Yes** or **No** to answer each question in the questionnaire.

How to Gain a Competitve Edge

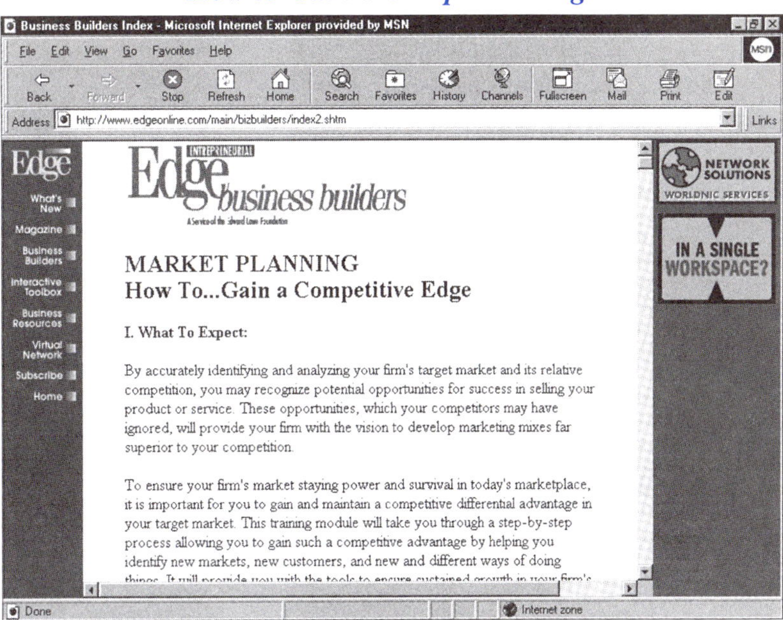

Global Best Practices Interactive Tool

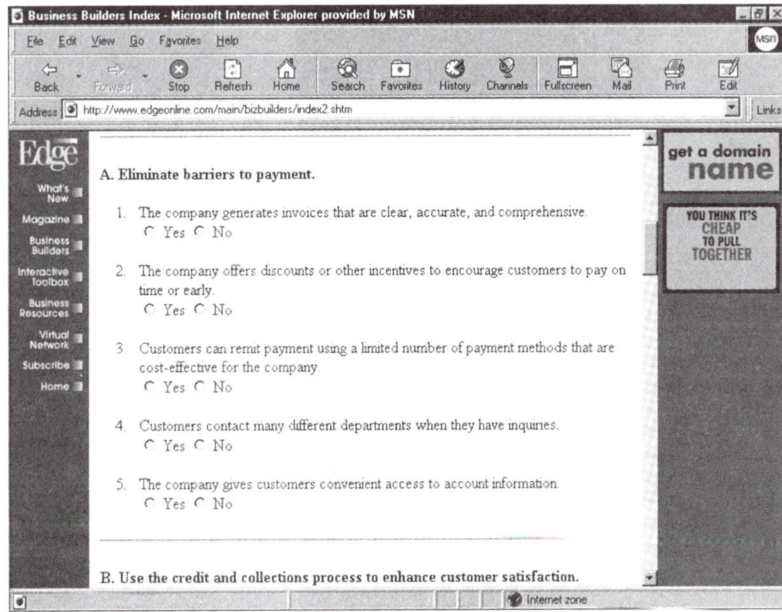

25. Click Generate Report.

   ➲ *A report showing your survey results opens. Note which areas of accounts receivable management require attention and improvement.*

26. Continue on to the next exercise.

   OR

   Exit from the simulation.

Accounts Receivable Survey Results

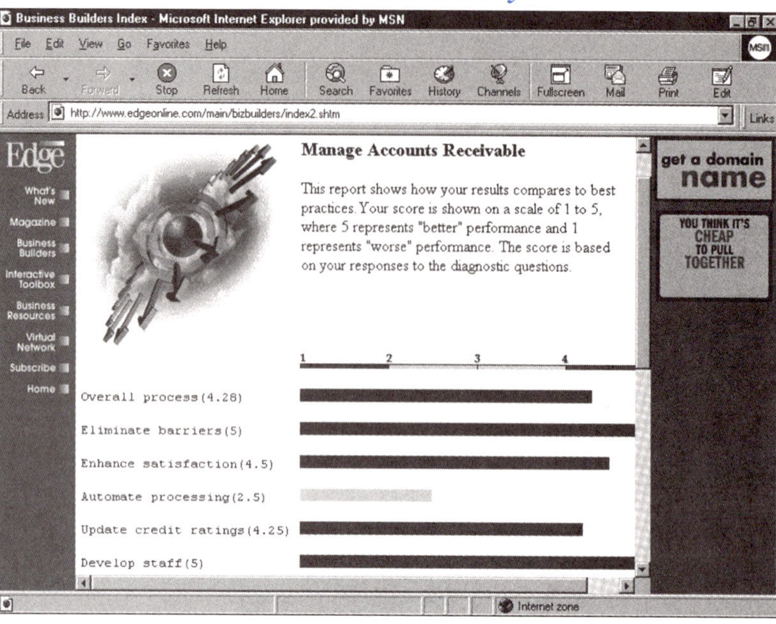

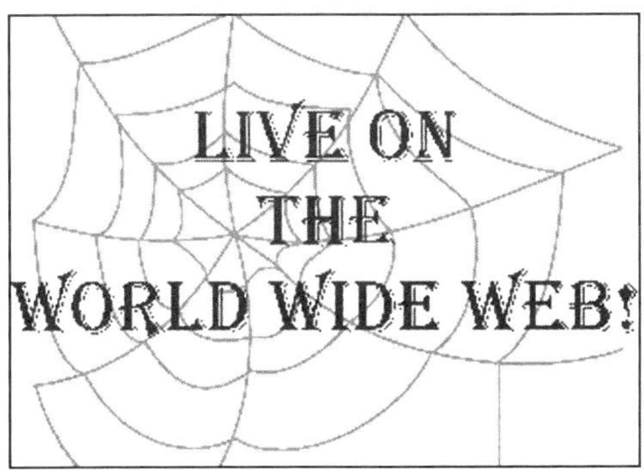

Small Business Administration Home Page
http://www.sba.gov/

Entrepreneurial Edge Online Home Page
http://www.edgeonline.com/

Exercise 4

- Research Computer Purchases with CNET
- Purchase a Computer Online
- Troubleshoot Computer Problems with The Tech Support Guy

NOTES

Research Computer Purchases with CNET

- Dozens of technology Web sites make fin
- ding computer bargains online easy. Search tools available at these sites enable you to compare a wider variety of makes and models than you can find at a consumer electronics megastores.
- One of the most complete resources for buying and learning about computers is the CNET Web site. This site has excellent new product reviews, price and performance comparison charts, software downloads, and feature columnists who keep you up to date about computer and technology trends.

CNET Home Page

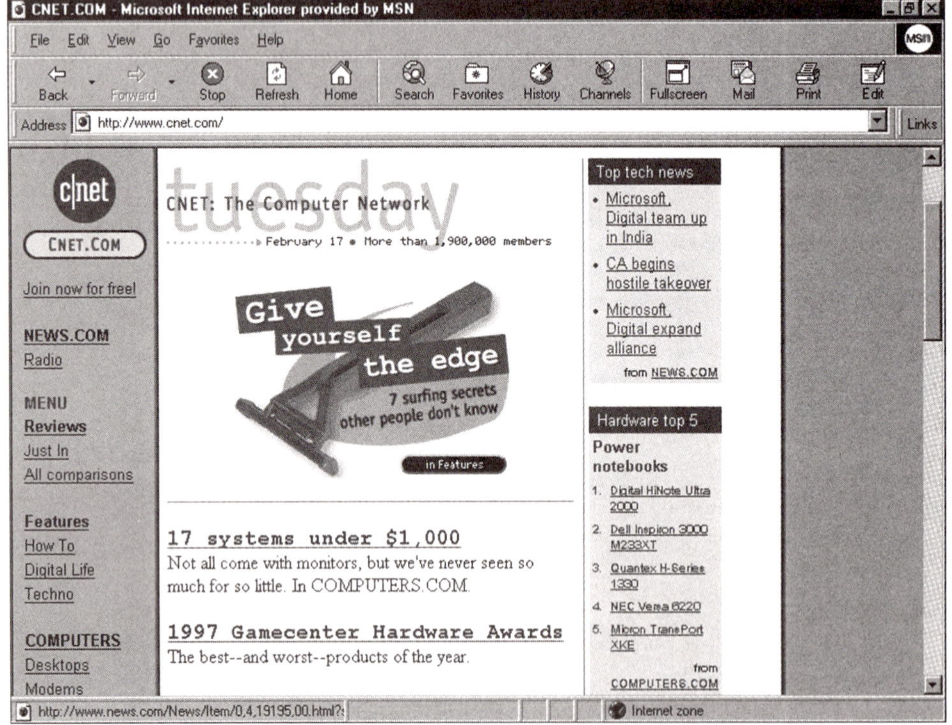

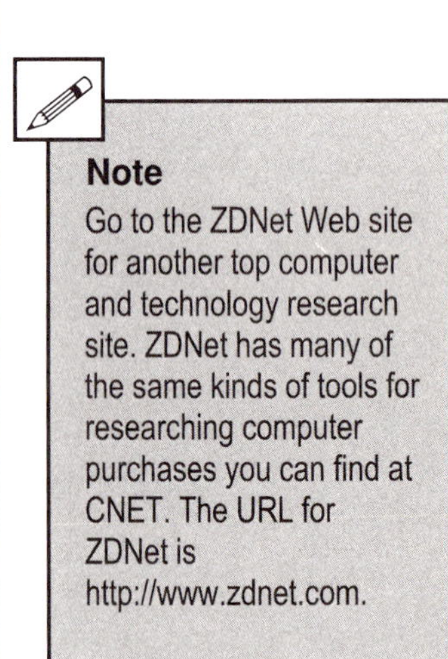

Note

Go to the ZDNet Web site for another top computer and technology research site. ZDNet has many of the same kinds of tools for researching computer purchases you can find at CNET. The URL for ZDNet is http://www.zdnet.com.

- To make an educated purchasing decision, click on the Reviews link or click on one of the product links featured on the CNET home page. Click the Just In link under Reviews to find reviews of the newest products on the market. Click the All comparisons link under Reviews to see a directory of links to reviews that discuss all types of computer products, from Web browsers to image editors to notebook computers.
- In addition, hardware reviews for specific product categories are featured in the Hardware top 5 box at the right of the CNET page. Top 5 lists feature reviews of products that CNET editors have selected as best in their category.
- Use the Features link on the CNET home page to keep up to date on trends in computer technology, find out how to maximize your time on the Web, and improve your computing skills with helpful tips and pointers.
- You can continue your research by clicking the Computers link on the CNET home page. Here you can select a product category such as desktop PCs and then view comparison charts for all products in the category.

Note
Click the Personalities link at the CNET home page to read the opinions of top-flight columnists. Click the Resources link for technical information and troubleshooting help online.

CNET Product Comparison Table

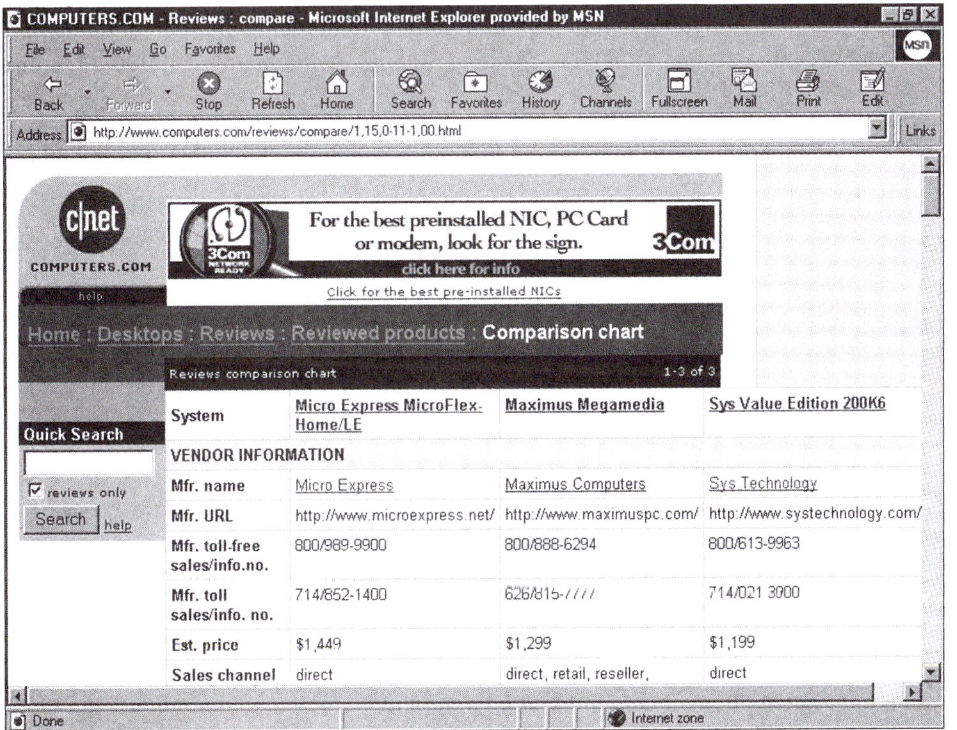

System	Micro Express MicroFlex-Home/LE	Maximus Megamedia	Sys Value Edition 200K6
VENDOR INFORMATION			
Mfr. name	Micro Express	Maximus Computers	Sys Technology
Mfr. URL	http://www.microexpress.net/	http://www.maximuspc.com/	http://www.systechnology.com/
Mfr. toll-free sales/info.no.	800/989-9900	800/888-6294	800/613-9963
Mfr. toll sales/info. no.	714/852-1400	626/815-7777	714/021 3000
Est. price	$1,449	$1,299	$1,199
Sales channel	direct	direct, retail, reseller,	direct

- Products are presented in a table listing price and performance. You can then click specific products for more detail. A custom fact sheet appears listing all relevant features for the product you select.
- Click a product's name to see the CNET review of the product, then click the manufacturer name at the bottom of the review to go directly to the manufacturer Web site and order online.

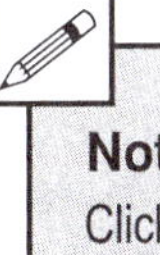

Note
Click Download.com to search for and download software. Click Shareware.com to search for and download top shareware programs. Use the Browser.com link to download the latest Web browser software upgrades.

Purchase a Computer Online

- After selecting a computer (or other piece of hardware) you want to purchase, you can often go directly to the manufacturer's Web site to buy the item online.

Maximus Computers Online Order Form

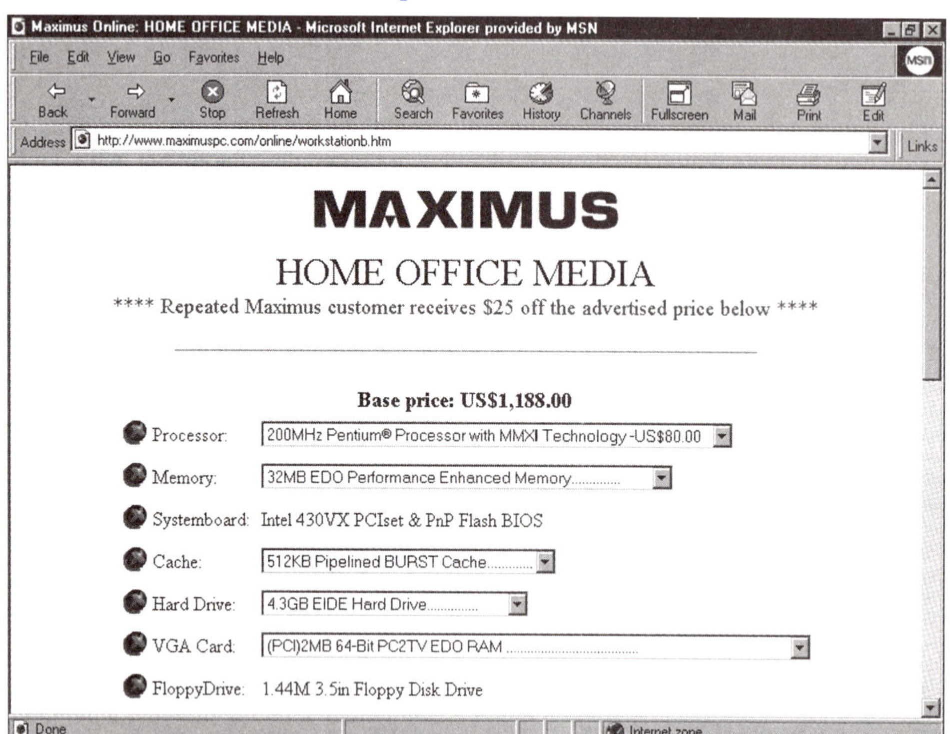

- For example, the Maximus Computers home page features best value systems, listing their specifications and price. Click the link for one of these systems to place an online order.
- Click the Maximus Systems link to view more featured computer systems. Click one of the systems links to go to an online order form where you can customize the system's configuration. For example, you may want to add more memory to the base system or change the type of keyboard that ships with the base system.
- Use the Check Total button at the bottom of the order form to see how your custom changes affect the base price. Click Reset Configuration if you want to cancel custom changes and return to the base system. If you are satisfied with the system configuration and price, click Order Now to place your order online.

Note

Web sites such as Internet Shopping Network and Insight Direct are devoted to computer shopping online. Some don't have detailed product reviews like CNET or ZDNet, but they feature bargain prices and enable you to buy online at their sites.

Troubleshoot Computer Problems with the Tech Support Guy

- What do you do when you receive the dreaded "not enough memory to perform operation" error message? How do you open a Zip file? When you need answers to questions such as these, you can turn to a number of tech support Web sites. These sites provide detailed information that can help you troubleshoot computer hardware and software problems.

Answers from The Tech Support Guy

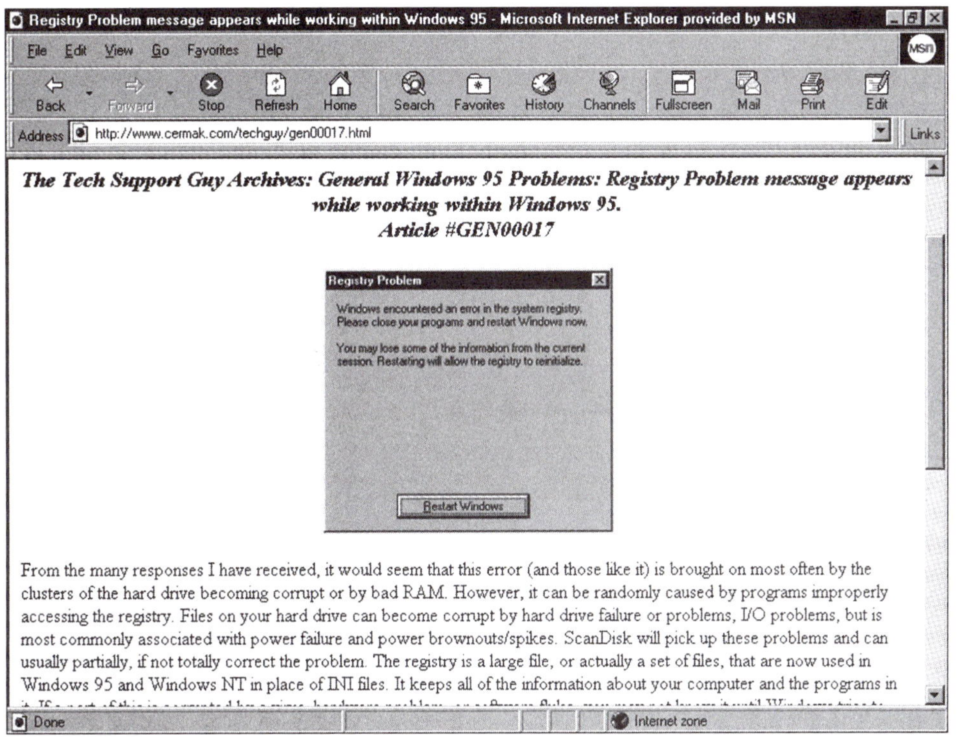

- In addition to tech support sites from hardware and software giants such as Microsoft, there are a number of independent sites dedicated to helping you solve your problem. The Tech Support Guy Web site provides answers to many common computing obstacles.
- The Tech Support Guy home page features two ways to find a quick answer. You can enter a topic into the site's search engine or click The Archives link.
- At The Archives page you can select from a directory of major categories. Click a category link to see links to solutions for the most frequently encountered problems. Articles are concise and aimed at the moderately experienced computer user.
- If you don't find the answer you need, you can also click the Submit link to send a question to the site. Either The Tech Support guy himself (yes, he is a real person, named Michael J. Cermak, Jr.) or other visitors to the site will attempt to answer your question.

Note

Click the Most Requested Utilities link at The Archives page to download useful utilities such as a security fix for Internet Explorer 4 and Microsoft emergency recovery tools for backing up system files.

In this exercise, you will search for a computer system online using the CNET Web site and then purchase a custom computer system at the Maximus Computers Web site. You will also troubleshoot common computer problems using the archives at The Tech Support Guy Web site.

Note: To ensure consistent results, this exercise uses simulated sites. The real URLs appear at the end of the exercise.

Web Search

Search for answers to the following questions using the Web sites you will visit in the Web simulation exercise.

1. What are the topics of the 5 computer buying tips?

   ____

2. What is the most expensive computer listed in the Comparison Guide? What is its price?

   ____

3. What is the least expensive computer listed in the Comparison Guide? What is its price?

   ____

4. Which computer ranks lowest in the Cheap PC performance comparison?

   ____

5. Which of the three computers listed in the Comparison Chart has the longest parts warranty?

   ____

6. What is the Windows 95 Registry?

   ____

EXERCISE DIRECTIONS

1. Launch the Internet simulation. From the Main Menu, select Lesson 6, then select Exercise 4.
2. On the Address line, type the following and press Enter:

   http://www.cnet.com/

   ➲ *The CNET home page opens.*

CNET Home Page

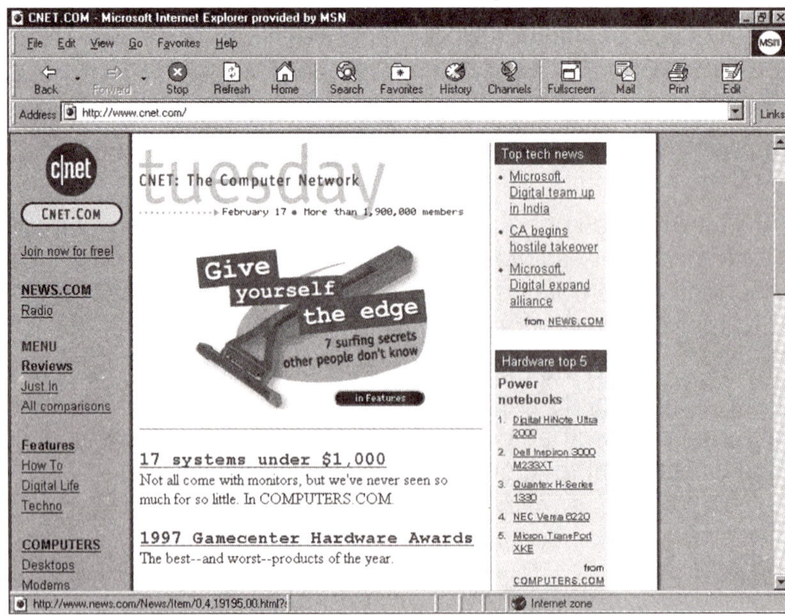

3. Click the 17 systems under $1,000 link.

   ➲ *The CNET Computers.com review of the cheapest PCs opens.*

CNET Computer Reviews

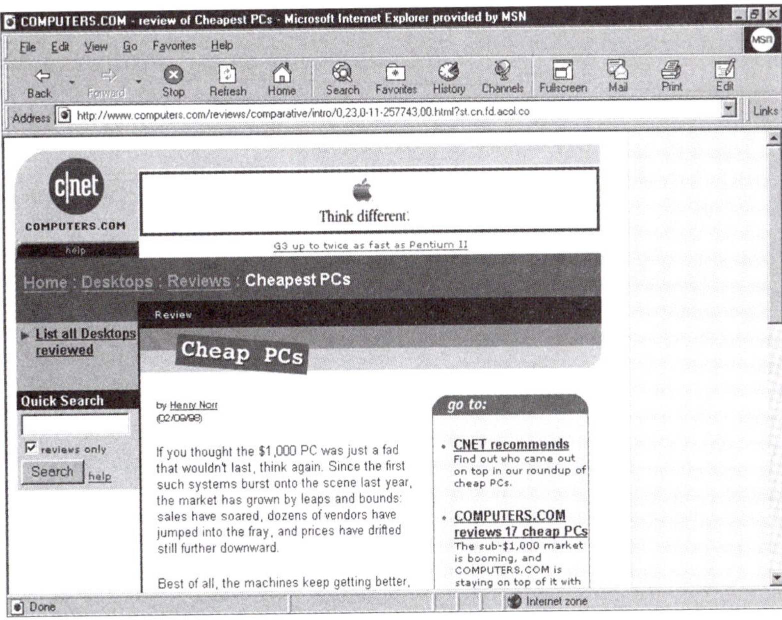

Computer Buying Tips

4. Click the Buying Tips link.

   A page listing computer tips for effective computer shopping opens.

5. Scroll down and read the suggestions CNET provides for finding the best value when shopping for computers.

6. Click the Comparison guide link near the top of the page.

   ➲ *A table comparing the 17 computer systems reviewed by CNET appears.*

7. Scroll down and review the various PCs listed in the comparison table.

   ✓ *Note the relationship of price to features included in the various models.*

Computer Comparison Guide

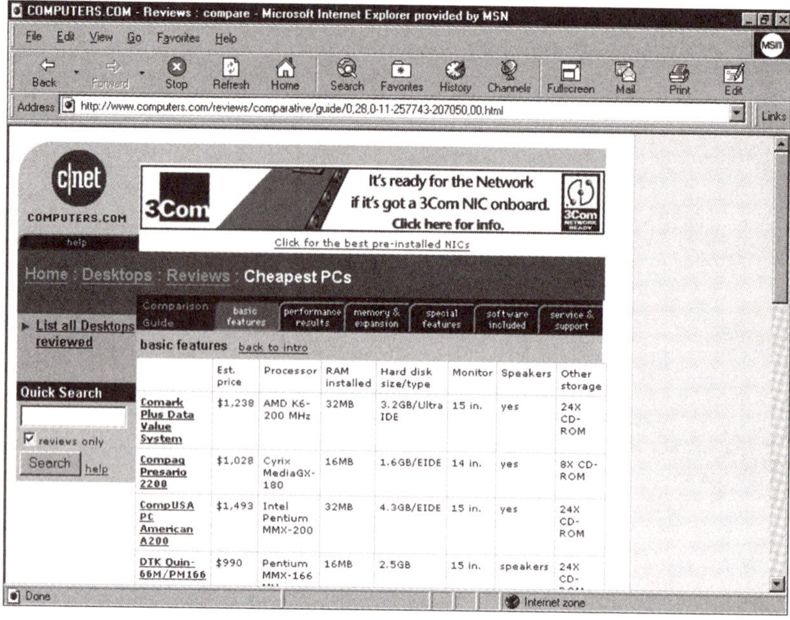

8. Click the performance results tab at the top of the Comparison Guide.

   ➲ *A table ranking the computer systems by performance opens.*

9. Scroll down to review how the various PCs rank in the performance comparison.

10. Read the general description of the performance test results at the bottom of the page, then click the How we tested link.

11. Read the description of the test CNET used to assess performance of the sub-$1,000 machines.

Computers Ranked by Performance

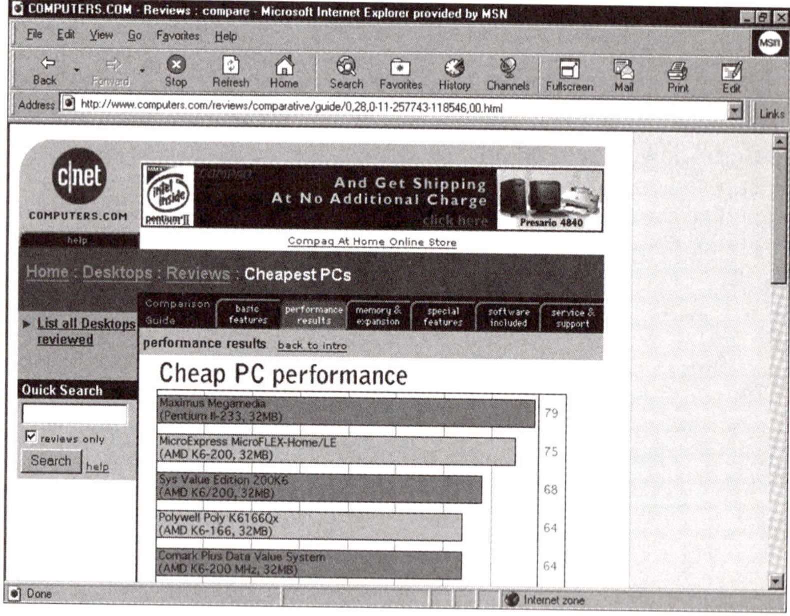

12. Click the List all Desktops reviewed link.
    - ➲ *A table listing all desktop PCs currently reviewed by CNET opens.*
13. Scroll down the page and click in the check boxes to select the following low-cost, high-performance PCs:

    Maximus Megamedia

    Micro Express MicroFlex-Home/LE

    Sys Value Edition 200K6
14. Click Compare.
    - ➲ *A table opens comparing in detail the three machines you selected.*
15. Scroll down the page to review the comparison.
    - ❓ *Which system do you think provides the best value?*
16. Return to the top of the page and click the Maximus Megamedia link.
    - ➲ *A review of the Maximus computer system opens.*

Table of All Reviewed PCs

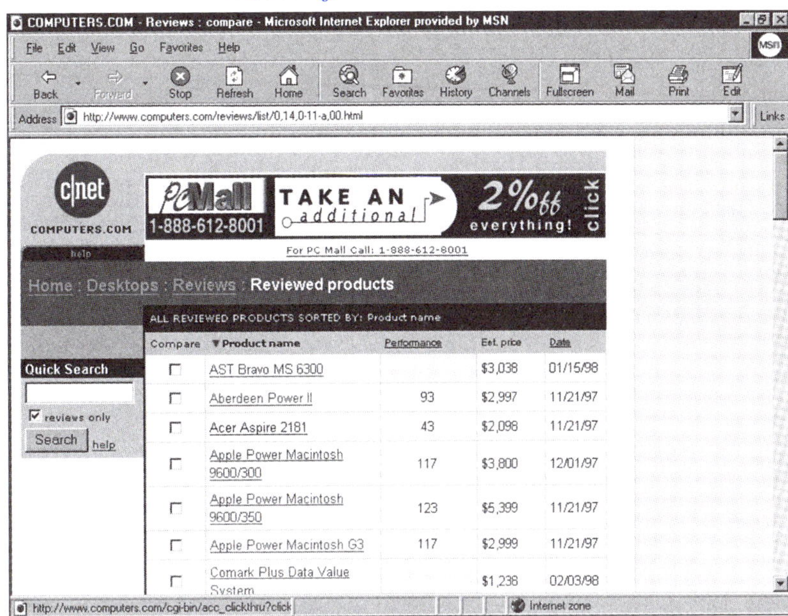

Head-to-Head Product Comparison

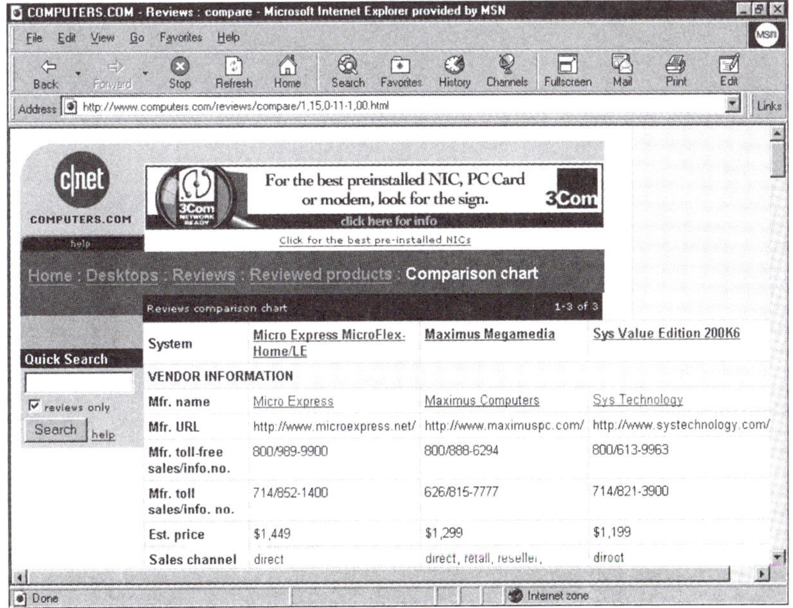

17. Scroll down to read the CNET review of the Maximus Megamedia system. Click the Maximus Computers link at the bottom of the page.

   ➲ *The Maximus Computers Web site opens.*

18. Click the Maximus Systems link.

   ➲ *A page listing the featured Maximus computer systems opens.*

CNET Computer Review

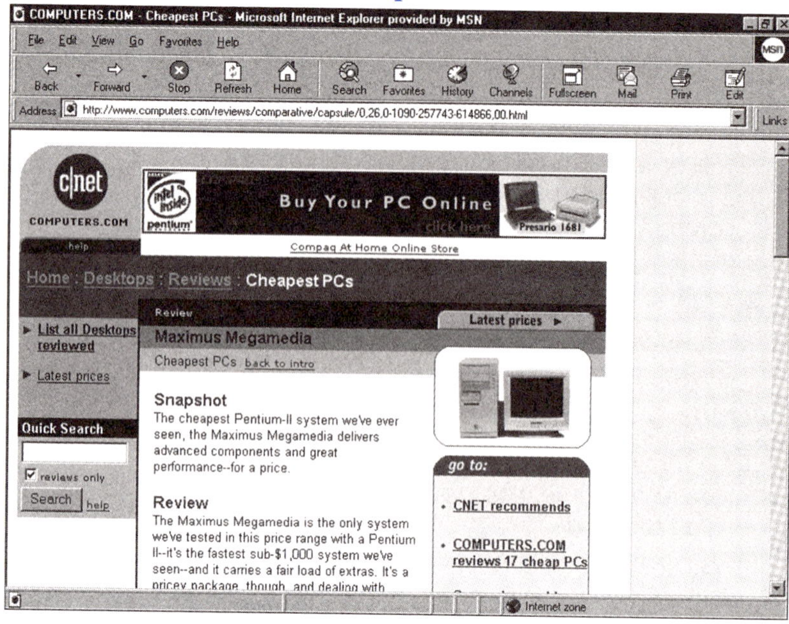

Maximus Computers Home Page

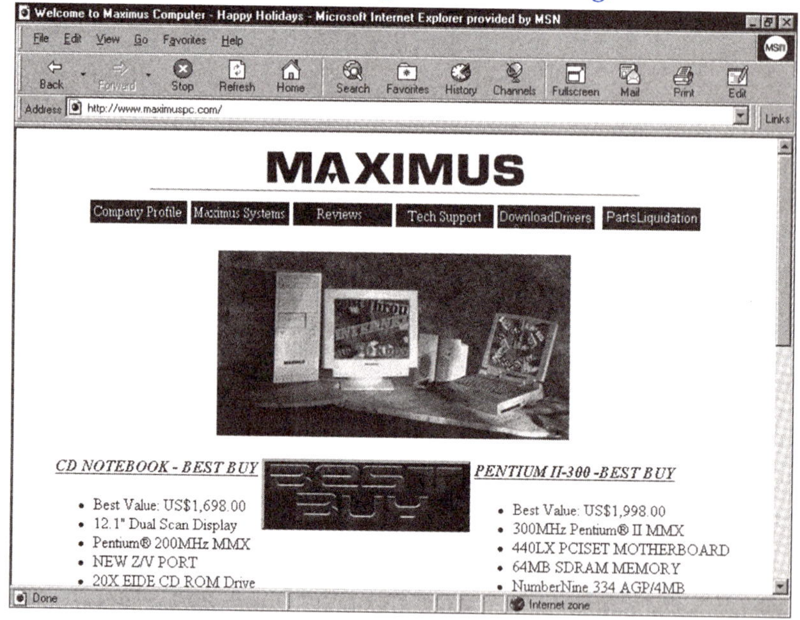

19. Click the Home Office Media link.
    - ➲ *A page for customizing the Home Office Media system appears.*
20. Select **200MHz Pentium Processor with MMX Technology-US$80.00** from the Processor menu. Click Check Total at the bottom of the page.
    - ➲ *A page confirming the system configuration and price for your order appears. Note that choosing the slower processor subtracts $80 from the listed base price.*
    - ✓ *If you were doing this exercise live on the Web, you could click Order Now to fill out an online order form and purchase the computer.*

Customize a Computer System

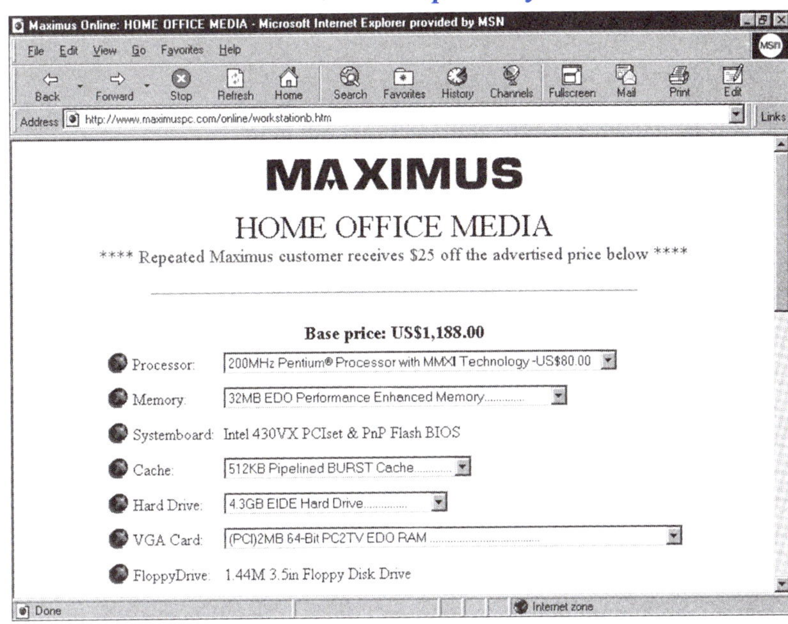

Confirm System Configuration and Order Price

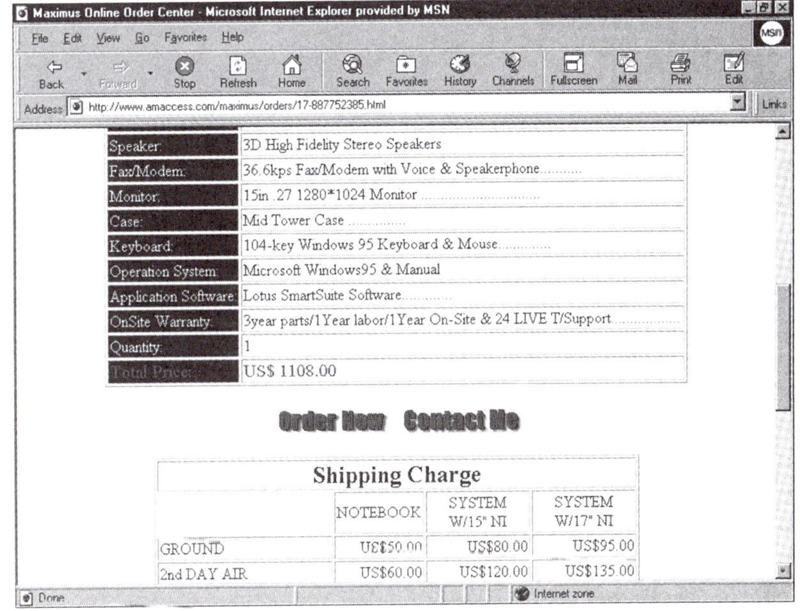

21. On the Address line of your browser, type the following URL and press Enter:

    http://www.cermak.com/techguy/

    ➲ *The Tech Support Guy home page opens.*

22. Click The Archives link.

    ➲ *A directory of category links for the Tech Support Guy archives opens.*

23. Click the General Microsoft Windows 95 Problems link.

    ➲ *A directory of Windows 95 and system problem links opens.*

Tech Support Guy Home Page

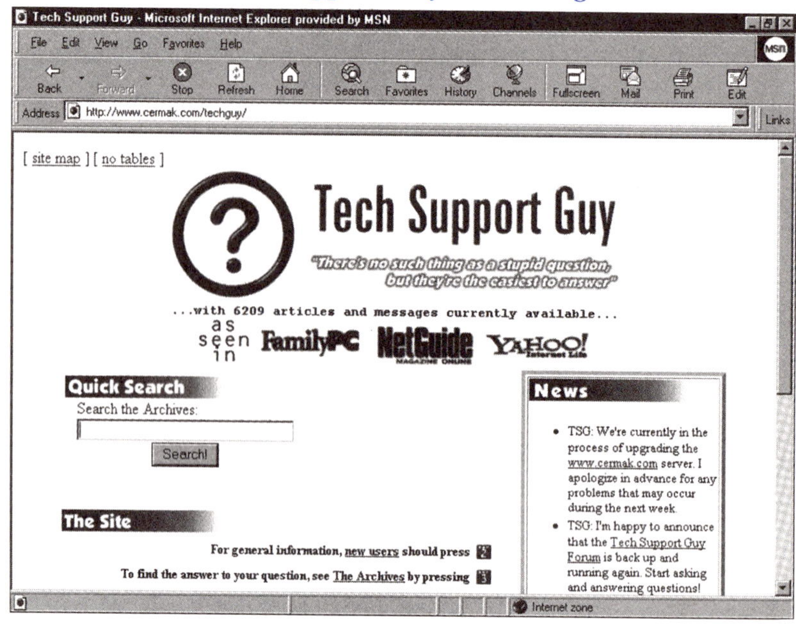

24. Click the Article #GEN00011 – ScanDisk won't scan all my hard disk link.

25. Read the article about problems with running ScanDisk while running Windows.

26. Click your browser's Back button to return to the Windows 95 Problems page.

Windows 95 Problem Links

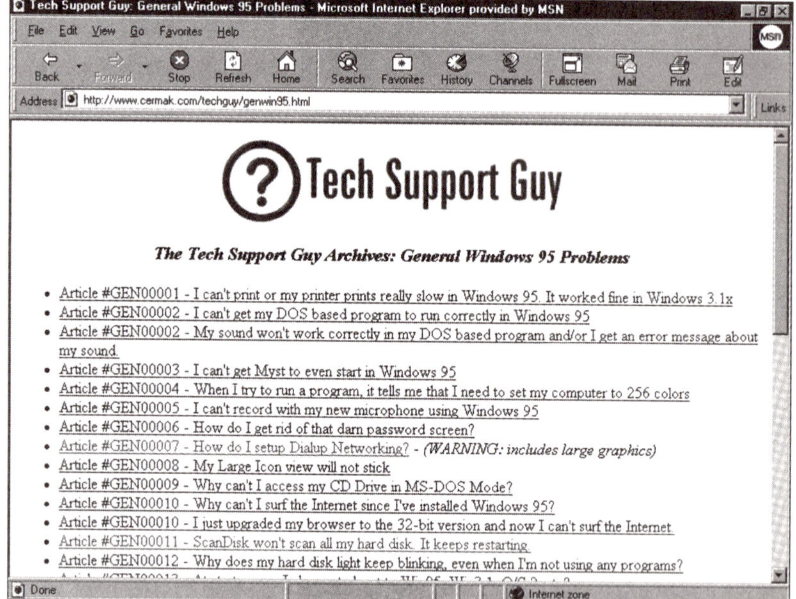

27. Click the Article #GEN00017 – Registry Problem message appears while working within Windows 95 link.
28. Read the solution provided by The Tech Support Guy.
29. Click your browser's Back button to return to the Windows 95 Problems page.
30. Click the Article #GEN00024 – What is the Windows 95 registry? link.
31. Read the description of the Windows 95 Registry.

    ✓ *Note the advice about how to prevent problems with the Registry.*

32. Continue on to the next exercise.

    OR

    Exit from the simulation.

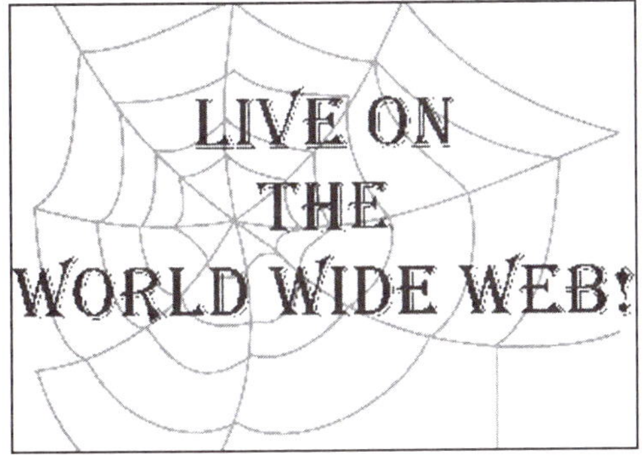

CNET Home Page
http://www.cnet.com/

Maximus Computers Home Page
http://www.maximuspc.com/

The Tech Support Guy
http://www.cermak.com/techguy/

Solution to Registry Error Message

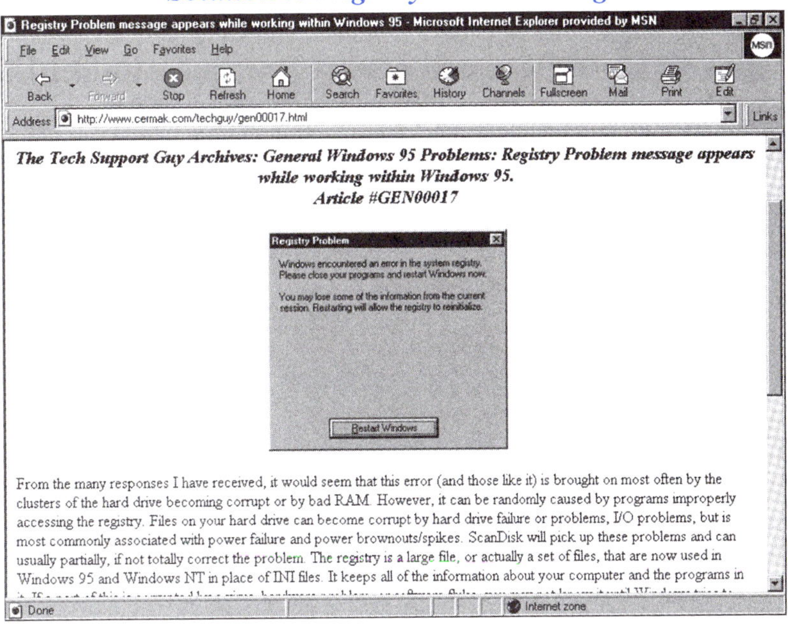

Exercise 5

- Send and Track Packages with the United States Postal Service
- Cut Your Phone Bill with TRAC

NOTES

Send and Track Packages with the United States Postal Service

- Track your business shipments using the United States Postal Service (USPS) Web site. The USPS site can help you choose the most cost-effective way to send your packages and track packages en route.
- The USPS Web site is simple and well organized. Click Express Mail Tracking, enter a package tracking number, and then click Enter to find the current location of a package.

USPS Home Page

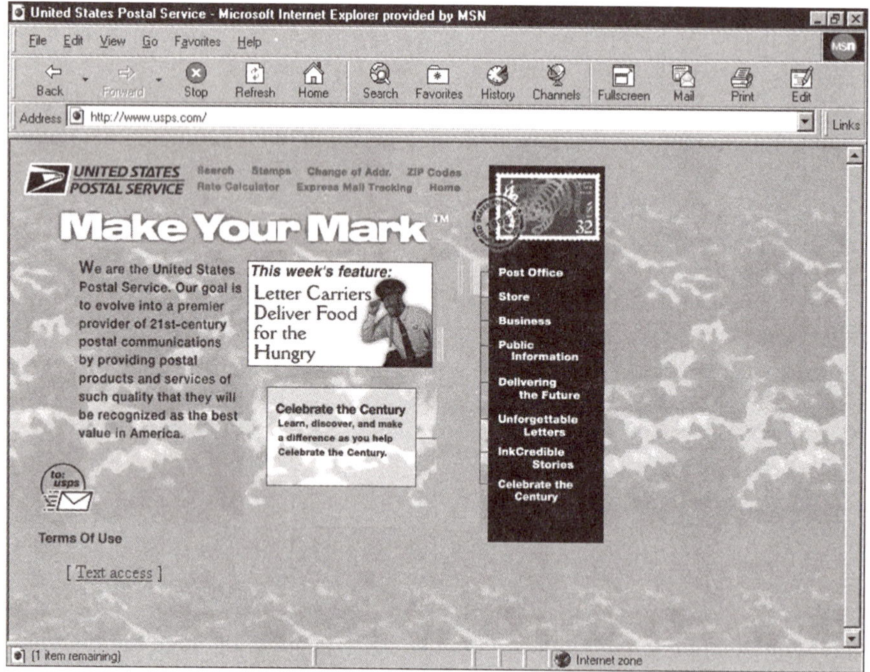

- Click Rate Calculator and enter a delivery address and package information to find out the cost of shipping a package via a particular USPS service. A list of costs for other delivery services such as registered mail, certified mail, and insurance is also supplied so that you can add those using the calculator as well.
- Click Post Office and then click Post Office Locator to find the nearest post office to you. Enter the location you want to check and then click Locate.

Note

Click the State Dept. Passport Info link from the Post Office page to download printable passport applications online. Click the IRS Tax Forms link from the Post Office page to download tax forms from the IRS Web site.

- Click ZIP Codes from the Post Office page to find the correct ZIP Code for any address in the U.S. You can also use this tool to find what ZIP Codes are associated with a city or town.
- Enter a city and state (such as Memphis, TN) and click Process to find out what ZIP Codes are associated with it. Enter a ZIP Code and click Process to find out what city or town is associated with it.

Cut Your Phone Bill with TRAC

- You can cut your phone costs by comparing long-distance phone service prices at the TRAC Web site. TRAC, the Telecommunications Research & Action Center, is a non-profit organization dedicated to helping telecommunications customers reduce their phone bills.

TRAC Long Distance Service Comparison

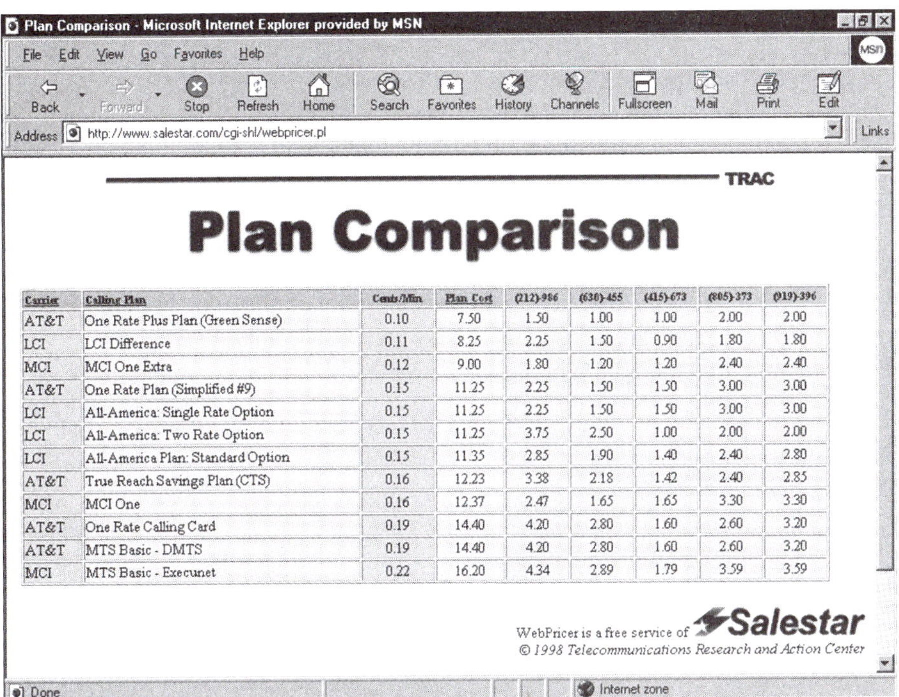

Carrier	Calling Plan	Cents/Min	Plan Cost	(212)-986	(630)-455	(415)-673	(805)-373	(919)-396
AT&T	One Rate Plus Plan (Green Sense)	0.10	7.50	1.50	1.00	1.00	2.00	2.00
LCI	LCI Difference	0.11	8.25	2.25	1.50	0.90	1.80	1.80
MCI	MCI One Extra	0.12	9.00	1.80	1.20	1.20	2.40	2.40
AT&T	One Rate Plan (Simplified #9)	0.15	11.25	2.25	1.50	1.50	3.00	3.00
LCI	All-America: Single Rate Option	0.15	11.25	2.25	1.50	1.50	3.00	3.00
LCI	All-America: Two Rate Option	0.15	11.25	3.75	2.50	1.00	2.00	2.00
LCI	All-America Plan: Standard Option	0.15	11.35	2.85	1.90	1.40	2.40	2.80
AT&T	True Reach Savings Plan (CTS)	0.16	12.23	3.38	2.18	1.42	2.40	2.85
MCI	MCI One	0.16	12.37	2.47	1.65	1.65	3.30	3.30
AT&T	One Rate Calling Card	0.19	14.40	4.20	2.80	1.60	2.60	3.20
AT&T	MTS Basic - DMTS	0.19	14.40	4.20	2.80	1.60	2.60	3.20
MCI	MTS Basic - Execunet	0.22	16.20	4.34	2.89	1.79	3.59	3.59

- The primary benefit at the TRAC Web site is the WebPricer Long Distance Plan Comparison. The WebPricer enables you to compare seven major long distance carriers (AT&T, MCI, Sprint, LCI, Matrix, Excel, and GTE) based on calling patterns you enter.
- Use the Plan Comparison form to enter how much you spend on long distance calling each month, your area code and three-number prefix, as well as the interstate numbers you want to compare (including, the time of day you call). After entering your calling pattern information, click Submit Calls to see the results.
- Comparison results are displayed in an easy-to-read table, with calling plans listed from the lowest rate to the highest. Special promotion plans are also noted in the comparison results.
- You can click the Plan Comparison column headings to change the order in which results are displayed. For example, click the Carrier heading if you want to see the comparison results in alphabetical order by long-distance carrier.

Note

Click the Choosing Your Long Distance Calling Plan link at the TRAC home page to get helpful advice about topics such as Top Ways to Save Money on Your Long Distance Bill, Time Periods, and Telephone "Slamming."

Note

The WebPricer compares only interstate long distance calls.

In this exercise, you will use the US Postal Service Web site to check the cost of shipping a package. You will also use the USPS site to find a location to drop off the package and to track the package. Finally, you will use the TRAC Web site to get tips on choosing a long-distance phone service and to compare long-distance calling plans.

Note: *To ensure consistent results, this exercise uses simulated sites. The real URLs appear at the end of the exercise.*

Web Search

Search for answers to the following questions using the Web sites you will visit in the Web simulation exercise.

1. What is the ZIP+4 Code for the DDC Publishing office in New York?

   ____

2. What is the Carrier Route for this address?

   ____

3. What is the cost of shipping the package by Express Mail?

   ____

4. What is the location of the nearest post office, as shown by the Post Office Locator?

   ____

5. According to the Tracking Information, when was the first attempted delivery of the Express Mail package?

   ____

6. On the Taking Charge of Your Telephone Bill page, what does LATA stand for?

   ____

7. What does the Telephone "Slamming" page say can be used by phone companies to obtain a customer's written authorization to change phone companies?

   ____

8. With the Plan Comparison table sorted by Calling Plan, what is the most expensive call on the fifth line down of the table?

   ____

EXERCISE DIRECTIONS

1. Launch the Internet simulation. From the Main Menu, select Lesson 6, then select Exercise 5.
2. On the Address line, type the following and press Enter:

   http://www.usps.com

   ➲ *The United States Postal Service home page opens.*

US Postal Service Home Page

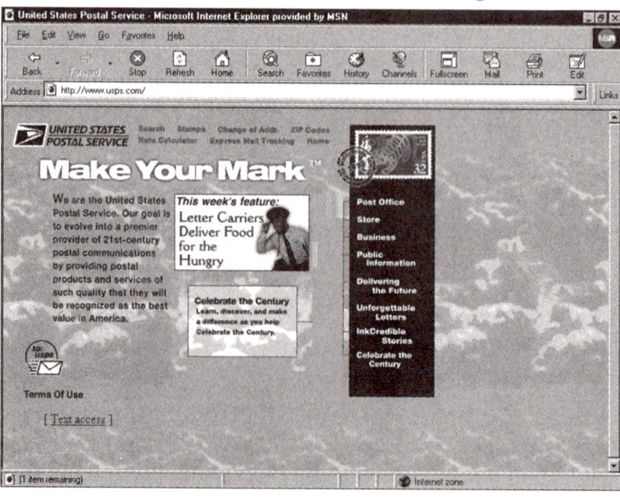

3. Click the Post Office link.
   - ➲ *The USPS Post Office page opens.*
4. Click the ZIP Codes link.
   - ➲ *The ZIP Code Lookup and Address Information page opens.*
5. Click the ZIP+4 Code Lookup link.
   - ➲ *The ZIP+4 Code Lookup page opens.*
6. Enter the following information in the text boxes on the Lookup page.

   Company: DDC Publishing

   Delivery Address: 275 Madison Avenue

   City: New York

   State: NY

   ✓ *Your form should look like the one shown in the illustration at right.*
7. Click Process Address.

   A page appears showing the ZIP+4 code for the address you entered.

   ✓ *You don't need to enter more specific information such as a suite number.*

USPS Post Office Page

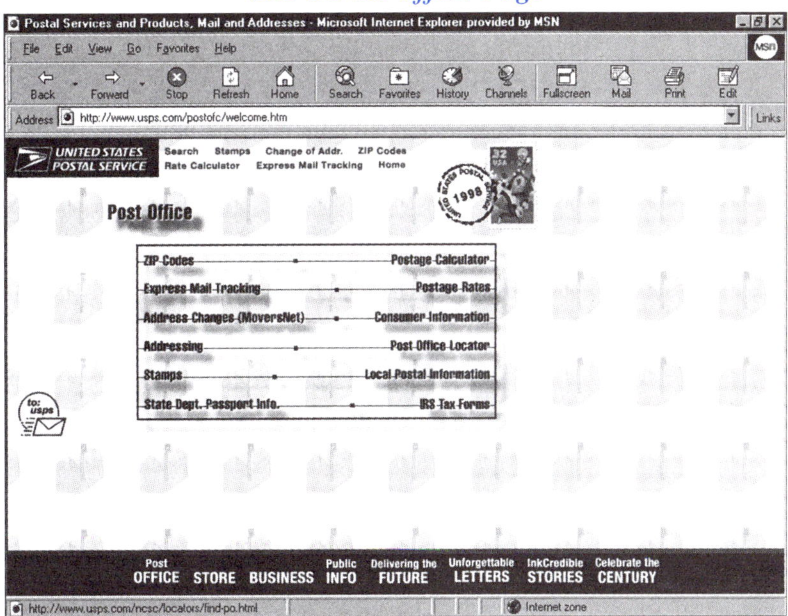

Look Up ZIP Code Form

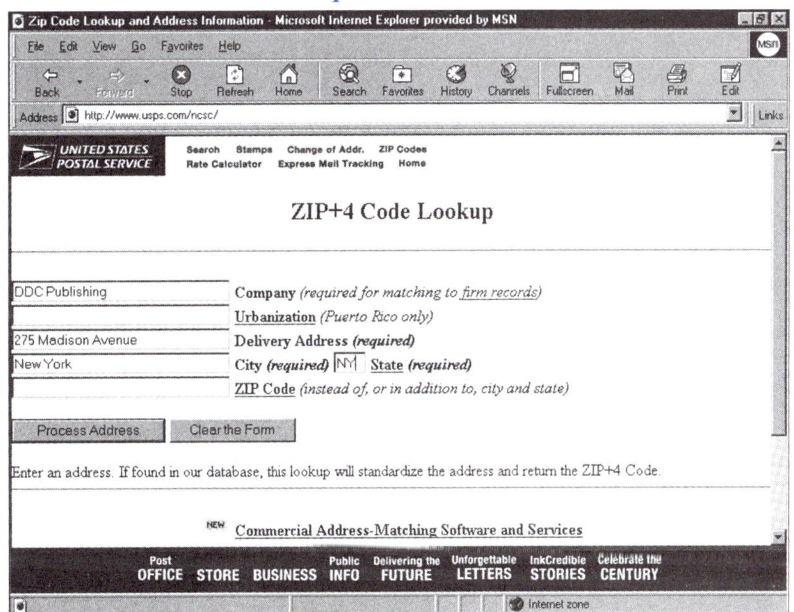

8. Click the Post OFFICE link at the bottom of the page.

   ➲ *The Post Office main page opens again.*

9. Click Postage Calculator.

   ➲ *The USPS Rate Calculators page opens.*

10. Click Domestic Rate Calculator.

    ➲ *The Domestic Rate Calculator page opens.*

11. Click A Large Envelope.

    ➲ *A form opens for you to enter shipping information.*

12. Enter the following information in the form:

    From ZIP Code: 46220

    To ZIP Code: 10016

    Pounds: 0

    Ounces: 4

    ✓ *Your form should look like the illustration at right.*

13. Click OK.

    ➲ *A page opens showing the cost of sending this package using different types of shipping.*

Domestic Rate Calculator Page

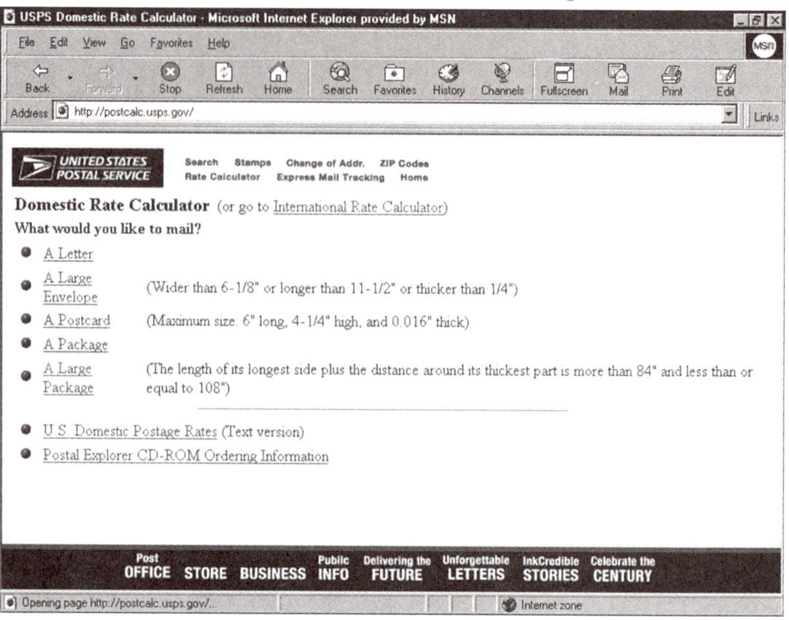

Enter Shipping Information

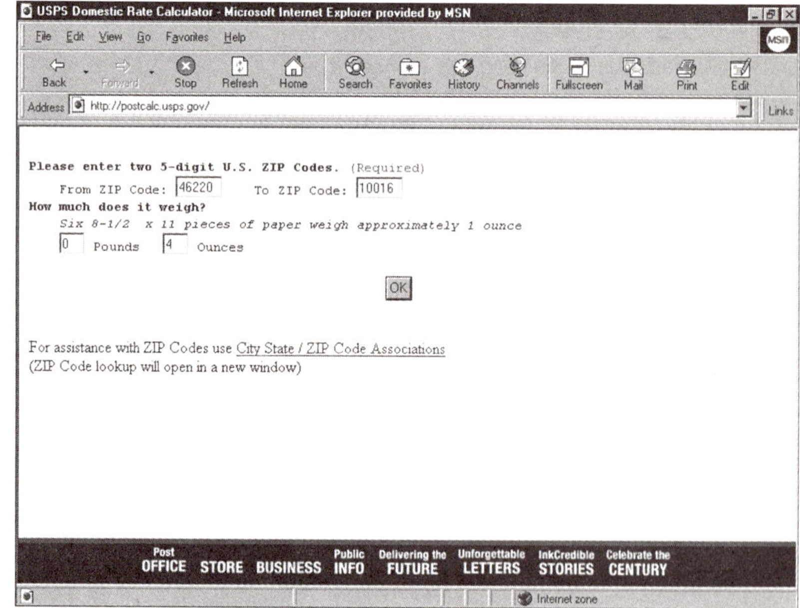

14. Click the Post OFFICE link again to return to the Post Office main page.
15. Click the Post Office Locator link.
    - *The Post Office Locator page opens.*
16. Enter the following information in the form:

    Delivery Address: 532 East 58th Street

    City: Indianapolis

    State: IN

    ZIP Code: 46220
17. Click Locate.
    - *The Post Office Locator page shows which post office delivers mail to the address. Nearby post offices are also shown.*
18. Click the Express Mail Tracking link at the top of the page.
    - *The Express Mail Tracking page opens.*
19. Enter the following package tracking number in the text box:

    EE347279042US
20. Click Enter.
    - *The package tracking results page appears.*
21. Click the See what happened earlier? button.
    - *A page showing the shipping history for the package appears.*

Enter Express Mail Tracking Number

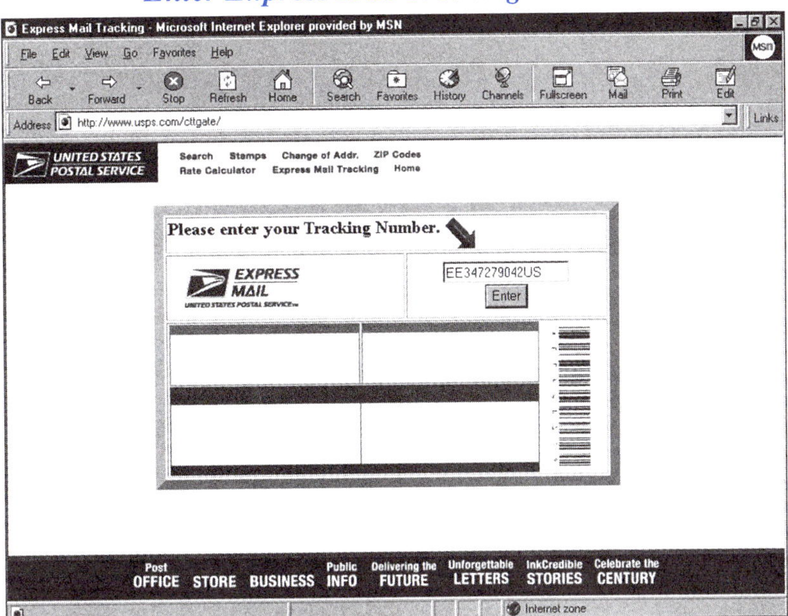

Package Tracking Results

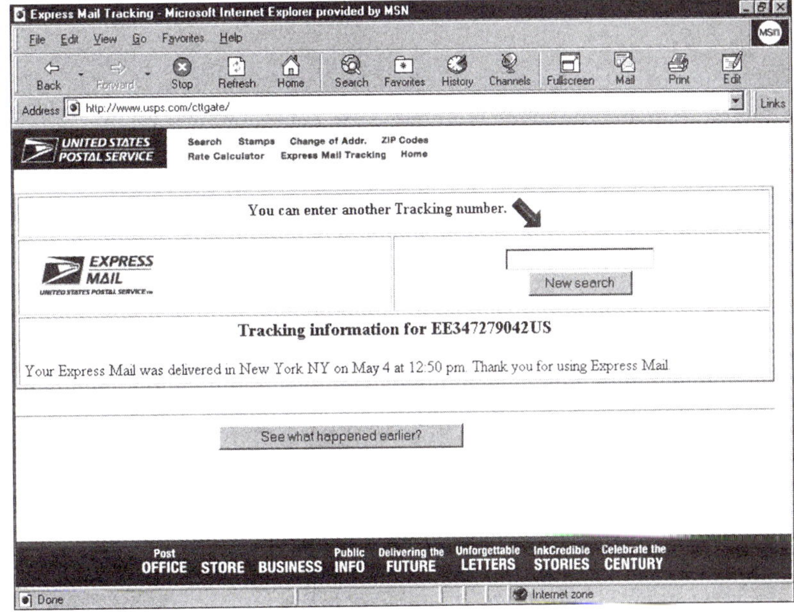

22. Type the following URL in your browser's Address line and press Enter:

    http://www.trac.org/

    ➲ *The TRAC home page opens.*

23. Click the Taking Charge of Your Telephone Bill link.

    ➲ *A checklist of advice for saving money on your long-distance phone bill opens.*

24. Scroll down to read the checklist of tips for making smart long-distance telephone service choices.

    ❓ *Have any of the problems described on this page happened to you?*

25. Click the Home link at the bottom of the page to return to the TRAC home page.

26. Click the Choosing Your Long Distance Calling Plan link.

    ➲ *A list of tips on choosing calling plans opens.*

TRAC Home Page

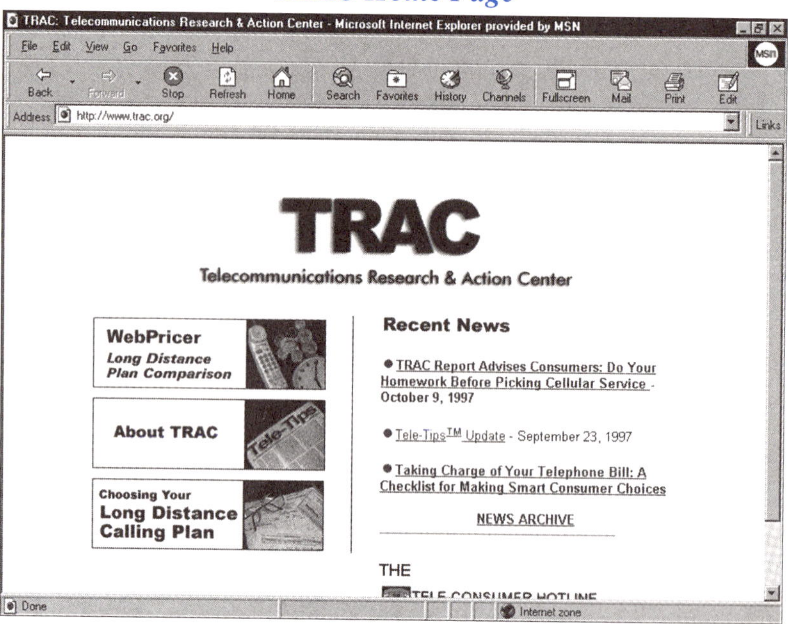

Phone Bill Consumer Checklist

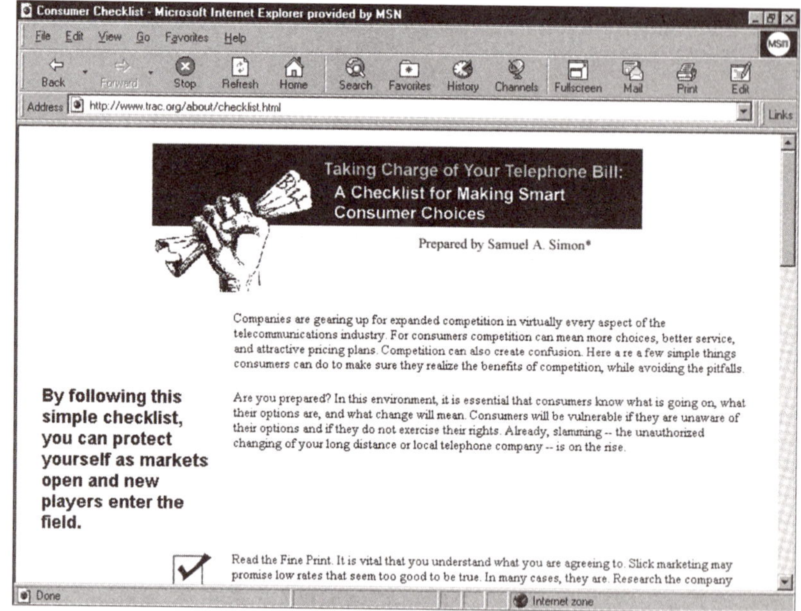

27. Click the Pre-Paid Calling Cards link.

   ➲ *A page describing pros and cons of using pre-paid calling cards opens.*

28. Read the calling cards page and then click your browser's Back button to return to the tips list.

29. Click the Telephone "Slamming" link.

   ➲ *A page describing the illegal practice of telephone "slamming" opens.*

30. Read the slamming page and then click the WebPricer link at the bottom of the page.

   ➲ *A page describing the TRAC Web Pricer opens.*

31. Click Get Me to the WebPricer at the bottom of the page.

   ➲ *The WebPricer Plan Comparison form opens.*

32. Click to select the following telephone companies to compare:

   AT&T, **MCI**, **LCI**

33. Enter the following sample information in the text boxes for questions 2 – 4:

   Question 2: 150, Question 3: 317, Question 4: 259

34. Enter the sample information shown in the illustration at right into the calling pattern text boxes for Area Code, Prefix, Calling Time, and Call Duration.

   ✓ *Click to select calling times.*

Tips for Choosing Long Distance Service

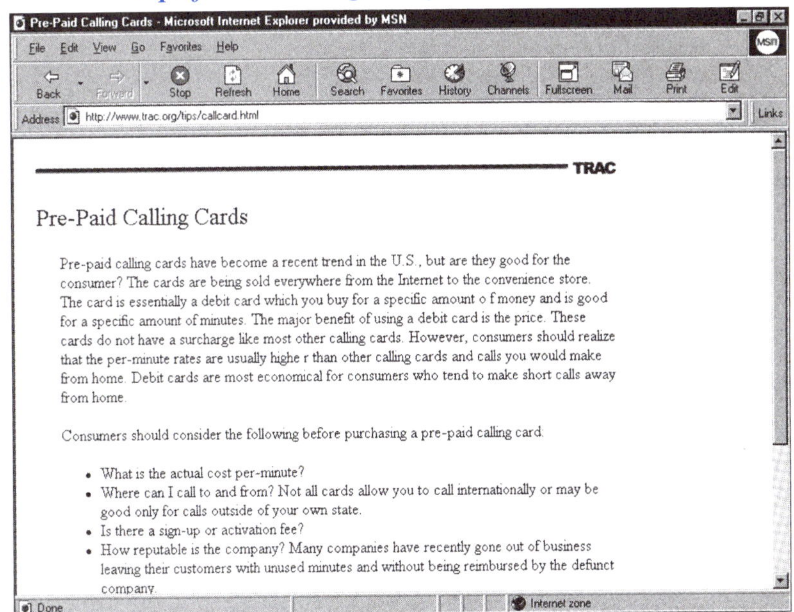

Pre-Paid Calling Cards - Microsoft Internet Explorer provided by MSN

Address: http://www.trac.org/tips/callcard.html

TRAC

Pre-Paid Calling Cards

Pre-paid calling cards have become a recent trend in the U.S., but are they good for the consumer? The cards are being sold everywhere from the Internet to the convenience store. The card is essentially a debit card which you buy for a specific amount o f money and is good for a specific amount of minutes. The major benefit of using a debit card is the price. These cards do not have a surcharge like most other calling cards. However, consumers should realize that the per-minute rates are usually highe r than other calling cards and calls you would make from home. Debit cards are most economical for consumers who tend to make short calls away from home.

Consumers should consider the following before purchasing a pre-paid calling card:

- What is the actual cost per-minute?
- Where can I call to and from? Not all cards allow you to call internationally or may be good only for calls outside of your own state.
- Is there a sign-up or activation fee?
- How reputable is the company? Many companies have recently gone out of business leaving their customers with unused minutes and without being reimbursed by the defunct company.

Enter Call Comparison Information

Area Code	Prefix	Day/Evening/Night	Call Duration (Minutes)
212	986	Day	15
630	455	Day	10
415	673	Evening	10
805	373	Night	20
919	396	Evening	20

TRAC Call Comparison Form

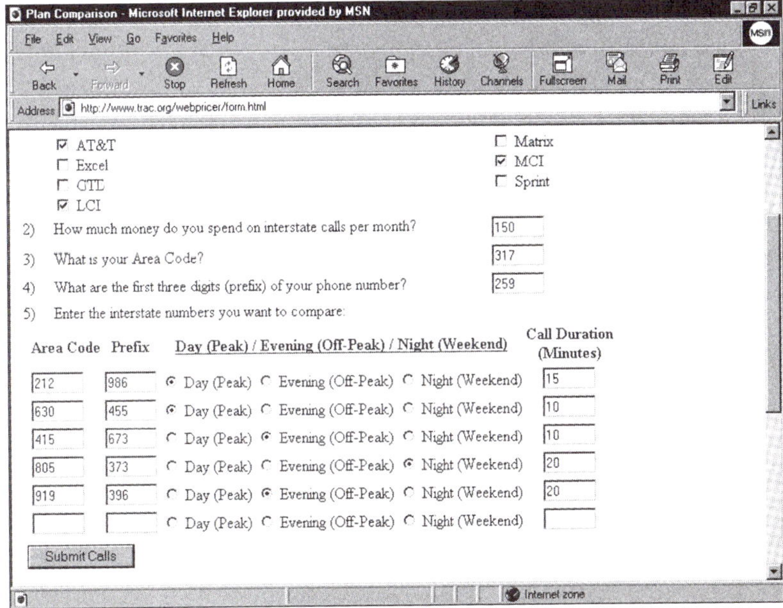

Plan Comparison - Microsoft Internet Explorer provided by MSN

Address: http://www.trac.org/webpricer/form.html

☑ AT&T ☐ Excel ☐ GTE ☑ LCI ☐ Matrix ☑ MCI ☐ Sprint

2) How much money do you spend on interstate calls per month? 150

3) What is your Area Code? 317

4) What are the first three digits (prefix) of your phone number? 259

5) Enter the interstate numbers you want to compare:

Area Code	Prefix	Day (Peak) / Evening (Off-Peak) / Night (Weekend)	Call Duration (Minutes)
212	986	● Day (Peak) ○ Evening (Off-Peak) ○ Night (Weekend)	15
630	455	● Day (Peak) ○ Evening (Off-Peak) ○ Night (Weekend)	10
415	673	○ Day (Peak) ● Evening (Off-Peak) ○ Night (Weekend)	10
805	373	○ Day (Peak) ○ Evening (Off-Peak) ● Night (Weekend)	20
919	396	○ Day (Peak) ● Evening (Off-Peak) ○ Night (Weekend)	20
		○ Day (Peak) ○ Evening (Off-Peak) ○ Night (Weekend)	

Submit Calls

35. Click Submit Calls.

➲ *A table showing calling plan comparison results appears. Note the wide range of charges for each of the calls you selected.*

36. Click the Calling Plan link.

➲ *The table is now sorted alphabetically by calling plan.*

37. Continue on to the next exercise.

OR

Exit from the simulation.

TRAC Calling Plan Comparison Table

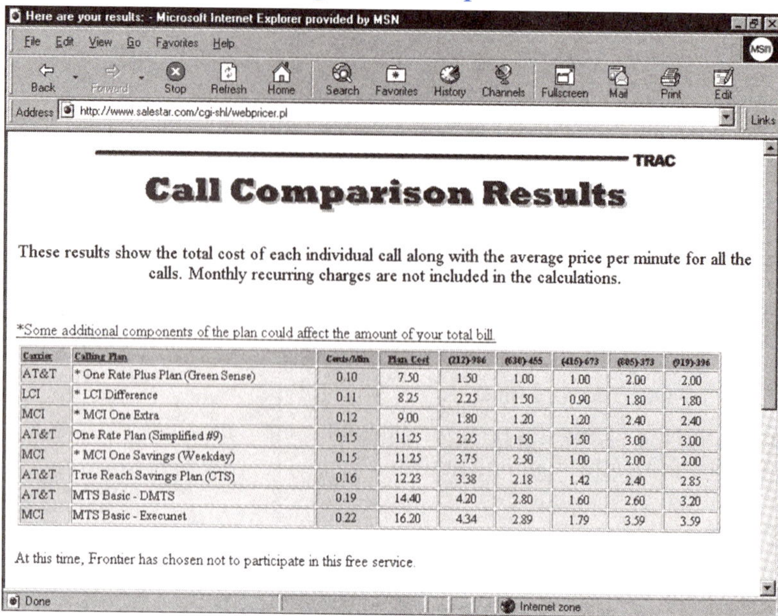

Call Comparison Results

These results show the total cost of each individual call along with the average price per minute for all the calls. Monthly recurring charges are not included in the calculations.

*Some additional components of the plan could affect the amount of your total bill

Carrier	Calling Plan	Cents/Min	Plan Cost	(212)-986	(630)-455	(416)-673	(805)-373	(919)-396
AT&T	* One Rate Plus Plan (Green Sense)	0.10	7.50	1.50	1.00	1.00	2.00	2.00
LCI	* LCI Difference	0.11	8.25	2.25	1.50	0.90	1.80	1.80
MCI	* MCI One Extra	0.12	9.00	1.80	1.20	1.20	2.40	2.40
AT&T	One Rate Plan (Simplified #9)	0.15	11.25	2.25	1.50	1.50	3.00	3.00
MCI	* MCI One Savings (Weekday)	0.15	11.25	3.75	2.50	1.00	2.00	2.00
AT&T	True Reach Savings Plan (CTS)	0.16	12.23	3.38	2.18	1.42	2.40	2.85
AT&T	MTS Basic - DMTS	0.19	14.40	4.20	2.80	1.60	2.60	3.20
MCI	MTS Basic - Execunet	0.22	16.20	4.34	2.89	1.79	3.59	3.59

At this time, Frontier has chosen not to participate in this free service.

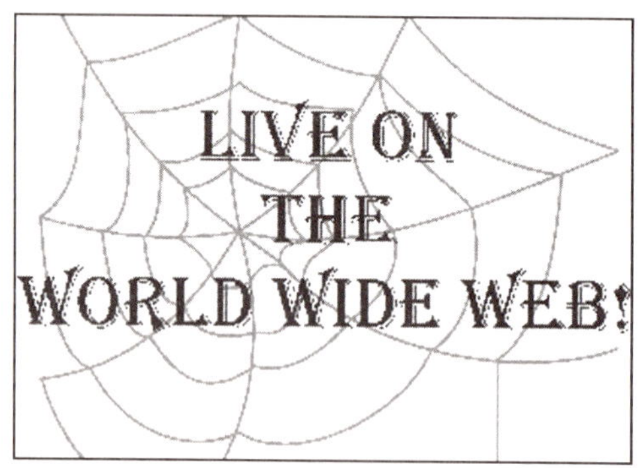

United States Postal Service Home Page

http://www.usps.com/

TRAC Home Page

http://www.trac.org/

NEXT EXERCISE

Exercise 6

- Master Common Tasks with Learn2
- Look up Words with Merriam-Webster Online
- Find Historical Documents at the National Archives
- Find the Correct Time for Any City in the World
- Use Financial Calculators

NOTES

Master Common Tasks with Learn2

- Learn2.com bills itself as "the ability utility." This is a Web site where you can learn how to do a thousand and one common and practical tasks. Use the search engine to find what you want to do or click one of the category links at the left of the home page.

Learn2 Home Page

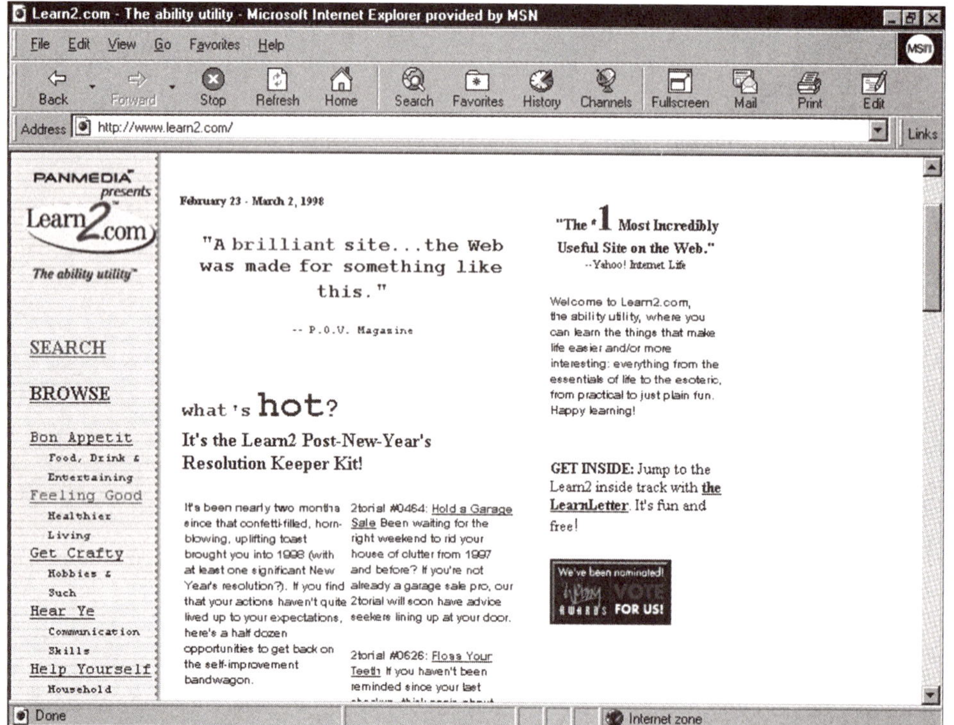

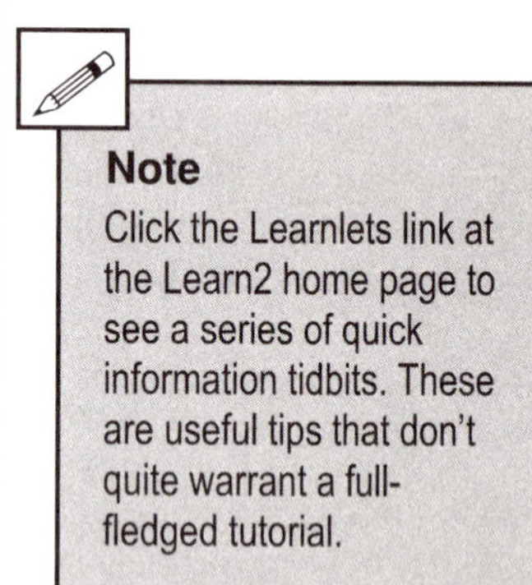

Note

Click the Learnlets link at the Learn2 home page to see a series of quick information tidbits. These are useful tips that don't quite warrant a full-fledged tutorial.

- Learn2 tutorials are quick, concise, and easy to understand. Ever wonder how to create hack-proof computer passwords? Check the Technowise page and then click the page links to read a ten-minute tutorial that tells you how to choose and use passwords that will keep your information safe.
- Other Learn2 category links include everything from Bon Apetit for food, drink, and entertaining to Your Turn, tutorials about sports, games, and recreation.

Look up Words with Merriam-Webster Online

- One of the most common office reference tasks is looking up words in a dictionary or thesaurus. Use Merriam-Webster Online to type a word in a text box and find its meaning or to find similar words.

Merriam-Webster Online Dictionary

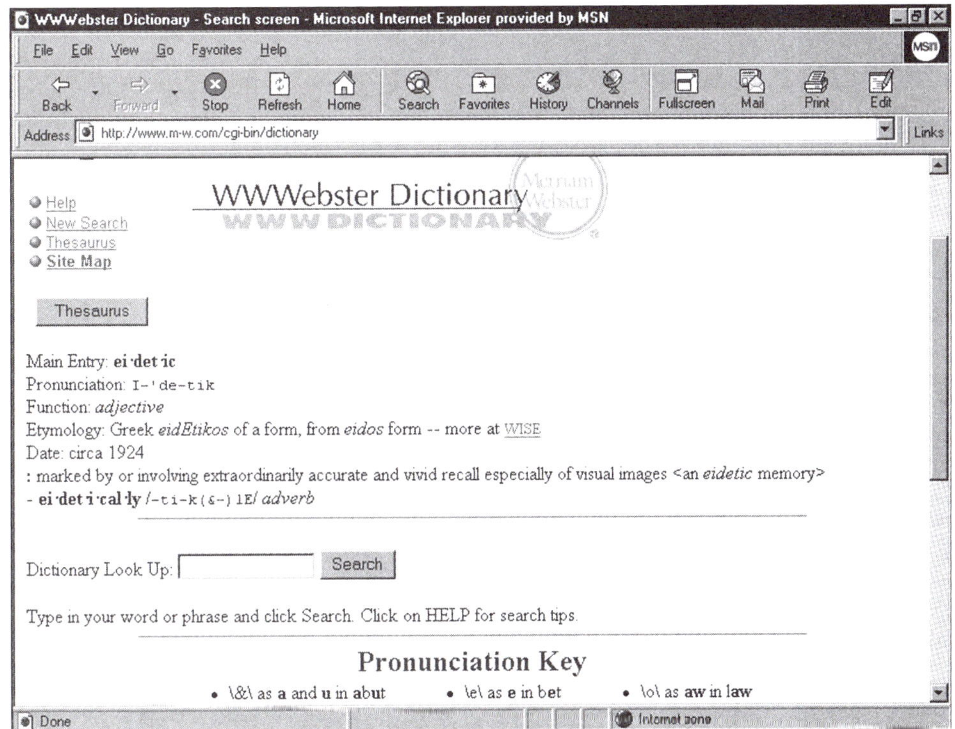

- Click the WWWebster Dictionary link to go to the dictionary page, then type the word you want to find and click Search. Dictionary search results show pronunciation, word origin, part of speech, date the word entered the language, and word definition.
- Go to the WWWebster Thesaurus page to look up words that have similar meanings. Several synonyms will be listed. The most similar in meaning to the lookup word are linked to their dictionary entry.
- Click the Word of the Day link to see the definition and interesting trivia for a new featured word each day. Click the Word Game of the Day to challenge yourself with a word game online.

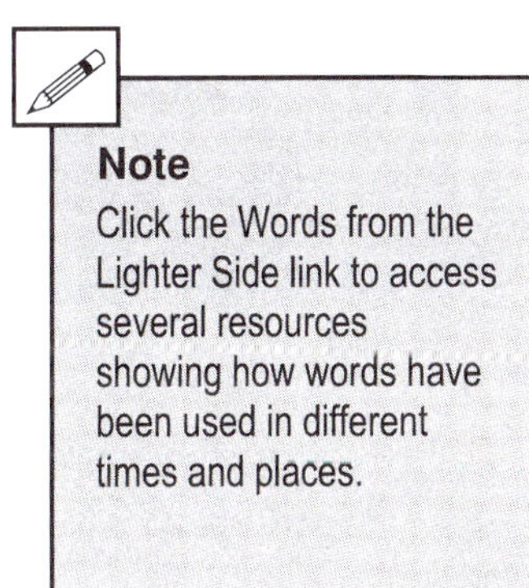

Note

Click the Words from the Lighter Side link to access several resources showing how words have been used in different times and places.

Find Historical Documents at the National Archives

- There are a number of Web sites that offer less commonplace reference materials. These may come in handy when you're preparing for a presentation or doing background research for a project.
- The Web site of the National Archives and Records Administration provides access to many featured government records and historical documents.
- Also available at this site, and well worth the visit, are the ever-changing online exhibits. Click the Online Exhibit Hall link to find special collections of documents, photographs, artwork, and other featured exhibits. In many cases you can download digital copies of archived documents. Online exhibits often include photos, video clips, and sound.

National Archives Online Exhibit

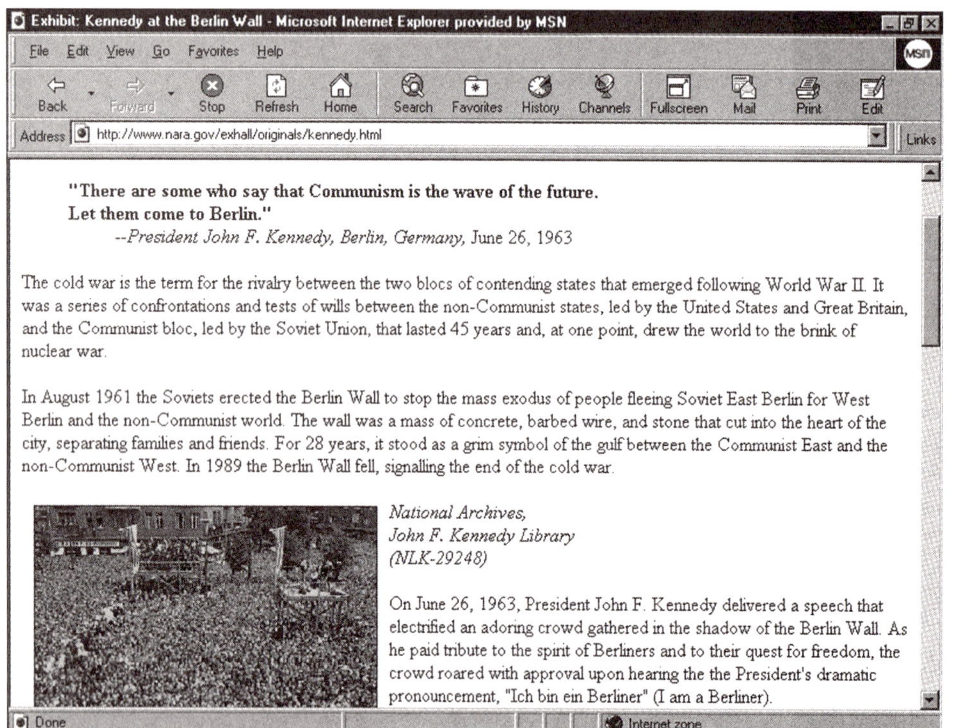

Note

Click The Digital Classroom link to find ideas for classroom use of National Archive materials.

Note

If you have an interest in tracing your ancestry, click The Genealogy Page link for quick guides to doing your own research as well as links to helpful sources of genealogy archive information.

Find the Correct Time for Any City in the World

- Finding the local time for any city in the world is another quick lookup on the Web. Go to the Time Zone Page and enter the city or cities you want to find, then click Get the Time!. If you enter more than one city, be sure to separate the city names by commas.
- The Time Zone Page displays the current time for all cities you enter as well as the Greenwich Mean Time, which is used as the standard "zero hour" for calculating time zones.

The Time Zone Page

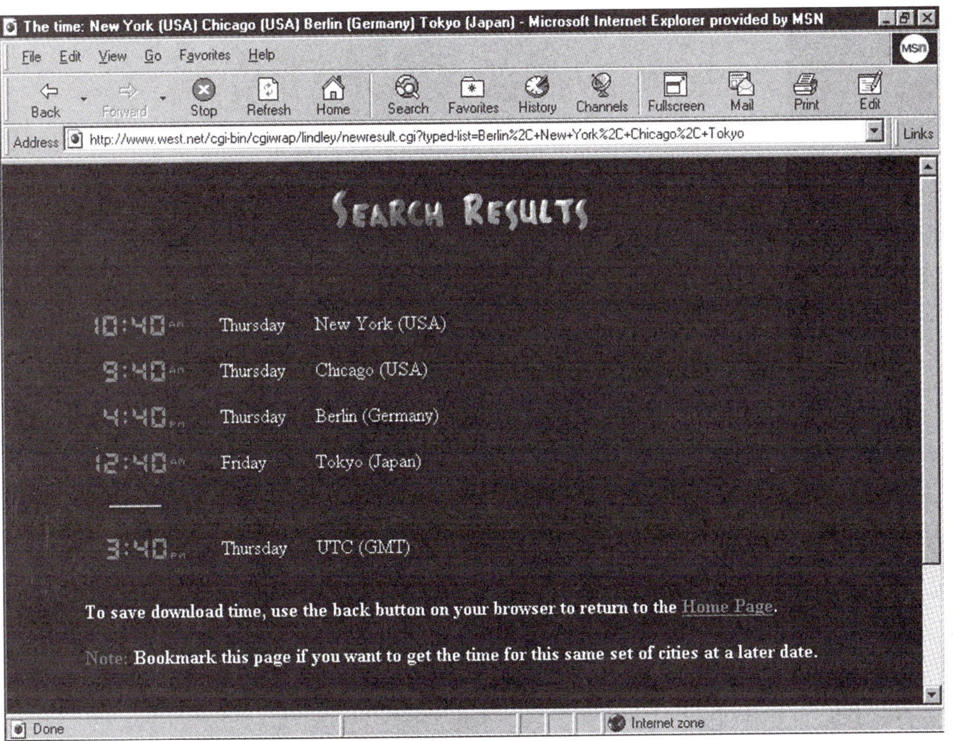

Use Financial Calculators

- The MoneyAdvisor directory has numerous links to financial calculators to help make solving business math problems easier. Click a link at the MoneyAdvisor directory to find several dozen calculators on the Web.

MoneyAdvisor Directory of Financial Calculators

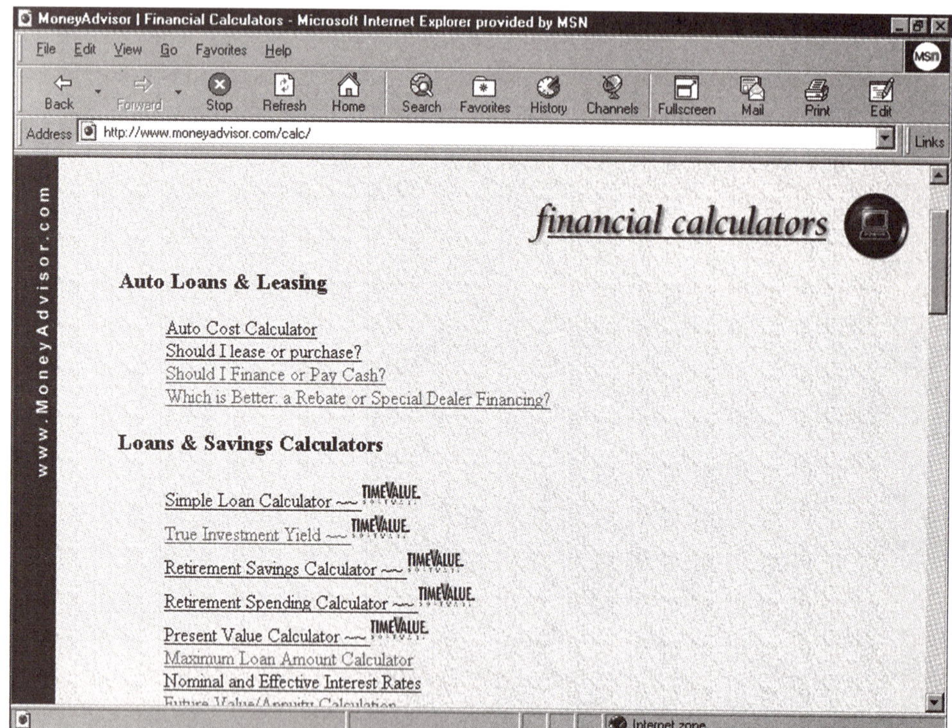

- These calculators address many of the most common business financial calculations, including present value, loan amortization, future value, and nominal versus effective interest rates. Specialty calculators include a graduated payment loan calculator, a retirement savings calculator, and a mortgage payment table calculator.
- Insurance and tax calculators let you figure out how much insurance coverage you need and estimate how much tax you may owe.
- Many of the links at this directory take you to other Web sites, so be prepared for a change of scenery when you skip from page to page. All of these calculators, however, are easy to use and very practical.

Note

Try the Just for Fun Calculators to check your body mass ratio, do weight and temperature conversions, and play the longevity game, which predicts your lifespan based on a survey of your lifestyle and health habits.

In this exercise, you will learn how to create and use a hack-proof computer password at the Learn2 Web site. You will then look up word definitions and use the thesaurus at Merriam-Webster Online. Next, you will find historical documents at the National Archives and check the local time for several cities around the world. Finally, you will use financial calculators from the MoneyAdvisor Web site.

Note: *To ensure consistent results, this exercise uses simulated sites. The real URLs appear at the end of the exercise.*

Web Search

Search for answers to the following questions using the Web sites you will visit in the Web simulation exercise.

1. What password does the tutorial suggest as "best choice" in the Pick a Winner example?

   ____

2. What language does the word arduous come from? What is the meaning of the word in that language?

   ____

3. What other language besides English and German did President Kennedy use in his speech?

   ____

4. What was the date of President Reagan's speech at the Berlin wall?

   ____

5. What year had the highest Rate of Inflation? What was the rate?

   ____

6. What year had the lowest Rate of Inflation (a negative number)? What was the rate?

   ____

EXERCISE DIRECTIONS

1. Launch the Internet simulation. From the Main Menu, select Lesson 6, then select Exercise 6.
2. On the Address line, type the following URL and press Enter:

   http://www.learn2.com/

   ➲ *The Learn2 home page opens.*

Learn2 Home Page

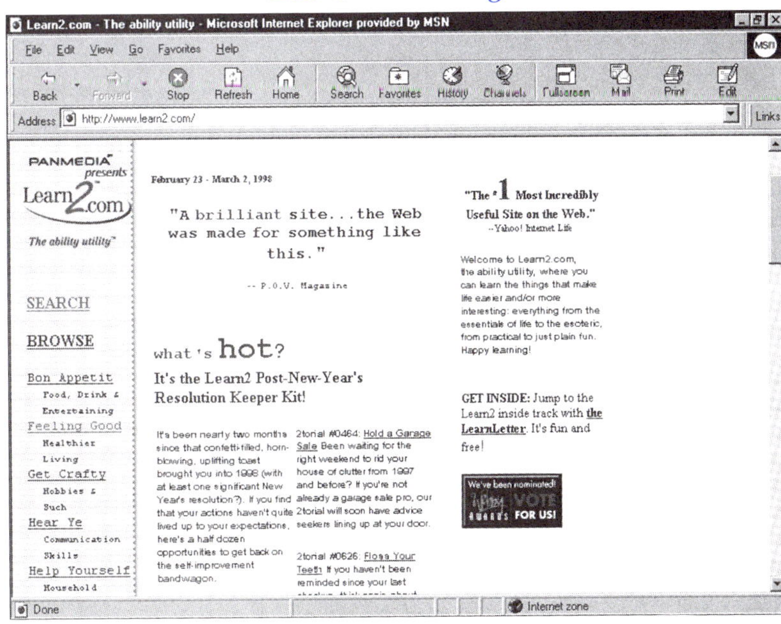

3. Scroll down the page and click the Technowise link in the left-hand column.

   ➲ *The Learn2 Technowise page opens.*

Learn2 Technowise Page

4. Scroll down and click the Choose and Use a Password link.

   ➲ *The "2torial" for choosing a computer password opens.*

5. Scroll down and read the introduction to the tutorial, then click the Step 1 link at the bottom of the page.

   ➲ *The first step of the tutorial opens.*

6. Read the first page of the tutorial, then click the link to the next page. Read each page of the tutorial.

   ❓ *Have you been choosing passwords for your computer that will be difficult for hackers to decode?*

How to Choose a Password

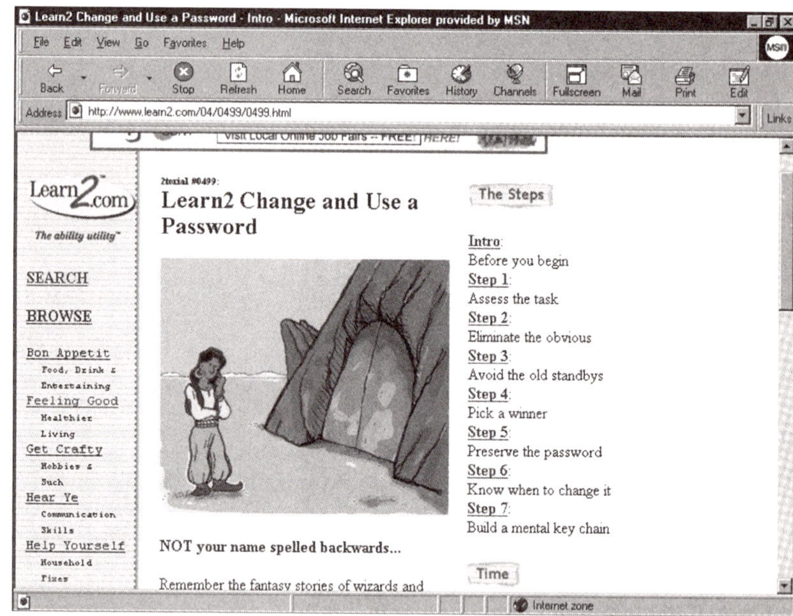

7. Type the following URL in your browser's Address line and press Enter:

   http://www.m-w.com/

   ➲ *The Merriam-Webster Online home page opens.*

8. Click the WWWebster Dictionary link in the left-hand column.

   ➲ *The Merriam-Webster Online Dictionary page opens.*

Merriam-Webster Online Home Page

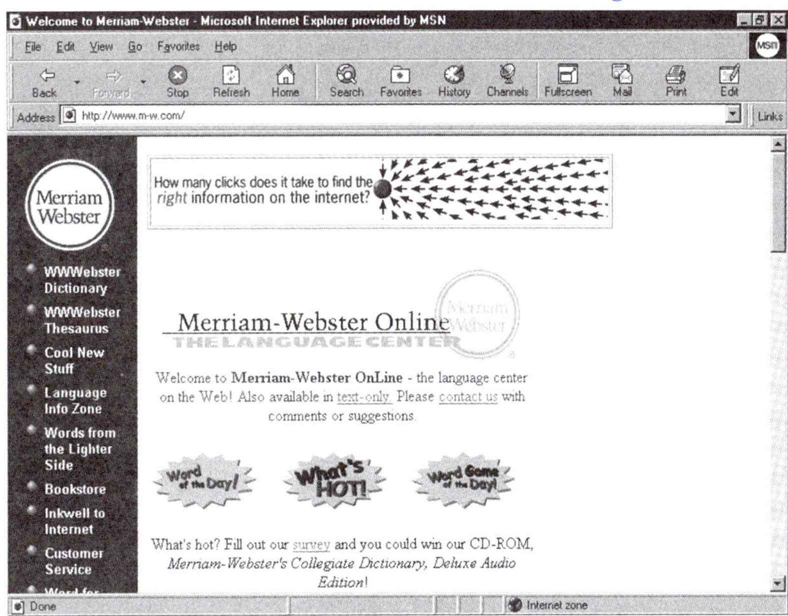

9. Enter the word *eidetic* in the Word to Look Up text box, then click Search.

Look up a Word's Definition

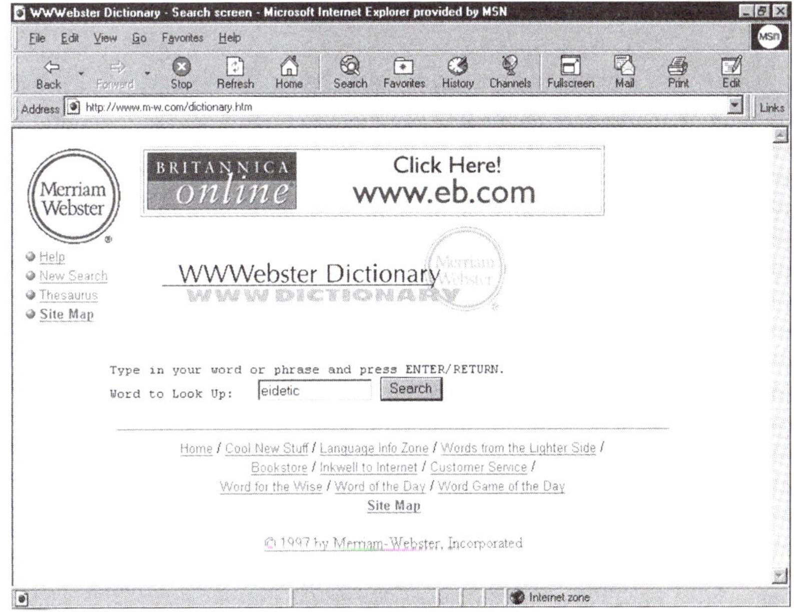

10. Read the definition, pronunciation, and word origin supplied by the Web site, then scroll down and click the Word of the Day link at the bottom of the page.

   ➲ *The Word of the Day page opens.*

Definition of Eidetic

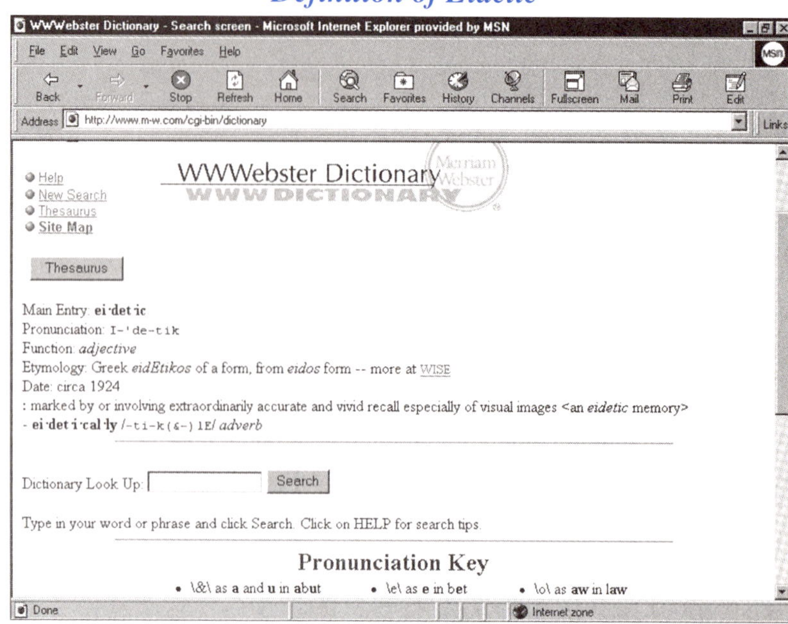

11. Read about the word *arduous*, then click the WWWebster Thesaurus link at the bottom of the page.

   ➲ *The Webster Thesaurus page opens.*

Webster's Word of the Day

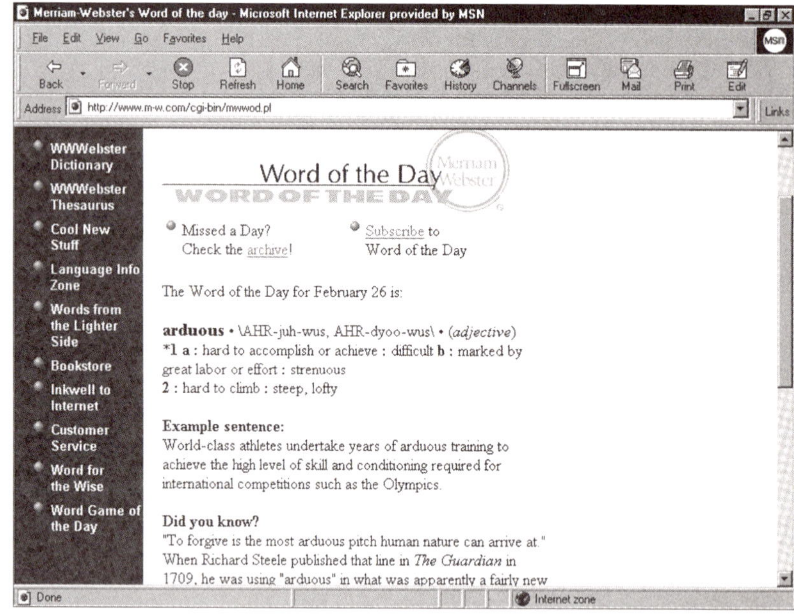

12. Enter the word *arduous* in the Word to Look Up text box, then click Search.
13. Read the synonyms for arduous.

❓ *Which set of synonyms has the most to do with the word from which arduous is derived.*

Synonyms for Arduous

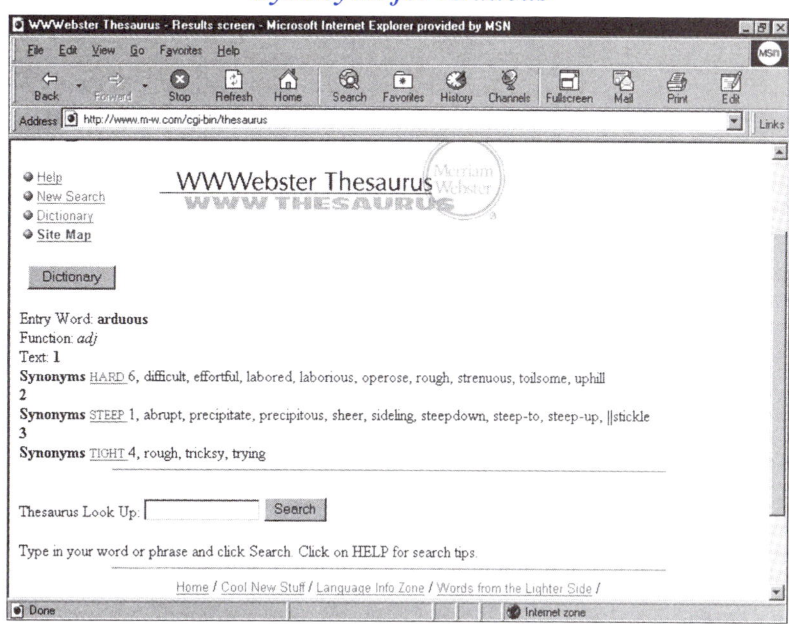

14. Type the following URL in your browser's Address line and press Enter:

    http://www.nara.gov/

    ➲ *The National Archives and Records Administration home page opens.*

National Archives Home Page

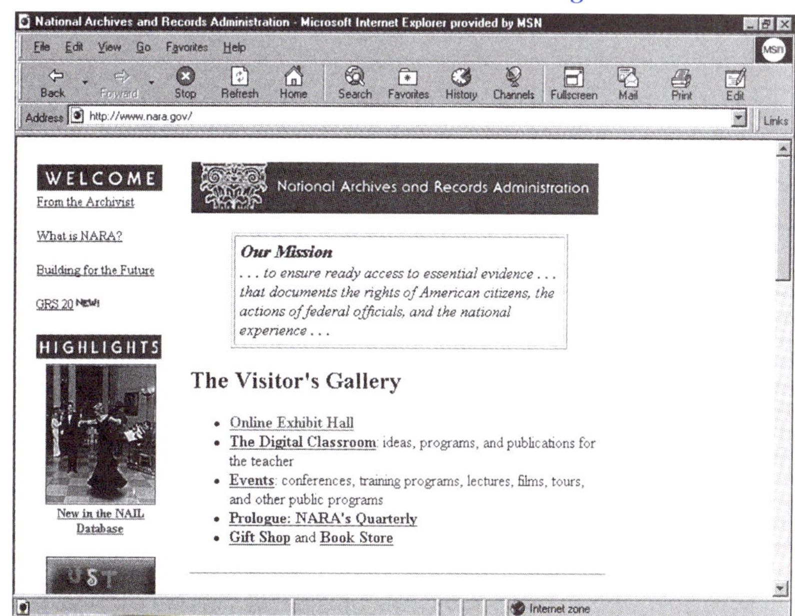

15. Click the Online Exhibit Hall link.

➲ *The Exhibit Hall page opens.*

National Archives Online Exhibit Hall

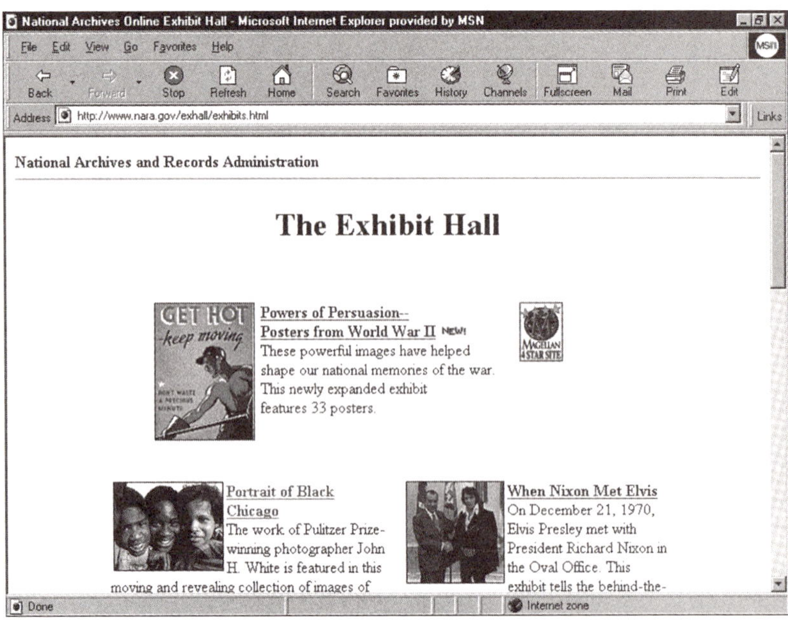

16. Scroll down and read about the many types of exhibits available at the site. Click the American Originals link.

➲ *The American Originals page opens.*

American Originals Page

Exhibit: American Originals - Microsoft Internet Explorer provided by MSN

File Edit View Go Favorites Help

Back Forward Stop Refresh Home Search Favorites History Channels Fullscreen Mail Print Edit

Address http://www.nara.gov/exhall/originals/original.html

Links

National Archives and Records Administration

AMERICAN Originals

Here will be preserved all . . . the records that bind State to State and the hearts of all our people in an indissoluble union.

—President Herbert Hoover, upon laying the cornerstone of the National Archives Building, February 20, 1933

Original documents are the raw stuff of history. They are physical links to the past. The original documents of the United States government--those that have been identified as having permanent value--are preserved and made available to the public by the National Archives. This online exhibit is based on one currently on display in the Rotunda of the National Archives Building in Washington, DC. **American Originals** presents a selection of some of the most significant and compelling documents from the National Archives holdings.

On July 2, 1776, Congress approves a Resolution for Independence, severing ties to Great Britain.

A U.S. district court renders its verdict against gangster Al Capone, October 17, 1931.

Done

Internet zone

17. Scroll down and read about the documents available at the American Originals page. Click the President John F. Kennedy's link.

   ➲ *A page describing Kennedy's historic visit to Berlin opens. Notice his handwritten notes, including the famous phrase "Ich bin ein Berliner."*

   ✓ *Also, note President Reagan's speech card at the bottom of the page, calling for Soviet leader Gorbachev to tear down the Berlin wall.*

18. Type the following URL in your browser's Address line and press Enter:

   http://www.west.net/~lindley/zone/

   ✓ *Be sure to type the tilde character (~) in the URL.*

   ➲ *The Time Zone Page opens.*

19. Scroll down and type the following cities in the text box:

   Berlin, New York, Chicago, Tokyo

   ✓ *Be sure to separate the cities with commas.*

20. Scroll down and click Get the time!.

   ➲ *The times for each city are displayed. Note that these are example times, not necessarily the current time.*

Kennedy's Visit to Berlin

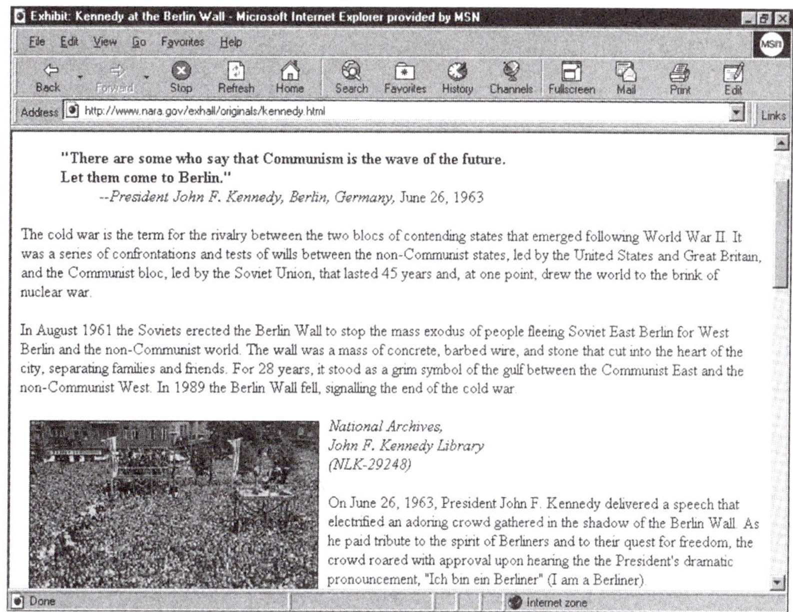

Time Zone Page

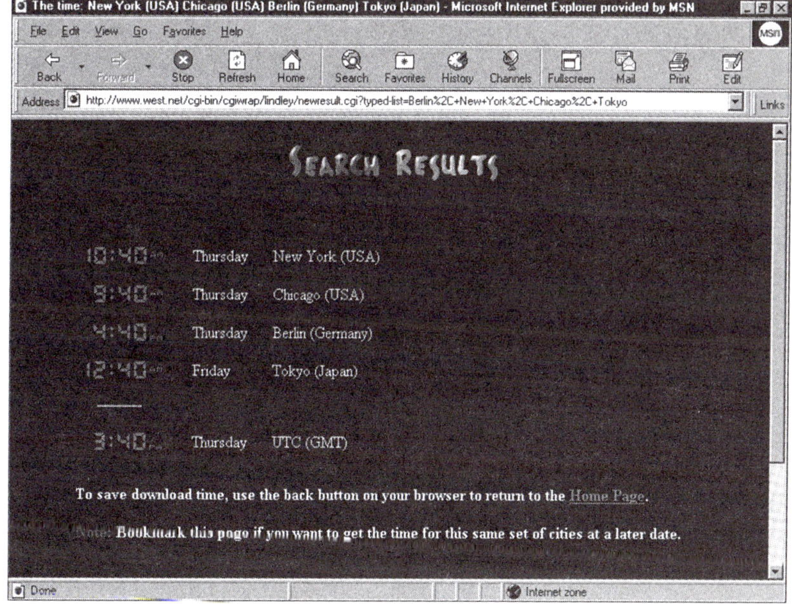

21. Type the following URL in your browser's Address line and press Enter:

    http://www.moneyadvisor.com/calc/

    ➲ *The MoneyAdvisor Financial Calculators page opens.*

22. Scroll down and view the wide variety of links to financial and other calculators available at this page. Click the Retirement Savings Calculator link under Loans & Savings Calculators.

    ➲ *The Retirement Savings Calculator page opens.*

23. Enter and/or select the following amounts in the text boxes:

    Deposit frequency: Monthly

    Deposit amount: 400

    Number of years to make deposits: 40

    Nominal annual interest rate: 7

24. Click Submit.

    ➲ *The calculator states that you would have $1,049,925.36 available for retirement if you make the deposits in this example.*

25. Click the Calculators icon at the bottom of the page (it looks like a computer).

Financial Calculators Page

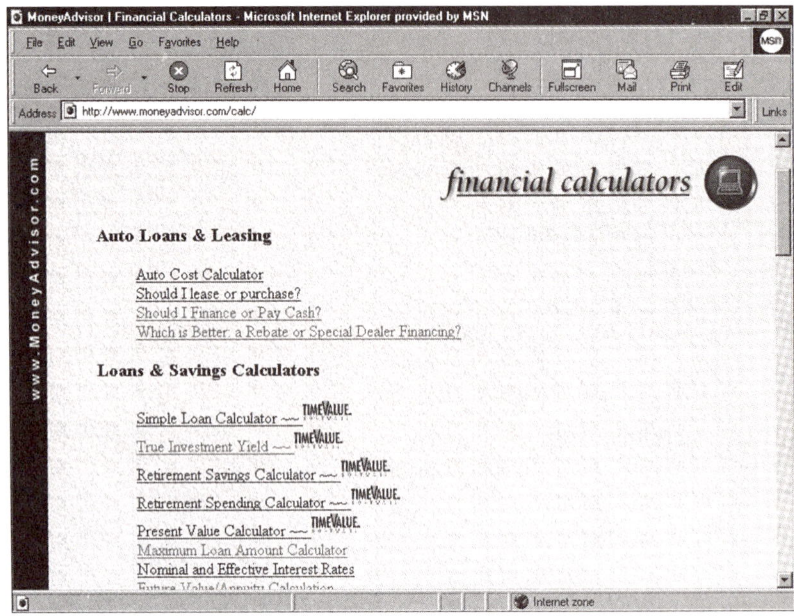

Retirement Savings Calculator

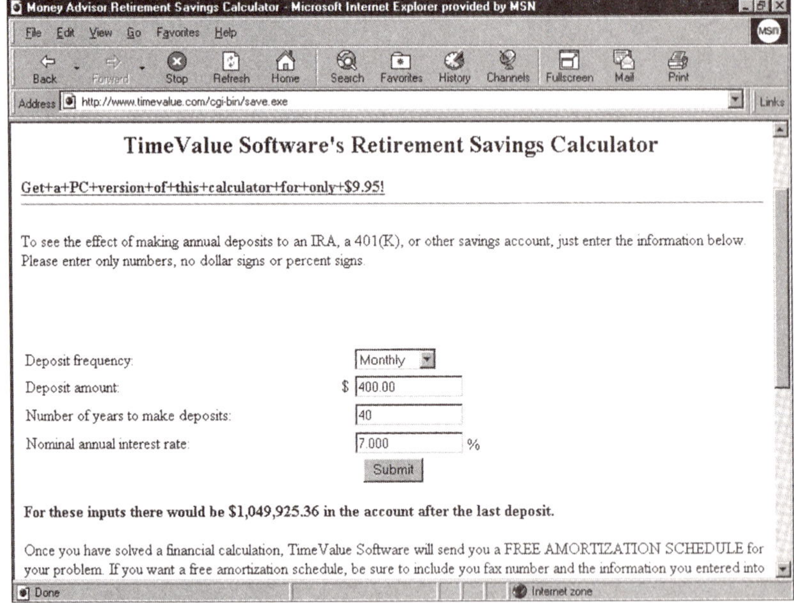

26. Scroll down and click the Consumer Price Index and Inflation Rates, 1913 link under the General Financial Calculators heading.
27. Enter the following amounts in the What is a dollar worth? calculator:

    *If in **1963** I bought goods or services for $1.00, in **1997** the same goods or services would cost*
28. Click Calculate.

    ➲ *The calculator states that one dollar's worth of goods or services purchased in 1963 would cost $5.25 in 1997.*
29. Click the Consumer Price Index and Inflation Rates, 1913- link on the What is a dollar worth? page.

    ➲ *A page showing the Consumer Price Index opens.*
30. Scroll down to view the inflation rates and Consumer Price Index (CPI).

    ✓ *Note the swings in the inflation rate as well as the general upward trend.*
31. Continue on to the next exercise.

    OR

    Exit from the simulation.

Gauging the Effects of Inflation

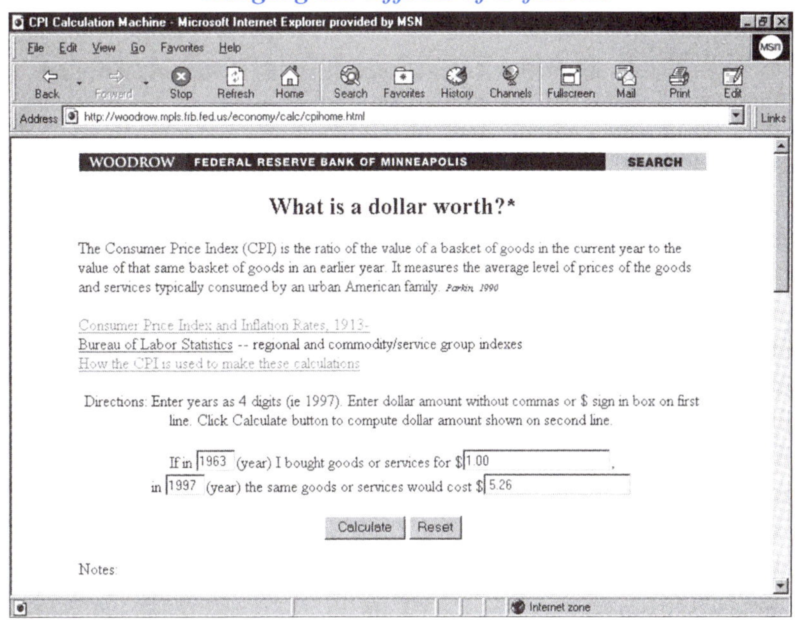

Consumer Price Index and Inflation

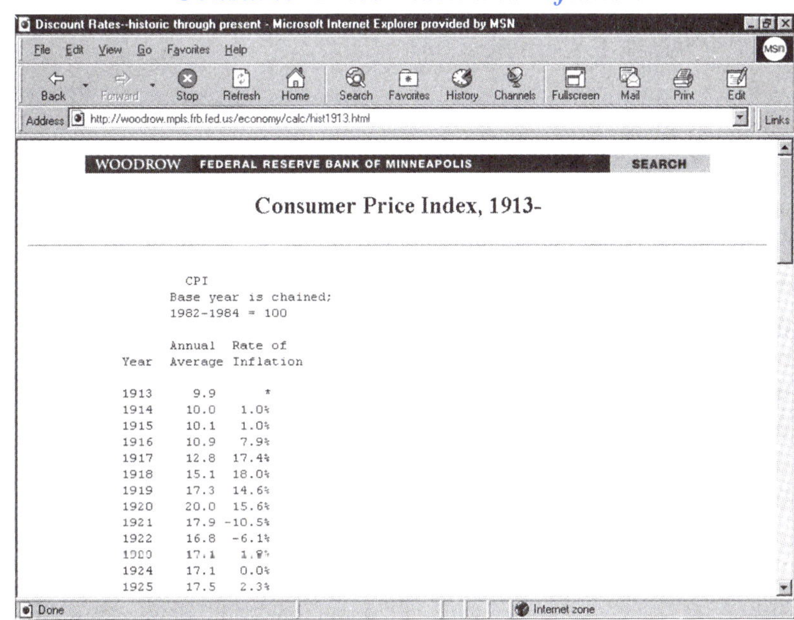

Year	Annual Average	Rate of Inflation
1913	9.9	*
1914	10.0	1.0%
1915	10.1	1.0%
1916	10.9	7.9%
1917	12.8	17.4%
1918	15.1	18.0%
1919	17.3	14.6%
1920	20.0	15.6%
1921	17.9	-10.5%
1922	16.8	-6.1%
1923	17.1	1.8%
1924	17.1	0.0%
1925	17.5	2.3%

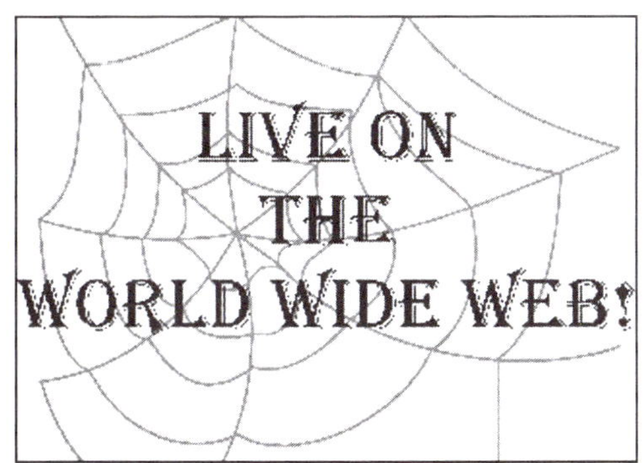

Learn2 Home Page

http://www.learn2.com/

Merriam-Webster Online Home Page

http://www.m-w.com/

National Archives and Records Administration

http://www.nara.gov/

The Time Zone Page

http://www.west.net/~lindley/zone/

MoneyAdvisor Calculators Page

http://www.moneyadvisor.com/calc/

Exercise 7

- Plan Travel with Microsoft Expedia
- Book Travel with Expedia's Travel Agent

NOTES

Plan Travel with Microsoft Expedia

- You can use the Web to make business trips more enjoyable and more cost effective. There are dozens of excellent travel-related sites that can help you plan your trip, search for travel bargains, and book tickets online.
- Microsoft Expedia is the award-winning travel Web site produced by Microsoft as part of its Microsoft Network online service. Awards and accolades include The Best of the Web top 100 Web sites by PC Magazine, Yahoo! Internet Life Five-Star Award (one of only 12 per year), and PCWeek E-Commerce Top Ten.

Microsoft Expedia Home Page

Note

To access Expedia quickly, add its URL to your browser favorites (bookmarks).

Note

Click the Mungo Park link to take a virtual expedition to any one of a dozen locations around the world.

- The site receives these awards with good reason: The Web page design is rich, interesting, and a pleasure to view. It's also easy to navigate and full of information about where to go and what to do.
- Click on Magazine to read travel articles, news briefs, and bargain updates, as well as featured columnists and ideas about fresh approaches to travel. Also, don't miss the Full Circle link, which offers spectacular 360-degree photographic views of top destinations around the world.
- To start planning a trip, click the Resources link. From the Resources page you can browse the World Guide, a complete online travel guidebook, check weather, use a currency converter, and find links to other travel Web sites.

Plan a Trip with Expedia Resources

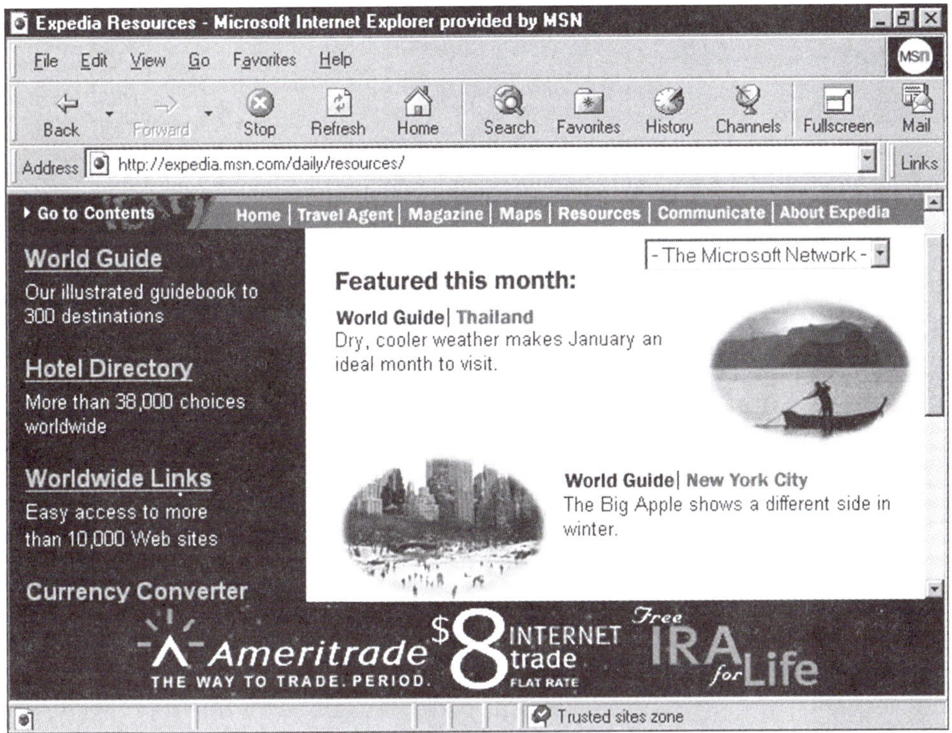

- Click the World Guide link on the Resources page to see an alphabetical index of links to guidebook listings for 300 destinations around the world. To find a World Guide listing, click on a letter at the top of the page for a list of cities that begin with that letter. Then click the name of the city you want to research.
- Use World Guide listings to learn about your destination and plan what you want to do while you visit. Each destination profiled in World Guide includes hotel and restaurant listings, complete background information about the location, descriptions of top attractions, travel essentials, and links to other Web sites.

Use World Guide Listings to Learn about a Destination

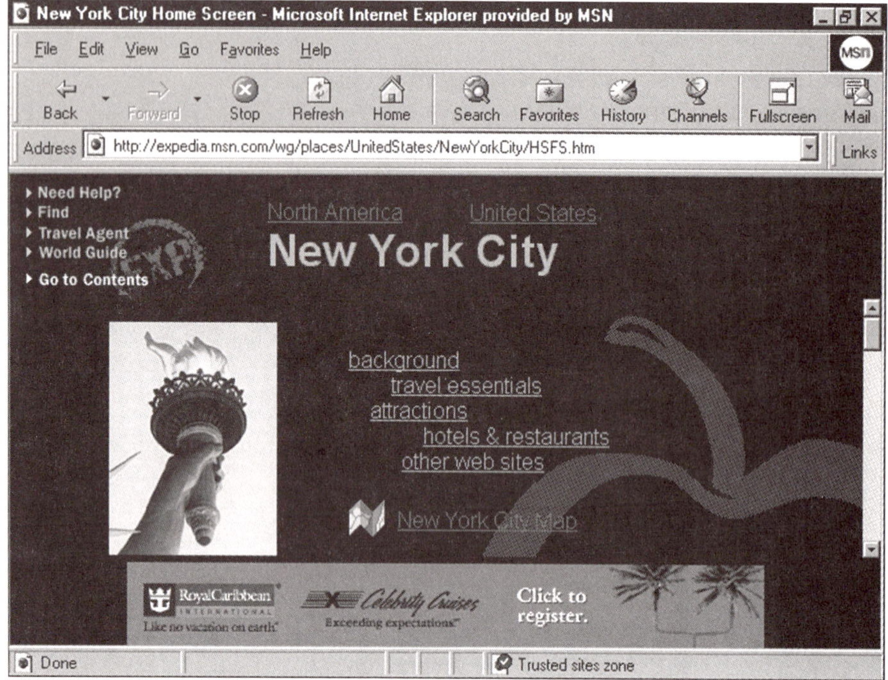

Book Travel with Expedia's Travel Agent

- The beauty of most travel Web sites is the capability to book travel online. Expedia's Travel Agent feature offers a number of powerful search and booking tools.
- From the home page, click the Travel Agent link to find low airfares and book airline tickets. You can also search for available hotel rooms at your destination and reserve rooms. If you need a rental car, simply find and reserve one using Travel Agent.

Expedia Travel Agent

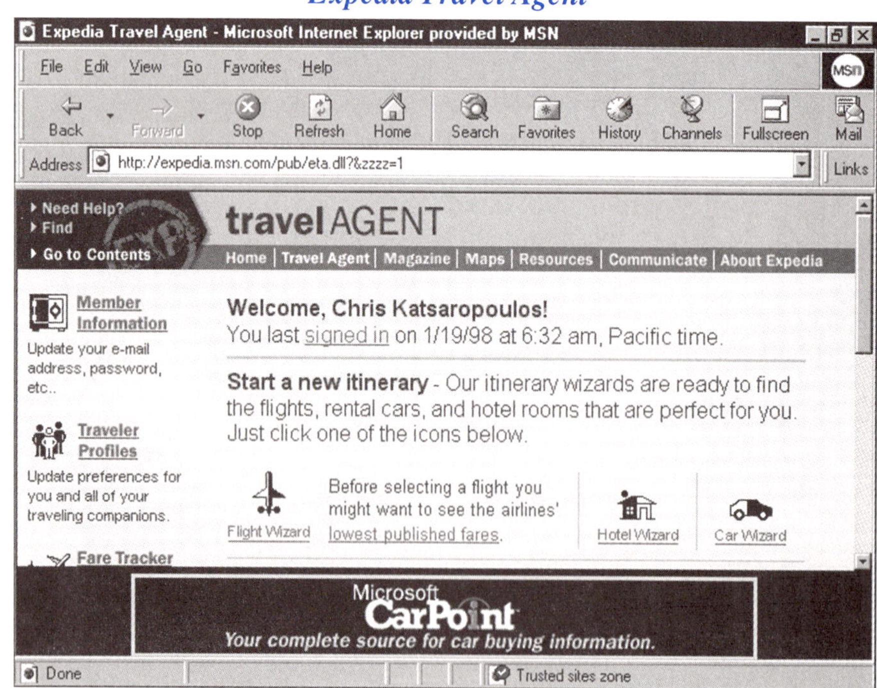

Note

To use Expedia's Travel Agent, you must first fill out and submit an online registration form. The Travel Agent service is available free of charge.

- Click on Flight Wizard to book an airline ticket using the Web. After the Flight Wizard starts, enter information about your departure and destination cities, when you want to travel, as well as airline, seating, and route preferences.
- You can choose to search by lowest fare or by schedule, then click Continue to see the search results. Review search results and click the Choose and Continue link next to the flight you want to book. Click the Change Search button at the bottom of the page if you want to modify search criteria.
- After choosing a flight, you can review flight details and then either reserve a seat on the flight, purchase a ticket for the flight, or add the flight to an itinerary for the trip.

Note
Reserving a seat only holds the seat for approximately 24 hours from the time of the reservation. You must purchase a ticket to hold the seat for your flight.

Enter Flight Wizard Search Information

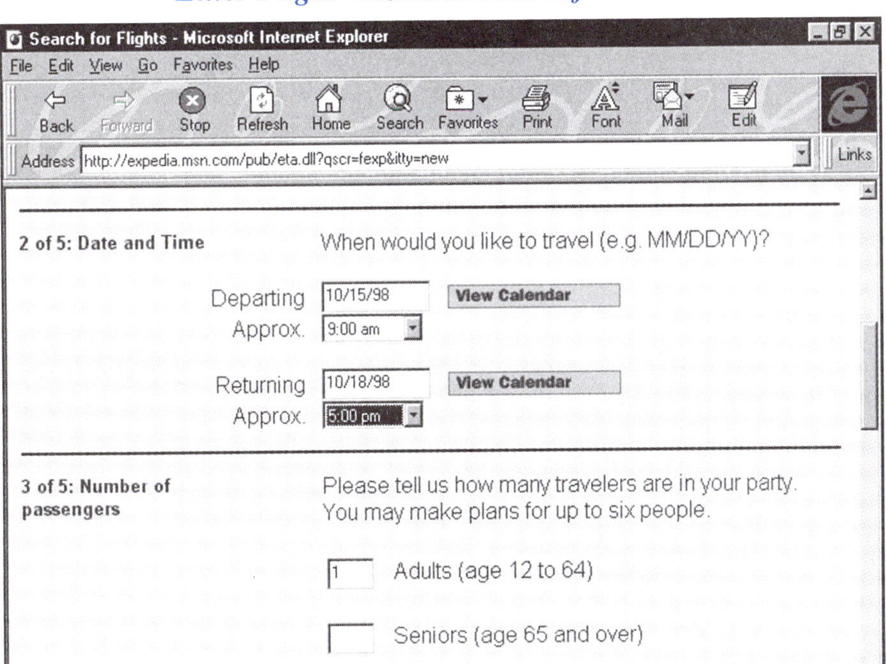

- Click on Car Wizard or Hotel Wizard from the Travel Agent page to search for and reserve cars or hotel rooms. Both wizards work in much the same way as the Flight Wizard. Simply enter information about the type of room or car you want to reserve and click Continue to view search results.
- Once you have selected the travel services you want to purchase, you must enter and submit credit card information using online forms provided by the various Expedia wizards. Credit card information is transmitted by a secure site to keep security risks to a minimum.

Note
You can start Flight Wizard, Hotel Wizard, and Car Wizard from your trip itinerary.

Enter Hotel Wizard Search Information

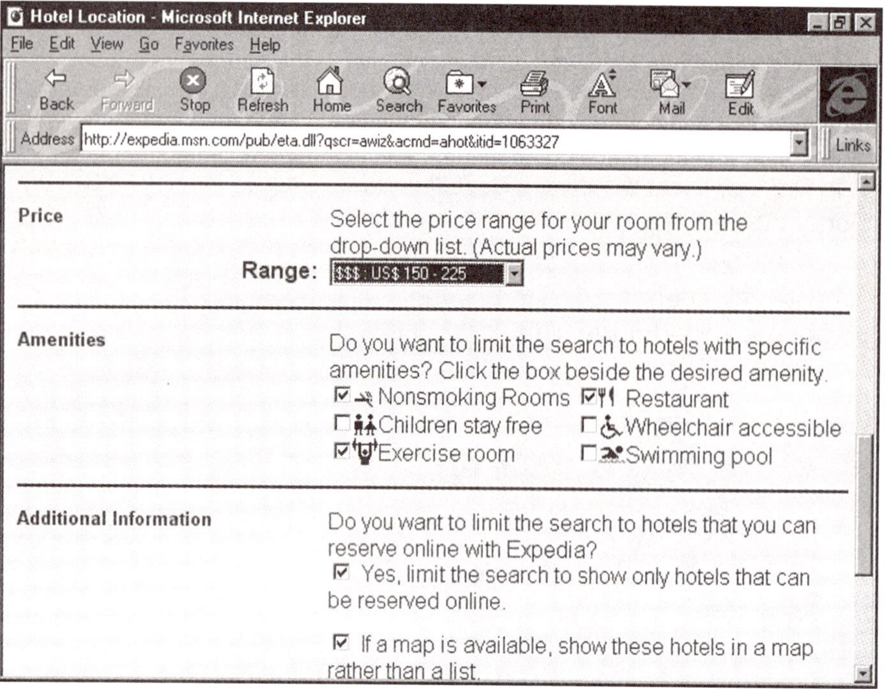

Travel Itinerary Showing Flight Information

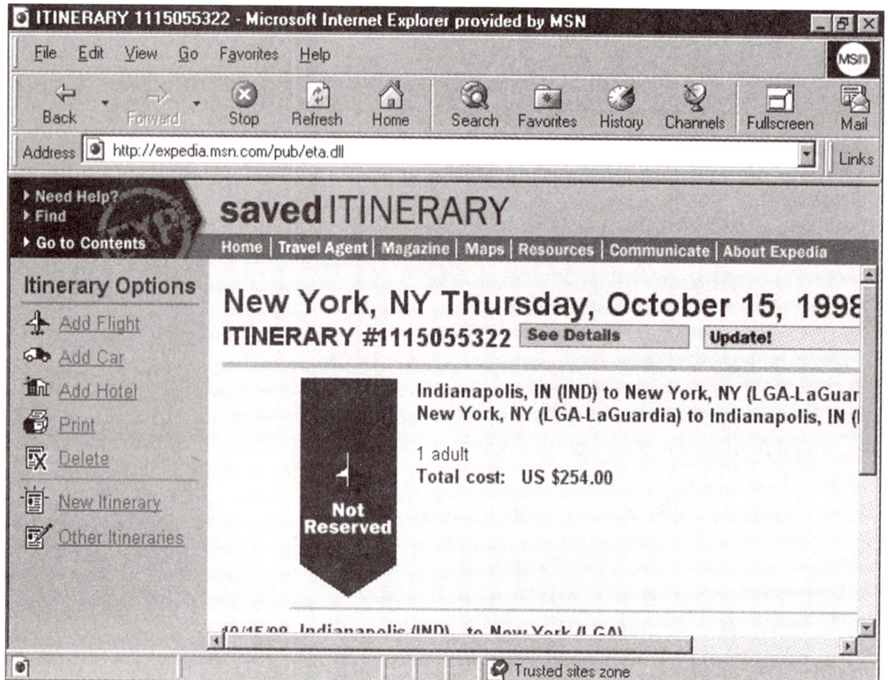

In this exercise, you will research a travel destination using the Expedia World Guide. You will then search for a flight to the destination and add the flight to your trip itinerary. Finally, you will search for a hotel room and add a room to your trip itinerary.

Note: *To ensure consistent results, this exercise uses simulated sites. The real URLs appear at the end of the exercise.*

Web Search

Search for answers to the following questions using the Web sites you will visit in the Web simulation exercise.

1. List five New York City attractions that Expedia recommends.

   ____

   ____

   ____

   ____

   ____

2. How much is the tax on the US AIR flight from Indianapolis to New York?

   ____

3. What is the distance of the flight between Indianapolis and New York?

   ____

4. How long is the return flight to Indianapolis?

   ____

EXERCISE DIRECTIONS

1. Launch the Internet simulation. From the Main Menu, select Lesson 6, then select Exercise 7.
2. On the Address line, type the following and press Enter:

   http://www.expedia.com

   ➲ *The Microsoft Expedia home page opens.*

Microsoft Expedia Home Page

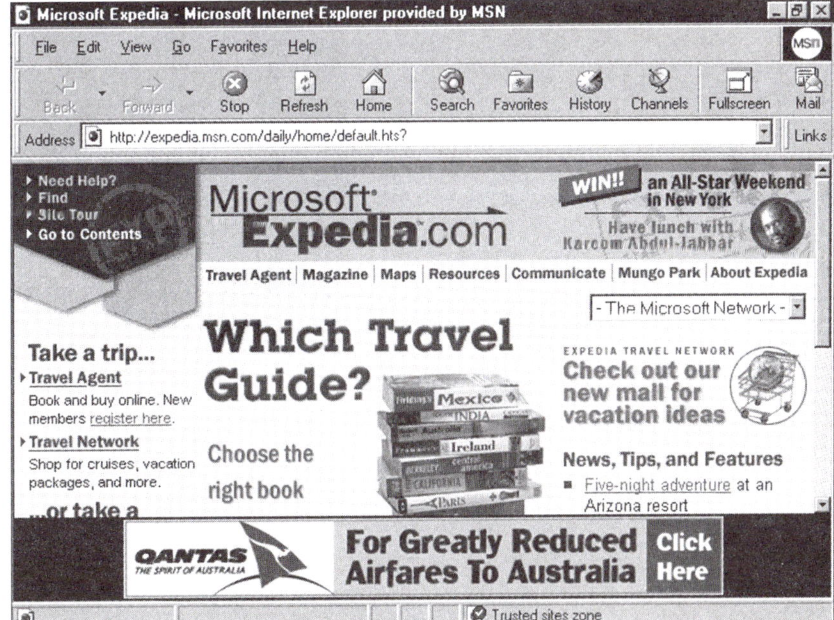

3. Click the Resources link near the top of the home page.

   ➲ *The Expedia Resources page opens.*

4. Scroll down and click the picture of New York City's Central Park.

   ➲ *The Expedia World Guide page for New York City opens.*

5. Click the background link, and then click the Highlights link.

Expedia Resources Page

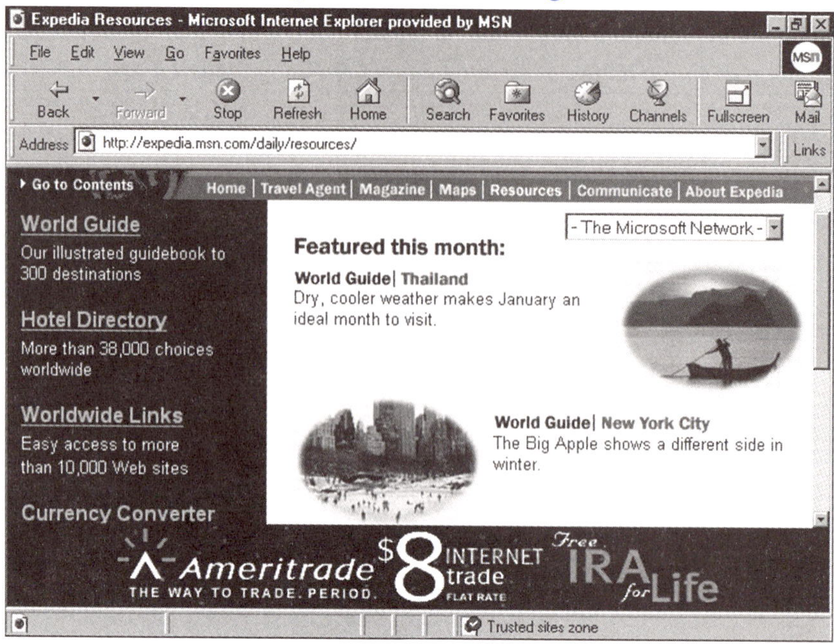

6. Read the article describing some of New York's top attractions.

World Guide Page for New York City

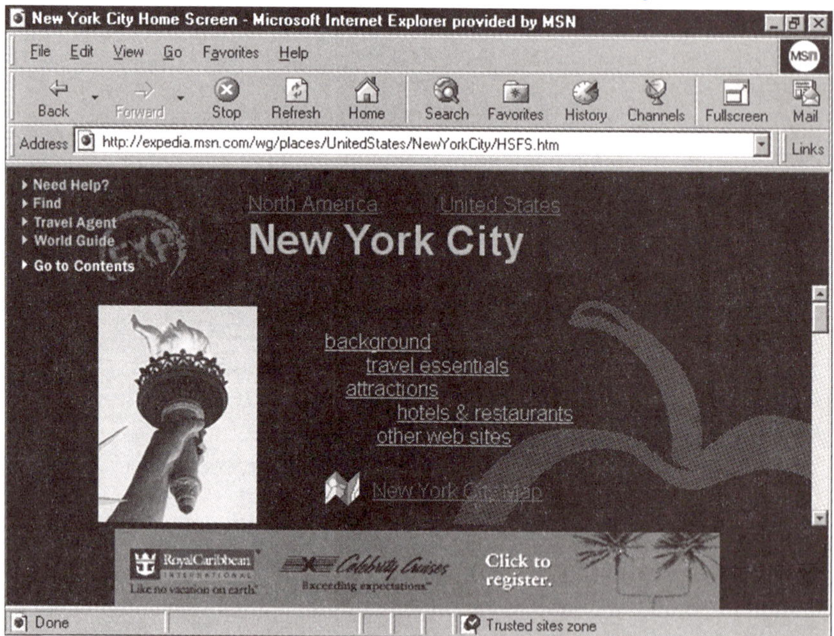

7. Click the browser's Back button until you return to the Expedia home page.
8. Click the Expedia Travel Agent link near the top of the page.

   ✓ *If you were visiting Expedia online for the first time, you would have to complete a registration form to use the Travel Agent service.*

Highlights of New York's Top Attractions

New York City Highlights - Microsoft Internet Explorer

Address http://expedia.msn.com/wg/places/UnitedStates/NewYorkCity/BGHIFS.htm

Highlights

Overview Neighborhoods Vicinities Highlights

Attraction Highlights

What would you do if you had only one day in New York?

You might start with a "power" breakfast in the Edwardian Room at the Plaza Hotel to get a taste of New York City in all its pretension and luxury. Or you might go to Chinatown for dim sum at the Silver Palace, or just a comforting bowl of *congee* from a street vendor.

9. Click the Flight Wizard link.

   ➲ *The Flight Wizard page opens.*

Expedia Travel Agent

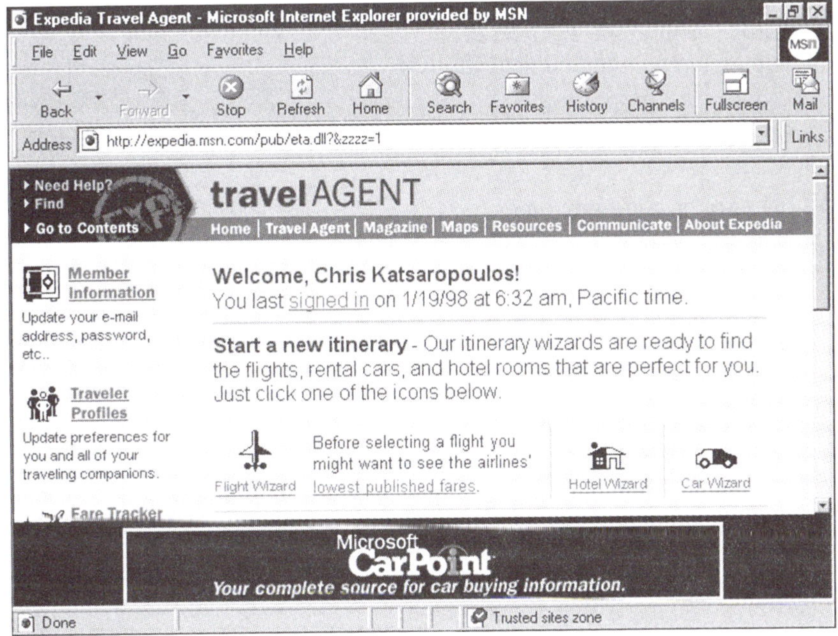

10. Type *Indianapolis, IN (IND)* in the From text box.
11. Type *New York, NY (LGA-LaGuardia)* in the To text box.

    ✓ *Use these two cities as a sample trip.*

Enter Departure and Destination Cities

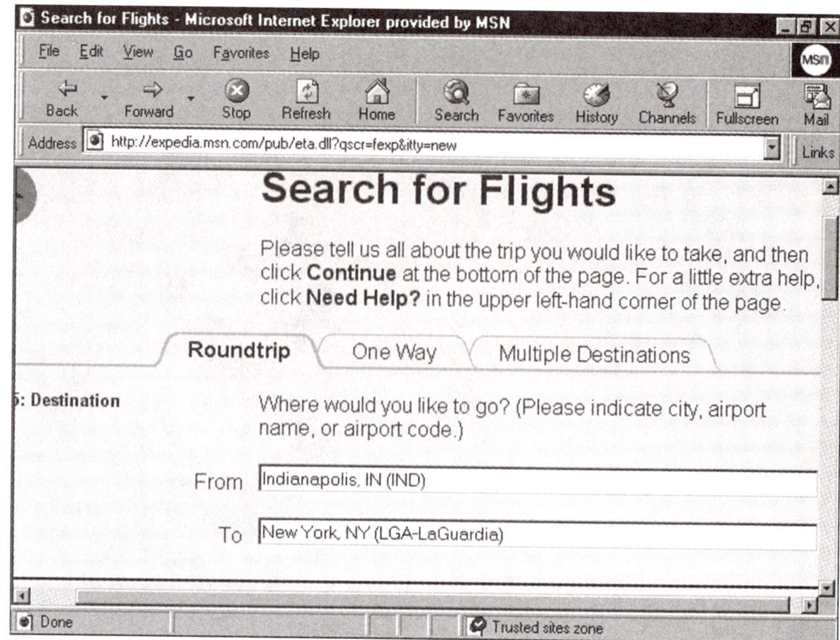

12. Enter *10/15/98* in the Departing text box. Click on the Approx. drop-down list box and select **9:00 AM**.
13. Enter *10/18/98* in the Returning text box. Click on the Approx. drop-down list box and select **5:00 PM**.
14. Do not change any other information on the Search for Flights form. Scroll down to the bottom of the page and click Continue.

Enter Trip Date and Time

Search for Flights - Microsoft Internet Explorer
File Edit View Go Favorites Help
Back Forward Stop Refresh Home Search Favorites Print Font Mail Edit
Address http://expedia.msn.com/pub/eta.dll?qscr=fexp&itty=new
Links

2 of 5: Date and Time
When would you like to travel (e.g. MM/DD/YY)?
Departing 10/15/98 View Calendar
Approx. 9:00 am
Returning 10/18/98 View Calendar
Approx. 5:00 pm

3 of 5: Number of passengers
Please tell us how many travelers are in your party. You may make plans for up to six people.
1 Adults (age 12 to 64)
Seniors (age 65 and over)

15. Scroll down the page to view the best-priced trips Flight Wizard found in its search. Click the Choose and Continue link for the first flight listed at the top of the page.
16. Read the details for the flight you selected. Scroll down to the bottom of the page and click on the check box to indicate you accept the conditions of the fare.
17. Click the Add to Itinerary button.

   ➲ *The flight you chose is added to a new itinerary.*

View Flight Wizard Search Results

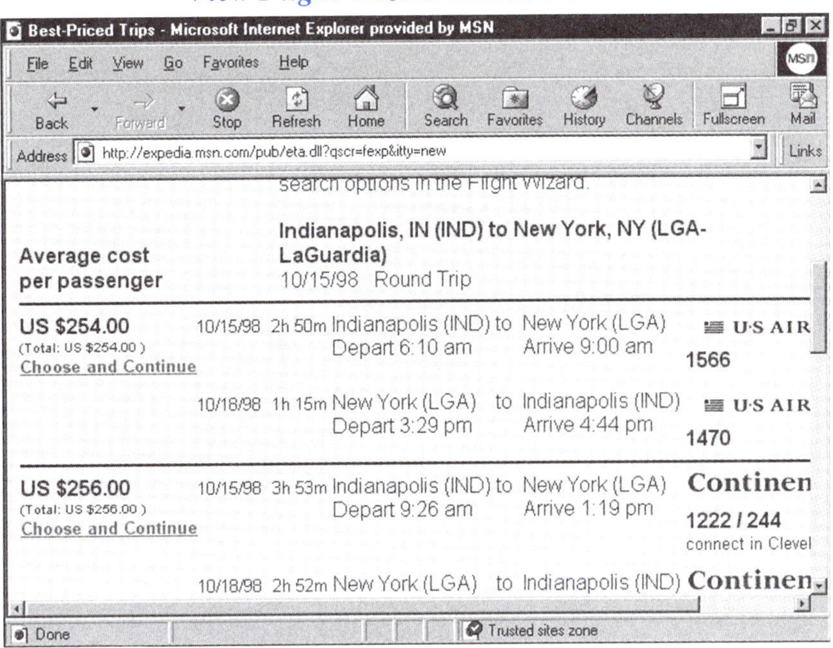

Flight Added to Your Itinerary

18. Click the Add Hotel link.

   ➲ *The Hotel Wizard opens. Because you are adding a hotel to the itinerary for your sample New York trip, Expedia automatically enters your destination in the Search for a Hotel form.*

19. Scroll down the page and select the **$$$ US$ 150-225** option from the Price Range drop-down list menu.
20. Click to select the following options in the Amenities section:

   Nonsmoking Rooms

   Exercise room

   Restaurant

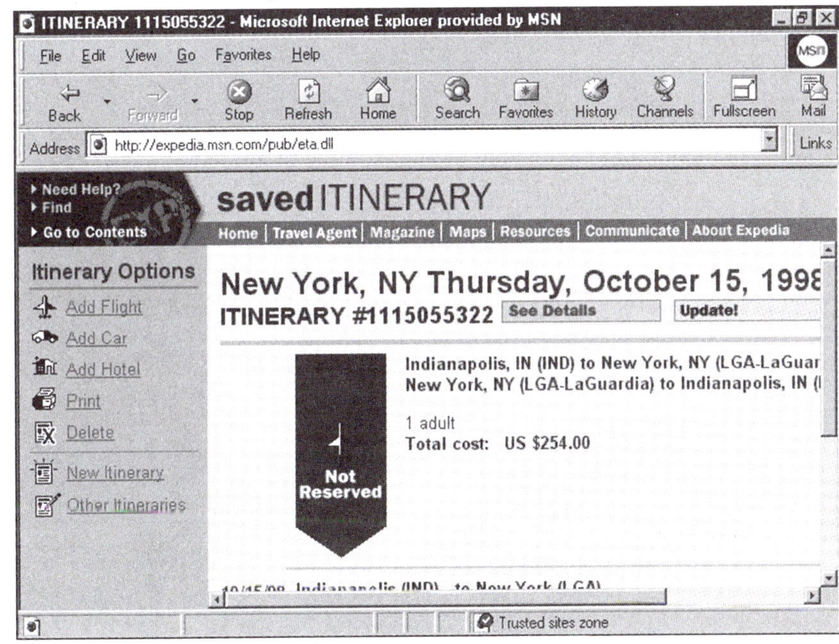

21. Click to select both of the options in the Additional Information section. Click the Continue button at the bottom of the page.
22. The Hotel Wizard needs more specific information about your location. Click **New York, New York, United States of America** on the list of options presented, then scroll to the bottom of the page and click Continue again.

   ➲ *Eight hotels will be listed when your search results appear on the Hotel Pinpointer. The Crowne Plaza at The United Nations will be highlighted.*

Select Hotel Search Options

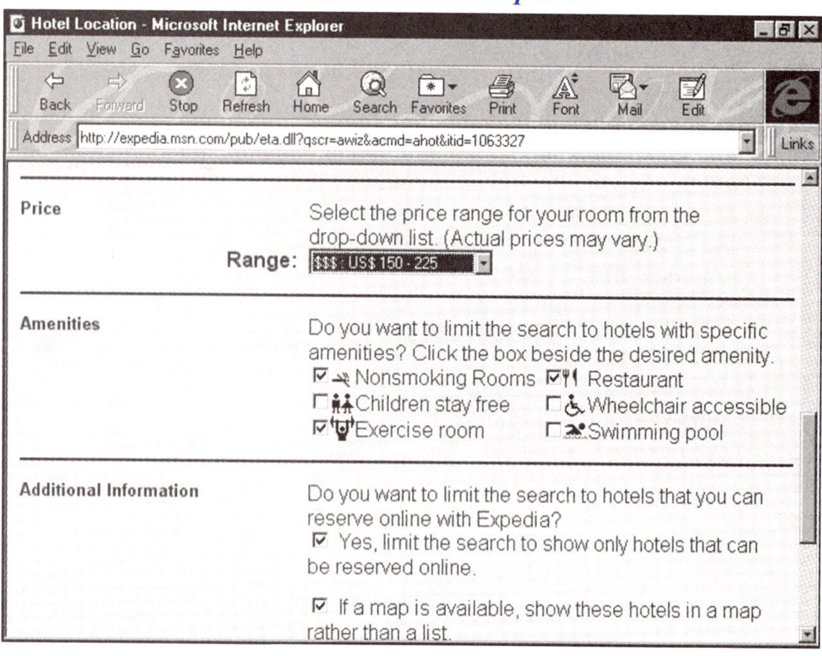

23. Click Continue. Scroll down to review the information displayed about the Crowne Plaza at The United Nations.
24. Click Check Room Availability.

Hotel Search Results

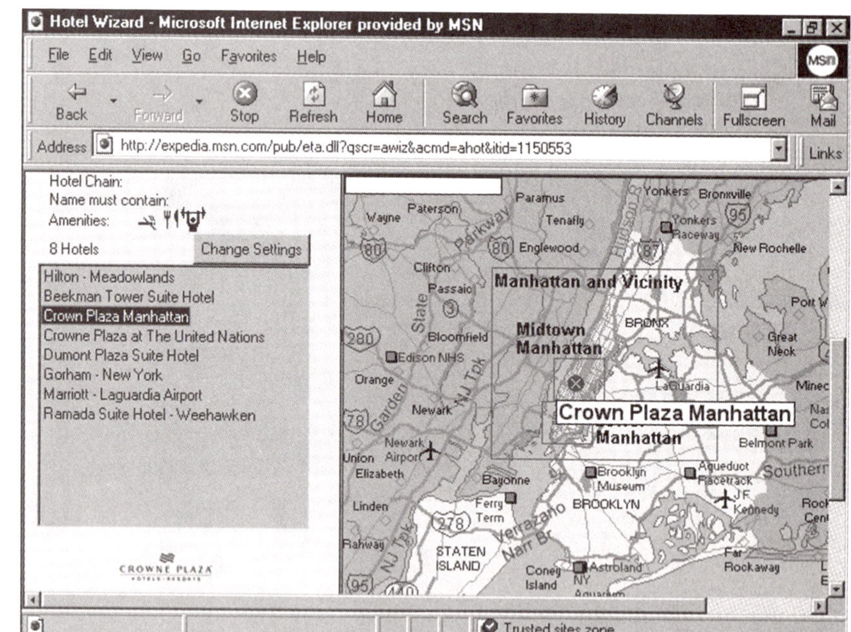

25. Scroll down to see the descriptions of available rooms, then click the price link next to the 1 Double Bed Non-smoking Great Rate Promotional Rate (the sixth room listing from the top).

View Hotel Description

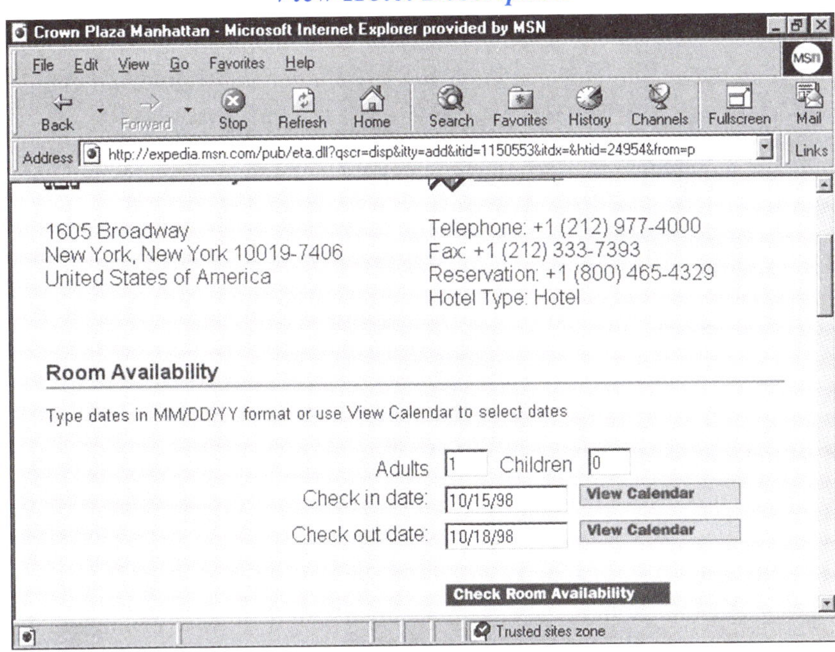

26. Scroll down to read the Hotel Room Details page, then click Add to Itinerary.
27. On the Itinerary page, scroll down to see the hotel room added to your itinerary for this trip.
28. Continue on to the next exercise.

OR

Exit from the simulation.

Hotel Room Added to Itinerary

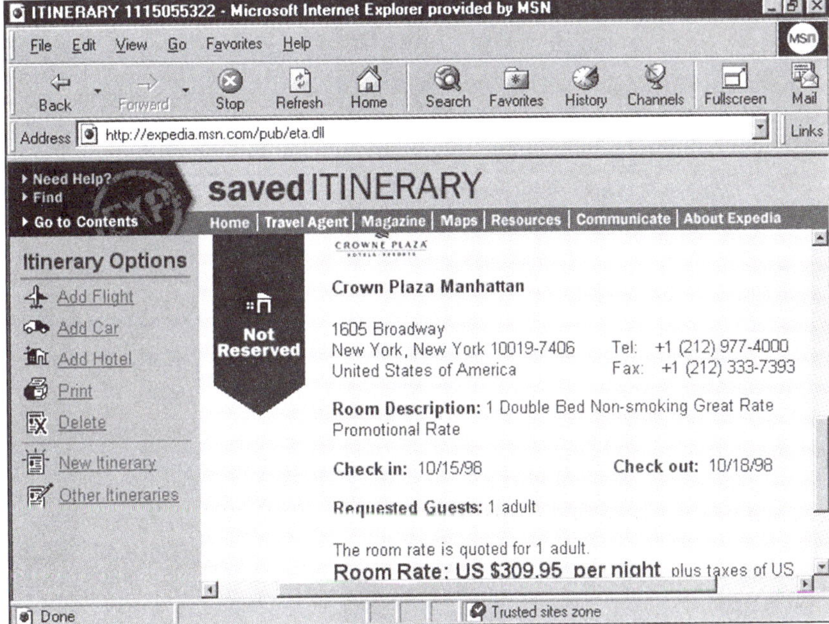

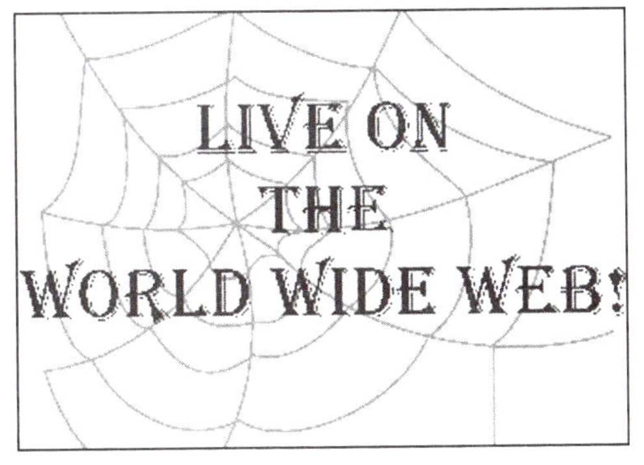

Microsoft Expedia Home Page

http://www.expedia.com/

Exercise 8

- Find a Restaurant with Zagat Survey
- Get Directions with MapQuest
- Check the Travel Forecast with Intellicast

NOTES

Find a Restaurant with Zagat Survey

- Consult the Zagat Survey Web site to find great restaurants when you travel.
- The Zagat Survey is widely recognized as the leading guide to fine dining across the country. Click on a city link to view an alphabetical index of restaurant listings for the city. You can also search the listings directory by cuisine, by food ranking, or by best deals.

Zagat Survey Home Page

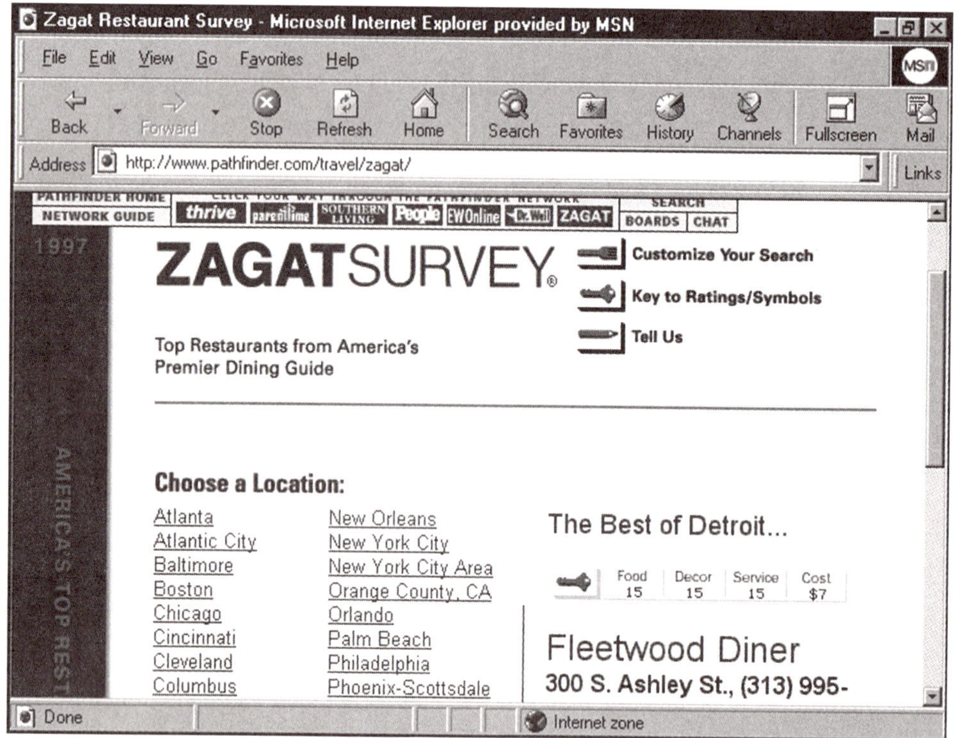

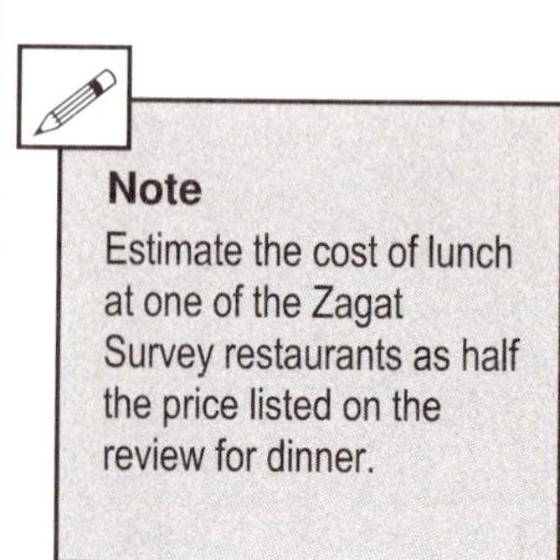

Note

Estimate the cost of lunch at one of the Zagat Survey restaurants as half the price listed on the review for dinner.

- If you already know the name of the restaurant you want to find, just type it into the search engine text box and click Find It!.
- Each link to a restaurant listing has a one- or two-word description of the type of restaurant (such as French, vegetarian, or Tex-Mex) to help you sift among the many possibilities.

- Click on a restaurant link to read the Zagat review. The survey rates each restaurant by food, décor, and service on a scale of 0 to 30, and include the cost of an average dinner plus drink and tip.

Get Directions with MapQuest

- If you need to know how to get to a business appointment, the MapQuest Web site can help you find the route to your destination.

MapQuest Home Page

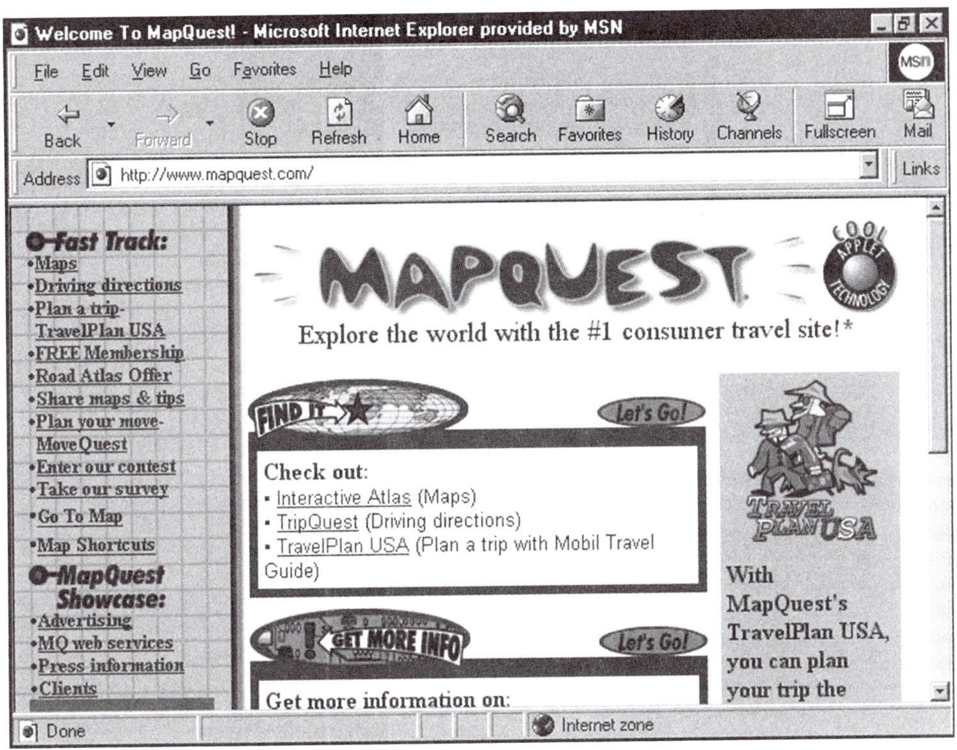

- Click the TripQuest link to find driving directions from point A to point B. Simply type the address of your starting point in the TripQuest form, then type the address of your destination.
- You can choose several mapping options for your directions, including city-to-city or door-to-door with an overview map, turn-by-turn maps with text, or text only.
- If you want to find your own way, click on the Interactive Atlas link at the MapQuest home page. At the Interactive Atlas page, you can enter a point of interest or an address to view a map of that location. You can zoom in or zoom out to view more or less detail on the maps.
- Click the TravelPlan USA link at the MapQuest home page to plan your next trip using the Mobil Travel Guide.

Note

MapQuest provides door-to-door directions for 29 major metro areas and city-to-city routing for any town or city within the continental U.S. and some parts of Mexico and Canada.

Check the Travel Forecast with Intellicast

- What will the weather hold for you on your next trip? Will driving conditions be hazardous? Should you expect weather-related flight delays? What clothes should you pack if you're flying from Chicago to Los Angeles or vice versa? Intellicast provides the answers to these questions at one very informative Web site.

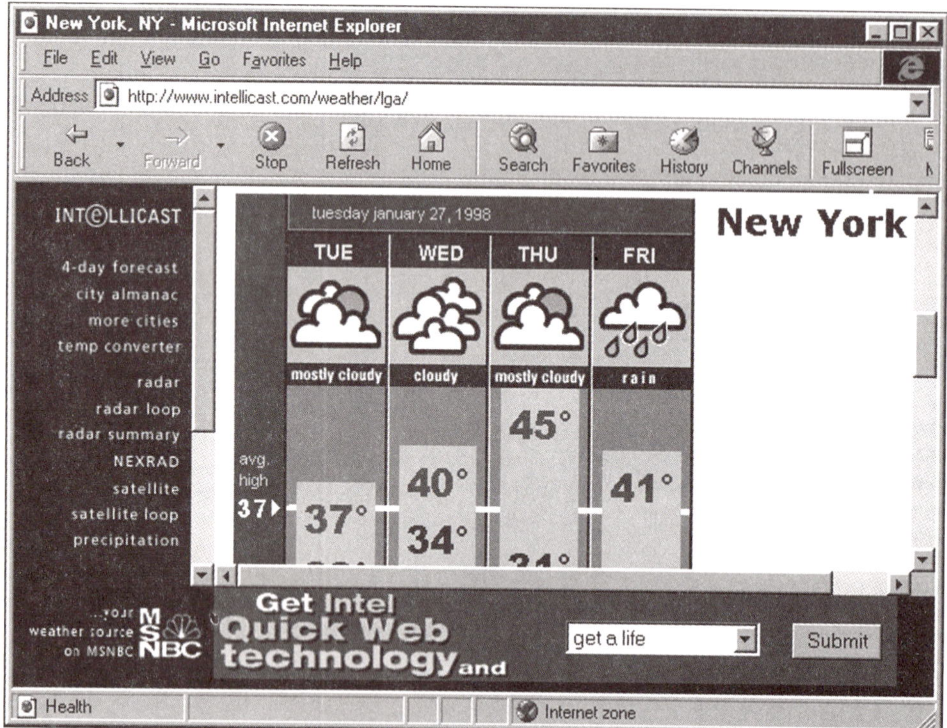

- Click the 4-day forecast to get the local four-day forecast for cities around the world. You can also click the Radar Loop link to check local radar loops, which update every 15 minutes, and see where stormy weather is heading. Click the Radar link to see a radar map for the surrounding region.
- Use the Travel Weather feature to check national maps for various types of inclement weather, including PrecipCast, FogCast, WindCast, SolarCast, and ThunderstormCast.
- Intellicast has extensive background information on weather phenomena and long-term forecasting. Other useful features include an influenza map, the Dr. Dewpoint question and answer service, as well as ski, tropical, and national park reports.

Note

Click the Intellicast Travel link and then click the flightcast link to find the current city forecast, flight status, and estimated departure and arrival times for flights currently in progress. Simply enter the flight's departure and arrival cities along with either the departure or arrival time to find the information you need.

In this exercise, you willl find restaurants for an upcoming trip using the Zagat Survey Web site. You will then use the MapQuest site to get directions from your hotel to the restaurants. Finally, you will check the four-day weather forecast for your travel destination using the Intellicast Web site.

Note: To ensure consistent results, this exercise uses simulated sites. The real URLs appear at the end of the exercise.

Web Search

Search for answers to the following questions using the Web sites you will visit in the Web simulation exercise.

1. What is the name of the last restaurant in the Zagat alphabetical listing of New York restaurants?

   ____

2. What food rating did the Gramercy Tavern receive?

   ____

3. How many listings are there for Chinese restaurants on the Zagats By Cuisine page?

   ____

4. What is the total distance from the Crowne Plaza hotel to the Union Square Café?

   ____

5. What is the average high temperature for New York during the last week of January?

   ____

EXERCISE DIRECTIONS

1. Launch the Internet simulation. From the Main Menu, select Lesson 6, then select Exercise 8.
2. On the Address line, type the following and press Enter:

   http://www.pathfinder.com/travel/zagat

   ➲ *The Zagat Survey home page opens.*

Zagat Survey Home Page

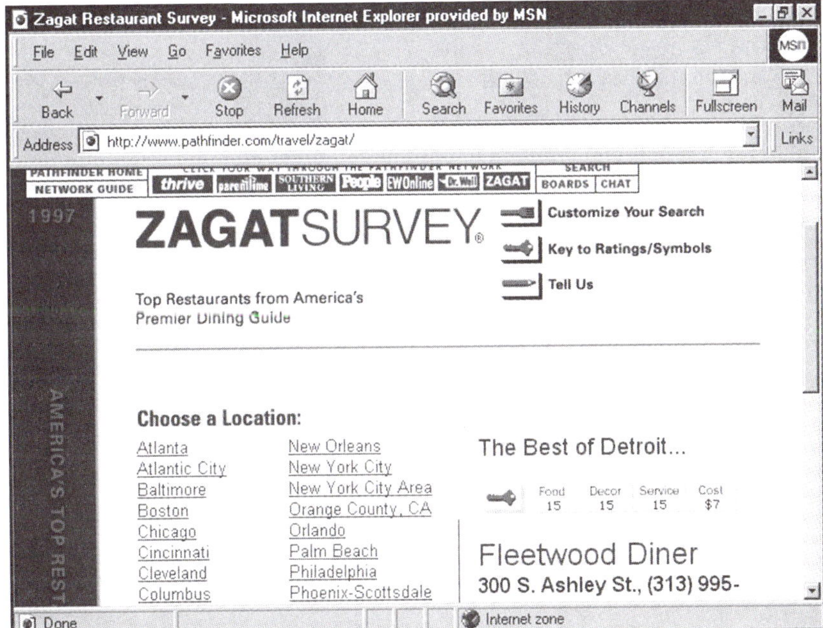

3. Click the New York City link.

   ➲ *An alphabetical directory of Zagat Survey restaurant reviews for New York opens.*

4. Scroll down the page to see the names of the reviewed restaurants.
5. Click the By Food Ranking icon.

   ➲ *A page listing review links for the top-rated restaurants in the city opens.*

Links to Reviews of Top New York Restaurants

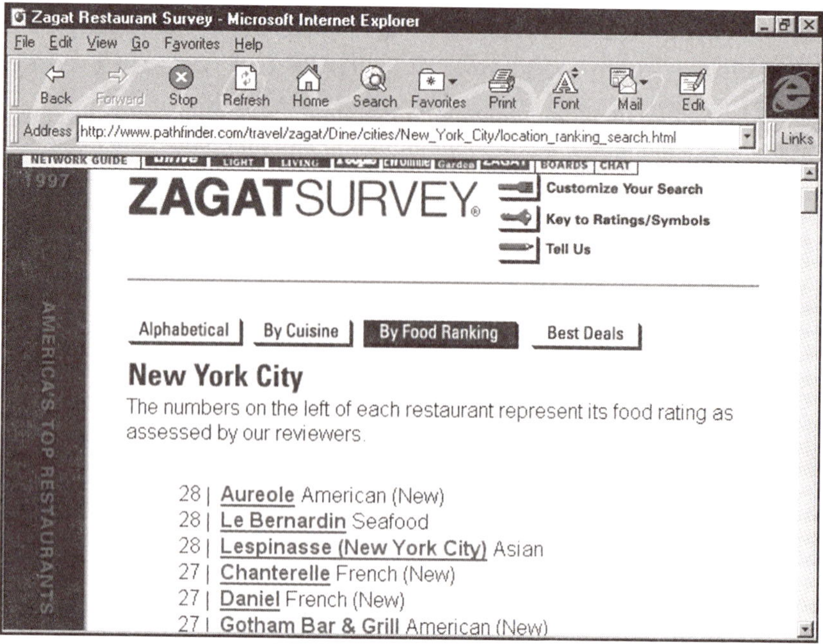

6. Scroll down and click the Union Square Cafe link and then read the review of this restaurant.
7. Scroll back up the page and then read more reviews of top restaurants. Click the By Cuisine link at the top of the page.
8. Scroll down and click the link for the Rainbow Room under the American (New) heading.
9. Read the Zagat review of the Rainbow Room.

Zagat Survey Review of Union Square Cafe

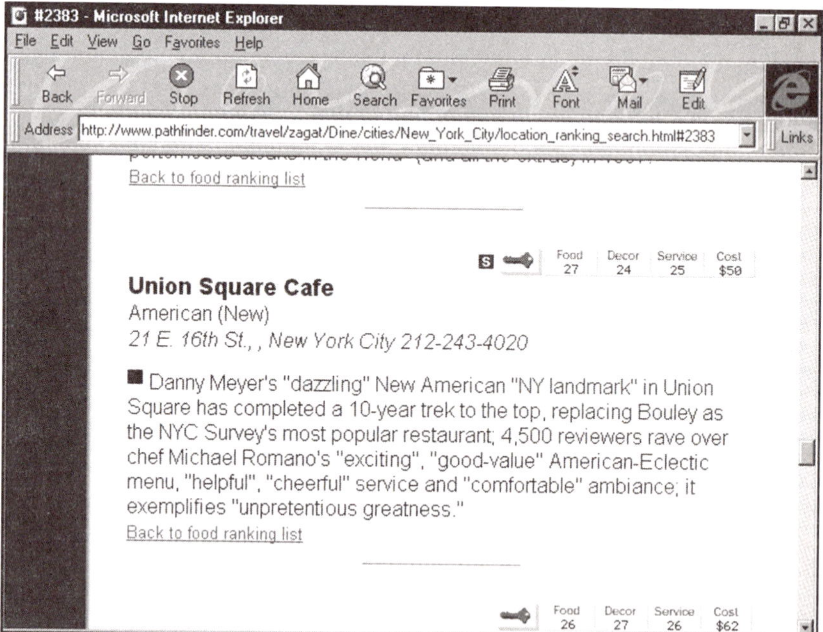

10. On the Address line of your browser, type the following URL and press Enter:

    http://www.mapquest.com

    ➲ *The MapQuest home page opens.*

11. Click the TripQuest link.

MapQuest Home Page

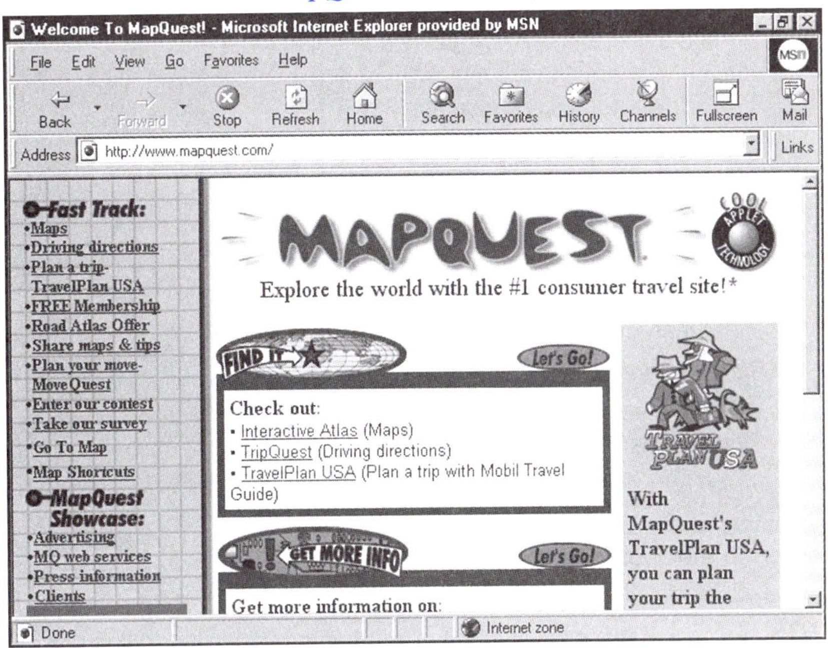

12. Enter the address for the Crowne Plaza hotel in the starting point text boxes of the TripQuest form:

    Street Address: 1605 Broadway

    City: Manhattan

    State: NY

13. Enter the address for the Union Square Cafe in the destination text boxes of the TripQuest form:

    Street Address: 21 East 16th Street

    City: Manhattan

    State: NY

14. Accept the default Route Type and Route Mapping Options and click Calculate Directions.

Enter Starting Point and Destination

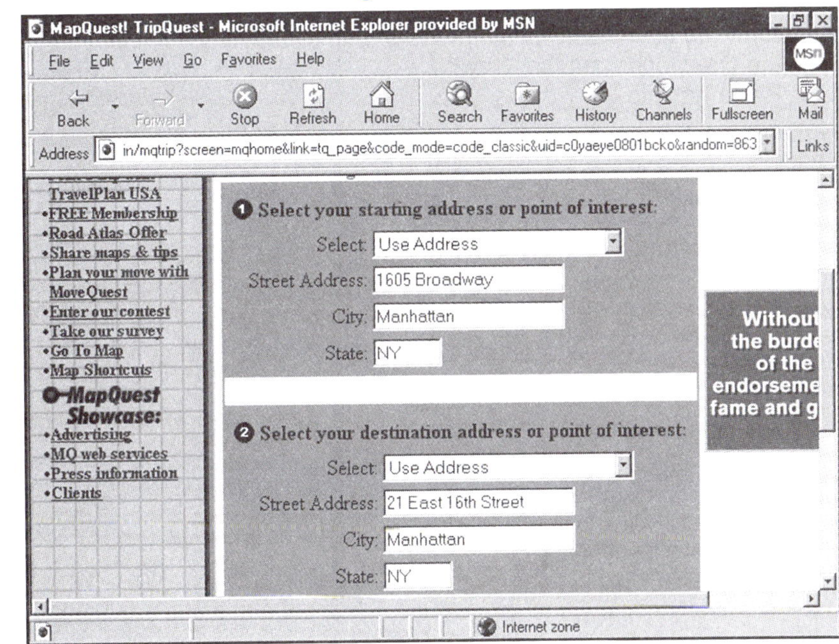

15. View the MapQuest maps and read the directions from the Crowne Plaza hotel to the Union Square Café.
16. Scroll down and click Calculate New Directions.
17. Enter the address for the Crowne Plaza hotel again as the starting point (see step 12), then enter the address for the Rainbow Room in the destination text boxes of the TripQuest form:

    Street Address: 30 Rockefeller Plaza

    City: Manhattan

    State: NY
18. Accept the default Route Type and Route Mapping Options and click Calculate Directions.

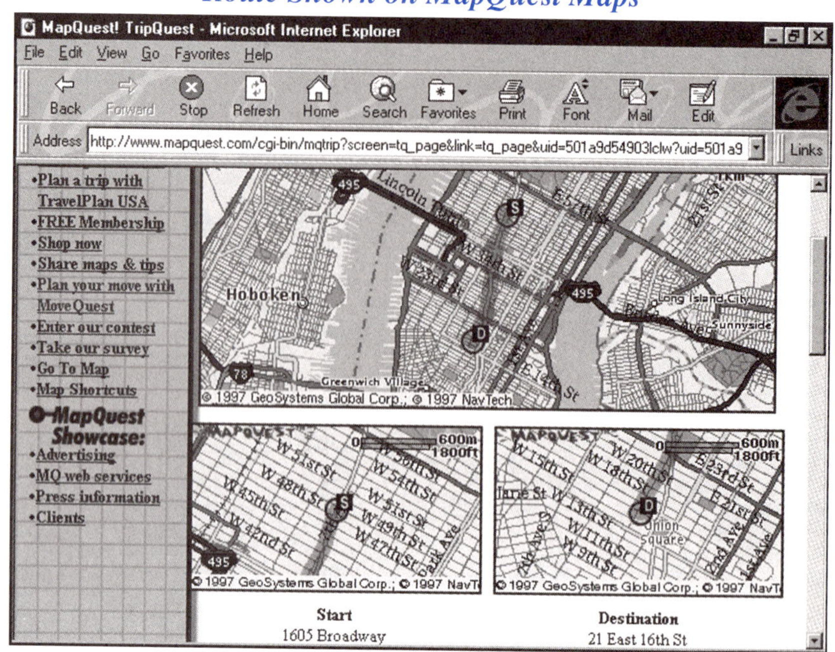

Route Shown on MapQuest Maps

19. View the MapQuest maps and read the directions from the Crowne Plaza hotel to the Rainbow Room.
20. On the Address line of your browser, type the following URL and press Enter:

    http://www.intellicast.com

    ➲ *The Intellicast home page opens.*

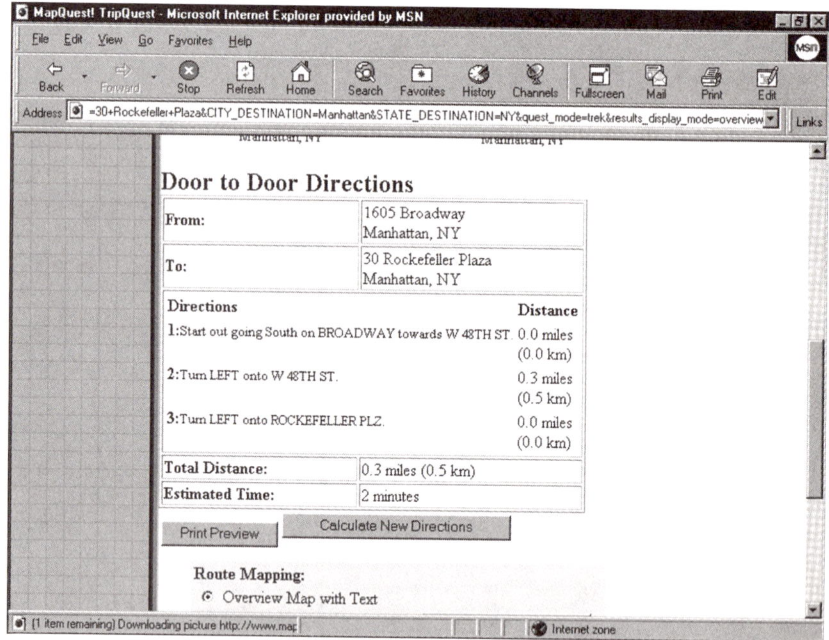

Door to Door Directions to the Rainbow Room

21. Click the usa link to see a map of United States weather.

Intellicast Home Page

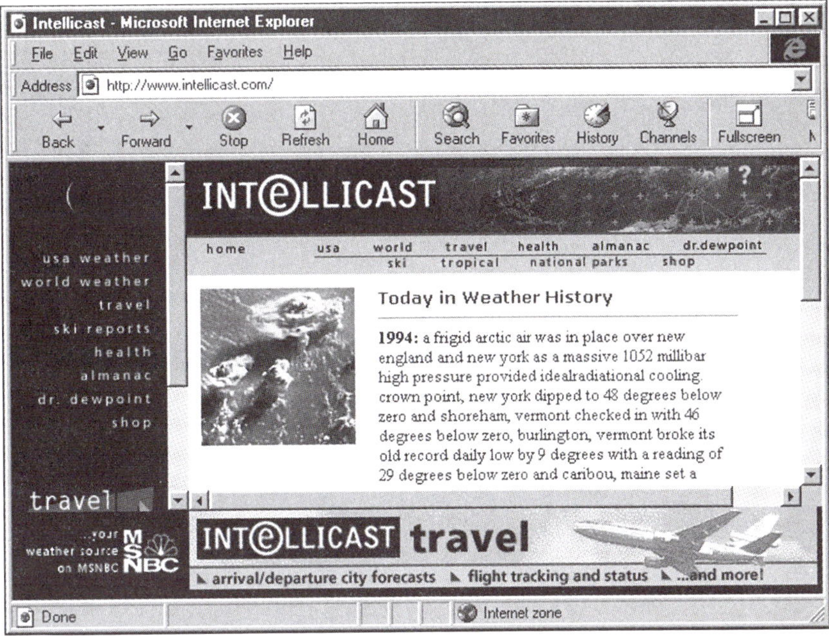

22. Click on the weather icon for New York.

➲ *A sample four-day forecast for New York City opens.*

United States Forecast Map

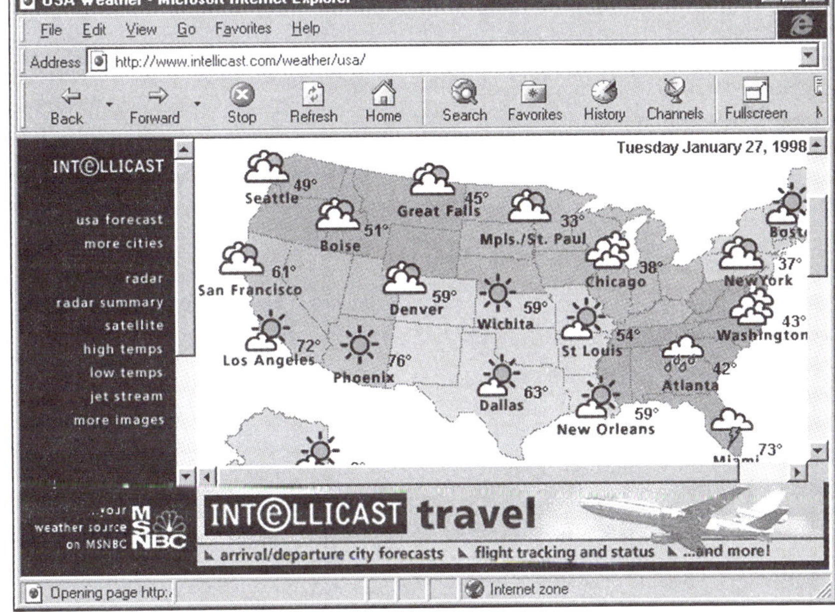

23. Click the radar link in the left column.

   ➲ *A sample radar map opens showing weather systems in the region surrounding New York City.*

24. Continue on to the next exercise.

   OR

   Exit from the simulation.

Four-Day Forecast for New York City

Radar for New York Region

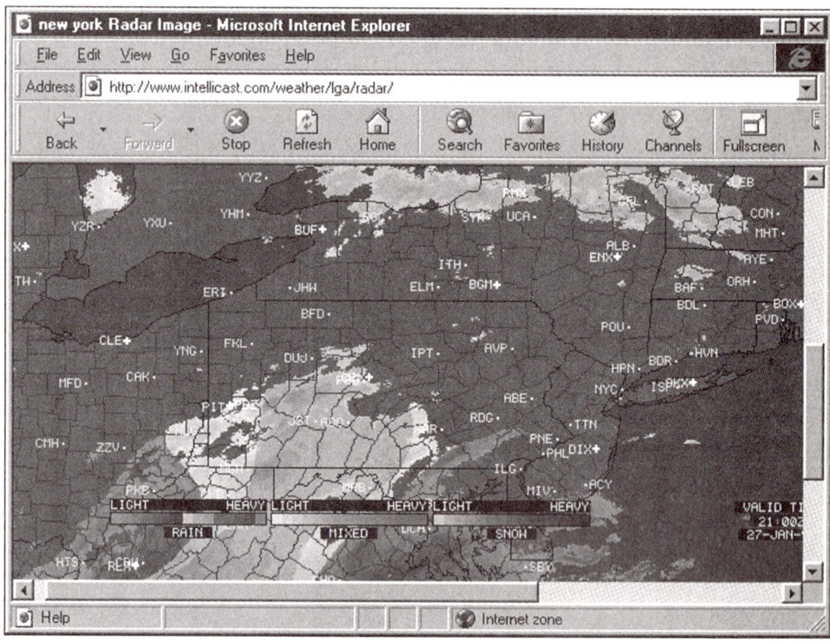

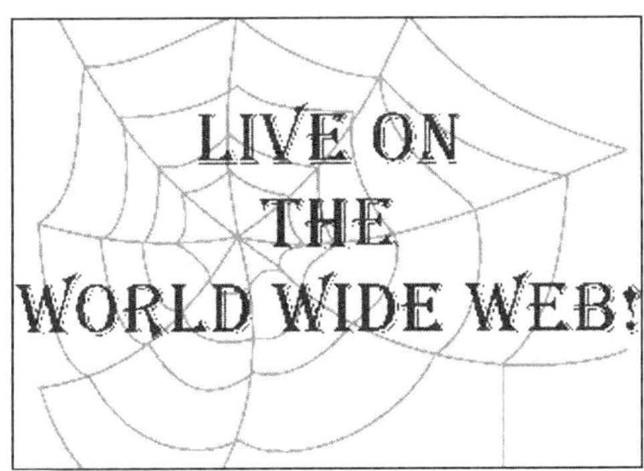

Zagat Survey Home Page

http://www.pathfinder.com/travel/zagat

MapQuest Home Page

http://www.mapquest.com

Intellicast Home Page

http://www.intellicast.com

NEXT LESSON

Lesson 7: Sales and Marketing

Exercise 1

- Improve Target Marketing with American Demographics
- Research Target Markets with U.S. Census Bureau

Exercise 2

- Develop Sales Leads with SalesLeads USA
- Research Companies with Hoover's Online

Exercise 3

- Locate Clients with BigBook
- Find People with Four11
- Find Company Web Sites with WebSitez

Exercise 4

- Improve Sales Techniques with SalesDoctors Magazine
- Get the Most out of Trade Shows with Trade Show News Network

Exercise 5

- Develop a Target Mailing List with List Merchant
- Search for Mailing Lists and Market Online with American List Council

Exercise 6

- Sell to the Government with Commerce Business Daily

Exercise 7

- Find International Sales Resources with MSU-CIBER
- Find Trade News with Trade Information Center
- Locate Trade Leads with Global Marketplace
- Translate Foreign Languages with travlang

Exercise 1

- Improve Target Marketing with American Demographics
- Research Target Markets with U.S. Census Bureau

NOTES

Improve Target Marketing with American Demographics

- You can improve your target marketing techniques by reading the publications featured at the American Demographics and Marketing Tools Web site. The Web site provides quick access to articles from American Demographics and Marketing Tools magazines, as well as a bookstore page where you can browse and purchase marketing titles.

American Demographics Home Page

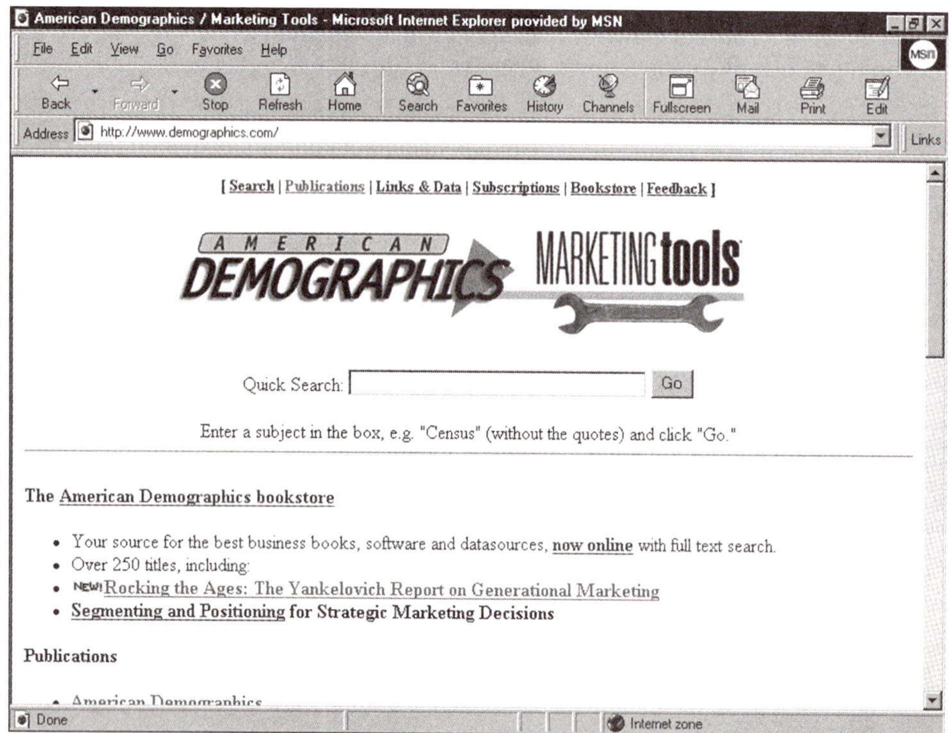

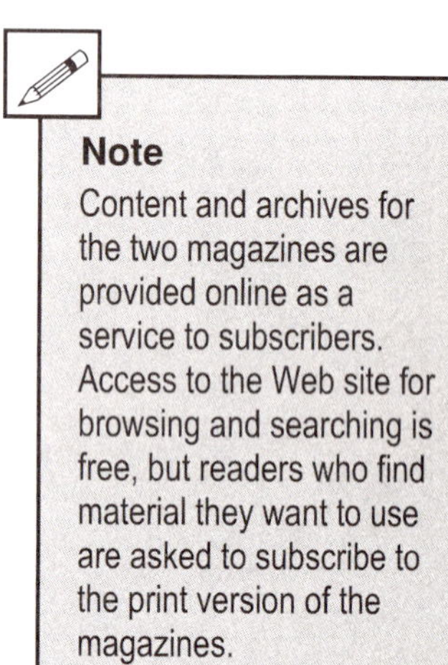

Note

Content and archives for the two magazines are provided online as a service to subscribers. Access to the Web site for browsing and searching is free, but readers who find material they want to use are asked to subscribe to the print version of the magazines.

- Click links for American Demographics or Marketing Tools to go to the respective magazines. A contents page for the magazine you select will open. Here you can click links to current or archive issues and browse the magazine's content by reading article summaries.
- Click the link for an article title to read the entire article. American Demographics magazine focuses on tracking consumer demographic trends. Marketing Tools magazine focuses primarily on marketing tactics and techniques.

Research Target Markets with U.S. Census Bureau

- Research a target market on the Web by searching the United States Census Bureau Web site for statistical and demographic information. The statistics available at this site can tell you a lot about your potential customers and how to reach them.
- Find out how many people live in a particular city, state, county, or town. Check the gender and age makeup of a certain area and find out about the inhabitants' economic resources. Monitor national, regional, and local economic trends, as well as business and economic trends by market sector.

Census Bureau Home Page

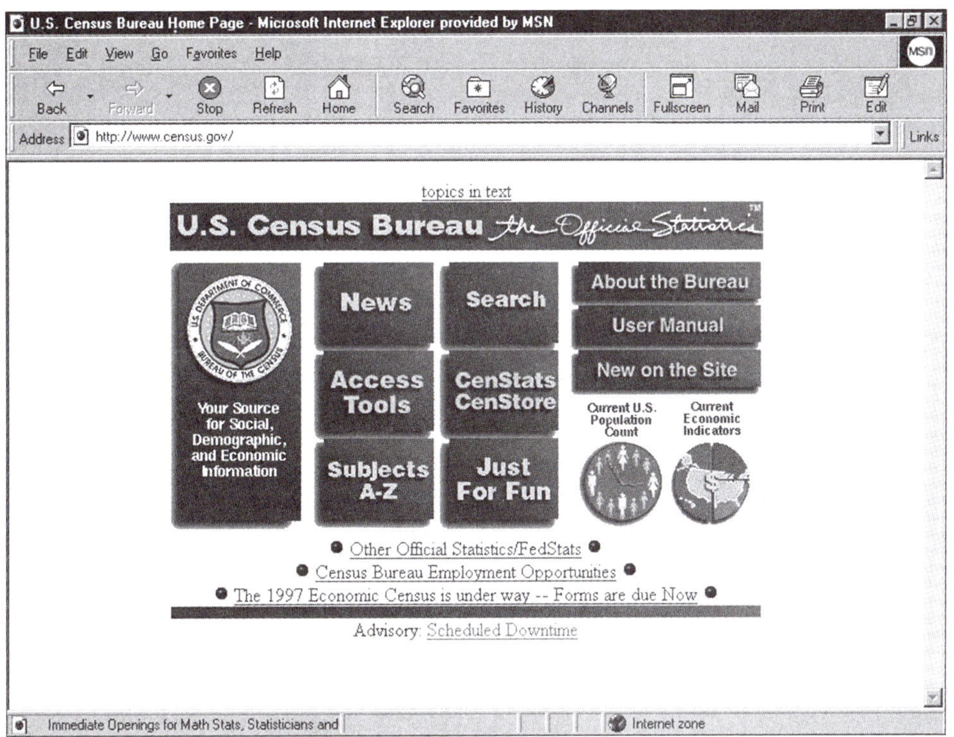

- A good place to start is the Current Economic Indicators icon, one of two pie charts at the right of the Census Bureau home page. The link takes you to a page that includes a series of links organized into categories such as About businesses, About people, Tools and tidbits, and Data elsewhere—links to other statistical and demographic pages on the Web.
- The About businesses category includes links to various types of business and industry. The About people category includes links to Income, Labor Force, and Households' statistics. You can also check the Census Economic Briefing Room for updates on the latest economic indicators.
- If you're looking for specific information, click on the Subjects A-Z link at the Census home page. Here you will find an alphabetical index of links to Census Bureau information and statistics.

Note

Click the Current U.S. Population Count icon on the Census Bureau home page to see population clocks for the United States and the World. The clocks show the estimated U.S. population at the current moment and an estimate of the World population.

Note

Click on the Access Tools link at the Census home page to see a listing of tools for downloading Census information and viewing Census data online. The Map Stats link takes you to an extensive gallery of interesting and useful Census Bureau maps.

- For example, if your market or sales territory is Cincinnati, you can go to the Metropolitan Areas link from the Subjects A-Z page and then click the link under 1990 Census Data for Metropolitan Areas. Select the area you want to search—nation, state, county, zip codes, or, in this case, metropolitan area. Then select the type of information you want and click Submit. The Census Bureau retrieves the information and presents it in list format.

Census Bureau Statistical Data

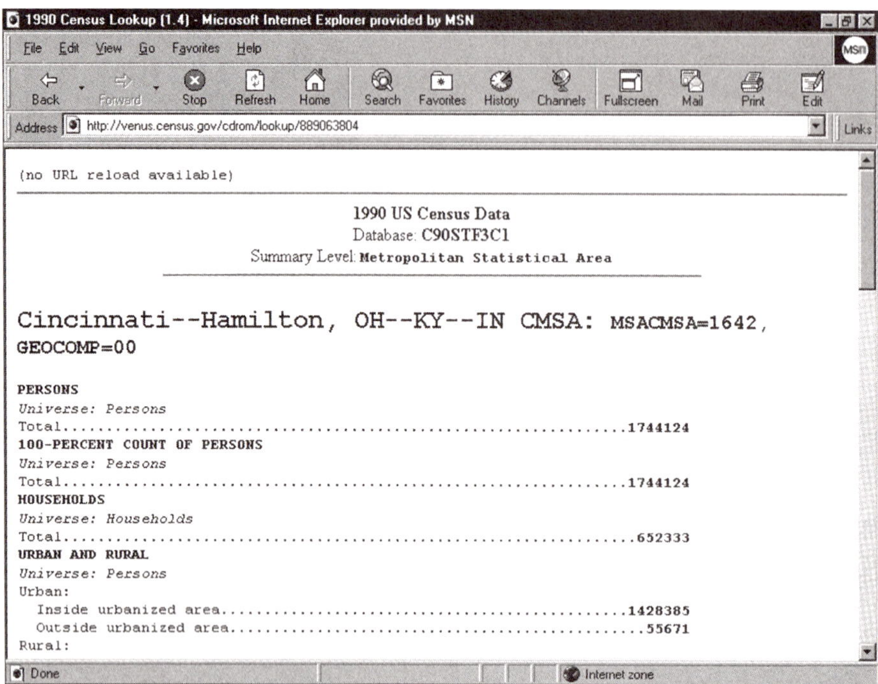

In this exercise, you will read articles from the American Demographics Web site describing target marketing trends and techniques. You will then search for statistical data for a sample target market at the U.S. Census Bureau Web site. You will also check the Census Bureau population clocks and a map of U.S. population distribution.

Note: *To ensure consistent results, this exercise uses simulated sites. The real URLs appear at the end of the exercise.*

Web Search

Search for answers to the following questions using the Web sites you will visit in the Web simulation exercise.

1. According to the article "College Come-Ons," what is the estimated spending power of college students?

   ____

2. According to the article "How to Measure Local Incomes," what is the Census Bureau's popular income estimate called?

   ____

3. How many 16 year olds lived in the Cincinnati metropolitan area in 1989?

   ____

4. What was the largest household income group (dollar range) in Cincinnati in 1989?

   ____

5. What was the median household income in Cincinnati in 1989?

   ____

6. What is the projected world population on July 1, 1998?

   ____

EXERCISE DIRECTIONS

1. Launch the Internet simulation. From the Main Menu, select Lesson 7, then select Exercise 1.
2. On the Address line, type the following URL and press Enter:

   http://www.demographics.com/

   ➲ *The American Demographics home page opens.*

American Demographics Home Page

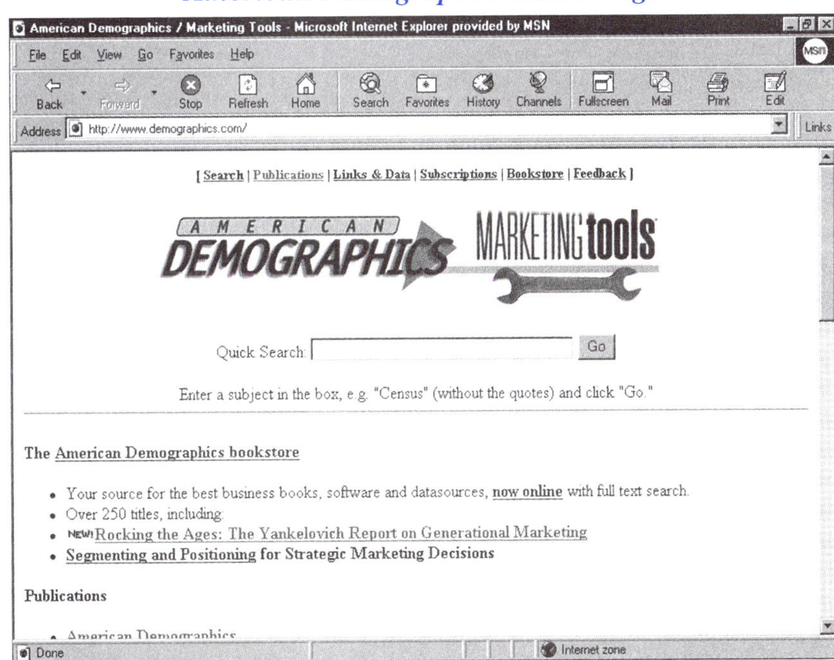

3. Click the American Demographics link under the Publications heading.

   ➲ *The American Demographics Magazine Web Archive opens.*

4. Click the March link next to the 1998 heading.

   ➲ *The Table of Contents Web page for the March 1998 edition of the magazine opens.*

5. Click the link for the Cover story, College Come-Ons.

   ➲ *The article opens.*

American Demographics Magazine

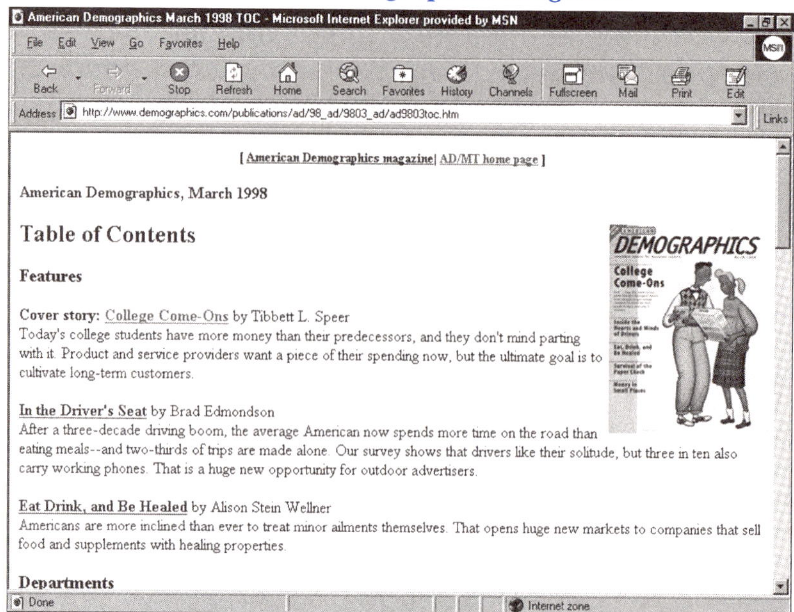

American Demographics March 1998 TOC - Microsoft Internet Explorer provided by MSN

File Edit View Go Favorites Help

Back Forward Stop Refresh Home Search Favorites History Channels Fullscreen Mail Print Edit

Address http://www.demographics.com/publications/ad/98_ad/9803_ad/ad9803toc.htm

[American Demographics magazine | AD/MT home page]

American Demographics, March 1998

Table of Contents

Features

Cover story: College Come-Ons by Tibbett L. Speer
Today's college students have more money than their predecessors, and they don't mind parting with it. Product and service providers want a piece of their spending now, but the ultimate goal is to cultivate long-term customers.

In the Driver's Seat by Brad Edmondson
After a three-decade driving boom, the average American now spends more time on the road than eating meals--and two-thirds of trips are made alone. Our survey shows that drivers like their solitude, but three in ten also carry working phones. That is a huge new opportunity for outdoor advertisers.

Eat Drink, and Be Healed by Alison Stein Wellner
Americans are more inclined than ever to treat minor ailments themselves. That opens huge new markets to companies that sell food and supplements with healing properties.

Departments

Done Internet zone

6. Scroll down and read the article.

   ❓ *How receptive do you think college students are to marketing efforts targeted at them?*

Target Marketing to College Students

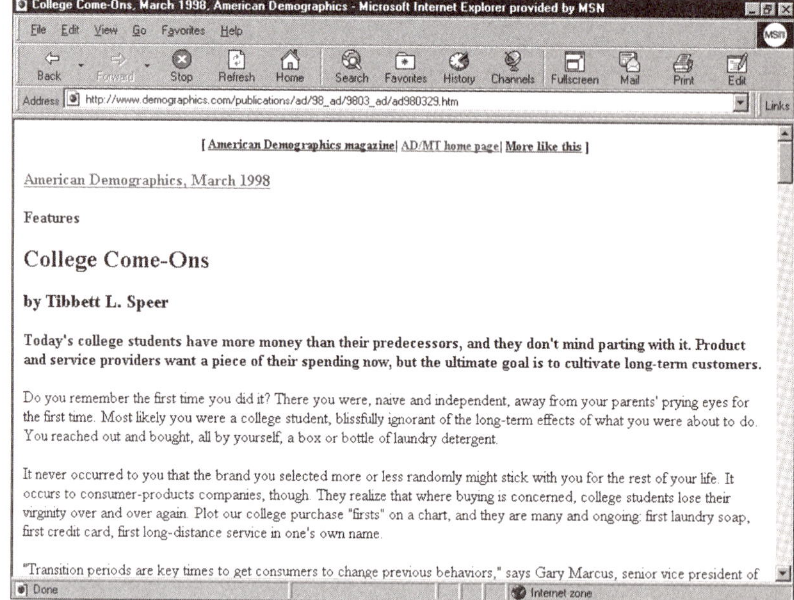

College Come-Ons, March 1998, American Demographics - Microsoft Internet Explorer provided by MSN

File Edit View Go Favorites Help

Back Forward Stop Refresh Home Search Favorites History Channels Fullscreen Mail Print Edit

Address http://www.demographics.com/publications/ad/98_ad/9803_ad/ad980329.htm

[American Demographics magazine | AD/MT home page | More like this]

American Demographics, March 1998

Features

College Come-Ons

by Tibbett L. Speer

Today's college students have more money than their predecessors, and they don't mind parting with it. Product and service providers want a piece of their spending now, but the ultimate goal is to cultivate long-term customers.

Do you remember the first time you did it? There you were, naive and independent, away from your parents' prying eyes for the first time. Most likely you were a college student, blissfully ignorant of the long-term effects of what you were about to do. You reached out and bought, all by yourself, a box or bottle of laundry detergent.

It never occurred to you that the brand you selected more or less randomly might stick with you for the rest of your life. It occurs to consumer-products companies, though. They realize that where buying is concerned, college students lose their virginity over and over again. Plot our college purchase "firsts" on a chart, and they are many and ongoing: first laundry soap, first credit card, first long-distance service in one's own name.

"Transition periods are key times to get consumers to change previous behaviors," says Gary Marcus, senior vice president of

Done Internet zone

7. Click the American Demographics, March 1998 link at the top of the page.
   ➲ *You return to the Table of Contents Web page for the March 1998 edition.*
8. Scroll down and click the How to Measure Local Incomes link.
   ➲ *The article opens.*
9. Scroll down and read the article.
   ✓ *Note the importance of collecting sound statistical information about a market's economic potential.*

Census Bureau Home Page

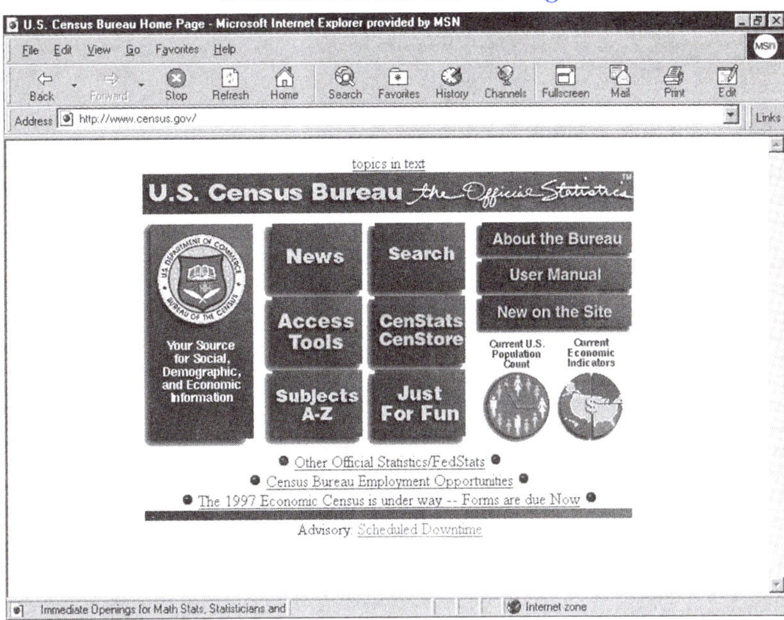

10. Type the following URL in your browser's Address line and press Enter:
    http://www.census.gov/
    ➲ *The U.S. Census Bureau home page opens.*
11. Click the Subjects A-Z icon.
    ➲ *The Subjects A to Z index and search page opens.*
12. Click the M link in the subject grid.
    ➲ *The index page moves to the topics that begin with M.*
13. Click the Metropolitan Areas link.
    ➲ *The Metropolitan Areas page opens.*

Subjects A to Z Index and Search Page

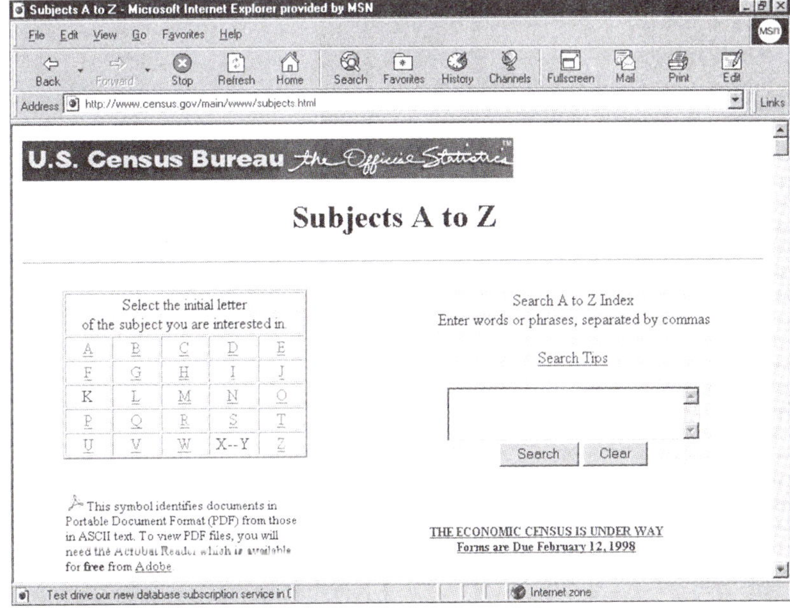

14. Click the STF3C-part 1 link.

    ➲ *The 1990 Census Lookup page opens.*

15. Scroll down and click the STF3C-part 1 link.
16. Choose the **Go to level Metropolitan Statistical Area** option, then click Submit.

1990 Census Lookup Page

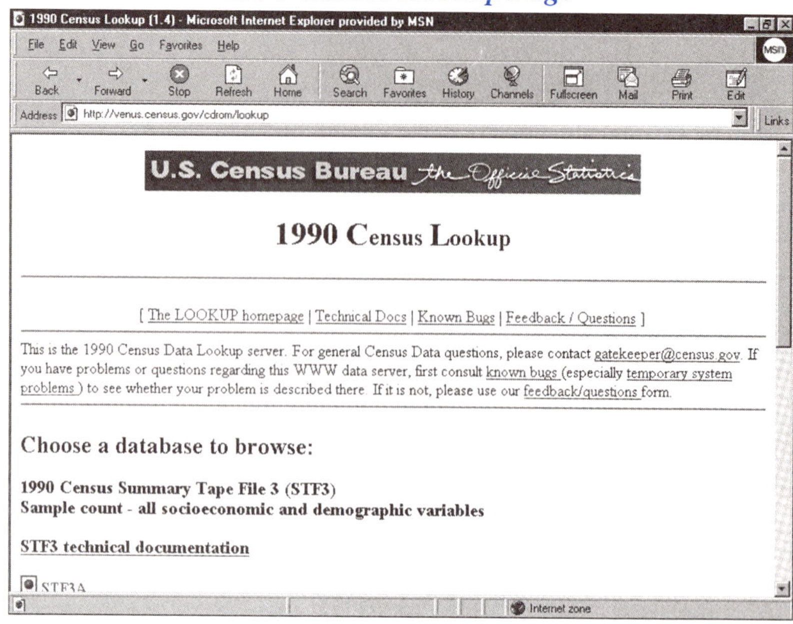

17. On the *Current Level*: Metropolitan Statistical Area page, choose the first option, **Retrieve the areas you've selected below** if it is not already selected.
18. Scroll down and click to select **Cincinnati-Hamilton, OH-KY-IN CMSA**, then click Submit.
19. Select the **Choose TABLES to retrieve** option if it is not already selected, then click Submit.

    ➲ *A menu of tables for you to select opens.*

Metropolitan Statustical Area Menu

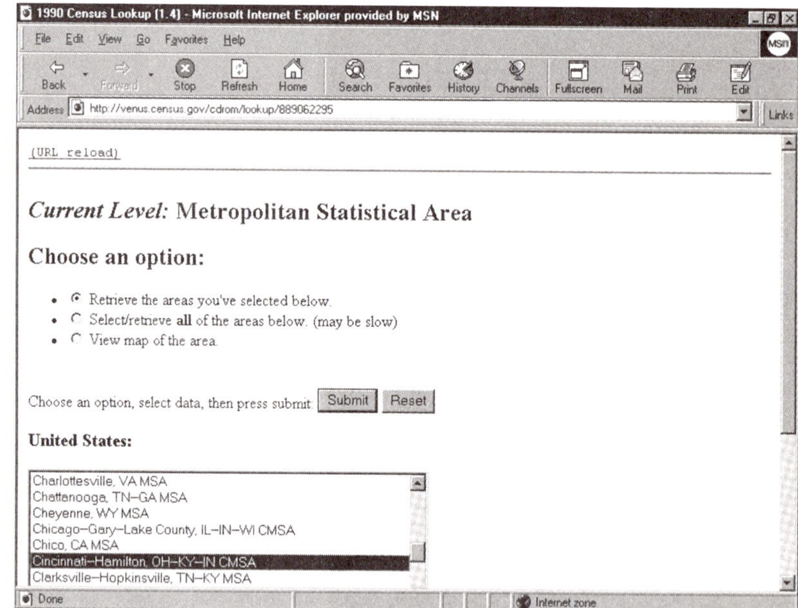

20. Click to select the following tables:

    P1. Persons

    P5. Households

    P6. Urban and Rural

    P7. Sex

    P8. Race

    P13. Age

    P80. Household Income in 1989

    P80A. Median Household Income in 1989

    P114A. Per Capita Income in 1989

    ✓ *You will have to scroll down the page to select the menu items.*

21. After you have selected the above menu items, return to the top of the page, then click Submit.
22. Choose the **HTML** format, then click Submit.

    ✓ *The Census Web site builds a report page that includes the data tables you chose.*

23. Scroll down to review the statistical data.

    ❓ *Why do you think this kind of information would be useful to sales and marketing professionals?*

Select Tables from This Menu

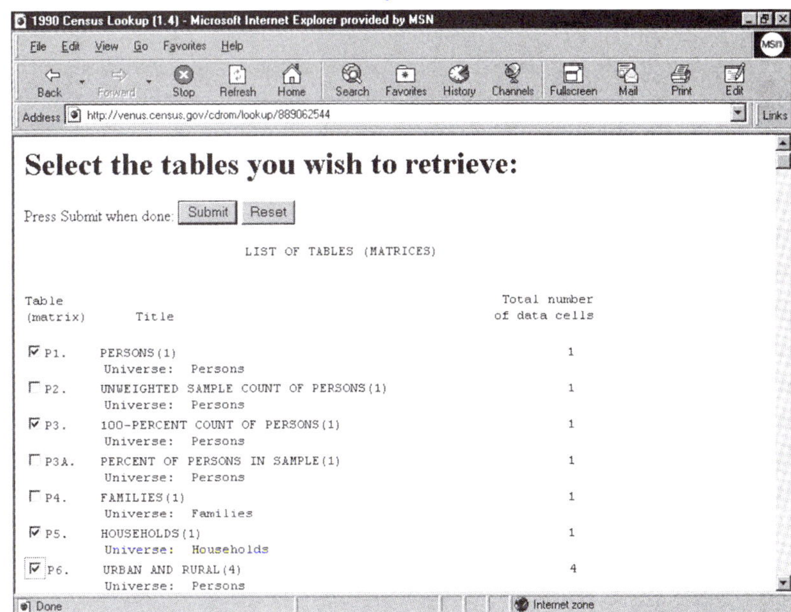

Statistical Data for Cincinnati Metropolitan Area

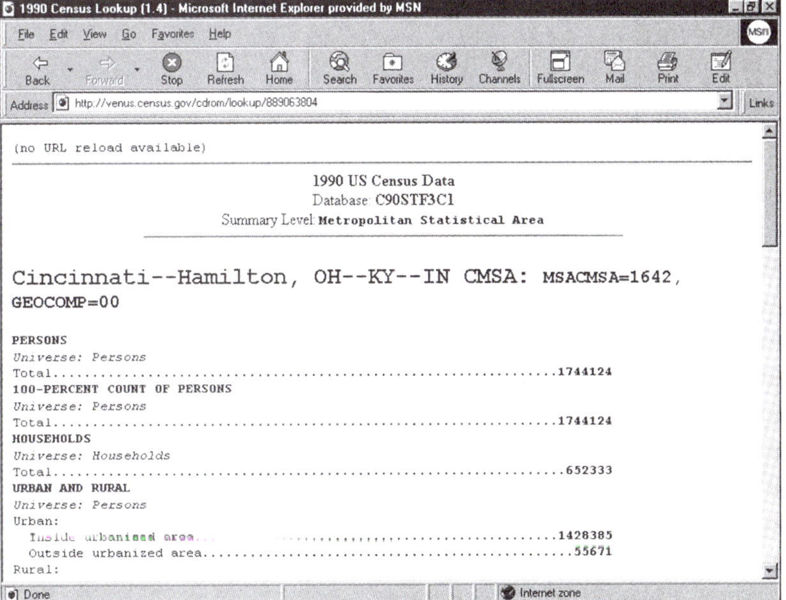

24. Type the following URL in your browser's Address line and press Enter:

    http://www.census.gov/

    ➲ *The U.S. Census Bureau home page opens again.*

25. Click the Current U.S. Population Count icon.

    ➲ *The Pop Clocks page opens.*

26. Click the United States link.

    ➲ *The Population Clock projection for the United States opens.*

27. Click your browser's Back button to return to the Pop Clocks page, then click the World link.

    ➲ *The Population Clock projection for the world opens.*

    ✓ *Notice that the world population is expected to increase by almost 100 million people during the year shown.*

28. Click on U.S. Census Bureau icon at the top of the page.

    ➲ *You return to the Census Bureau home page.*

29. Click the Just for Fun link.

30. Scroll down and click the Map Gallery link.

    ➲ *The Geography Division Map Gallery page opens.*

United State Population Clock

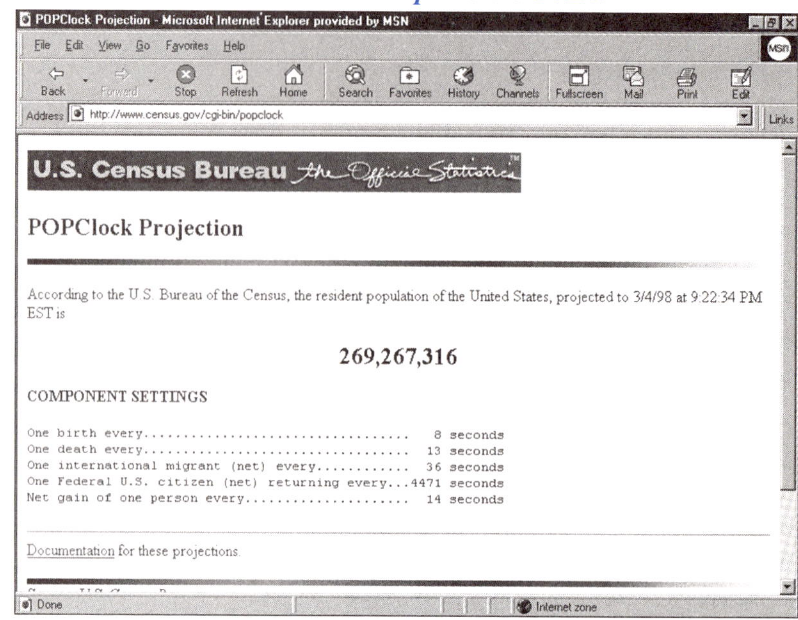

World Population Clock

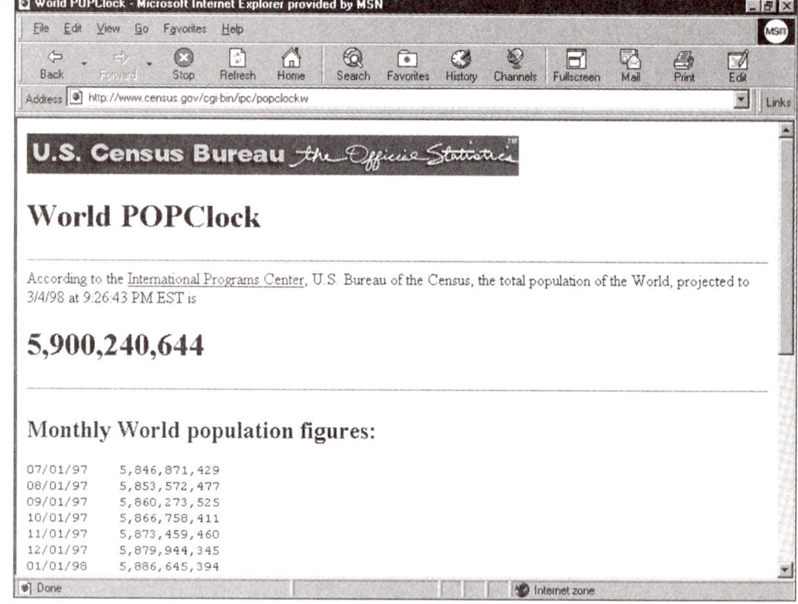

31. Scroll down and click the 1990 Population Distribution in the United States link.

   ➲ *The Popluation Distribution map page opens.*

32. Click on the map to view it on the full screen.

33. Continue on to the next exercise.

   OR

   Exit from the simulation.

Geography Division Map Gallery

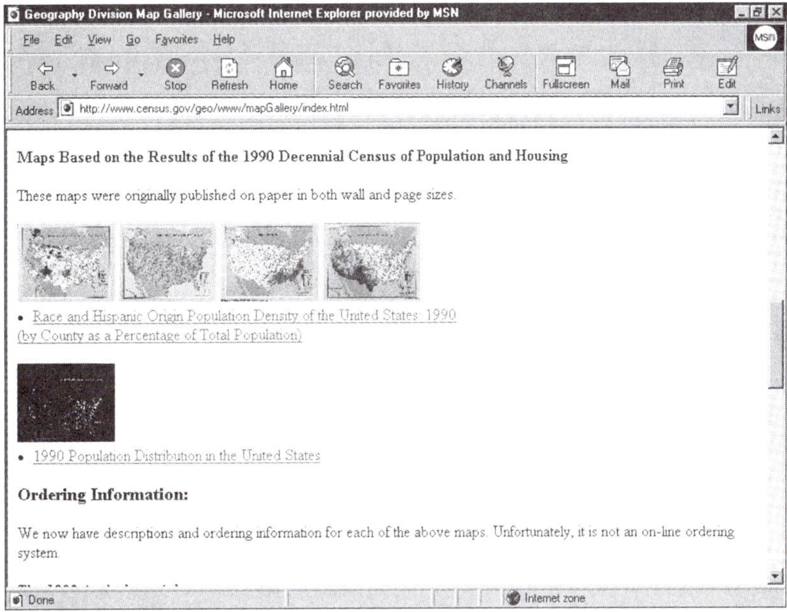

United States Population Distribution

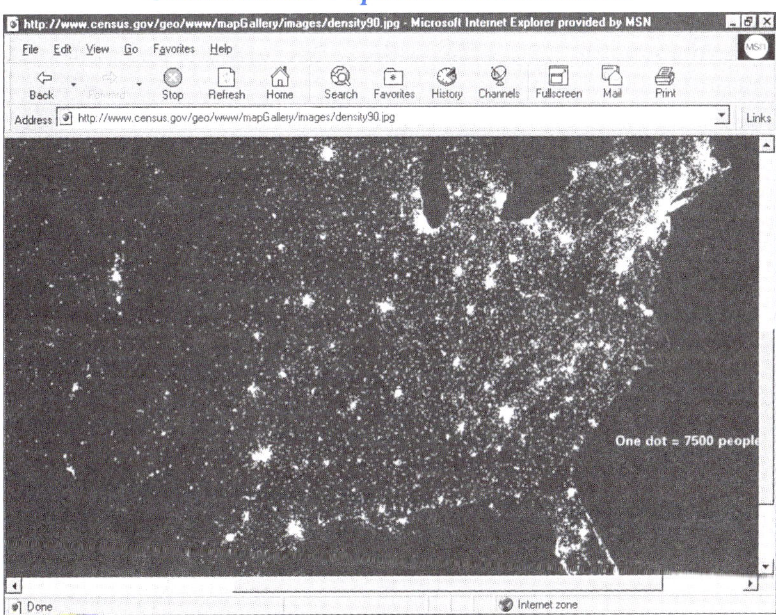

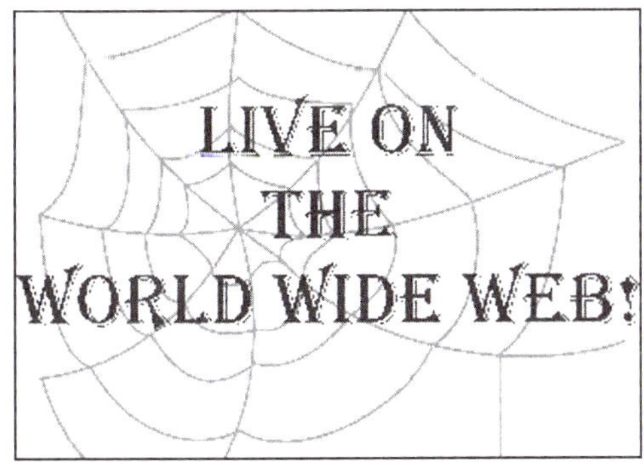

American Demographics Home Page
http://www.demographics.com/

United States Census Bureau Home Page
http://www.census.gov/

Exercise 2

- Develop Sales Leads with SalesLeads USA
- Research Companies with Hoover's Online

NOTES

Develop Sales Leads with SalesLeads USA

- You can use the Web to help you develop sales leads. Many sites include searchable databases of U.S. and international corporations, including company financial information and key contacts. The large databases and powerful search engines at these sites help you quickly zero in on the types of businesses you want to find.
- SalesLeadsUSA offers a searchable database of more than 10 million businesses and more than 100 million households. A search of businesses in a single ZIP code can return a result of more than 2,400 businesses.

SalesLeads USA Home Page

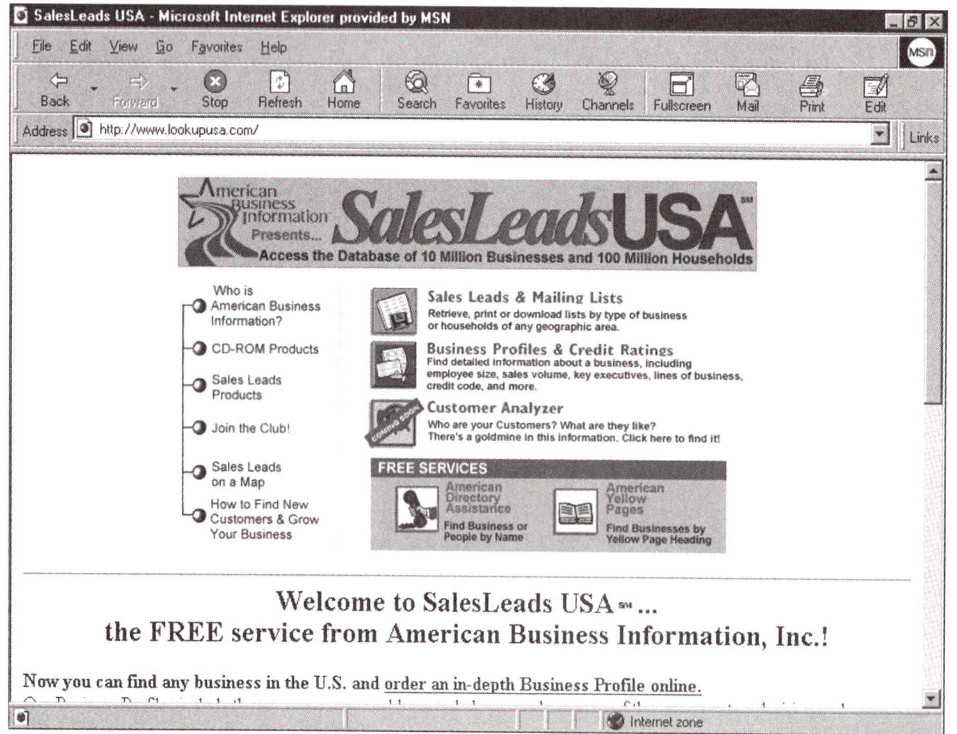

Note

Sales lead lists available for free at the SalesLeadsUSA Web site include only company names. You can purchase complete sales lead lists and company information for the amount stated on the search results screen.

- Click the Sales Leads and Mailing Lists icon to access a search engine that you can use to search by type of business, by state, county, metropolitan area, city, ZIP code, or company name. After you receive initial search results, you can further narrow your search by a number of different criteria, and then choose whether you want to pay for the list of business information at the quoted price.
- For example, if you have a three-state sales territory in the pharmaceutical industry, you can search using *pharmaceuticals* as your keyword, then narrow the search results to only those firms in your three-state territory. Finally, you can further narrow the search by using criteria such as number of employees or sales revenue.

Sales Leads Search Results

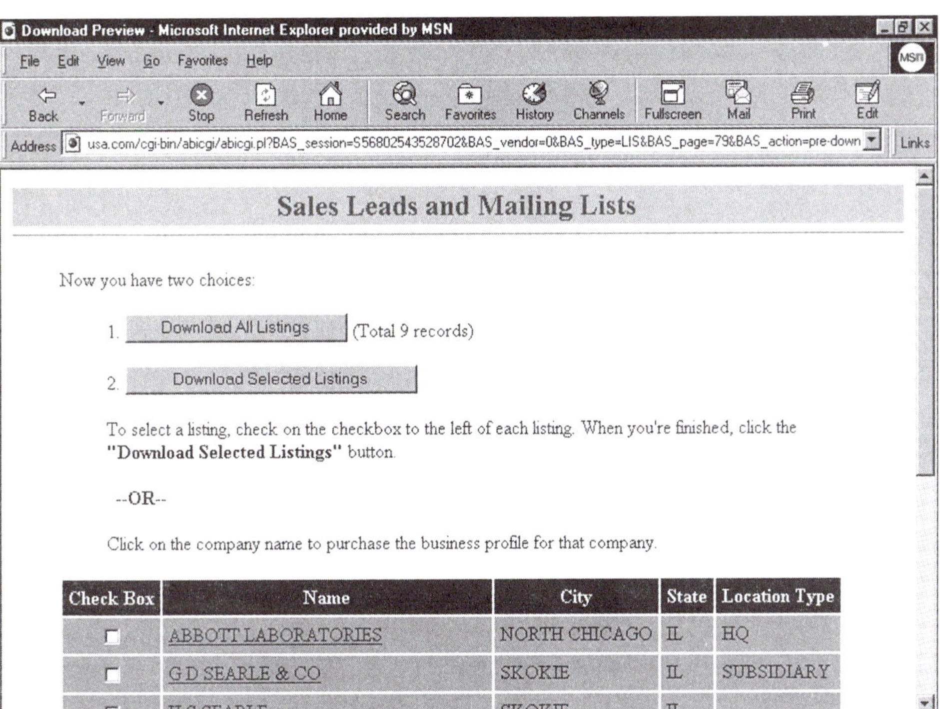

- Click the Business Profiles and Credit Ratings icon to search the SalesLeadsUSA database of company profiles. This is an excellent source of corporate information, including estimated annual sales, name of owner or top decision-maker, credit rating code, and number of employees.

Note

Click on the Sales Leads Products link at the home page to see a directory listing of links to each of the site's sales lead formats, including prospect lists, mailing labels, diskettes and magnetic tape, and monthly sales lead updates.

Research Companies with Hoover's Online

- Hoover's, Inc., is well known as a publisher of company capsules on more than 11,000 public and private companies around the world. The Hoover's Online Web site provides an outstanding source of free company data.

Hoover's Online Home Page

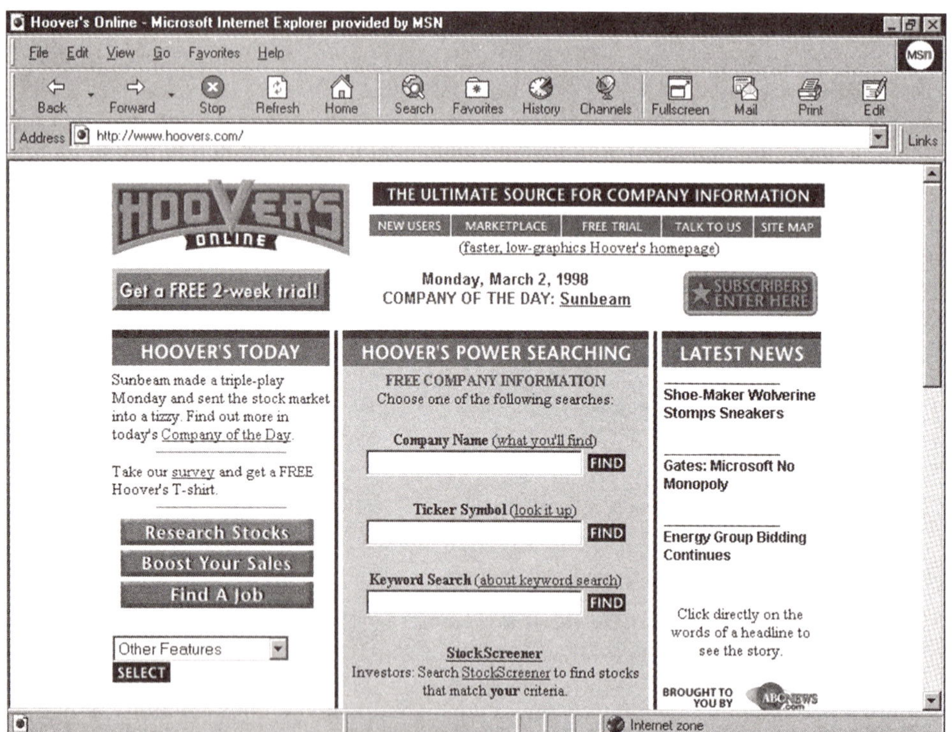

- At Hoover's Online you can search for company information by name or ticker symbol. Subscribers can also sort companies based on industry, location, and/or sales. Each company capsule contains basic information you can use to locate, communicate with, and analyze a company.
- To search the Hoover's list of company capsules, go to the home page and enter the company name, a stock ticker symbol, or a keyword. A business news ticker on the home page keeps you up to date while you search.
- Search results include a wealth of company information, including a description of the company's major markets and competitors, top decision-makers, and financial information. Click the Company Capsule tab to see a brief overview of the information, including contact information, links to the company Web site, and links to current stock ticker and stock trend charts.

Note

Click the Research Stocks link to go to a full-feature investor research page. Click the Boost Your Sales link to see a page that has sales resources such as articles, tips, and links to top sales Web sites.

- Click the Financials tab to see a complete financial report. Hoover's Online subscribers can click the Company Profile tab to read more in-depth analysis of the company and its business strategies.

Hoover's Online Home Page

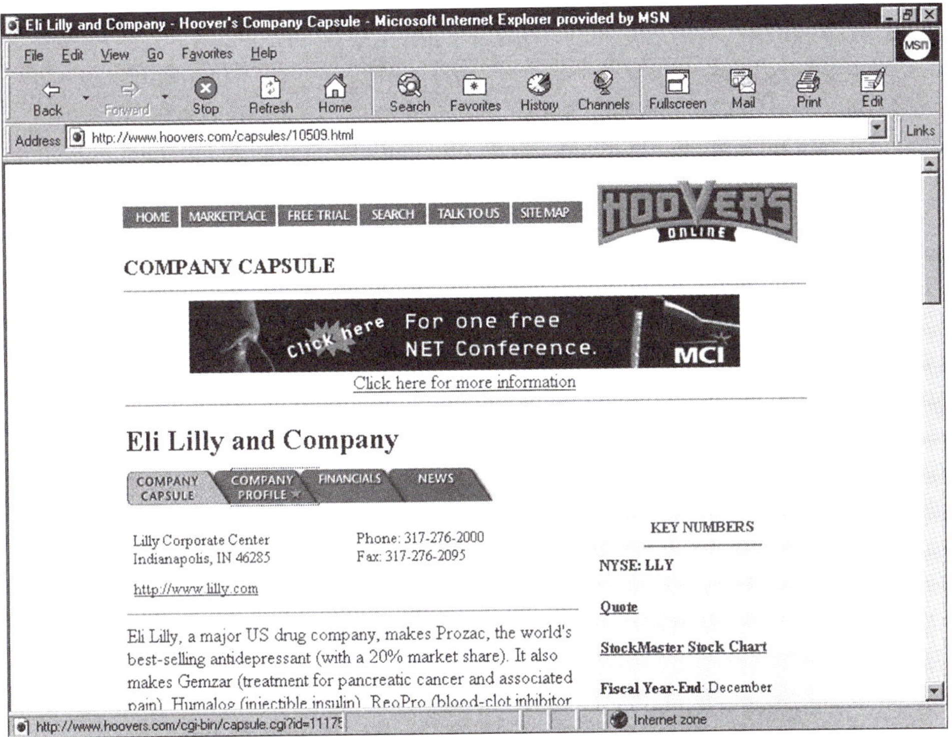

- For more company research and some fun reading, select List of Lists from the Other Features menu on the Hoover's home page. The List of Lists page includes links to sites that rank businesses and people in many different categories, including The Biggest & Richest Companies & People, Top Brands, Top Salaries, and Stock Market Performance.

In this exercise, you will use the SalesLeadsUSA Web site to search for pharmaceutical company sales leads in a three-state territory. You will then use the Hoover's Online Web site to search for companies that produce insulin or insulin-related products. You will also review sample company profiles from both Web sites.

Note: To ensure consistent results, this exercise uses simulated sites. The real URLs appear at the end of the exercise.

Web Search

Search for answers to the following questions using the Web sites you will visit in the Web simulation exercise.

1. What is the name of the last of the 9 businesses shown on the Sales Leads and Mailing Lists page?

   ____

2. What is the SIC code for Redfield Business Forms' primary line of business?

   ____

3. What is the last company listed on the Keyword Search Results page?

   ____

4. What was Eli Lilly and Company's 1997 Sales in millions of dollars?

   ____

5. Who is Amazon.com's chief competitor in the online bookselling market?

   ____

6. What was Amazon.com's December 1997 net income in millions of dollars?

   ____

EXERCISE DIRECTIONS

1. Launch the Internet simulation. From the Main Menu, select Lesson 7, then select Exercise 2.
2. On the Address line, type the following URL and press Enter:

   http://www.lookupusa.com/

   ➲ *The SalesLeadsUSA home page opens.*

SalesLeadsUSA Home Page

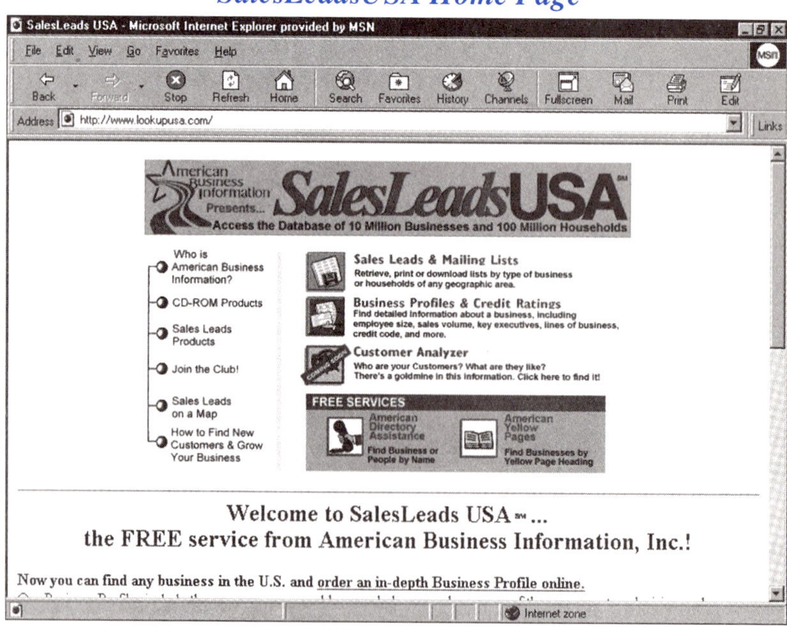

3. Click the Sales Leads & Mailing Lists link.
   ➲ *The Sales Leads & Mailing Lists page opens.*
4. Accept the default selection **Type of Business**, then click Next.
5. Accept the default selection **Yellow Page Headings**, then click Next.
6. Type *pharmaceuticals* in the search text box, then click Next.
   ➲ *A search results page opens.*
7. Click to select the **Pharmaceuticals (Wholesale)** check box, then click Next.
   ➲ *A Criteria Review page opens, showing the search criteria you have selected so far as well as the number of business listings your search yields.*
8. Click the Next button at the bottom of the page.
   ➲ *A page opens with a selection of geographical search areas opens.*

Yellow Page Heading Search Result

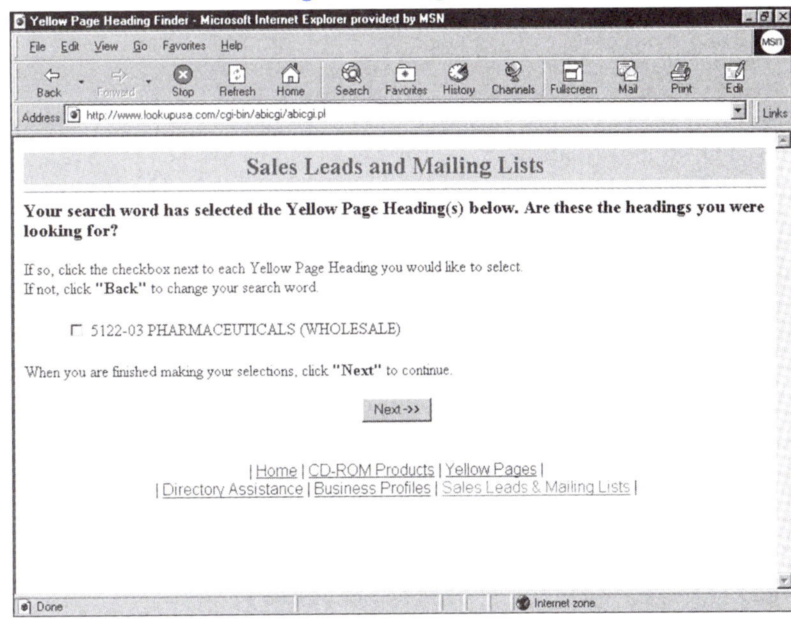

Search Criteria Review Page

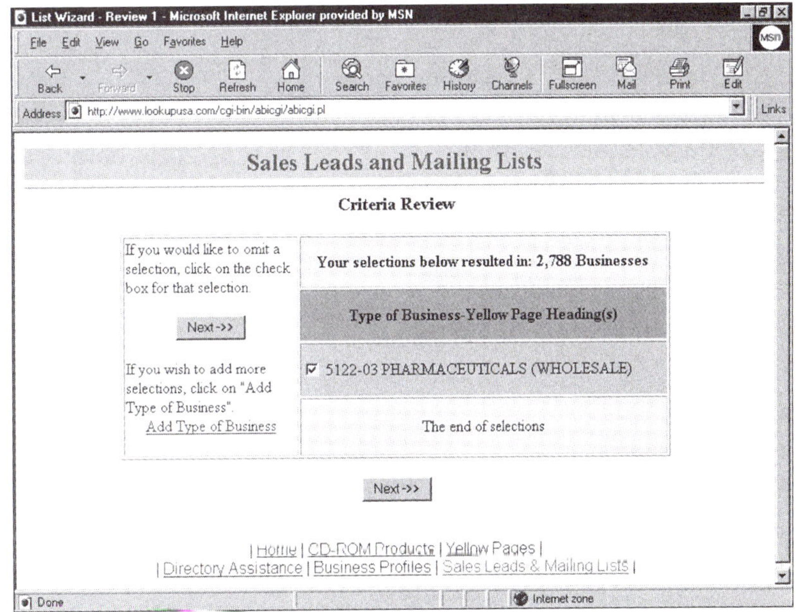

9. Click to select **State(s)**, then click Next.

   ➲ *The Search by State page opens.*

10. Click to select **Illinois**, **Indiana**, and **Ohio**, then click Next.

    ➲ *Another Criteria Review page opens, showing the search criteria you have selected as well as the number of business listings your search yields.*

    ✓ *Notice that the number of businesses in the search results has decreased from more than 2,700 businesses to 303.*

11. Click the Next button at the bottom of the page.

    ➲ *A Search by Size of Business page opens.*

12. Click to select **Sales Volume**, then click Next.

13. Click to select **Over $1 billion**, then click Next.

    ➲ *Another Criteria Review page opens, showing the search criteria you have selected as well as the number of business listings your search yields. The number of businesses in the search results has decreased to 9.*

14. Click the Next button at the bottom of the page.

    ➲ *A Final Criteria Review page opens, providing one more chance to change your search and also showing the cost for ordering the mailing list.*

15. Again, click the Next button at the bottom of the page to continue.

16. Click Preview Your List.

17. Click Preview Your List and Download Selected Listings.

    ➲ *A table listing the businesses in your search results opens.*

Select Size of Business by Sales Volume

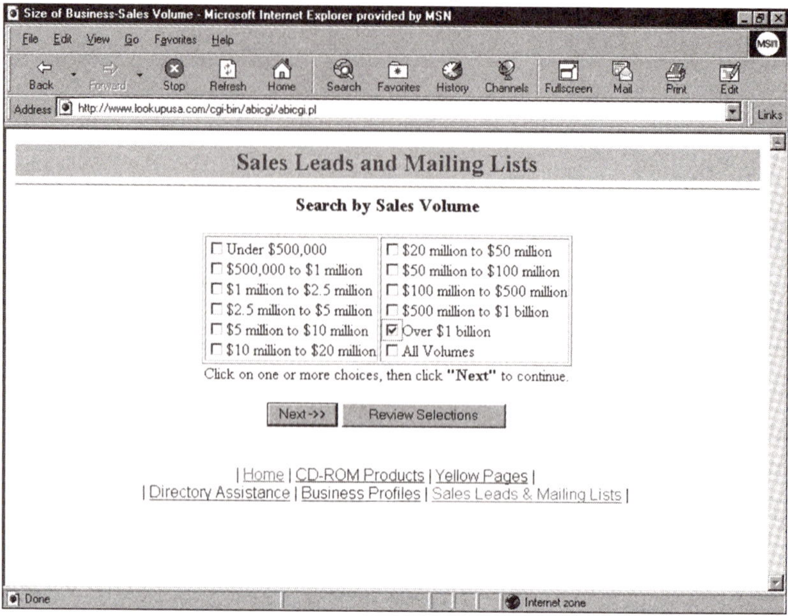

Final Search Criteria Review Page

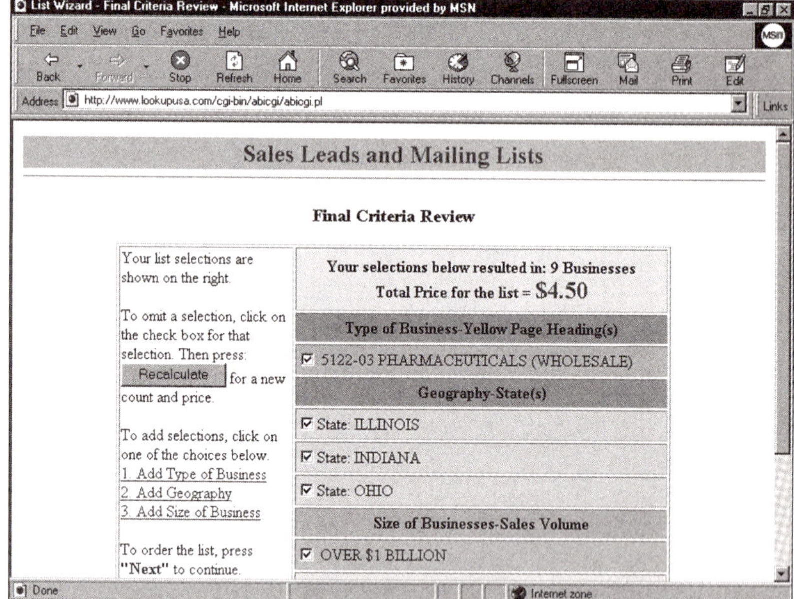

18. Scroll down and click the Eli Lilly & Co link.

    ➲ *A page appears describing the type of information you can get for Eli Lilly & Co if you click Order the Profile. You cannot get any further information for free.*

19. Click the 'click here!' link to see a sample business profile.

    ➲ *A sample Company Profile Report opens.*

20. Scroll down and read the report.

    ❓ *What information about this business do you think would be most valuable to you as a sales person?*

Sales Leads Search Results

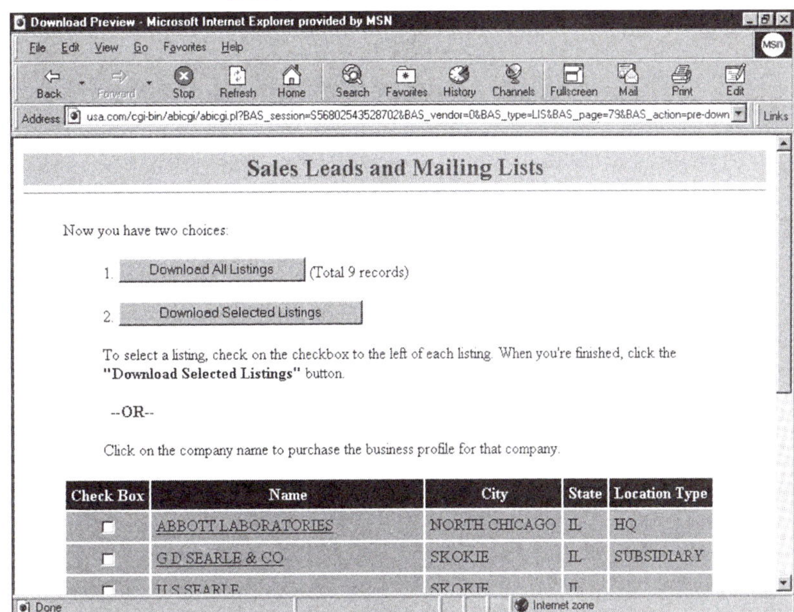

Sample Business Profile

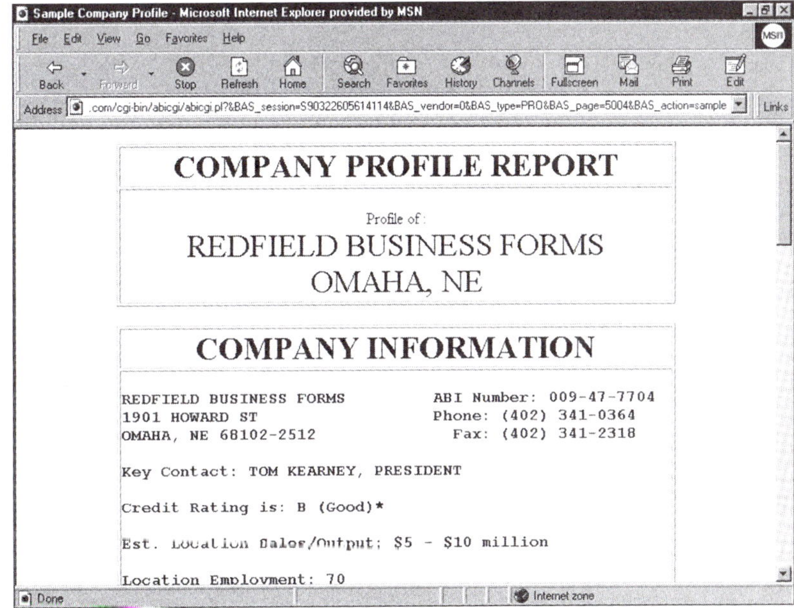

21. Type the following URL in your browser's Address line and press Enter:

    http://www.hoovers.com/

    ➲ *The Hoover's Online home page opens.*

22. Enter the word *insulin* in the Keyword Search text box on the Hoovers Online home page. Click Find.

    ➲ *The Hoover's search engine displays company listings containing the word insulin.*

Hoover's Online Home Page

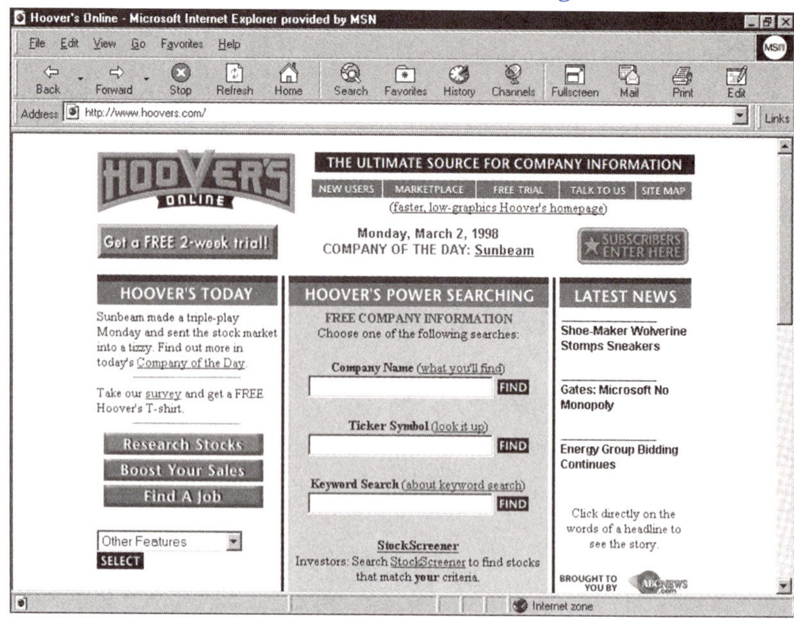

Hoover's Keyword Search Results

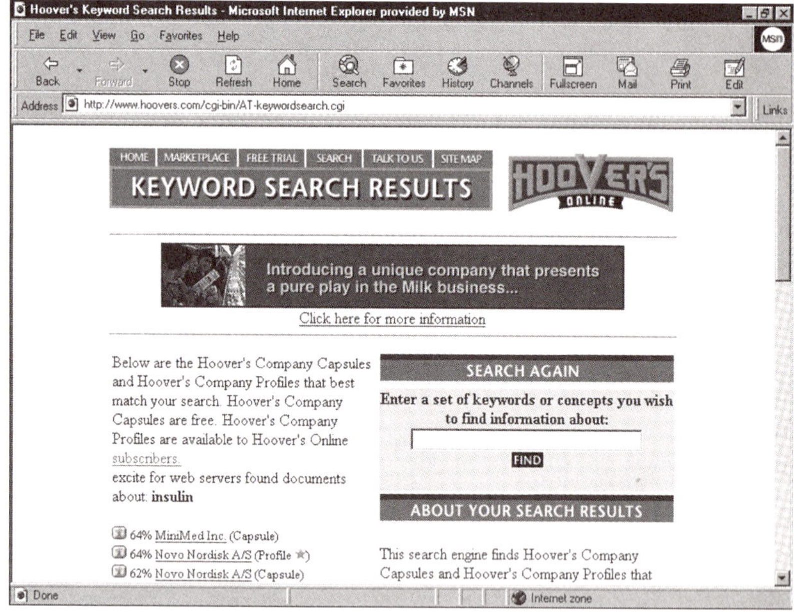

23. Scroll down and click the link for <u>Eli Lilly and Company (Capsule)</u>.

    ➲ *The Hoover's Company Capsule for Eli Lilly opens.*

24. Scroll down and read the description of this leading pharmaceutical firm.

25. Click the <u>Samples</u> link under the Hoover's In-Depth Company Profile heading.

    ➲ *A page of links to sample company profiles opens.*

26. Click the <u>Amazon.com, Inc.</u> link.

    ➲ *A sample company profile for Amazon.com, Inc. opens.*

27. Scroll down to read about this leading online book seller.

    ❓ *What opportunities do you think might exist for selling to this online company?*

Company Capsule for Eli Lilly

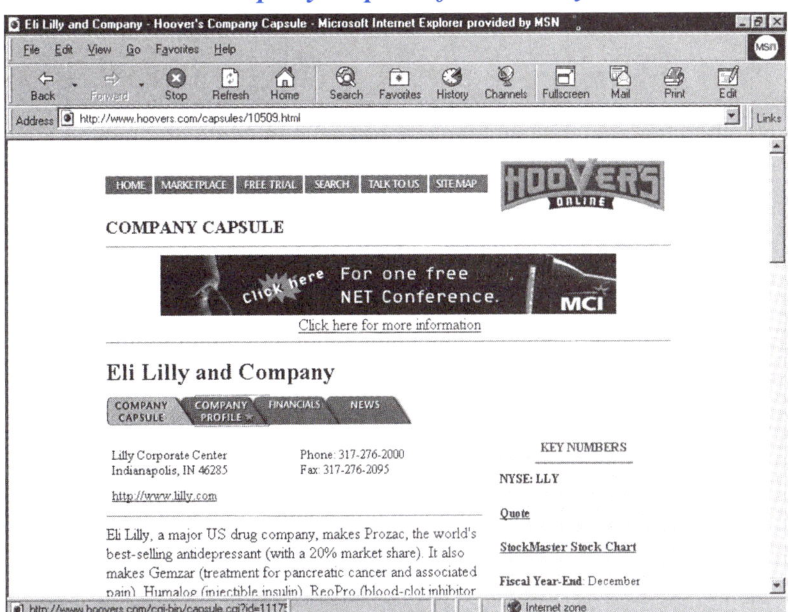

Sample Company Profile

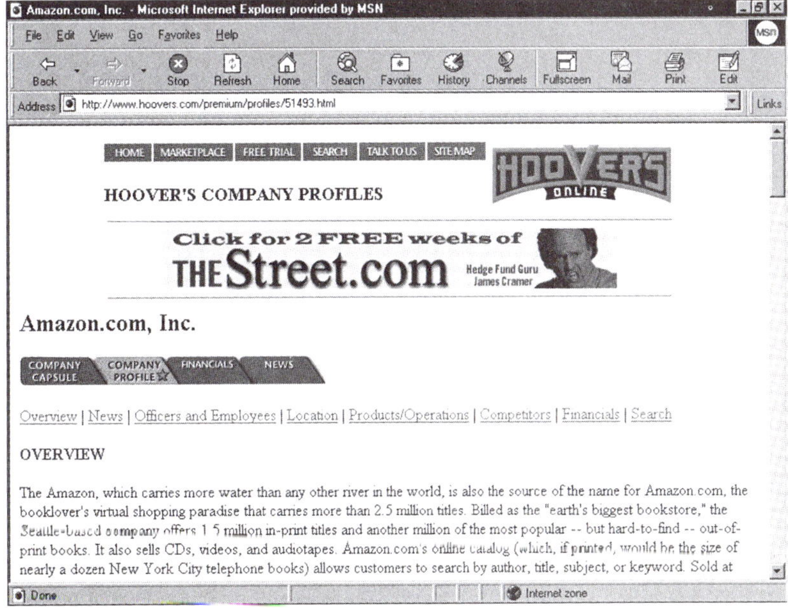

28. Click the Financials tab.

➲ *A page showing the financial information for Amazon.com, Inc. opens.*

29. Read the income statement and balance sheet for Amazon.com.

30. Continue on to the next exercise.

OR

Exit from the simulation.

Amazon.com Financial Information

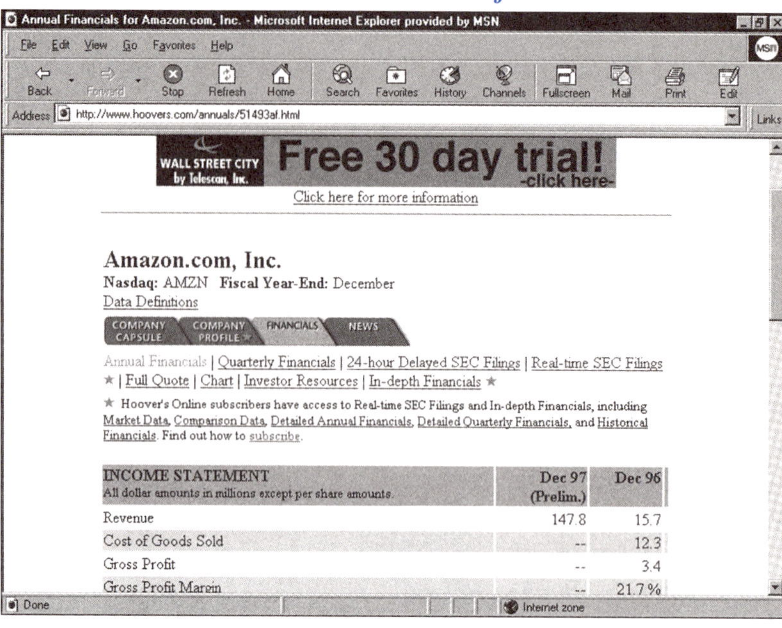

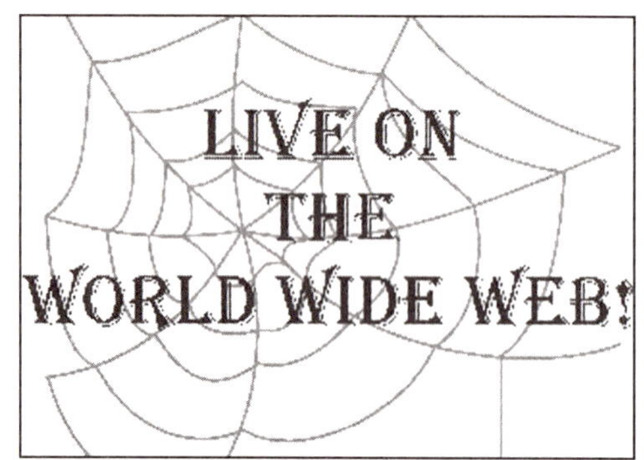

SalesLeads USA Home Page

http://www.lookupusa.com/

Hoover's Online Home Page

http://www.hoovers.com/

NEXT EXERCISE

Exercise 3

- Locate Clients with BigBook
- Find People with Four11
- Find Company Web Sites with WebSitez

NOTES

Locate Clients with BigBook

- Find potential customers and clients with BigBook, one of the leading online yellow pages sites. BigBook offers a number of added value services that can help you find the business or professional service firm you're looking for quickly and easily.
- Use BigBook's geographic search capability to build a list of potential customers. You can search for businesses several ways. Enter either a business (e.g. Microsoft) or a category (e.g. Computer Software) in the search text box on the Quick Search page (the home page) and then enter a city and/or state to search.

BigBook Home Page

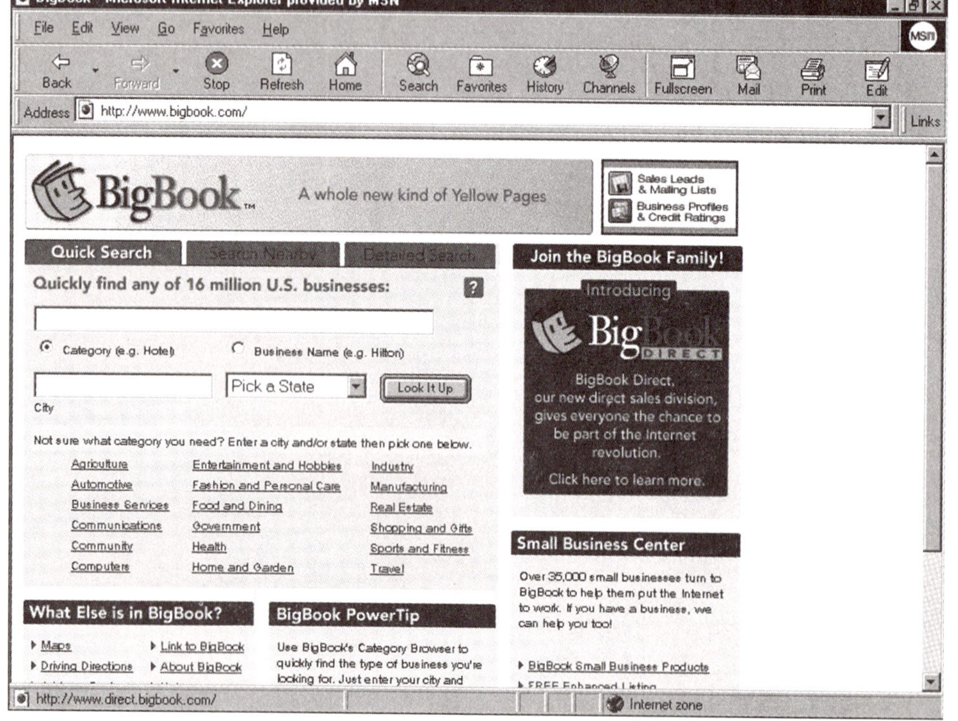

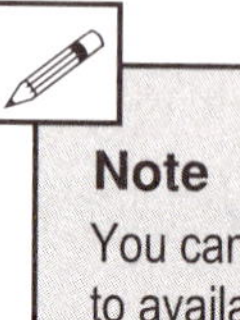

Note

You can also click on links to available search categories to find the subcategory you need.

Note

BigBook also includes links to sales leads, mailing lists, business profiles, and credit ratings provided by American Business Information.

- If you want to find nearby businesses, you can use either the Search Nearby tool or the Detailed Search tool. With Search Nearby, you can specify a business or category and then a distance from a specific address. For example, a BigBook search shows that there are 11,894 lawyers and 143 pizza shops within a 1 mile radius of the DDC Publishing home office in Midtown Manhattan.
- With Detailed Search, you specify a business or category and then a specific street name, area code, city, state, or ZIP code to search. The search results list all of the businesses you asked for in that specific location.
- Detailed Search and Search Nearby are outstanding tools for building sales lead lists for a geographic sales territory. For example, if you are a computer software sales representative and your territory includes the states of Louisiana, Mississippi, and Alabama, you can enter those states and the category *computer software* in the Detailed Search form. BigBook compiles a complete listing of potential customers for your entire territory.
- After you receive the search results page, which includes addresses and phone numbers, you can click on a specific listing to see a map showing the business location.

Map Showing Business in Search Results

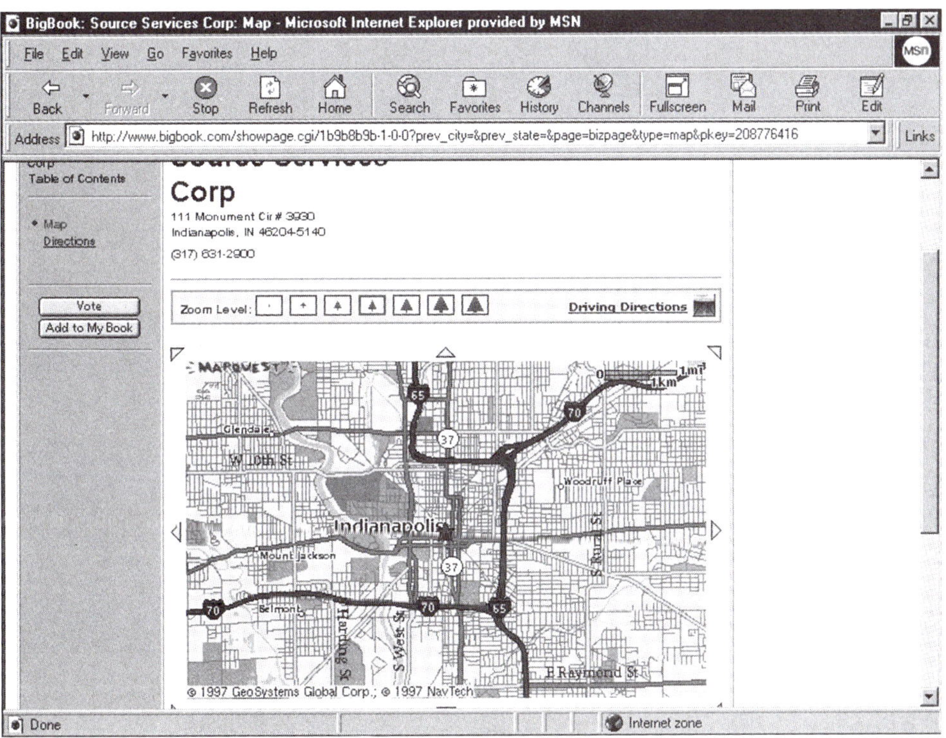

Note

From a BigBook map page, click on the Driving Directions icon and enter your location to find out how to get to the business you've found.

Find People with Four11

- Four11 has been recognized as the leading Internet people finder site for some time and has become part of the Yahoo! search and directory site.
- Using Four11, you can enter the name of a person you wish to find along with any additional address information you know about the person and then click Search.

Four11 Home Page

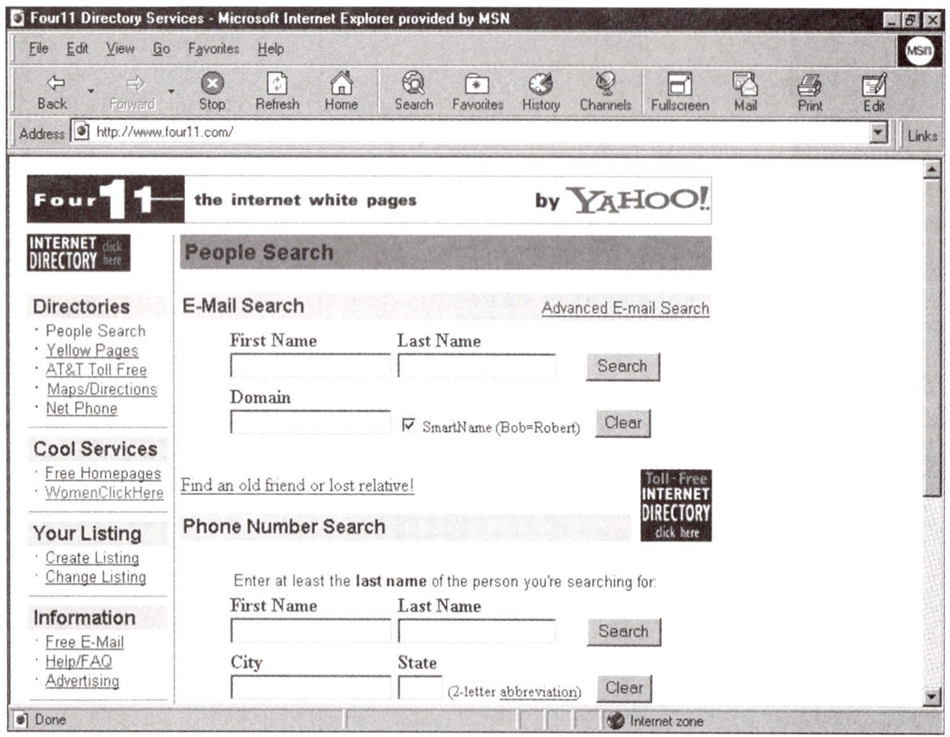

- Use the Phone Number Search text boxes on the home page to find phone numbers. The Four11 search engine looks for the person in its database of phone directories from across the United States.
- Use the E-Mail Search to find e-mail addresses. Searching for someone by e-mail address can often prove more successful than searching for phone numbers because you can click on the Advanced E-Mail Search link to add personal interests and/or previous contact locations that will enhance your search.
- After your search results appear, click on the link for the name that best fits the person you want to find. A page showing detailed phone, address, and e-mail information opens.

Note

If you are concerned about your privacy, you can click Change Your Listing to change how your information appears on Four11.

Find Company Web Sites with WebSitez

- If you want to contact a prospective client and all you know is the company name (or even part of the company name), try a search at the WebSitez home page.
- Because thousands of Web sites are added to the Internet each day and because many company names are similar, Web addresses often do not seem logical. They may be shortened versions of the company name, they may include hyphens, or they may, by necessity or by choice, use a word that is altogether different than the company name.
- By using WebSitez, you can avoid trying to guess a company's URL. Simply enter the company name in the WebSitez search form and let WebSitez find the URL for you.

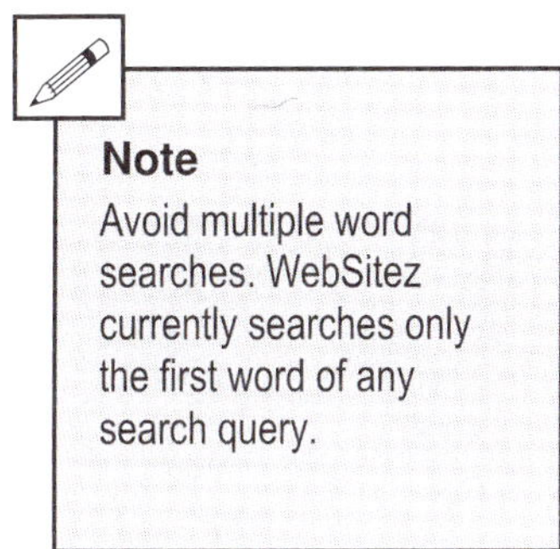

Note

Avoid multiple word searches. WebSitez currently searches only the first word of any search query.

WebSitez Home Page

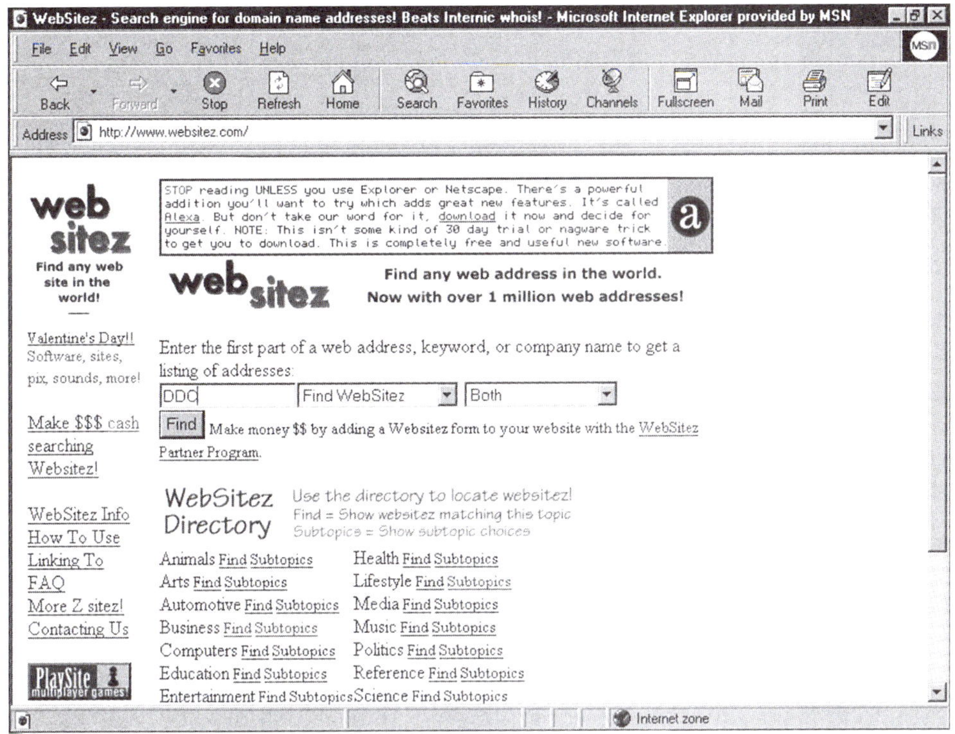

- To search for a site, enter what you know about the company you want to find, choose whether you want to find Web sites, files, or FTP sites, and then choose whether you want to see Web site names, company names, or both displayed in the search results. WebSitez searches a database of more than 1 million Web addresses, and its fast servers return results quickly.

WebSitez Search Results

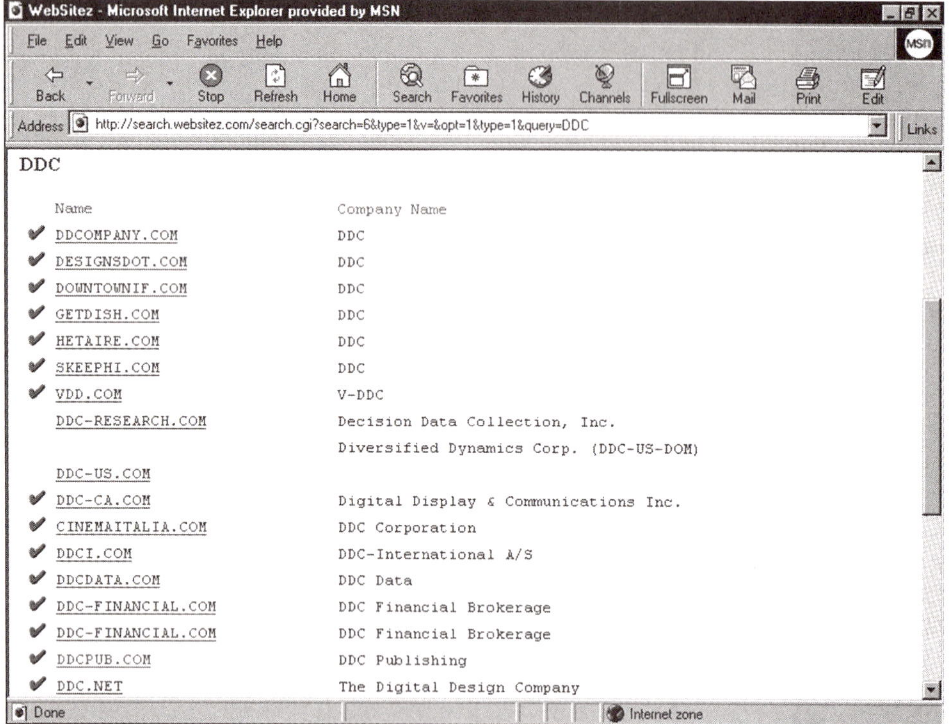

- Search results display categories that match or nearly match your search criteria. The number of site or name matches within each category also appears. Click on a category to see links to Web sites and/or company names. Click a company link to go directly to the company's Web site.
- WebSitez comes in handy if you have forgotten a Web address or if you simply want to enter keywords to find sites that match your interest.

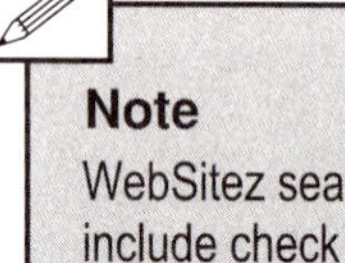

Note

WebSitez search results include check marks showing which sites were active as of the last WebSitez test of the site.

In this exercise, you will use BigBook to search for businesses by city, within a distance from a certain location, and by ZIP code. You will also view business locations on BigBook maps. You will then search for a person's phone number and e-mail address at the Four11 Web site. Finally, you will look for a company Web site using the WebSitez search engine.

Note: To ensure consistent results, this exercise uses simulated sites. The real URLs appear at the end of the exercise.

Web Search

Search for answers to the following questions using the Web sites you will visit in the Web simulation exercise.

1. What is the address of the Banyan Systems office in Indianapolis?

    ____

2. What is the name of the business immediately following Microsoft Corp in the search results?

    ____

3. What is its address?

    ____

4. How far away is Strategic Information Mgmt from 115 East Michigan St.?

    ____

5. How many computer software businesses are found between 5 and 10 miles from 115 East Michigan St? How many are found between 10 and 25 miles?

    ____

6. What is the name of the company or Web site following DDC's on the WebSitez search results page?

    ____

EXERCISE DIRECTIONS

1. Launch the Internet simulation. From the Main Menu, select Lesson 7, then select Exercise 3.
2. On the Address line, type the following URL and press Enter:

    http://www.bigbook.com/

    ➲ *The BigBook home page opens.*

BigBook Home Page

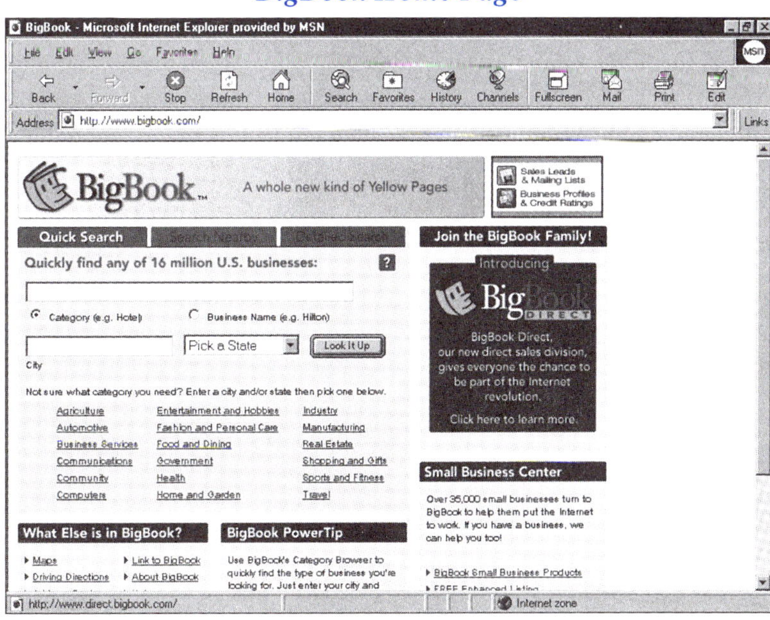

3. Type *Computer Software* in the first text box on the home page.
4. Type *Indianapolis* in the City text box.
5. Select **Indiana** from the State menu, then click Look It Up.
   ➲ *BigBook displays a listing of all computer software businesses in Indianapolis.*
6. Click the M link at the bottom of the page.
   ➲ *The businesses in the listing that begin with the letter M are shown.*

Enter Quick Search Criteria

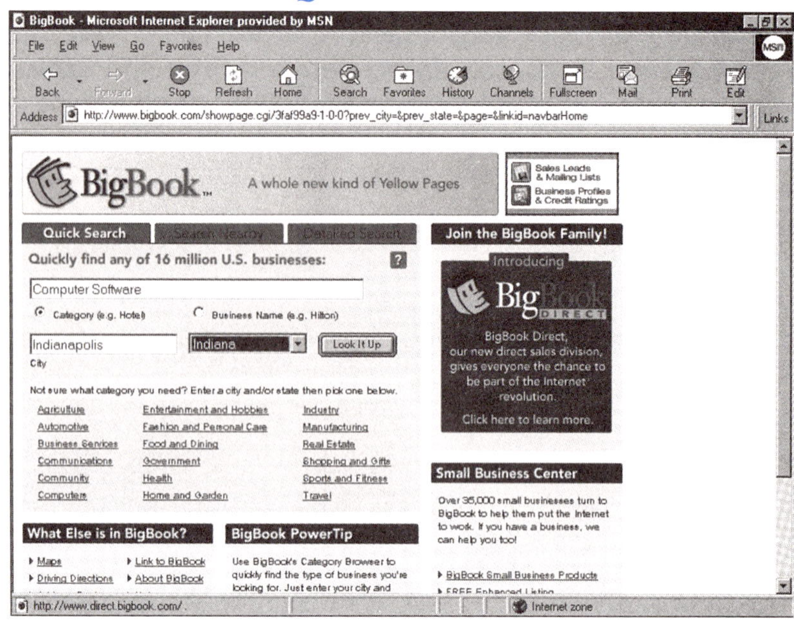

Quick Search Results

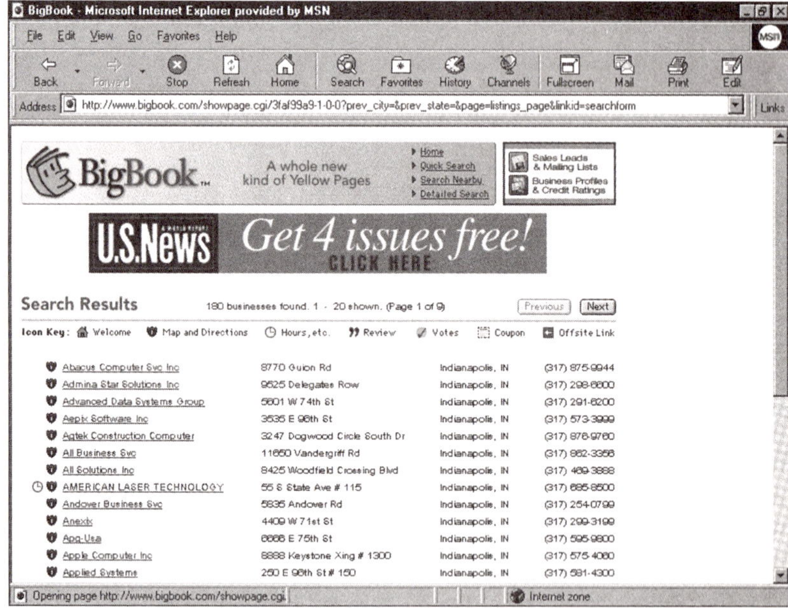

7. Click the Microsoft Corp link.

   ➲ *A map showing the location of the Microsoft office in Indianapolis opens.*

8. Click the middle "tree" icon on the Zoom Level bar.

   ➲ *A wider area of the city near the office location appears.*

9. Click the Search Nearby link at the bottom of the page.

   ➲ *A new search form opens.*

10. Type *Computer Software* in the first text box on the Search Nearby page.

11. In the Street Address text box, type: *115 East Michigan St.*

12. In the City text box, type: *Indianapolis*

13. Select **Indiana** from the State menu, then click Look It Up.

    ➲ *BigBook displays a listing of all computer software businesses within 1 mile of the address you entered.*

14. Click the Source Services Corp link. Zoom the map to different levels by clicking on the tree icons.

15. Click your browser's Back button to return to the Search Results page. Scroll to the bottom of the page and click the Jump To 5-10 link.

    ➲ *A listing opens showing computer software businesses found within a 5-10 mile radius of the address you entered.*

16. Click the Jump To 10-25 link.

    ➲ *A listing of software businesses within a 10-25 mile radius appears.*

17. Click the Detailed Search link at the bottom of the page.

    ➲ *A new search form opens.*

18. Delete **Indianapolis** and **IN** from the search form.

Map Showing Microsoft Corp

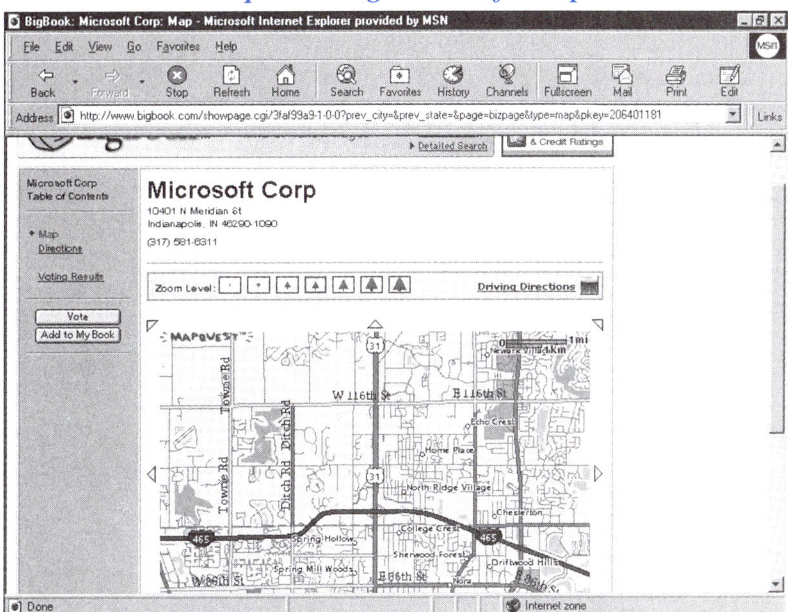

Map Showing Source Services Corp

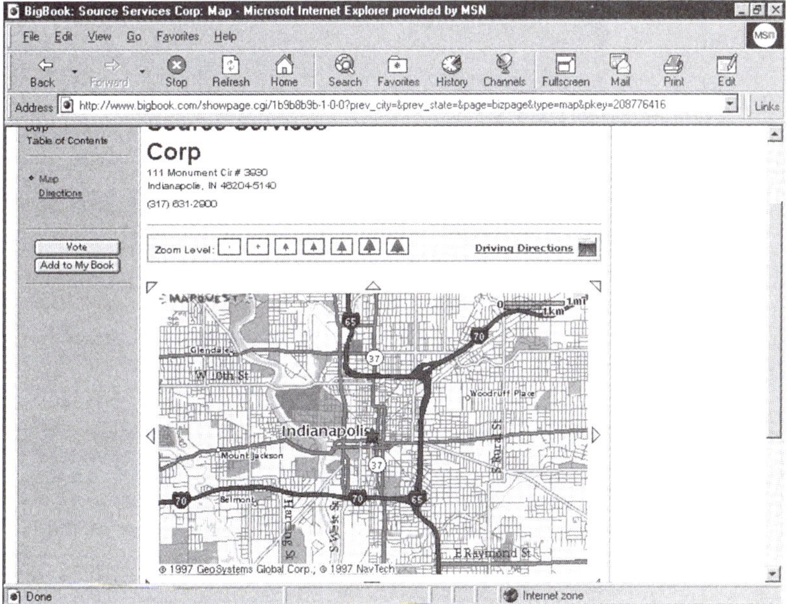

19. Type *Computer Software* in the Category text box. Type *10016* in the Zip Code text box, then click Look It Up.

    ➲ *BigBook displays a listing of all computer software businesses in the 10016 Zip Code.*

20. Click the link for Ad Value Media Tech.

    ➲ *A map showing the location of the business opens.*

Map Showing Ad Value Media Tech

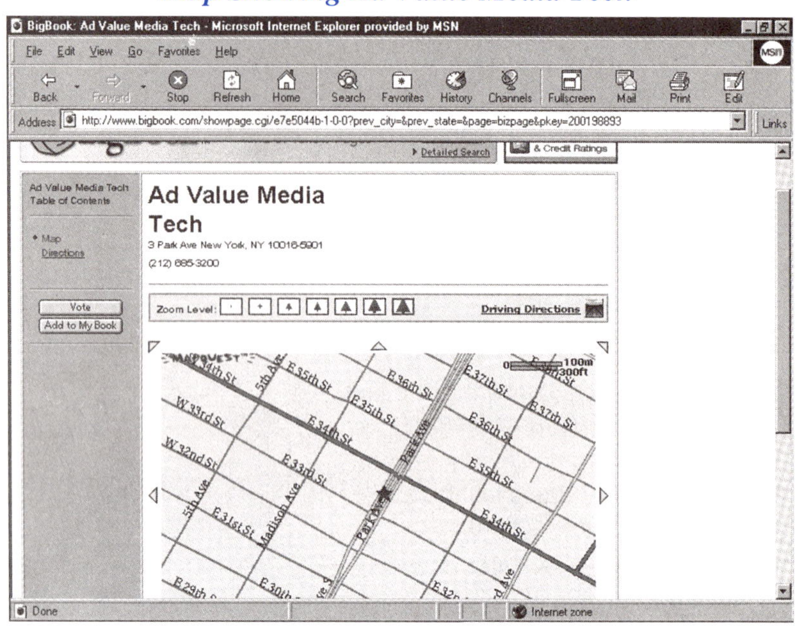

21. Type the following URL in your browser's Address line and press Enter:

    http://www.four11.com/

    ➲ *The Four11 home page opens.*

Four11 Home Page

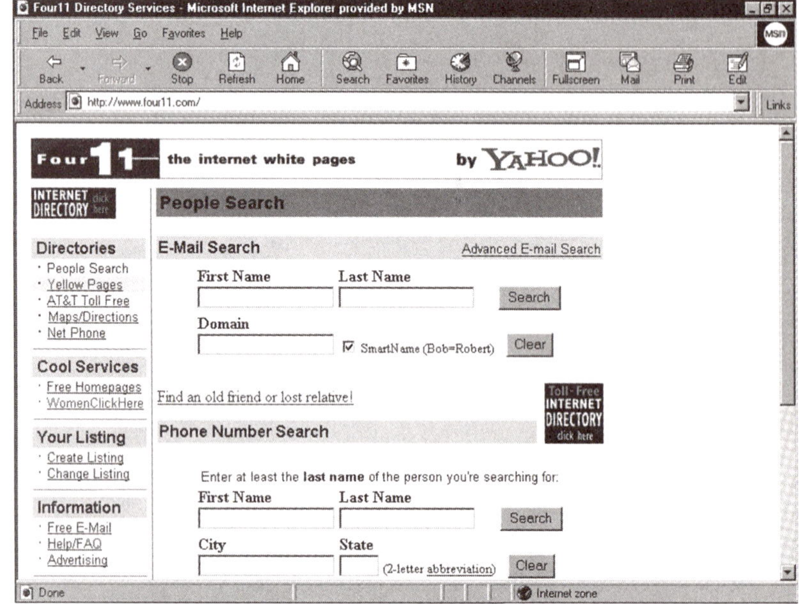

22. Scroll down and type *Katsaropoulos* in the Last Name text box of the Phone Number Search. Click Search.

    ➲ *Four11 opens a search results page with one match.*

    ✓ *Check your spelling of the name if you don't come up with a match.*

23. Click the Chris Katsaropoulos link.

    ➲ *Four11 displays complete address and phone number information in the People Search Result page.*

    ✓ *If you are doing this exercise live on the Web, try using your name in the search.*

24. Click the Search for E-Mail Address link.

    ➲ *Four11 opens a search results page with one match.*

25. Click the Chris Katsaropoulos link.

    ➲ *Four11 displays the complete e-mail address.*

    ✓ *If you are doing this exercise live on the Web, you can click on the E-Mail Address link and send the author a message.*

Four11 People Search Result

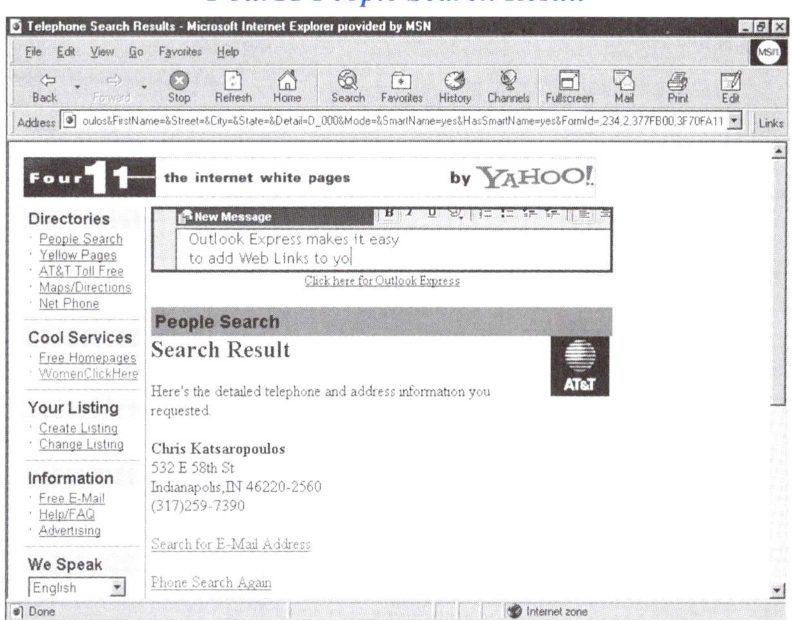

E-Mail Search Result

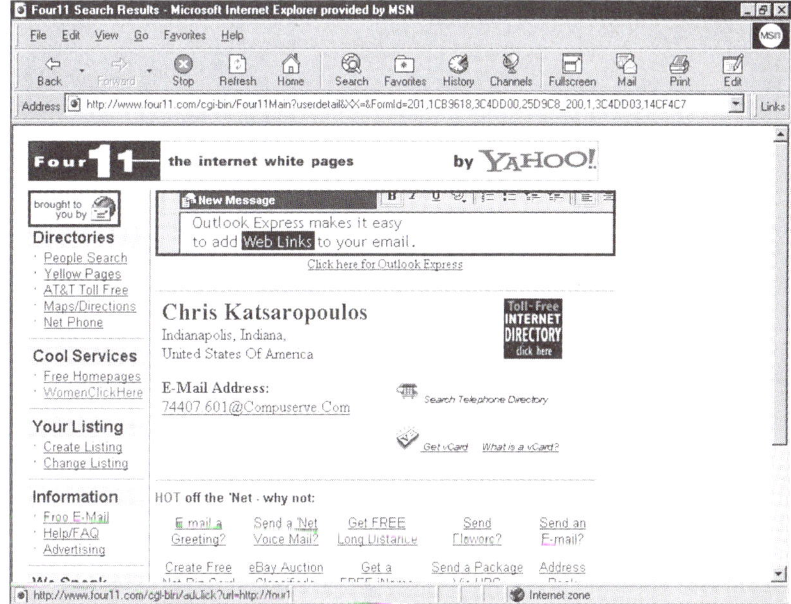

26. Type the following URL in your browser's Address line and press Enter:

http://www.websitez.com/

➲ *The WebSitez home page opens.*

27. Type *DDC* into the left-most text box on the WebSitez home page. Click Find.

➲ *WebSitez displays company names and Web site names that contain the letters DDC.*

WebSitez Home Page

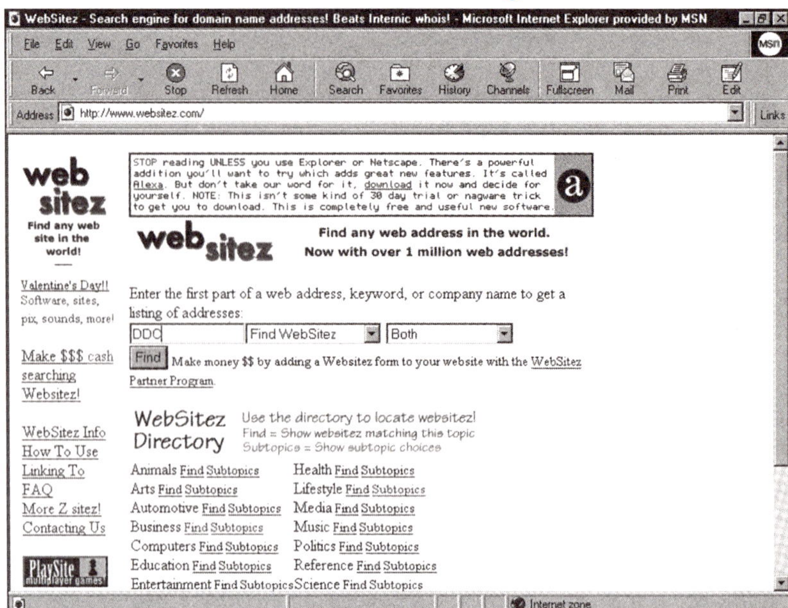

WebSitez Search Results

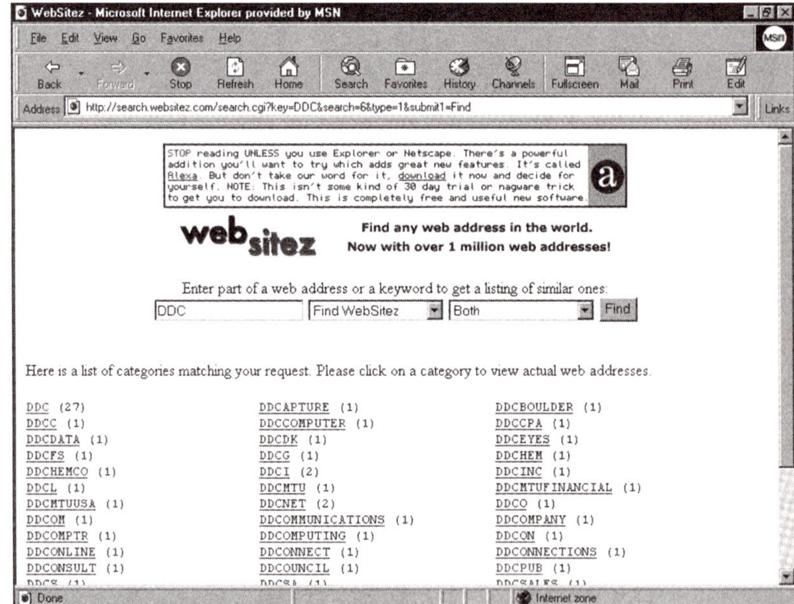

28. Click the DDC link.

   ➲ *A page listing companies or Web sites with DDC in the name appears.*

   ✓ *Note also that DDCPUB appears on the search results page as a separate entry.*

Companies or Web Sites that Include DDC in Their Names

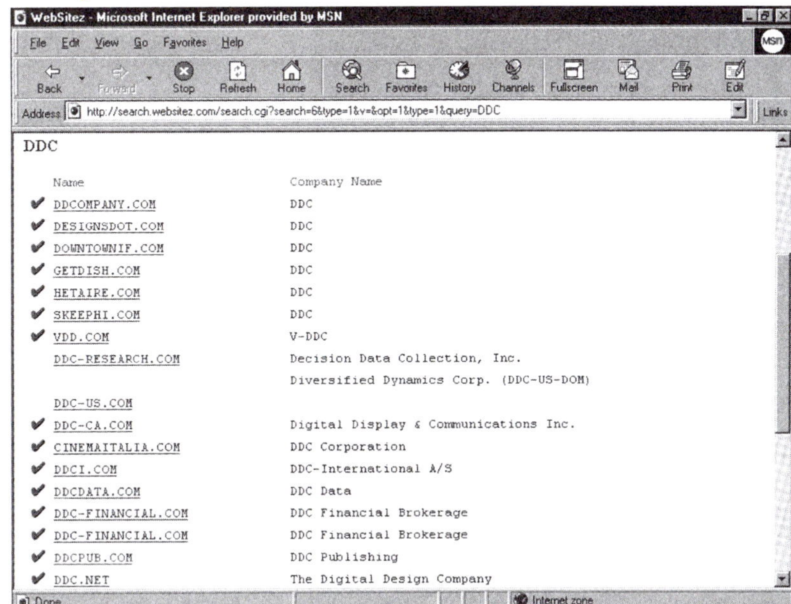

29. Click the DDCPUB.COM link.

   ➲ *The DDC Publishing Web site opens.*

30. Continue on to the next exercise.

   OR

   Exit from the simulation.

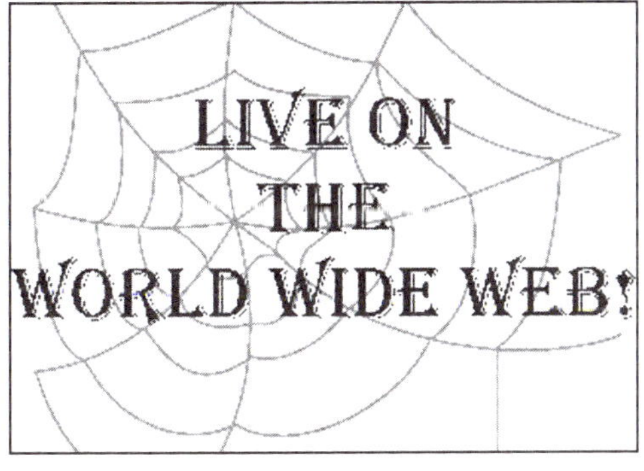

BigBook Home Page

   http://www.bigbook.com/

Four11 Home Page

   http://www.four11.com/

WebSitez Home Page

   http://www.websitez.com/

Exercise 4

■ Improve Sales Techniques with SalesDoctors Magazine
■ Get the Most out of Trade Shows with Trade Show News Network

NOTES

Improve Sales Techniques with SalesDoctors Magazine

- Constant effort is required to improve your sales results. Use the SalesDoctors Magazine Web site to learn new selling techniques that can make you more successful.
- SalesDoctors Magazine has been named the number one sales Web site by Entrepreneur Magazine, and with good reason. This site is the most complete resource available online for sales professionals, offering practical, how-to information and access to tools that can help you close sales.

SalesDoctors Home Page

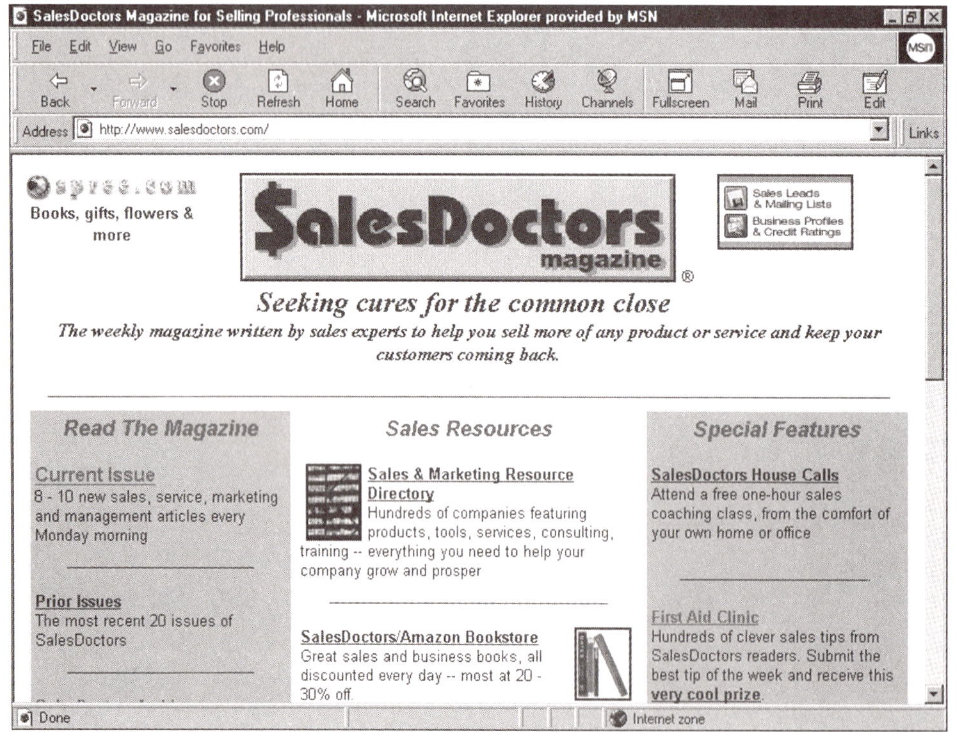

Note

Click on the Managers and Trainers link to get ideas for using SalesDoctors articles and features in your company's training programs. Click the Mental Health link for motivational articles dealing with bumps along the road to success.

- The SalesDoctors Web site is filled with useful tips, selling strategies, and sales resources. You can click on links to related sites and you can browse the magazine archives in addition to current content for the information you need.
- From the SalesDoctors home page, click on the Current Issue link to read new articles on sales, service, management, and marketing. A new issue appears with updated content every Monday morning.
- Click on the Prior Issues link to review the preceding 20 weeks of the magazine. Click on the Archives link to search more than 600 articles from leading sales experts.
- The Special Features column of the home page contains links to House Calls (an online sales coaching class), First Aid Clinic (hundreds of tips from SalesDoctors readers), Laser Surgery (quick cures for sales ailments), and Featured Sales Experts.

Note

The Sales and Marketing Resource Directory contains links to hundreds of tools and services that can make your life as a sales professional easier. The SalesDoctors Free link offers a directory of links to sites, business tools, software, and services that are free on the Web.

Laser Surgery Provides Quick Cures for Sales Challenges

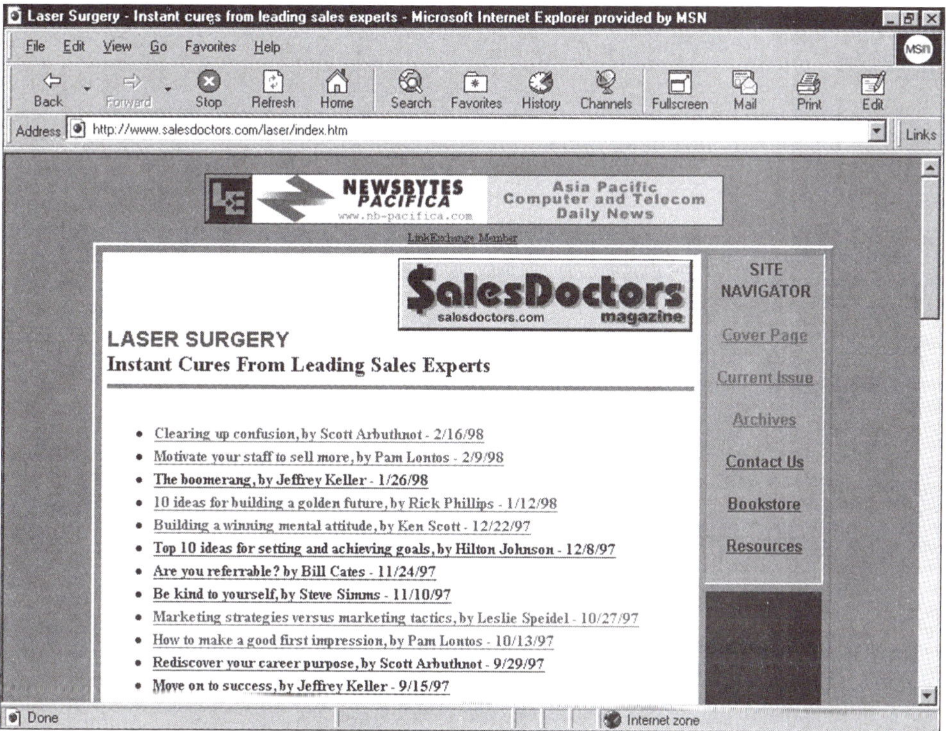

Get the Most Out of Trade Shows with Trade Show News Network

- Trade shows can provide a focused, high-visibility means of connecting with your customers, but without effective exhibit planning and booth selling techniques, your trade show presence can do more harm than good.
- Before you spend a big chunk of your marketing budget on a show, use the Trade Show News Network (TSNN) to help plan your trade show selling strategy.

Trade Show News Network Home Page

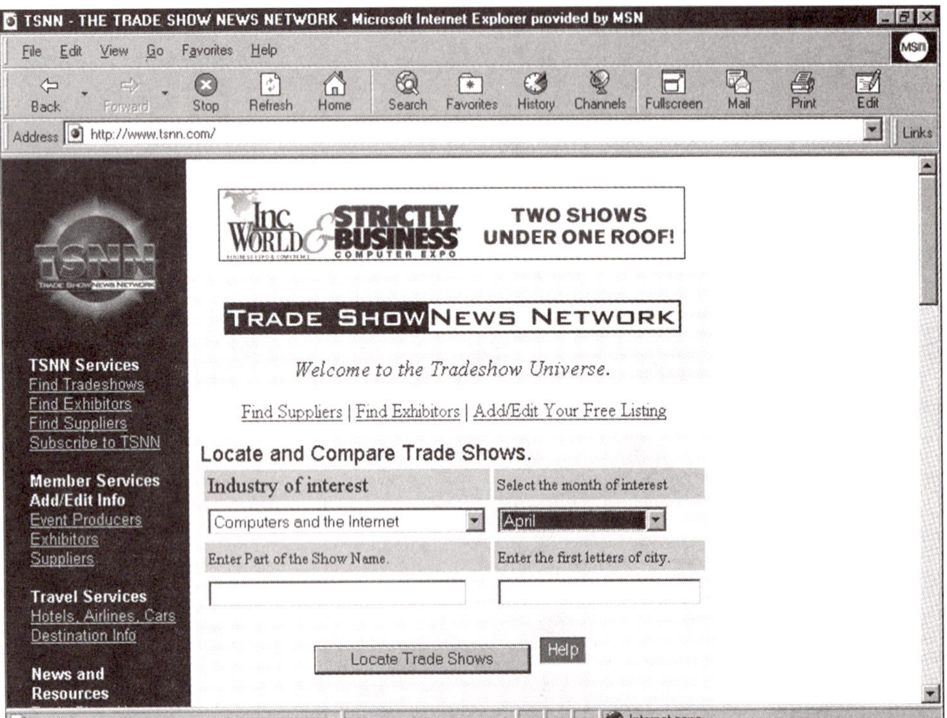

- The TSNN Web site provides outstanding practical information whether you plan, present, or attend trade shows. Check the News and Resources links to find out what's happening in the world of exhibitors. The Trade Show News link takes you to news from around the industry, the Related Industry Jobs link connects you to several searchable job databases, and the EventWeb Newsletter link offers current and past issues of the weekly newsletter.
- Home page news stories and features such as "The Psychology of Handshakes," exhibitor tips, and an Ask the Expert column provide practical how-to information to improve your performance in the booth.
- Click on the Find Tradeshows link to search for the type, time, and location of a trade show you want to attend, or simply use the search engine text boxes available on the home page. Links to trade show organization sites on the Web are included in the search results.
- Click the Find Exhibitors link to search for companies participating in the trade show industry. Click Find Suppliers to locate exhibit supply companies.

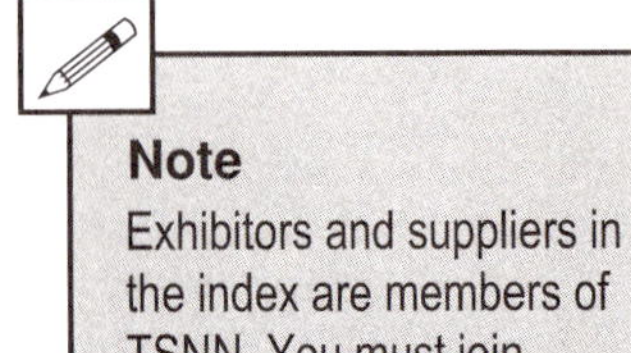

Note
Exhibitors and suppliers in the index are members of TSNN. You must join TSNN if you wish to be included in the database.

In this exercise, you will read tips and advice about how to improve sales at the SalesDoctors Web site. You will then search for a trade show and read tips about working a trade show booth from the Trade Show News Network Web site.

Note: To ensure consistent results, this exercise uses simulated sites. The real URLs appear at the end of the exercise.

Web Search

Search for answers to the following questions using the Web sites you will visit in the Web simulation exercise.

1. In the First Aid Clinic, what does Calvin Coolidge say is the most important element of success?

2. What is the sixth way to discover a gold mine of prospects?

3. What is the first suggestion for a way to motivate salespeople?

4. According to the 10 Ideas for Building a Golden Future article, worry is a misuse of what?

5. In addition to *60 Minutes*, what other TV news program has Leslie Stahl hosted?

6. What is the ninth guideline for engaging prospects at a trade show booth?

EXERCISE DIRECTIONS

1. Launch the Internet simulation. From the Main Menu, select Lesson 7, then select Exercise 4.
2. On the Address line, type the following URL and press Enter:

   http://www.salesdoctors.com/

   ➲ *The SalesDoctors home page opens.*

SalesDoctors Home Page

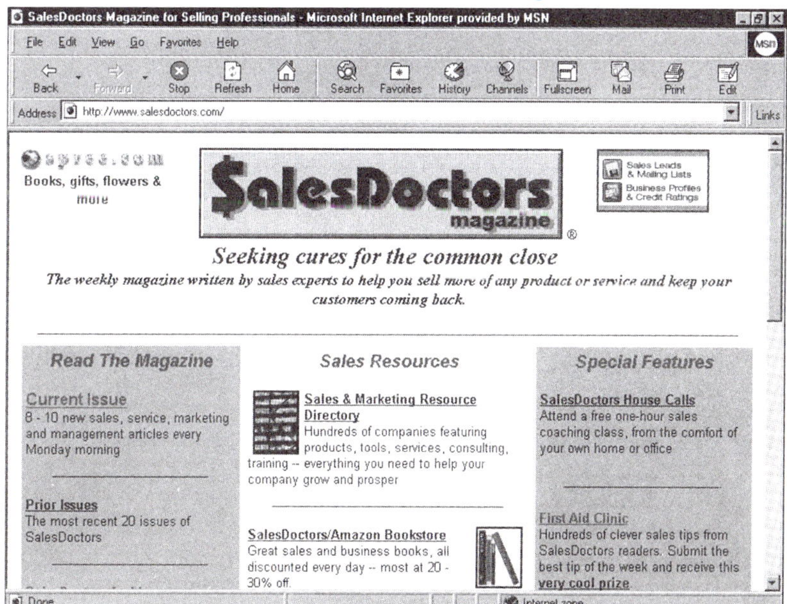

3. Click the First Aid Clinic link.

   ➲ *The First Aid Clinic page opens.*

4. Click the Quick selling ideas you can use today—2/23/98 link.

   ➲ *The First Aid Clinic tips page opens.*

5. Scroll down and read sales tips on this page.

   ❓ *Which of these tips would you find most useful as a sales representative?*

6. Click the SalesDoctors Magazine icon at the top of the page.

   ➲ *The SalesDoctors home page opens again.*

First Aid Clinic Tips

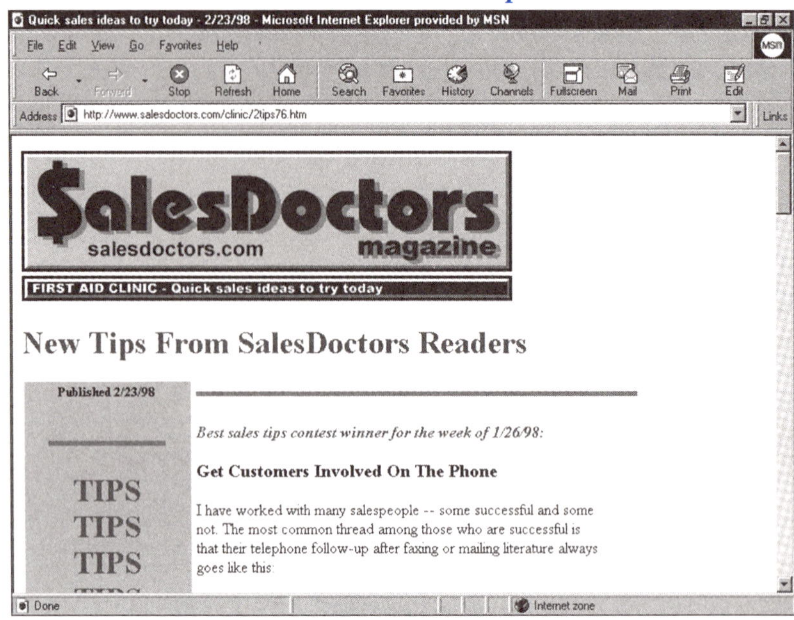

7. Click the Current Issue link.

   ➲ *The current issue of SalesDoctors Magazine opens.*

Current Issue

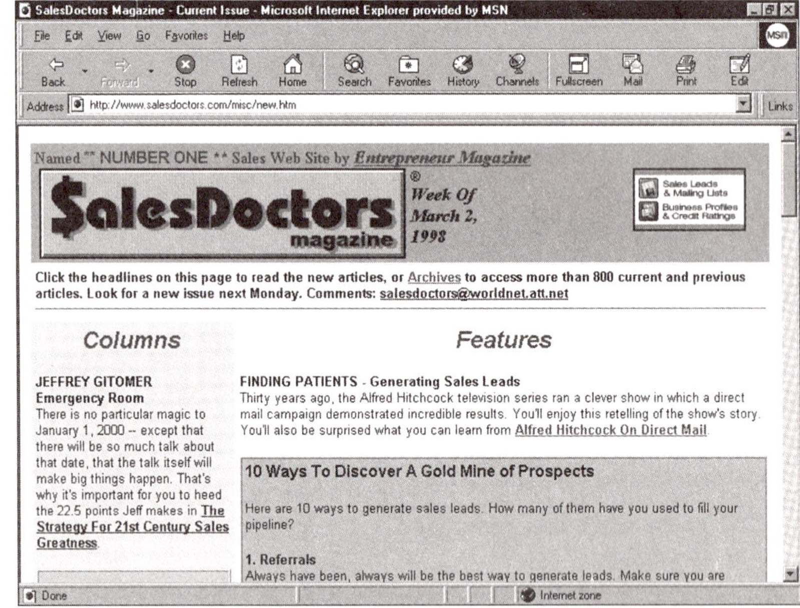

8. Scroll down and read 10 Ways to Discover a Gold Mine of Prospects.
9. Click the A Bad Call, Start to Finish link at the left side of the Current Issue page.

   ➲ *The Business By Phone page opens.*
10. Scroll down and read the advice of Art Sobczak about what to avoid in a phone sales call.

    ❓ *As a salesperson, how would you have presented the sales call?*
11. Click your browser's Back button to return to the Current Issue page.

Hone Your Telephone Sales Technique

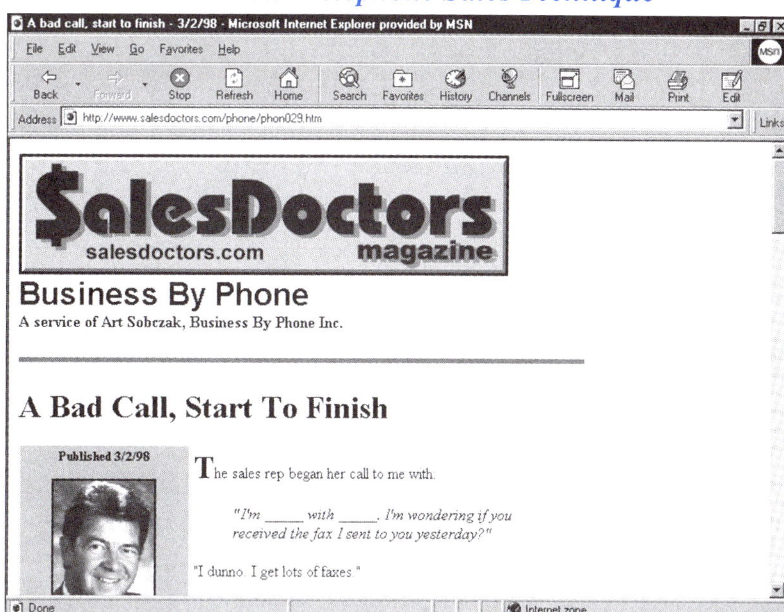

12. Scroll down to the bottom of the page and click the LASER SURGERY link.

    ➲ *The Laser Surgery page opens.*

Laser Surgery Page

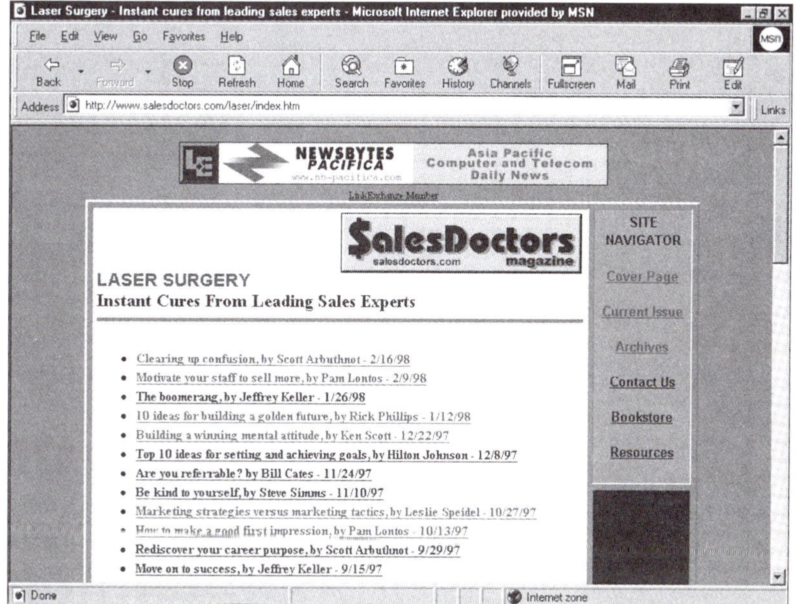

13. Click the Motivate your staff to sell more link.

   ➲ *The Laser Surgery article opens.*

14. Scroll down and read the article.

   ❓ *Which of the suggestions for ways to motivate salespeople would motivate you the most?*

15. Click your browser's Back button to return to the Laser Surgery page.

16. Click the 10 ideas for building a golden future link.

   ➲ *The Laser Surgery article opens.*

17. Scroll down and read the article.

   ❓ *Note how many of the 10 ideas are focused on the customer.*

18. Type the following URL in your browser's Address line and press Enter:

   http://www.tsnn.com/

   ➲ *The Trade Show News Network home page opens.*

19. Select **Computers and the Internet** from the Industry of Interest menu.

20. Select **April** from the month of interest menu.

Laser Surgery Article

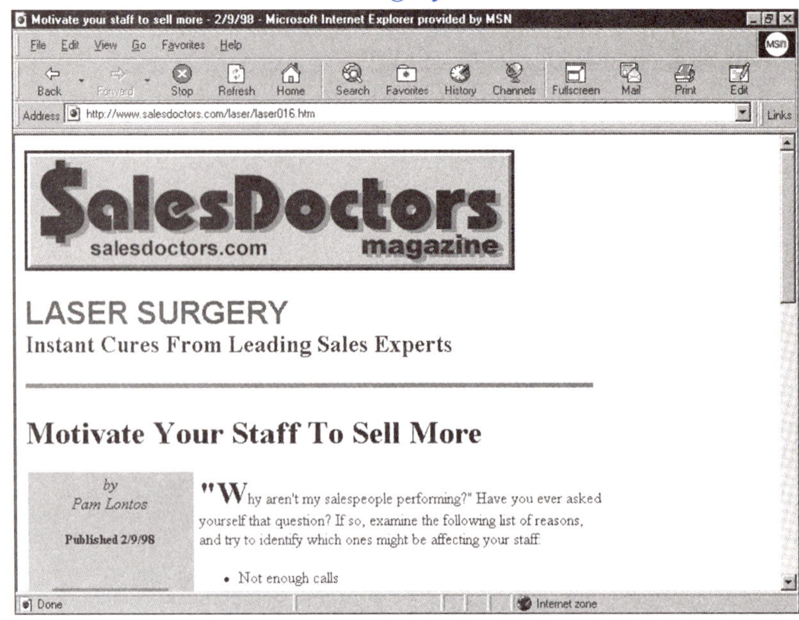

Trade Show News Network Home Page

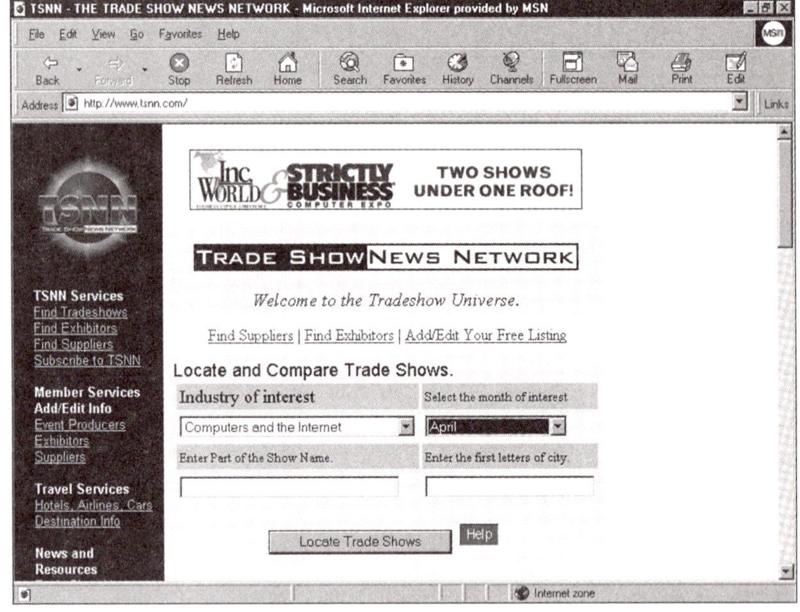

21. Click Locate Trade Shows.
    ➲ *The search results page opens.*
22. Scroll down and read the search results. Click the Campus Market Expo link.
    ➲ *A page describing this trade show opens.*

Trade Show Search Results

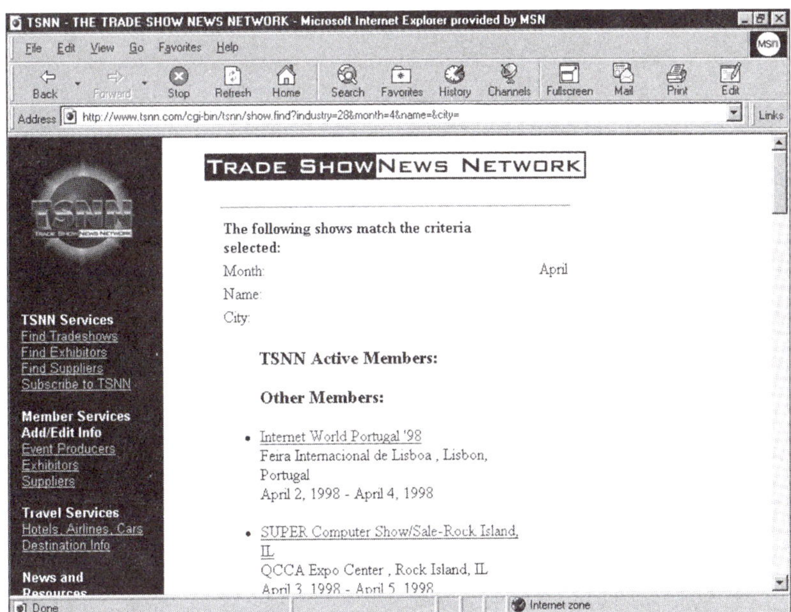

Trade Show Description

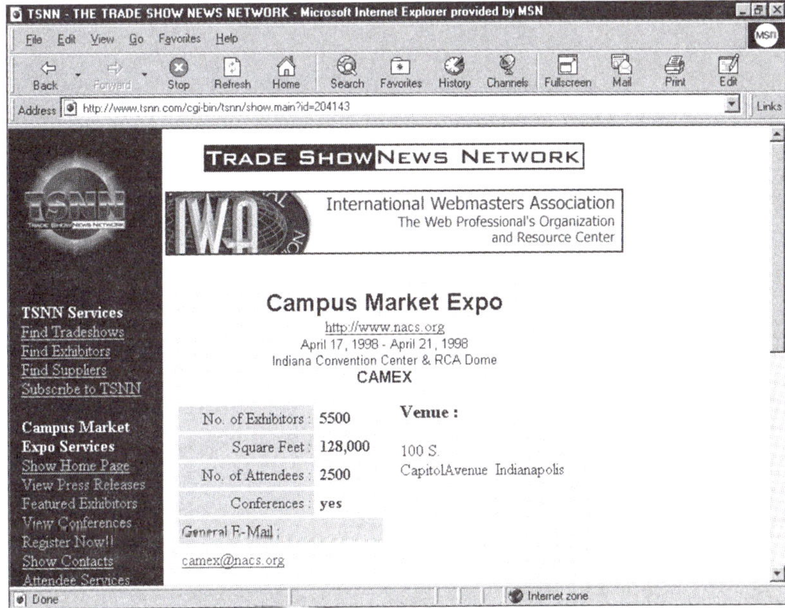

23. Click the http://www.nacs.org link.

   ➲ *The National Association of College Stores (NACS) home page opens. The Campus Market Expo is the NACS annual meeting.*

24. Click the Lesley Stahl To Address First General Session link.

   ➲ *A news update page for the NACS Annual Meeting opens.*

25. Scroll down and read the news updates.

26. Type the following URL in your browser's Address line and press Enter:

   http://www.tsnn.com/

   ➲ *The Trade Show News Network home page opens again.*

NACS Home Page

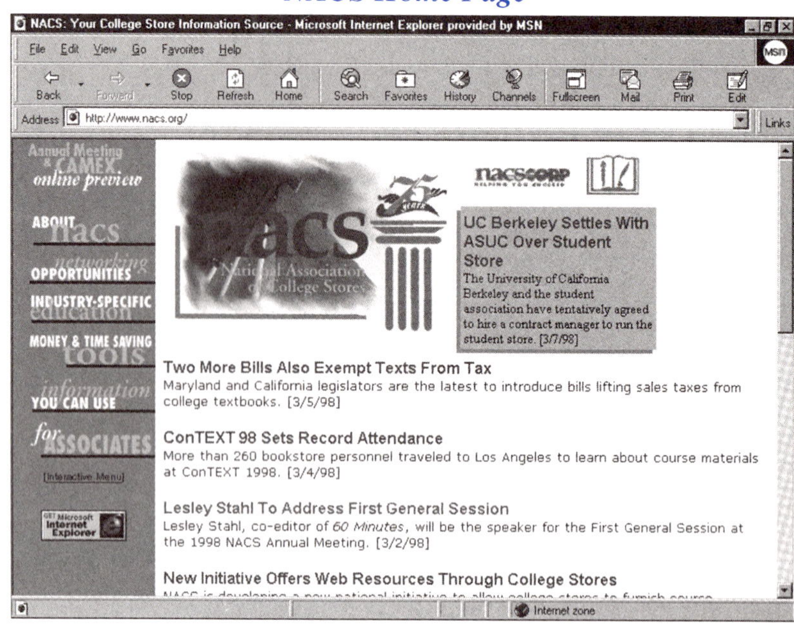

News Updates for NACS Annual Meeting

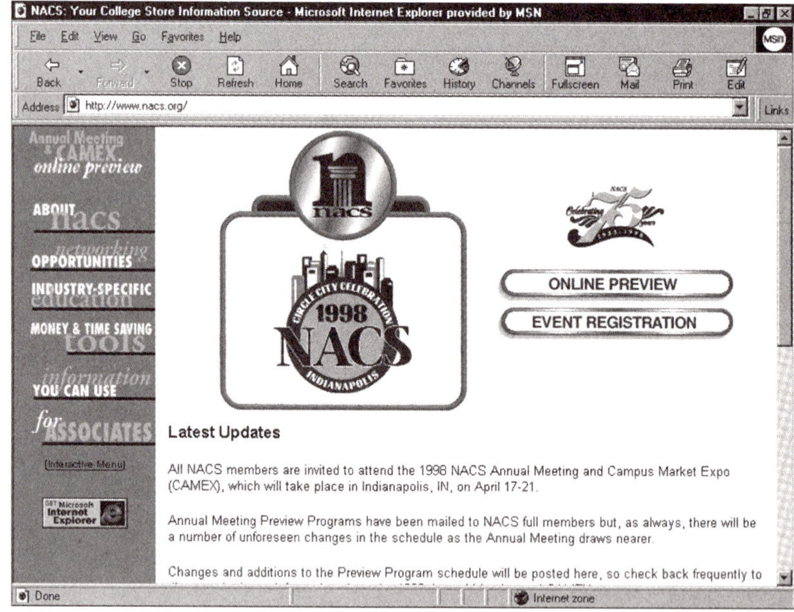

27. Scroll down and click the Tips on Exhibiting link.

   ➲ *The Exhibitor Tips page opens.*

28. Click the Boothmanship—Part I link.

   ➲ *The Exhibitor Tips page opens.*

29. Scroll down and read the tips.

   ✓ *Be sure to read the Guidelines for Engaging Prospects.*

30. Continue on to the next exercise.

   OR

   Exit from the simulation.

Trade Show Exhibitor Tips

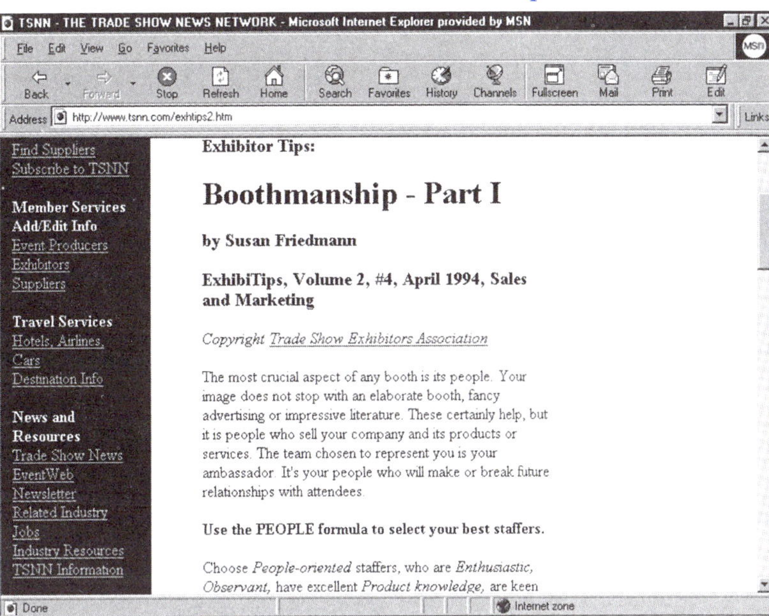

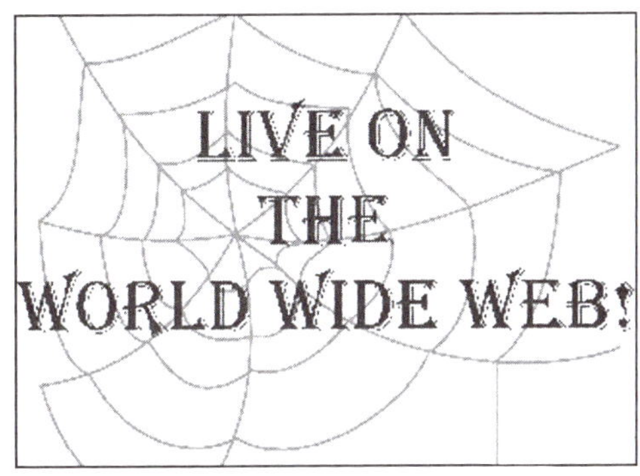

SalesDoctors Magazine Home Page

   http://www.salesdoctors.com/

Trade Show News Network Home Page

   http://www.tsnn.com/

National Association of College Stores Home Page

   http://www.nacs.com/

Exercise 5

- **Develop a Target Mailing List with List Merchant**
- **Search for Mailing Lists and Market Online with American List Council**

NOTES

Develop a Target Mailing List with List Merchant

- The capability to search databases and send messages online makes the Web a perfect place to develop direct marketing campaigns. The List Merchant Web site enables you to develop custom mailing lists online by selecting geographic and demographic criteria.
- You can develop a custom list by narrowing the list of targeted consumers to those who are most likely to be interested in your product or service. This means more "hits" and a more cost-effective use of your marketing budget.

List Merchant Home Page

- From the List Merchant home page, click the TRY listM link to conduct a sample search of a List Merchant database according to criteria you enter.

Note

You can use List Merchant to search and narrow lists for free. Then, when you have a custom list that meets your needs, you can register and pay only for the number of names you have selected. This way, you don't pay for an entire pre-built list that includes names you may not need.

- You can search either the Polk consumer database or the Dun & Bradstreet business database. Click Search and then follow the easy steps to define and narrow your list.
- For the consumer database, click a state you want to search. Select the entire state or select a metropolitan area to narrow the search. You can also narrow the geographic area even further by selecting cities or zip codes within a metropolitan area.
- Next, you can click Niches to select from a menu of pre-built demographic patterns such as Big Spender Parents, Feathering the Nest, and Rocky Road. A description of the Niche you select appears on the selection Web page. Click the Build Profile button to finish building your list and download it to your computer.

Note

The Polk database has information on more than 95 million households and more than 175 million individuals (two-thirds of the U.S. population). The Dun & Bradstreet database has information on more than 11 million businesses.

Define Demographic Patterns for a Mailing List

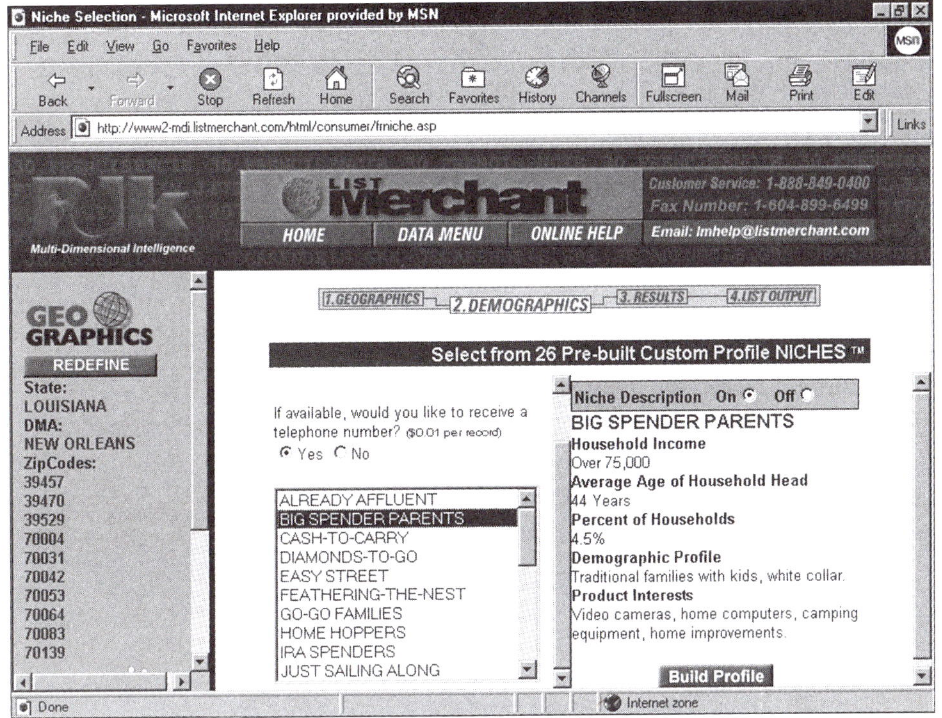

Note

If you don't want to use List Merchant's pre-defined demographic Niches, you can click Create Profile to create a custom demographic profile that better fits your needs.

Search for Mailing Lists and Market Online with American List Council

- The American List Counsel (ALC) provides a complete online marketing Web site. Though you can't customize mailing lists at the ALC site, you can quickly search and browse a wide variety of very effective pre-built lists.
- Click the ALC List Directory icon to see a directory of links to available lists or click the ALC List Search icon to perform a keyword search of the lists. Search results show ALC lists that match your entry.

American List Council Home Page

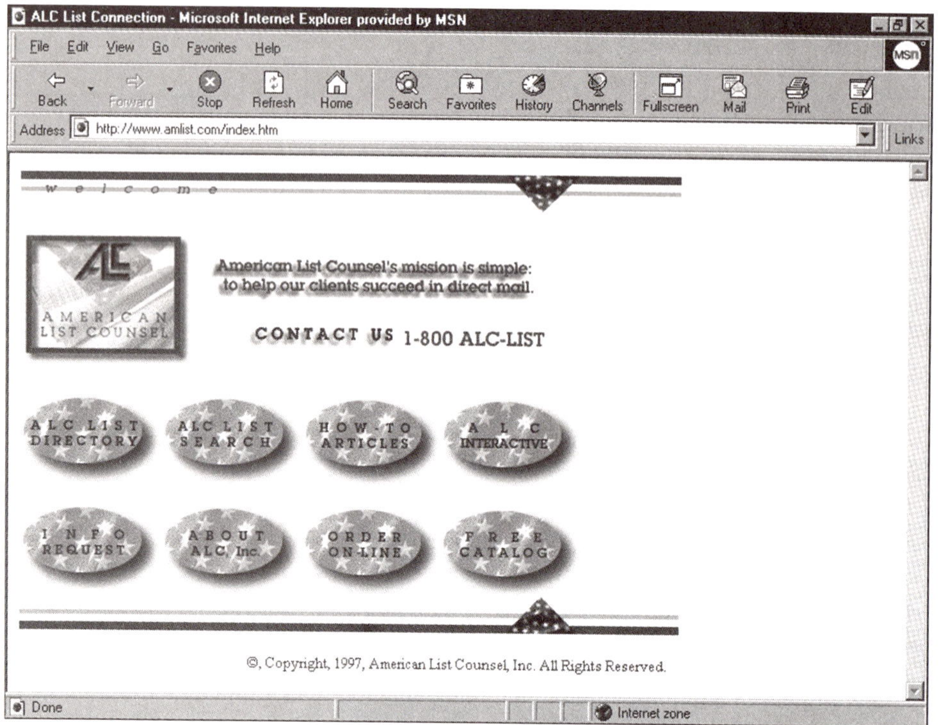

- Click on a list link to see a detailed description of the list, including demographic information, purchasing habits, and list pricing. If you want to order the list, click ORDER ON-LINE to access an order form you can submit to the ALC Web site.
- You can also do direct marketing online using the ALC Web site. Just be careful to avoid what's commonly called "spamming" on the Web. Spamming is the unsolicited delivery of e-mail sales messages to a wide target audience.
- Spamming tends to generate a vehement backlash from some members of the Internet community, and it certainly is less effective than a well-targeted electronic mailing.
- Click the ALC Interactive link to find out more about what are called "opt-in" e-mail lists—lists of people who voluntarily request information about a particular topic online. Messages sent from these lists are received in a kinder light than unsolicited e-mail, and they receive a better response rate.
- ALC Interactive provides a complete online marketing management service, which can help you launch and manage an e-mail marketing campaign or a Web site banner advertising campaign. Web site banner advertising involves placing ads for your business on Web sites in exchange for a fee or in exchange for placing the other Web sites' ads on your own site.

Note

Click on the How-To Articles link to see a listing of links to information and tips about direct mail marketing.

In this exercise, you will develop a custom mailing list using the List Merchant Web site. You will then search for a mailing list and find out more about online marketing at the American List Council Web site.

Note: *To ensure consistent results, this exercise uses simulated sites. The real URLs appear at the end of the exercise.*

Web Search

Search for answers to the following questions using the Web sites you will visit in the Web simulation exercise.

1. What is the average age of the Diamonds-to-Go Niche household head?

    ____

2. What is the household income range for the Go-Go Families Niche?

    ____

3. What is the demographic profile of the Loose Change Niche?

    ____

4. What are the product interests of the Totebaggers Niche?

    ____

5. What percentage of Inc. Magazine readers use a computer at work?

    ____

6. What is the median household income of Wired Magazine readers?

    ____

7. Name the four types of e-mail messages sent by online marketers.

    ____

EXERCISE DIRECTIONS

1. Launch the Internet simulation. From the Main Menu, select Lesson 7, then select Exercise 5.
2. On the Address line, type the following URL and press Enter:

    http://www.listmerchant.com/

    ➲ *The List Merchant home page opens.*

List Merchant Home Page

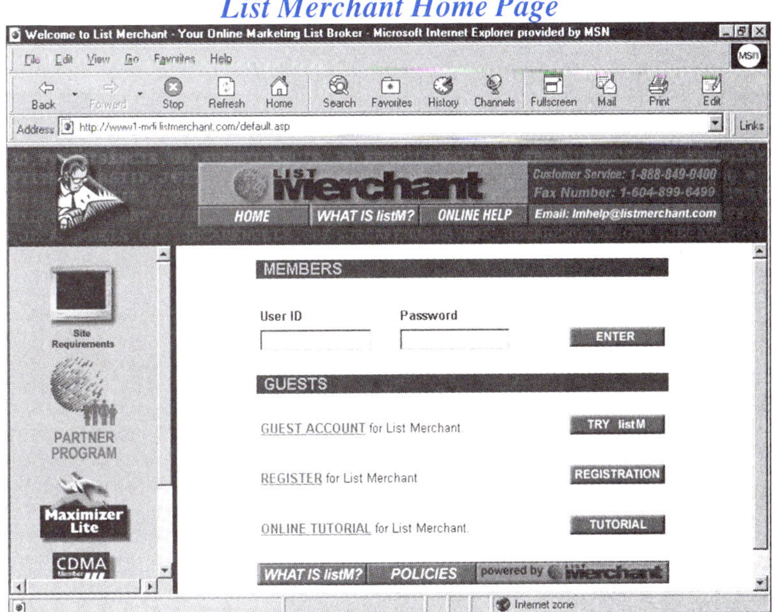

3. Click the TRY listM link.

   ➲ *The List Merchant Guest page opens.*

4. Click the Consumer Data Options Search button.

   ➲ *The Polk consumer database search tool opens.*

5. Click LA (Louisiana) on the United States map.

   ➲ *Louisiana is defined as your search state.*

List Merchant Guest Page

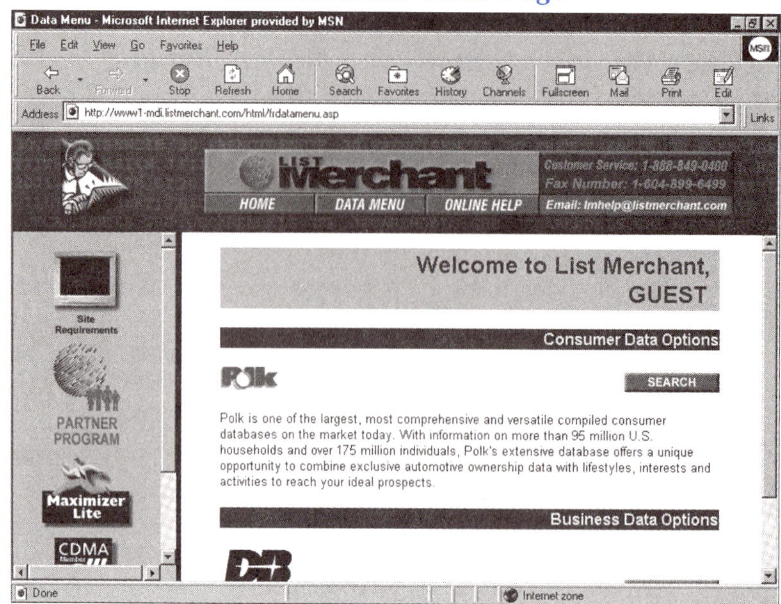

Select a State to Search

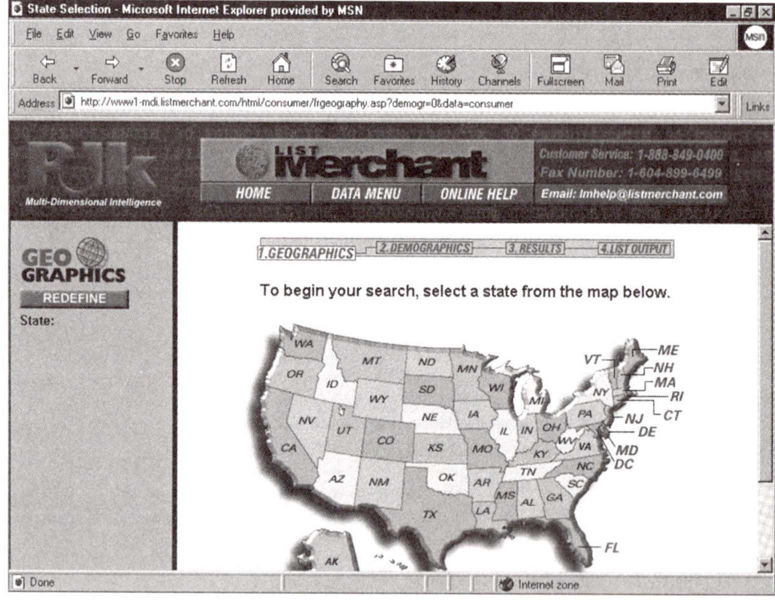

6. Click 622 on the map of Louisiana to select the New Orleans metropolitan area.
7. Click to select **Search by Zip Codes Within Selected DMA**, then click Next.

   ➲ *The Zip Code selection page opens.*

8. Select the following Zip Codes from the Selection List menu. Click Add after clicking each Zip Code to add it to your search criteria.

   39457

   39470

   39529

   70004

   70031

   70042

   70053

   70064

   70083

   70139

Select a Metropolitan Area

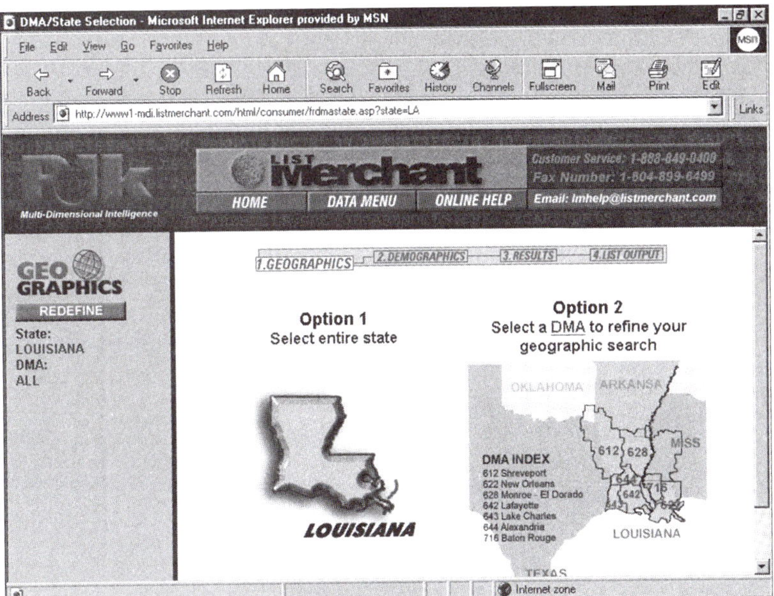

Select Zip Codes

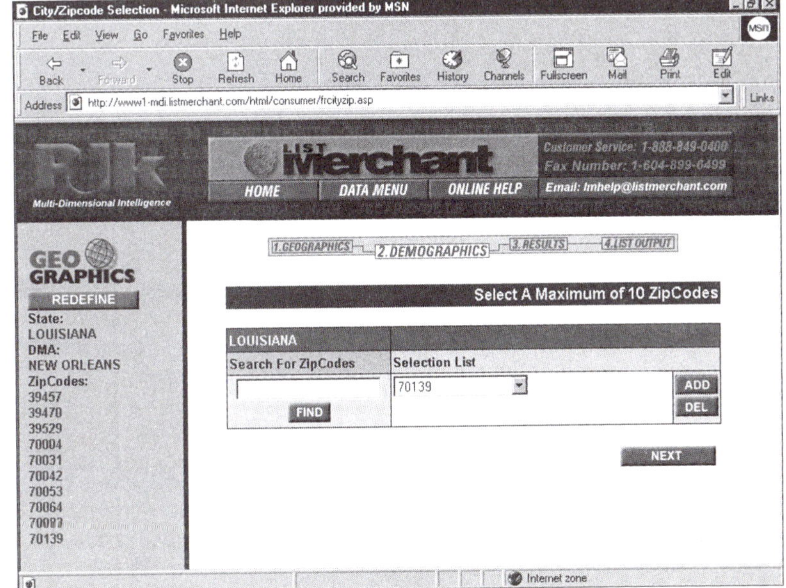

9. After you have made your Zip Code selections, click Next.

   ➲ *The customer profile selection page opens.*

10. Scroll down and click the Niches button.

   ➲ *The Niches selection page opens.*

11. Click to select each of the **Niches** from the menu. Read the descriptions of each Niche.

12. Click to select the **Big Spender Parents Niche**, then scroll down and click the Build Profile button.

   ➲ *The search Results page opens. Your search results in a list of 829 records.*

Select a Market Niche

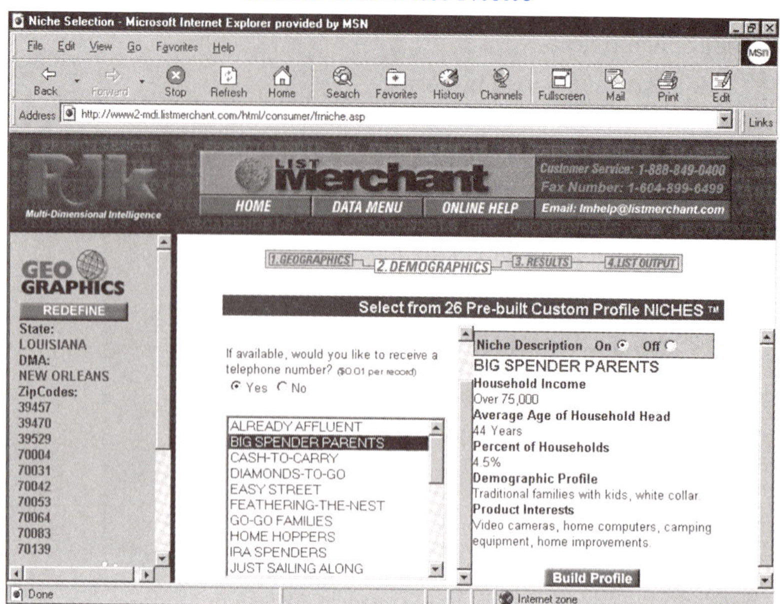

List Search Results

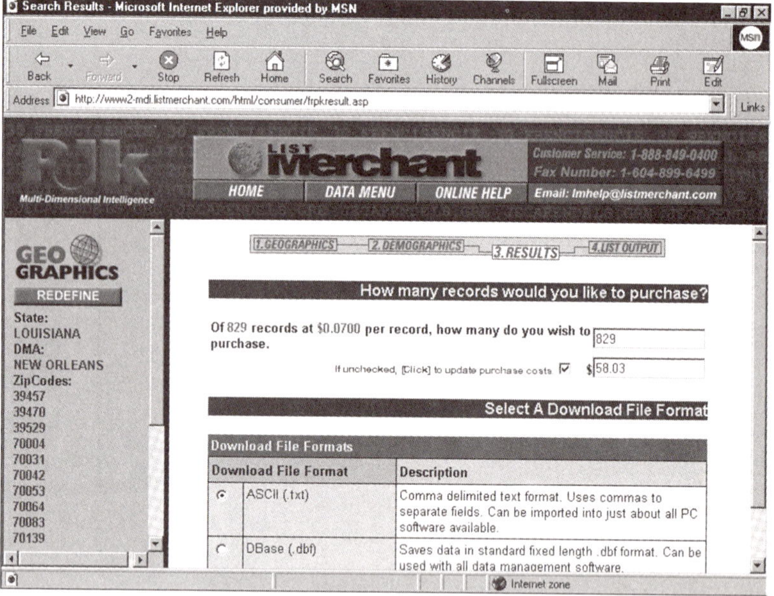

13. Make sure the ASCII (.txt) option is selected, then click Next.

   ➲ *The List Output page opens.*

14. Use the scroll bar at the left portion of the screen to review the geographic and demographic criteria for your list.

15. Review the Purchase Summary, then scroll down and click the checkbox next to **I accept the above terms**.

16. Select **Direct Mail/Advertising** from the Intended Use menu.

17. Type *New Orleans Big Spender* in the Naming your list text box.

   ✓ *If you were completing the exercise online, you could click Download to download the mailing list to your computer.*

18. Enter the following URL in your browser's Address line:

   http://www.amlist.com/

   ➲ *The American List Council home page opens.*

Complete the List Purchase Information

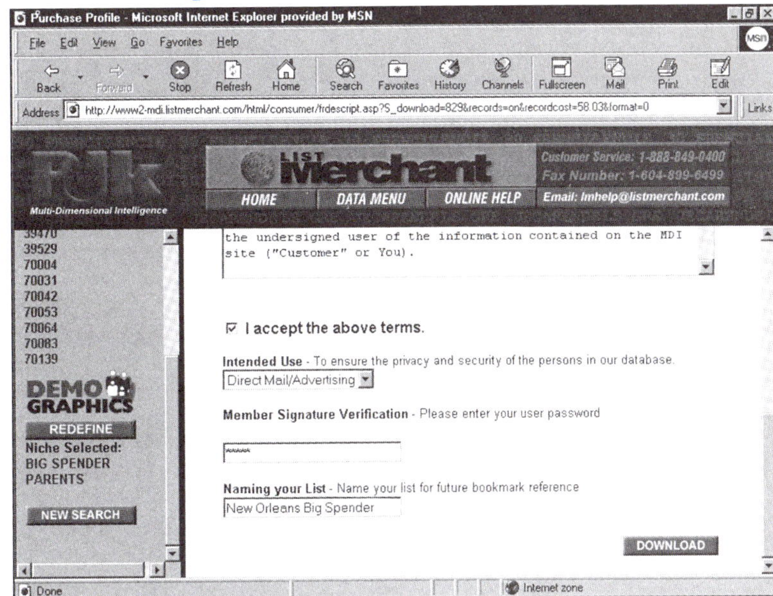

American List Council Home Page

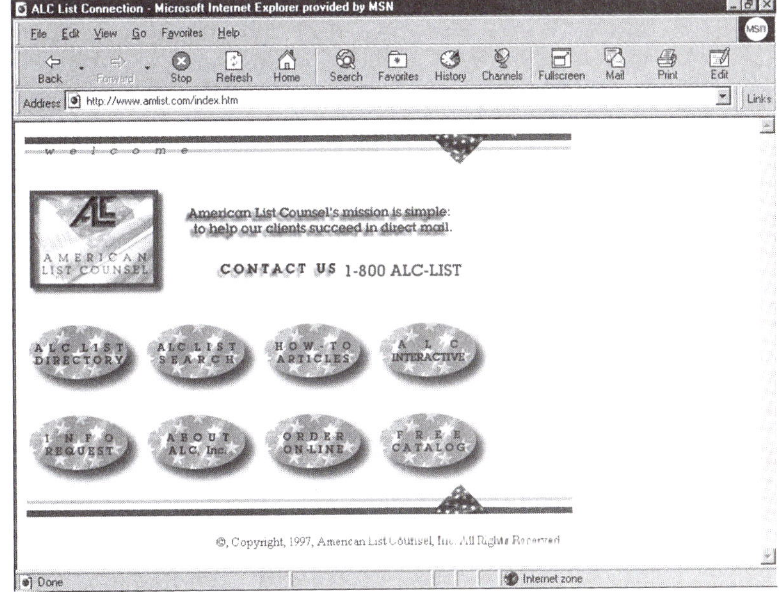

19. Click the ALC List Directory icon.

   ➲ *The ALC List Directory page opens.*

20. Click the browse by category link.

   ➲ *The List Directory Category Listing opens.*

21. Click the Computers & Data Processing link.

   ➲ *A page showing mailing lists targeted to computer users opens.*

ALC List Directory Categories

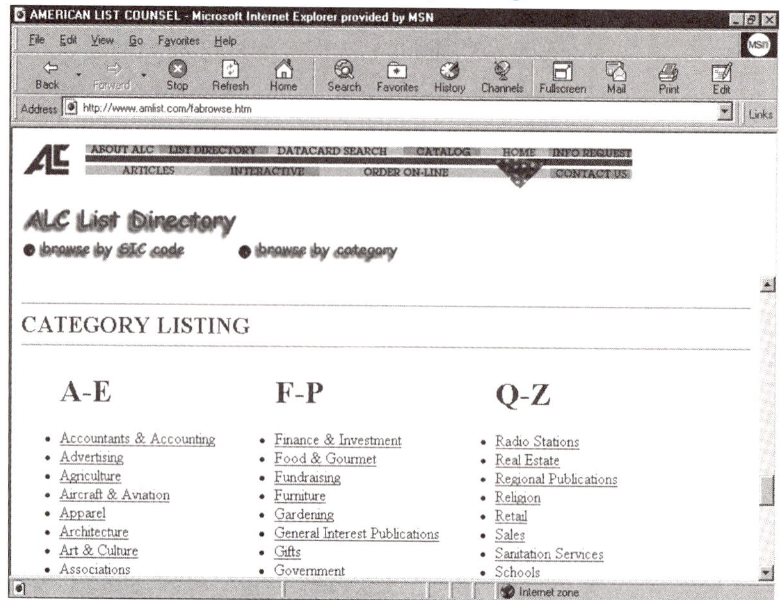

Mailing Lists Targeted to Computer Users

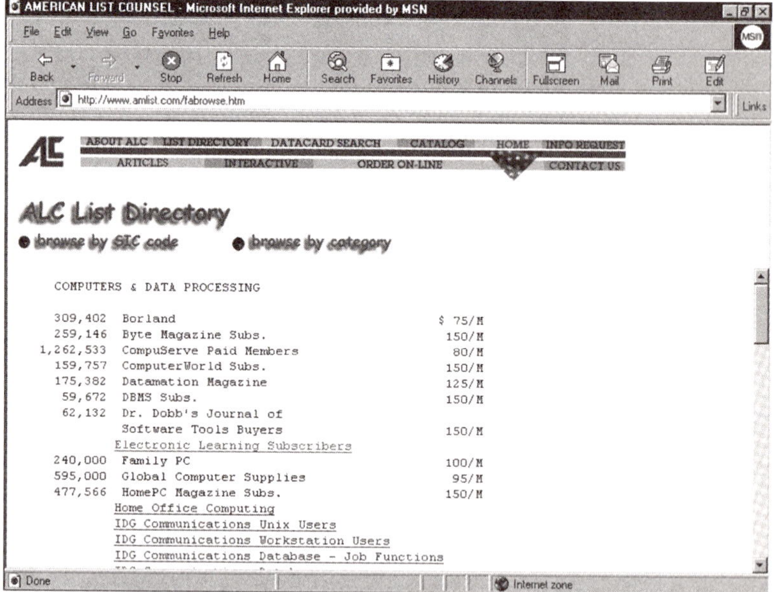

22. Click the Inc. Magazine link.
    - ➲ *The datacard for the Inc. Magazine mailing list opens.*
23. Scroll down and read the description of this mailing list.
    - ✓ *Note the demographic information about readers of the magazine as well as the various ways the list can be purchased and delivered.*
24. Use your browser's Back button to return to the Computers & Data Processing page.
25. Click the Wired Magazine Subscribers link, then read the description of this mailing list.
    - ✓ *Note the difference in demographics between readers of Wired Magazine and readers of Inc. Magazine.*
26. Click the Interactive link at the top of the page.
    - ➲ *The ALC Interactive Media page opens.*
27. Scroll down and click the E-Mail Marketing Guidelines link.
    - ➲ *The E-Mail Marketing Guidelines page opens.*
28. Scroll down and read the marketing guidelines.
    - ✓ *Note the four types of e-mail messages online marketers send.*
29. Use your browser's Back button to return to the ALC Interactive Media page.
30. Click the Understanding Banner Placement link.
    - ➲ *The Understanding Banner Placement page opens.*
31. Read the description of Web site banner advertising strategy.
    - ❓ *How does Web site banner advertising differ from other forms of advertising?*
32. Continue on to the next exercise.

    OR

    Exit from the simulation.

Datacard for Inc. Magazine List

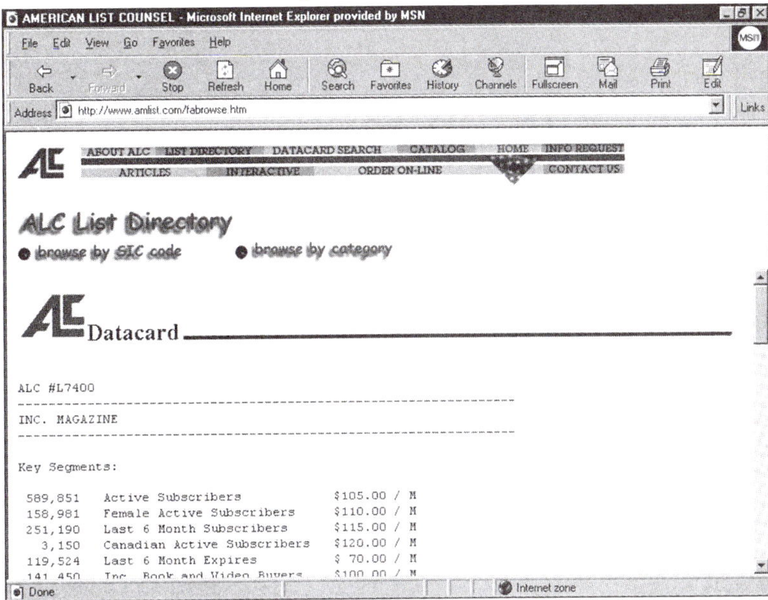

ALC Interactive Media Page

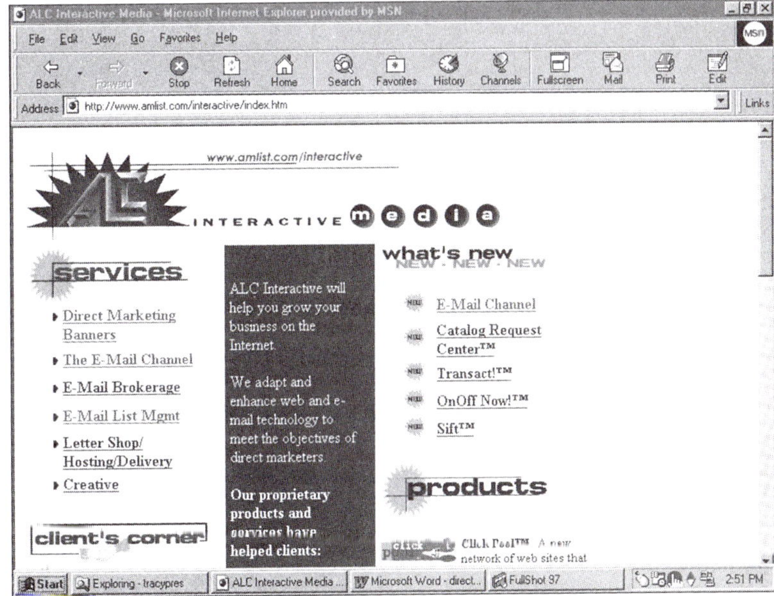

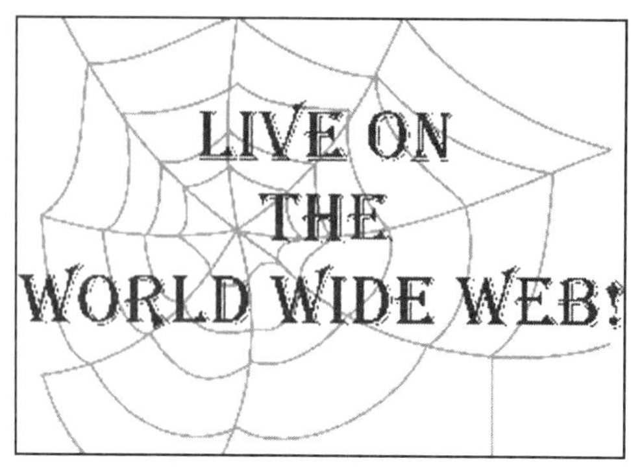

List Merchant Home Page

http://www.listmerchant.com/

American List Council Home Page

http://www.amlist.com/

NEXT EXERCISE

Exercise 6

Sell to the Government with Commerce Business Daily

NOTES

Sell to the Government with Commerce Business Daily

- The federal government can be the source of millions of dollars of potential sales, but you often need to cut through a maze of bureaus, agencies, departments, and red tape to close a government sale.
- You can find government sales and business opportunities online at the Commerce Business Daily (CBD) Web site, called CBDNet, part of the Department of Commerce Web site. CBD updates a database of government procurements, contract awards, and sales of government property daily.

Commerce Business Daily Home Page

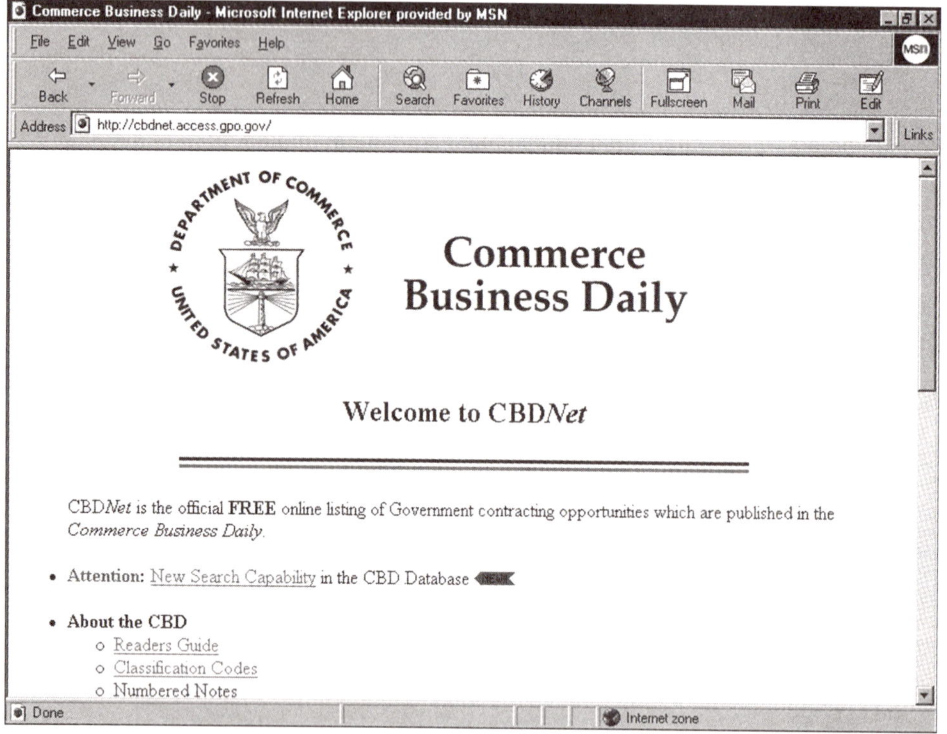

- Search CBD to find your best opportunities for doing business with the federal government. All proposed government contracts and procurements over $25,000 are required by law to be listed in the CBD database.

Note

Click the Classification Codes link at the CBD home page to see a page listing classification codes and their meanings. Classification codes are divided into two primary groups, services and supplies. Services are assigned alphabetic codes. Supplies are assigned numeric codes.

- You can conduct either a Simple Search or a Fielded Search of the CBD database. The Simple Search requires you only to enter a keyword or keyword(s). Use the Fielded Search if you want to look at specific segments of the CBD database or if you want to use and/or statements to narrow your search criteria.
- The CBD database contains all active notices of government contract requisitions. The database is updated continuously as new requisitions are added to it. Notices of requisition remain in the active database for 15 days, after which the notices are moved permanently to an archive database. You can also include the archive database in your searches.
- After you receive search results, click links to see the actual procurement notice.

Note

You can also use Fielded Search criteria such as Classification Code, Subject, Response Date, Point of Contact, Description, Award Amount, and Cite code.

Procurement Notice Posting

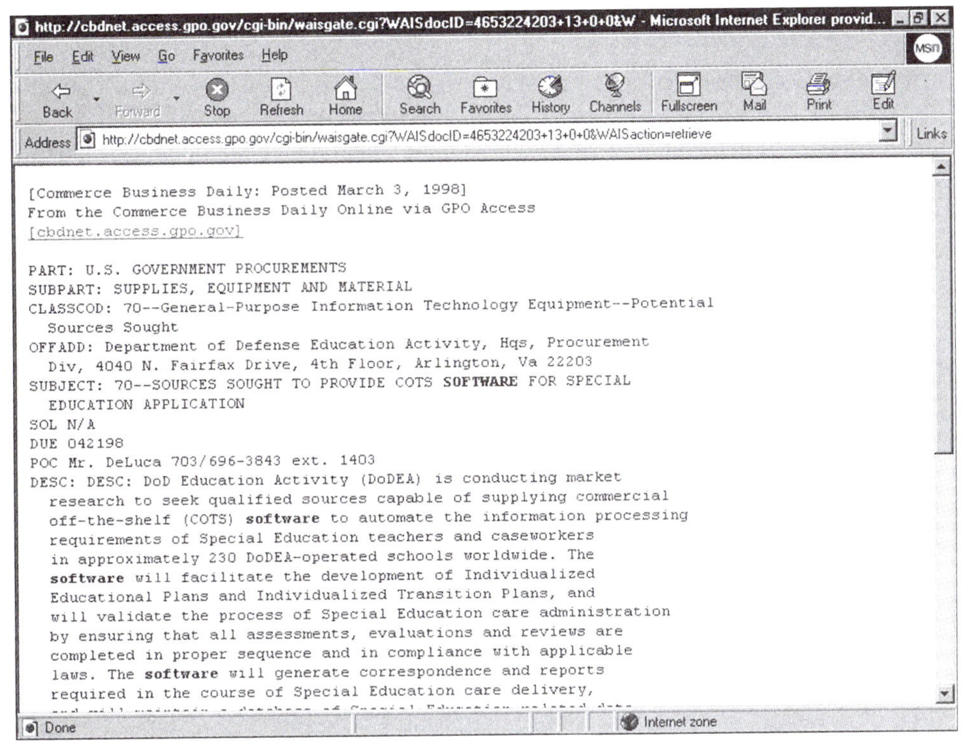

```
[Commerce Business Daily: Posted March 3, 1998]
From the Commerce Business Daily Online via GPO Access
[cbdnet.access.gpo.gov]

PART: U.S. GOVERNMENT PROCUREMENTS
SUBPART: SUPPLIES, EQUIPMENT AND MATERIAL
CLASSCOD: 70--General-Purpose Information Technology Equipment--Potential
  Sources Sought
OFFADD: Department of Defense Education Activity, Hqs, Procurement
  Div, 4040 N. Fairfax Drive, 4th Floor, Arlington, Va 22203
SUBJECT: 70--SOURCES SOUGHT TO PROVIDE COTS SOFTWARE FOR SPECIAL
  EDUCATION APPLICATION
SOL N/A
DUE 042198
POC Mr. DeLuca 703/696-3843 ext. 1403
DESC: DESC: DoD Education Activity (DoDEA) is conducting market
  research to seek qualified sources capable of supplying commercial
  off-the-shelf (COTS) software to automate the information processing
  requirements of Special Education teachers and caseworkers
  in approximately 230 DoDEA-operated schools worldwide. The
  software will facilitate the development of Individualized
  Educational Plans and Individualized Transition Plans, and
  will validate the process of Special Education care administration
  by ensuring that all assessments, evaluations and reviews are
  completed in proper sequence and in compliance with applicable
  laws. The software will generate correspondence and reports
  required in the course of Special Education care delivery,
```

In this exercise, you will search the Commerce Business Daily Web site for procurement notices that may yield business or sales opportunities. You will also browse the Commerce Business Daily site by service code for sales opportunities.

Note: To ensure consistent results, this exercise uses simulated sites. The real URLs appear at the end of the exercise.

Web Search

Search for answers to the following questions using the Web sites you will visit in the Web simulation exercise.

1. What are the minimum computer hardware requirements for the Special Education software?

 ____

2. What is the CITE number for this posting?

 ____

3. What SIC code applies to the Develop Software Application posting?

 ____

4. What is the last posting link on the Fielded Search Results page?

 ____

5. What experience is required for the developer of the NAFTA Web site?

 ____

6. What is the format required for documents posted to the NAFTA Web site?

 ____

EXERCISE DIRECTIONS

1. Launch the Internet simulation. From the Main Menu, select Lesson 7, then select Exercise 6.
2. On the Address line, type the following URL and press Enter:

 http://cbdnet.access.gpo.gov/

 ➲ *The Commerce Business Daily (CBD) home page opens.*

Commerce Business Daily Home Page

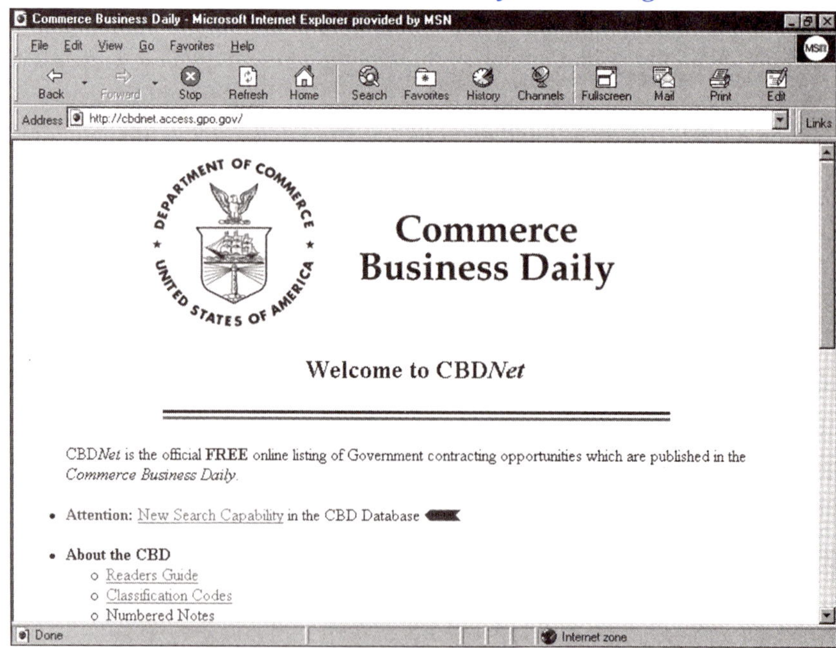

3. Click the Simple Search of the CBD link.

   ➲ *The CBD Simple Search page opens.*

4. Type *Computer Software* in the Search Terms text box, then click SUBMIT.

   ➲ *The Simple Search Results page opens.*

CBD Simple Search Page

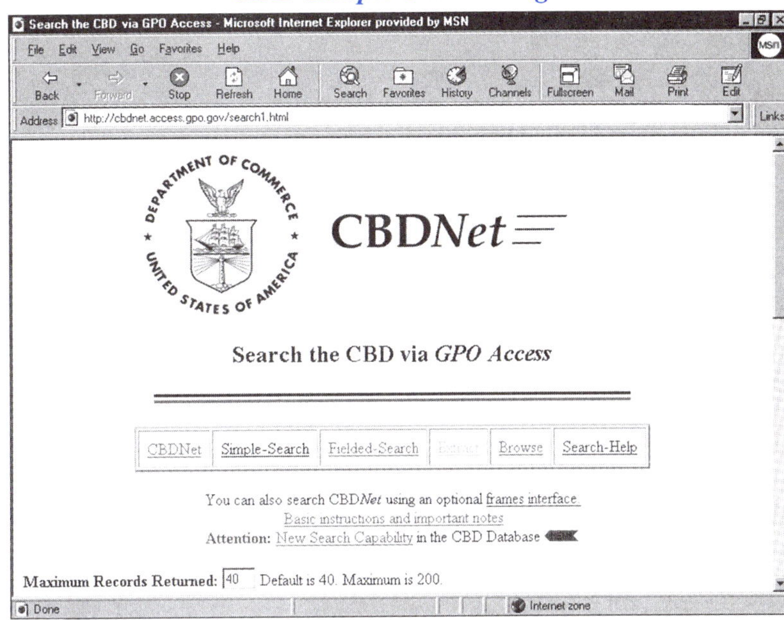

Simple Search Results

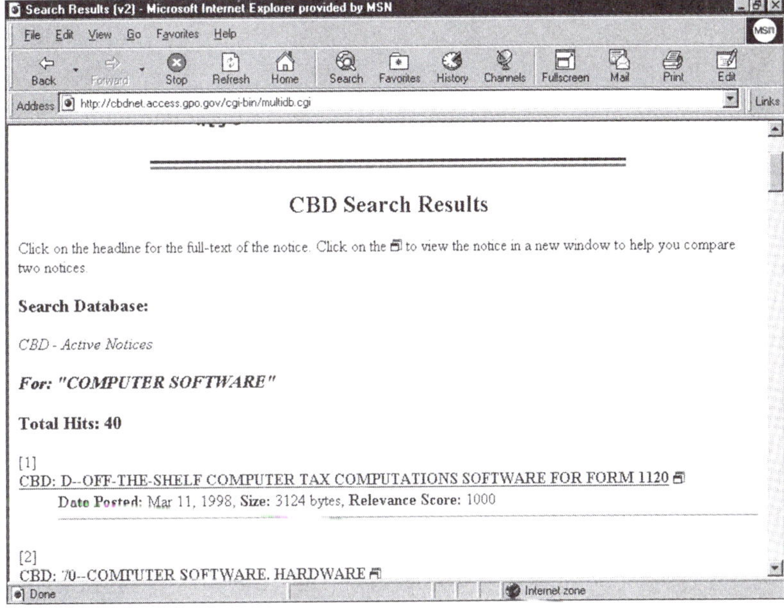

5. Click the CBD: 70—SOURCES SOUGHT TO PROVIDE COTS SOFTWARE FOR SPECIAL EDUCATION APPLICATION link.

   ➲ *The CBD posting opens.*

6. Scroll down and read the posting.

   ✓ *Note the hardware requirements for the proposed software package.*

7. Use your browser's Back button to return to the Simple Search Results page.

8. Click the CBD: D—Develop Software Application link.

   ➲ *The CBD posting opens.*

9. Scroll down and read the posting.

10. Click the cbdnet.access.gpo.gov link at the top of the page.

    ➲ *The Commerce Business Daily home page opens.*

Government Procurement Posting

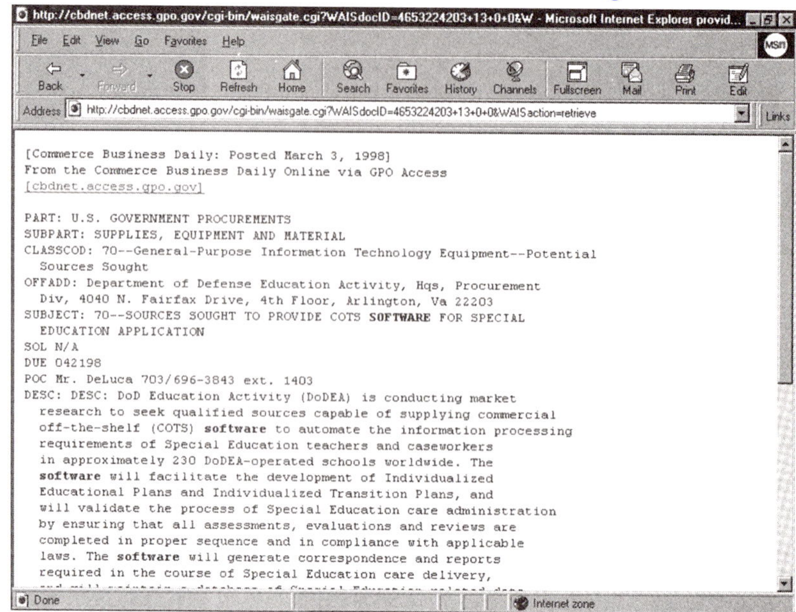

[Commerce Business Daily: Posted March 3, 1998]
From the Commerce Business Daily Online via GPO Access
[cbdnet.access.gpo.gov]

PART: U.S. GOVERNMENT PROCUREMENTS
SUBPART: SUPPLIES, EQUIPMENT AND MATERIAL
CLASSCOD: 70--General-Purpose Information Technology Equipment--Potential Sources Sought
OFFADD: Department of Defense Education Activity, Hqs, Procurement Div, 4040 N. Fairfax Drive, 4th Floor, Arlington, Va 22203
SUBJECT: 70--SOURCES SOUGHT TO PROVIDE COTS **SOFTWARE** FOR SPECIAL EDUCATION APPLICATION
SOL N/A
DUE 042198
POC Mr. DeLuca 703/696-3843 ext. 1403
DESC: DESC: DoD Education Activity (DoDEA) is conducting market research to seek qualified sources capable of supplying commercial off-the-shelf (COTS) **software** to automate the information processing requirements of Special Education teachers and caseworkers in approximately 230 DoDEA-operated schools worldwide. The **software** will facilitate the development of Individualized Educational Plans and Individualized Transition Plans, and will validate the process of Special Education care administration by ensuring that all assessments, evaluations and reviews are completed in proper sequence and in compliance with applicable laws. The **software** will generate correspondence and reports required in the course of Special Education care delivery,

Posting for Software Developer

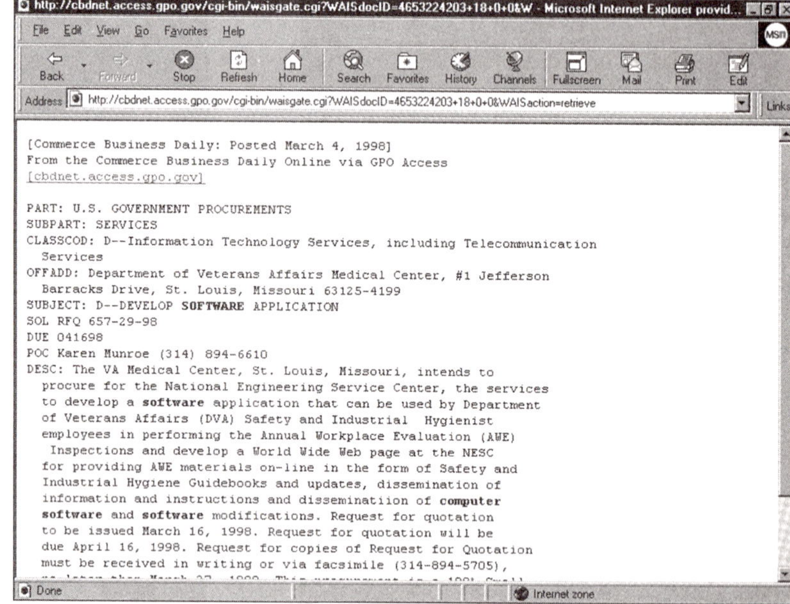

[Commerce Business Daily: Posted March 4, 1998]
From the Commerce Business Daily Online via GPO Access
[cbdnet.access.gpo.gov]

PART: U.S. GOVERNMENT PROCUREMENTS
SUBPART: SERVICES
CLASSCOD: D--Information Technology Services, including Telecommunication Services
OFFADD: Department of Veterans Affairs Medical Center, #1 Jefferson Barracks Drive, St. Louis, Missouri 63125-4199
SUBJECT: D--DEVELOP **SOFTWARE** APPLICATION
SOL RFQ 657-29-98
DUE 041698
POC Karen Munroe (314) 894-6610
DESC: The VA Medical Center, St. Louis, Missouri, intends to procure for the National Engineering Service Center, the services to develop a **software** application that can be used by Department of Veterans Affairs (DVA) Safety and Industrial Hygienist employees in performing the Annual Workplace Evaluation (AWE) Inspections and develop a World Wide Web page at the NESC for providing AWE materials on-line in the form of Safety and Industrial Hygiene Guidebooks and updates, dissemination of information and instructions and disseminatiion of **computer software** and **software** modifications. Request for quotation to be issued March 16, 1998. Request for quotation will be due April 16, 1998. Request for copies of Request for Quotation must be received in writing or via facsimile (314-894-5705),

11. Click the Fielded Search of the CBD link.
    - ➲ *The CBD Fielded Search page opens.*
12. Click to select **Archive of Notices** next to the Database to Search heading.
    - ✓ *Active Notices should also be checked.*
13. Type *Computer Software* in the FIELDS: Full text of the *CBD text* box.
14. Select **AFTER** under the Posted Date heading, then type *010197* in the text box next to AFTER.
15. Click to select the following under the Part heading:

    U.S. Government Procurements
    Sources Sought
16. Scroll down and click the SUBMIT button.
    - ➲ *The Fielded Search Results page opens.*
    - ✓ *Note that while many of the postings are the same as in the Simple Search, several different postings are also shown.*
17. Click the CBD Home icon at the bottom of the page.
    - ➲ *The Commerce Business Daily home page opens.*

Enter Fielded Search Criteria

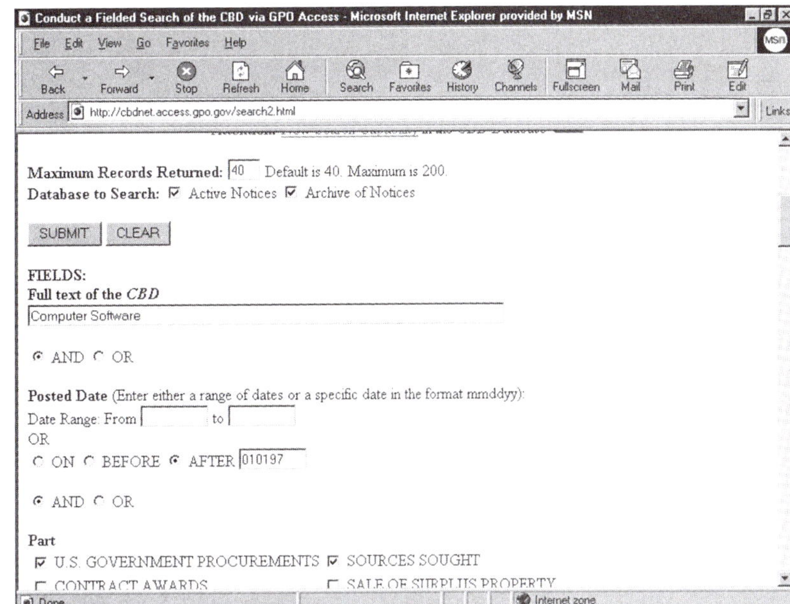

Fielded Search Results

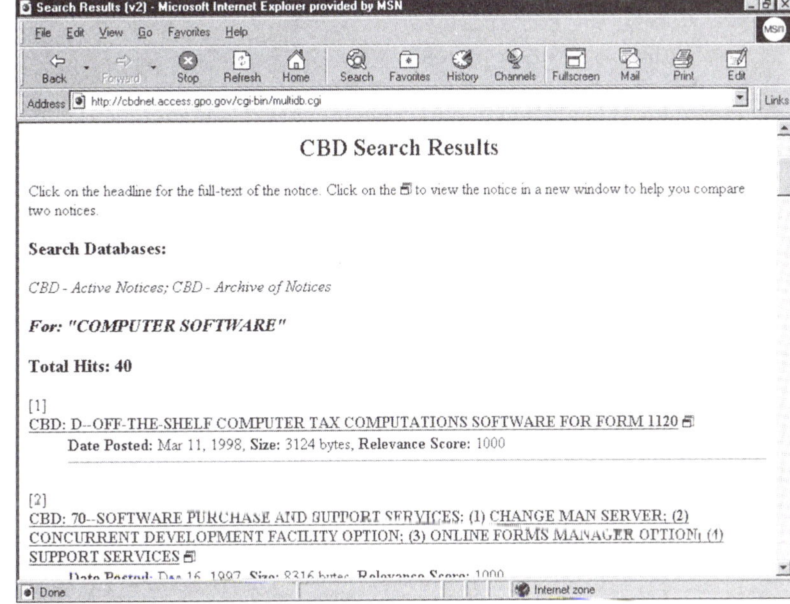

18. Scroll down and click the Browse the CBD link.

   ➲ *The Browse CBD Notices page opens.*

19. Click the U.S. Government Procurements link.

   ➲ *You move to the Procurements section of the Browse page.*

20. Click the D link next to the SERVICES Class Code heading.

   ➲ *The page listing class D services links opens. Class D is defined as Information Technology Services, including Telecommunication Services.*

Browse CBD Notices

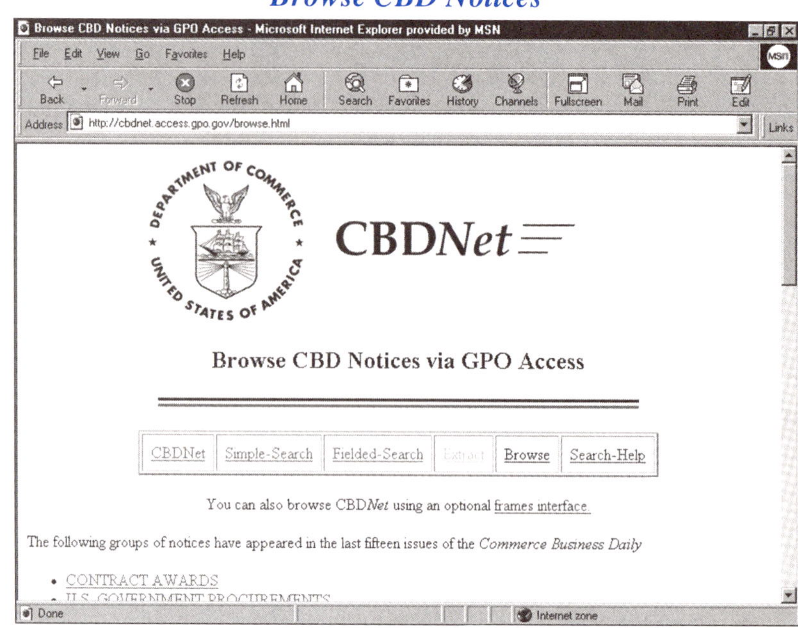

21. Click the CBD: D--NAFTA CUSTOMS WEB SITE link.

   ➲ *The posting opens.*

22. Scroll down and read the posting.

   ✓ *Note that the posting is in English, French, and Spanish.*

23. Continue on to the next exercise.

   OR

   Exit from the simulation.

Posting for NAFTA Web Site Developer

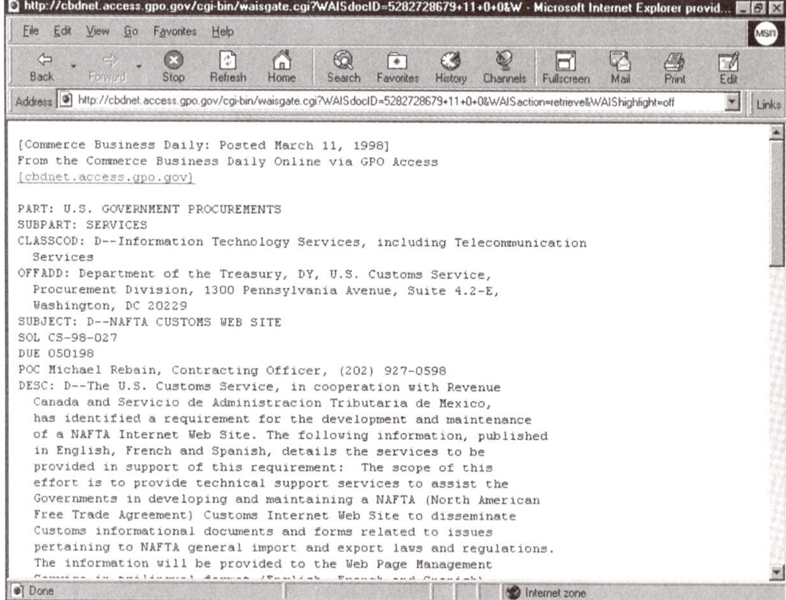

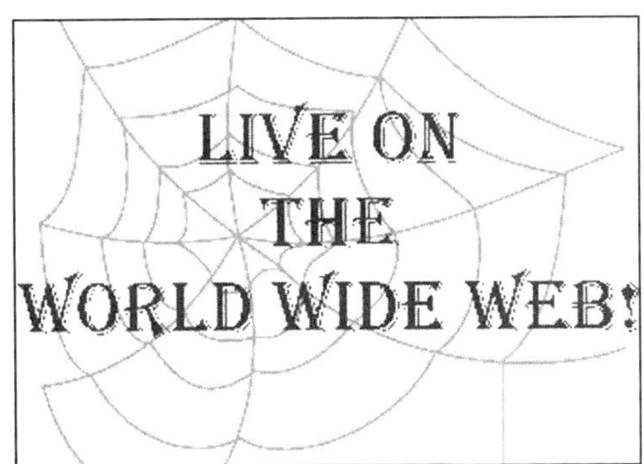

Commerce Business Daily Home Page
http://cbdnet.access.gpo.gov/

Exercise 7

- Find International Sales Resources with MSU-CIBER
- Find Trade News with Trade Information Center
- Locate Trade Leads with Global Marketplace
- Translate Foreign Languages with travlang

NOTES

Find International Sales Resources with MSU-CIBER

- Expand your markets by exporting your product to other countries with the help of Web sites. The MSU-CIBER Web site provides excellent search and directory starting points for finding international trade resources online.

MSU-CIBER Home Page

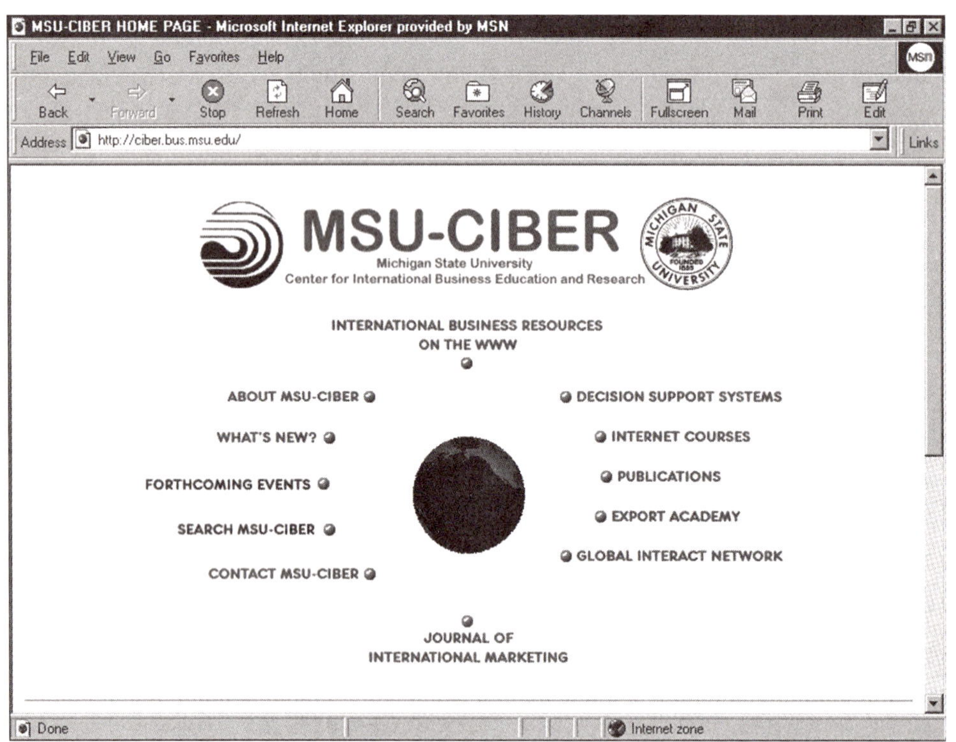

- From the MSU-CIBER home page, click the International Business Resources on the WWW link. This opens a superb directory site for finding online information and business links about international trade. The site has received a number of awards from online and computer magazines.
- Like most good directory sites, you can either search or browse to find what you want. Type keywords in the Search IBR on the WWW textbox and click the Search button.

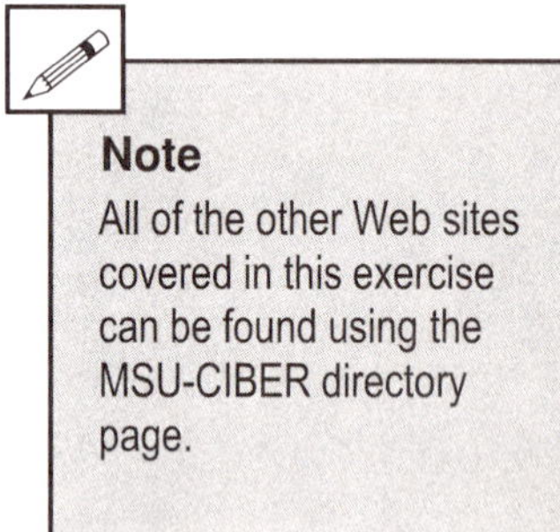

Note

All of the other Web sites covered in this exercise can be found using the MSU-CIBER directory page.

- Scroll down the International Business Resources home page to browse an index of about 20 category links. Click on a link that interests you to see a page of Web site links for that topic along with a brief description of each site.
- For example, click the International Trade Information link to find sites such as Trade Information Center that provide information about trade in various countries and regions around the world.
- Use the International Trade Leads link from the Business Resources home page to find sites such as Global Marketplace that provide a wealth of international sales leads. Click the Various Utilities and Useful Information link to find sites that help make selling overseas easier.

Note
Click the Statisitcal Data and Information Resources link to find government, statistical, and market indicators.

Find Trade News with Trade Information Center

- The Trade Information Center (TIC) is operated by the International Trade Administration of the U.S. Department of Commerce to provide a comprehensive resource for exporters. The TIC Web site is one of the top sources of information for exporters on topics such as government assistance, export financing, regulations, and sales leads.

Trade Information Center Home Page

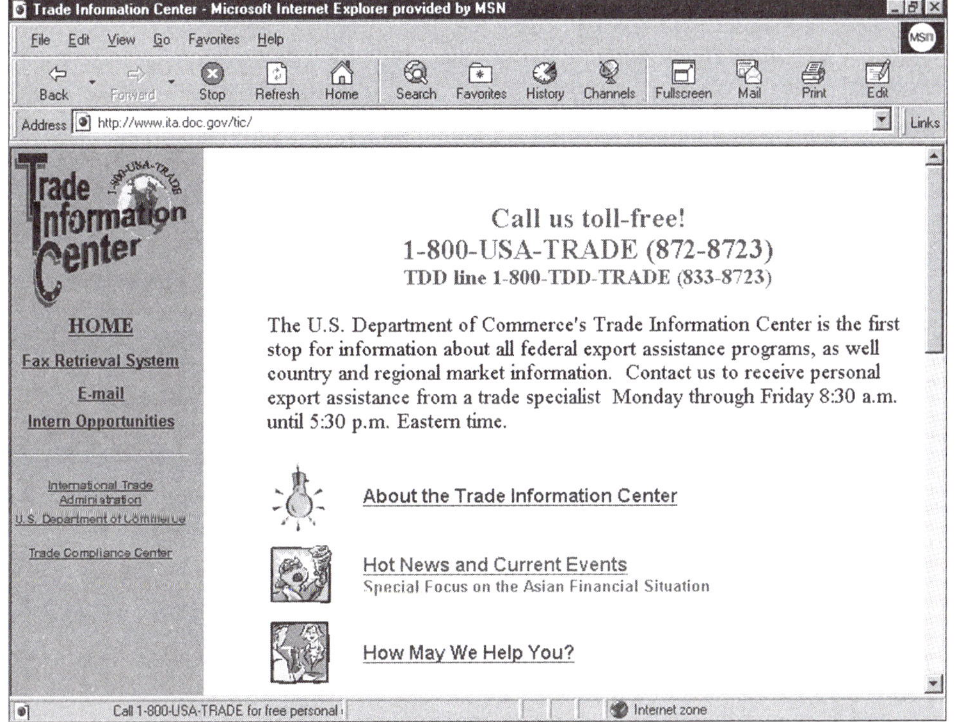

Note
The TIC recently won Vice President Al Gore's "Hammer Award" for helping to create a government that works better and costs less.

Note
Click the Trade Lead Information link at the TIC home page to access a guide to Web sites that provide trade leads.

- Click the Hot News and Current Events link to read about the latest trade news. From the Hot News and Current Events page, click the Asian Financial Situation link to get updates on the Asian financial crisis and its effects on trade. Click The Pressroom to see the official news source of the International Trade Administration, including trade statistics by state and by industry sector.

- Click the Country and Regional Market Information link to find trade information for various countries and regions around the world. This information includes answers to frequently asked questions about doing business in specific countries, which can help you avoid common pitfalls businesses face in expanding sales overseas.

Locate Trade Leads with Global Marketplace

- There are scores of Web sites devoted to international trade leads. The Global Marketplace trade bulletin board, part of the Word Business Network Web site, provides one of the largest and most current databases of trade leads online.

Global Marketplace Trade Leads

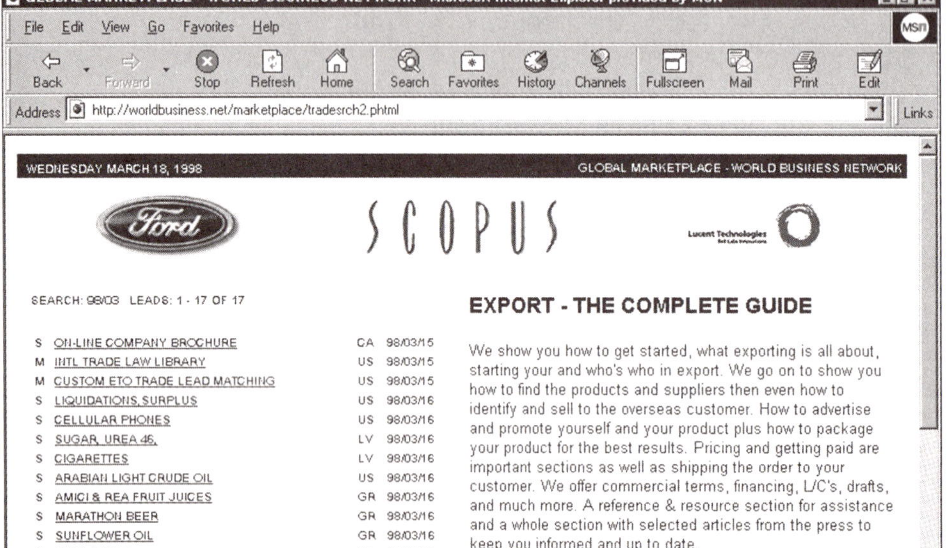

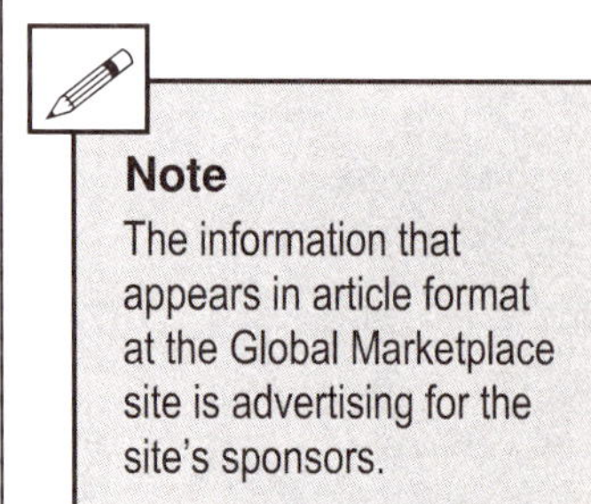

Note
The information that appears in article format at the Global Marketplace site is advertising for the site's sponsors.

- At the Global Marketplace home page, simply click the Trade Leads Today button to see links to all trade leads posted on the current day. Click Trade Leads This Month to see all leads posted in the current month.
- Click the name of a lead to see the lead, including contact information and a brief description of the product available for import or export.
- You can also click the Old Trade Leads link to see leads from previous months. The Global Marketplace search engine allows you to search the trade lead database by selecting a field (such as Products or Company) and then entering a keyword.

Translate Foreign Languages with travlang

- One of the obstacles to doing business in foreign countries is communicating in foreign languages. You can use the travlang Web site to learn the basics of new languages quickly and to translate from English to another language (and vice versa).

Travlang Home Page

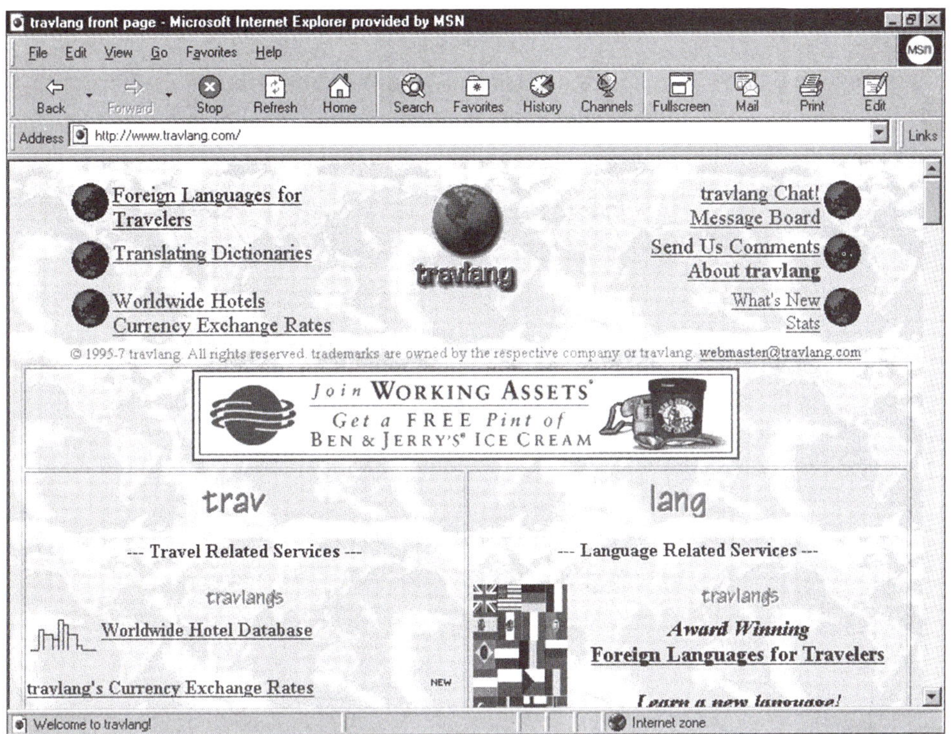

- Travlang is a valuable directory Web site that includes links to dozens of language and international travel Web resources. Language resources include links to online translating dictionaries, translating software, and translation services.
- Also included among the language resources are links to Web sites that provide introductory-level instruction in many languages. For example, click the Travelers' Japanese with Voice link to begin learning Japanese pronunciation and essential phrases online.
- To draft a business letter for an international client or for quick translation of a document you receive from an overseas business partner, click the Translating Dictionaries link. A page listing links to travlang's many translating dictionaries opens.
- Click the link for the dictionary you want, then type a word or phrase in the search text box and click Submit. A translation of the word or phrase appears on the Search Results page.

Note

Click the travlang Word of the Day link to see a word translated into dozens of languages from around the world.

In this exercise, you will search for international trade Web sites using the MUS-CIBER directory Web site. You will find trade news at the Trade Information Center Web site, then search for trade leads at the Global Marketplace site. Finally, you will find translations for English words using the travlang Web site.

Note: To ensure consistent results, this exercise uses simulated sites. The real URLs appear at the end of the exercise.

Web Search

Search for answers to the following questions using the Web sites you will visit in the Web simulation exercise.

1. What is the literal translation for the Chinese word "crisis"?

   ____

2. What is the date for the ITALIAN WINES FOR SALE trade link on the February trade links page?

   ____

3. What is the name of the export manager for the Instant Soluble Coffee trade lead?

   ____

4. What is the company name and address for the Instant Soluble Coffee trade lead?

   ____

5. What is the Greek word for "stamps"?

   ____

6. What is the Swahili word for "stamps"?

   ____

7. What is the Czech word for "information"?

   ____

EXERCISE DIRECTIONS

1. Launch the Internet simulation. From the Main Menu, select Lesson 7, then select Exercise 7.
2. On the Address line, type the following URL and press Enter:

   http://ciber.bus.msu.edu/

   ➲ *The MSU-CIBER home page opens.*

MSU-CIBER Home Page

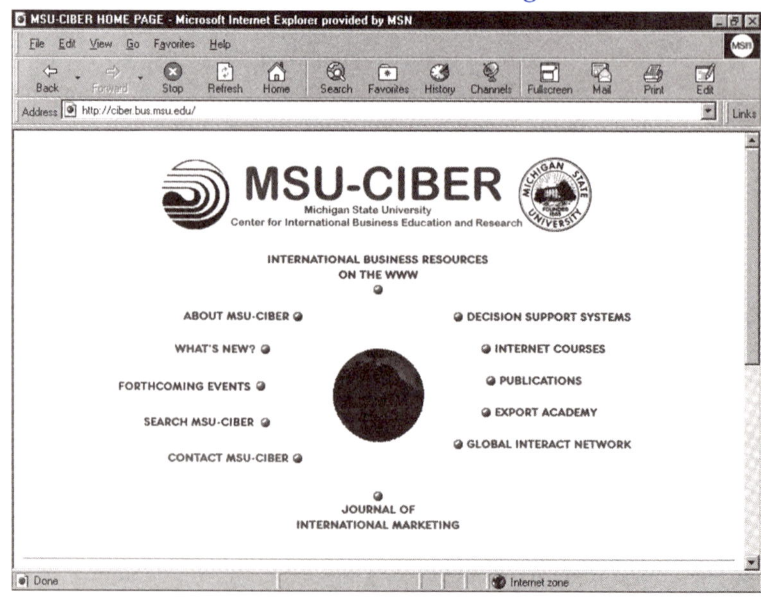

3. Click the International Business Resources On The WWW link.

   ➲ *The International Business Resources page opens.*

4. Scroll down and click the International Trade Information link.

   ➲ *The International Trade page opens.*

International Business Resources

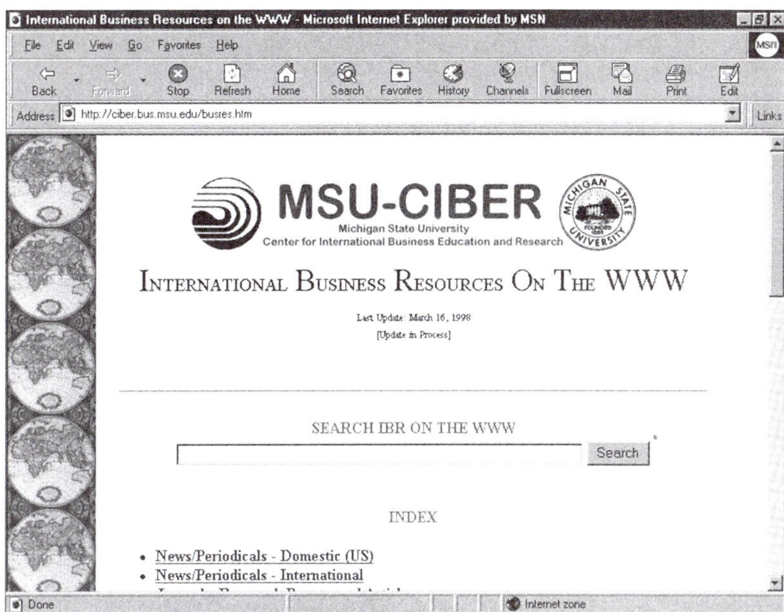

International Trade Links

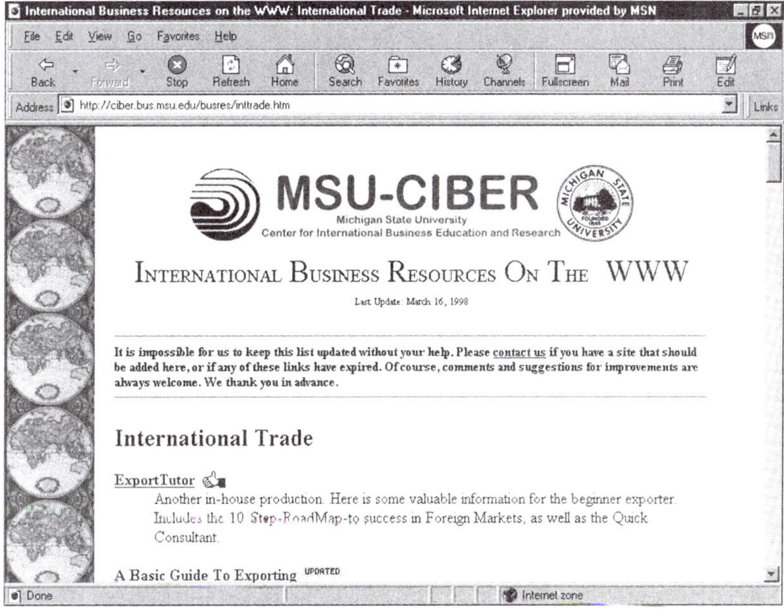

5. Scroll down and click the Trade Information Center link.

   ➲ *The Trade Information Center home page opens.*

6. Click the Hot News and Current Events link.

   ➲ *The Hot News and Current Events page opens.*

7. Click the Asian Financial Situation link.

8. Click the Impact of Korean Financial Crisis on U.S. Food and Beverage Exports link.

   ➲ *The news article page opens.*

Trade Information Center Home Page

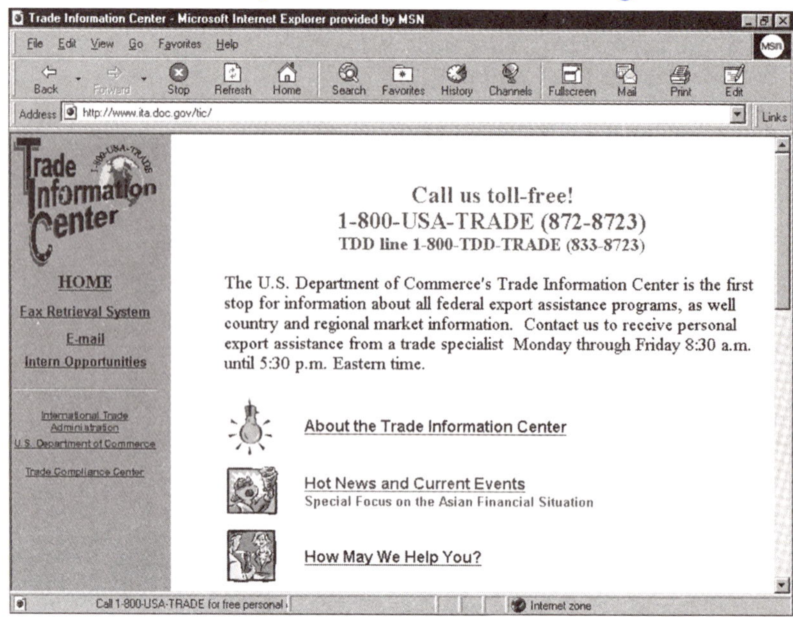

9. Scroll down and read the article about the Korean financial crisis.

   ✓ *Note the article's emphasis on viewing the financial crisis as an opportunity for exporters.*

Asian Trade News

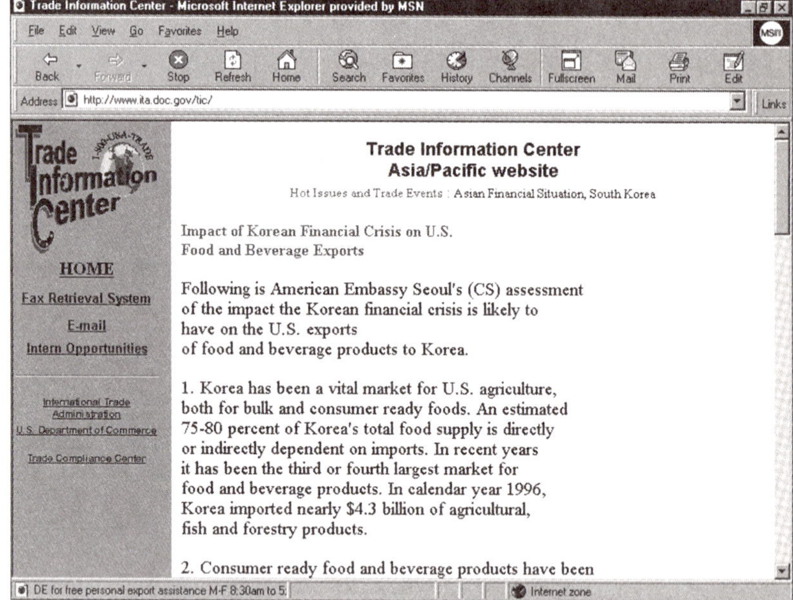

10. Click the HOME link.
    - ➲ *The Trade Information Center home page opens again.*
11. Click the Country and Regional Market Information link.
12. Click the Western Europe link.
13. Click the Frequently Asked Country Export Questions and Answers link.
14. Click the Search all the Questions and Answers link.
15. Type *France* in the Enter Keyword text box, then click Start the Search.
    - ➲ *A page displaying your search results opens.*
16. Click the France link next to question number 8: What are the labeling requirements for products I wish to sell in the French market?
    - ➲ *The answer page opens.*

Trade Information Search Results

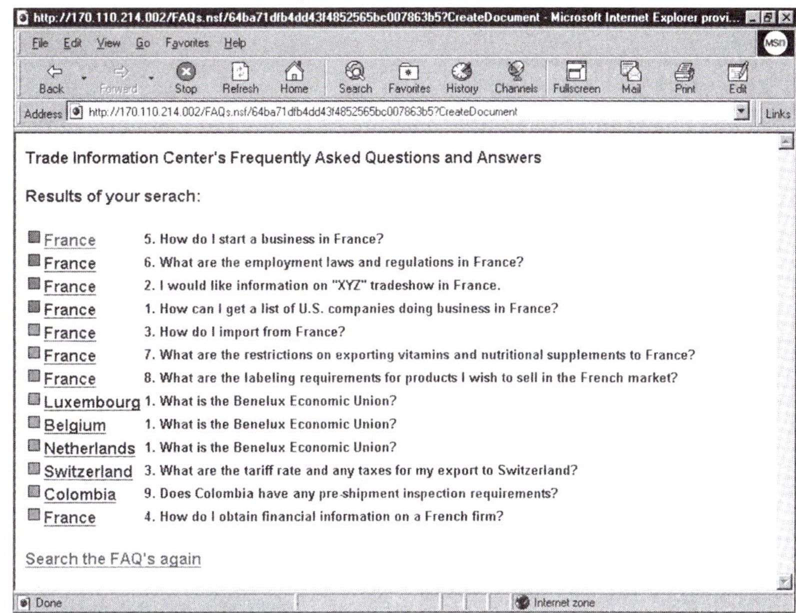

Information About Product Labeling in France

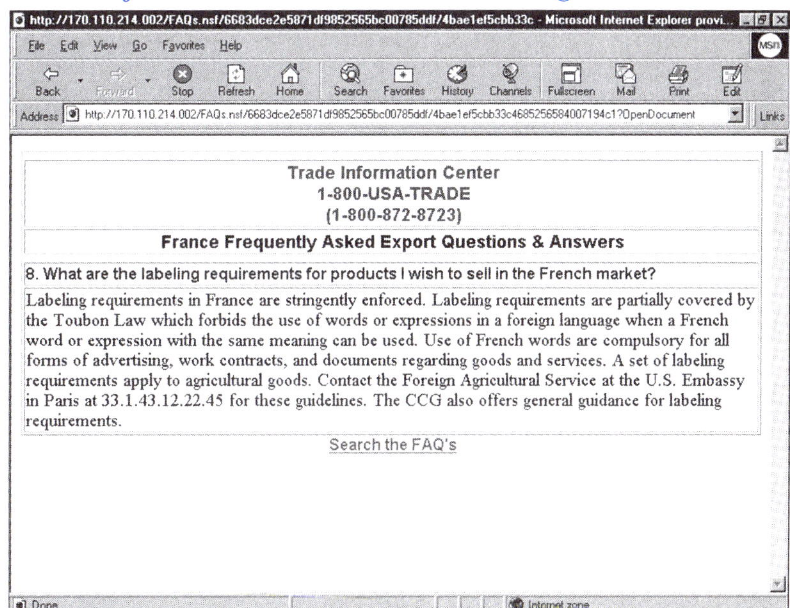

17. Read the answer, then click the arrow next to your browser's Back button. From the Back button drop–down menu, select **MSU-CIBER HOME PAGE**.

   ➲ *The MSU-CIBER home page opens again.*

18. Click the International Business Resources on the WWW link.

   ➲ *The International Business Resources on the WWW index page opens.*

19. Click the International Trade Leads link.

   ➲ *The International Trade Leads index page opens.*

20. Click the Global Marketplace – World Business Network link.

   ➲ *The Global Marketplace home page opens.*

Use the Back Menu to Return to MSU-CIBER

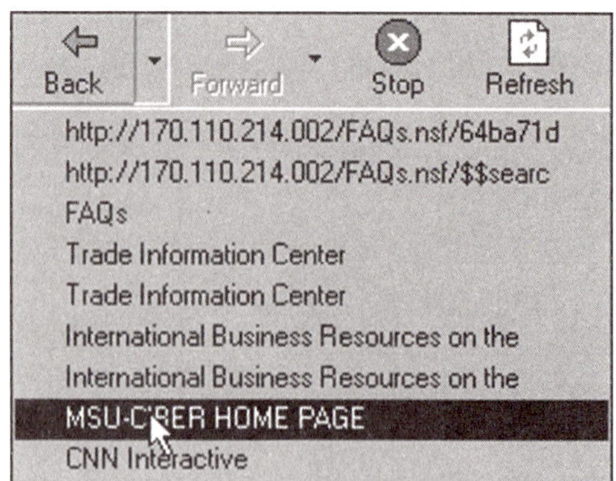

Global Marketplace Home Page

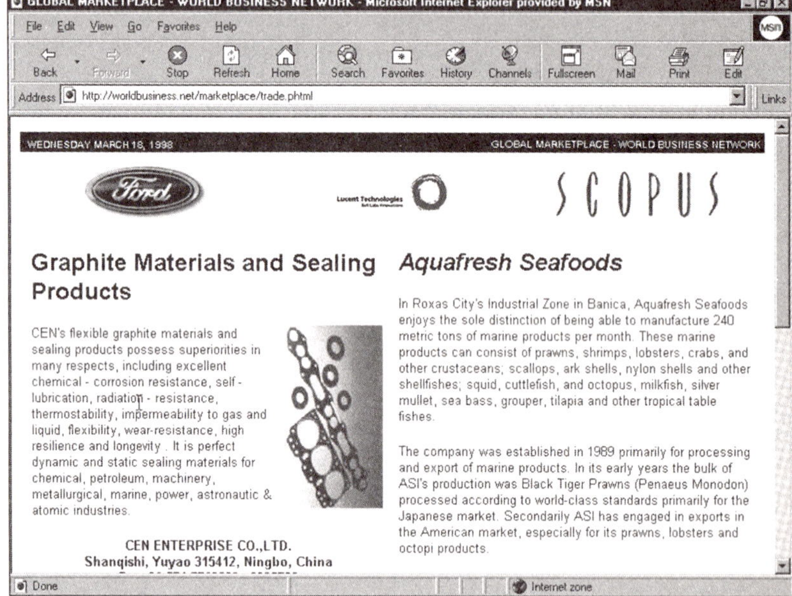

21. Click the Trade Leads This Month button.
    - ➲ *A page showing links to trade leads for March 1998 opens.*
22. Click the ATHLETIC SHOES link.
    - ➲ *Contact information and a description of the athletic shoes trade lead appears.*
    - ✓ *Note that other information on the page is advertising for the page's sponsors.*
23. Click the OLD TRADE LEADS link near the bottom of the page.

Trade Leads for the Current Month

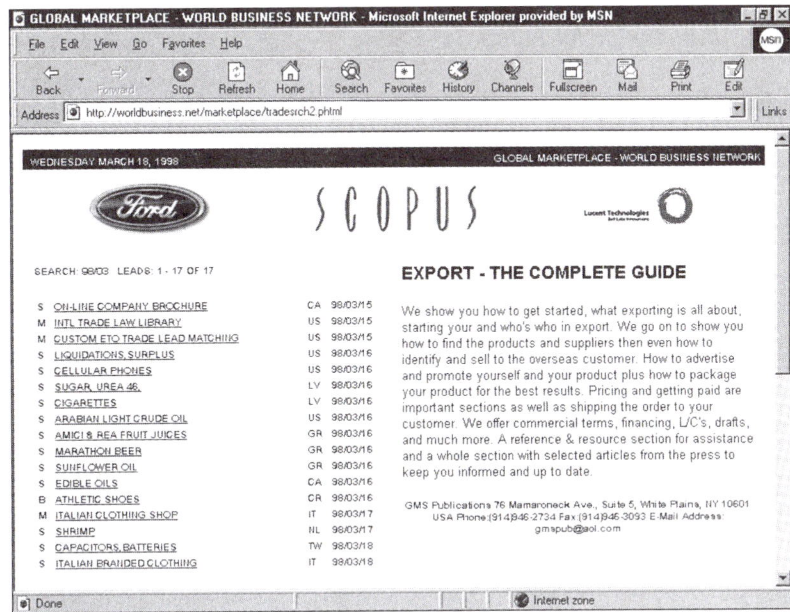

Trade Lead for Athletic Shoes

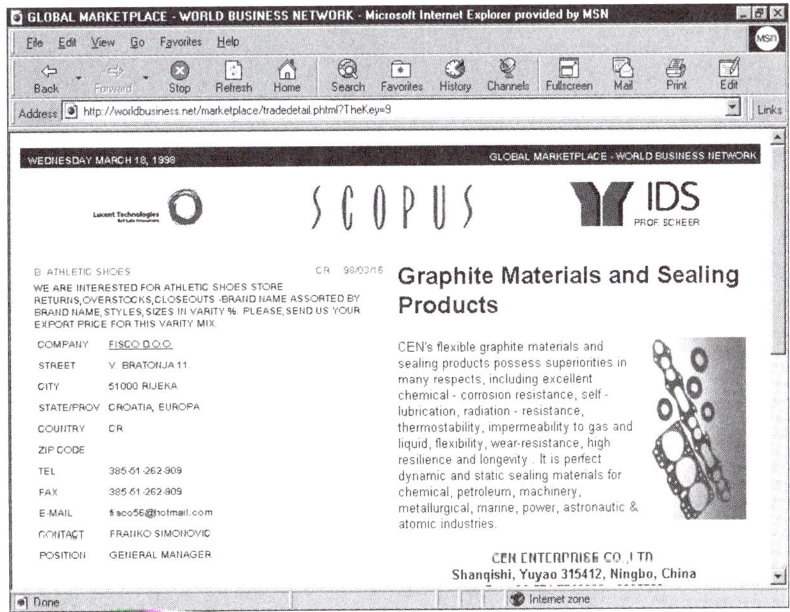

24. Click the FEB 98 link.

 ➲ *A page showing links to trade leads for February 1998 opens.*

 ✓ *Note that the date is shown in dd/mm/yy format at this Web site.*

25. Scroll down and read the various trade links, then click the INSTANT SOLUBLE COFFEE link.
26. Read the trade lead, then use your browser's Back menu to return to the **MSU-CIBER HOME PAGE**.
27. Click the International Business Resources On The WWW link and then scroll down and click the Various Utilities and Useful Information link.
28. Click the Travlang Site link.

 ➲ *The travlang home page opens.*

29. Click the travlang's Word of the Day link.

 ➲ *The Word of the Day page opens.*

30. Scroll down and read the translations for the word "stamps" in the various languages.

Travlang Home Page

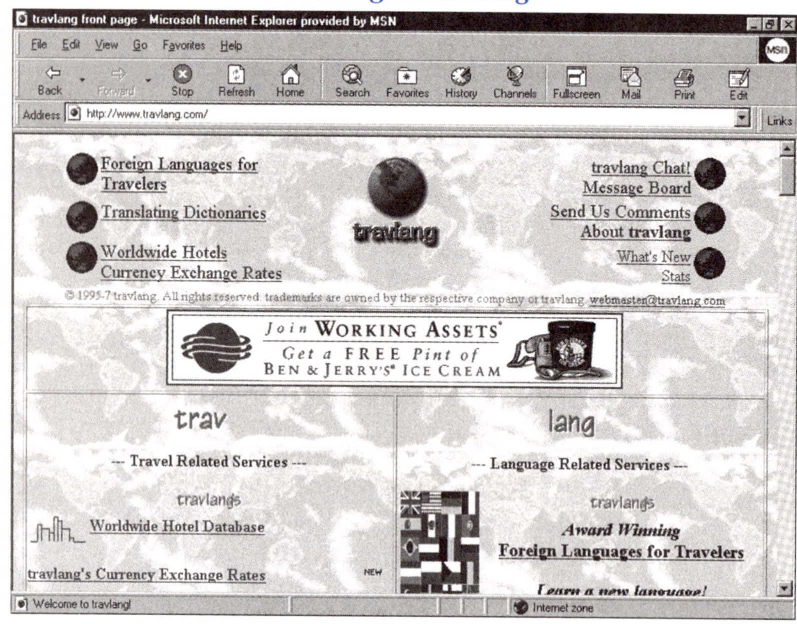

Travlang Word of the Day

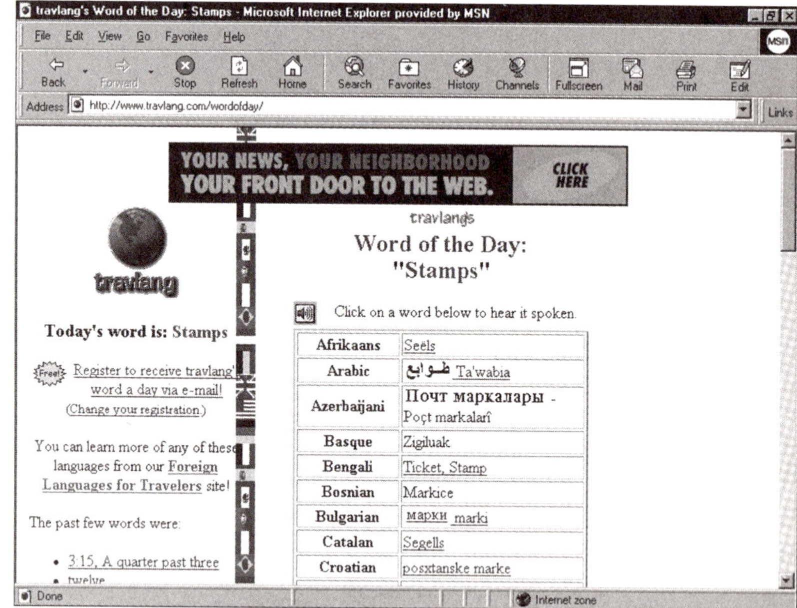

31. Click the travlang globe icon to return to the travlang home page.
32. Click the Translating Dictionaries link.
33. Scroll down and click the English→Czech Dictionary link.
    ➲ *The English-Czech On-line Dictionary page opens.*
34. Type the word *information* in the search text box, then click Submit.
    ➲ *The dictionary displays the results of its search for the Czech word for information.*
35. Continue on to the next exercise.

    OR

    Exit from the simulation.

English-Czech Dictionary

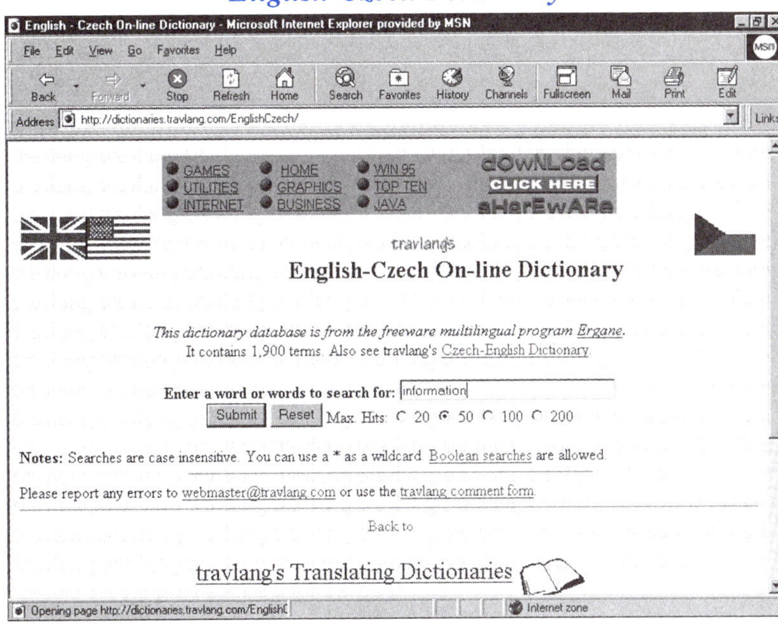

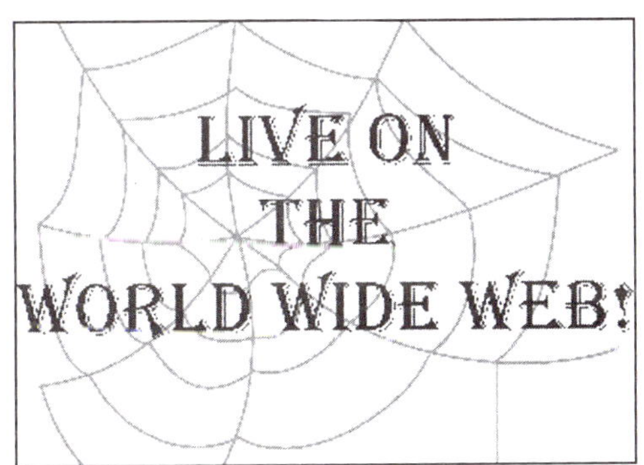

MSU-CIBER Home Page

http://ciber.bus.msu.edu/

Trade Information Center Home Page

http://www.ita.doc.gov/tic/

Global Marketplace—World Business Network Home Page

http://worldbusiness.net/marketplace/trade.phtml

Travlang Home Page

http://www.travlang.com/

NEXT LESSON

Lesson 8: Creating a Company Web Page

Exercise 1

- Use Word's Web Publishing Tools
- Design Your Web Site
- Word 97 Web Page Templates
- Create a Basic Home Page

Exercise 2

- Enter New Text in a Web Page
- Work with Tables
- View Table Borders
- Insert Table Rows or Columns

Exercise 3

- Character Formatting
- Change Text Colors
- Paragraph Formatting
- Online Layout View
- Web Page Preview
- Use Web Page Styles

Exercise 4

- Save a Document as a Web Page
- Create Bulleted Lists
- Create Numbered Lists

Exercise 5

- Create and Insert Hyperlinks
- Edit Hyperlinks

Exercise 6

- Copy Hyperlinks
- Paste as Hyperlink

Exercise 7

- Create a Web Page with the Blank Web Page Template
- Create a New Table
- Merge and Split Cells

Exercise 8

- Work with Horizontal Lines
- Add Colors to Tables
- Add Background Textures

Exercise 9

- Create a Feedback Form
- Work in Form Design Mode
- Add Controls to Forms
- Modify Controls and Control Properties

Exercise 10

- Insert Graphics Files
- Use the Clip Gallery
- Supply Alternate Text
- Exercise 11
- Add Marquees
- Add Animation

Exercise 12

- Insert Videos
- Add Background Sound

Exercise

1

■ Use Word's Web Publishing Tools
■ Design Your Web Site ■ Word 97 Web Page Templates
■ Create a Basic Home Page

NOTES

Use Word's Web Publishing Tools

- Microsoft Word 97 provides a full range of powerful Web page authoring features you can use to create professional, fully-functioning Web pages. Web publishing has in the past been a daunting technical task due to the HTML programming and network administration skills it required. However, Word 97 provides a wealth of easy-to-use tools, such as wizards and templates, that make Web publishing easy for anyone with basic word processing skills.

Note
Make sure all the Web publishing features of Word 97 are loaded on your system. See Appendix G, Troubleshooting, to learn how to check for and load these components.

Design Your Web Site

- Designing and creating a Web page is only one step in creating a successful Web site, and each page you create must be designed with the purpose, visual style, and content of the entire Web site in mind. Most Web sites consist of several Web pages connected by hyperlinks, which allow visitors to jump from one page to the next and back again as they choose.
- Typically, the first page visitors see when they view a Web site is the **home page**. The home page provides an introduction to the site with summaries of information included on other pages within the site and hyperlinks to the major Web pages within the site. Most of the Web pages within the site include hyperlinks back to the home page.
- You can design your Web site in one of two basic patterns. The site can be set up in a linear design similar to a book in which the home page serves as a table of contents with links to each of the individual Web pages. Each individual page has links to the home page and the pages immediately before and after it. For example, a visitor to a linear site might jump from the home page to Page 4. From Page 4, the visitor could then jump either to Page 3, to Page 5, or back to the home page.
- Because you can create hyperlinks to any page in your site or on the Internet, a more common Web site organization is a tree-like hierarchy. In this design, the home page has links to several main category pages, each of which in turn contains links to several subcategory pages.

Template
A Word document that includes pre-set formatting and styles.

Home Page
The starting point for a Web site. A home page acts as a table of contents for the Web site and includes links to the various related pages in the site.

Word 97 Web Page Templates

- Word 97's built-in Web page templates are a major advantage of using Word to build your Web pages. You can access Web page templates any time you open a new document in Word using the File, New command. Templates provide a basic layout, sample text, and in some cases simple instructions for creating the new document. Templates can be used to create many different types of regular Word documents or Web pages.

Web Pages Tab of the New Dialog Box

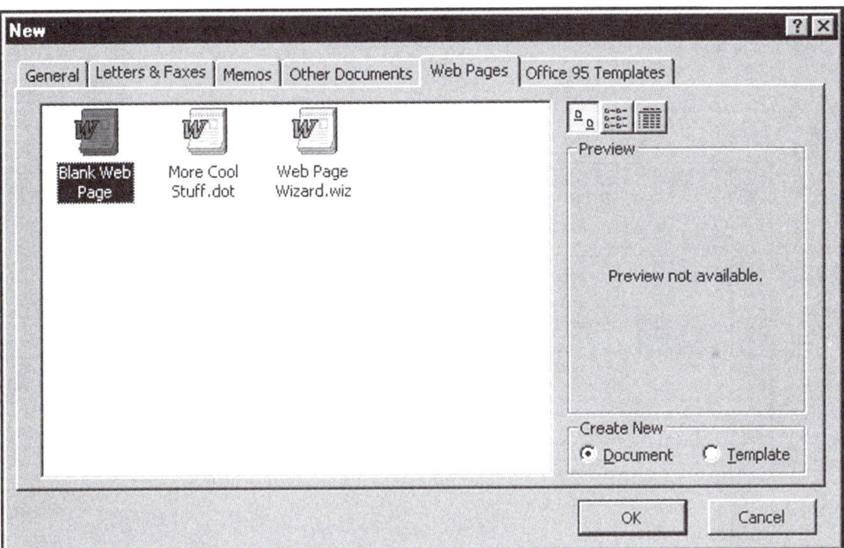

Create a Basic Home Page

- The easiest way to jump start your Web publishing effort is to create a basic home page using one of the Web page templates Word provides. Select the Web Page Wizard in the Web Pages tab of the New dialog box to have Word walk you through the steps of creating a first home page. The wizard will provide you with options for choosing the type of content and visual style of your page.
- After you create the basic Web page using the wizard, you can modify the content and design of the page to suit your specific needs. You will create several different types of Web pages using the wizard in the Exercises of this Lesson.

Web Page Wizard Dialog Box

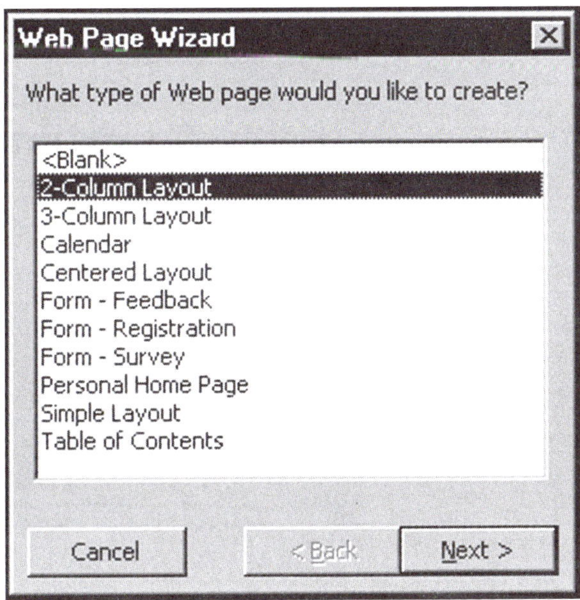

In this exercise, you will create a new HTML Web home page for Verity Books, a chain of bookstores, using the Word 97 Web Page Wizard. You will enter new text into the home page and save your work.

EXERCISE DIRECTIONS

1. Click Start on the Windows 95 Taskbar.
2. Click Programs.
3. Click Microsoft Word. Microsoft Word 97 starts.
4. Open a new Word document by selecting File, New. The New dialog box appears.
5. Click the Web Pages tab of the New dialog box to view Word's built-in Web page templates.

   ✓ *If a dialog box opens asking if you want to connect to the Internet, click No.*

6. Click the Web Page Wizard.wiz. Make sure the Document option is selected in the Create New group of the dialog box.

   ✓ *You should be able to view file name extensions in the dialog box. If not, open Windows Explorer, then select View, Options, then deselect Hide MS-DOS file extensions for file types that are registered.*

7. Click OK. The first dialog box of Word's Web Page Wizard appears. Notice the various types of Web page templates provided.
8. Select 2-Column Layout in the wizard's list box. Notice that a sample of the 2-Column Layout appears under the wizard dialog box.
9. Click Next>.

Click the Web Page Wizard in the New Dialog Box

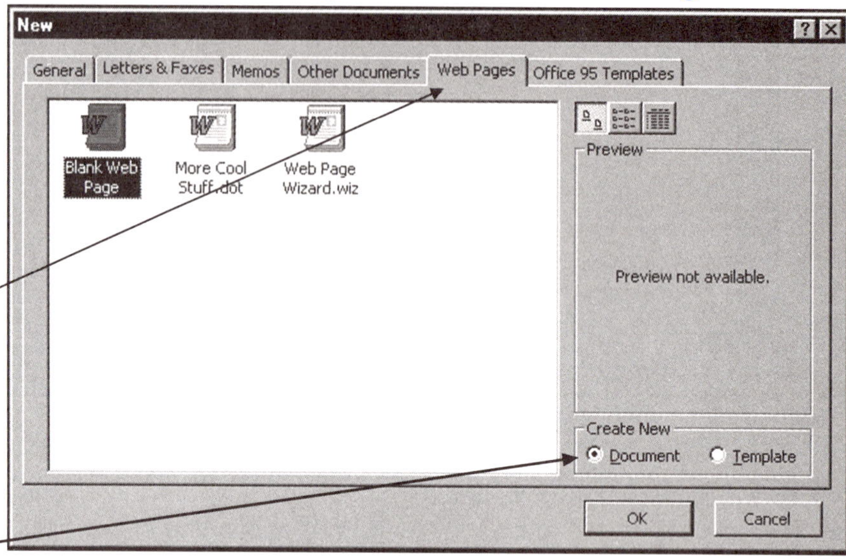

Web Page Wizard Dialog Box

10. The second dialog box of the Web Page Wizard appears. Notice the various visual styles from which you can choose.

    ✓ *To preview a visual style, select it and then wait for the selection to be applied.*

11. Select Elegant from the list box, if it's not already selected.

12. Click Finish to create your first Web page. If you want to change any of your selections in the wizard, you can return to a previous page using the <Back button before you click Finish.

Web Page Wizard Styles Dialog Box

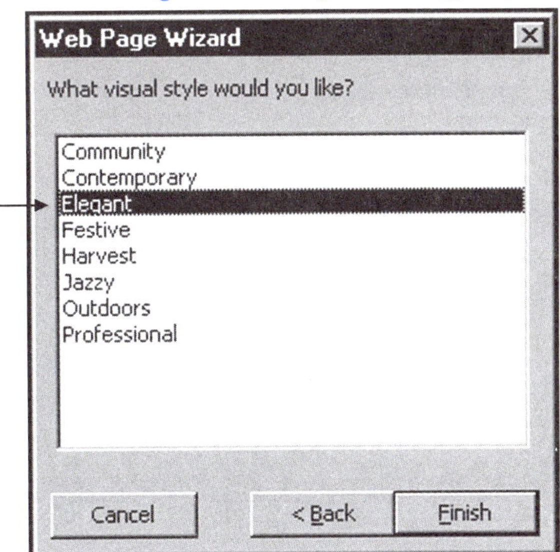

➲ *The new Web page document should look like the one shown here.*

New 2-Column Web Page

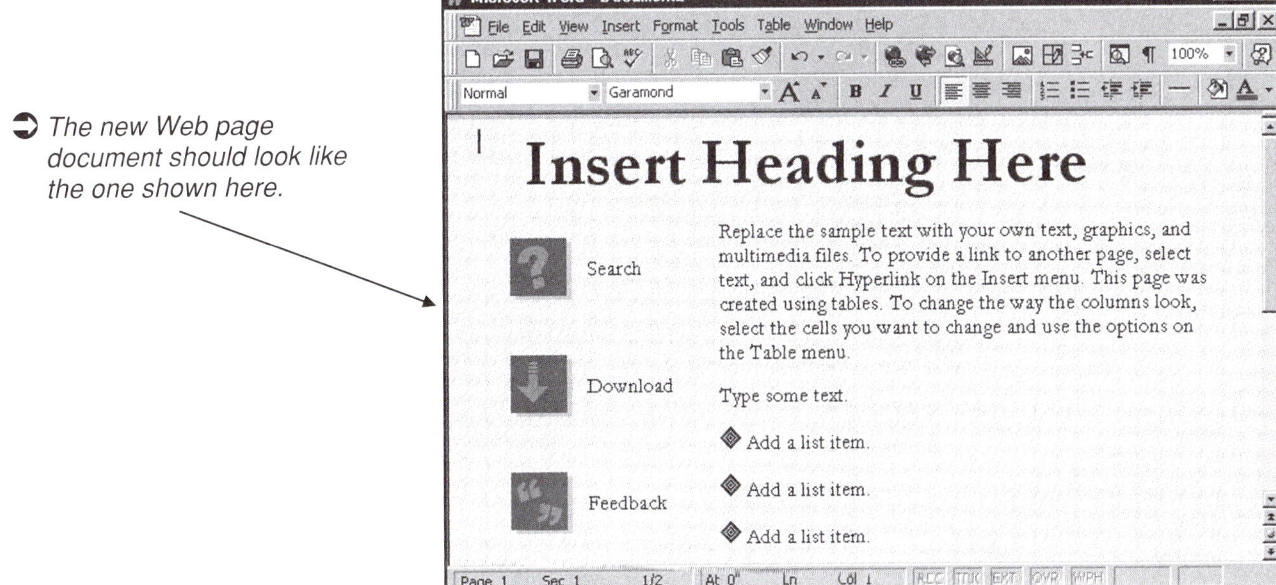

13. Now create a basic home page for Verity Books by clicking the text in the web page template and then entering the new text as shown in the Verity Books Home Page illustration below.

Verity Books Home Page

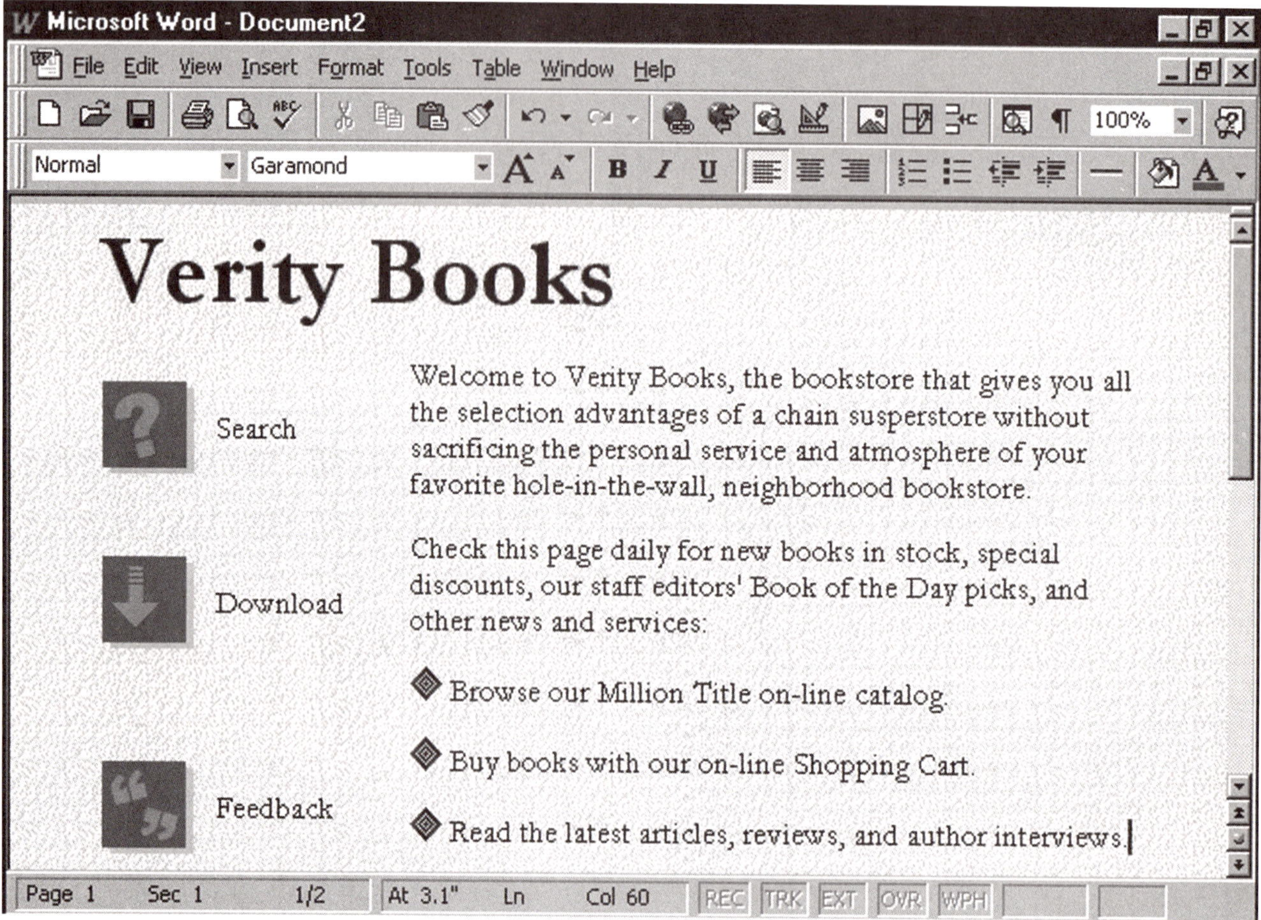

14. Select File, Save As to save your new Web page. The Save As dialog box opens.
15. Use the Save in drop-down list to find the appropriate location for a new folder you will now create. You will use this folder to store all the Web page files you create for the exercises in this book.

    ✓ *If necessary, consult your instructor or system administrator for the proper location.*

16. Click the button to create the new folder. In the New Folder dialog box, enter a file such as **CDKWEB** for this folder. Use **your own initials** + **WEB** for your Web site folder name.
17. Click OK.
18. Enter **VERITY.HTML** in the File name list box. Make sure HTML Document (*.html; *.htm; *.htx) appears in the Save as type list box.

    ✓ *If you are saving your files to a network drive, enter the extension .htm. Networks only allow three-letter extension names.*

19. Click Save.
20. Select File, Close to close the Web page.

Save As Dialog Box

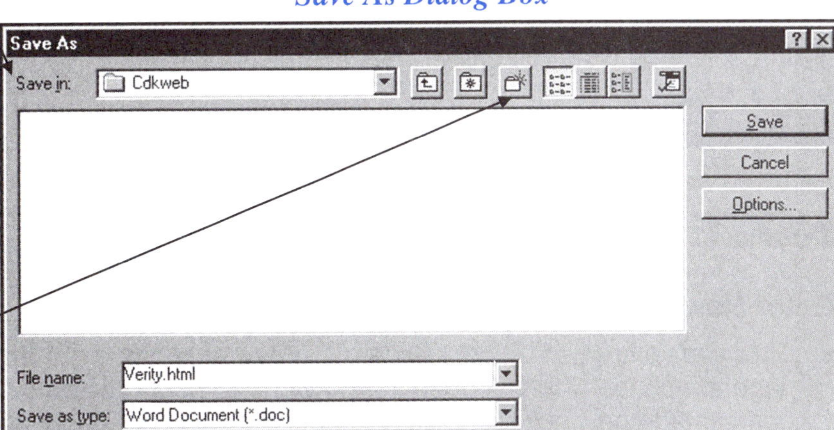

New Folder Dialog Box

Exercise 2

■ Enter New Text in a Web Page ■ Work with Tables ■ View Table Borders ■ Insert Table Rows or Columns

NOTES

Enter New Text in a Web Page

- After you've created a home page using one of Microsoft Word's Web page templates, you can open the HTML Web page document in Word again to add new text to the page. Select File, Open to view the Open dialog box, then select the appropriate drive and folder where the HTML file is located.

Open Dialog Box

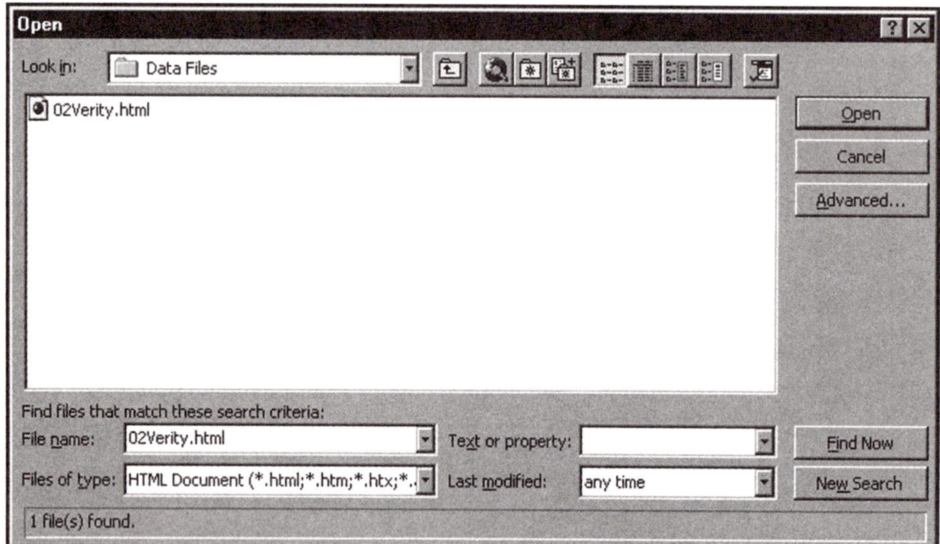

- Because you are opening an HTML document, Word displays a special interface designed to help you edit and format Web pages. Special features of this interface include menus, toolbars, and shortcut keys tailored to creating Web pages as well as formatting styles and macros suitable for working with HTML documents.
- After the Web page document is open, you can work with it in much the same way as a normal Word document. You can cut, copy, and paste text within the Web page as well as from other documents and even pages located on the Internet. To add new text, you simply position the insertion point where you want it and type.

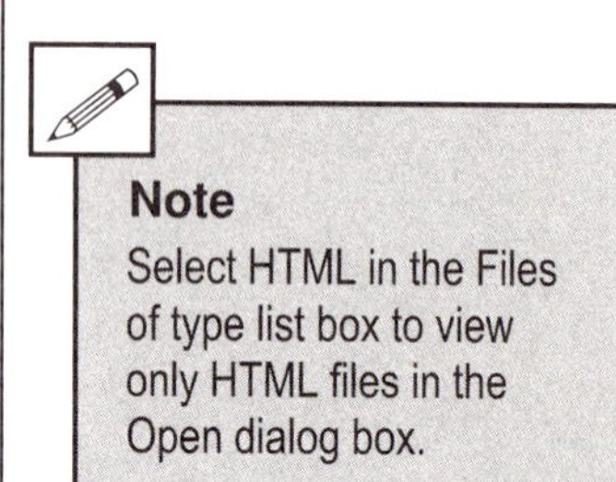

Note
Select HTML in the Files of type list box to view only HTML files in the Open dialog box.

- Note that some standard features, commands, and formats you find in working with a normal Word document are not available when you work with Web pages in Word. This is because HTML files cannot support or create all of Word's various formats and features. Conversely, Word does not support all of the features present in HTML. Therefore, it may be helpful to edit and format HTML documents created in an application other than Word with more advanced Web publishing software such as FrontPage 97.

Work with Tables

- Because of the formatting limitations in HTML documents, it is often necessary to use tables to create more complex and attractive Web page layouts. You can use tables to organize information into separate columns and areas on the page in which you place different text styles and graphics.

Note

The 2-Column template you used to create your first home page uses columns to organize the various elements on the page.

View Table Borders

- The cells, rows, and columns of a table are outlined by gridlines, which you can choose to view or hide by selecting Table, Borders and then selecting Grid in the Presets area of the Table Borders dialog box. The Table Borders dialog also lets you select the border width you want to display.

Insert Table Rows or Columns

- You can change the layout of a Web page table and add new text or graphics to the table by inserting table rows or columns. Select a position in the table where you want to insert a new row or column. Then select Table, Insert Rows to insert a new row above the insertion point. Select an entire column of the table (Table, Select Column) and then select Table, Insert Columns to insert a new column to the left of an existing column.

Note

You will learn more about creating a new table in a Web page in Exercise 7.

In this exercise, you will create and add new text to the Verity Books home page, view table borders, and insert a new table row in the home page to hold new text.

EXERCISE DIRECTIONS

1. Select File, Open. The Open dialog box appears.
2. Use the Look in list box to select the Web site folder you created in Exercise 1.
3. Select HTML Document (*.html; *.htm; *.htx) in the Files of type list box.
4. Type **VERITY.HTML** in the File name text box, then click Open.

   ✓ *If the Convert File dialog box opens at this point, click OK. See the Appendix G, Troubleshooting, if you don't want to view this dialog box each time you open an HTML file.*

5. Select the text "hole-in-the-wall" in the first paragraph of the document body. Delete this text and the comma that follows it.
6. Position the insertion point after the period at the end of the final bulleted point. Press enter to add another bullet, then add the following bulleted points to the list:
   - Sign up for our on-line contests and submit customer feedback or book reviews.
   - Check the Verity Books monthly Calendar of special events.
   - Check the menu and place a food order at one of our Verity Books Cafés nationwide.

Open Dialog Box

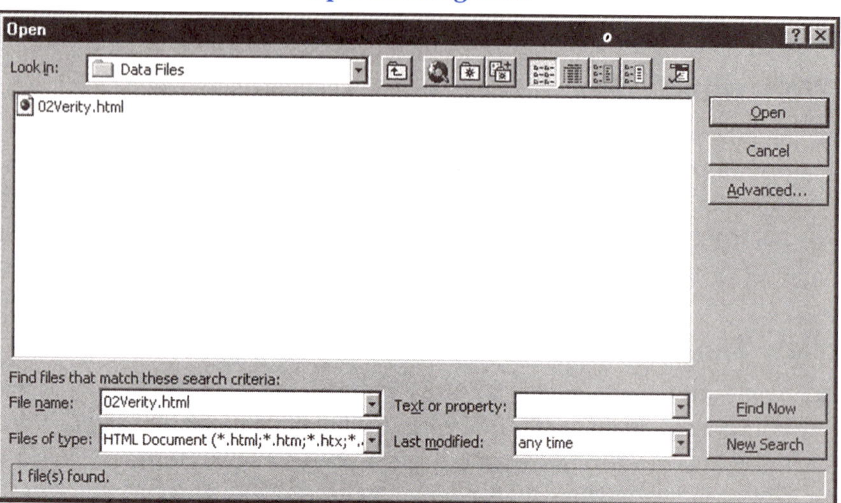

Add Bulleted Points to Home Page

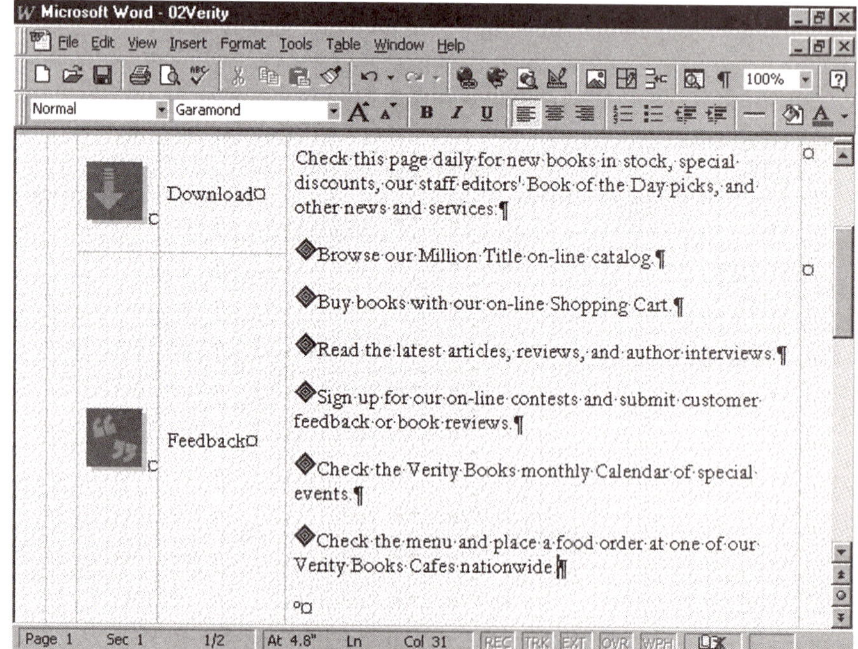

7. Select Table, Borders. The Table Borders dialog box opens.
8. Click Grid in the Presets section of the dialog, then click OK to close the Table Borders dialog box. Notice the gridlines for the table displayed in the document.
9. Move down the page and select the line between the bulleted list and the Related Pages.

Table Borders Dialog Box

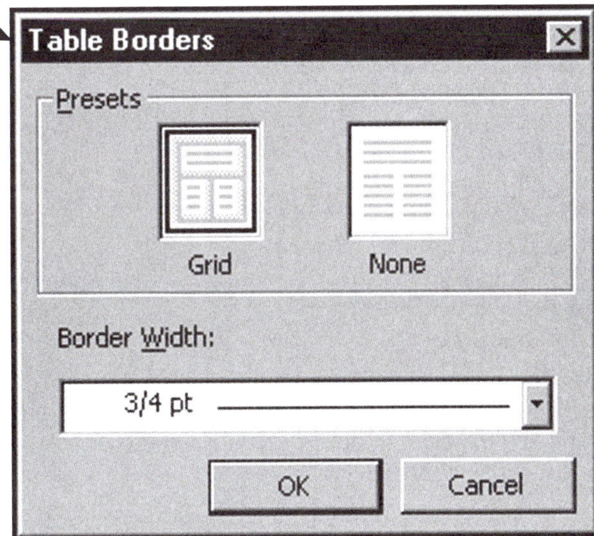

10. Select Table, Insert Cells. The Insert Cells dialog box opens. Select Insert entire row and click OK.

   ➲ *Word inserts a new row above the row containing the line. The cursor should be in the new row ready for you to enter text.*

Insert Cells Dialog Box

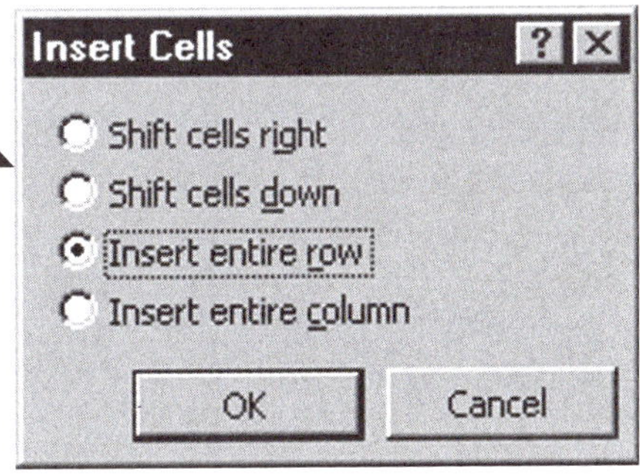

11. Insert the following text into the new row:

    Page Turners

    Here's the latest information on books and authors in the news: Nancy Davolio's new thriller has Dirk Luchte, her famous hard-boiled gumshoe, convicted of a crime he didn't commit and sent to a prison camp in another country... Read The Atlantic Journal's review of My Family, a biographical novel about the exploits of three generations of the illustrious Leverling family.

12. Change the text next to the square icons in the left column of the Web page as follows. Note the position for the text in the figure at right:

    Search the Million Title Catalog

    Buy Books

    Send Us Feedback & Reviews

13. Select Table, Borders and click None in the Table Borders dialog box. Click OK. When finished, your home page should look like the one shown in the figures at right.

14. Save your work to **VERITY.HTML** in your Web site folder, then close the document.

Verity Books Home Page with New Text

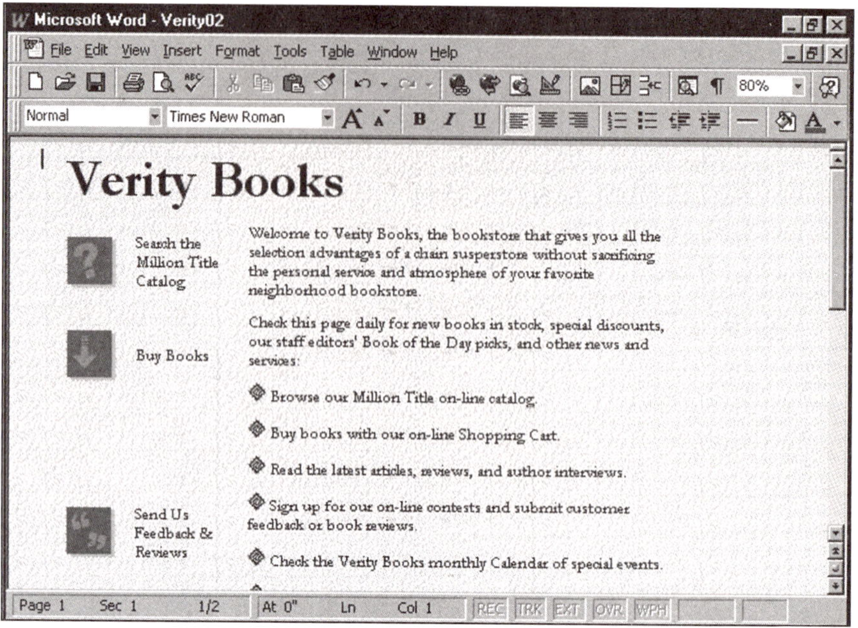

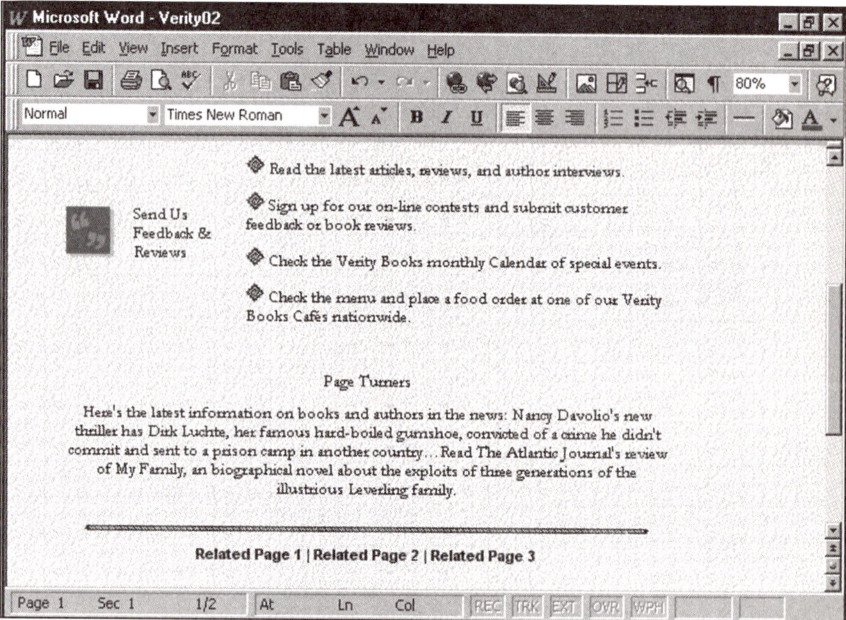

NEXT EXERCISE

Exercise 3

- Character Formatting
- Change Text Colors
- Paragraph Formatting
- Online Layout View
- Web Page Preview
- Use Web Page Styles

Formatting Toolbar

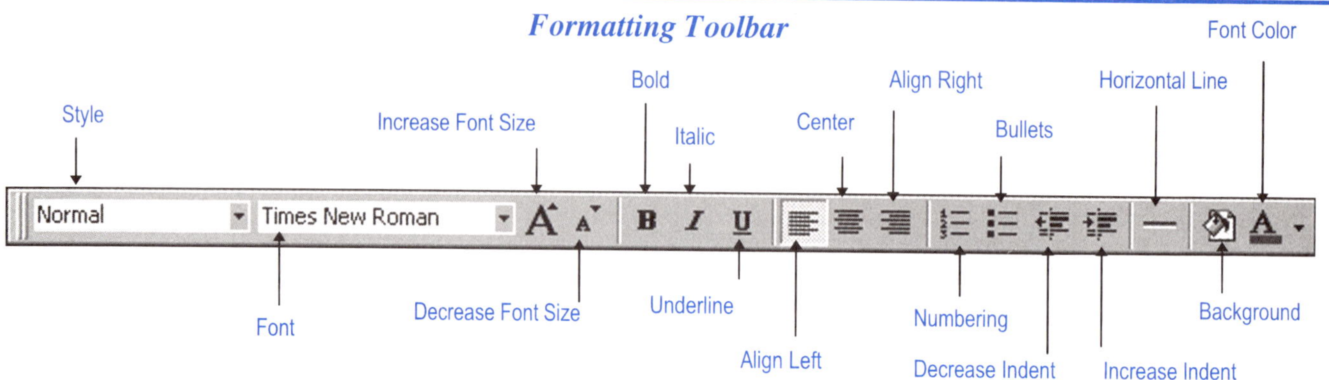

NOTES

Character Formatting

- Word's basic Web page templates are a good place to start building your Web site, but they can go only so far towards creating a customized look and feel for your Web site. After you've created a Web page using a template and added the basic text for your page, you can enhance the page with character formatting.
- Character formatting enables you to add emphasis to various elements on the page and provide a distinctive look and feel for the page that visitors will recognize and remember.
- You can use most of Word's standard character formatting features to format text on your Web pages. You can quickly add emphasis to text by selecting the text and clicking the B or I buttons on the Formatting toolbar. Avoid formatting text as underlined, because hypertext links are typically formatted using underline and a second color.
- You can also change the font and size of text to vary the appearance of the page. Use the Font drop-down list box to quickly select a new font. Use the A and A buttons on Word's special Web Formatting toolbar to quickly change font size.

Note

Once you have created a particular visual style for your Web page, you should strive to maintain a similar style across all the pages of your Web site. This serves as a visual reminder for visitors to your site that they are still looking at your pages.

Change Text Colors

- In addition to changing text fonts, size, and emphasis, you can add color to headings and text that will increase the visual interest in your page. You can select text and apply color by clicking the A button on the Web Formatting toolbar. A palette of sixteen colors appears for you to choose from when you click the arrow next to the button, or simply click the button to add the color currently displayed.

- Select Format, Text Colors to view the Text Colors dialog box. Here you can choose default colors for body text, hyperlinks, and followed hyperlinks.

Note

Remember to follow a consistent and restrained color scheme throughout the pages in your Web site to maintain an attractive, recognizable look for your site.

Paragraph Formatting

- Word enables you to employ paragraph formatting to change the alignment of your text elements. You can click the , , or buttons to change text alignment quickly. You can also press Ctrl+L to left align, Ctrl+E to center, and Ctrl+R to right align text. By default, paragraphs are not indented. You can increase indents by clicking the button. Decrease indents by clicking the button.
- The HTML standard is designed so that browser software will format your Web page in the best way for each viewers computer and operating environment. Because of this, many other paragraph formatting features are not available to you as you create Web pages in Word. This is why it is best to create complex Web page layouts using tables.

Online Layout View

- Due to the differences between HTML and Word, Word provides a special view called Online Layout view, which is the default view for working with Web pages. If Online Layout view is not on, select View, Online Layout. Use this view when changing text and paragraph formatting because it provides a **WYSIWYG** editing environment, showing what your page will look like when viewed on a Web browser.

WYSIWYG

An acronym for "What You See Is What You Get."

Web Page Preview

- Another way to check the appearance of your Web page is to view the finished product by selecting File, Web Page Preview. The browser software installed on your system automatically starts and opens your Web page for viewing. You must have browser software installed on your system to use Web Page Preview.

Use Web Page Styles

- Another way to apply character and paragraph formatting to your Web page is to use predefined styles. Word styles quickly apply a set of predefined formats to a block of text. For example, you can easily format a line of text as Heading 3 to apply an appropriate typeface, font size, character enhancements and other features rather than setting each of these formats individually. You can modify preset styles or create your own custom styles.
- To apply a style, select the text you want to format, then select a style from the drop-down list at the far left of the Web Formatting toolbar. You can also press Ctrl+Shift+S to access the styles list.

Styles Drop-Down List

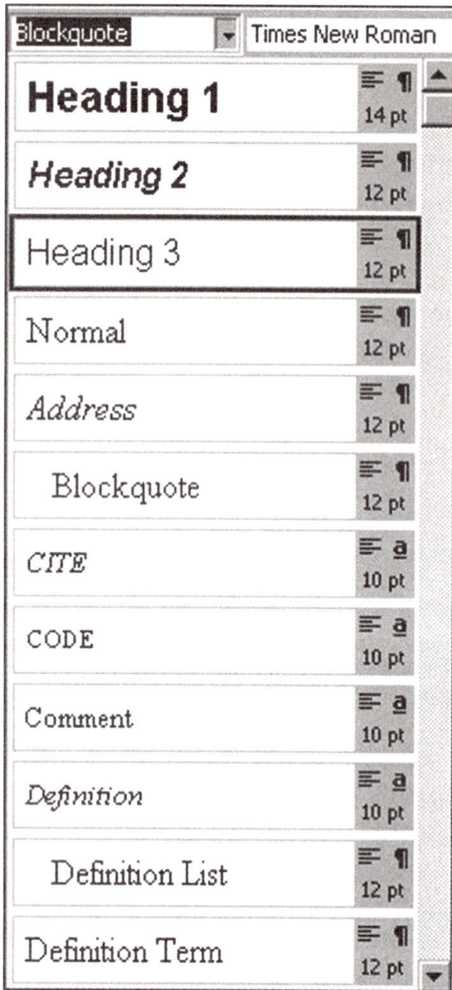

- When you apply Word's standard styles to Web page text, the HTML file created for the page will not record the style, only the individual formatting characteristics applied to the text.
- Word also includes a set of special Web Page Styles that do not apply specific formatting characteristics to text. Instead, these styles label the general purpose of the text and allow the individual Web browsers to interpret the actual formatting as they read the page.
- For example, applying the H1 Web Page Style will display the text as a rather generic-looking heading in Word. A person viewing the page over the Web using Internet Explorer will then see the heading as Explorer chooses to display a first-level heading. All headings marked as H1 will be displayed consistently by Explorer.
- The advantage of using Web Page Styles is that it enables the browser software to display your pages in the best way possible for viewing on a visitor's particular system.

CAUTION

Remember that the appearance of your Web page will vary when viewed using different browser software, so try to view your pages using as many different browsers as possible, and especially the two most widely used browsers, Microsoft Internet Explorer and Netscape Navigator, before publishing to the World Wide Web.

Note

You give up some degree of specific control over your site's appearance using Web Page Styles but ensure that your pages are displayed in the best way for everyone who visits your site.

In this exercise, you will add character and paragraph formatting to the Verity Books home page, change text colors, view the results using Web Page Preview, then format the page using Web Page Styles.

EXERCISE DIRECTIONS

1. In Word, Select File, Open to open **VERITY.HTML** from your Web site folder.
2. Select the Verity Books heading.
3. Click the arrow to the right of the font drop down list box on the Formatting toolbar, then scroll up and click on Copperplate Gothic Light, if available; otherwise, select any appropriate serif font. The heading font changes.
4. Select the six text items in the bulleted list then press Ctrl+B to format the text as bold.
5. Select the Page Turners heading and change the font to Copperplate Gothic Light, if available; otherwise, select any appropriate serif font.
6. Click the A button three times to increase the Page Turners heading's font size. Then, with the heading still selected, press Ctrl+I to change the heading to italic.
7. Select the heading text next to each of the graphic icons and change the font for this text to Impact, if available; otherwise, select any appropriate sans serif font.
8. Select the body text under the Page Turners heading and click [align left button] to change the text alignment to flush left. Press Ctrl+R to change the alignment to flush right, then press Ctrl+E to change it back to centered.
9. Change the following text in the Page Turners section to italic:
   - Dirk Luchte
   - The Atlantic Journal's
   - My Family

Font Drop-Down List

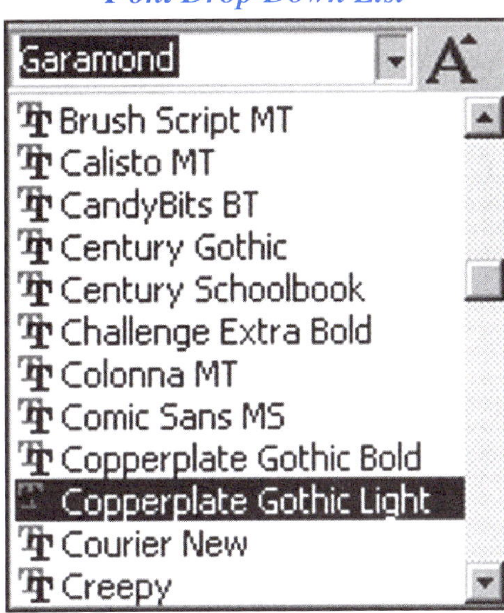

10. Select Format, Text Colors. The Text Colors dialog box opens.

    ✓ *These changes to the default colors will not be visible until Exercise 6, where you add hyperlinks to the home page.*

11. Change the Hyperlink color to Teal and change the Followed hyperlink color to Dark Red. Click OK.

12. Select the home page heading Verity Books. Click the A scroll arrow to display the font color palette, then click the Dark Blue color, the second from the right on the top row of the palette.

13. Select the Page Turners heading and use the font color palette to change its color to Dark Blue.

14. Use the font color palette to change the color of the headings next to the icons in the left column of the home page to Red.

15. Save your work to **VERITY.HTML** in your Web site folder. Keep the file open.

16. Select File, Web Page Preview to view the revised home page as it appears in a Web browser. The illustrations at right show the page as it appears in Internet Explorer.

17. Select File, Close to close your browser and return to viewing the home page in Microsoft Word. Commands for closing Web browsers may vary.

18. Create a new file by saving the **VERITY.HTML** Web page as **WEB.HTML** in your Web site folder (File, Save As).

19. Select the Verity Books heading and press Ctrl+Shift+S. Use the Up and Down arrows on your keyboard to find and select the H1 Web page style from the drop-down list of HTML compatible styles, then press Enter.

20. Format the Page Turners heading with the H2 Web page style.

21. Format the headings next to the icons in the left column with the H3 Web page style.

Text Colors Dialog Box

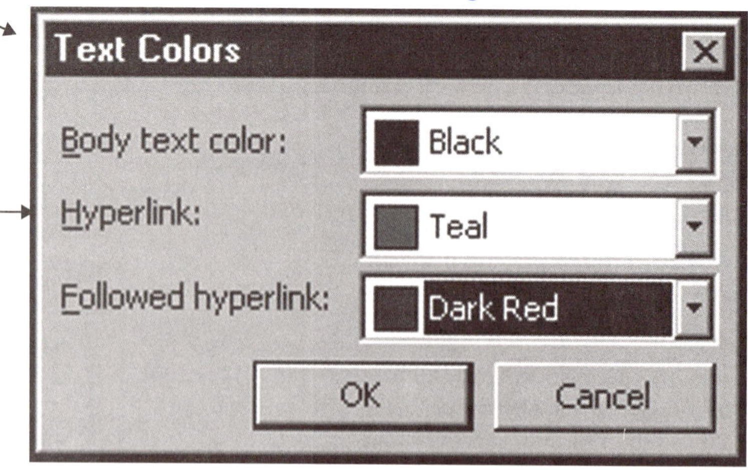

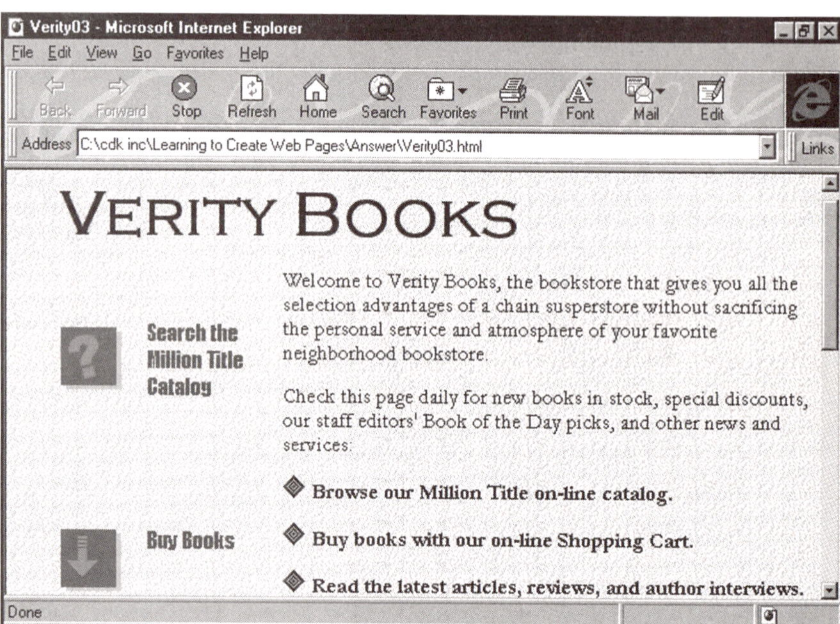

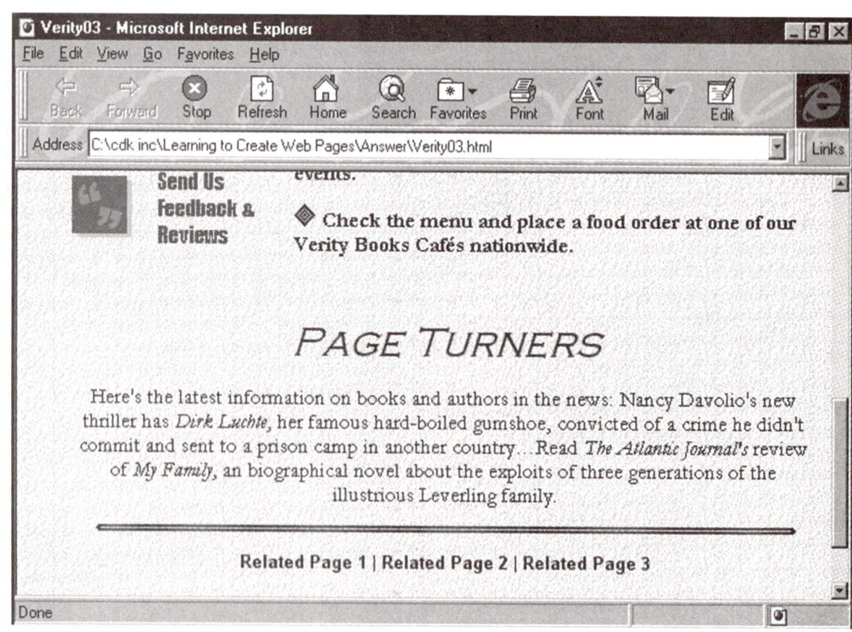

22. Format the book and magazine titles in the Page Turners body text with the Emphasis Web page style.
23. Format the bulleted list text with the Strong Web page style.
24. View the changes to the home page in a Web browser using Web Page Preview. Note the difference in formatting as shown in the illustration at right.

   ✓ *Click Yes if you are asked to save changes before opening the file in a browser.*

25. Close your browser to exit Web Page Preview.
26. In Word, save your changes to **WEB.HTML** and close the file.

Home Page with Web Page Styles in Internet Explorer

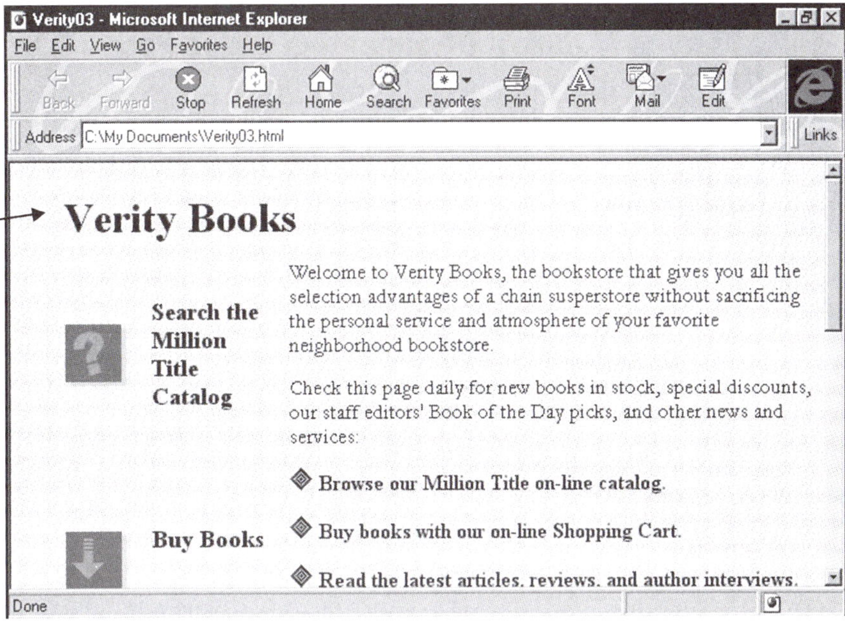

Exercise 4

■ Save a Document as a Web Page ■ Create Bulleted Lists
■ Create Numbered Lists

NOTES

Save a Document as a Web Page

- In addition to creating Web pages using Word's Web page templates, you can save an existing Word document as a Web page using the Save as HTML feature. Simply open the document you want to save as a Web page, then select File, Save as HTML.
- The Save as HTML dialog box is very similar to the normal Save As dialog box, providing text boxes and drop-down lists in which you can choose the location where the file will be saved, the file name, and the type of file, which should display HTML Document (*.html; *.htm; *.htx).

Save as HTML Dialog Box

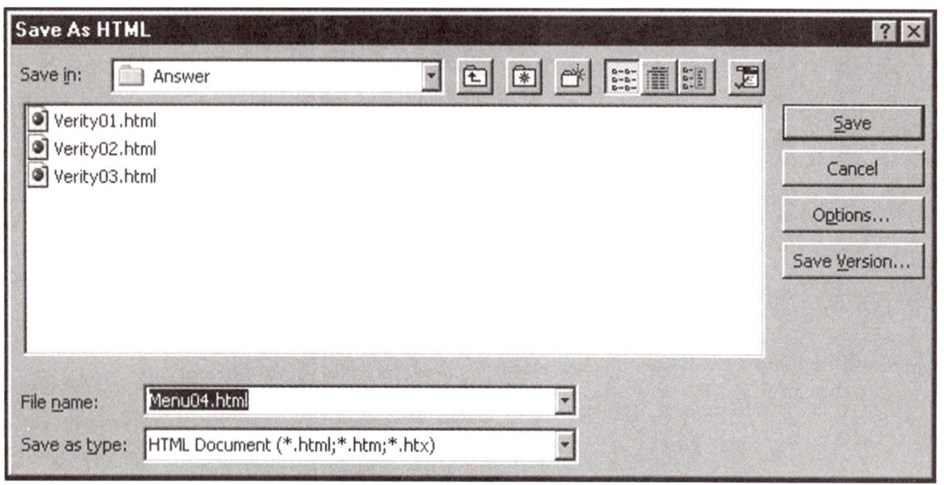

- After you have entered the desired file name and selected the drive, folder, and file type, click Save. The document is converted to an HTML Web page and appears on screen with Word's Web page features active.
- Standard Word features not supported by HTML will either be discarded or converted to the closest feature that is supported by HTML. Review the new Web page document carefully after conversion and be prepared to make formatting changes and/or insert text or graphics that have been lost.

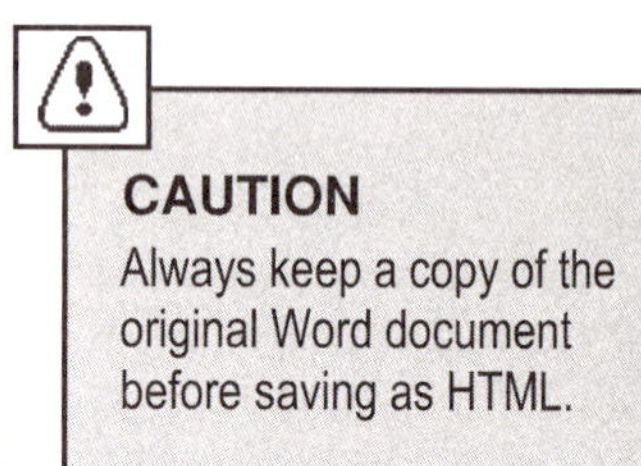

CAUTION

Always keep a copy of the original Word document before saving as HTML.

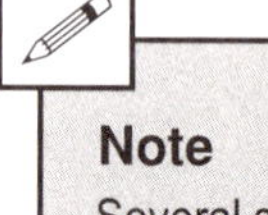

Note

Several standard Word features are not supported by HTML, including WordArt, AutoShapes, and text boxes.

Create Bulleted Lists

- Each item in a bulleted list begins with a dot or other graphic symbol to separate the items in the list and make them easier to read. Bulleted lists are common elements of Web pages. Select the text or list you want to format as a bulleted list, then select Format, Bullets and Numbering to open the Bullets and Numbering dialog box.

Bullets and Numbering Dialog Box

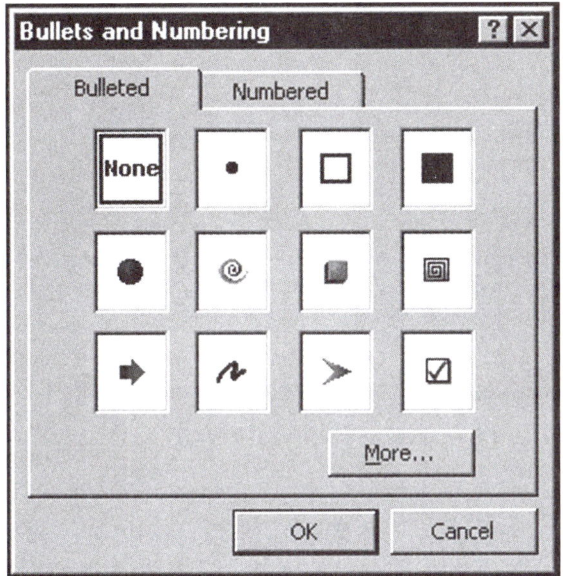

- From the Bulleted tab, click the bullet style you want to use, then click OK. If you want to view other bullet styles or use a graphic image of your own, click the More button. The Insert Picture dialog box enables you to select a graphics file to use as a bullet.
- You can also create a bulleted list by clicking the button on the Web Formatting toolbar. Word will use the default bullet, a black dot, or will automatically use the bullet style you last selected from the Bullets and Numbering dialog box, if you have selected a different style from the default.

Note

By default, the Insert Picture dialog box opens to the Bullets folder in the Microsoft Office directory, which contains a number of graphics from which you can choose.

Create Numbered Lists

- You can create a numbered list by selecting the Numbered tab of the Bullets and Numbering dialog box and then clicking the numbering style you desire. You can resume a previous numbered list of the same style by selecting Continue previous list in the Bullets and Numbering dialog box.
- To quickly create a numbered list using the default style or the preceding style you selected, click the button.

Numbered Tab of the Bullets and Numbering Dialog Box

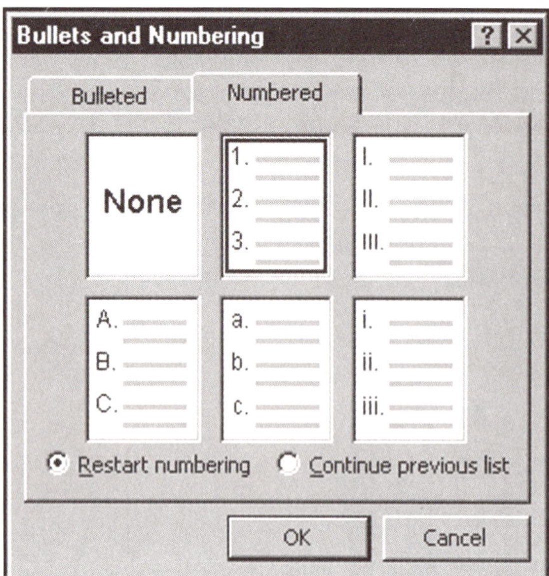

- You can make the numbered list a multi-level list, like an outline, by increasing the indentation of a given set of items in the list using the  button.
- Press Enter twice at the end of a numbered or bulleted list to stop the list formatting and create a normal paragraph. Remove a *standard* bullet or number from an item by selecting the text item, opening the appropriate tab of the Bullets and Numbering dialog box, selecting None, and clicking OK. You must select and delete *graphic* bullets individually.

Note

You cannot create a Web page numbered list using different numbering styles in succeeding levels of a numbered list (Roman numerals and then Arabic numerals, for example).

As the person in charge of creating and managing the Verity Books Web page, you have been asked to create a Web page for the Verity Books Café menu using a standard Microsoft Word document. You will save the document as an HTML Web page and format the menu items using bulleted and numbered lists.

EXERCISE DIRECTIONS

1. In Word, open **04MENU.DOC** from the folder containing the data files for this book.
   ✓ *If necessary, ask your instructor for the location of the data files folder.*
2. Select File, Save as HTML. The Save as HTML dialog box opens.
3. Select your Web site folder from the Save in drop-down list box.
4. Enter the file name **MENU.HTML** in the File name text box.
5. Make sure the Save as type text box says HTML Document, then click Save. Word saves the document as a Web page and displays it with the Web page toolbars.
6. Select the Verity Books Café heading and change the font to Copperplate Gothic Light, if available, or to the heading font that you used in Exercise 3. Format the heading as bold and increase the font size by clicking the A button three times.
7. Format the word Menu as Copperplate Gothic Light, Bold, if available. Format the text Week of June 23, 1997 as Copperplate Gothic Light, if available. If Copperplate Gothic Light is not available, use the heading font you used in Exercise 3.
8. Format the headings such as Soups and Salads in the rest of the menu as Copperplate Gothic Light, Bold, if available, or use the same font as you used in Exercise 3. Delete any extra line spaces between the heads and between the menu items.

Save as HTML Dialog Box

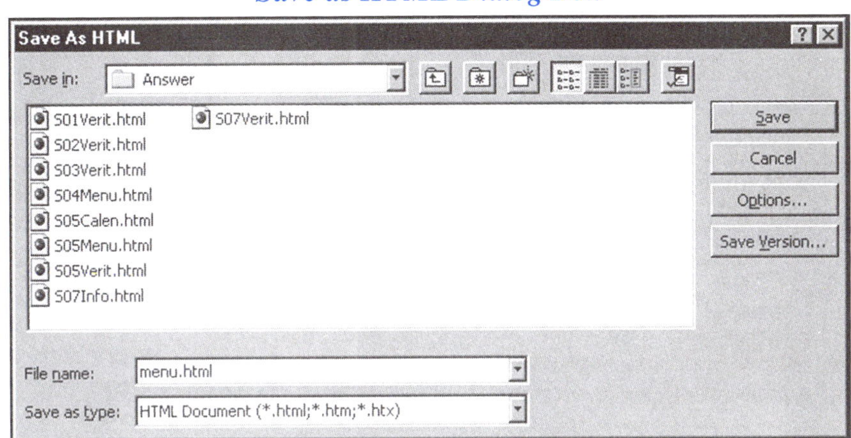

Menu Saved as HTML and Formatted

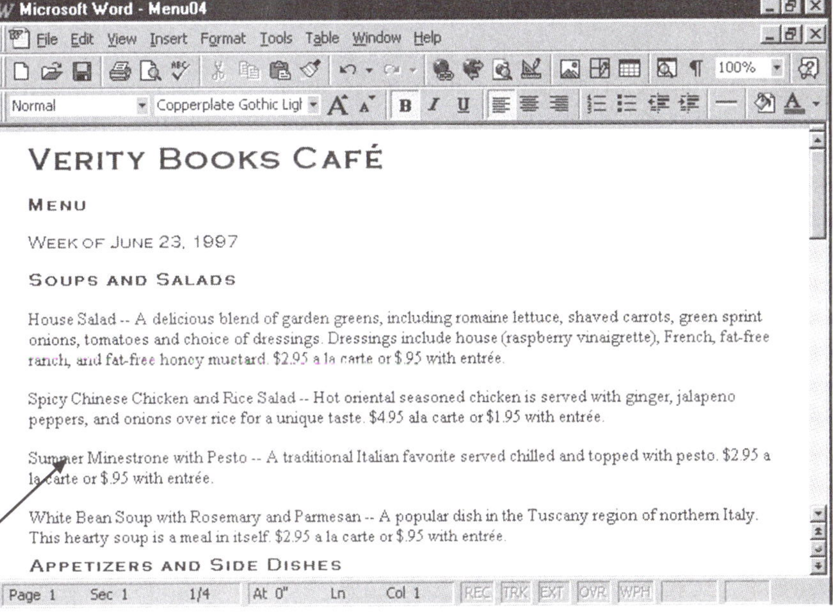

9. Correct text alignment as needed.
10. Select the menu items in the Soups and Salads section, then select Format, Bullets and Numbering. The Bullets and Numbering dialog box appears.
11. Click the More button, then select GREEN AND BLACK **DIAMOND.GIF** from the Insert Picture dialog box that appears.
12. Click [Insert]. The menu items are formatted as a bulleted list. The black and green diamonds appear as bullets.
13. Format the Appetizers and Side Dishes menu items as a bulleted list using the green square bullet.
14. Format the Entrees menu items as a bulleted list using the black squiggle bullet.
15. Format the names of all dishes in the menu's bulleted lists in bold. Adjust the spacing between bullet list items as needed. Your Web page should look like the one shown in the illustration at right.

Bullets and Numbering Dialog Box

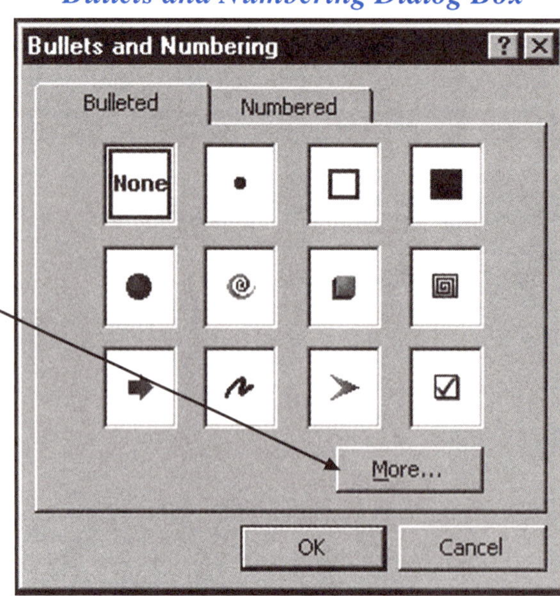

Web Page Menu with Bulleted Lists

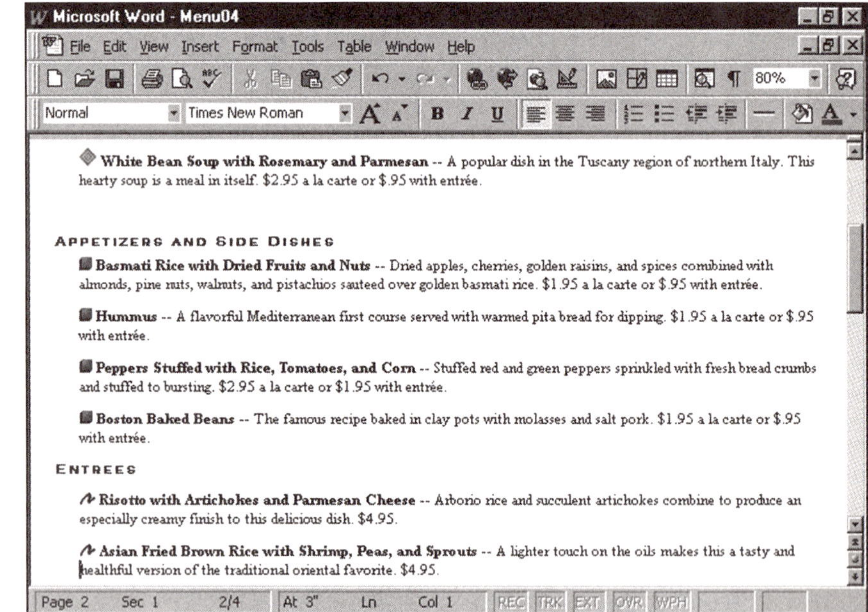

16. Select the Weekly Specials menu items, then select Format, Bullets and Numbering.
17. Select the Numbered tab of the Bullets and Numbering dialog box and click the Arabic numerals sample.
18. Click OK. The menu items are formatted as a numbered list, as shown in the illustration at right.
19. Save your work to **MENU.HTML** in your Web site folder.
20. Preview **MENU.HTML** in your browser.
21. Close your browser and then close the Web page in Word.

Web Page Menu with Numbered List

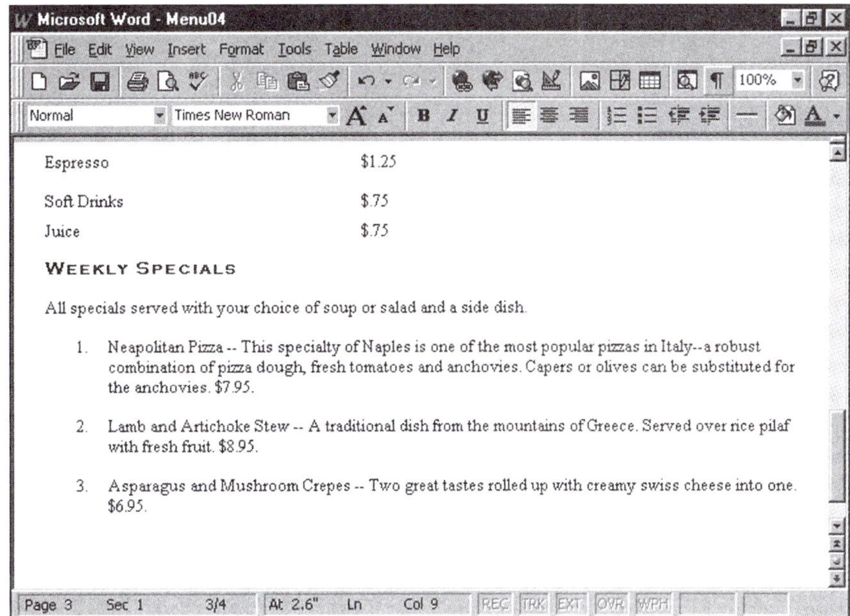

Exercise 5

■ Create and Insert Hyperlinks ■ Edit Hyperlinks

NOTES

Create and Insert Hyperlinks

- Now that you have built a couple of Web pages, you can begin creating a Web site by adding hyperlinks to the Web pages. Hyperlinks are specially formatted blocks of text, graphics, or other objects that you click to move to another document or a different location in the same document.
- Select Insert, Hyperlink to open the Insert Hyperlink dialog box. You can also click the button on the Standard toolbar or press Ctrl+K to open the dialog box.
- Once the Insert Hyperlink dialog box is open, you can click the Browse button to open the Link to File dialog box and select the file you wish to link (see illustration on next page). You can also simply type the address of the **target document** in the Link to file or URL text box.

Insert Hyperlink Dialog Box

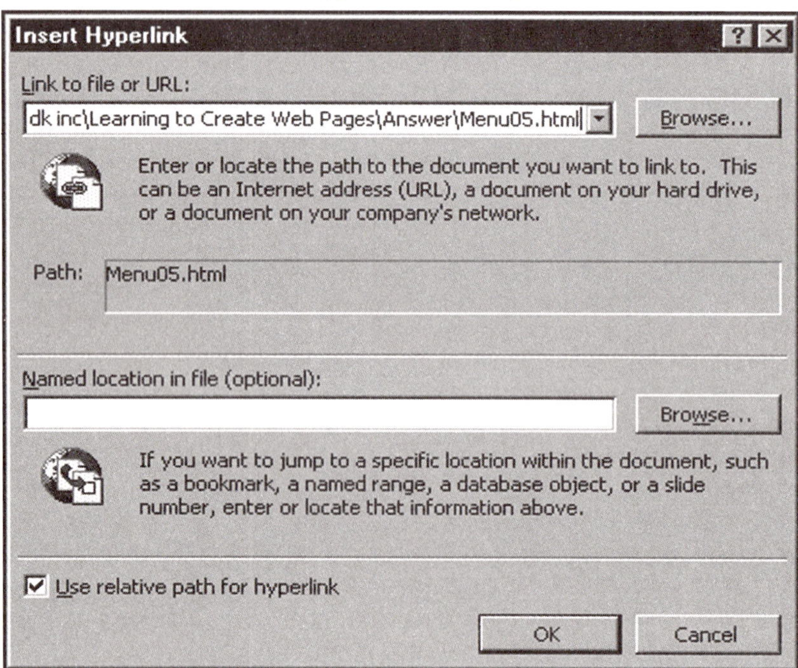

- You must specify either the full file path, the full path for documents on a network disk, or the full URL of an Internet document. (See next page for examples of each.)
- You may also enter a partial file path in the Link to file or URL text box if the target document is located on the same disk as the document that

contains the hyperlink. However, if you enter a partial file path, you must select the Use relative path for hyperlink option.

Link to File Dialog Box

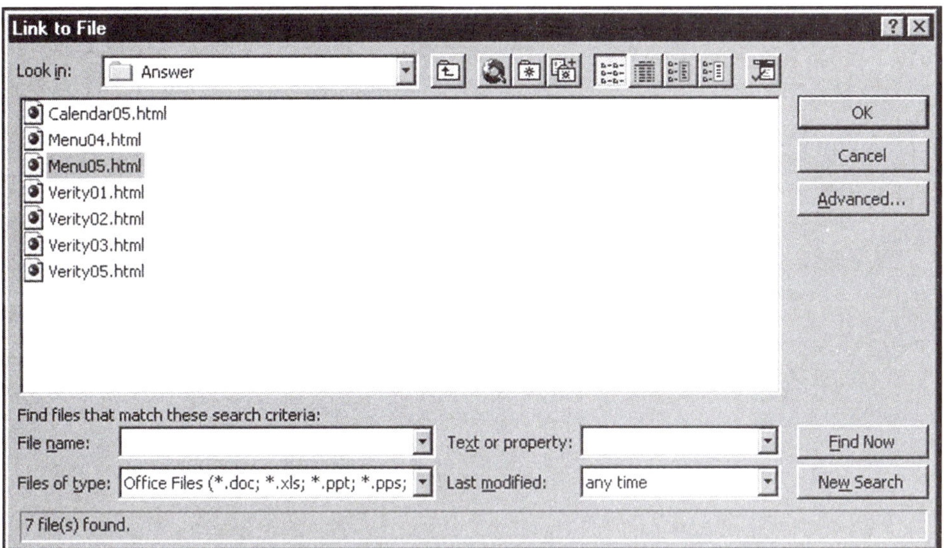

- Following are examples of each method of specifying a file location.
  - Full File Path:
    c:\My Documents\Verity Books\Verity05.html
  - Network Path:
    \\verity\c\webpages\verity.html
  - Full URL:
    http://www.verity.com/default.html
  - Partial File Path:
    Verity05.html
- When you create a Web site in Word 97, you should store all the files for your site in the same folder and use relative file links. That way, if you need to move the folder containing the Web site files, you can easily do so and keep all the site's hyperlinks intact.
- You can also indicate a specific location within the target document in the Named location in file text box.

Note

Entering the partial file path at left would open VERITY05.HTML from within the same folder as the document in which the hyperlink is being inserted.

Relative link

A hyperlink that still works as long as the relative locations of the target document and source document remain the same.

Edit Hyperlinks

- After creating a link, you can change the text or formatting of the link by right-clicking the link. Click Hyperlink on the pop-up menu that appears and then click Select Hyperlink. After the link is selected, type the new text you want or make any formatting changes you desire.
- Right-click a hyperlink and select Hyperlink, Edit Hyperlink from the pop-up menu to remove the hyperlink or make changes to the definition of the hyperlink.

In this exercise, you will create hyperlinks among several Web pages to build a basic Web site for Verity Books.

EXERCISE DIRECTIONS

1. Open **VERITY.HTML** and **MENU.HTML** from your Web site folder.
2. Open **05CALEND.HTML** from the folder containing the data files for this book.
3. Save **05CALEND.HTML** as **CALENDAR.HTML** in your Web site folder.
4. In **VERITY.HTML**, the Verity Books home page, capitalize the word "menu" in the final item of the bulleted list. Select the word "MENU."
5. Select Insert, Hyperlink. The Insert Hyperlink dialog box opens.
6. Click Browse... to locate **MENU.HTML** in your Web site folder.
   - ➲ *The Link to File dialog box appears as shown at the top of the next page.*

Insert Hyperlink Dialog Box

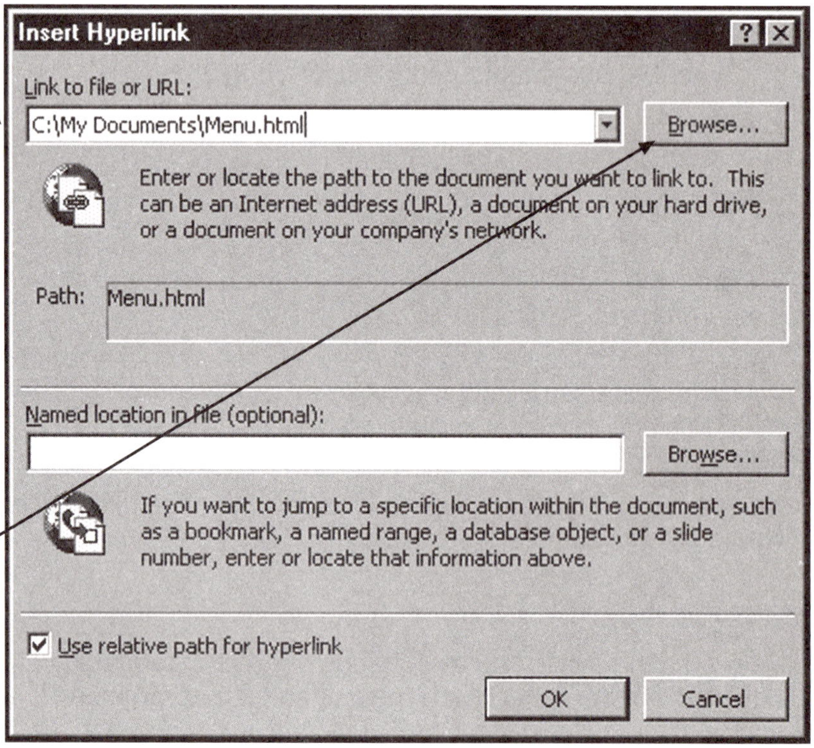

7. Use the Look in drop-down list box to select your Web site folder. Click on **MENU.HTML**, then click OK.

   ➲ *The file name and path appears in the Link to file or URL text box of the Insert Hyperlink dialog box, as shown on the preceding page. Because **MENU.HTML** is in the same folder as **VERITY.HTML**, the file name alone appears in the Path box.*

Link to File Dialog Box

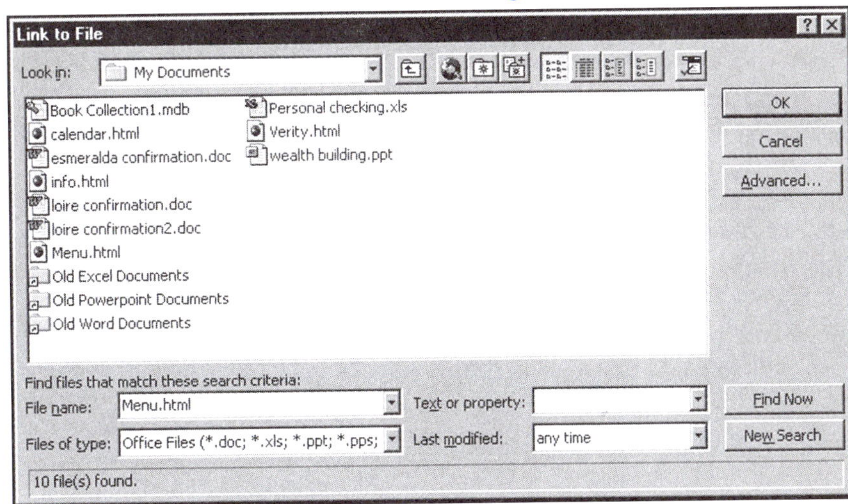

8. Make sure the Use relative path for hyperlink option is checked, then click OK. The word Menu appears in **VERITY.HTML** formatted as a hyperlink.
9. Select Format, Text Colors and change the Hyperlink color to Blue. This makes the link more visible against the page's background.

Text Colors Dialog Box

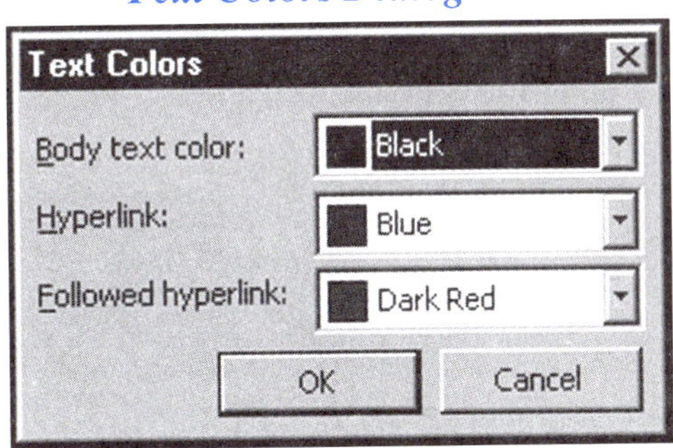

10. Now select the word Calendar in the preceding bulleted text item. Click the insert hyperlink button, to change this word to a hyperlink to the Verity Books Calendar page.
11. Select **CALENDAR.HTML** in the Link to file or URL text box.

    Hint: Click Browse to select the file in the Link to File dialog box. Make sure you are creating a relative link to the file located in your Web site folder.
12. Click OK. The word Calendar appears in **VERITY.HTML** as a hyperlink.
13. Click the word Calendar. The **CALENDAR.HTML** Web page appears.
14. Select the words "Related Page 1" at the bottom of the page. Press Ctrl+K.
15. The Insert Hyperlink dialog box opens. Create a link to **VERITY.HTML** (located in your Web site folder).

Home Page with Hyperlinks

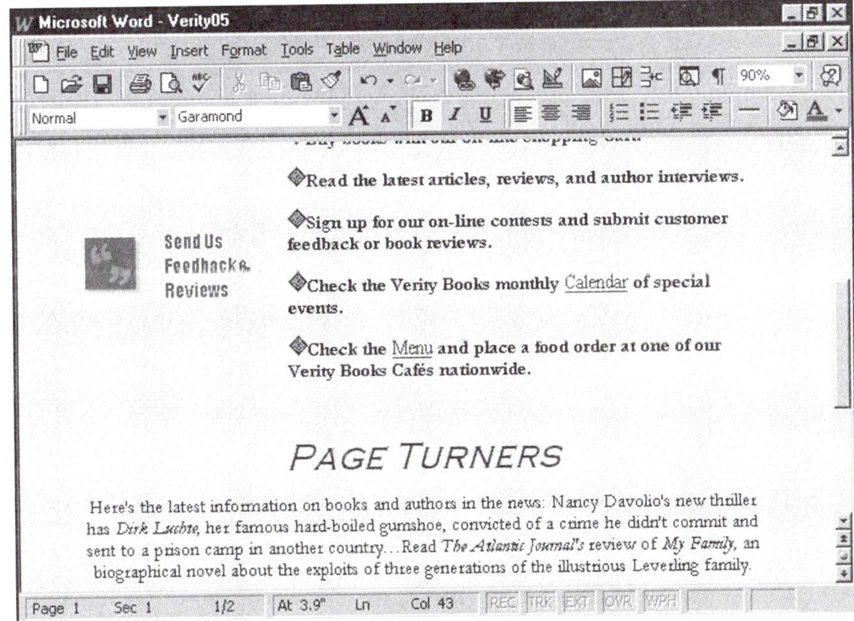

16. Right-click the new hyperlink, then select Hyperlink from the pop-up menu that appears. Click Select Hyperlink from the submenu that appears.
17. With the hyperlink selected, type Verity Books Home Page. Click elsewhere on the Calendar page to deselect the edited hyperlink.
18. Select "Related Page 2" and create a hyperlink to **MENU.HTML** (located in your Web site folder). Edit the new hyperlink to read Verity Books Café Menu.
19. Go to **MENU.HTML** using the hyperlink.
20. Move to the bottom of the Menu page and insert a hyperlink to **VERITY.HTML** (located in your Web site folder). Edit the hyperlink text to read Verity Books Home Page.
21. Start a new line and insert another hyperlink, this one to **CALENDAR.HTML** (located in your Web site folder). Edit the hyperlink text to read Calendar of Events.
22. In Word, save your work in each file.
23. Preview the Web pages in your browser.
24. Close your browser and close each file in Word.

Calendar Web Page with Hyperlinks

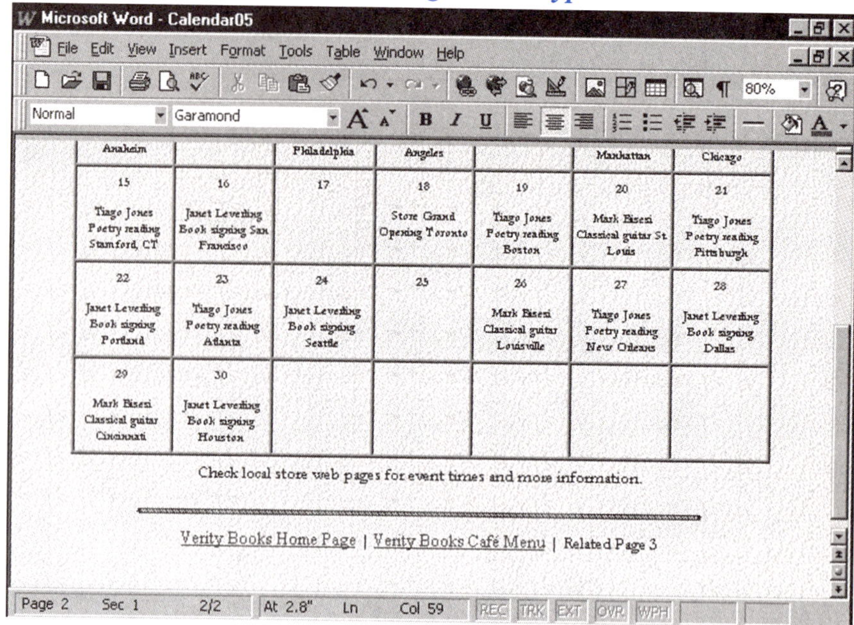

Menu Web Page with Hyperlinks

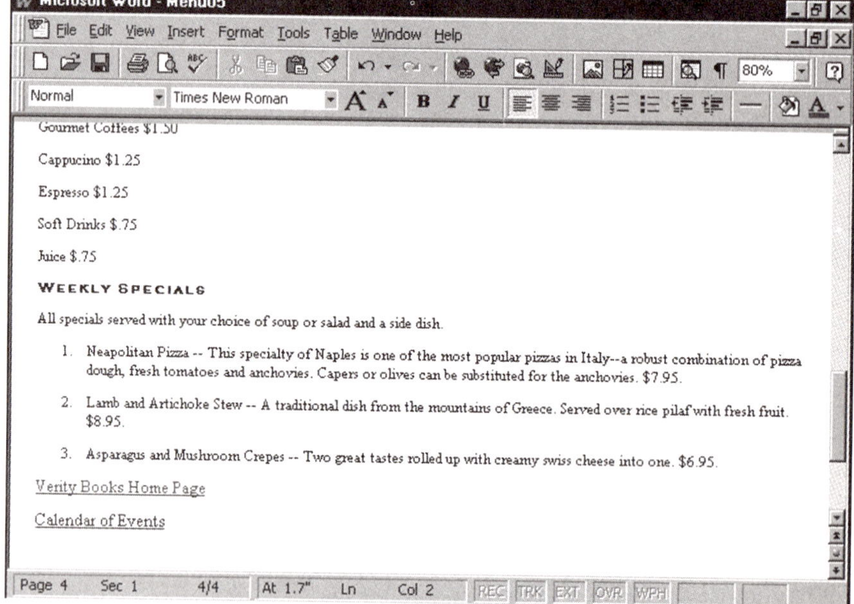

NEXT EXERCISE

Exercise 6

■ Copy Hyperlinks ■ Paste as Hyperlink

NOTES

Copy Hyperlinks

- After you have created a hyperlink to another document, you can copy and paste the hyperlink using special commands. Right-click the hyperlink you want to copy, then select Hyperlink, Copy Hyperlink from the pop-up menus.

Copy a Hyperlink with the Pop-Up Menu

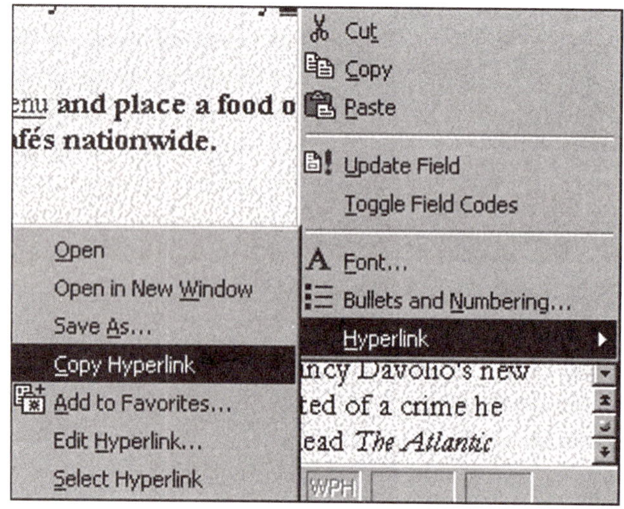

- Next, position the cursor at the point where you want a copy of the hyperlink to appear. Select Edit, Paste as Hyperlink. A copy of the hyperlink is pasted into the document at the new position.
- You can also copy a hyperlink by selecting the link and then using Word's standard copy and paste tools. Position the cursor on the link you want to copy, then right-click and select Hyperlink, Select Hyperlink. Next, select Edit, Copy or press Ctrl+C. You can also click to copy the link.
- Position the cursor where you want the copy of the hyperlink to appear, and select Edit, Paste or press Ctrl+V. You can also click to paste the link.

Paste as Hyperlink

- Note that the Paste and Paste as Hyperlink commands can be used interchangeably when pasting a hyperlink you have copied. However, the Paste as Hyperlink command is also useful in creating new hyperlinks.

Note

The hyperlink is copied to the Clipboard. The original hyperlink remains in place.

- Select the block of text, graphic, or object you want to be the *target* of the hyperlink and copy it. Then, position the cursor in the location for the new hyperlink you want to create. Select Edit, Paste as Hyperlink. The copied text, graphic, or object appears in the new location formatted as a hyperlink back to the original text, graphic, or object.

In this exercise, you will copy two hyperlinks on the Verity Books home page using various methods.

EXERCISE DIRECTIONS

1. Open **VERITY.HTML** from your Web site folder.
2. Right-click on the Calendar hyperlink in the bulleted list. A pop-up menu appears.
3. Select Hyperlink, Copy Hyperlink.
4. Select the text "Related Page 1" at the bottom of the web page.
5. Select Edit, Paste as Hyperlink. The new hyperlink appears.
6. Click the new hyperlink to test it.
7. Return to **VERITY.HTML** by clicking the Back button on the toolbar.
8. Right-click on the Menu hyperlink in the bulleted list.
9. Click Hyperlink, Select Hyperlink. The Menu hyperlink is selected.
10. Press Ctrl+C.
11. Select the text "Related Page 2" at the bottom of the web page.
12. Press Ctrl+V. The new Menu hyperlink appears, as shown in the illustration at right.
13. Click the new hyperlink to test it.
14. Return to **VERITY.HTML**.
15. Save your work and close all open files.

Copy a Hyperlink with the Pop-Up Menu

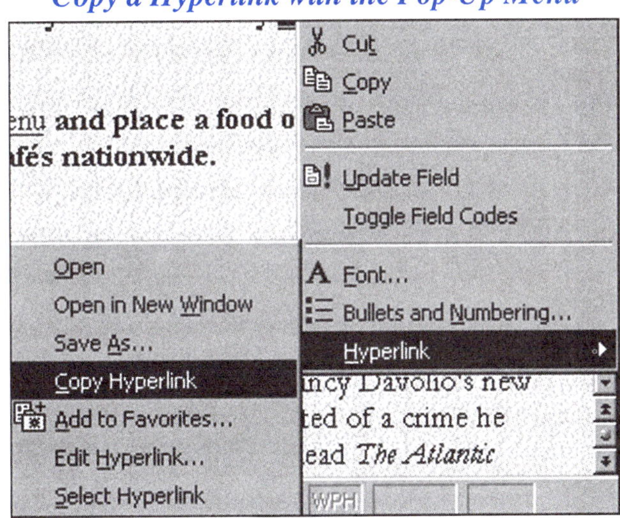

Home Page with Copied Hyperlinks

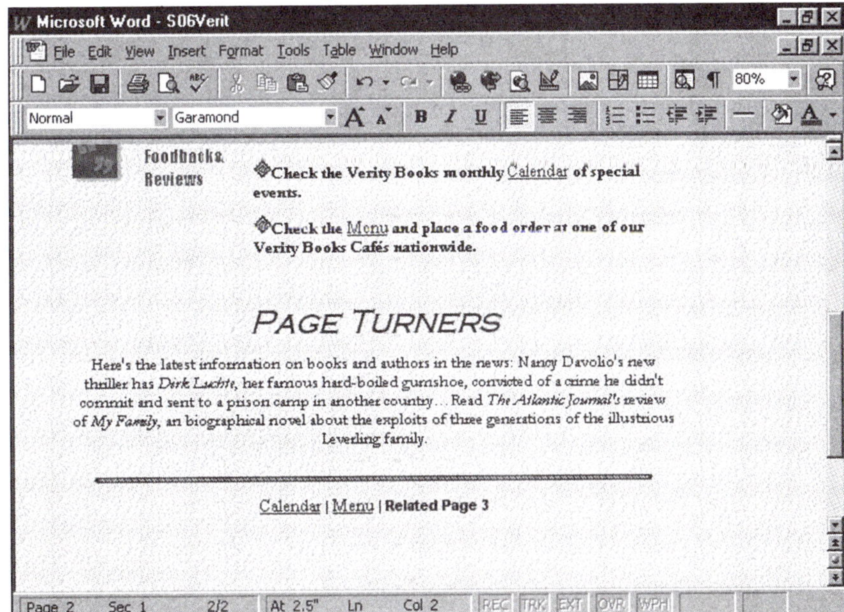

Exercise 7

- Create a Web Page with the Blank Web Page Template
- Create a New Table
- Merge and Split Cells

NOTES

Create a Web Page with the Blank Web Page Template

- There may be occasions when you want to create a new Web page that doesn't fit the mold provided by the available Web Page Wizard templates. In such cases, you can simply choose Word's Blank Web Page template by selecting File, New.
- In the New dialog box, select the Web Pages tab, click the Blank Web Page template, then click OK. Select the Document option if you want to open the new Web page as a document, or select Template if you want the new Web page to serve as a template upon which other documents are based.

Create a Blank Web Page

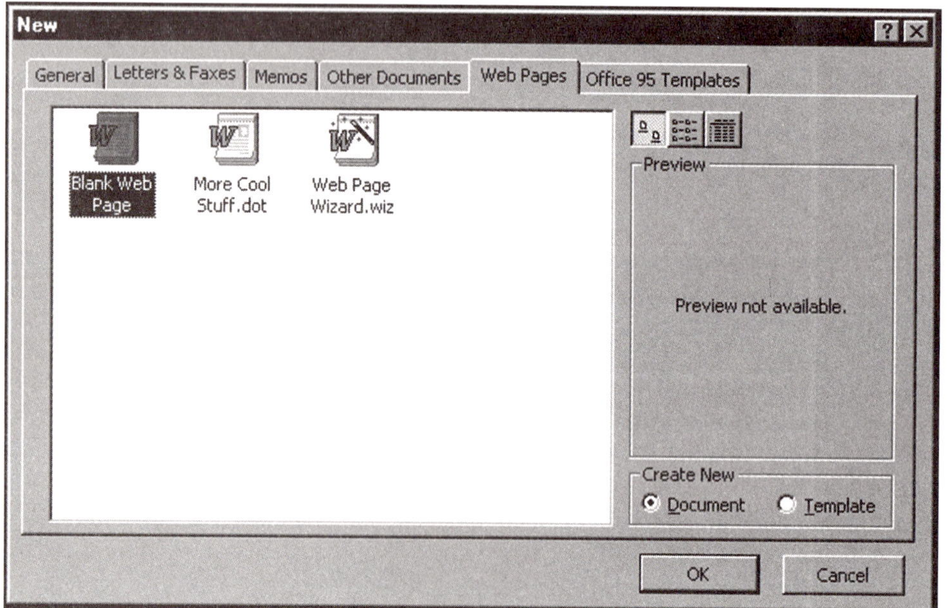

- After you click OK, Word opens a new, blank HTML Web page document. You can now create a new Web page by adding any new content and formatting you want.

Create a New Table

- You can use the same basic techniques to create a Web page table as you would normally use in Word. Click the button on Word's Standard Web page toolbar or select Table, Insert Table.
- When you click the Insert Table button, a grid appears on which you can drag your mouse pointer to select the number of rows and columns you want. Click the grid to create the new table.

The Insert Table Grid

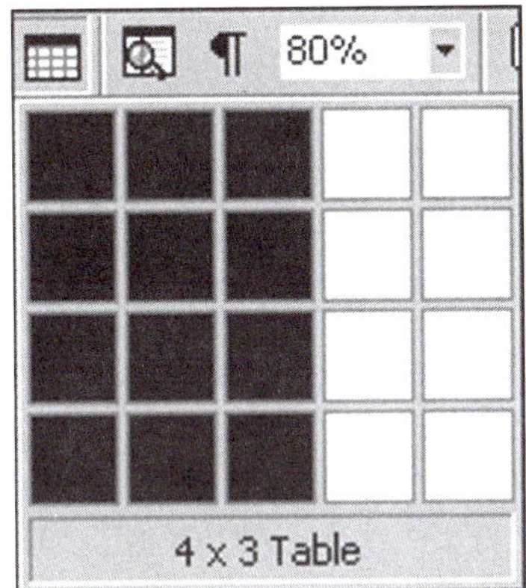

Note

The Insert Table Grid also appears when you select Table, Insert Table. In a normal Word document the Insert Table dialog box would appear. Select the number of rows and columns you want for your table on the grid and click the grid to create the new table.

- Click the cell you want to work in and enter text in the new table as you would in a normal Word table. Click or select View, Toolbars, Tables and Borders to display the Tables and Borders toolbar. Click the appropriate tools on this toolbar to work with your table as you normally would in Word.

Tables and Borders Toolbar

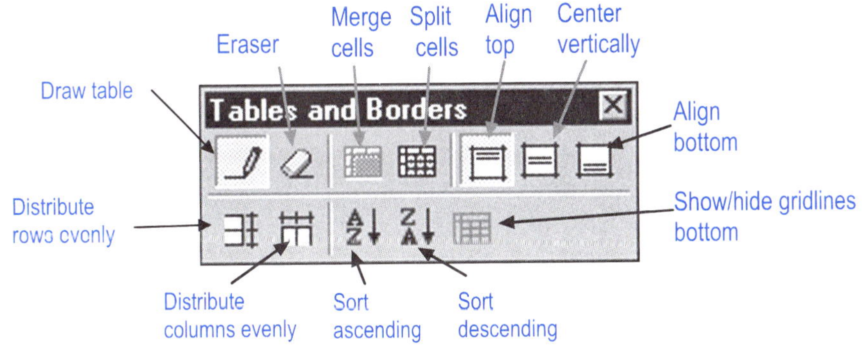

Merge and Split Cells

- An interesting way to alter the design of your table is to merge cells or split cells.
  - To merge cells, select the cells you want to merge, then click the Merge Cells button on the Tables and Borders toolbar or select Table, Merge Cells.
  - To split cells, click the Split Cells button on the toolbar or select Table, Split Cells. The Split Cells dialog box opens. Select the number of rows and/or columns you want, then click OK.

The Split Cells Dialog Box

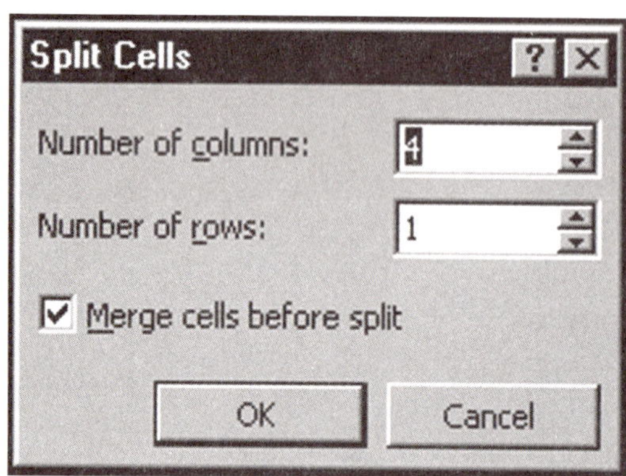

In this exercise, you will create a new Web page using the Blank Web Page template, then add content to the page by creating and formatting new tables on the page. You will also link the new page to the Verity Books home page.

EXERCISE DIRECTIONS

1. Select File, New. The New dialog box opens.
2. Select the Web Pages tab of the New dialog box, then click Blank Web Page. Make sure the Document option is selected, then click OK.
3. Word opens a new, blank Web page. Save the file as **INFO.HTML** in your Web site folder.
4. Enter the following text at the top of the page:
   Verity Books
   Store Information

Select Blank Web Page Template

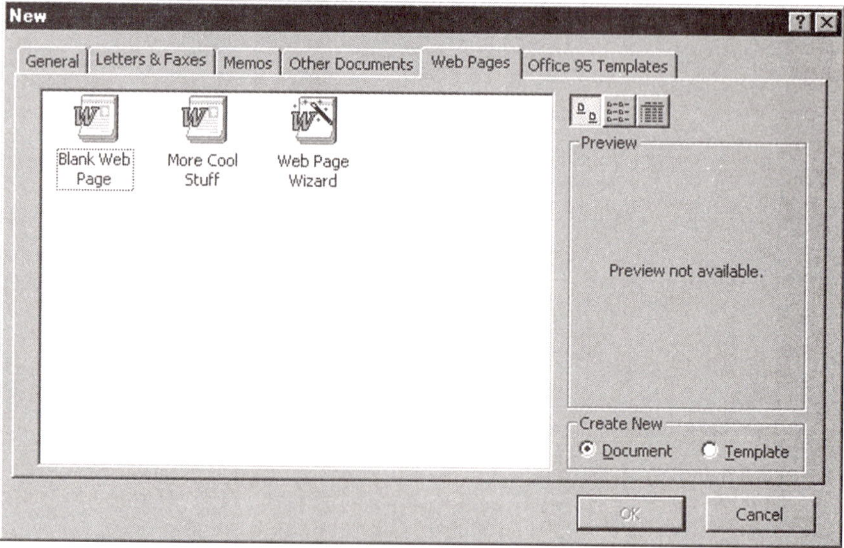

5. Format Verity Books in Copperplate Gothic Light Bold, if available, or use the heading font you used in previous exercises. Increase the font size three times.
6. Format Store Information in Copperplate Gothic Light, if available, and press Enter to go to the next line.
7. Click on the Web toolbar to display the Insert Table grid.
8. Drag down and to the right to highlight grid cells until the grid shows at bottom that you will create a 4 x 3 table, then click on the grid.
   ➲ *Word creates a 4 x 3 table.*

The Insert Table Grid

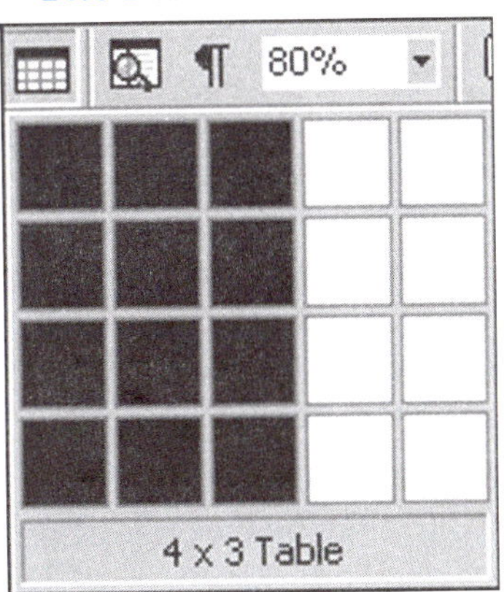

9. If gridlines are not displayed, select Table, Show Gridlines to view the table's cells.
10. Click on the Formatting toolbar five times to insert five additional rows.
11. If necessary, select the entire first row, then select Table, Merge Cells.
12. Insert the following text in the first row:
    Verity Books store hours are as follows:
13. Press Ctrl+E to center the new text across the table.
14. Select Tables, Borders and click Grid to show the table borders. Enter the table text as shown in the illustration at right. Format headings in bold.

Table Inserted in New Web Page

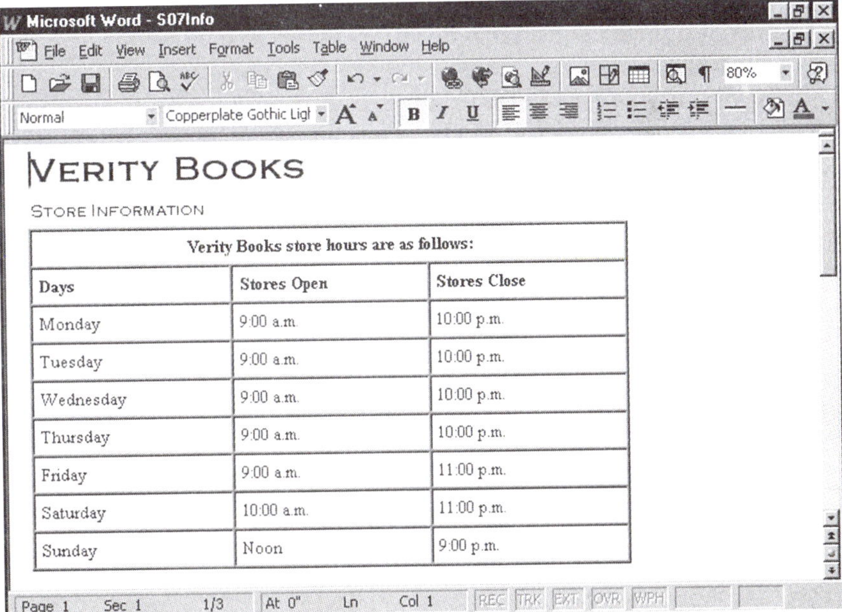
Microsoft Word - S07Info

File Edit View Insert Format Tools Table Window Help

Normal | Copperplate Gothic Ligl | 80%

VERITY BOOKS

STORE INFORMATION

Verity Books store hours are as follows:		
Days	**Stores Open**	**Stores Close**
Monday	9:00 a.m.	10:00 p.m.
Tuesday	9:00 a.m.	10:00 p.m.
Wednesday	9:00 a.m.	10:00 p.m.
Thursday	9:00 a.m.	10:00 p.m.
Friday	9:00 a.m.	11:00 p.m.
Saturday	10:00 a.m.	11:00 p.m.
Sunday	Noon	9:00 p.m.

Page 1 Sec 1 1/3 At 0" Ln Col 1 REC TRK EXT OVR WPH

15. In a new line beneath the Store Hours table, type Store Locations. Format the text as Copperplate Gothic Light, if available.
16. Create a new 4 x 5 table beneath the words Store Locations.
17. Add 9 new rows to the table. Show table borders.
18. If necessary, select the entire first row of the table and merge cells.
19. Type Northeast in the first row and center it. Change the font to Copperplate Gothic Light, if available, or use the heading font you have been using.
20. Enter these cities in the following two rows of the table, as shown in the illustration at right:

    Baltimore, Boston, Hartford, Manhattan, Philadelphia, Pittsburgh, Princeton, Providence, Stamford, Washington

21. Select the next row of the table and merge cells. Type South in the row, center it, and change font to Copperplate Gothic Light, if available, or use your heading font. Enter these cities in the following three rows of the table:

    Atlanta, Birmingham, Charlotte, Dallas, Houston, Memphis, Miami, Mobile, Nashville, New Orleans, Richmond, Tampa

22. Merge cells in the next row, type Central, and center it. Change the font to Copperplate Gothic Light, if available, or use your heading font. Enter these cities in the next two rows:

    Chicago, Cincinnati, Cleveland, Detroit, Indianapolis, Kansas City, Louisville, Milwaukee, Minneapolis, St. Louis

23. Merge cells in the next row, type West, and center it. Change the font to Copperplate Gothic Light, if available, or use your heading font. Enter these cities in the next two rows:
    Albuquerque, Anaheim, Denver, Los Angeles, Phoenix, Portland, Salt Lake City, San Diego, San Francisco, Seattle

Verity Books Store Locations

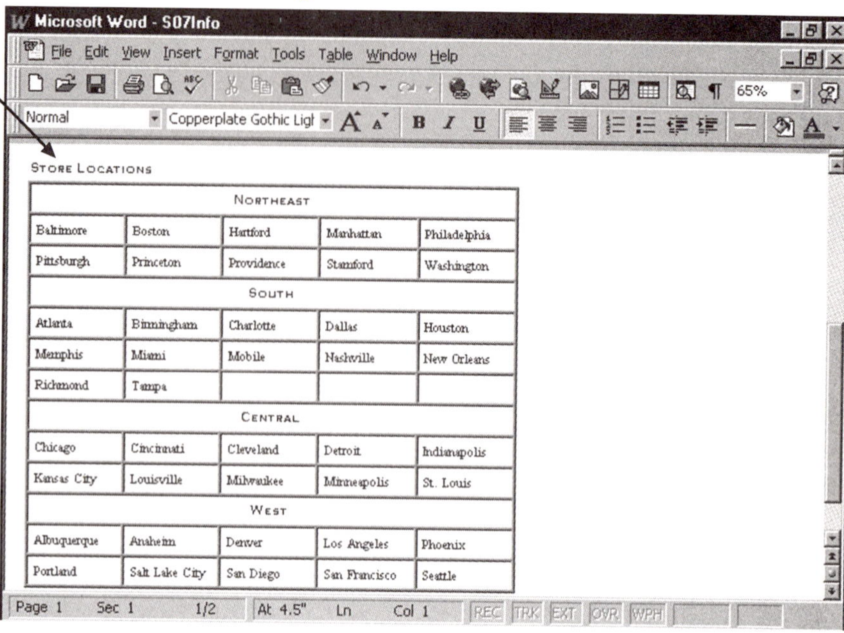

STORE LOCATIONS

NORTHEAST				
Baltimore	Boston	Hartford	Manhattan	Philadelphia
Pittsburgh	Princeton	Providence	Stamford	Washington
SOUTH				
Atlanta	Birmingham	Charlotte	Dallas	Houston
Memphis	Miami	Mobile	Nashville	New Orleans
Richmond	Tampa			
CENTRAL				
Chicago	Cincinnati	Cleveland	Detroit	Indianapolis
Kansas City	Louisville	Milwaukee	Minneapolis	St. Louis
WEST				
Albuquerque	Anaheim	Denver	Los Angeles	Phoenix
Portland	Salt Lake City	San Diego	San Francisco	Seattle

24. Open VERITY.HTML from your Web site folder.
25. Select Window and choose INFO.HTML from the drop-down list.
26. Insert a hyperlink to the Verity Books Home Page (VERITY.HTML) at the bottom of the Store Information page. See illustration at right.
27. Click the hyperlink to go to VERITY.HTML.

Hyperlink to Verity Books Home Page

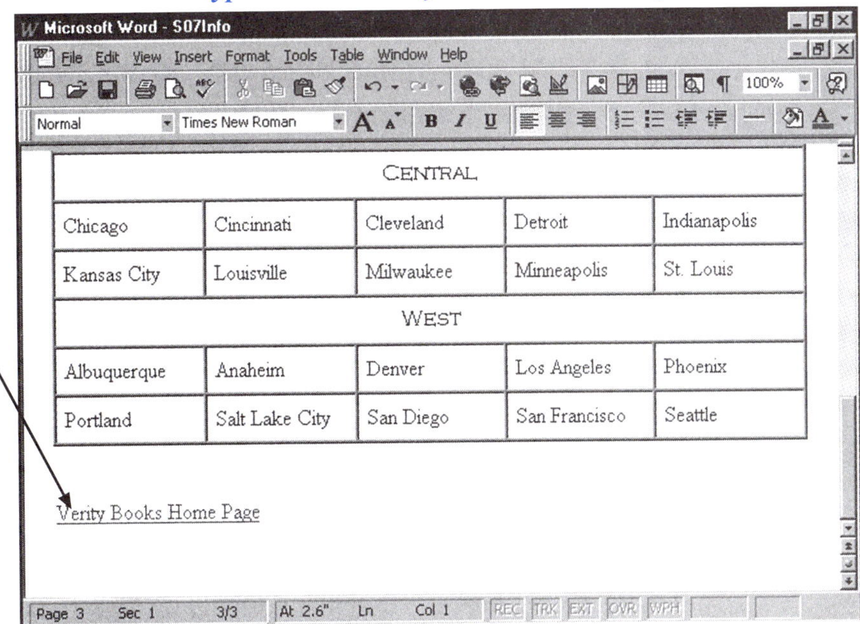

New Hyperlink to Information Page

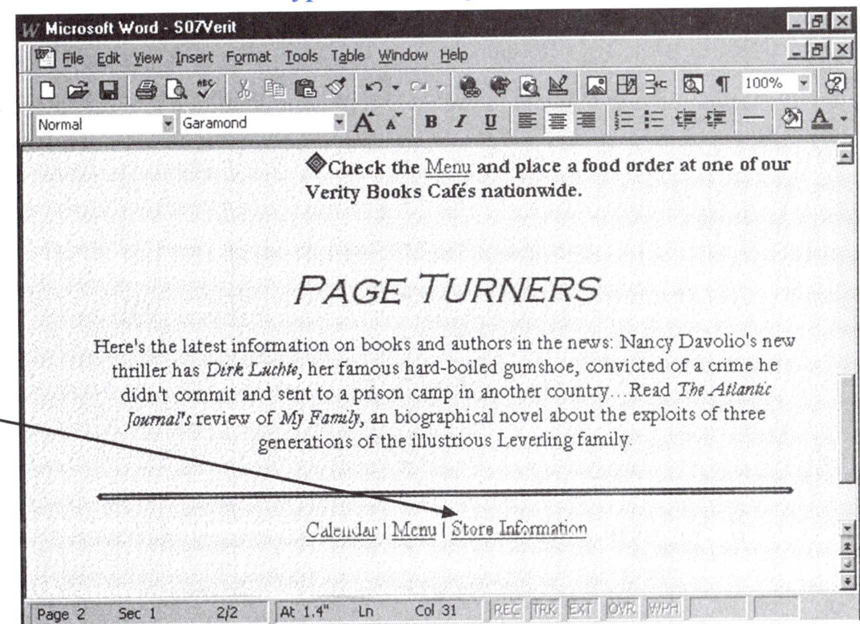

28. Replace the text "Related Page 3" at the bottom of VERITY.HTML with a hyperlink to INFO.HTML. Edit the link to read Store Information as shown in the illustration at right.
29. Click the hyperlink to go to INFO.HTML.
30. Save your work in both files and close them.

Exercise 8

- Work with Horizontal Lines
- Add Colors to Tables
- Add Background Textures

NOTES

Work with Horizontal Lines

- Horizontal lines help you divide various elements of your Web page and add visual interest to your page. Word provides a variety of line styles you can use to liven up your page.
- Position the cursor where you want the new line to appear, then select Insert, Horizontal Line. The Horizontal Line dialog box opens, providing a selection of different line styles.
- The top line displayed in the Style list is the Standard line, which inserts a standard HTML line. This line is displayed according to how each individual browser interprets the HTML standard horizontal line element.
- Selecting any of the other lines inserts a GIF graphic file of the decorative line into the Web page. The GIF file will be stored in the same folder as the Web page document file. Such graphic lines are displayed exactly as shown in Word when the Web page is viewed by any browser software.

Horizontal Line Dialog Box

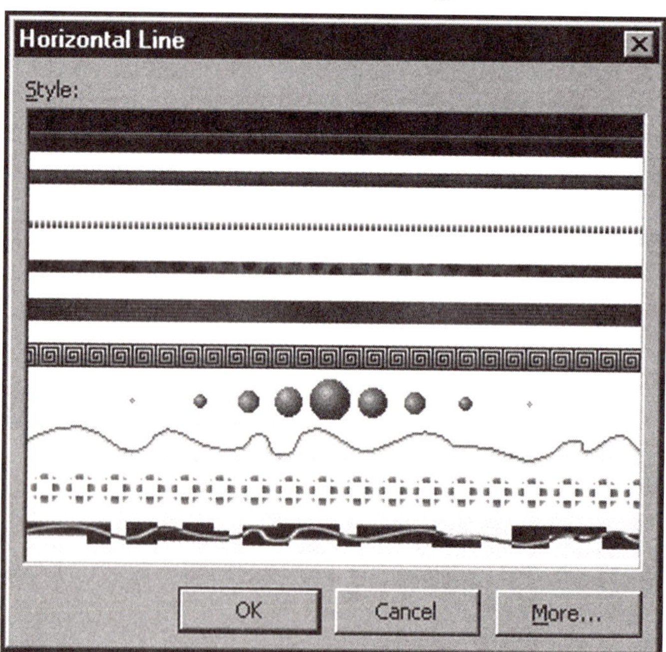

GIF (Graphics Interchange Format)
A graphics file format commonly used in creating Web pages.

- Click the More button in the Horizontal Line dialog box to view the Insert Picture dialog box, which contains additional graphical line files.

Add Colors to Tables

- Tables can be formatted with a color background to add visual interest. Select Table, Table Properties to open the Table Properties dialog box. Click Background to display a drop-down list of colors from which you can choose. Select a color and then click OK.
- Select Auto from the Background list to blend the table background with the background of the Web page.
- The Table Properties dialog box also allows you to wrap text around the table, adjust the distance of text surrounding the table, and adjust space between table columns.

Table Properties Dialog Box

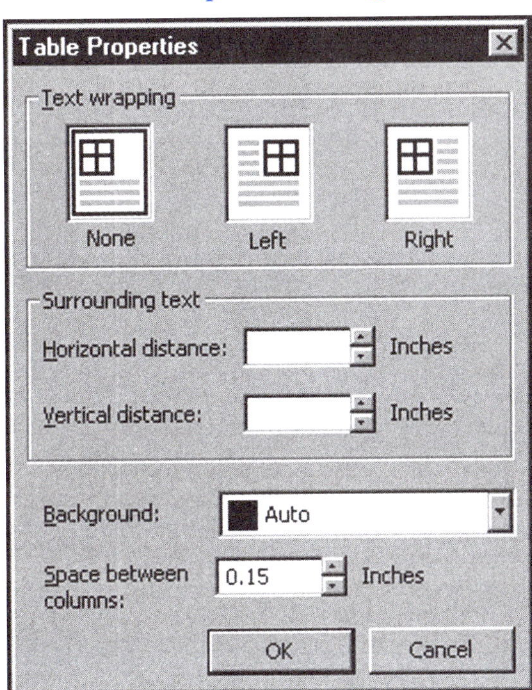

Note

You can cut, copy, paste, and move horizontal lines the same way you would any other graphic object.

Add Background Textures

- Web pages created with the Blank Web Page template or saved as HTML from a standard Word document typically have a plain white background. Adding a background texture to the page gives it a rich look and adds depth to the page.

Fill Effects Dialog Box

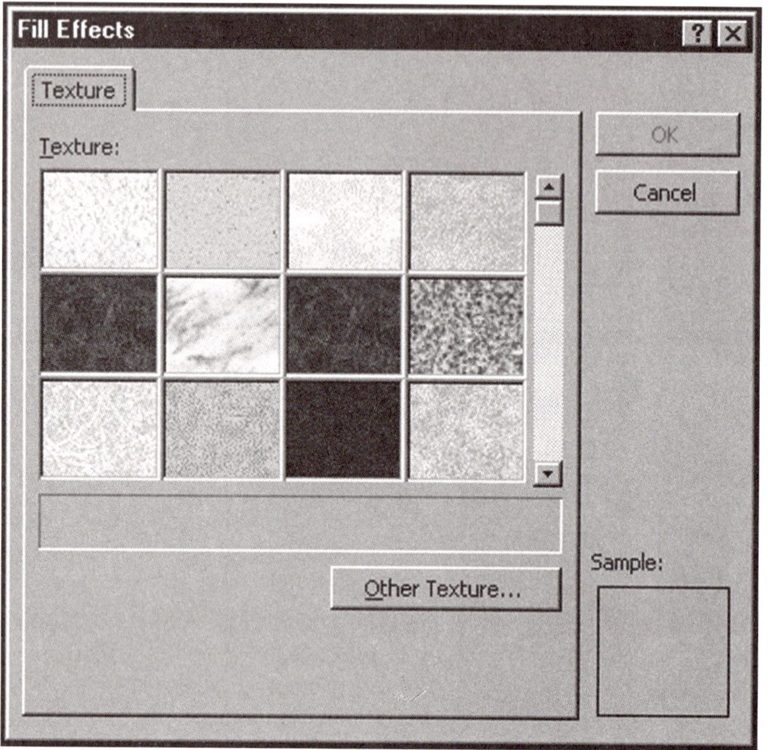

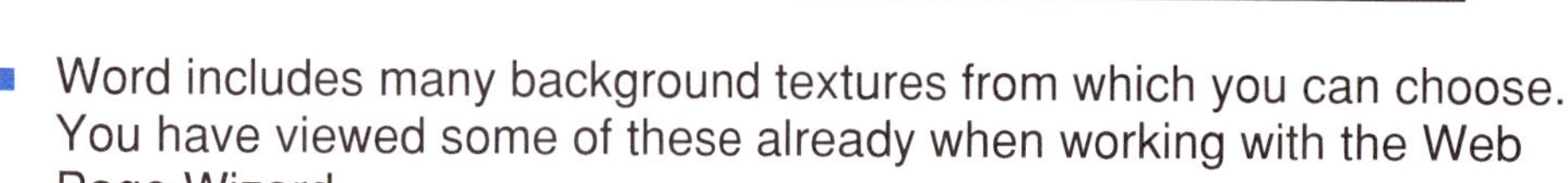

- Word includes many background textures from which you can choose. You have viewed some of these already when working with the Web Page Wizard.
- Select Format, Background to display a palette of background colors. Click a color to use as a background, or click Fill Effects to view the Fill Effects dialog box. This dialog box provides a selection of textures. Click one to see a sample in the dialog box, then click OK to add the background to your page.
- Remember to avoid a background that is too dark or too busy for your text. Choose a background that provides strong contrast with your text so that the text can be read easily.

Note

It's always best to keep your layouts simple and to exercise restraint in adding graphical elements such as backgrounds and lines.

Note

You can also click Other Texture to view the Select Texture dialog box. Select the Backgrounds folder of the Office 97 Clipart folder, select a texture, and click OK.

In this exercise, you will add a horizontal line to the Verity Books store information page, add a background color to the Store Information table, then create a background texture for the entire Web page.

EXERCISE DIRECTIONS

1. Open INFO.HTML from your Web site folder.
2. Position the cursor in the blank line between the Store Information table and the Store Locations heading. If there is no blank line, create one by positioning the cursor and pressing Enter.
3. Select Insert, Horizontal Line. The Horizontal Line dialog box opens. Select the wavy line, third from the bottom, then click OK.
   ✓ *Notice that this line does not fit the style of the Verity Books Web site. Click on the line to select it, then press Delete.*
4. Delete any additional lines between the Store Information table and the Store Locations heading. There should be only one blank line between the two.
5. Position the cursor again in the blank line between the Store Information table and the Store Locations heading.
6. Open the Horizontal Line dialog box, then click More.
7. The Insert Picture dialog box opens, displaying the Lines folder of the Office Clipart directory.
8. Select Etched Double Line, then click Insert.

Horizontal Line Dialog Box

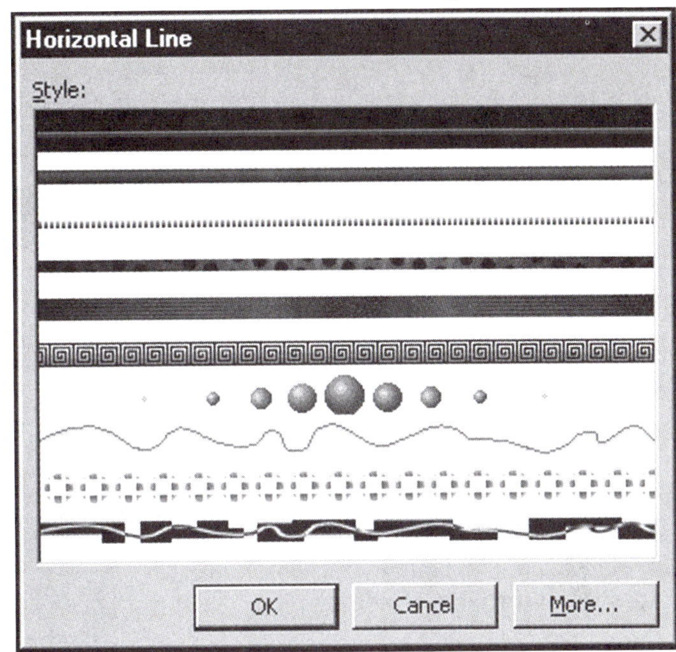

Insert Picture Dialog Box

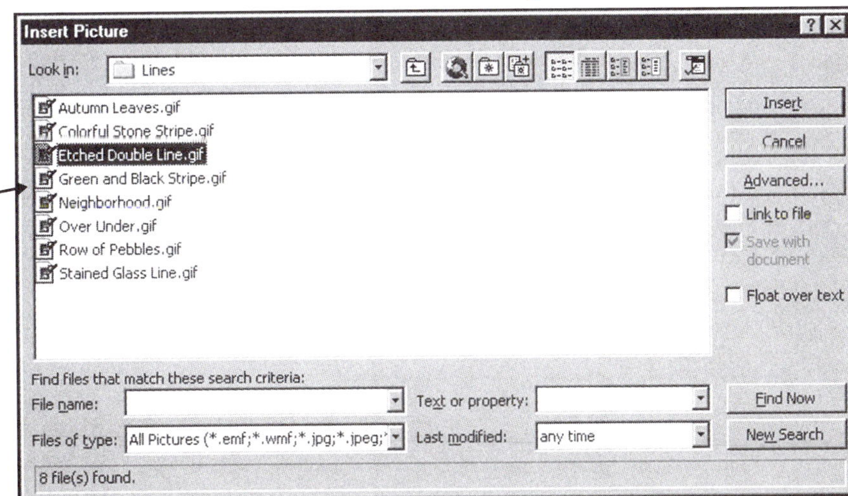

9. Word inserts a new line.

   ✓ *This line is the same as the one used in the* ***VERITY.HTML*** *home page.*

10. Click the line to select it, then press Ctrl+L to align it flush left.
11. Position the cursor anywhere in the Store Information table.

Information Page with New Line

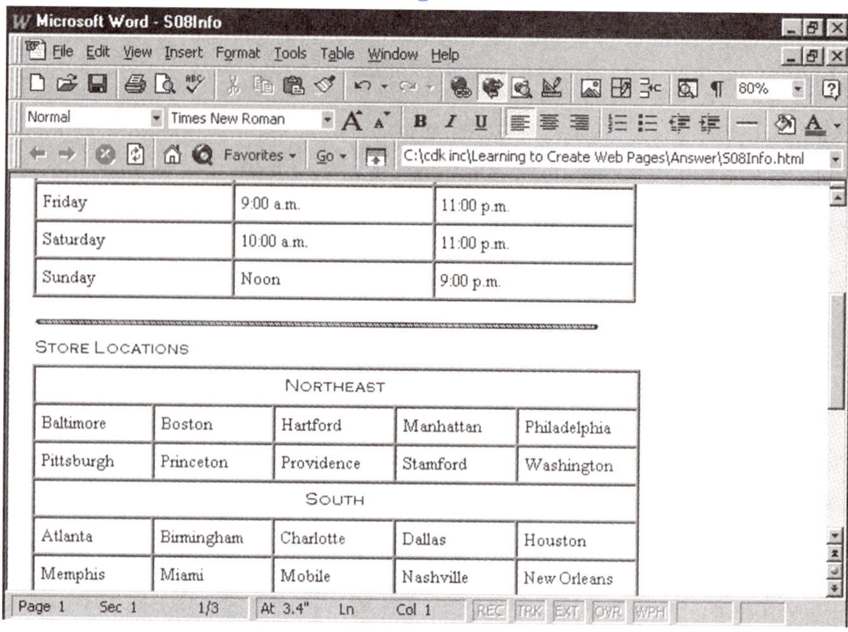

12. Select Table, Table Properties. The Table Properties dialog box opens.
13. Select Background, then select any color you wish to use for the background of the table.

    ✓ *Remember to make sure that the table's text will be readable against the background color you choose.*

14. Click OK. The table appears with the color background.

Table Properties Dialog Box

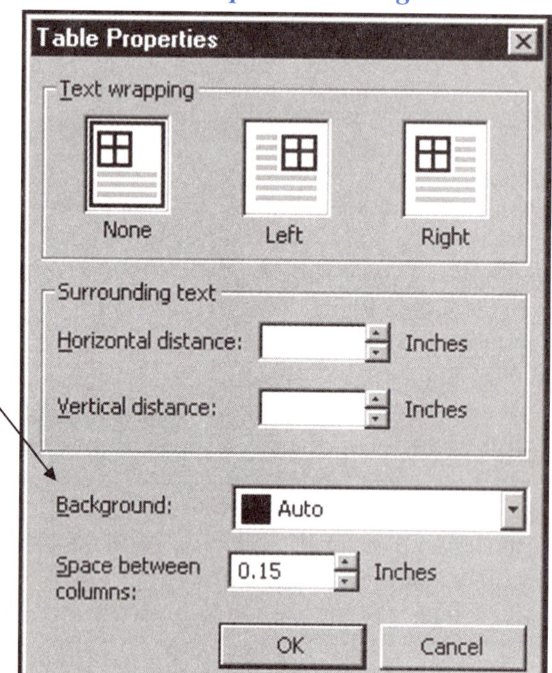

15. Select Format, Background. Select Fill Effects from the palette. The Fill Effects dialog box appears, as shown at right.
16. Click several of the textures displayed to view a sample of each in the dialog box.
17. Click Other Texture.

Fill Effects Dialog Box

18. The Select Texture dialog box opens, as shown in the illustration at right.
19. Make sure the Backgrounds folder of the Office Clipart directory is displayed in the Look in list box.
20. Select Off Yellow Bookcover, then click OK.
21. The Off Yellow Bookcover texture is displayed in the Texture list of the Fill Effects dialog box. Select it, then click OK.
22. The **INFO.HTML** Web page's background changes to the new texture.

    Notice that this is the same background used on the ***VERITY.HTML*** *home page.*
23. If necessary, move the cursor to the Store Information table. Change the table's background color to Auto.
24. The Store Information table's background now matches the Web page's background, as shown in the illustration at right.
25. Save your work to **INFO.HTML**, then close the file.

Select Texture Dialog Box

Information Page with New Background and Line

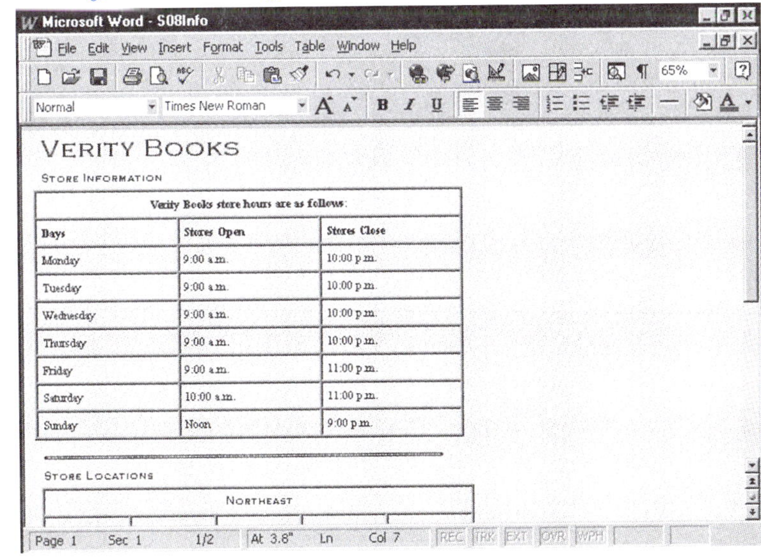

VERITY BOOKS

STORE INFORMATION

Verity Books store hours are as follows:		
Days	Stores Open	Stores Close
Monday	9:00 a.m.	10:00 p.m.
Tuesday	9:00 a.m.	10:00 p.m.
Wednesday	9:00 a.m.	10:00 p.m.
Thursday	9:00 a.m.	10:00 p.m.
Friday	9:00 a.m.	11:00 p.m.
Saturday	10:00 a.m.	11:00 p.m.
Sunday	Noon	9:00 p.m.

STORE LOCATIONS

NORTHEAST

Exercise 9

- Create a Feedback Form
- Work in Form Design Mode
- Add Controls to Forms
- Modify Controls and Control Properties

NOTES

Create a Feedback Form

- One of the best uses for your Web site is gathering information from the people who visit the site. **Forms** are the best type of Web page for gathering this information. Word provides three forms in the Web Page Wizard from which you can choose to quickly get started with a basic form layout.
- These Web pages are created like any other page using the Web Page Wizard. You can add text and format the form page using the basic Web page techniques you have learned in the previous Exercises.

Form
A document that includes controls that enable users to enter and submit information.

Work in Form Design Mode

- You can also create a form by adding **controls** to a standard Web page or to an existing form. Various types of controls let the user enter information on the form. Controls that collect information include:
  - Check boxes and option buttons for choosing options
  - Drop-down boxes and list boxes for selecting items from lists
  - Text boxes for entering text.
- You must select View, Form Design Mode to add controls to a Web page. Working in Form Design Mode enables you to select a control and modify its **properties** or insert a new control from the Control Toolbox.

Control
An object such as a check box or text box that can be added to a document in Form Design Mode.

Properties
The elements of an object or control that define its various aspects such as how it appears on screen and how it functions.

Working in Form Design Mode

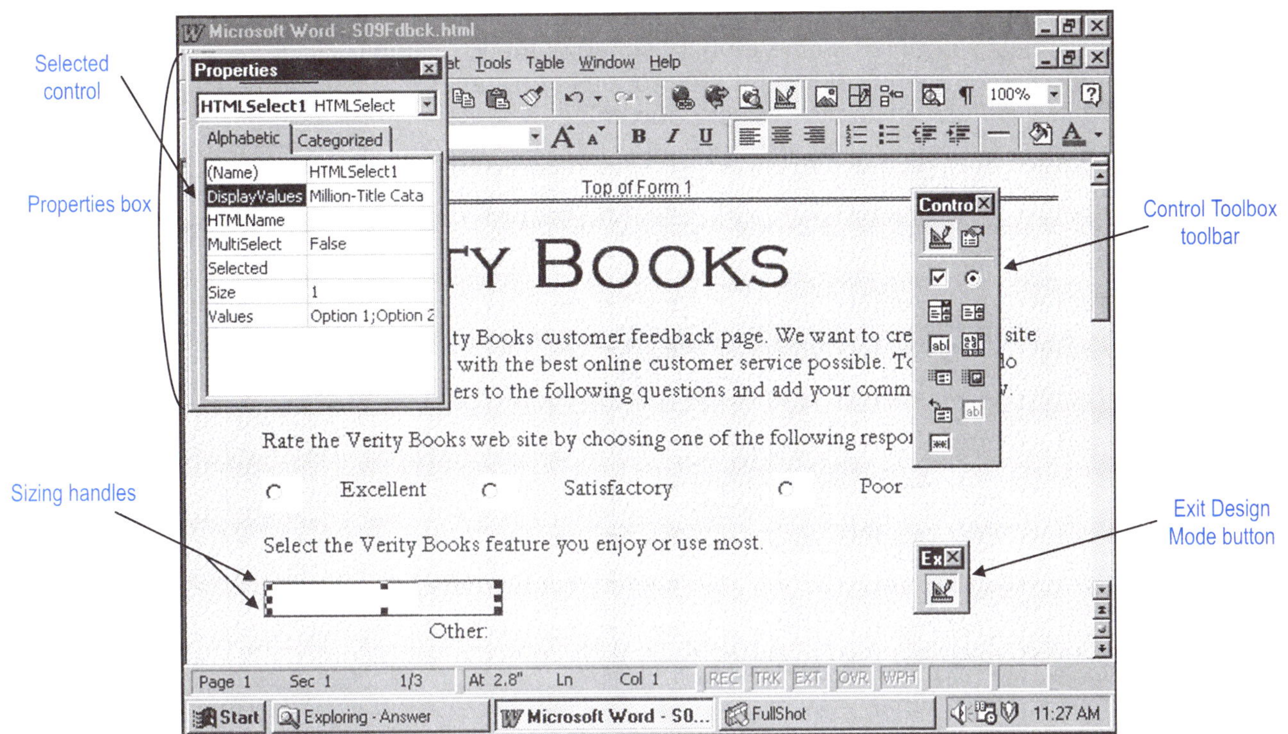

Control Toolbox Toolbar

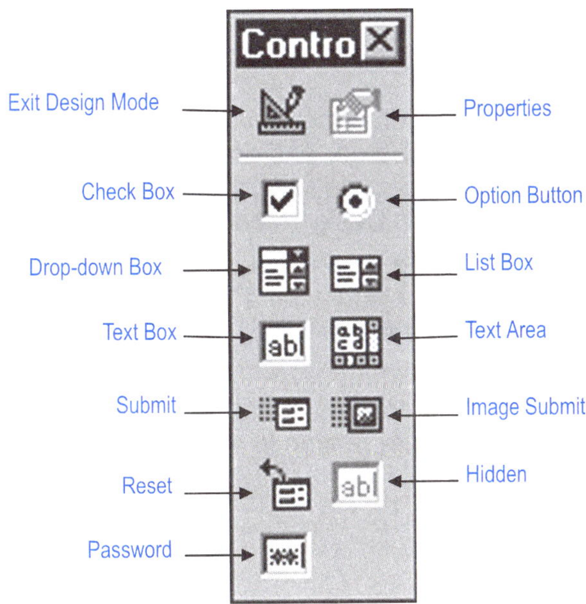

Add Controls to Forms

- To add a control to a form, simply click the control you want to add on the Control Toolbox toolbar. Word automatically inserts the control at the location of the insertion point.

Modify Controls and Control Properties

- After inserting the new control on the form, you must then double-click the control to set its initial properties. In the Alphabetic tab of the Properties window, click on the right-hand column for the property you want to modify, then enter the new value over the existing value.
- Be sure to give new controls a name in the HTMLName property. The browser and server software must be able to read a name and values for each control on the Web page to display the page properly.

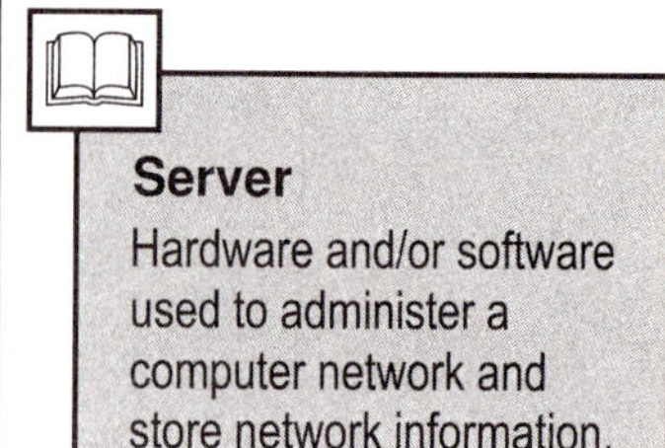

Server
Hardware and/or software used to administer a computer network and store network information.

Properties Window

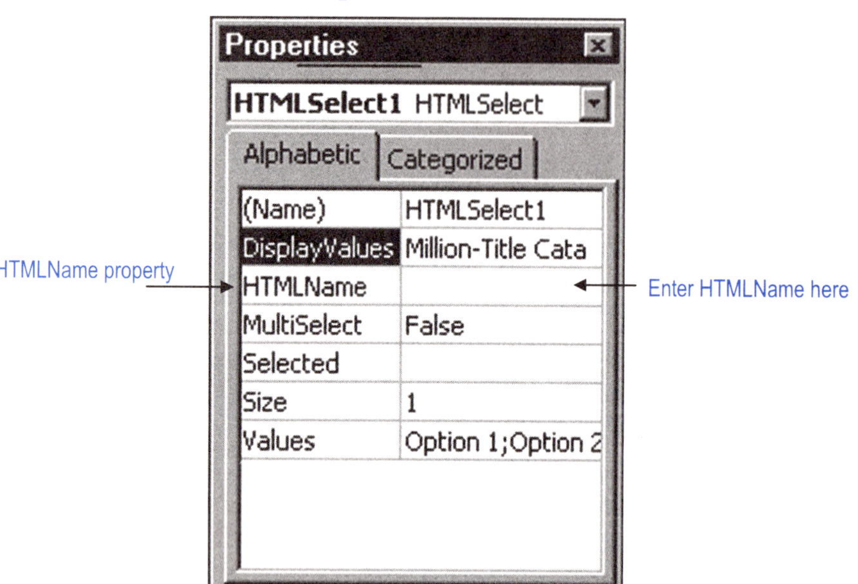

- After defining the control's properties, you can click and drag the control's sizing handles to resize the control or click the control's border and drag it to reposition the control. You can also use standard editing tools such as cut, copy, paste, and delete to work with controls in Form Design Mode.
- Note that Word includes tools and templates, such as the Web Page Wizard, for designing forms, but Word doesn't include tools to write a program for the Web server to receive, process, or store such information.
- Writing such programs is beyond the scope of this book, but you can create Excel forms that automatically collect and store information in a database on a server.

In this exercise, you will create a new Web page using the Form - Feedback Web Page template, then add content to the page, change a control's properties, and change the control's format.

EXERCISE DIRECTIONS

1. Select File, New. The New dialog box opens.
2. Select the Web Page Wizard template from the Web Pages tab, then click OK. Be sure to create the Web page as a document, not a template.
3. The Web Page Wizard opens. Select Form - Feedback, then click Next>.
4. Select the Elegant style from the next wizard dialog box, then click Finish.
5. Word creates a new feedback form Web page. Save the new Web page in your Web site folder as **FEEDBACK.HTML**.

Form - Feedback Web Page Wizard

6. Insert the following new text for the Web page as shown in the illustration at right. Format the page heading in Copperplate Gothic Light, if available, or use the heading font you have used in previous exercises.

   Verity Books

   Welcome to the Verity Books customer feedback page. We want to create a Web site that will provide you with the best online customer service possible. To help us do this, enter your answers to the following questions and add your comments below.

   Rate the Verity Books Web site by choosing one of the following responses.

   Excellent, Satisfactory, Poor

   Select the Verity Books feature you enjoy or use most.

   Type in any other comments or suggestions you have in the following text box.

The New Feedback Form

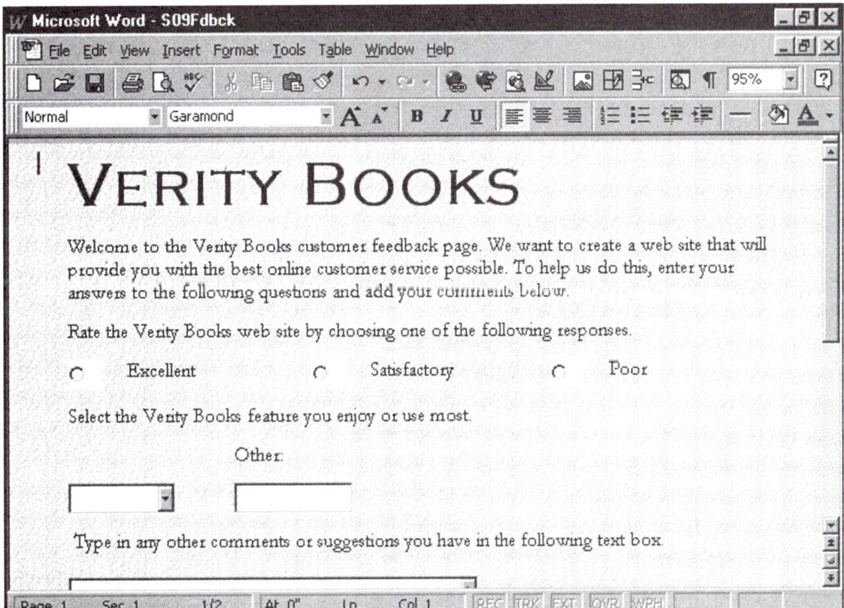

7. Select View, Form Design Mode. The view changes to Form Design Mode. The Control Toolbox and the Exit Form Design Mode toolbar button appear on screen.
8. Double-click the drop-down list box under the sentence "Select the Verity Books features you enjoy or use most."

   ✓ *The drop-down list box is to the left of the box titled "Other."*

9. The Properties window for the drop-down list control opens. Double-click the word "Option" to the right of the Display Values property, then type the following text options:

   Million-Title Catalog;Book Reviews;Café Menu

   Be sure to type the new options exactly as shown above, including semi-colons, with no space between them and the text they separate.

10. Click the empty text box to the right of the HTMLName property, then type List Box.
11. Click [X] to close the Properties window.
12. Open the Properties window for each of the other controls on the form and enter a name for the HTMLProperty in each.
13. Click [¶] to display paragraph marks and other hidden characters.
14. Select Table, Show Gridlines.
15. Click on the right gridline of the table cell containing the drop-down list control. Drag the cell gridline to the right, beyond the right edge of the control.
16. In the next cell, delete the paragraph mark to the right of the word Other. Enter a space between the colon and text box.
17. Select Table, Cell Properties. The Cell Properties dialog box appears.
18. Select the Top Vertical alignment, then click [OK].

Changing a Control's Properties

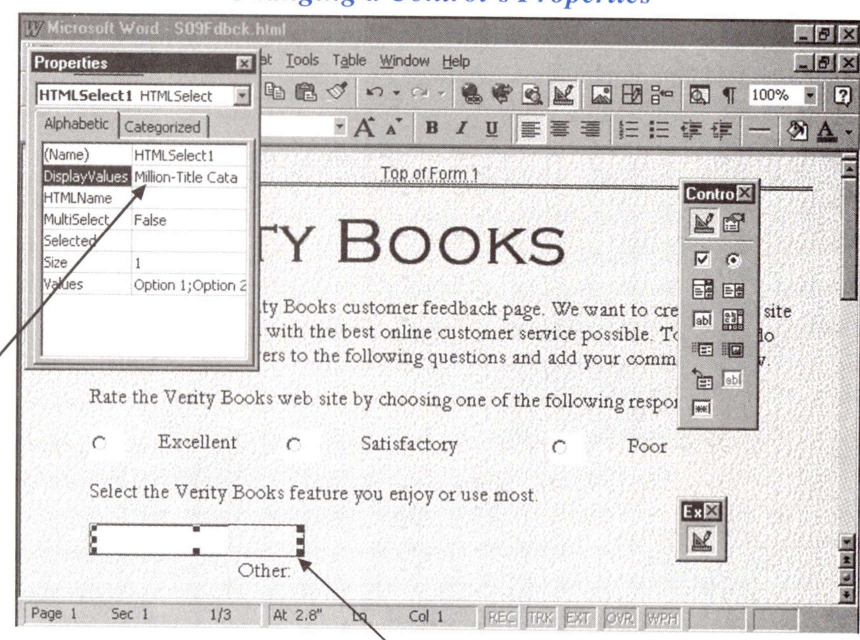

Click and drag right control border here to resize.

Cell Properties Dialog Box

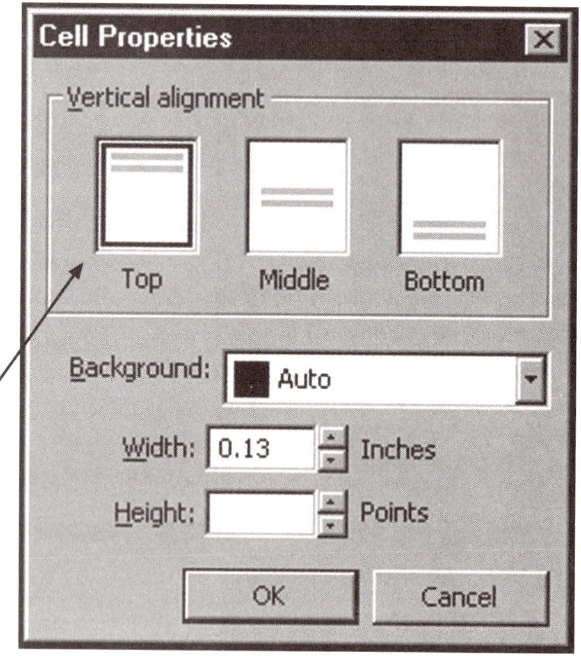

19. Select View, Form Design Mode to return to the standard Online Layout view.
20. Click X to close the Control Toolbox. Your Web page should look similar to the one shown at right.
21. Save your work on **FEEDBACK.HTML** in your Web site folder, then close the file.
22. Open **FEEDBACK.HTML** in your browser to practice entering information into the form. Select choices and enter responses in the text boxes.

    ✓ *Click drop-down list box arrow to view choices. Click in text box to enter text.*

23. Click Submit at the bottom of the feedback form, then click Reset to practice using the form to submit information.

    ✓ *If the form were set up to load data to a server, information you entered into the form would be sent to the server when you clicked the Submit button.*

24. Close your browser.

Feedback Form with New Control and Responses

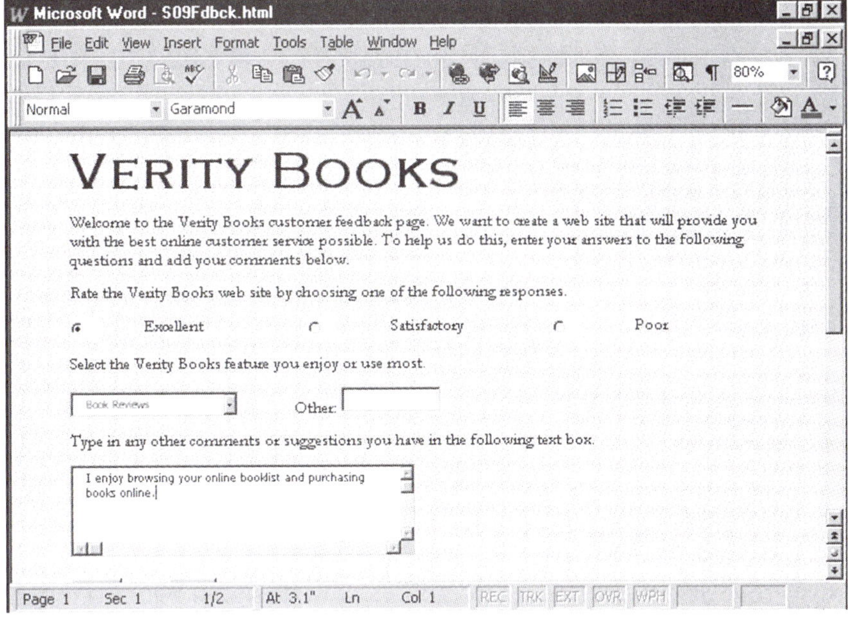

Exercise 10

■ Insert Graphics Files ■ Use the Clip Gallery
■ Supply Alternate Text

NOTES

Insert Graphics Files

- Perhaps the easiest way to liven up your Web page is to insert graphics files. You can insert files from the Microsoft Clip Gallery 3.0, graphics copied from another program, or any other graphics files you have stored on your system.
- Remember to use graphics sparingly in designing your page, as graphics files tend to be large and take a long time to download, especially for someone with a slow-speed modem.
- To insert a graphics file you have stored on your system, select Insert, Picture, From File or click . The Insert Picture dialog box works similar to the File Open dialog box. Select the drive and folder where the graphics file is stored using the Look in drop-down list box. Then select the file you want and click Insert.
- Click the Preview button to see a sample of the file you've selected before inserting.

Insert Picture Dialog Box

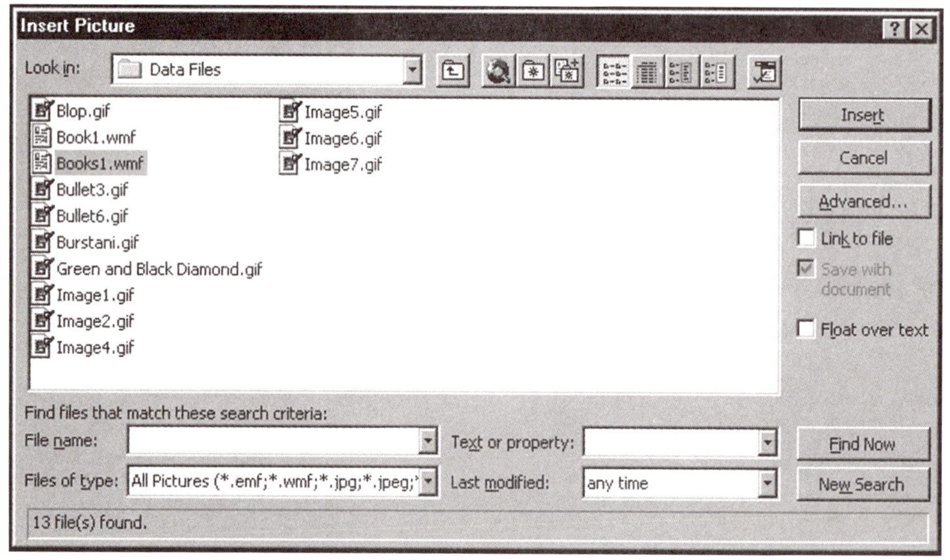

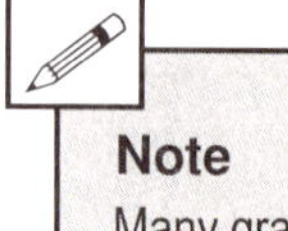

Note
Many graphics files can be found in the Office Clipart folder.

CAUTION
In the Insert Picture dialog box, be sure *not* to select the Float over text option. It can result in the loss of Web page text when the graphics file is inserted.

Use the Clip Gallery

- Microsoft Clip Gallery is a quick source for graphics files you can insert on your Web pages. Select Insert, Picture, Clip Art to open the Clip Gallery. Next, select the appropriate category to view the graphics, select the object you wish to insert, and click .

Microsoft Clip Gallery 3.0

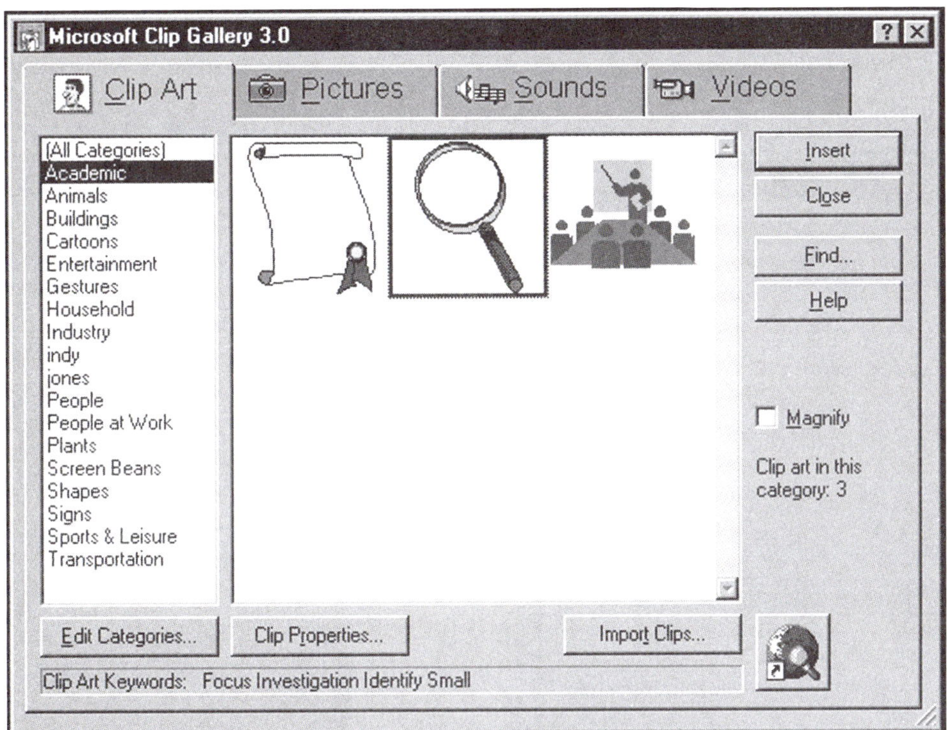

- Word inserts the Clip Art graphic you selected at the insertion point. Often, you will have to resize the graphic. To do so, click the graphic to select it. Then, click and drag one of its sizing handles.
- After a graphic has been inserted, you can copy, cut, paste, and move the graphic as you would any other object in a Word document.

Supply Alternate Text

- Because graphics files take a long time to download, many users will turn off the graphics display on their browsers to increase viewing speed. Keep this in mind when you design your page. If you use large graphics files, you can supply text that will display instead of a graphic when a browser's graphic display is turned off.
- To assign alternate text, click the graphic to select it. Then select Format, Picture to display the Picture dialog box. Go to the Settings tab and enter the Picture placeholder text, then click OK.

Picture Dialog Box

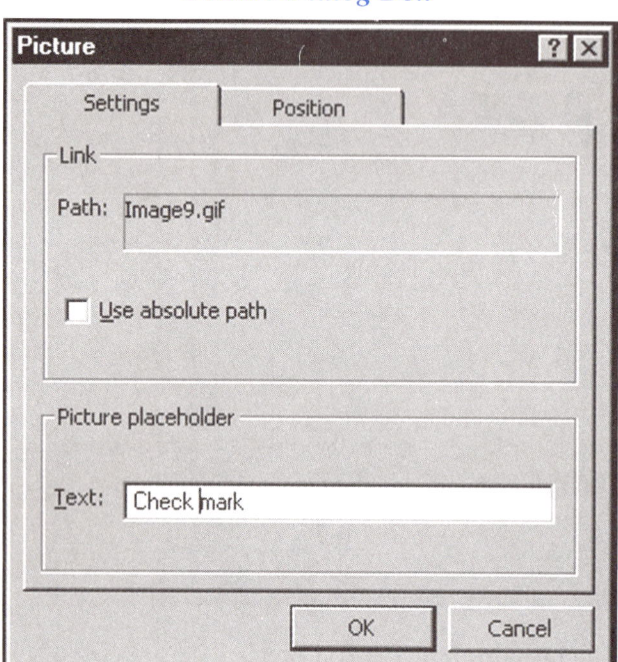

Note

You can also create a hyperlink to a graphics file to provide users a choice of whether or not to view the graphic. Simply create a link from the Web page to the graphics file and make sure the graphics file is stored in the same folder as the Web page. Use a relative link to the graphics file.

In this exercise, you will add graphics to the Verity Press home page from the Clip Gallery and from data files. You will also resize graphics and format a graphic as a hyperlink.

EXERCISE DIRECTIONS

1. Open **VERITY.HTML** from your Web site folder.
2. Select the question mark graphic next to Search the Million-Title Catalog by clicking on it. Press Delete.
3. Select Insert, Picture, Clip Art. The Microsoft Clip Gallery 3.0 opens.
4. Select the Clip Art tab, then select the Academic category.
5. Click the Magnifying Glass graphic, then click Insert. Word inserts the Magnifying Glass graphic in the Web page.
6. Click the Magnifying Glass graphic and drag its top-right or bottom-right corner sizing handles toward the center of the graphic to resize it. Resize the graphic so it matches the size of the question mark graphic you deleted and the down arrow icon below it.

   ✓ *When the picture is inserted, it may be partially hidden.*
7. Delete the down arrow graphic next to Buy Books.
8. Insert the Check Mark graphic from Clip Gallery's Shapes category.
9. Resize the Check Mark graphic to match the size of the arrow graphic you deleted.
10. Delete the quotation marks graphic next to Send Us Feedback & Reviews.
11. Insert the Light Bulb graphic from Clip Gallery's Industry category.
12. Resize the Light Bulb graphic to match the size of the quotation marks graphic you deleted. The home page should now look like the one shown in the illustration at right.
13. Select the Light Bulb graphic, then press Ctrl+K to format the graphic as a hyperlink.

Microsoft Clip Gallery

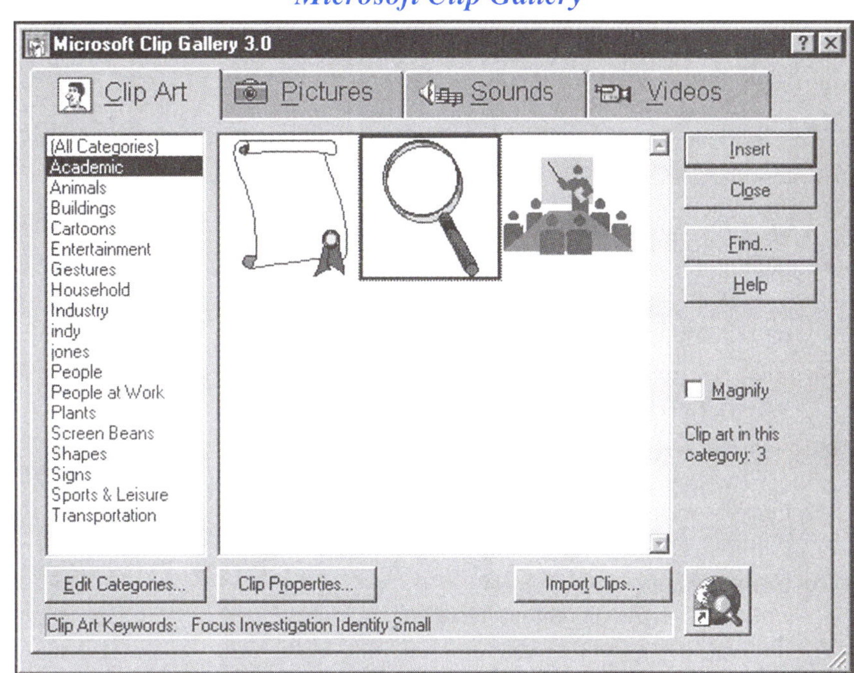

Home Page with New Graphics

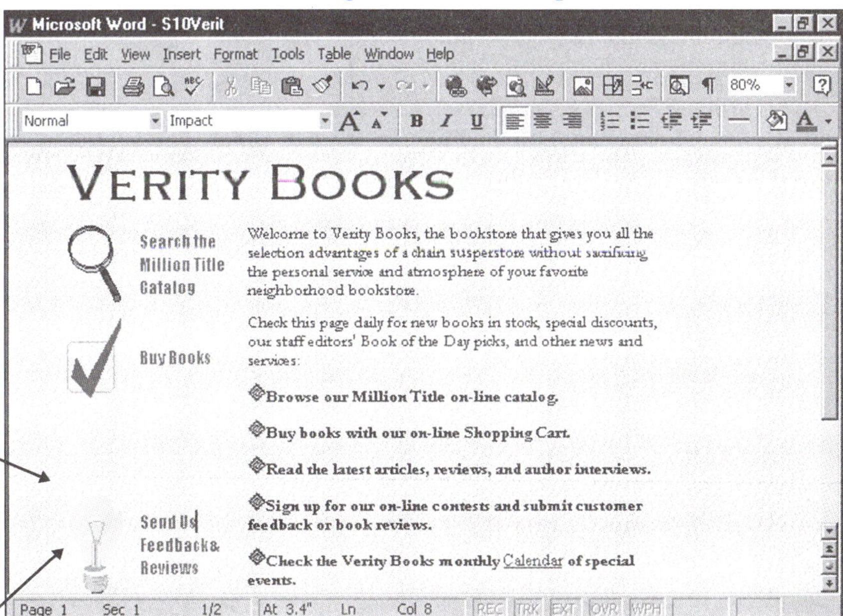

14. The Insert Hyperlink dialog box opens. Link the Light Bulb graphic to **FEEDBACK.HTML** in your Web site folder.

    ✓ *Be sure to select Use relative path for hyperlink.*

15. Click the Light Bulb to go to **FEEDBACK.HTML**.
16. At the bottom of **FEEDBACK.HTML**, insert a hyperlink to **VERITY.HTML** in place of the text "Related Page 1." The hyperlink should say Verity Books Home Page, as shown in the illustration at right.
17. Remember that you need to select the link by right-clicking on the line and selecting Hyperlink before you can change the text.
18. Click the hyperlink to return to **VERITY.HTML**.
19. Select the text "Send Us Feedback & Reviews." Change this text into a hyperlink to **FEEDBACK.HTML** (Ctrl+K).
20. Right-click the new Send Us Feedback & Reviews text hyperlink, then select Hyperlink, Select Hyperlink from the pop-up menu.
21. Change the hyperlink's font to Impact, if available, or choose an appropriate sans serif font.
22. Position the insertion point to the left of the Page Turners heading.
23. Select Insert, Picture, From File. The Insert Picture dialog box opens. Select **BOOK1.WMF** from the drive and folder containing this book's data files. The new graphic appears next to the Page Turners heading.
24. Position the insertion point to the right of the Verity Books heading at the top of page 2 and insert the **BOOKS1.WMF** graphic from the drive and folder containing this book's data files.

    ➲ *The Verity Books home page should now look like the illustration at right.*

25. Save your work on **VERITY.HTML** and **FEEDBACK.HTML** in your Web site folder, then close both Web pages.

New Hyperlink in Feedback.HTML

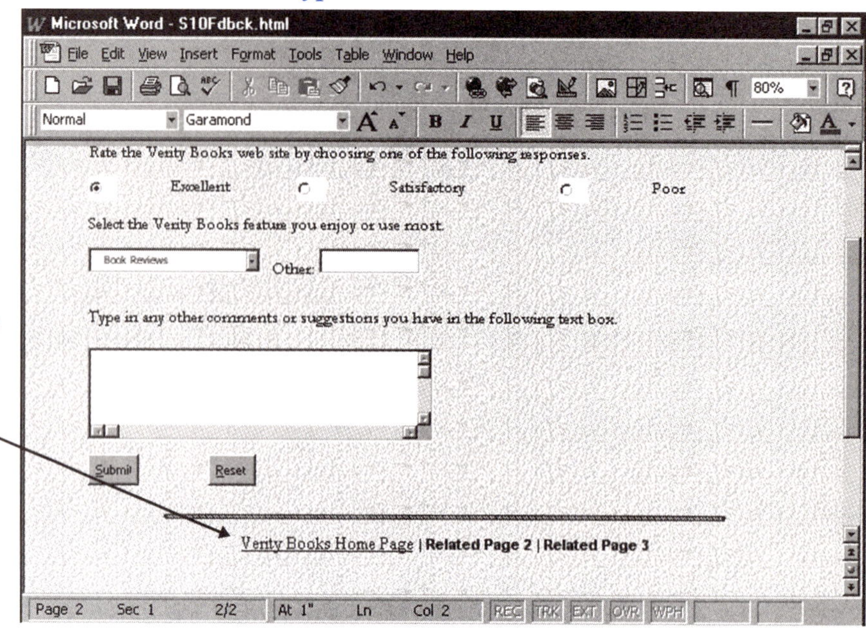

Home Page with More Graphics

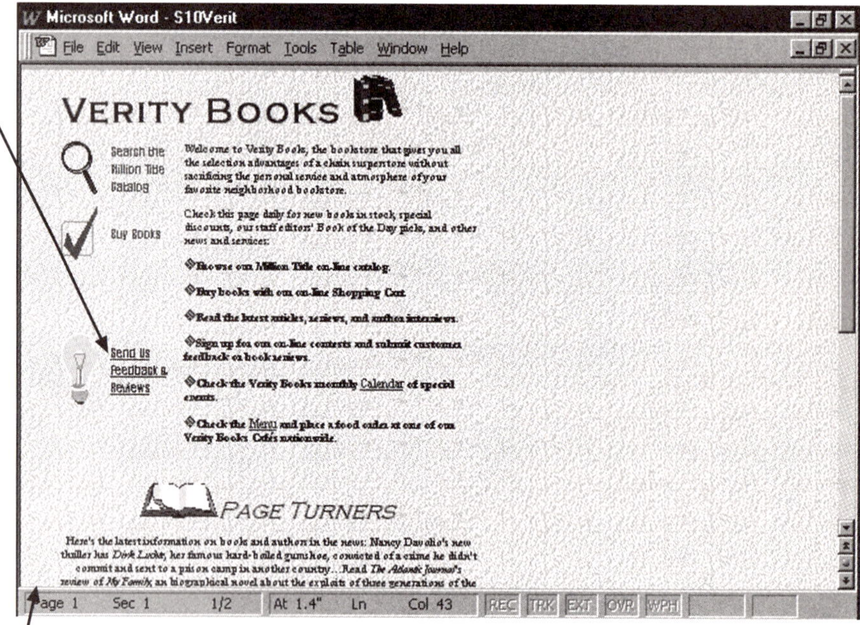

NEXT EXERCISE

Exercise 11

■ Add Marquees ■ Add Animation

NOTES

Add Marquees

- Marquee text is a unique formatting feature you can add to your Web pages to highlight a message. Marquee text can scroll across the page in a variety of ways, moving from left to right, from right to left, or back and forth. You can also choose the number of loops, or times, the text moves across the page, as well as the speed of the movement.
- To insert marquee text, select Insert, Scrolling Text. The Scrolling Text dialog box opens. Here you can select the Behavior, Direction, and Loops number, as well as a text box for entering the text to be scrolled.
- View an example of your text in the Preview window before clicking OK to insert the marquee.

Scrolling Text Dialog Box

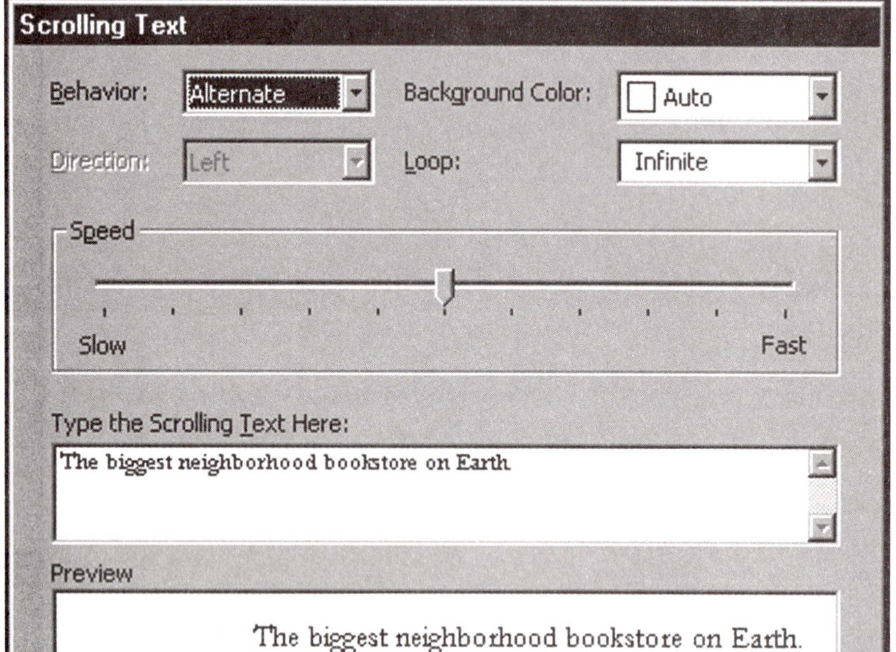

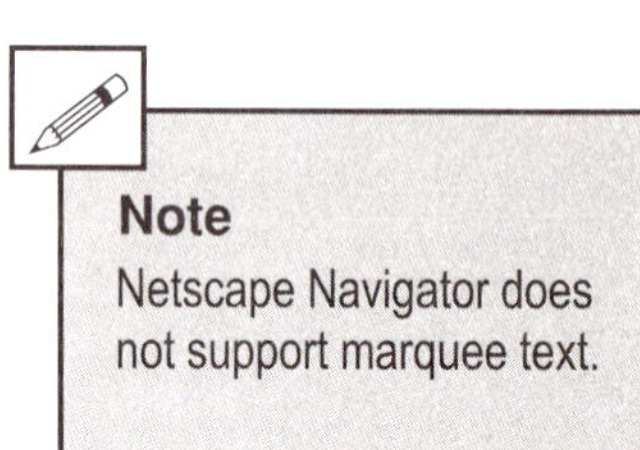

Note

Netscape Navigator does not support marquee text.

Add Animation

- Another simple way to jazz up your Web page is to add animated graphics files. Microsoft Office 97 includes a variety of animation graphics in the GIF file format in the \Office\Valuepack\Animgifs folder.
- These animation files can be inserted just as you would insert any other graphics files. Select Insert, Picture, From File, then select the appropriate drive, folder and file name in the Insert Picture dialog box.
- The new graphics file will be inserted as a static image in your Word Web page. When the page is viewed using a browser, the graphic will display as a continuous animation effect.

Note

Keep in mind that you should not overload your pages with special effects such as marquees, graphics, and animations. Using such effects sparingly increases their impact on the page and ensures a reasonable downloading time for the people who visit your Web site.

In this exercise, you will add a marquee and an animation graphic to the Verity Books home page, then view the new effects in Web Page Preview.

EXERCISE DIRECTIONS

1. Open VERITY.HTML from your Web site folder.
2. Select Table, Show Gridlines.
3. Click in the cell containing the text "Search the Million-Title Catalog."
4. Select Table, Insert Rows. A new row is inserted above the current row.
5. Select all the cells in the new row, then select Table, Merge Cells. The new, blank row now spans the width of the table.
6. Position the mouse pointer on the bottom gridline of the new row so that the pointer changes to a two-headed arrow ÷.
7. Click and drag the gridline up to decrease the height of the new, blank row. The table should look like the one shown in the illustration at right.
8. Place the cursor at the far left side of the new row, then select Insert, Scrolling Text. The Scrolling Text dialog box opens.
9. Select Alternate from the Behavior drop-down list box.
10. Select Yellow from the Background Color list box.
11. Enter the following text in the Type the Scrolling Text Here text box:

    The biggest neighborhood bookstore on Earth.

    ✓ *If you are using Netscape Navigator as your browser, you will be able to preview the scrolling text in Word, but the text will not scroll in your browser.*
12. View the Preview of the marquee text and experiment with the Speed and Behavior of the text if you like.
13. Click OK. The marquee text is inserted into the Web page.

New Row Added to Table

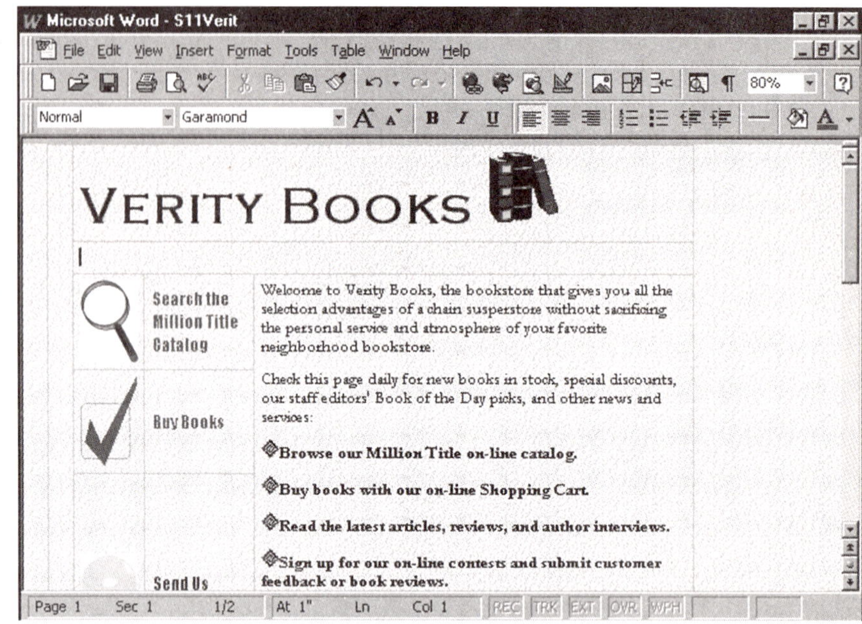

Scrolling Text Dialog Box

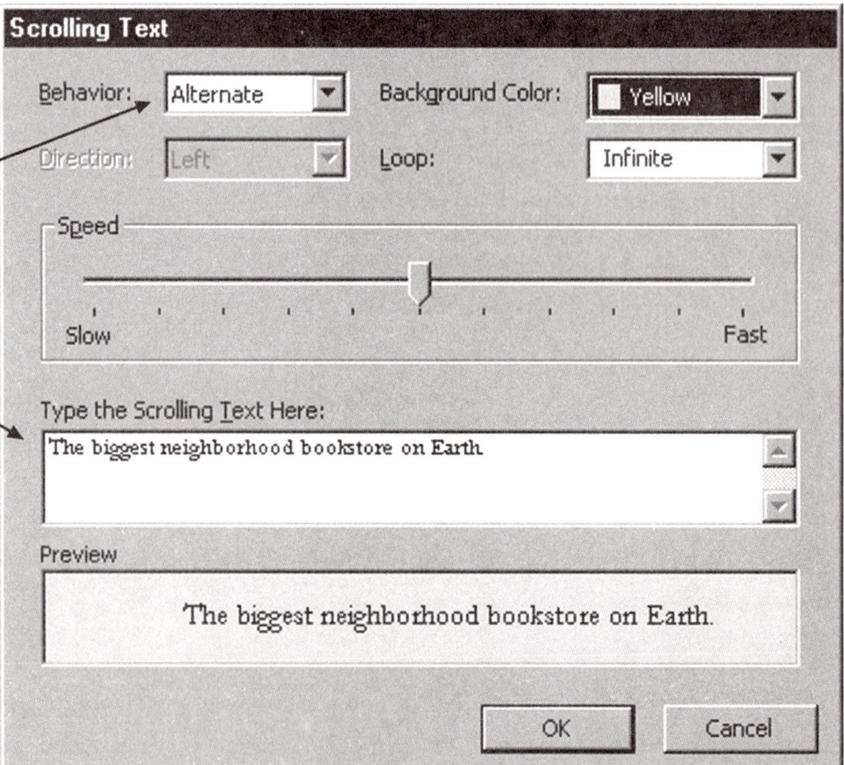

14. With the marquee object selected, click one of the sizing handles on the right side of the marquee and drag the marquee border to fit within the width of the table row.
15. Click outside the marquee cell to deselect the marquee and view the scrolling text on the Web page, as shown in the illustration at right.
16. Select the line between the Page Turners text and the hyperlinks at the bottom of the page.
17. Delete the line.
18. Select Insert, Picture, From File.
19. In the Insert Picture dialog box, select the **BURSTANI.GIF** file from the folder for this book's data files. Click Insert. The animation graphic is inserted into the Web page.
20. Hide table gridlines.
21. Save your work on **VERITY.HTML** in your Web site folder.
22. Select File, Web Page Preview to view the animation and marquee text on your system's Web browser. The Web page is shown in Microsoft Explorer in the illustration at right.
23. Click ☒ to close Web Page Preview.
24. Close **VERITY.HTML** in Word.

Scrolling Text Added to the Home Page

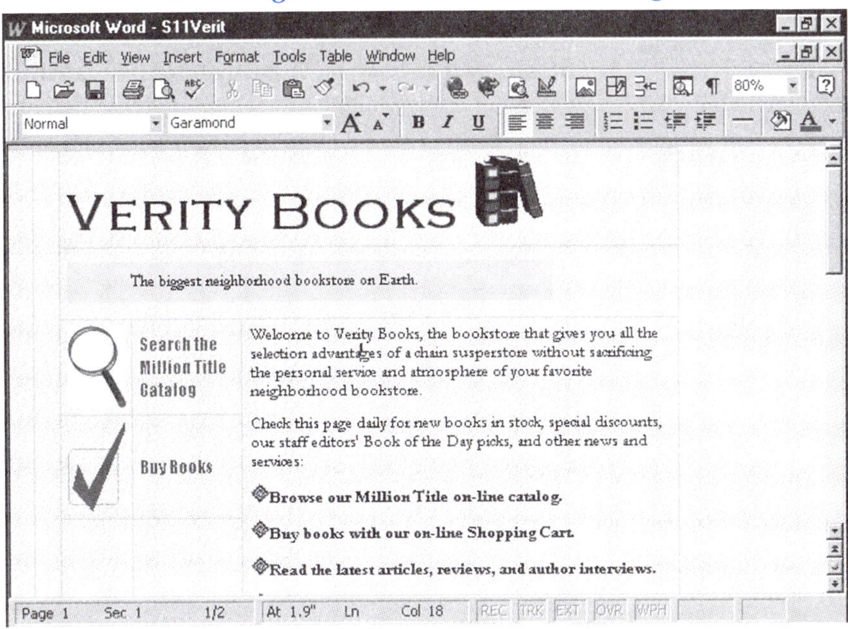

Animation Viewed in Internet Explorer

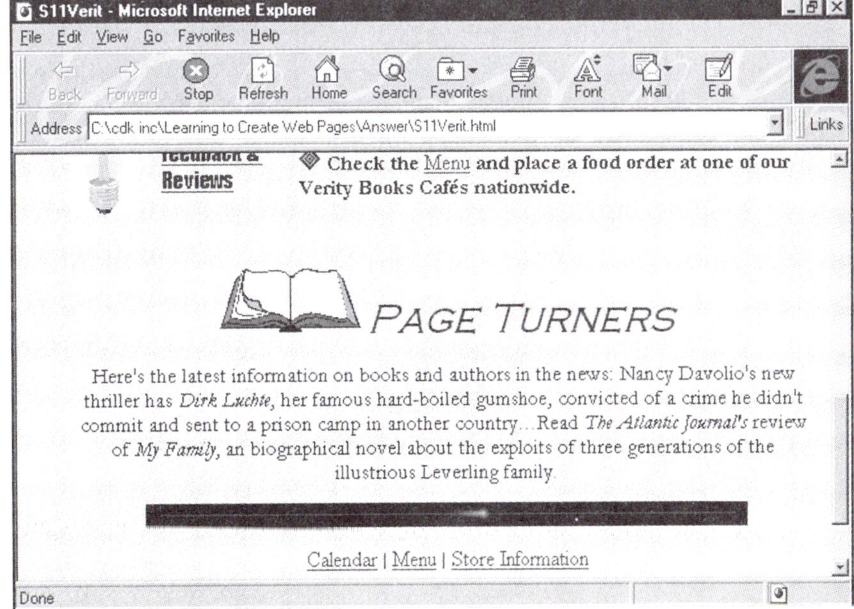

Exercise 12

■ Insert Videos ■ Add Background Sound

NOTES

Insert Videos

- You can create full-blown multimedia Web pages in Word 97, including video clips and background sound. The limitations on what you can do when adding multimedia to your Web pages are not in Word, but in the technology that currently transfers the Web page files to a browser's computer.
- Video files of any length can be extremely large and, therefore, can take a long time to download—even longer than graphics or sound files. For this reason, many people who view your Web page may choose to turn off video display in the browser software. Also, many browsers do not support video.
- For this reason, you should always supply alternate text and perhaps even an alternate graphic image when you insert video clips in your Web pages. Keep the length and number of video clips you use to a minimum. Choose your spots wisely and the video you display will have more impact.

Video Clip Dialog Box

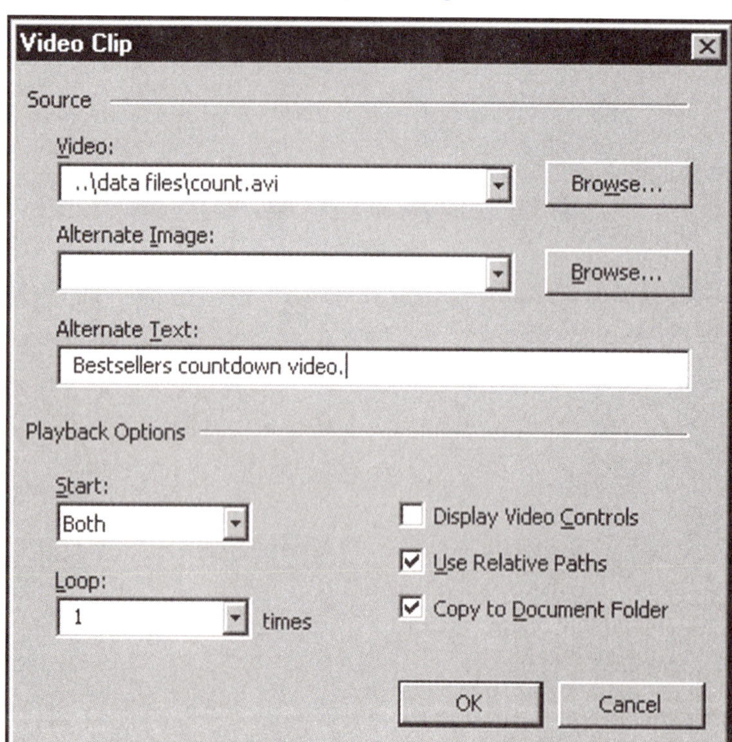

Note

Your computer system must have a sound card installed to experience the Web page sound file in this Exercise.

- To insert a video clip, select Insert, Video. The Video Clip dialog box enables you to search for the file you want to insert by clicking the Browse... button. After you have selected the video clip, you can select an alternate graphic image and insert alternate text that will be displayed if a user elects not to view the video.
- Select Display Video Controls to display a VCR-like interface for controlling play of the video when the clip runs. You should typically choose Use Relative Paths and Copy to Document Folder when inserting a video into a Web page.

Note
You can also select the action that starts the video and how many times to loop the clip in the Video Clip dialog box.

Add Background Sound

- Background sound can be added to your Web page to literally jazz up the page. Background sound files begin playing as soon as the Web page opens and can range from a short sound effect to a favorite piece of music.
- Sound files can be looped to play continuously while your page is being viewed. Because sound files are not nearly as large as video files, length of sound files is less of a concern.
- To insert a sound file, select Insert, Background Sound, Properties. The Background Sound dialog box opens. In it you can click Browse... to select the file you want to add. Next, click the Loop drop-down list box to select how many times you want the file to repeat.
- You should typically choose Use Relative Paths and Copy to Document Folder when inserting a sound into a Web page. Click OK to insert the file. It will be added to the folder in which your Web page is stored. A reference to the file will be added to the Web page.

Background Sound Dialog Box

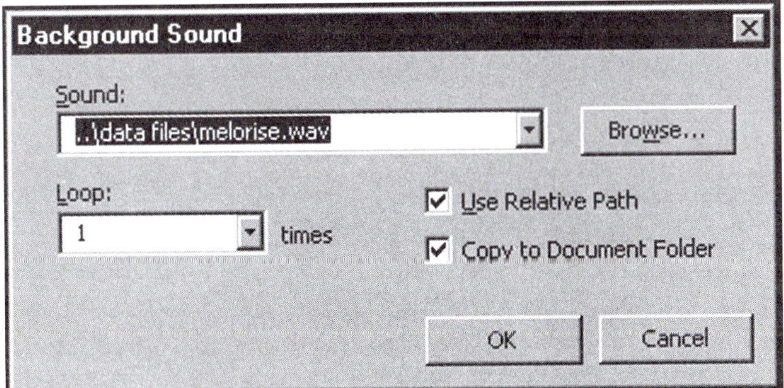

Note
Keep in mind that many users may not have computers equipped with a sound card and speakers to enable them to hear your sound files. Convey important Web page information using text.

In this exercise, you will add a video clip and a background sound file to the Verity Books home page, then view the new effects in Web Page Preview.

EXERCISE DIRECTIONS

1. Open **VERITY.HTML** from your Web site folder.
2. Point to the Light Bulb graphic, then right-click to display the pop-up menu.
3. Click Hyperlink, Select Hyperlink.
4. With the Light Bulb selected, press Delete.
5. Select Insert, Video. The Video Clip dialog box opens.
6. Select Video, then click Browse... to the right of the Video text box. The File Open dialog box appears, as shown in the illustration at right.
7. Select the drive and folder containing this book's data files. Click **COUNT.AVI**, then click Open.
8. The complete file name and path is inserted in the Video text box.
9. Select Alternate Text, then type *Bestsellers countdown video.* in the text box.
10. Select Start, then click the Both option from the drop-down list.
11. Check to be sure the other options are as shown in the illustration at right, then click OK.
    ✓ *You may see a dialog box asking you to insert an alternate image file after you click OK. If so, click Continue to proceed with inserting the video file.*
12. The brief video file is inserted into the Web page. It will begin playing as soon as it is inserted. Watch the video play.

Browse to Select Video Files

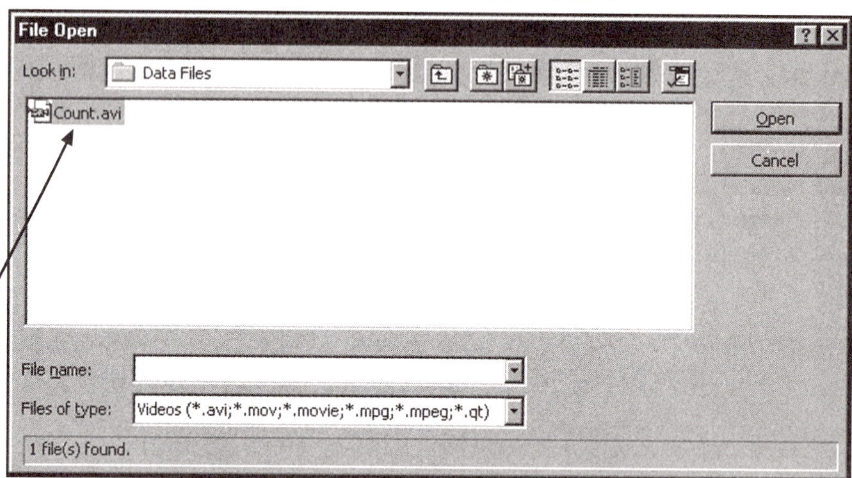

Video Clip Dialog Box

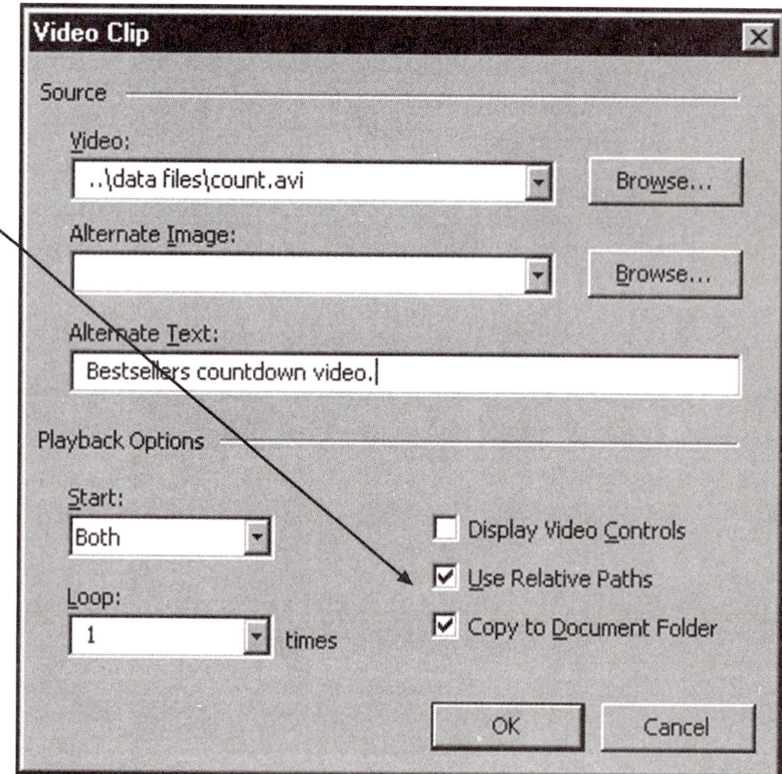

13. Click either the top-right or bottom-right corner sizing handle and drag to reduce the size of the video window. The window should fit into the space previously occupied by the Light Bulb graphic.
14. Click on the Verity Books heading at the top of the page, then select Insert, Background Sound, Properties. The Background Sound dialog box opens.
15. Click Browse... . The File Open dialog box appears, as shown in the illustration at right.
16. Select the drive and folder containing this book's data files. Click **MELORISE.WAV**, then click Open .
17. The complete file name and path is inserted in the Sound text box.
18. Click OK .
19. The new sound file is inserted into the folder containing **VERITY.HTML** (your Web site folder) and a reference to the sound file is inserted into the Web page. The brief sound file will play as the dialog box closes.
20. Save your work on **VERITY.HTML** in your Web site folder.
21. Select File, Web Page Preview to open the Web page in your system's browser.
22. The new sound file and the video clip should play as the browser opens the Web page.
23. Point to the video window to see the video again. Refresh the page if you want to hear the sound file again.
24. Click ☒ to close Web Page Preview.
25. Close the Web page.

Browse to Select Sound Files

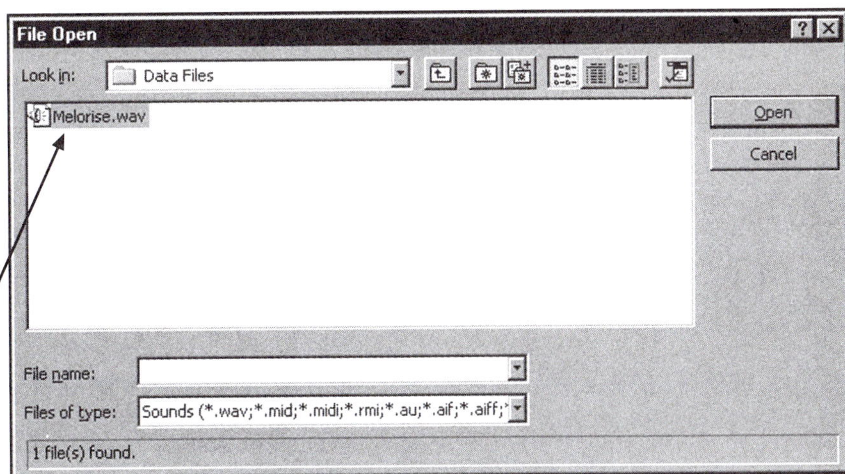

Background Sound Dialog Box

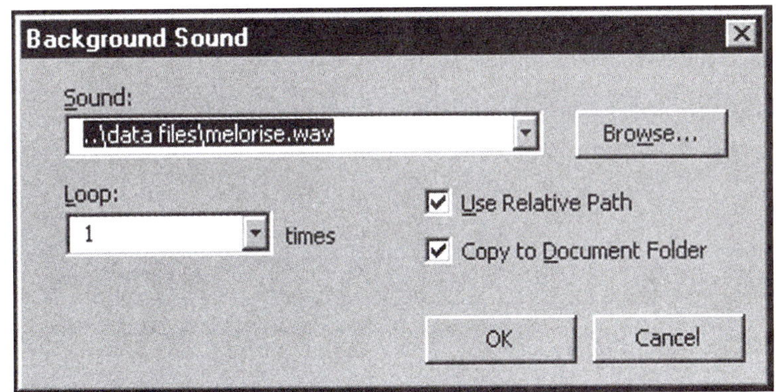

Video Clip Viewed in Internet Explorer

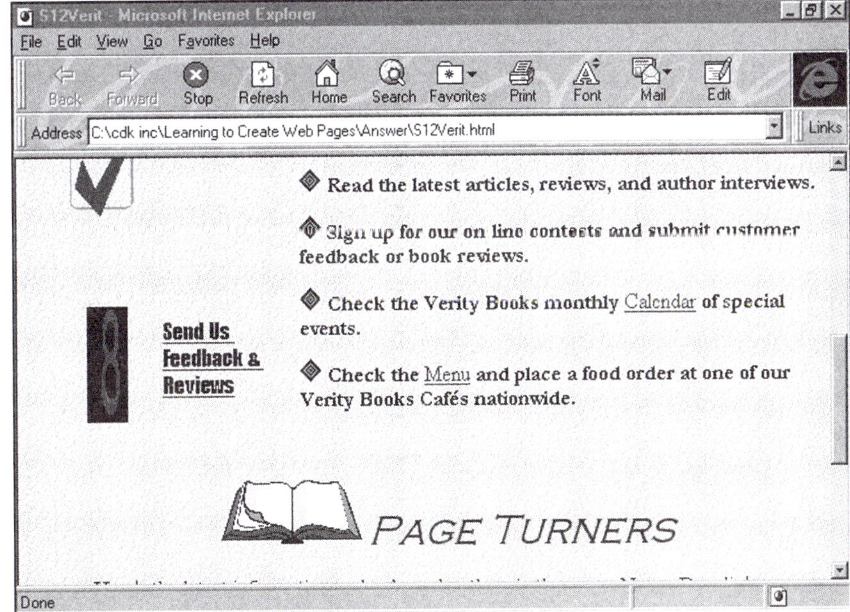

Appendixes

Appendix A: Viruses

Appendix B: Essential Downloads

Appendix C: Glossary

Appendix D: Publish Your Web Page

Appendix E: Troubleshooting

Appendix A

■ Introduction ■ Origins of Viruses ■ Categories of Viruses
■ Virus Symptoms

Viruses

Introduction

Viruses are malicious software written to deliberately cause some form of destruction to someone's computer. They are instructions or code that have been designed to reproduce as they attach themselves to other programs without the user's knowledge. Viruses are a nuisance, but if you know how they work and take the necessary precautions, they can be manageable. No one is exempt from viruses; strict precautions and anti-virus programs are the answer.

Viruses are potentially destructive to one file or to an entire hard disk, whether the file or hard disk are used on a standalone computer or on a multi-user network. Like biological viruses, computer viruses need a host, or a program, to infect. Once infection has been transferred, the viruses can spread like wildfire through the entire library of files. Like human sickness, viruses come in many different forms; some are more debilitating than others.

Origins of Viruses

Viruses can be acquired in a variety of ways:

- An infected diskette
- An infected file downloaded from a bulletin board, the Internet, or an online service.
- A file or program shared across a network

Knowing where viruses are likely to be introduced will make you sensitive to the possibility of getting one.

Categories of Viruses

Viruses come in two categories:

- Boot Sector Viruses
- File Viruses

Boot Sector Viruses may also be called System Sector viruses because they attack the system sector. System or boot sectors contain programs that are executed whenever the PC is booted. Because these sectors are vital for PC operation, they are prime areas for a target by viruses. Viruses that attach to these areas are seriously damaging ones.

File Viruses are more commonly found. Characteristically, a file virus infects by overwriting part or all of a file.

Virus Symptoms

How can you tell if you have a virus? Hopefully, you will install anti-virus software in your PC that will identify viruses and make you aware immediately upon entry to your system. Otherwise, you may experience different symptoms such as:

- Slow processing
- Animation or sound appears out of nowhere
- Unusually heavy disk activity
- Odd changes in files

Appendix B

Essential Downloads

■ **Internet Explorer** ■ **Netscape Navigator** ■ **TUCOWS**
■ **Shareware.Com** ■ **The Jumbo Download Network**
■ **VDOLive Video Player** ■ **Adobe Acrobat Reader** ■ **Shockwave**

Essential Downloads

- The Internet can be a convenient source for downloading valuable software. Log on to the following URLs to download Web and multimedia software, much of which is available free of charge or as shareware, which requires a minimal registration fee.

Internet Explorer

http://www.microsoft.com/ie/download/

- Internet Explorer 4.0 is the latest version of Microsoft's Internet browser software. It has attracted a lot of attention for both it's powerful new features and it's role in the Department of Justice investigation of Microsoft for antitrust violations.
- Explorer 4.0's active desktop features allow the browser software to be much more integrated into the Windows operating system you use to run your computer.
- You can also receive active content from the Web using Explorer's "push" technology. Active content lets you choose from among several Web content "channels" to receive automatic information updates to your desktop.
- Other Explorer 4.0 tools include NetMeeting virtual conferencing software and FrontPage Express. NetMeeting helps facilitate virtual meetings held via the Internet and one-to-one telephone calls from your computer. FrontPage Express enables you to create and post your own Web pages.
- Whatever the outcome of the legal wrangling, Explorer is rapidly gaining market acceptance as the leading Web browser. Get your copy free of charge at this site.

Netscape Navigator

http://home.netscape.com/download/index.html

- Netscape Navigator 4.0 is the other major Web browser on the market today and the direct descendant of the Mosaic browser that first swept many users into the world of surfing the Web.
- Netscape Communicator includes Navigator 4.0 and a complete suite of Internet tools, including Messenger for e-mail, Collabra for newsgroups, and Composer for creating Web pages.
- You can also download a complete installation of Netscape Communicator which includes Netscape Netcaster for receiving active

channel content, Netscape Conference for online collaboration and the capability to handle rich multimedia content as well as bitstream fonts.

- Though you must pay for Netscape products available at this download site, you can download evaluation versions of new software free of charge. Educational institutions and nonprofit organizations can download a number of Netscape products at no charge.

TUCOWS

http://www.tucows.com

- TUCOWS stands for The Ultimate Collection Of Winsock Software. The site bills itself as the world's best collection of Internet software.
- After logging on to the TUCOWS home page, click the appropriate link for your geographical location (such as United States, Europe, Canada), then click the appropriate state (or other area) link. These geographical links are used to produce faster and more reliable software downloads.
- Next click the appropriate link for your computer's operating system. You will see a directory page listing links for more than 60 different types of Internet software.
- Click on a category link to see a listing of software available in that category for downloading. Listings include a complete description of the software, its hardware requirements, and a rating of the software (by number of cows). Click the Download button next to a particular listing to start downloading.
- Most software available at TUCOWS is either shareware or freeware, though some products offered are only demo versions that may have limited features or time restraints.

Shareware.Com

http://www.shareware.com

- Shareware.Com is another great site for downloading software via the Web. The site is a service of the C/Net Web page, noted for its computer and technology news coverage.
- You can browse the site by clicking on the New Arrivals or Most Popular links, or you can simply enter the name of the software you hope to find in the search engine text box.
- Highlights of available shareware are shown on the home page. Click on a link to go to a description of the shareware and a link to the download page.

The Jumbo Download Network

http://www.jumbo.com

- Yet another great software downloading site is The Jumbo Download Network, which lists more than 250,000 shareware programs and links. Available software is conveniently organized by channels, including Business, Desktop, Internet, Utilities, Games, Entertainment, Developer, and Demo City, which offers the latest commercial demos so you can try before you buy.

VDOLive Video Player

http://www.vdo.net/download/

- Download VDOnet Corporation's VDOLive Video Player 3.0 free of charge at this site. VDOLive is the top software for broadcasting and receiving video content over the Internet and is used by many major television networks, including CBS News, MTV, and PBS.
- Click on the VDOLive 3.0 link to begin downloading the software. You must register to download, but otherwise the procedure is free and relatively easy. Only the VDOLive Player software is available for free download. VDOLive server software must be purchased.
- You can also download a trial version of VDOPhone, touted as the first full-color video telephone available for either regular telephone lines or the Internet. VDOPhone lets you see and hear anyone over the Internet with no additional phone charges.
- VDOPhone is currently available for Windows 95 users only. The trial version expires after 5 hours of video reception.

Adobe Acrobat Reader

http://www.adobe.com

- Adobe Acrobat Reader lets you view, navigate, and print many document files available on the Web for downloading.
- To download the Acrobat Reader free of charge, click the Free Plug-Ins and Updates link at the Adobe home page. The link takes you to a file library page that displays a list of nearly thirty software products you can download. Links to download sites for each type of software are displayed by operating system.
- Click the Acrobat Reader link for your computer's operating system. The reader is available for Windows, Macintosh, DOS, UNIX, and OS/2. You will go to a page including short description links and download links for the available versions of Acrobat Reader. Click the Download link to register and begin downloading.
- You can also click the Tryout Software link at the Adobe home page to see descriptions of Adobe's latest multimedia and graphics products as well as download links for trial versions.

Shockwave

http://www.macromedia.com/shockwave/download/

- Macromedia Shockwave facilitates smooth viewing of animation and multimedia over the Internet. Many Web browsers and online services such as Internet Explorer, Netscape Navigator, and AOL include Shockwave with their software.
- If you want to download Shockwave, go to the Shockwave Download Center at the above URL, and click the Get Shockwave link.

Appendix C

Glossary

address book An application where you can store and access frequently used e-mail addresses.

anonymous FTP A special kind of FTP service that allows any user to log on. Anonymous FTP sites have the predefined user named "anonymous" that accepts any password.

Archie A database system of FTP resources that helps you find files that exist anywhere on the Internet.

ARPAnet (Advanced Research Projects Administration Network) Ancestor to the Internet: ARPAnet began in 1969 as a project developed by the US Department of Defense. Its initial purpose was to enable researchers and military personnel to communicate in the event of an emergency.

ASCII (American Standard Code for Information Interchange) A computer code that represents text as numbers that can be transferred and read by nearly any computer in the world. ASCII text is often called plain text.

ASCII file Also called plain text file. A file containing ASCII-formatted text only; can be read by almost any computer or program in the world. Only ASCII files can be sent through the e-mail system.

attachment A file or Web page sent with an e-mail message.

Base64 (MIME) encoding One of the encoding schemes, used in the MIME (Multipurpose Internet Mail Extensions) protocol.

baud The number of signals sent per second by a communication device. Usually used to measure the speed of file transfer over a modem.

bps (bits per second) The speed of file transfer measured in bits of data per second.

BCC (Blind Carbon Copy A copy of an e-mail message sent to a recipient without the recipient's address appearing in the message.

binary file A file containing more than just plain text, such as images, media clips, programs, or formatted text files such as spreadsheets or word-processor documents. A binary file must be encoded (converted to ASCII format) before it can be passed through the e-mail system.

BinHex An encoding scheme for the Macintosh platform that allows a file to be read as text when passed through the e-mail system.

bookmark (called a *favorite* in Internet Explorer) A browser feature that memorizes and stores the address of a certain Web site. Creating bookmarks enables a quick return to favorite sites.

browser A software program that allows you to locate and display documents on the World Wide Web. Browser programs such as Netscape Navigator and Microsoft Internet Explorer provide simple searching techniques and create paths that can return you to sites you visited previously.

CC (Carbon Copy) A copy of an e-mail message sent to a person(s) who is not the primary recipient.

CDF (channel definition format) A system developed by Microsoft that allows Web publishers to use push technology to broadcast Web content to users on a "channel." Users who subscribe to a channel can be automatically notified of updates to channel content, which can then be automatically downloaded to the user's system.

Channel Web sites designed for subscription access that predefine what pages should be downloaded and how often updates should occur. Channels work using CDF, a type of Push technology, which allows Web publishers to broadcast information to you without your having to go to the Web site or even be connected to the Internet.

chat (Internet Relay Chat) A live "talk" session with other Internet or network users in which a conversation is exchanged back and forth.

client program A computer program designed to talk to a specific server program. An e-mail client, for example, is designed to connect to a mail server and request and download incoming messages from it. Client programs usually run on your own computer and talk to server programs on remote computers on a network.

client A computer that signs onto another computer, usually referred to as the server.

complex search Uses a text string of multiple words, and may also use operators that modify the search string, to search for matches in a search engine's catalog.

connect time The amount of time you are connected to an Internet server or other remote computer.

cookie A text message sent by a Web server when you access a Web site for the first time. Cookies are stored on your hard drive by your browser and sent back to the Web server each time your browser requests a page from that server. Cookies are used primarily to identify and track users for the purpose of customizing Web content to suit particular users.

copyright The legal right of ownership of published material. E-mail messages are covered by copyright laws. In most cases, the copyright owner is the writer of the message.

crawler See *spider.*

digital signature A digital code attached to an e-mail message that uniquely identifies the sender. Digital codes are used to enhance e-mail security by ensuring that the sender is who he or she claims to be.

directory 1. Also referred to as a folder. Directories are lists of files and other directories. They are used for organizing and storing computer files. 2. A menu-based hierarchical listing of Web sites that you can browse by clicking links to increasingly specific topics.

domain The portion of an Internet address that follows the @ symbol and identifies the computer you are logging onto.

download Copy files (e-mail, software, documents, etc.) from a remote computer to your own computer.

e-mail (electronic mail) A communication system for exchanging messages and attached files. E-mail can be sent to anyone in the world as long as both parties have access to the Internet and an Internet address to identify themselves.

e-mail address An address that identifies an electronic post office box where e-mail can be sent. All Internet e-mail addresses have the form: <name>@<domainname > For example, nmckay@morgan.edu

e-mail client A program that lets you to send and receive e-mail, such as Outlook Express or Netscape Messenger.

encoding A method of converting a binary file to ASCII format for e-mail purposes. Common encoding schemes include UUencoding and MIME (Base64) encoding.

encryption The conversion of data into a secret code meant to prevent unauthorized access to confidential information transferred over the Internet or any network. To translate encrypted data, you must have the necessary password or code key.

fair use The right to use short quotes and excerpts from copyrighted material such as e-mail messages.

FAQ (Frequently Asked Questions document) A text document that contains a collection of frequently asked questions about a particular subject. FAQs on many subjects are commonly available on the Web.

favorite See *bookmark*.

file A general term usually used to describe a computer document. It may also be used to refer to more than one file, however, such as groups of documents, software, games, etc.

file compression A file storage format that uses less computer memory than regular file formats. To compress and decompress files you need a file compression application, such as WinZip or PKZip, installed on your computer. Compressed files are easier to send across the Internet, since they take less time to upload and download.

folders/directories Folders, also referred to as directories, are organized storage areas for maintaining computer files. Like filing cabinets, they help you manage your documents and files.

font A typeface that contains particular style and size specifications.

freeware Software that can be used for free forever. No license is required, and the software may be copied and distributed legally.

FTP (File Transfer Protocol) The method of transferring files from one computer to another over a network (or across the Internet). It requires that both the client and server computers use special communication software to talk to one another.

FTP site An Internet site that uses File Transfer Protocol and enables files to be downloaded and/or uploaded. When you access an FTP site through a browser application, however, your log-in is considered "anonymous" and will not allow uploading.

FTP software A computer program used to move files from one computer to another. The FTP program usually comes in two parts: a server program that runs in the computers offering the FTP service, and a client program running in computers, like yours, that wish to use the service.

Gopher A browsing system for Internet resources that predates the World Wide Web. Gopher works much like a directory or folder, listing Internet sites in a hierarchical menu of files.

heading fields (headings) Individual fields, like To and From, in the header of an e-mail message.

hierarchically structured catalog A catalog of Web sites that is organized into a few major categories that have sub-categories under them. Each sub-category has additional sub-categories under it. The level of detail in this structure depends on the particular Web site.

Home page A Web site's starting point. A Home page is like a table of contents. It outlines what a particular site has to offer, and usually contains connecting links to other related areas of the Internet as well.

host A central computer that other computers log onto (usually via a modem connection) for the purpose of sharing and exchanging information.

hot lists Lists of Web sites that you have visited or "ear-marked" and wish to return to later. Your browser program will store the paths to those sites and generate a short-cut list for future reference.

HTML (HyperText Mark Up Language) The programming language used to create Web pages so that they can be viewed, read, and accessed from any computer running on any type of operating system.

HTTP (HyperText Transfer Protocol) The communication protocol that allows for Web pages to connect to one another, regardless of what type of operating system is used to display or access the files.

hyperlinks Specially formatted text or graphics that you can click to jump to another location on the Web, in the current Web site, or on your own computer.

hypertext or hypermedia A database system in which related documents or sites on the Internet can be linked to each other. The clickable text and objects (pictures, sound, video, etc.) that activate the links are called hyperlinks.

image map A graphic image on a Web page containing multiple hyperlinks.

IMAP (Internet Message Access Protocol) A communications protocol used to transfer incoming messages from e-mail servers to your system.

inbox Where incoming e-mail messages are stored and retrieved.

Indexer A program that indexes Web sites collected by a spider program for use in a search engine's database.

Information Superhighway Nickname for the Internet: a vast highway by which countless pieces of information are made available and exchanged back and forth among its many users.

Internet A world-wide computer network that connects millions of users working out of businesses, schools, research foundations, private homes, and other networks. Anyone with access can log on, communicate via e-mail, and search for various types of information.

Internet address The user ID utilized by an individual or host computer on the Internet. An Internet address is usually associated with the ID used to send and receive e-mail. It consists of the user's ID followed by the domain.

Internet Protocol The method of communication which allows information to be exchanged across the Internet and across varying platforms that may be accessing or sending information.

intranet A network that functions like the Internet but is accessible only by members of the sponsoring organization.

ISDN (Integrated Services Digital Network) A protocol for sending data over special digital telephone lines that transmit data faster than regular modem lines do.

ISP (Internet Service Provider) A private or public organization that offers access to the Internet. Most ISP's charge a monthly or annual fee and generally offer such features as e-mail accounts, a predetermined number of hours for Internet access time (or unlimited access for a higher rate), etc.

Java A programming language often used on the World Wide Web. Small Java applications are called Java applets. Java applets are often included in Web pages and can be downloaded and run on your computer by a Java-compatible Web browser, such as Netscape Navigator or Microsoft Internet Explorer.

KBPS (Kilobits Per Second) A unit of measurement often used to calculate the speed of data transfer using a modem. A kilobit is made up of 1,024 bits.

LAN (Local Area Network) A network confined to a small area that allows several computers to share data and devices, such as printers and modems.

links Hypertext or hypermedia objects that, when clicked selected, will connect you to related documents or other areas of interest. See *hyperlink*.

login A process by which you gain access to a computer by giving it your username and password. If the computer doesn't recognize your login, access will be denied.

macro virus A virus written in the macro language of a particular program (such as Word) and contained in a program document. When the document is opened, the macro is executed, and the virus usually adds itself to other, similar documents. Macro viruses can be only as destructive as the macro language allows.

message header The group of heading fields at the start of every e-mail program used by the e-mail system to route and otherwise deal with your mail.

meta-tree structured catalog Another term for a hierarchically structured catalog.

MIME (Multipurpose Internet Mail Extension) An Internet protocol that encodes and decodes binary files sent over the Internet as e-mail attachments.

modem A piece of equipment (either internal or external) that allows a computer to connect to a phone line for the purpose of dialing into the Internet, another network, or an individual computer.

modem speed (baud rate) Indicates at what speed your computer will be able to communicate with a computer on the other end. The higher the rate, the quicker the response time for accessing files and Web pages, processing images, downloading software, etc.

multimedia The process of using various computer formats: pictures, text, sound, movies, etc.

multithread search engines Software that searches the Web sites of other search engines and gathers the results of these searches for your use.

Netiquette (network etiquette) The network equivalent of respectfulness and civility in dealing with people and organizations.

network A group of computers (two or more) that are connected to one another through various means, usually cable or dial-in connections.

newsgroup An online discussion group. Users specify which news topic they are interested in and subscribe to receive information on that topic. To read and post messages to a newsgroup, you must have a newsreader application installed on your computer.

newsreader A program that allows you to connect to a news server and read and respond to Usenet newsgroups.

offline The process of performing certain tasks, such as preparing e-mail messages, prior to logging onto the Internet.

online Connected to the Internet.

online services Organizations that usually offer Internet access as well as other services, such as shareware, technical support, group discussions, and more. Most online services charge a monthly or annual fee.

operators Words or symbols that modify a search string instead of being part of it.

outbox Where offline e-mail messages are stored. The contents of an outbox are uploaded to the Internet once you log on and prompt your e-mail program to send them.

packet A body of information that is passed through the Internet. It contains the sender's and receiver's addresses and the item that is being sent. Internet Protocol is used to route and process the packet.

platform Refers to the type of computer and its corresponding operating system, such as PC, Macintosh, UNIX. The Internet is a multi-platform entity, meaning that all types of computers can access it.

plug-ins Programs that enable a Web browser of e-mail application to view files they cannot run on their own.

POP (Post Office Protocol) A communications protocol used to transfer incoming messages from e-mail servers to your system.

protocol A standardized format for transferring data between computers on a network. Your computer must support a particular protocol if you want to communicate with other computers using that protocol.

public domain freeware Software that can be used for free; usually the author is anonymous.

pull To request data from another computer on a network. Clicking a hyperlink for a Web page you want to view on your screen is an example of pulling data.

push To send data to a computer(s) on a network without the recipient computer(s) having first requested it. Sending e-mail is an example of pushing data. Internet channel broadcasts are an example of the increasing use of push technology by Web page providers to send information to users on a regular basis, without the recipients having to request the data or be connected to the site.

quote format A way of displaying text quoted from other e-mail messages, most frequently used in replies. Quoted text usually has a character like ">" at the start of each line. Some e-mail programs let you set the style of quoted material.

search engine A program that searches a database of Web documents for specified keyword(s) and then returns a list of Web sites containing the keyword(s).

search sites Web sites that contain catalogs of Web resources that can be searched by headings, URLs, and key words.

self-extracting archive Macintosh-platform compressed file that does not require external software for decompression. These files usually end with an .sea extension.

self-extracting file PC-platform compressed file that does not require external software for decompression. These files usually end with an .exe extension.

server program A program located on a remote computer that offers a service to other programs called client programs. An e-mail server program, for example, stores incoming e-mail messages until e-mail client programs connect to it and download the messages.

server A computer that is accessed by other computers on a network. It usually shares files with or provides other services to the client computers that log onto it.

shareware Computer programs, utilities and other items (fonts, games, etc.) that can be downloaded or distributed free of charge, but with the understanding that if you wish to continue using it, you will send the suggested fee to the developer.

signature A few lines of text automatically appended to the body of an e-mail message. Signatures usually include the sender's address plus other information.

simple search Uses a one- or two-word text string without any operators to search for matches in a search engine's catalog.

.sit file A Macintosh file compressed by using a compression application called StuffIt.

SLIP (Serial Line Internet Protocol) Software that allows for a direct serial connection to the Internet. SLIP allows your computer to become part of the Internet – not just a terminal accessing the Internet. If your computer is set up with SLIP, you can Telnet or FTP other computers directly without having to go through an Internet provider.

SMTP (Simple Mail Transfer Protocol) The method used to transfer e-mail messages between servers and from your system to your mail server.

snail mail Mail sent by the United States Postal Service.

spider A program that crawls all over the Web seeking new Web pages for a search engine. The collected Web pages are then indexed according to the text they contain. This index is added to the search engine's database, which users can search by keyword to find sites of interest. Other terms for these programs are robot and webcrawler.

standalone FTP client program A standalone computer program designed to talk to an FTP server program running at a remote computer site that offers FTP services. The FTP client program can ask for the files you want and send files you wish to deliver. The client program runs in your computer; the server program runs at the site.

start page The opening page within a browser application. This is the page from which all other Web site links are built. A browser's start page is its Home page by default, but you can customize your browser to begin with any Web site as your start page.

subject-structured catalog A catalog organized under a few broad subject headings. The number and names of these headings depend on the Web site.

surfing the Internet Moving from site to site on the World Wide Web by clicking hyperlinks of interest.

TCP/IP (Transmission Control Protocol/ Internet Protocol) The communication system that is used between networks on the Internet. It checks to make sure that information is being correctly sent and received from one computer to another.

Telnet A program that allows one computer to log on to another host computer. This process allows you to use any of the features available on the host computer, including sharing data and software, participating in interactive discussions, etc.

text format file Same as the ASCII format file: a document that has been formatted to be read by almost any computer or program in the world.

text string A string of ASCII characters. The text string may or may not contain operators.

threaded messages Messages grouped so that replies to a message are grouped with the original message. When threaded messages are sorted, threads are kept together.

uploading The process of copying computer files (e-mail, software, documents, etc.) from one's own computer to a remote computer.

URL (Uniform Resource Locator) An address that identifies the location of a particular document on the World Wide Web.

Usenet A world-wide discussion system, operating on linked Usenet servers, consisting of a set of newsgroups where articles or messages are posted covering a variety of subjects and interests. You can use your browser or a newsreader program to access the newsgroups available from your Internet provider's Usenet server.

UUencoding (UNIX-to-UNIX encoding) An Internet protocol that enables transport of binary files over the Internet. UUencoding is common on all platforms, not just UNIX.

virus A small, usually destructive computer program that hides inside innocent-looking programs. Once the virus is executed, it attaches itself to other programs. When triggered, often by the occurrence of a date or time on the computer's internal clock/calendar, it executes an annoying or damaging function, such as printing a message or reformatting your hard disk.

WAIS (Wide Area Information Servers) A system that allows for searches for information based on actual contents of files, not just file titles.

Web server A computer that posts Web pages.

Web site A location on the Internet that represents a particular company, organization, topic, etc. It normally contains links to more information within a site, as well as suggested links to related sites on the Internet. Each Web site is identified by a unique Internet address, or URL.

Web TV A group of products that let you access the World Wide Web on your TV and navigate through it using a remote control.

Webcast To use the Web to broadcast or push Web data to users without their having to request it or be connected to the host site.

Webmaster The person in charge of creating, updating, and monitoring a Web site.

World Wide Web (WWW) A graphical, user-friendly way to find information on the Internet through the use of hypertext or hypermedia linking. Hypertext and hypermedia consist of text and graphic objects that, when you click on them, automatically link you to different areas of a site or to related Internet sites.

zip file PC file compressed with a file compression program, such as WinZip or PKZip. Zipped files usually need to be unzipped with a file compression program before they can be used.

Appendix D

- Post Web Sites to a Server
- Save All Your Web Site Files in One Folder
- Use Relative Hyperlinks ■ Contact Your Internet Service Provider
- Use Personal Web Server

NOTES

Post Web Sites to a Server

- Creating Web pages in Office 97 is only the first part of the Web publishing process. After creating your Web site you must then post it to a Web server. In order for others to access your Web site via the Internet and the World Wide Web, the site's files must be saved on a Web server machine that can deliver the files to browsers that request them.
- Posting Web sites to a server is beyond the scope of this book and of necessity involves consultation with your Internet Service Provider and/or the system administrator for your network. However, following the procedures in this Appendix as you create your Web site in Office 97 will make posting your site to a server much smoother.

Save All Your Web Site Files in One Folder

- The most important thing to keep in mind about posting to a server as you create Web pages in Office 97 is simply to save all your files in *one* working folder. That means all Office documents and HTML Web pages you create as well as all the associated graphics, template, sound, animation, and video files should be stored in the one working folder.
- Typically, the Office 97 wizards used to create Web pages do this by default.
- Then, when you have completed your work on the Web site in Office and you want to post the site to a server, you can copy and transfer the working folder to the Web server. Storing all your files in one folder, both in the working folder while you're developing your Web site and in the "live" folder on the server, ensures that all the necessary files along with their associated graphics, scripts, and mutlimedia files will be available for testing and for access by browsers visiting your site.

Use Relative Hyperlinks

- Another important step to take as you prepare your Web site is to use relative hyperlinks among the files in your Web site folder. The major advantage of this is that you won't have to manually update in HTML the hyperlinks among the various Web pages within the folder.
- When you transfer your working Web site folder to the Web server, all the relative hyperlinks will remain active and correct because they still refer to locations within the working folder.

SERVER
Can mean both the actual machine hosting a Web site as well as the server software used to administer a Web site.

SCRIPT
A file defining the procedure used by the Web server for accepting and sending network data and/or executing programs over the network.

CAUTION
Some Internet Service Providers will not allow you to have execute permission when posting to their servers due to the security risks involved. In such cases, you cannot post Word and Excel Web forms that receive information or Access dynamic Web databases.

Contact Your Internet Service Provider

- Creating your Web site with the previous steps in mind will make life easier when it comes time to post your Web site to a server. When you are ready to post your site, you should contact your Internet Service Provider or the system administrator of your network.
- If you are posting to a network Intranet or your local computer, you may be able to simply copy the folder to the location indicated by the system administrator.
- If you use an independent Internet Service Provider, the file posting procedure may prove to be more complex. You will need to contact the Service Provider and ask for the proper location for your Web site folder as well as detailed instructions for transferring the folder to the Service Provider's Web server machine. Some Service Providers have software programs you can use to help automate the transfer procedure.

Use Personal Web Server

- In addition to the other Web-friendly features you have learned about in this book, Office 97 also includes a program called Microsoft Personal Web Server. This software enables you to set up a Web server on your own computer.
- Setting up a Web server using Personal Web Server is beyond the scope of this book, but it's relatively simple to use if you're linked to a school or company Intranet and want to set up your own server.
- Personal Web Server is designed specifically to run on Windows 95 and to support all the Office 97 Web features, including Excel Web forms and dynamic Access databases. This means you can set up the server as you wish and freely install the executable scripts needed to handle these interactive Web pages.
- The other major advantage of using a Personal Web Server on your own machine is that you can post your Web site simply by copying your site folder to the appropriate location on your hard drive.

NOTE

If you want to set up your own server for the Internet via your Internet Service Provider, you will have to have a very fast Internet connection and you will probably need a more robust server program such as Microsoft Internet Information Server.

Appendix E

Troubleshooting

NOTES

- This appendix contains information that you may find useful in resolving problems that arise while you are creating a Web page with Office 97. This appendix covers the following topics:

  - Install Internet Explorer 3.0, below
  - View File Extensions, page 491
  - Network File Extension Names, page 491
  - Install Office 97 Web Publishing Tools, page 492
  - Turn off HTML Source View, page 492
  - Turn off Word Fields, page 492
  - Confirm Conversion at Open, page 493
  - **Error! Reference source not found.**, page **Error! Bookmark not defined.**
  - **Error! Reference source not found.**, page **Error! Bookmark not defined.**
  - **Error! Reference source not found.**, page **Error! Bookmark not defined.**
  - **Error! Reference source not found.**, page **Error! Bookmark not defined.**

Install Internet Explorer 3.0

- Not all Web browsing software is created equal, and some browsers will work better than others for completing the exercises in this book. All the exercises and illustrations involving Web browsers in the book were created using Microsoft Internet Explorer 3.0, which is included with Office 97.
- If not already on your system, it is recommended that you install Internet Explorer 3.0. You will achieve the best results in viewing and running the Office Web pages you create if you use Explorer. To install Explorer, run the program \Valupack\Iexplore\MSIE301.exe on the Office 97 CD.
- If you use another browser such as Netscape Navigator or NCSA Mosaic to complete the exercises in the book, you may not be able to view some of the graphics and multimedia features created using Office 97. In many cases your Web pages when viewed in your browser will look different from the book illustrations.

CAUTION

Check with your instructor or system administrator if you are not sure about the procedures you should use when installing programs on your school or company network.

- Formatting features such as center and right alignment, wrapping around graphics and other objects, as well as special formatting such as marquees may not be handled by many browsers. In such cases, the browser will display the affected text according to its own interpretation of the formatting. For example, marquee text will be presented as static text. Center-aligned text will be shifted to left alignment.

View File Extensions

- Viewing file extensions is important for identifying the many different types of files you use in creating Web pages. It is recommended that you have file extensions visible as you work through the Exercises in this book. If they are not visible, you may have problems when files of the same file name but different file type are used.
- To view file extensions, open Windows Explorer and select View, Options. Select the View tab, then deselect the Hide MS-DOS file extensions for file types that are registered option.

Network File Extension Names

- If you are saving your files to a network drive, you must limit the file extensions to three characters. For example, save your files with the .HTM extension, not the full .HTML extension.
- If you try and save to a network drive with a four-character file extension, you will receive an error message that your file name is invalid on an 8.3 system and will be unable to save the file. Rename the file with the three-character file extension.

Install Office 97 Web Publishing Tools

- Many of the procedures and tools described in this book will not work unless the Office 97 Web publishing tools are available. If you have problems performing any of the Web publishing activities in the Exercises, run Office 97 setup again and install the Web tools to your system.
- To run setup, insert the Office 97 CD into your CD-ROM drive, then double-click the Setup.exe icon. The Microsoft Office 97 Setup dialog box appears. Click the Add/Remove button, then check the Web Page Authoring (HTML) and Converters and Filters components. Continue through the end of the installation process following the on-screen instructions.

Double-Click Setup.exe to Install Office Web Components

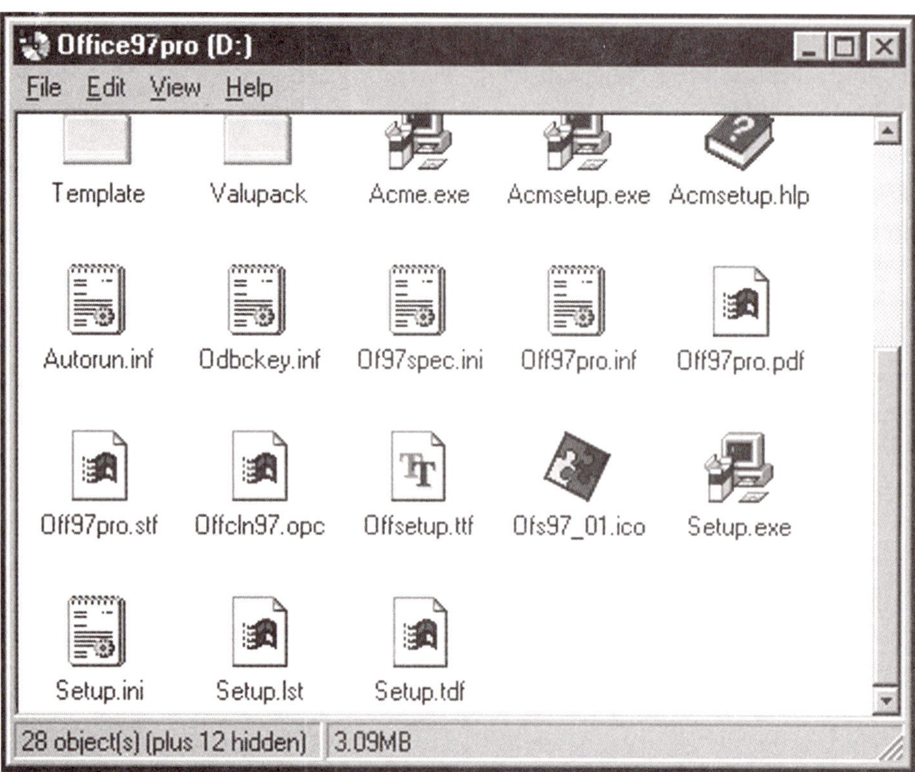

Turn off HTML Source View

- If you open a Web page in Word and see the HTML source code instead of the document itself, select View, Exit HTML Source. Word will change the view to Online Layout view.

Turn off Word Fields

- If you open a Web page in Word and see Word fields (text and formatting codes in curly brackets), press Alt+F9 to switch off viewing the Word fields. Pressing Alt+F9 again will turn the fields view back on.

Confirm Conversion at Open

- If you want to confirm the conversion of a Web page file you're opening in Word, select Tools, Options to open Word's Option dialog box. Go to the General tab and select Confirm conversion at Open, then click OK. With this option selected, Word displays the Convert File dialog box each time you open a file of type other than Word documents and templates. The dialog box shows you what type of file you are converting and opening. Click OK to confirm the file type and opent the document.

General Tab of the Options Dialog Box

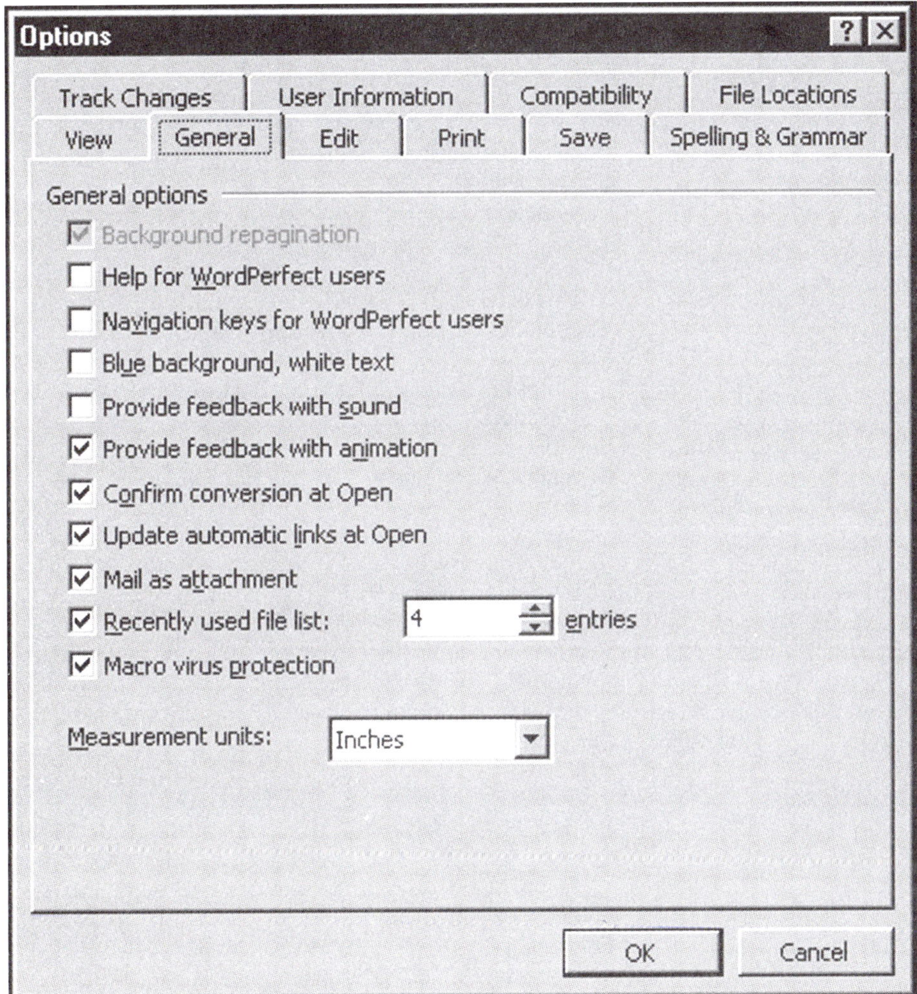

- If you don't want to see this dialog box when opening files, go to the General tab of the Options dialog box and deselect the Confirm conversion at Open option.

Index

A

Adobe Acrobat Reader 480
America Online Home Page 192
America's Job Bank 252
America's Job Bank Home Page 261
American Demographics 332
American Demographics Home Page 341
American List Council Home Page 386
American List Counsel (ALC) 377
Animation
  add 467
AOL.com 180

B

Back button
  Netscape 62
Background sound
  add 471
Bank Rate Monitor 208, 215
BigBook 354
BigBook Home Page 365
Bookmark
  Netscape 71
Bookmarks
  create from history list 74
  edit in Netscape 44
Bulleted list
  create 429
Bullets and Numbering
  Word 429
BusinessWeek Online 194, 205

C

Cell
  merge and split 444
Chicago Tribune Home Page
  http://www.chicago.tribune.com 76
Clip Gallery 461
CNET 272
CNET Home Page 283
CNN Interactive
  http://www.cnn.com 76
Commerce Business Daily 388
Commerce Business Daily Home Page 395
Control
  add to form 455
  for form 454
  modify 456
Copy
  hyperlink 440

D

DDC Publishing Home Page
  http://www.ddcpub.com 69
Delete a bookmark
  Netscape 40, 73
Disconnect
  from service provider 59
Dun & Bradstreet business database 377

E

Edge Online Business Tools 263
Edit bookmarks
  Netscape 44
E-mail
  how it works 117
  uses of 116
Entrepreneurial Edge Online Home Page 271
Exit
  Internet Explorer 18
  Netscape 59
Expedia 182
Expedia's Travel Agent 310

F

Fast Company Home Page 192
Favorites folder
  create new in Internet Explorer 41
  Internet Explorer 38
  organize in Internet Explorer 41
File extensions
  network 491
  view 491
Forbes Digital Tool 195, 205
Form
  Design Mode 454
  feedback 454
Format
  Character 422
  Paragraph 423
Forms
  Add Controls 455
Fortune Home Page 192
Forward button
  Netscape 62
Four11 356
Four11 Home Page 365

G

Global Marketplace trade bulletin board 398
Global Marketplace—
  World Business Network Home Page 407

Glossary of terms 481
Graphic Files
insert 460

H

History
Netscape 70
Home page
create a basic 411
defined 410
Homebuyer's Fair 241
Homebuyer's Fair Home Page 251
HomeScout 239
HomeScout Home Page 251
Hoover's Online 344
Hoover's Online Home Page 352
Horizontal Lines
Work with 448
http://www.chicago.tribune.com
Chicago Tribune Home Page 76
http://www.cnn.com
CNN Interactive 76
http://www.ddcpub.com
DDC Publishing Home Page 69
http://www.microsoft.com
Microsoft Corporation Home Page 11
http://www.microsoft.com/ie/
Internet Explorer Home Page 11
http://www.netscape.com
Netscape Navigator's Home Page 69
http://www.si.edu
Smithsonian Instituition Home Page 29, 69
Hyperlink
copy 440
create/insert 434
edit 435
target document 434
use relative 488
Hypertext Links 58

I

Insert
table rows or columns 417
Insert Graphics Files 460
Intellicast 322
Intellicast Home Page 329
Internet
basics x
browsers x
cautions xi
common uses x
e-mail xi
glossary of terms 481
history x
home page x
how to access x
network x
requirements vi
search engines xi
terms x
URLs x
viruses xi
Word Wide Web x
Internet Explorer 478
about 2, 13
Internet Explorer Home Page
http://www.microsoft.com/ie/ 11
Internet Service Provider (ISP) xi
IRS Digital Daily 227
IRS Digital Daily Home Page 236

L

Learn2 294
Learn2 Home Page 307
Legal Information Institute 224, 236
List Merchant 376
List Merchant Home Page 386
Locate button
Netscape 134, 159, 163
Location Field
Netscape 54

M

MapQuest 321
MapQuest Home Page 329
marquee text 466
Maximus Computers 274
Maximus Computers Home Page 283
Menu bar
Netscape 54
merge cells 444
Merriam-Webster Online 295
Merriam-Webster Online Home Page 307
Microsoft Corporation Home Page
http://www.microsoft.com 11
Microsoft Expedia 308
Microsoft Expedia Home Page 319
Microsoft Internet Explorer
see Internet Explorer /n 13
Microsoft Internet Explorer 3.0
install 490
Microsoft Network Home Page 192
Mining Company 182
MoneyAdvisor Calculators Page 307
MoneyAdvisor directory 298
MoneyHunt TV Show 217
MoneyHunter 216
MoneyHunter Home Page 223
Morningstar 206
Morningstar.Net 215
MSN.com 181
MSU-CIBER 396
MSU-CIBER Home Page 407
Multimedia
add 470

N

National Archives 296
National Archives and Records Administration 307

National Association of College Stores Home Page 375
Net Properties Home Page 251
NetProperties 238
Netscape
  home page 53
  location field 81
  main search page..78
  start search..81
Netscape Navigator...478
Netscape Navigator's Home Page
  http://www.netscape.com 69
Netscape Toolbar.......................................62, 129, 141, 159
NewsHound...196, 205
Numbered list
  create 429

O

Open a web site
  Netscape 63
Operators 90
OSHA
  Occupational Safety and Health Administration 226
OSHA (Occupational Safety and Health Administration) ...226
OSHA Home Page 236

P

Paste as Hyperlink 440
Pathfinder Network..183
Pathfinder Network Home Page..192
Preview
  Web Page...423
Print button
  Netscape 62, 159
Progress bar
  Netscape 55
Properties
  for form 454
Purchase a Computer Online..274

R

Reply
  Internet Mail..146
Results
  of search..95
Return home page
  Netscape 65

S

SalesDoctors Magazine 366
SalesDoctors Magazine Home Page 375
SalesLeads USA 342
SalesLeads USA Home Page 352
Save
  Word document as Web page...428
Search engine 86
Search Engines xi
  multi-threaded 88
Search results 95
Search sites..89
  Boolean operators 106
  grouping operators 108
  operators 90
  results..94
  search basics 90
  text string...90
Shareware.Com 479
Shockwave 480
Small Business Administration (SBA) 262
Small Business Administration Home Page......................271
Smithsonian Instituition Home Page
  http://www.si.edu 29, 69
Sound
  add background...471
Split
  cells 444
Status indicator
  Netscape 55
Stop a load or search
  Netscape 64
Stop button
  Netscape 163

T

Table
  create new in Word 443
Tables
  Add Background Textures 450
  Add Colors...449
  work with 417
Target document 434
Tech Support Guy 275
Telecommunications Research & Action Center...............285
Template
  Web Page Wizard 442
Templates
  Word Web page 410
Text
  enter in Web page 416
  marquee 466
  scrolling (marquee)...466
Text Colors
  Change...422
Text string..90
Time Zone Page..297
Title bar
  Netscape 54
Toolbar
  Netscape 54, 62, 129, 141, 159
TRAC...285
TRAC Home Page...292
Trade Information Center (TIC) 397
Trade Information Center Home Page 407
Trade Show News Network...368
Trade Show News Network Home Page...........................375
Travlang 399
Travlang Home Page 407
Troubleshooting..490
TUCOWS 479

U

U.S. Census Bureau 333
Uniform Resource Locator
  see URL 54
United States Census Bureau Home Page 341
United States Postal Service 284
United States Postal Service Home Page 292
URL (Uniform Resource Locators)
  defined x
Use Web Page Styles 423
Use Word's Web Publishing Tools 410

V

VDOLive Video Player 480
Video clips
  add 470
View
  Online Layout 423
View
  table borders 417
Viruses 476
  origins 476
  symptoms 477

W

Web page
  save Word document as 428
  Word templates 410
Web Page Wizard 442
Web publishing tools
  install 492
Web server
  post Web site to 488
Web site
  designing 410
  post to server 488
  save files in one folder 488
WebSitez 357
WebSitez Home Page 365
Word document
  save as Web page 428

Z

Zagat Survey 320
Zagat Survey Home Page 329

NOTES

NOTES

FREE CATALOG
AND
UPDATED LISTING

We don't just have books that find your answers faster; we also have books that teach you how to use your computer without the fairy tales and the gobbledygook.

We also have books to improve your typing, spelling and punctuation.

Return this card for a free catalog and mailing list update.

275 Madison Avenue,
New York, NY 10016

❑ Please send me your catalog and put me on your mailing list.

Name ______________________

Firm (if any) ______________________

Address ______________________

City, State, Zip ______________________

Phone (800) 528-3897 ***Fax (800) 528-3862***

SEE OUR COMPLETE CATALOG ON THE INTERNET @: http://www.ddcpub.com

FREE CATALOG
AND
UPDATED LISTING

We don't just have books that find your answers faster; we also have books that teach you how to use your computer without the fairy tales and the gobbledygook.

We also have books to improve your typing, spelling and punctuation.

Return this card for a free catalog and mailing list update.

275 Madison Avenue,
New York, NY 10016

❑ Please send me your catalog and put me on your mailing list.

Name ______________________

Firm (if any) ______________________

Address ______________________

City, State, Zip ______________________

Phone (800) 528-3897 Fax (800) 528-3862

SEE OUR COMPLETE CATALOG ON THE INTERNET @: http://www.ddcpub.com

FREE CATALOG
AND
UPDATED LISTING

We don't just have books that find your answers faster; we also have books that teach you how to use your computer without the fairy tales and the gobbledygook.

We also have books to improve your typing, spelling and punctuation.

Return this card for a free catalog and mailing list update.

DDC Publishing

275 Madison Avenue,
New York, NY 10016

❑ Please send me your catalog and put me on your mailing list.

Name ______________________

Firm (if any) ______________________

Address ______________________

City, State, Zip ______________________

Phone (800) 528-3897 Fax (800) 528-3862

SEE OUR COMPLETE CATALOG ON THE INTERNET @: http://www.ddcpub.com

NO POSTAGE
NECESSARY
IF MAILED
IN THE
UNITED STATES

BUSINESS REPLY MAIL
FIRST CLASS MAIL PERMIT NO. 7321 NEW YORK, N.Y.

POSTAGE WILL BE PAID BY ADDRESSEE

275 Madison Avenue
New York, NY 10157-0410

NO POSTAGE
NECESSARY
IF MAILED
IN THE
UNITED STATES

BUSINESS REPLY MAIL
FIRST CLASS MAIL PERMIT NO. 7321 NEW YORK, N.Y.

POSTAGE WILL BE PAID BY ADDRESSEE

275 Madison Avenue
New York, NY 10157-0410

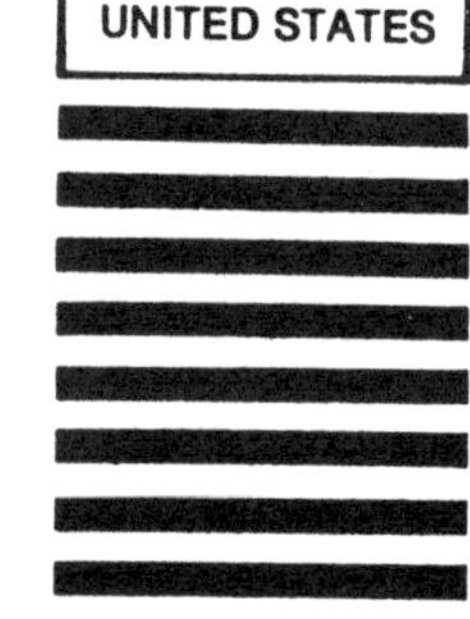

BUSINESS REPLY MAIL
FIRST CLASS MAIL PERMIT NO. 7321 NEW YORK, N.Y.

POSTAGE WILL BE PAID BY ADDRESSEE

275 Madison Avenue
New York, NY 10157-0410